Implanting Strategic Management

H. Igor Ansoff · Daniel Kipley
A. O. Lewis · Roxanne Helm-Stevens
Rick Ansoff

Implanting Strategic Management

Third Edition

H. Igor Ansoff
Strategic Management
Alliant International University
San Diego, CA, USA

Roxanne Helm-Stevens
Strategic Management
Azusa Pacific University
Azusa, CA, USA

Daniel Kipley
Strategic Management
Azusa Pacific University
Azusa, CA, USA

Rick Ansoff
Alliant International University
San Diego, CA, USA

A. O. Lewis
Strategic Management
National University
San Diego, CA, USA

H. Igor Ansoff is Deceased

ISBN 978-3-319-99598-4   ISBN 978-3-319-99599-1   (eBook)
https://doi.org/10.1007/978-3-319-99599-1

Library of Congress Control Number: 2018956581

This Palgrave Macmillan imprint is published by the registered company Springer Nature Switzerland AG
The registered company address is: Gewerbestrasse 11, 6330 Cham, Switzerland

In appreciation and gratitude to H. Igor Ansoff, "The Father of Strategic Management"—a giant in the field. Whose Strategic Success Hypothesis and numerous other contributions in strategic management progressed the study of management to a state where organizations can succeed in turbulent, changing, and surpriseful environment. Your legacy of brilliance and foresight continues on in this updated manuscript so that future generations of scholars and managers can benefit from the 'Ansoff approach.'

Acknowledgements

The authors of this book give special thanks to the significant contributions made by Prof. Steve Gabriel, senior adjunct instructor at Azusa Pacific University School of Business and Management whose professional insights and active participation helped shape and develop this book through data interpretation, writing, editing, and evaluation of the manuscript.

Contents

List of Figures

List of Tables

Part I

Original Concepts of Strategic Management and the Evolution of Management Systems

1

Epistemological Underpinnings and Original Concepts of Strategic Management

Archimedes is reported to have said: 'Give me an [appropriate] point of leverage and 1 will turn the world.' The remark highlights a fundamental truth that the picture of strategic behavior obtained by an observer depends on the knowledge-seeking model (paradigm) through which he perceives reality.

At the present time, study of management is in the midst of a 'paradigmatic revolution.' In this chapter, we explore two aspects of this revolution.

The Contingency Perspective

The major aim of an effort to understand a previously unstudied part of reality is to reduce the complexity of the real world to a model which is comprehensible and manipulable by man. But experience shows that complexity, like Salome's seven veils, must be peeled off one layer at a time. First to be perceived is a highly smoothed and aggregated shape of the underlying reality. Then come models of increasing complexity and sophistication which deepen the observer's understanding.

As is typical of all young sciences, the first step in the study of organizations was directed to identifying the typical behavior of organizations.

Sociologists, who studied response of complex organizations to environmental change, came to the conclusion that organizations are myopic, resistant to change, bureaucratic, inertial. They adapt to environment in a reactive, incremental manner. When hit by a sudden discontinuity, they go into a cataclysmic crisis.

© The Author(s) 2019
H. I. Ansoff et al., *Implanting Strategic Management*,
https://doi.org/10.1007/978-3-319-99599-1_1

Economists, who undertook to study a subclass of complex organizations, called the business firm, arrived at a totally different perception. For them, the firm was an aggressive, perpetual seeker of maximum profit.

The picture became complicated when sociologists joined economists to formulate a behavioral theory of the firm. The firm that emerged from this research was very close to the original model of the sociologists: Its behavior had to be triggered by problems; it could handle only one goal at a time; and it engaged in 'local search' for solutions to problems. The choice of the preferred solution was 'satisficing,' which meant that the firm accepted the first satisfactory solution that came along.

A matter of central importance to the present discussion is that the authors of this research labeled their results in the singular: *A behavioral theory of the Firm* (Cyert and March 1963-G), implying that *all* firms exhibit the same change-denying conservative behavior.

This conclusion is in direct contradiction to the equally singular 'economic theory of *the* firm,' in which all firms are seen as aggressive profit maximizers.

Nor is it possible for a manager in Google, Apple, Amazon, Microsoft, and numerous Chinese firms to recognize themselves in the mirror held up to them by the behavioral theory.

But, if the next of Salome's veils is removed, at the higher level of understanding it becomes apparent that the contradiction is only apparent and not real. There are, in fact, numerous firms which are accurately described by the behavioral theory. There are also profit maximizers, and there are restless entrepreneurial firms described by the economist Schumpeter, who are creators of novel technologies, markets, and industries.

Thus, when the second veil is peeled off, managerial reality appears to consist of a range of different behaviors. Under this paradigm, attention is no longer focused on the average aggregate behavior of firms, but on the variety of behaviors, and on conditions under which they are appropriate.

The study of management is currently in a transition to this second level. A new paradigm, rather grandiosely described as *contingency theory*, is rapidly becoming the epistemological leverage in studies of both management and of business firms.

Readers of Ansoff's prior work—*Strategic Management*—will recall that it was rooted in the contingency approach. As a rough approximation, of the order of two thousand different strategic behaviors were explored in the book.

This book is in the same tradition. The major contingent variables are: key success factors, turbulence levels in the environment, strategic aggressiveness of the firm, and its capability profile. Unlike the preceding book, which studied the full range of behaviors which are observed in practice, this book is focused on behaviors which should be chosen in light of the environmental imperatives, on the one hand, and the objectives and resources of the firm, on the other.

This book is a step in the emergence of practical management technology from a 'single Model T' age. Until recently, a manager seeking help was offered a variety of competing approaches by consulting firms and by academics, each claiming that his approach was the best. In this book, we have related the merits of different approaches to the needs and circumstances of the firm.

Simplicity, Complexity, and Requisite Variety

As the succeeding veils are peeled off, the researcher comes closer and closer to perceiving the shape of Salome. But the complexity of the picture also increases. In the later stages, as minor details and undulations are added, the researcher is in danger of losing perception of the shape and grace of the beautiful dancer, because of his preoccupation with anatomical details. Thus, at a certain point, further proliferation of complexity (removal of the final veils) becomes dysfunctional. To use another analogy, the researcher can no longer see the wood for the trees.

How much complexity is enough for an effective response to the environmental challenges is today one of the central and vexing questions, not only in strategic management, but also in society as a whole. One answer, which had President Reagan for its patron saint, is that the responses have become too complex and that complexity should be rolled back.

An eloquent call for a return to simplicity in management was made in a 1960s *Fortune* magazine by Theodore Levitt who accused the railroad and the petroleum industries of having an over simplistic perception of the boundaries of their respective businesses.

As the reader has seen in the preceding chapters, the position taken in this book is that simplicity is not a 'free good,' as the economists would say, and that the price of oversimplicity is a failure to make a timely and effective response to environmental challenges and opportunities.

For example, use of control and extrapolative budgeting systems as the primary management tools was not only adequate but appropriate in the 1920s. But in the last quarter of the twentieth century, a firm whose management persists in the belief that the future is extrapolative, and the prospects are for a 'resumption of growth,' is, as a minimum, headed for surprises and, as a maximum, for extinction. (Recall the statement by the current chairman of General Motors, when he took office several years ago: 'General Motors has unlimited growth horizons and it is the world's best managed company,' and compare this statement to the declining trend in the company's market share.)

Instead of minimal complexity, this book is based on the *requisite variety principle* which was enunciated by Roy Ashby. Paraphrased into the language of management, the principle may be stated as follows:

> To assure success and continuity, the speed, subtlety, and complexity of a firm's response must be in tune with the critical success factors and the turbulence level in the environment.

When low price and reliable products determine the market share, the firm will succeed by keeping its products undifferentiated and focusing its energies on minimizing production costs. But when turbulence is high and product innovation is frequent, success depends on product differentiation and aggressive marketing, and adherence to the single product strategy leads to a loss of competitive position.

When environmental discontinuities are infrequent, and change is slow relative to the speed of response by the firm, management can succeed by responding to discontinuities after they have surfaced and impacted on the firm. But on turbulence levels above 4, when discontinuities are frequent and fast, management must begin listening to complex weak signals.

But it must also be recognized that complexity is no more of a 'free good' than is simplicity. In the first place, complexity is expensive. Thus, as we have discussed, issue management places a much smaller workload on the firm than does the more complex strategic position management. But beyond the cost, there are limits to the complexity which an organization can manage.

Through the years, aggressive and successful firms not only welcomed, but sought complexity. In the last quarter of the twentieth century, there are increasing signs that the complexity of some large diversified firms has become both incomprehensible and unmanageable. When this occurs, the only way a firm can practice the requisite variety principle is not by increasing further the complexity of its response, but by reducing the range of environmental challenges which it undertakes to handle. In other words, the firm must '*undiversify.*' Recent and frequent reports in the business press have been reporting of contractions in scope and divestments by some of the world's leading companies. This is a weak signal which suggests that, in the future, management will increasingly put limits on the complexity of their firms to preserve their manageability.

The Original Concepts of Strategic Management

This chapter is based on Ansoff's research (1972-F) which was the first to introduce the concepts of strategic management. Ansoff argued that operating and strategic behaviors call for substantially different 'organizational architecture' and that when both behaviors have to be accommodated in the same firm, the two architectures conflict. It may be of benefit to the reader to review Ansoff's 1972-F tentative insight into the nature of strategic management with the practical methodology discussed in this chapter.

Two Styles of Organizational Behavior

Environmental serving organizations (ESOs) such as the business firm exhibit a variety of behavioral styles. This discussion will focus on two typical contrasting styles: the *incremental* and the *entrepreneurial*.

Incremental behavior is exhibited by a large percentage of business firms and virtually by all nonbusiness, purposive organizations such as hospitals, churches, and universities. As the name implies, the incremental mode is directed toward minimizing departures from historical behavior, both within the organization and between it and the environment. Change is not welcome, rather it is to be either controlled, 'absorbed,' or minimized.

Since social change is inexorable, few organizations succeed in containing it fully. In the incremental style, the response to change is *reactive* in which action is taken after the need for change has become clear and imperative. This is what Cyert and March have aptly called a *'problemistic search'* for solutions (Cyert and March 1963-G). The solutions are sought locally: through minimizing the increments of change from the previous status quo. The search for alternatives is sequential, and the first satisfactory solution is acceptable (*satisficing* behavior in Simon's terms: March and Simon 1958-F).

Both profit and nonprofit organizations exhibit incremental behavior. However, there is a significant difference between the business firm and the other environment-serving organizations. A majority of firms which behave in the incremental mode are also efficiency seeking. The minority that ceases to seek efficiency do not survive in the long run. Conversely, the nonbusiness organizations tend to be bureaucratic. Rather than seek efficiency, they tend to develop set rules and procedures for 'how business is done.' Thus, while incrementalism in the firm is used to enhance the effective utilization of resources, in other organizations it is directed to the maintenance of the organizational status quo.

The incremental mode is widely observable. As a result, it has been the focus of research on organizational behavior.

Entrepreneurial Behavior

The second mode of behavior is *entrepreneurial*. It entails a drastically different attitude toward change rather than suppresses and minimizes it an entrepreneurial organization seeks change. Instead of reacting to problems, future threats and opportunities are anticipated; instead of local solutions, global search is conducted for alternative courses of action; instead of a single alternative, multiple ones are generated; instead of satisficing, the decision process is to choose the best from among available alternatives. Rather than seek to preserve the past, the entrepreneurial organization strives for a continuing change in the status quo.

Entrepreneurial behavior is much less frequently observable than incremental. In nonbusiness organizations, it usually occurs when the organization is first created and the early post-birth period is devoted to definition of the organizational purposes and to the creation of the administrative structure. Following the creative period, the organization progressively settles into the incremental mode. Entrepreneurial behavior does not occur except under conditions of extreme crisis caused by severe erosion of the social utility of the organization.

In the business sector, the birth of a firm is an entrepreneurial creative act. The fact that in the 200 years of industrial history birth and death of firms has been a much more frequent phenomenon than birth and death in the public sector (with the exceptions of the periods during World War I and World War II in which the frequencies were reversed) is one reason why entrepreneurial behavior is usually ascribed to the business firm.

Another reason is that the occurrence of crises that threatens the survival if the organization persists in the incremental mode is much more frequent in the business firm. This can be traced to the fact that the firm, uniquely among purposive organizations, depends on its continued ability to make a profit. The nonprofit firms are not subject to the direct market test: The funds that support their operations are not coupled in a direct and measurable way to the continued utility of their products or services.

Among firms, frequency of concern with survival is determined by the life span of its technology-demand life cycle. This can vary from less than one year (for a typical video game), to less than five years (for a cell phone), to half a century (for the fax machine), to a century (for aircraft manufacturers), and to millennia (the demand for coal and natural gas).

The average life span of products, markets, and entire industries has been steadily and dramatically decreasing during the past 100 years. The resulting frequent threats to survival have been increasingly forcing some firms into *continual entrepreneurial behavior.*

The third reason why entrepreneurial behavior is more frequently observable in business is the fact that a small minority of firms (e.g., Berkshire Hathaway, Royal Dutch Shell, HSBC Holdings, GE, and many of the so-called conglomerates) are observed to behave *entrepreneurially continuously* in a deliberate search for growth through change.

However, if the entire spectrum of modern business firms were to be analyzed, the occurrence of entrepreneurial behavior would still constitute a relatively small percentage of the total. When this small percentage is added to the totality of nonprofit organizations, the incremental mode appears predominant.

This is probably the reason why entrepreneurial behavior has received relatively little attention from organizational theorists. This is also the reason why some students of organizational theory have argued that not only is the incremental mode the only observable one but that it also should be consciously and deliberately followed by organizations.

During the last fifty years, while students of organizational theory have focused their attention on the incremental mode, an increasing number of firms have been forced to turn entrepreneurial in order to assure success and survival. As a result, a large body of business-generated literature has appeared which recommends the entrepreneurial mode as not only feasible but the preferred way to deal with the increasing rate of environmental change.

Differences in Organizational Profiles

In Table 1.1, we illustrate the differences in organizational profiles appropriate to incremental and entrepreneurial behavior. A comparison of the profiles shows that an incremental organization will be ineffective in handling entrepreneurial behavior and vice versa.

Table 1.1 Comparison of organizational profiles

Behavior / Profile attribute	Incremental	Entrepreneurial
Objective goals	Optimize profitability extrapolation of past goals	Optimize profitability potential determination through interaction of opportunities and capabilities
Constraints	1. Environment 2. Internal capability	1. Limitations on ability to affect change in the environment 2. Ability to acquire or develop requisite skills 3. Ability to accommodate differing modes of behavior
Rewards and penalty system	1. Rewards for stability, efficiency 2. Rewards for past performance 3. Penalties for deviance	1. Rewards for creativity and initiative 2. Penalties for lack of initiative
Information	1. Internal: performance 2. External: historical opportunity space	1. Internal: capabilities 2. External: global opportunity space
Problems faced leadership Style	Repetitive, familiar 1. Popularity 2. Skill to develop consensus	Nonrepetitive, novel 1. Charisma 2. Skill to inspire people to accept change
Organizational structure	1. Stable or expanding 2. Activities grouped according to resource conversion process 3. Search for economies of scale 4. Activities loosely coupled	1. Fluid, structurally changing 2. Activities grouped according to problems 3. Activities closely coupled
Management problem-solving: (a) Recognition of action need	1. Reactive in response to problem 2. Time-lagged behind occurence of problems	1. Active search for opportunities 2. Anticipatory
(b) Search for alternatives	1. Reliance on past experience 2. Incremental departures from status que 3. Single alternative generated	1. Creative search 2. Wide ranging from status quo 3. Multiple alternatives generated
(c) Evaluation of alternatives	Satisficing—first satisfactory accepted	Optimizing—best of a set of alternatives selected 1. Risk-seeking
(d) Risk attitude	1. Minimize risk 2. Consistency with past experience	2. Risk portfolio balance

Transitioning from one profile to the other involves far-reaching changes, is time-consuming, costly, psychologically disturbing to individuals, and frequently requires a realignment of power. An attempt to accommodate both styles within the same organization produces conflicts and strain. A natural question is, therefore, which of the two modes is appropriate to a particular organization. In business literature, recent concern with strategic planning, which is a systematic approach to entrepreneurial behavior, has tended to create the impression that the incremental mode is conservative and stagnant while the entrepreneurial mode is aggressive and growth oriented. On the other hand, as already mentioned, some organizational theorists argue that the incremental mode is organic and natural to complex organizations, and that in complex environments the entrepreneurial style is not possible because of limitations of human rationality.

In this book, we argue that while in the past the modes have alternated sequentially in response to changing environmental challenges, in the future business firms will have to learn to accommodate both at the same time.

Strategic and Operations Management

Environment-serving organizations such as the firm are in constant two-way interaction with the environment. They take in an assortment of resources from the environment, add value to them, and deliver them back to the environment in the form of goods and/or services.

The activity of the organization consists of time-phased flows of the various resources, buffered by reservoirs (stocks, money, people, and information) that help balance and maintain the flows. The flows are not unidirectional but are looped with both positive and negative feedback.

Successful environment-serving organizations are *open systems*. The 'open' property is made necessary by two factors: (1) Continued organizational survival depends on its ability to secure rewards from the environment which replenish the resources consumed in the conversion process, and (2) continued maintenance by the organization of its social legitimacy. This latter requirement arises from the fact that in addition to their products and services, organizations produce side effects on the environment (such as air pollution or student protests), which may socially be undesirable. *Inside* the organization, there are two major streams of activity (or two subsystems): (1) *logistics subsystem* that is engaged in conversion of the input resources into goods/services, and (2) *managerial subsystem* that is concerned with guidance and control of the activities of the organization.

While the logistic subsystem typically handles different assortments of resources (physical materials, money, information, and human resources), the 'working material' of the managerial subsystem is information. The body of information handled by the logistic subsystem overlaps but is distinct from information required for managerial activity.

Within the managerial subsystem, there are *two* principle managerial regimes: *strategic management* and *operations management*.[1]

The strategic management activity is concerned with establishing objectives and goals for the organization, and with maintaining a set of relationships between the organization and the environment which (a) enable it to pursue its objectives, (b) are consistent with the organizational capabilities, and (c) continue to be responsive to environmental demands.

One end product of strategic management is a potential for future fulfillment of the organization's objectives. *Within* the business firm, this consists of (a) the input to the firm: availability of financing, manpower, information, and 'raw' materials; (b) at the output end: developed products and/or services, tested for their potential profitability; and (c) a set of social behavior rules that permit the organization *to* continue to meet *its* objectives.

In addition to the future performance potential, another end product of strategic management is an internal structure and dynamics capable of continued responsiveness to changes in the external environment. In the business firm, this requires (a) a managerial capability to sense and interpret environmental changes, coupled to a capability to conceive and guide strategic response and (b) logistic capability to conceive, develop, test, and introduce new products and services.

These respective capabilities are determined in part by the *organizational architecture*:

- Physical facilities, their capacities, and capabilities, and technology.
- Information processing and communication capacities and capabilities.
- Organizational tasks assigned to individuals and groups of individuals.
- Rewards and punishments for the performance of assigned tasks.
- Power structure and dynamics.
- Systems and procedures.
- Organizational culture, norms, values, and models of reality that guide organizational behavior.

---

[1]In subsequent chapters, which will be focused on the business firm, Ansoff sometimes uses 'competitive' to describe the 'operational' activity.

In part, the strategic capabilities of the organization are determined by the characteristics of the individuals *within it*.

- Attitudes toward change.
- Risk-taking propensity.
- Cognitive problem-solving skills appropriate to strategic activities.
- Social problem-solving skills appropriate to bringing about organizational change.
- Work skills (e.g., product design and development, pilot manufacturing, and test marketing).
- Motivation to engage in strategic activities.

In summary, the concerns of the strategic manager are the following:

- To determine and bring about strategic change in the organization.
- To build an organizational architecture conducive to strategic change.
- To select and develop individuals (both workers and managers) motivated and capable of creating strategic change.

While strategic management activity is concerned with creating a strategic position that assures future environmental viability of the organization, operations management is concerned with exploiting the present strategic position to achieve the organizational objectives. In the business firm, the strategic manager is concerned with continued profitability potential; the operations manager is concerned with converting the potential into actual profits.

In operations management, the major activity is to establish and bring about levels of organizational output that will best contribute to the objectives.

The end product of operations activity is delivery of products/services to the environment in exchange for rewards. In the firm, the contributing activities are purchasing, manufacturing, distribution, and marketing. The managerial roles include determination of overall operating goals, motivation, coordination, and control of others in the firm (both managers and workers) in the process of achieving the goals.

Just as in strategic management, operations management involves creation and maintenance of appropriate organizational architecture and selection and development of individuals with the appropriate motivations and skills. But these are quite different for the two types of management.

Table 1.2 Comparison of organizational architectures

	Operating	Strategic
Culture	Production/marketing orientation:	Strategic/flexibility orientation:
	Success = aggressive competition + efficient production	Success = invention + anticipation/creation of needs
Manager	1. Profit maker	1. Entrepreneur
	2. Goal achiever	2. Innovator
	3. Controller	3. Charismatic leader
Management system	1. LRP/budgetin	1. Strategic planning/SIM*
	2. Historical performance control	2. Strategic management
		3. Strategic control
Information	Demand profitability trends	New threats, opportunities
Structure	1. Functional/divisional	1. Project/matrix
	2. Stable	2. Dynamic
Power	1. Decentralized	1. In general management
	2. In production/marketing	2. In R&D
		3. In new ventures
		4. In strategic planning

* SIM - 'Strategic Issue Management'

Strategic social architecture is change seeking, flexible, and loosely structured, while the operations architecture is change resistant, efficiency seeking, and highly structured.

While the strategic manager is a change seeker, risk-propensive, divergent problem solver, skillful in leading other into new and untried directions, the operations manager is a change absorber, cautious risk-taker, convergent problem solver, skillful diagnostician, coordinator, and controller of complex activities. His leadership skills are different from those of the strategic manager. Rather than change direction of the organization, he provides motivation to excel and improve over past performance.

This is illustrated in Table 1.2. As the figure shows, strategic culture is open, flexible, and inventive; the operations culture is change controlling, efficiency seeking.

Table 1.2 further shows that systems, information, organizational, and power structures are also significantly different between strategic and operations management.

A comparison of Tables 1.1 and 1.2 shows that there is a close affinity between the organizational behavior profiles and the respective management regimes: strategic management calls for the entrepreneurial profile and operations management for the incremental profile.

The problem that we face in this book is threefold:

1. How to determine the combination profile that will optimize the firm's chances of success. This problem is handled in Part II.
2. How to assure an effective transition from one profile to another. This problem is handled in Chapters 18 and 20.
3. How to assure a happy coexistence of a combination of profiles. This is addressed in Chapter 20.

Summary

Behavioral science literature describes two types of organizational behavior: incremental and entrepreneurial. Management of the business firm involves two complementary activities: strategic, which develops the firm's future potential; operating behavior, which converts the existing potential into profits and growth.

Strategic management requires entrepreneurial organizational behavior, and operating management succeeds through incremental behavior.

During the first half of the twentieth century, strategic behavior and operating behavior were alternate efforts of the firm. During the second half of the twentieth century, firms increasingly needed to accommodate both behaviors at the same time. But the social architects required by the respective behaviors are distinct and different. Therefore, firms will need to develop complex architectural designs that can accommodate both.

Exercises

1. What kinds of obstacles and difficulties would you expect in trying to accommodate both incremental and entrepreneurial behaviors within the shell of a single firm?
2. What solutions would you suggest for overcoming the obstacles?
3. Why does a great majority of nonprofit organizations behave incrementally? Is it possible to make them behave in the entrepreneurial change-seeking mode? Can you provide recent examples of such organizations? What made them behave entrepreneurially?
4. What are the differences between strategic planning and strategic management?

2

Why Make Strategy Explicit?

In the 1950s, when the response to environmental discontinuities became important, the concept of strategy entered into the business vocabulary. In the early days, the meaning of strategy was not clear. The dictionaries did not help, since following military usage they still defined strategy as 'the science and the art of deploying forces for battle.'

At first, many managers and some academics questioned the usefulness of the new concept. Having witnessed half a century of miraculous performance by American industry without the benefit of strategy, they asked why it had suddenly become necessary, and what it could do for the firm. This chapter is based on Ansoff's early writings in which he addressed these pertinent questions.

Concept of Strategy

Basically, a strategy is a set of decision-making rules for guidance of organizational behavior. There are four distinct types of such rule:

1. Yardsticks by which the present and future performance of the firm is measured. The quality of these yardsticks is usually called *objectives* and the desired quantity called *goals*.
2. Rules for developing the firm's relationship with its external environment: What products-technology the firm will develop, where and to whom the

© The Author(s) 2019
H. I. Ansoff et al., *Implanting Strategic Management*,
https://doi.org/10.1007/978-3-319-99599-1_2

products are to be sold, how will the firm gain advantage over competitors. This set of rules is called the product-market or *business strategy*.
3. Rules for establishing the internal relations and processes within the organization; this is frequently called the *organizational concept*.
4. The rules by which the firm conducts its day-to-day business called *operating policies*.

A strategy has several distinguishing characteristics:

1. The *process* of strategy formulation results in *no immediate action*. Rather it sets the general directions in which the firm's position will grow and develop.
2. Therefore, strategy must next be used to generate strategic projects through a *search process*. The role of strategy in search is first to focus on areas defined by the strategy, and second, to filter out and uncover possibilities that are consistent/inconsistent with the strategy.
3. Thus, strategy becomes *unnecessary whenever the historical dynamics of an organization will take it where it wants to go.* This to say, when the search process is already focused on the preferred areas.
4. At the time of strategy formulation, it is not possible to enumerate all the project possibilities that will be uncovered. Therefore, strategy formulation must be based on *highly aggregated, incomplete, and uncertain information* about the various classes of alternatives.
5. When search uncovers specific alternatives, the more precise, less aggregated information that becomes available may cast doubts on the wisdom of the original strategy choice. Thus, successful use of strategy requires *strategic feedback*.
6. Since both strategy and objectives are used to filter projects, they appear similar. Yet they are distinct. *Objectives* are a set of higher-level decision rules and represent the *ends* that the firm is seeking to attain, while the *strategy is the means to these ends.* A strategy that is valid *only* under one set of objectives may lose its validity when the objectives of the organization are changed.
7. Strategy and objectives are interchangeable; both at different points in time and at different levels of organization. Thus, some attributes of performance (such as market share) can be an objective of the firm at one time and its strategy at another. Further, as objectives and strategy are elaborated throughout an organization, a typical hierarchical relationship results: *elements of strategy at a higher managerial level become objectives at a lower one.*

Thus, strategy is an elusive and a somewhat abstract concept. Its formulation typically produces no immediate productive action in the firm. Above all, it is an expensive process both in terms of money and managerial time and effort.

Strategy and Performance

Since management is a pragmatic results-oriented activity, the question needs to be asked whether an abstract concept, such as strategy, can usefully contribute to the firm's performance.

In the business firm, concern with explicit formulation of strategy still exists. However, history of business abounds with clear examples of deliberate and successful use of strategy. Two well-known examples of strategic success include DuPont's deliberate and successful move from explosives into chemicals in the 1920s and Henry Ford's concentration on the Model T for the emerging mass market, although Ford's strategy of vertical integration was a failure. More recently, Larry Page and Sergey Brin's farsighted yet simple design for a web search was the basis for Google. In another instance of success, Apple's Steve Wozniak and Steve Jobs developed the first 'personal computer' to a market that did not know that it needed it. Apple just became the first US company with a $1 Trillion-dollar market cap.

A trained business observer can discern a unique strategy in a majority of successful firms. However, while discernible in most cases, strategies are frequently not made explicit. They are either a private concept shared only by the key management, or a diffuse, generally understood but seldom verbalized sense of common purpose throughout the firm.

It has been argued by some managers, and with good reason, that this is a desirable state of affairs: Because it represents a unique competitive advantage of the firm, strategy should not be made explicit and must be kept private. However, since the 1960s, American business literature has increasingly reflected an opposing view in favor of a carefully and explicitly formulated strategy. This view favors not only making strategy a matter of concern to many managers throughout the firm, but also to many of the relevant 'workers,' particularly in marketing and R&D, since they are not only making important contributions to strategy formulation but are also the principal agents of its implementation.

If the value of a concept is to be measured by its contribution to success, one would have to admit that both of the above views are correct: Many firms have succeeded and are succeeding without the benefit of an explicitly enunciated strategy, while a growing number have benefited from a deliberate strategy formulation.

An explanation can be sought through resolution of another apparent paradox: Strategy is a system concept that gives coherence and direction to growth of a complex organization. How is it possible then for a large and complex organization, such as a business firm, to attain coordination and coherence without making strategy explicit?

The answer is to be found in the nature of the firm's growth. If a firm is operating in growing markets, if the characteristics of demand change slowly, if the technology of products and processes is stable, if all these conditions exist, strategy needs to change slowly and incrementally. Coherence of behavior and organizational coordination are attained through informal organizational learning and adaption. New managers and workers are typically given long indoctrination periods into the nature of the business; their careers are shaped by gradual progression through the firm. In the process they acquire an experiential, almost intuitive, awareness of the firm's strategic guidelines. When environment, technology, or competitors change in an orderly manner, these managers are able to adapt their responses incrementally, using their accumulated knowledge and experience. A manger in R&D can be expected to act coherently with managers in marketing and production. The result is reasonably coherent organizational growth. The strategy remains stable and implicit.

It can be questioned whether such loosely coordinated behavior produces the best possible growth, but it works demonstrably. The first half of the twentieth century was a period of relatively stability with continued growth, and the absence of concern with strategy is not surprising. However, the second half of the century, particularly the 90s and on, is a new 'ball game.' In many cases, the historical organizational dynamics arc a path to stagnation and/or decline. Therefore, strategy has emerged as a tool for reorienting the organizational thrust. Given this fact, several questions need to be asked concerning the utility of having a strategy.

The first is whether a systematic, explicit strategy is a viable concept. Some writers (significantly observers not of the firm but of decision processes in the government) have argued that organizational complexity; uncertainties of information and limited human cognition make it impossible to approach strategy formulation in a systematic manner. Their argument is that strategy formulation must of necessity, proceed in the adaptive, unsystematic, informal way observed in most organizations. The answer to this contention is that the proof of the pudding is in the eating. Numerous business firms, which in recent years formulated and announced their strategies, have laid this argument to rest.

Given that systematic strategy formulation is feasible, the second question to ask is whether it produces improvement in organizational performance if used as an alternative to adaptive growth. Several pieces of evidence support this statement.

One of these comes from an extensive study of American mergers and acquisitions. Among other significant results, we found that deliberate and systematic preplanning of acquisition strategy produces significantly better financial performance than an unplanned, opportunistic, adaptive approach. These results are valid under stringent tests of their statistic validity (Ansoff et al. 1970-B). A summary of these findings will be discussed in Part III. Since these earlier studies, a number of subsequent research studies confirmed our findings, namely that explicit strategy formulation can improve performance.

When to Formulate Strategy

The third question we need to ask is when does recourse to an explicit strategy become essential. One condition is when rapid and discontinuous changes occur in the environment of the firm. This may be caused by saturation of traditional markets, technological discoveries inside or outside the firm, and/or a sudden influx of new competitors.

Under these conditions, established organizational traditions and experiences no longer suffice for coping with the new opportunities and new threats. Without the benefit of a unifying strategy, the chances are high that different parts of the organization will develop different, contradictory and ineffective responses.

Marketing will continue struggling to revive historical demand; production will make investments in automation of obsolete production lines, while R&D develops new products based on an obsolete technology. Conflicts will result, and reorientation of the firm will be prolonged, turbulent, and inefficient. In some cases, the reorientation may come too late to guarantee survival.

When confronted with discontinuities, the firm is faced with two very difficult problems:

1. How to choose the right directions for further growth from among many and imperfectly perceived alternatives.
2. How to harness the energies of a large number of people in the new chosen direction.

Answers to these questions are the essence of strategy formulation and implementation. At this point, strategy becomes an essential and badly needed managerial tool.

Such conditions were the cause of interest in explicit strategy formulation in the USA during the mid-1950s when pent-up wartime demand began to reach saturation; and again, during 1990s when technology began to make obsolete some industries and to proliferate new ones; and when restructuring of international markets presented both new threats and new opportunities to business firms.

An explicit new strategy also becomes necessary when the objectives of an organization change drastically as a result of new demands imposed on the organization by society. This is precisely what is happening today in many nonbusiness purposive organizations: the church, the government, and universities.

Difficulties Encountered in Implanting Strategy Formulation

One major source of difficulty comes from the fact that in most organizations the pre-strategy decision-making processes are heavily political in nature. Strategy introduces elements of rationality that are disruptive to the historical culture of the firm and threatening to the political processes. A natural organizational reaction is to fight against the disruption of the historical culture and power structure, rather than confront the challenges posed by the environment. It is less visible, but nevertheless present and strong, during introduction of strategic planning into the business firm.

A no less important difficulty is that introduction of strategic planning triggers conflicts between previous profit-making activities and the new innovative activities. Organizations typically do not have the capability, the capacity or the motivational systems to think and act strategically.

Finally, organizations generally lack information about themselves and their environment that is need for managerial talents capable of formulating and implementing strategy.[1]

---

[1]The ideas in this brief section were written in 1972 and were central to theme of strategic management. They will be elaborated on in Parts II and V of this book.

Summary

Strategy is a potentially very powerful tool for coping with the conditions of change that surround the firm today; but it is complex, costly to introduce, and costly to use. Nevertheless, there is evidence that it more than pays for itself.

Strategy is a tool that offers significant helps for coping with turbulence confronted by business firms, loss of relevance by universities, breakdown in law enforcement, breakdown in health service system, urban congestion. Therefore, it merits serious attention as a managerial tool, not only for the firm but also for a broad spectrum of social organizations.

Exercises

1. Some senior managers have argued that even if made explicit and written down, strategy should be kept private to the very top managers of the firm in order to prevent competition from finding out about it. What are the merits and faults of this argument?
2. Other senior managers have argued that by focusing search, strategy restricts the entrepreneurial freedom to respond to whatever attractive opportunities may come along. What are the merits and faults of this argument?

3

Evolution of Management Systems

The management system used by a firm is a determining component of the firm's responsiveness to environmental changes because it determines the way that management perceives environmental challenges, diagnoses their impact on the firm, decides what actions to take, and implements the decisions.

Early in the twentieth century, in response to the increasing turbulence of the environment, systems have been forced to become progressively more responsive and more complex. In this chapter, Ansoff discusses the historical evolution of management systems and relates them to the respective turbulence levels.

Evolution of Management Systems

As the turbulence levels changed, management developed systematic approaches to handling the increasing unpredictability, novelty, and complexity. As the future became more complex, novel, and less foreseeable, systems became correspondingly more sophisticated, each complementing and enlarging upon the earlier ones.

The evolution of systems for general management is shown in Table 3.1. The figure suggests that the respective systems were responsive to the progressively decreasing familiarity of events and decreasing visibility of the future.

© The Author(s) 2019
H. I. Ansoff et al., *Implanting Strategic Management*,
https://doi.org/10.1007/978-3-319-99599-1_3

Table 3.1 Evolution of management systems

		Changeability					
		1900	1930	1950	1970	1990	2010
		Familiarity of Events					
		<Familiar><Extrapolable><Familiar discontinuity> <Novel discontinuity>					
Unpredictability of the Future	Recurring	>Systems and procedures manuals >**Management by Control** >Financial control					
	Forecastable by extrapolation	>Operations budgeting >Capital budgeting >**Management by extrapolation** >Management by objectives >Long Range Planning					
	Predictable threats and opportunities	>Periodic strategic planning >**Management by anticipation of change** >Strategic posture planning					
	Partially predictable opportunities/ Unpredictable surprises	>Contingency planning >Strategic Issue management >**Management by flexible/rapid response** >Weak signal Issue management >Surprise management					
	Turbulence Level	1 **Stable**	2 **Reactive**	3 **Anticipatin**	4 **Exploring**	5 **Creative**	

As shown in the figure, the systems can be grouped into four distinctive stages of evolution:

1. *Management by* (after-the-fact) *control* of performance, which was adequate when change was slow.
2. *Management by extrapolation*, when change accelerated, but the future could be predicted by extrapolation of the past.
3. *Management by anticipation*, when discontinuities began to appear but change, while rapid, was still slow enough to permit timely anticipation and response.
4. *Management through flexible/rapid response*, which is currently used by many firms, under conditions in which many significant challenges develop too rapidly to permit timely anticipation.

The earlier systems, up to and including long range planning (LRP), are now still widely practiced. Firms have adopted strategic planning and periodic strategic management has attracted interest from firms that encounter difficulties in implementing drastically new strategies. Strategic issue management is becoming more popular in the USA and Asia. Weak signal management is on the rise.

In the rest of the chapter, we shall compare the systems starting with LRP.

Long Range Planning and Strategic Planning

In this section, we assume that the reader is familiar with the concepts of LRP and strategic planning and focus attention on the distinctive differences between the two. Readers unacquainted with the two planning approaches can refer to extensive literature on the subject (see Bibliography Part C).

One basic difference between LRP (also known as corporate planning) and strategic planning is their respective view of the future.

In long range planning, the future is expected to be predictable through extrapolation of the historical growth. This is illustrated in the upper part of Fig. 3.1 by the wavy dashed line that is '*extrapolated*' forward. The jagged line, with the 'hockey-stick effect,' illustrates the typical goal-setting process that occurs in LRP.

Top management typically assumes that the future performance of the firm can and should be better than in the past, and it negotiates appropriately higher goals with lower level management. The process typically produces optimistic goals that are not fully met in reality (hence, the hockey

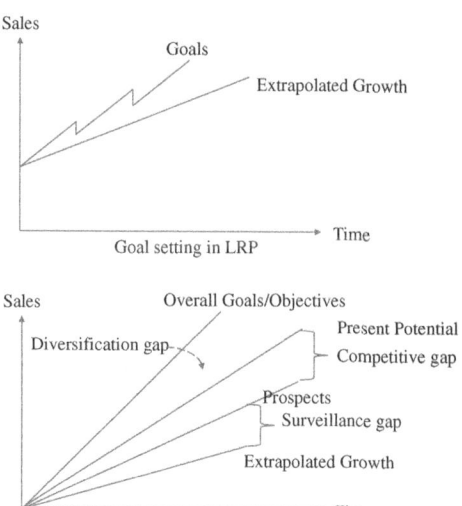

Fig. 3.1 Gap analysis in strategic planning

stick effect). In well-managed companies, the results are above extrapolation but follow the typical saw-tooth effect shown in the figure. In poorly managed companies the actual performance also follows the saw-tooth but falls below extrapolation.

In strategic planning the future is not necessarily expected to be an improvement over the past, nor is it assumed to be extrapolable. Therefore, as the first step, and *analysis of the firm's prospects* is made which identifies trends, threats, opportunities, and singular 'breakthrough' events which may change the historical trends.

The results of prospects analysis are shown in the lower half of Fig. 3.1. In the language first introduced in the 1960s by Robert Stewart of the Stanford Research Institute, determination of prospects closes the *surveillance gap* between extrapolation and the performance the firm is likely to attain if it follows its historical strategies.

The second step is a *competitive analysis* that identifies the improvement in the firm's performance that can be obtained from improvements in the competitive strategies in the respective business areas of the firm.

The competitive analysis typically shows that, even if the firm were to pursue optimal strategies in all of its business areas, some of the areas are more promising than others, and some areas may have a distinctly unpromising future. Therefore, the third step is a process which is called the *strategic portfolio analysis*: the firm's prospects in the different business areas are compared, priorities are established, and future strategic resources are allocated among the business areas.

The overall performance which can be obtained if the firm implements the results of the competitive analysis and of the portfolio balance is shown as the *present potential* line on Fig. 3.1. *This closes the competitive gap.*

The management may be willing to accept the present potential line as its goal. In this case, the gap analysis is completed and programs and budgets are developed for implementation.

In many cases though, the present potential line will be unacceptable either because of strategic vulnerability of the present portfolio or because the prospects line shows an imbalance between the long and short-term prospects or because the growth ambitions of management are substantially above the prospects line.

In such cases, the next step is a *diversification analysis* that diagnoses the deficiencies in the present portfolio and identifies new business areas into which the firm will seek to move.

When the performance expected from the new business areas is added to the present potential line, the results are the *overall goals and objectives* of the firm shown in the figure. These are determined by two factors: the ambitions and drive of the top management and by the strategic resources that will be available for diversification.

The differences in the process between LRP and strategic planning are illustrated in Fig. 3.2. In LRP, the goals are elaborated into action programs, budgets, and profit plans for each of the key units of the firm; these units next implement the programs and budgets.

Strategic planning replaces extrapolation by an elaborate strategy analysis that, as shown in the lower part of Fig. 3.2, balances the prospects against objectives to produce a strategy.

The next step is to establish two sets of goals: for the near-term performance goals, and strategic goals.

Operating programs/budgets guide the operating units of the firm in their continuing profit-making activity, and strategic programs/budgets generate the firm's future profit potential. The latter, as we shall be discussing in detail later, fit poorly into the operations implementation system and require a separate project management implementation system. Strategic implementation requires a separate and different control system, labeled *strategic control* in the figure.

LRP responds to the needs of a firm when the future is extrapolable from the past. In terms of Table 3.1, this means that LRP will effectively respond to environmental challenges of turbulence levels 2.0–3.0. Strategic planning becomes necessary on mid-level 3 when future challenges start to become discontinuous. Strategic planning will be discussed in Part II.

Fig. 3.2 LRP and strategic planning compared

Strategic Posture Management

When strategic planning was first invented, it was clear that the firm's ability to move into new business areas depended on its capability to perform successfully in these areas. Therefore, one of the key strategy selection criteria was that new competitive strategies in the historical business areas, as well as in new business areas, must match the historical strengths of the firm. Thus, analysis of the firm's strengths and weaknesses become an early step in strategic planning.

However, experience began to show that insistence on using historical strengths became a limitation on the strategic action by the firm. Frequently, firms could find few (or no) attractive business areas to which their historical strengths were applicable. To make matters worse, even in the updating of competitive strategies within the firm's historical businesses, the historical strengths frequently became weaknesses, and an obstacle to change. For example, in 1987 Nokia introduced the Mobira Cityman, the first handheld mobile phone becoming the industry first mover. In 1992 Nokia launches its first digital handheld GSM phone, the Nokia 1011 the then president and chief executive officer, Jorma Ollila, focuses the firm strategy on mobile phones becoming the industry leader and in 2005 Nokia sells its billionth phone. However, Nokia lost their leadership in the mobile industry beginning in 2007 when Steve Jobs introduced a wide-screen I-Pod with touch controls, Internet connection, and a revolutionary mobile phone; this was not three separate products but one, it was the iPhone. In other words, Nokia's historical focus on the standard mobile phone became a weakness when the market was shifted due to discontinuous product development.

As it became clear that reliance on historical strengths can be dangerous, the concept of strategic planning underwent a change in the manner illustrated in Fig. 3.3.

In an environment on turbulence level E, there is a range of success strategies from S^1_O to S^1_n. Through gap analysis shown in Fig. 3.1, the firm selects a strategy, S^1_F which best meets its objectives; but the success of the external strategy will depend on the internal capabilities of the firm. As shown in the figure, there are two, complementary types of capability: functional (R&D, marketing, production, etc.) and general management capability. Thus, so long as the environment remains on level E_1, the firm must have capabilities C^1_f and S^1_M assure success of its strategy S^1_F.

If, as the figure illustrates, turbulence analysis (see section Two) shows that the future turbulence will move to a (higher or lower) level E_2 the range

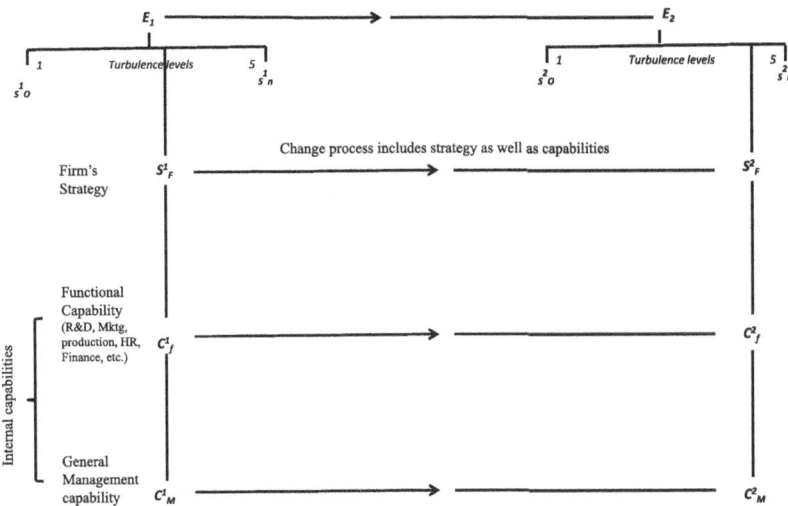

Fig. 3.3 Bird's eye view of strategic posture management

of effective strategies becomes S^2_O to S^2_n. As a result, not only will the firm's strategy have to change to S^2_F, but so will the capabilities to C^2_f and C^2_M. Thus, in strategic management, capability planning is added to strategy planning.

This new process is complex for two reasons:

1. Strategy and capability have a 'chicken and egg' relationship and must support each other. We shall discuss this interaction in detail in Parts II and III of this book.
2. While the concept of functional (R&D, production, marketing, etc.) capability planning is well understood today, and practice, the concept of general management capability planning is both new and complex. General management capability will be discussed in Part II.

For the present, it is sufficient to recognize that general management capability is determined by five mutually supporting components:

1. Qualifications and mentality of the key managers.
2. Social climate (culture) within the firm.
3. Power structure.
4. Systems and organizational structure.
5. Capacity of general management to do managerial work.

Thus, the first significant difference between strategic planning and strategic posture management is the *addition of capability planning to strategy planning*.

Experience has shown that when planning calls for a discontinuous change in general management capability (particularly in managers' mentality, culture, or power structure) implementation of the plan encounters strong organizational resistance to change. Unless measures are taken to reduce, overcome, and manage resistance during the implementation process, planning is likely to become a process of 'paralysis by analysis.'

The second difference between strategic planning and strategic posture management is the *addition of systematic management of the resistance to change during implementation of the strategy and capability plans*.

Management to resistance to change will be discussed in detail in Part V.

Strategic Issue Management

Table 3.1 shows that during the first seventy years of the twentieth-century systems evolved in response to two challenges: the increasing changeability of the environment on the one hand and the decreasing predictability of the future on the other.

At its introduction in the in the 1950s, the environment appeared to be predictable enough to confine strategic planning to a single most probable plan. As predictability became poorer, it became necessary to make multiple plans; the *basic plan* preparing the firm for the most probable future plus *contingency plans* for less probable events and futures in which the basic plan would become invalid. By the mid-1970s, however, contingency planes alone were insufficient preparation for the unpredictable future: the speed of change had increased to a point at which events surfaced and developed too rapidly to allow timely preparation of such plans.

The planning of positioning responses is an organization-wide process lasting several months and involving many levels of management. It is too slow and cumbersome to cope with unanticipated 'mid-year surprises' originating from government, foreign competition, breakthroughs in R&D, etc., whose speed is faster than that of the planning cycle.

As environmental turbulence has begun to approach level 4, firms have begun to use real-time systems, called *strategic issue management*, which is illustrated in Fig. 3.4.

The system is simple to install and manage and does not interfere with the existing structure and systems. Briefly, the ingredients of issue management are the following:

1. A continuous surveillance is instituted over environmental-business-technological-economic-social-political trends.
2. The impact and urgency of the trends are estimated and presented as key strategic issues to top management at frequent meetings and whenever a new major threat or opportunity is perceived.
3. Together with the planning staff, top management then sorts issues into one of four categories:

   a. Highly urgent issues of far-reaching effect that require immediate attention.
   b. Moderately urgent issues of far-reaching effect that can be resolved during the next planning cycle.
   c. Non-urgent issues of far-reaching effect that require continuous monitoring.
   d. Issues that are 'false alarms' and can be dropped from further consideration.

4. The urgent issues are assigned for study and resolution, either to existing organizational units, or whenever rapid cross-organizational response is essential to special taskforces.
5. Top management both for strategic and tactical implications monitors the resolution of issues.

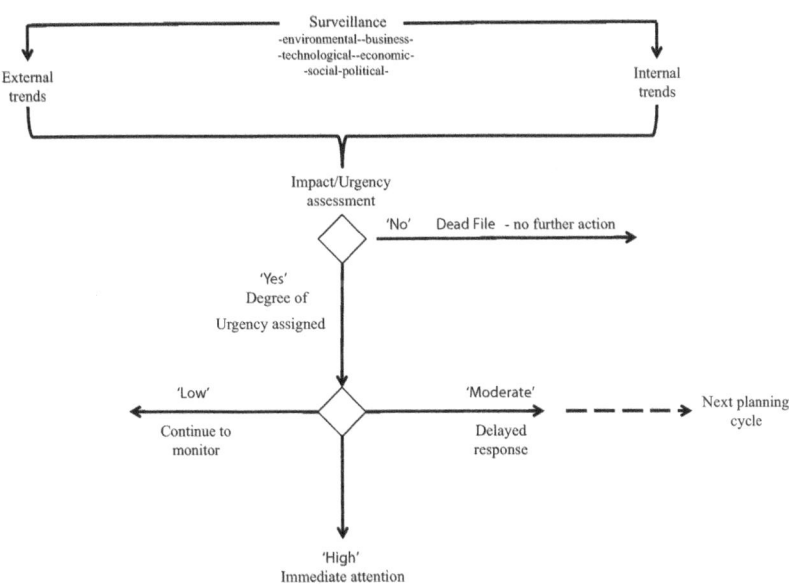

Fig. 3.4 Strategic issue management

6. The list of the issues and their priorities is kept up-to-date through periodic review by the top management.

Conceptually, strategic issue management is a very simple system, much simpler than either strategic planning or periodic strategic management. We shall discuss it in detail in Part IV.

Weak Signals and Graduated Response

Issues identified through environmental surveillance will differ in the amount of information they contain. Some issues will be sufficiently visible and concrete to permit the firm to compute their impact and to devise specific plans for response. We shall call these *strong signal issues*.

Other issues will contain *weak signals*, imprecise early indications about impending impactful events. For example, it is clear today that for the foreseeable future, the Middle East/Asia will be the source of important political upheavals, but it is not possible to predict with confidence where and when they will occur nor what specific shape they will take.

Such weak signals mature over time and become strong signals. When the turbulence level is around 3.5–4, the firm can afford to wait until such signals become strong, because enough time is left before impact to permit the firm to evaluate its impact and to mount a timely response.

But at levels 4–5, when the speed of change is fast, if the firm waits until a signal becomes strong, it will either be late in its response, or it will fail to respond until after the issue has impacted the firm. Therefore, *at high turbulence levels, it becomes necessary to start the firm response while the environmental signals are still weak*.

A method for doing this is illustrated in Table 3.2. The left-hand column identifies five stages in the evolution of information about a new issue. Proceeding from top to bottom, the originally weak signals become progressively strong. At the top (signal level I), the only information available is a certainty that the environment holds potential surprises. At the bottom (level V) enough is known to compute the profit consequences of both the impact and the response. On level IV, enough is known to launch a concrete response to the threat/opportunity, even though the firm is not able to estimate its financial consequences.

The column headings of Table 3.2, from the left to right, show progressively stronger responses that become possible as the strength of the signal

Table 3.2 Weak signals and generated response

Graduated response / Strength of Signal	A Environmental Surveillance	B Identification of relative strengths and weaknesses	C Reduction of external strategic vulnerability	D Increase of internal strategic flexibility	E Capability plans and response	D Action plans and response
I Sense of threat/opportunity						
II Sense of threat/opportunity is known						
III Shape of threat/opportunity is concrete		Feasible response area				
IV Response strategies and understood						
V Outcome of response is forecastable						

increases. The weakest (response A) is to start environmental surveillance of the field of turbulence. At the other extreme (response F), the strongest response is to develop and implement a direct response to the threat/opportunity, such as a new product line, new marketing strategy, and enter/leave a business area. The responses between the two extremes become more specific, but also more costly and irreversible, as one moves from left to right.

The shaded area inside the figure shows that, as the signals gain strength, information becomes available for progressively stronger responses. By the time the source of the threat/opportunity is identified (but not yet its actual shape) a substantial program can be launched which will reduce the firm's vulnerability and increase flexibility of response.

Table 3.2 can be used to sensitize the strategic issue management system to respond to weak signals. To provide an input to the system, the environmental surveillance process must be sensitized to warning signals of emerging issues. In addition, general management and other participants need to develop an attitude that welcomes a change, a decision-making behavior which accepts unfamiliar risks, and problem-solving approach which foregoes reliance on experience in favor of new learning. We shall be discussing the *weak signal issue management* in detail in Part IV, Chapter 20.

Strategic Surprise Management

Just as in a radar surveillance system, in spite of the best efforts, some issues will slip by the environmental surveyors and become strategic surprises. The strategic surprise has four factors:

1. The issue arrives suddenly, *unanticipated.*
2. It poses *novel* problems in which the firm has little prior experience.
3. Failure to respond implies either a *major financial reversal* or loss of a major opportunity.
4. The response is *urgent* and cannot be handled promptly enough by the normal systems and procedures.

There are numerous examples of strategic surprises that have had a major impact on international business activities over the past fifty years. Among them is the attack on the World Trade Centers, the formation of OPEC, the Arab Spring uprising, and the Tohoku 9.1 earthquake followed by 40.5-meter tsunami triggering a level-7 nuclear meltdown at the Fukushima Daiichi nuclear power plant.

The combination of the four factors creates major problems. The previous strategies and plans do not apply, the challenge is unfamiliar, and there is a flood of new information to process and analyze. Thus, the firm is in danger of information overload. The surprise element and the prospect of a major loss, usually widely perceived throughout the organization, create a danger of widespread panic. Perhaps most importantly, decentralization initiatives, which normally can expedite response, become ineffective and even potentially dangerous in a strategic surprise. Lacking a coherent strategy of response, local managers are likely to move the firm 'in all directions at the same time' and create havoc. Finally, preoccupation with morale and the surprise is likely to divert attention from the continuing operations of producing, selling, and distributing.

If the firm expects its environmental turbulence to be around level five, it needs to invest in yet another system, a *strategic surprise system.* The characteristics of such a system, which are illustrated in Table 3.3, are the following:

1. When strategic surprise arrives, an *emergency communication network* goes into effect. The network crosses normal organizational boundaries and rapidly communicates with the entire organization.

Table 3.3 Emergency response to strategic surprise

Problem	Response	Contingent response system
Perceived by entire organization	1	1. Emergency communication network
Danger of panic	2, 6	2. Information evaluation and assignement center
Information overload	2	3. Top management division of responsibility
Disruption of priorities	3	Contol and maintenance of morale
Simulataneous need to	3	Response to surprise
Reassure organization		Business as usual
Keep business going		4. Strategic task force network(s)
Develop straegic response		a. Leader selection and training
Contingent plans do not apply	4	b. Star communication network
Existing strategy does not apply	4	c. Centrally coordinated strategy
Structure and systems do not apply	4	d. Decentralized implementation
Decentralized response leads to havoc	4	5. Novel problem-solving capability
Severe time pressures	4c	Creativity
Experience does not apply	4d	Analytical skills
	5, 6	Team work
		6. Exercise networks under non-crisis conditions

2. Within the network information, *evaluation and assignment center* is established. This center evaluates the incoming information and passes it to parts of the network that are responsible for responding to it.
3. For the duration of the emergency, the *responsibilities of top management are repartitioned:*

   a. One group devotes its attention to control and maintenance of organizational morale.
   b. Another group assures continuance of 'business as usual' with a minimum of disruptions.
   c. A third group takes charge of response to the surprise.

4. For dealing with the surprises a *strategic taskforce network* is activated:

   a. Leaders and taskforce members cross normal organizational lines and constitute strategic action (not just planning) units.
   b. The communication is of the 'star shape' directly between the taskforces and the central to management group.
   c. The top management group formulates the overall strategy, assigns implementation responsibilities, and coordinates the implementation.

   d. The decentralized taskforces implement their components of the new strategy.

   e. Several networks may be designed in advance; one to deal with surprises in the marketplace, another with technological surprises, a third for political surprises, etc.

5. The taskforce and communication network members are *trained* in prompt response to novel problems that combine creativity, analytic techniques, and teamwork.

6. The networks are *exercised under non-crisis conditions* in addressing real strategic issues, as if they were surprises.

The cross-connecting lines in Table 3.3 show how the respective characteristics of the surprise management system respond to the problems and challenges posed by a strategic surprise.

Few firms, if any, seem to have developed and committed themselves to a formal surprise management system. The features incorporated in the system presented here are derived from a study of military surprises as well as histories of response to surprises that have struck business firms. Thus, the current system is only a proposal for handling surprises, and a prediction that firms on the turbulence level 5 will begin to adopt the surprise management systems, similar to the one described above.

Choosing the Management System for a Firm

A complication arises in diversified firms that do business in environments on different levels of turbulence. In such firms, *each environment must be diagnosed separately*. If the expected turbulence levels in the respective environments are different, the management needs to reconcile the consequent need for different systems.

Historically, firms solved this problem by using a system that was appropriate for the historical 'core' business of the firm. In recent years, however, some firms began to use different systems for different business areas.

The preceding discussion has shown that there are two types of systems that enable management to respond effectively to their environment(s): positioning and real-time systems.

At levels of turbulence 1–3, the positioning systems are adequate to assure an effective and timely response. At levels above 3, it becomes necessary to supplement the positioning system with a real-time system.

To identify the combination of systems that will be needed by the firm:

1. Use Table 6.1 to diagnose the future turbulence.
2. Use Table 3.1 to select the system(s) that will be needed by the firm.

Note Asterisked sections present technical procedures. A reader interested in the basic concepts and relationships may prefer to skip these sections.

Managing Complexity

As environments became ever more complex and unpredictable, progressive firms developed more subtle, complex, and rapid systems. At the same time, managers in many other firms, as well as some academics, proposed the opposite solution: reduction of complexity, 'keeping it simple,' reduction of LRP horizons, abandoning planning in favor of reliance on intuition and experience (Mintzberg 1976-C).[1]

Both approaches deserve attention. To support the builders of complex responses, we can paraphrase a basic theorem from the science of cybernetics proposed by an Englishman, Roy Ashby. Restated in business terminology, his *requisite variety* theory states that for a successful response to the environment; the complexity and speed of the firm's response must match the complexity and the speed of the environmental challenges. This is the theory that gave rise to the strategic success paradigm (see Chapter 6). The firm will not succeed either through simplistic or overelaborate responses. Thus, it is necessary that management build progressively complex systems in order to deal with progressively more complex environments.

To support the proponents of simplicity, we refer to the concept of *bounded rationality* advanced many years ago by American Nobel Prize winner, Herbert Simon. From his research in managerial behavior, Simon found that individuals, as well as organizations, couldn't handle problems when they pass a certain level of complexity. When this level is passed, managers can no longer understand what is going on in the environment nor manage rationally the firm's strategies.

There is much evidence today that the complexity of society has passed the understanding of those who are responsible for guiding it and the size

---

[1]Capital letters indicate in which part of the bibliography the cited reference may be found.

and complexity of some firms are already beyond the comprehension of their managers.

How to reconcile the conflict between the need for increased complexity, dictated by requisite variety, and the need for simplicity dictated by bounded rationality? On both the level of the firm and of the society, the answer appears to lie in reduction of complexity. It does not lie in using simplistic responses to complex challenges.

Thus, if management is reluctant to increase the complexity of the firm's systems to a level necessary to make them responsive to the environment, it should simplify the strategic position of the firm by exiting from turbulent business areas. Our research finding shows that failure to do so is an invitation to bankruptcy.

Summary

During the twentieth century, progressively increasing turbulence of the environment has led firms to invent progressively more complex and elaborate systems. Two different types of systems have evolved: *positioning* systems (LRP, strategic planning, strategic position management) which directs the firm's thrust in the environment; and *real-time systems* (strong signal issue management, weak signal issue management, surprise management) which respond one at a time to rapid and unpredicted environmental developments.

The choice of the system combination for a particular firm depends on the turbulence characteristics of the environments in which it participates and expects to enter. The choice of systems appropriate to the firm will be discussed in detail in Chapters 8, 19, and 20.

Exercise

1. Identify what you feel will be the turbulence-causing factors during the next five to seven years in the following industries: automotive, computer, food retailing, banking, healthcare, medical, and any other industries with which you are familiar. Be sure to include significant factors that are specific to an industry.

4

From Strategic Planning
to Strategic Management

Our previous discussion of the evolution of management systems easily gives the impression of a logical untroubled progression from one system to another. In fact, the progression was slow, turbulent, and accompanied by setbacks, whenever the new system disturbed what Machiavelli described as the 'historical order of things' within the firm. The evolution of first strategic planning and then the evolution of strategic management described in this chapter are examples of such disturbances.

Doubts About Strategic Planning

The history of management systems is a succession of inventions. As new challenges arose, progressive firms invented and tried new ways of managing. Some of the new systems failed, some succeeded, and other firms imitated successful systems. Out of such pragmatic trial and error processes grew the body of systems that we described in Chapter 3. As is typical of inventions, they were like a medicine man's potions, treating symptoms rather than the underlying causes. If the treatment worked, it was used until new symptoms appeared. If it did not work, the treatment was discredited and the search started again.

As discussed in Chapter 3, *long range planning* was the firm's response to the pressures of rapid growth, size, and complexity. In the 1950s, this configuration of factors reached a point where it was no longer possible to rely on budgeting for preparing the firm for its future competitive challenges and

© The Author(s) 2019
H. I. Ansoff et al., *Implanting Strategic Management*,
https://doi.org/10.1007/978-3-319-99599-1_4

expansion needs. Long range planning was the answer that quickly proved itself to be useful, and was accepted by most large firms and a substantial number of medium-sized ones.

Strategic planning, which was invented in the 1960s, less than ten years after long range planning, had a very different history. It will be recalled that the stimulus was saturation and decline of growth in a number of firms. At the time, reasons for the saturation/decline were poorly understood. But it was clear that it was both undesirable and dangerous to plan the firm's future on the basis of extrapolation of past trends, as is done in long range planning.

As the reader will see, strategic planning is a multifaceted, complex, and time-consuming process, much more so than long range planning. But it was just another in a series of inventions which, while superficially logical, offered no proof that the substantial investment of the firm's energy which it required would prove worthwhile.

Early results were discouraging. Usually imposed on the firm by an enthusiastic chief executive, strategic planning was poorly understood by the involved managers, perceived as 'another form-filling exercise' for the sole benefit of the corporate office. New strategies were slow to produce results; the new strategic investments turned out to be larger than anticipated. Strategic planning encountered resistance from the affected managers who tried to avoid and to sabotage it. When the enthusiasm of the chief executive manager waned, and he turned his attention to other matters, the sabotage frequently succeeded to the point of causing a regression to a previous (budgeting or long-range planning) system.

Does Planning Pay?

Among the many criticisms of strategic planning, the fundamental one was that it was a poor invention and that, even if well installed and used by the firm, it does not produce any improvement in the firm's performance. Critics who advanced this view argued that when the environment was extrapolated, long range planning produced no harm and might even do some good. But, when the environment turned turbulent, firms were advised to avoid formal planning and make their decisions 'organically' on the basis of managerial intuition and experience (Mintzberg 1973-C).

Proponents of strategic planning refused to accept this view and some of them turned to research in an effort to prove that properly installed strategic planning can more than pay for itself in terms of better performance.

One of the earliest research studies asked the question whether strategically planned mergers and acquisitions produced better results than ad hoc acquisitions based on intuitions and experience. The findings of this study are summarized in the next two sections (Ansoff et al. 1970-C).

Design of the Study

The study was designed to investigate the relationship between performance and the growth methods used by large US manufacturing firms during the twenty-year period 1947–1966. The study focused on firms that used acquisitions as a primary vehicle for growth. The first part of the study examined *behavioral characteristics* of acquisitions including planning, search, evaluation, and integration processes used by the different firms. These characteristics were investigated by means of an extensive questionnaire.

The behavioral characteristics were nest related to performance based on financial data furnished by the S&P Compustat tapes. The questionnaire and the financial performance analyses were structured to permit comparison of the pre-acquisition and post-acquisition performance. That is, the performances of firms before they entered a merger were compared to the post-acquisition performance. *Then, a correlation was made of the typical patterns of acquisition behavior with the changes in performance.*

The questionnaire was divided into two sections: The first part sought subjective descriptions of the acquisition activity, and the second requested objective information from company records. It was requested that the first part be completed by someone who was directly involved in the acquisition program, and the second part to be completed by a staff analyst.

Ninety-three responses were received from a mailing of 412 questionnaires, a response rate of 22.6%. These 93 firms had acquired 299 other firms during the acquisition programs under investigation. However, over 66% of the acquiring firms made only one or two acquisitions.

The questionnaire was designed to explore two different types of acquisition planning behavior. The first type, *strategic planning*, determines whether and what types of acquisition the firm should seek. This includes an explicit statement of objectives and of the diversification strategy. The second type is *operational planning*. This includes establishing procedures for search, standards for evaluation of candidates, procedures for post-acquisition integration, and allocation of responsibilities and resources to the acquisition activity. The study measured performance differences on thirteen variables. These are shown in Fig. 4.1.

1.	Sales	8.	Debt to equity
2.	Earnings	9.	Common equity
3.	Earnings per share	10.	Earnings/total equity
4.	Total Assets	11.	Price/earnings ratio
5.	Earnings/equity	12.	Dividends/earnings
6.	Dividends per share	13.	Price/equity ratio
7.	Stock price		

Fig. 4.1   Performance variables

Results of the Study

The questionnaire singled out eight characteristics of managerial behavior during acquisition activity. Four of the characteristics described the process of systematically establishing plans, and four described the systematic execution of plans such as search for opportunities, evaluation, and integration of acquisitions into the parent firm.

The results of the questionnaire revealed that firms that planned their acquisitions also planned their execution. On the other hand, firms that made acquisitions opportunistically did little or no execution planning. Therefore, it was possible to subdivide the sample into two categories: *planners* and *non-planners*.

Analysis of financial performance of planners vs. non-planners along with thirteen measures in Fig. 4.1 shows that planners performed overwhelmingly better than non-planners. This is demonstrated in Table 4.1 that shows the ratios of post-acquisition to pre-acquisition performance for the two groups. In particular, the planners notably outperformed the non-planners on sales growth, earnings growth rate, earnings/share growth rate, and earnings/common equity growth rate.

The principle findings may be summarized as follows:

1. Firms take two distinct approaches to acquisition planning. The first is an *un-planned opportunistic approach* and the other a *systematic planned approach*. If a firm fails to plan any phase of the program, it is likely to forego planning altogether. If a firm does plan a phase, it is likely to plan all phases.
2. Firms that do plan tend to use these plans and to exhibit deliberate and systematic acquisition behavior.
3. On all relevant financial criteria, planners significantly outperformed the non-planners.
4. Not only did planners do better on the average, they performed more predictably than non-planners.

Table 4.1 Performance variables pre-/post-acquisitions

Performance variables	Planners $n=22$	Nonplanners $n=41$
Sales growth	2.64	−6.08
Earnings growth	17.51	0.05
Earnings/share growth	16.70	−1.24
Total assets/growth	−1	−2.55
Earnings/common equity growth	12.08	3.43
Payout ratio growth	5.21	−3.14
Total equity growth	−0.86	−5.5
Earnings/total capital growth	10.97	4.47
Stock price growth	−0.03	7.33
Debt/equity growth	−2.11	−0.33
Price earnings growth	−0.28	−0.98
Debt/equity growth	0	−0.06
Payout ratio	−0.04	0.06
Price/equity ratio	0.18	0.52
Total equity	23.49	31.52
Earnings/total equity	−0.01	−0.03

The Chandlerian Perspective

Since the original study, which is summarized above, several other research studies arrived at substantially the same conclusion, which is that the difficulty encountered by strategic planning was not due to the fact that it is a poor instrument. On the contrary, once strategic planning is installed in a firm, it can help produce significant improvements in performance. As a result, attention began to shift from the question of ultimate effectiveness to the transitional difficulties encountered by strategic planning: the resistance to planning, the implementation delays, the chronic profitability lags.

In early planning literature, the prescriptive offered for overcoming the resistance was to secure enthusiastic support of top management. However, cumulative experience showed that while top management enthusiasm was essential for starting strategic planning, this enthusiasm was no reflected in the behavior of the affected managers. For all of the enthusiasm of Mr. McNamara, and Presidents Kennedy and Johnson, the generals and admirals in the Defense Department stubbornly continued to resist PPBS, making sure that PPBS was effectively rolled back to the antecedent politically based budgeting system once Mr. McNamara left the secretary's chair.

Thus, it became increasingly evident that top management support is a necessary but not sufficient condition of assuring the effectiveness of strategic planning within a firm. Fortunately, a basic insight into the other necessary conditions was provided by the seminal work of Alfred D. Chandler, Jr., an American business historian (Chandler 1962-F).

Professor Chandler focused his research on the first half of the twentieth century and on the manner in which firms responded to major discontinuities in their environments. As he studied in meticulous detail four very different, successful American firms, he began to perceive a very similar pattern in their responses. An extension of the study, in less detail, to another forty firms showed the same pattern. Later, other researchers replicated Chandler's findings in studies of European firms.

Although during Chandler's period of interest strategic planning did not yet exist, the typical response found in his studies sheds important light on the problems encountered by strategic planning.

1. Firms resisted discontinuous environmental strategic change by refusing to recognize it until after the change made a significant impact on their performance.
2. When the need for a new strategic response was finally recognized, the development of a new strategy was slow, through trial and error, taking as long as ten years.
3. After the new strategy was installed, the expected profits were slow to materialize, in spite of strong competitive efforts in the marketplace.
4. Management eventually arrived at the conclusion that the chronic unprofitability problem was due, not to a bad strategy, but to the mismatch between the historical organizational structure and the new strategy of the firm. This triggered a major reorganization.
5. Some researchers who sought to duplicate Chandler's results focused their attention on the strategy–structure sequence, perhaps because of the somewhat misleading title of Chandler's book: *Strategy and Structure*. But the process of internal adaptation to the new strategy did not stop with the organizational structure.
6. The new structure induced dysfunctions and tensions within the firm. Managers lacked skills and knowledge needed for performing in the new roles defined by the structure; the historical information system no longer served the needs of the new roles; the historical reward system did not encourage the new risk-taking that was now expected from managers. This historical management system was ineffective in solving the problems posed by the new strategy.
7. These deficiencies were discovered and remedied, one at a time, over a period of years.
8. The period of organizational adaptation to the new strategy could take as long as ten years, in addition to the preceding period of the development of the new strategy.

The total duration of strategic and organizational adaptation took from ten to twenty years. Once the dual adaptation was complete, the four major firms in Chandler's sample remained leaders in their respective industries for a long time.

Four Stages of Evolution

Using Chandler's findings, we can now explain the difficulties encountered by strategic planning and also show how they can be resolved through a broader concept of strategic management.

The historical evolution of the firm's strategic response is illustrated in Fig. 4.2. The first line of the figure is the reactive Chandlerian sequence that we have just described. An environmental discontinuity ΔE was followed by adaptation of a strategy ΔS, which took some five to ten years, and then by adaptation of capability ΔC (usually with a change in structure), which took another five to ten years.

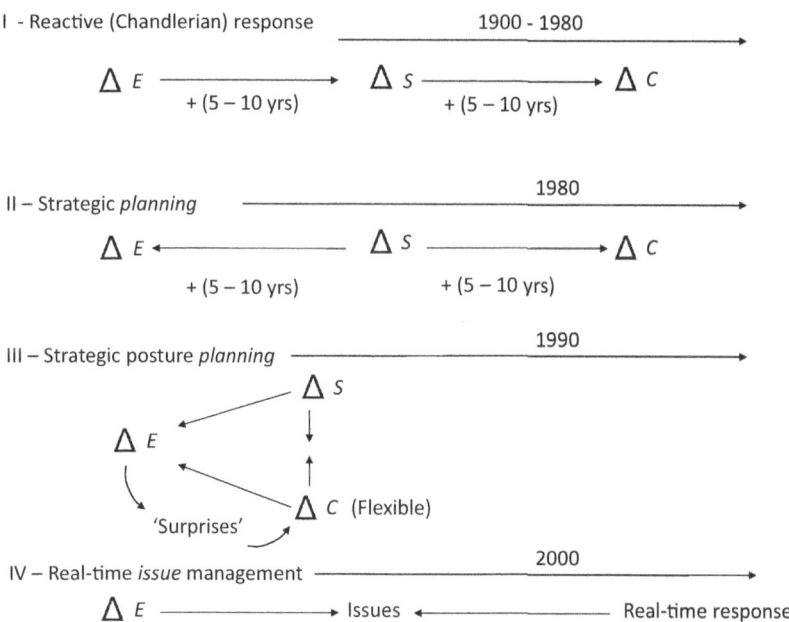

Fig. 4.2   Four stages of evolution

The companies studied by Chandler were among the most successful American firms: DuPont, General Motors, Sears, and Standard Oil of New Jersey. All of them emerged from the adaptation stronger than before and remained profitable for many years thereafter. Thus, it could be argued, together with some management researchers, that the reactive unguided Chandlerian process is the best way to adapt the firm to environmental discontinuities.

The counterargument is that Chandlerian adaptation, which was fast enough for the early days of the twentieth century, is too slow for the present. The frequency and speed of discontinuities both increased to a point where reactive, organic adaptation is now likely to leave the firm at least one adaptation cycle behind the external reality, somewhat like a dog trying to catch its tail.

'Smart' business firms perceived this difficulty in the 1960s and invented strategic planning which anticipates the environmental threats/opportunities and puts in place a responsive strategy in advance of their arrival. Thus, it can be said that strategic planning reversed the first Chandlerian gap (between environment and strategy) from reaction to anticipation.

However, strategic planning failed to address the problem of the second gap: between strategy and capability. It will be recalled that the original strategic planning approach was based on the assumption that new strategies should take advantage of the historical strengths and should avoid historical weaknesses of the firm. Thus, it was assumed that the historical capability could remain the same while strategy changed. This was not an unreasonable assumption in the early days of strategic planning, when the focus was on diversification by acquisition, because the new merger partners brought with them the capabilities needed for the new strategy. But even then, the problem of incompatibility between the management capabilities of the parent company and the subsidiary began to be recognized as a potential depressor of profitability of the firm (Ansoff 1988-B).

As the environment became progressively more turbulent and differentiated, reliance on historical strengths became further questionable for two reasons:

1. Some firms were unable to find diversification opportunities that made use of the firm's historical strengths.
2. Even more importantly, changing turbulence in the firm's historical business often turned its historical strengths into weaknesses.

Whenever the environment change was discontinuous (e.g., a replacement of the historical technology by a new and drastically different one, such as the evolution of the cell phone from its nascent beginnings in 1973 to the discontinuous development of the smartphone in 1992 when IBM introduced the Simon Personal Communicator).

In such cases, if strategic planning was used to determine a new strategy, as shown in the second time line of Fig. 4.2, the time gained through the planning of strategy was lost in the Chandlerian reactive adaptation of the capability, accompanied by resistance, delays, and chronic unprofitability of the new strategy. (It is of interest that the five-to-ten-year capability lag, found by Chandler early in the twentieth century, corresponds closely to the five-to-seven-year time delay that was found in the second half to the twentieth century, necessary to implant strategic planning into the firm.)

As previously discussed, until the 1970s, the successive management systems were invented within firms in response to pressing but poorly understood challenges. Consultants and academics had little to contribute to these inventions because the appropriate theoretical insights were lacking.

Since 1970, the post-strategic planning developments began to be influenced by the new understanding of strategic phenomena contributed by Chandler and other researchers, as well as by problem-solving technologies developed by leading management consulting companies.

This work led to the concept of strategic management, described in Chapter 1 and illustrated in line III of Fig. 4.2, which was a direct outgrowth of important theoretical contributions made by Herbert Simon and other researchers in organizational behavior. The first international conference on strategic management was held in 1973 in Nashville, Tennessee, with sponsorship from IBM and the General Electric Company. The first book on strategic management (Ansoff et al. 1976-F) was the outcome of this conference. A wide interest within academia in strategy formulation (particularly the work of Henry Mintzberg) and in the strategy–structure relationship began to offer new insights into the nature of strategic behavior and suggestions for improving its effectiveness.

Thus, the reversal of the second Chandlerian gap shown in line III of Fig. 4.2 can be said to come as much from new theoretical insights as from practical inventions within the firms.

Lines III and IV of the figure show two complementary forms of strategic management: strategic posture planning, which is a logical extension of strategic planning, and real-time issue management, developed in the late 1970s, which permits the firms to respond to surprising changes that are too fast to be captured by periodic strategic positioning exercises. In the rest of this chapter, we focus on strategic posture management. In Part IV, we shall deal with real-time strategic responses.

Theoretical Underpinnings of Strategic Posture Management

As line III of Fig. 4.2 shows, strategic posture management concerns itself simultaneously with both the strategy and the capability needs of the firm. Forecasts are made not only of future threats and opportunities, but also of the kind of capabilities that will be essential for success in the future environment.

As shown, the new capability is designed to support the future strategy. But, in turbulent environments, additional flexibility can be built into the new capability to provide an effective and timely response to surpriseful events.

The concepts of strategic management presented in this book are built upon a coherent and empirically supported theoretical foundation. This foundation was developed by Ansoff (1979d-F) who has expanded Chandler's findings into general theoretical propositions about strategic behavior of organizations. The key dimensions of the theory are the following:

The theory covers so-called environmental serving organizations (ESOs), including firms and nonprofit institutions. No generalizations are made about behavior of the ESOs as a class. The theory is contingent in the sense that it relates internal characteristics of ESOs to their external behavior on the one hand and success or failure or different behaviors to the levels of external turbulence on the other.

Propositions are developed that explain differences in strategic behavior between profit-seeking firms and nonprofit institutions.

Strategic behavior is explained in terms of three interacting rationalities: economic, behavioral, and political.

- The process of ESOs' response to discontinuities is explained in terms of interaction between the vital moving force, the general management, and internal resistance force of the organization.
- Managers are not idealized. A variety of behaviors by managers is described, ranging from change-generating to inert.
- The timeliness of response to external challenges is explained in terms of the environment, strategy, capabilities (ESCs) perceptions of the environment (myopic or foresight).
- The outcome (success or failure) of strategic response to discontinuous changes is explained by the ultimate match or mismatch of three variables: the level of environmental turbulence, the aggressiveness of the ESOs' strategy, and the responsiveness to change in the ESOs' internal capability.

- Scales of turbulence, aggressiveness, and responsiveness are developed which permit the ESO to determine the degree of match or mismatch.

In this book, we translate the theoretical propositions into practical tools for managing the firm's adaptation to discontinuities. These tools are based on the strategic success theorem that has been proven by empirical research.

I.   **For optimum potential profitability, the aggressiveness of the firm's strategy must match the turbulence of the environment.** By aggressiveness we mean the degree of discontinuity that the firm introduces into succeeding generations of its products, technologies, marketing concepts.

II.   **To assure optimal realization of the profitability potential, the responsiveness of the firm's general management capability must match the aggressiveness of its strategy.** By responsiveness we mean the degree of discontinuity in environmental changes that management is prepared to perceive, accept, and is capable of processing.

III.   **To assure optimal effectiveness of the new capability, the components of the capability must be supportive of one another.** By components we mean skills and mentality of managers, culture of the firm, its power structure, its information system, and structure.

IV.   **The resistance to strategy–capability change is proportional to the difference between the historical and the new capability profiles.**

V.   **To assure an optimal transition to the new strategy capability, the process should be managed in a way that anticipates, minimizes, and controls resistance.**

VI.   If a change in strategic aggressiveness of behavior is not accompanied by the appropriate capability change, there will be a tendency to reject and reverse the change. **The strength of this tendency will be proportional to the difference between the historical culture and power structure and the culture/power structure needed to support the new strategy.**

VII.   **To assure stable behavior under the new strategy, the capability components should be aligned with one another and with the firm's new strategy.**

Summary

Strategic planning, a logical, analytic process for choosing the firm's future position via-a-vis the environment, was invented by firms that sought to avert saturation of growth and technological obsolescence.

Unlike its predecessor, long-range planning, strategic planning is a much more complex and organization-disturbing process. On frequent early occasions, the introduction of strategic planning into the firm encountered resistance and failed to produce the desired improvements in the firm's performance.

This raised the question of whether strategic planning was useful, or whether organic adaptation, based on managerial intuition and experience, was not a better method for responding to strategic challenges.

A number of research studies showed that strategic planning, when properly installed and accepted by management, did produce superior improvements in performance.

Other research studies showed that resistance occurred when the firm made a discontinuous change in its strategy, and that the resistance was due to a mismatch between the new strategy and the historical management capability.

A new and research-proven approach called strategic management is now gaining acceptance in firms. It consists of two complementary management systems: strategic posture management and real-time issue management. Both of these will be discussed in detail in the remainder of the book.

Exercises

1. Having read this chapter, the director of planning in your firm reacts in the following manner: 'As I see it, this new label 'strategic management' simply means adding an implementation box to the strategic planning flowchart. We've always been implementing anyway, so I don't see what all this fuss is about.' He asks you to prepare a memorandum of two pages or less that will explain to him the differences between strategic planning and strategic management, and tell him why and when the latter should be used instead of the former. Prepare such a memorandum.

2. When change is slow and Chandlerian reactive trial and error adaptation will assure timely strategic adaptation, are there any reasons for replacing the trial and error process by a systematically planned process? If there are, prepare a list of the reasons.

5

Modes of Strategic Behavior

The following are different types of strategic behavior that are observed in practice today. In this section, we shall describe each and compare the conditions under which they are appropriate to the success of a firm.

Unmanaged Organic Adaptation

Sociologists and political scientists have studied organizations and firms as depersonalized homogeneous entities. As a result, their perception is that strategic change is unguided and unmanaged. Under certain conditions, changes are proposed by some part of the organization. Negotiations and political interactions occur, as a result of which the change is accepted or rejected. In the former case, implementation starts and proceeds, again unguided, by trial and error, to either a successful or unsuccessful conclusion.

Typically, the alternatives generated and accepted are incremental and logical extensions of historical dynamics. When the environment poses a discontinuous threat to the organization's survival, the response follows the reactive pattern which will be described in Chapter 18. The organization exhibits strategic myopia until the impact of discontinuity progresses to a point where it is perceived to threaten survival of the organization.

This perception triggers a crisis, and incremental adaptation is abandoned in favor of a frantic search for a discontinuous response which will assure survival. Typically, the first step is to replace the now discredited power structure and to bring in a savior from outside, who has an idea for rescuing the organization.

© The Author(s) 2019
H. I. Ansoff et al., *Implanting Strategic Management*,
https://doi.org/10.1007/978-3-319-99599-1_5

In Chapter 22, we will discuss how the organization closes ranks behind the savior until signs of recovery appear. At that point, pressures build up for a return to incremental unmanaged behavior.

The significance of the unmanaged adaptation has been variously interpreted by observers. Certainly, it is a behavior widely observable in nonprofits, particularly in bureaucracies. But observers have argued that it is not only a natural organic process but also a process which should not be tampered with, because it is the optimal way to adapt to change. It assures both learning and adaptation to environment in complex organizations; it is self-designing, similar to biological adaptation; and the final, strategic posture arrived at by unmanaged adaptation meets the needs of both the organization and its participants.

It has been further argued (Lindblom 1959-G) that in a complex environment, unmanaged adaptive learning is the only feasible method for changing complex organizations, because the organization lacks the intelligence to comprehend the world around it.

Students of the business firm agree that unmanaged adaptation is also observable in some firms. These are either firms with 'tired' management in which general management ceased managing, or large complex firms, described by Galbraith, in which management has become a captive of 'technocracy.' Such firms are typically mediocre performers and continue to survive only in environments which are noncompetitive. Intensification of competition, or environmental discontinuities, induces a crisis which follows a course very similar to the nonprofits.

No experienced management practitioner would prescribe such unmanaged behavior as an example to be imitated, and few security analysts would recommend to their clients that they invest money in an unmanaged firm. The reasons are simply that unmanaged firms are poor profit-makers and are prone to strategic surprises.

Systematic Planning

The planning profession, and scientists whose roots are in mathematics, recommend a behavior which is at the opposite extreme from the unmanaged. This is *planned behavior* in which management plays a vigorous and rational role by predetermining in a systematic manner the directions in which a firm will develop and then guides and controls the execution in accordance with the established plans.

The planners argue that unmanaged adaptation is inefficient, ineffective and that it became antiquated when managers have developed systematic planning procedures. Their view is that change must be managed and that management of change is, in fact, the *raison d'etre* of management.

According to the planner's view, whenever change is incremental and evolutionary, management of change should be delegated to the lower (divisional and functional) levels of management and corporate management should coordinate the functions.

In Chapter 16, a formal company-wide process called long range planning has been developed and used successfully in many firms, to guide decentralized incremental strategic adaptation.

For guiding and implementing discontinuous strategic change, practical planners have developed strategic planning in which guidance moves to the general management and corporate levels. But the process remains participative, involving all managers who have a responsibility for initiating and implementing change. Unlike LRP, early efforts to use strategic planning ran into serious difficulties.

This led proponents of unmanaged adaptation to argue that planning is artificial and unusable. In a classic article, Mintzberg (1976-C) joined Lindblom (1959-G) by arguing that, when environment is not complex or turbulent, planning will, at worst, do no harm; but, under high complexity/turbulence, planning no longer works, and managers must return to 'intuitive managing.'

As we will be discussing in this book, there is now both empirical and practical proof that an appropriate type of planning (not the LRP which Mintzberg apparently has in mind) does work, when it is properly installed in the firm. Furthermore, it substantially improves performance (see Chapter 7).

These results disprove Lindblom's assertion that firms are not sufficiently intelligent to comprehend and find their preferred paths in a complex environment.

But comprehensive organization-wide planning is costly and time-consuming. And comprehensive planning reactions become too slow when confronted with fast-maturing threats and opportunities. Therefore, there are numerous decision occasions in which comprehensive planning may be either ineffective or not worthwhile. These occasions are:

1. When the risk taken by foregoing planning is small, because the desirability and consequences of an action are clear and certain.
2. When the information necessary to formulate concrete plans is insufficient or unavailable (see Chapter 20).
3. When the cost of planning is so high that it is more cost-effective to take a direct plunge into action without the benefit of prior planning. It will

be review in Chapters 9 and 14 that this situation occurs in internationalization and diversification, when it is sometimes less expensive to try than to plan.

4. When the urgency is so high that there is no time to plan, this typically occurs during a crisis (see Chapter 2).

Under one or more of the above conditions, Mintzberg's advice to use 'plain managing' may indeed be the preferred course of action. We next explore what such managing means.

Ad hoc Management

As already mentioned, managers who let themselves be carried by the natural dynamics of the firm, or let themselves be manipulated by the firm's technocracy, can survive only in protected or noncompetitive environments. Managers who practice systematic strategic management are still few in number (see Chapter 7). Thus, the type of management behavior referred to by Mintzberg is the numerical majority. But, in literature on organizational behavior, this behavior, like the part of an iceberg below the water, had been hidden from view until a pioneering con tri but ion was made by Mintzberg (1973a-B) who studied how responsible managers manage when they do not use a formal planning system.

The behavior which we are about to discuss, and which, following the terminology of this book, is *ad hoc issue management* (or simply *ad hoc management*) falls between the unmanaged and the planned.

On the one hand, the manager does not let organic adaptation determine the strategic development of this firm. On the other hand, he does not provide comprehensive deliberate strategic guidance. Instead, he addresses strategic issues one at a time, as he perceives them himself, or as they are brought to his attention by his colleagues and subordinates. In Chapter 18, we will discuss how managers differ in the time frame within which they perceive issues. Some are reactive and delay response until after an issue has had a significant impact on the firm; others are decisive and confront issues when their impact is imminent.

A characteristic of ad hoc management, which makes it an important alternative to comprehensive planning, is its shorter reaction time. This does not mean that managers do not plan their responses. On the contrary, good managers consult experts, order studies of profitability, feasibility, and potential impact issues, and they convene problem-solving and decision-making groups. But, compared to the cumbersome company-wide planning, this process typically involves a small number of people, the time consumed in deliberation and decision making is short, and initiation of action is prompt.

As the preceding discussion indicates, ad hoc management is a cost-effective alternative to systematic planning, under the following conditions:

1. When issues develop slowly enough to permit a reactive or a decisive response (see Chapter 18).
2. When incidence of issues is infrequent enough so that a conflict of issue priorities does not arise.
3. When an issue is 'local' and does not affect other issues, or parts of the firm, other than the one in which the issue is being treated.
4. When the underlying evolutionary thrust of the firm's development will meet the objectives of the firm.

Whenever the first two conditions do not hold, the firm becomes an ineffective responder to the environment because of the lateness of response and issue overload. Under these conditions, systematic strategic issue management becomes necessary.

When conditions (3) and (4) do not hold, both ad hoc and systematic issue management become, at best, a means to help a firm to make corrections in its basic development thrust at a time when a revision of the thrust is necessary. At this point, comprehensive *strategic posture management* becomes necessary.

Choice of Strategic Behavior Mode

As the preceding discussion indicates, the unmanaged behavior has little interest for responsible managers. Among the managed behaviors, we have so far identified the following alternatives:

1. Ad hoc management which treats issues as they arise, one at a time.
2. Issue management which anticipates, assigns priorities, and systematically manages resolution of issue. It will be recalled that systematic issue management takes three forms:

   a. Strong signal issue management (Chapter 19).
   b. Weak signal issue management (Chapter 20).
   c. Strategic surprise management (Chapter 3).

3. Strategic posture management which provides comprehensive guidance to the firm's strategic development. This has three distinct forms:

    a. Long range planning (Chapters 3 and 16).
    b. Strategic posture planning (Chapter 3 and Part II).
    c. Strategic posture management (Chapter 3 and Part VI).

Thus, there are, in effect, at least seven distinct modes for managing the firm. As discussed in the preceding pages, each mode has its advantages and shortcomings, and each is optimal under different conditions. Further, as we shall see presently, the conditions frequently require a combination of two of the modes. This is illustrated in Table 5.1. The figure deals with three conditions: predictability of strategic challenges, their complexity, and their novelty. It will be recalled that *predictability* is a measure of the completeness and unambiguity of the information which is available to the firm by the time it must respond, if its response is to be on time. High predictability means that information is adequate to define and evaluate specific business alternatives. Low predictability means that information is partial, action alternatives are not yet clear, nor are their consequences (see Chapter 20).

    Complexity is a dual measure of the pervasiveness of the impact of a challenge on various parts of the firm, as well as the frequency of occurrence of challenges.

    Novelty is a measure of the extent to which knowledge gained from experience can be extrapolated to responses to new challenges.

Table 5.1 Modes of strategic development appropriate under different conditions of predictability/complexity/novelty

Predictability	Appropriate development nodes			
Low	Weak signal issue management	Quasistrategic planning: LRP + issue management	Strategic posture planning + issue management	Strategic learning[a]
Moderate	Strong signal issue management			Strategic posture management + issue management
High	Ad hoc management	Long range planning	Strategic posture planning	Strategic posture management
Complexity	Low	High	High/low	High/low
Novelty	Low/high	Low	Moderate	High

[a]Strategic learning = strategic posture management + issue management + gradual commitment + parallel planning/implementation

Table 5.1 shows that, when complexity is low and predictability is high, ad hoc management is the suitable approach for dealing with strategic challenges.

As predictability decreases (left-hand column), ad hoc management must be progressively replaced by strong signal issue management (Chapter 19) and weak signal issue management (Chapter 20), both of which anticipate the challenges, assign priorities, and manage them systematically.

As complexity and then novelty increase (bottom line), ad hoc management must be replaced, first by long range planning, then by strategic posture planning, and finally by strategic posture management.

As shown in the figure, other combinations of predictability/complexity/novelty make it necessary to use a combination of an issue management system and of a comprehensive planning approach. The manner in which they can be related within a firm is illustrated in Figs. 5.1 and 5.2.

The combination of LRP with issue management, shown in Fig. 5.1, is called *quasi-strategic planning*, because it is a half-way point between LRP and strategic planning. As is seen from the figure, the extrapolative LRP system, shown on the left, is left undisturbed. But a parallel issue management system permits the firm to make a strategic response to the episodic strategic issues. Thus, a quasi-strategic planning system does not change the basic course of strategic development of the firm, but its issue management provides an autopilot which helps maintain this course.

Figure 5.2 shows that strategic planning and issue management must be linked together in three ways. The first is through inclusion of issues of moderate urgency into the annual planning process (see Chapter 19).

The second is through combining the projects generated by the annual planning and by the issue management system within an overall project

Fig. 5.1   Quasi-strategic planning: LRP + issue management

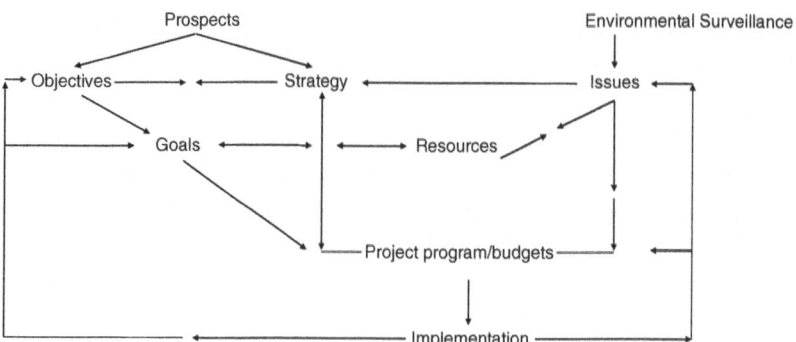

Fig. 5.2 Strategic planning and issue management

management system (see Chapter 25). A third important connection, not visible in the figure, is a need to set aside, during annual planning, a reserve strategic issue budget which can be applied to resolution of new issues as they surface in the course of the year (see Chapter 25).

Strategic Learning

The upper right-hand box of Table 5.1 represents a condition which requires a management approach which goes beyond a combination of issue and position management. The reason is that, when low predictability is coupled with high novelty and complexity, information is inadequate for formulation of strategies. This occurs when a clear description of future prospects in an SBA cannot be made, either because such description would require prohibitively costly market research, or because the SBA is in the early stages of emergence and information about its future prospects is still imperfect.

We have already encountered this condition on the following occasions (Chapter 12):

1. In developing and implementing the diversification strategy for the firm.
2. In developing pioneering products and technologies.
3. In diversifying a firm into poorly known foreign markets.
4. In dispersed SBA positioning.

On all of these occasions, a complex approach, which combines the planning and action in a novel way, becomes necessary. We shall refer to it as the *strategic learning mode*:

1. The usual single-step (go-no-go) strategic decision process should be replaced by a subtler *progressive commitment process* (see Chapter 13).
2. Each commitment decision should be designed to keep open as many options as possible, until a stage is passed at which the firm is prepared to make a firm commitment to the new strategic move (see Chapter 19).
3. Each commitment decision should be designed to maximize strategic learning which will contribute to the next commitment decision (see Chapter 12).
4. Implementation should be launched after each commitment decision and conducted in a way which will maximize strategic learning. Thus, as discussed in Chapter 25, planning and implementation cease to be sequential and become parallel processes.
5. At each step in the decision process, a 'to plan or to act' decision should be taken. This choice will depend on three factors:

   a. Which of the alternatives is most cost-effective for strategic learning?
   b. The urgency of response which may make it necessary to launch action without a preceding detailed planning exercise.
   c. The risk incurred in launching direct action. If the risk is small, direct action becomes preferable. Direct action does not mean that the decision analysis is dispensed with altogether, and a snap decision 'to go' is made by the 'seat of the pants.' But it does mean that a careful and time and money consuming decision analysis exercise is foregone in favor of a quick decision, made on the basis of the best readily available information.

It can be seen from the preceding discussion, and particularly from Table 5.1, that we arrive at a conclusion altogether different from Mintzberg's. Ad hoc managing is recommended when environment is on a low turbulence level. As turbulence increases, various ways of assisting managers to react promptly, systematically, and to master novelty and complexity of challenges becomes progressively necessary.

One explanation for the disagreement arises from the fact that Mintzberg does not make a clear differentiation between the various types of planning. Certainly, in the early days of planning when extrapolative long-range planning was the only alternative to ad hoc management, Mintzberg's advice was well given. In those days, when environment turned turbulent, it was better to revert to unassisted, unstructured but flexible managing than to assume (as is done in long range planning) that the future will be an extrapolation of the past.

A Map of Strategic Management

Figure 5.3 presents a global perspective on strategic management in the form of a logically connected tree of events which transpires subsequently to a major environmental challenge. The brackets adjacent to each branch contain references to the part of this book in which the relevant subject is discussed.

The appearance of a major threat or opportunity may at first be disregarded in some firms and eagerly anticipated in others. Thus, the triggering event, which starts the process of response, determines its timing. The *trigger* will depend on the environmental surveillance mechanism of the firm, on the techniques used for analysis and estimation of impact, on the mentality of key managers, and on the power structure within the firm. In this book, we have suggested that assuring change-receptive mentality/power structure is the key to assuring a timely trigger.

Beyond the trigger, strategic management branches, depending on whether it is managed or unmanaged.

In some firms, and most nonprofits, strategic change is not managed and occurs through organic adaptation. In most firms, combinations of different types of manager response are used.

In firms which do not have systematic planning analysis, the first step in the managed response is to act: Limited decision analysis is quickly followed by implementation. Firms with systematic planning may also choose to act, rather than to plan, when predictability is low and urgency is high.

Having chosen to forego decision planning, management may choose to continue with ad hoc implementation, or it may make a systematic choice of

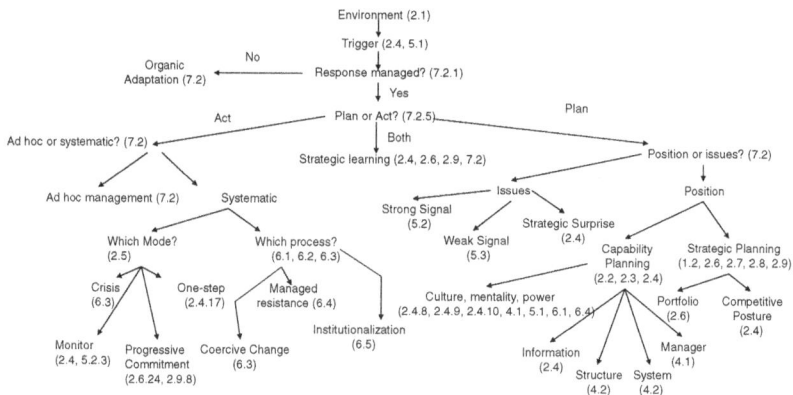

Fig. 5.3 Tree of strategic management

the action mode. In the latter case, urgency and predictability will determine the desirability of one of the four responses: crisis management, continued monitoring of the challenge, stepwise progressive commitment, or one-step decisive strategic response.

In the use of the systematic action mode, another important choice is made about the manner in which the change will be introduced into the firm. The choice is between rapidly forcing the change into *the* firm (coercion), managing resistance on a project by project basis, or institutionalizing within the firm a change-receptive culture, power structure, and competence. This choice is determined by the discontinuity of challenges, their frequency, and their urgency.

Returning to the 'plan or act' line, the prescription in the planning literature is to plan first. The validity of this prescription depends on the complexity, novelty, predictability, and the speed of the challenges.

If predictability is high enough to permit meaningful decision analysis, and if the challenges require a basic reorientation of the firm's strategic development, position planning is necessary. This is a comprehensive, firmwide process which consists of strategic planning and capability planning. The former is again in two parts: competitive posture planning for each of the firm's distinctive businesses and portfolio planning for the totality of the businesses. The capability planning assures that the components of general management are mutually consistent and supportive or the chosen strategy. These include culture/mentality, information, structure, systems, and the personality and qualifications of the general managers.

In addition to or in lieu of positioning planning, the firm may need to engage in issue management. This will be undertaken when challenges are frequent and fast developing. When the challenges are predictable, strong signal issue management will suffice. Response to challenges of low predictability should be handled by weak signal issue management. In environments in which some challenges are unpredictable, the firm should expect to be periodically surprised. In this case, a built-in crisis preparedness system becomes desirable.

It goes without saying that, having planned, the firm must act. Thus, there should be an arrow leading from all of the planning branches back to ad hoc or systematic action choice of the method to be used for implementation. The arrow is omitted for lack of space in the figure.

Returning to 'act or plan' at the top center of Fig. 5.2, in some cases, the answer is both. This occurs when urgency of response is high, predictability is low, complexity is pervasive, and novelty is high. The firm needs to reorient its strategic development, but the information and time are insufficient to prepare a complete position plan. As the figure shows, in this case response is the preferred strategic learning described in the preceding section.

The tree of strategic management presented in Fig. 5.3 can be used in three ways:

1. As a descriptive diagnostic tool to identify the approach to strategic management being used within a firm.
2. As a prescriptive design tool to select the approach needed by the firm in view of future environmental challenges.
3. To identify the strategic mode preferred by the firm's management.

Historical Development

The evolution of strategic management (SM) can be traced back to the contributions based on the seminal works of Andrews (1980), Ansoff (1965), Chandler (1962), Schendel and Hofer (1979), Miles and Snow (1978), Mintzberg (1979), Porter (1985), among others.

H. I. Ansoff (1979) defined strategic management as a process for managing a firm's relationship with its environment, composed of strategic planning, capability planning, and management of change. Chandler (1972) provided generalizations about growth and management of certain large industrial firms which he examined. He posited that the fundamental purpose of structure is to integrate all the different activities of the firm in order to meet market demands; structure was examined as the combination of organizational structure, systems, and planning.

J. K. Galbraith (1973), in reference to the American industry, noted that change has always occurred and will continue to occur as a result of the inapplicability of traditional economic models; hence, new developments were needed in order to respond to these changes. He furthermore maintained that firms face technological consequences which are brought about by technological innovations which impact the relationships between other organizations, customers, and the state.

Hatten (1982) defined strategic management as a process which '(1) determines and maintains a viable set of relationships between the organization and its environment, (2) systematizes the evaluation of organizational performance, (3) sets directions for the organization's long-term development, (4) uses major resource allocation programs to pursue the organization's objectives, matching capabilities with the opportunities and threats of the environment, (5) provides guidelines for any appropriate change in the organizational structure to implement further development, (6) gives diverse participants, from varied and sometimes contentious functional areas, a common experience and concepts on which to base discussions of future development, (7) explicitly matches strategies and situations in an active and administrative process, and (8) requires a systematic evaluation of the position of the organization in its environment (p. 102).'

It should be noted that various studies use strategic planning and strategic management interchangeably. For the sake of clarity, strategic planning is the analytical process whereas strategic management is the systems perspective defined by Ansoff as consisting of strategic planning, capability planning, and the management of change.

Ackoff (1974) proposed a philosophy of planning which focuses more on the objectives and logic of the planning process than on planning techniques. Strategic planning was distinguished from tactical planning, the former being long-range corporate planning that is ends-oriented but not exclusively so. Three philosophies of planning were analyzed: satisficing, optimizing, and adaptivizing. The latter adaptivizing signaled a new planning concept requiring scientific methods, tools, and techniques. Planning is divided into five 'parts,' including ends—specification of objectives and goals; means—selection of policies; programs; resources—determining needs, and how they can be attained and allocated; implementation; or detecting and correcting failures in the plan.

D. Channon (1973) focused on the sequence of strategy, and structure in order to achieve normative performance. His study was based on the pioneering work by Chandler (1962). Based on a survey on British enterprises, Channon wrote that the adoption of new strategy, caused by changes in the environment, resulted in a dramatic change in the administrative structure of large corporate enterprise. The reorganization of the enterprises into various divisions provided the administrative mechanism to control, consolidate, and institutionalize the new strategy (Channon 1973: 238).

Thorelli (1977) discussed the issues of strategy, structure and performance. He made the distinction between the internal and external environment of the firm. He talked about performance but did not mention how the performance is affected when changes occurred in strategy and structure and furthermore mentioned bargaining power/'politics' in achieving the goals of the firm.

E. H. Schein (1980) emphasized 'organizational effectiveness.' He stressed that 'good communication, flexibility, creativity, and genuine psychological commitment,' are the background for effectively organizing the firm, and coping with environmental changes.

Ackoff (1981) emphasized four basic traits in strategic planning:

1. Reactive: typifies those who avoid change, respect history, as well as preserve tradition.
2. Inactive: typifies those who have stability and survival as their objectives. Their response to crises is delayed until their objectives are threatened. They want things to be like in the past.
3. Proactive: typifies those who anticipate the future, are willing to minimize the impact of predicted threats, and take advantage of predicted future opportunities. They are change seekers who like to detach from the past.
4. Interactive: typifies those who bring about the future, learn new developments, adapt to sudden changes. They are highly capable of responding to high levels of environmental turbulence.

H. I. Ansoff (1965, 1979, 1984) analyzed the relationship of capability, strategy, environment, and performance and presented theoretical propositions; whereby for different types of environments, different solutions are applied. Various studies have attempted to examine the relationships between strategic planning and performance. Two groups have emerged as a result of their findings:

1. Strategic planning does contribute to a better performance (Ansoff et al. 1970; Burt 1978; Herold 1972; Kager and Malik 1975; Rue and Fulmer 1973; Rhyne 1986; Wood and LaForge 1979; and others).
2. Strategic planning does not contribute to better performance (Kudla 1980; Leontiades and Tezel 1980; and others).

Five weaknesses were pointed out by Greenly (1986) regarding studies concerning strategic planning and performance as follows:

1. Not identifying other variables associated with the implied relationships.
2. Subjectivity in paradigmic conceptualization.
3. Personal and methodological bias.
4. Uncommon parameters of assessments were evident.
5. Statistical significance of results varied and was not reported in some cases.

Day (1983) suggested that institutions have employed various strategy analysis instruments. Furthermore, he noted that a skillful combination of the various theories and models would aid in clarifying even the most complex strategy. In 'the stages of planning,' he classified strategy analysis in four steps. The first step is situation assessment, whereby business definition, current position, assumptions, and issues represent the variables to be examined. The second step is strategy generation evaluation, which is composed of alternatives ("directional indicators"), objectives, and the allocation of resources. The third step is the implementation of the generated strategy—programs, budgets, and timetables. The final step is the monitoring of the above.

Environment

Modern firms and organizations operate in a highly competitive and dynamic environment. Additionally, the traditional role of the firm is being challenged by society which places many conflicting demands on organizations. As such, the environment could thus be classified as being very turbulent. The fundamental ability of top management's accurate anticipation or perception of future turbulence would enhance the firm's ability to survive in such turbulent environments.

R. M. Steers (1977) asserted that the capability of an organization to adapt to its environment is facilitated to a great extent by its ability to know what the external environment is going to be like in the future. Aguilar (1967) identified the environment as an important variable for a firm's survival. Adapting to the environment is the core of survival. He divided the environment into four elements: social, economic, political, and technological. Stodgill (1966) asserted that the survival of an organization is based on the relationships it maintains with its external environment in which it exists. The organization must be capable of coping with environmental discontinuity by providing the mechanisms to identify and evaluate the present and trend of environmental change in relation to its internal condition.

Duncan (1972) defined the environment of a firm as being physical as well as social. These two elements are directly considered when decision making arises in the firm, according to Duncan. Furthermore, he maintained that the environment is divided into internal and external components. The internal is composed of social and physical elements inside the firm, while the external is composed of the same two elements outside the firm. In conclusion, he emphasized the importance of environment when decisions are made. Furthermore, he maintained that as the turbulence of the environment increases, the level of uncertainty increases, and as the environmental turbulence decreases, the level of uncertainty decreases likewise.

Jurkovitch (1974) suggested that the rate of change of the environment can be defined by measuring the amount of changes and alternatives to major goals in a given period. He found that the higher the change rate of the environment, the higher the number of major organizational goals that must be altered and vice versa.

Miles et al. (1974: 263) addressed the extent to which the environment shapes the organization. In their article on organizational environment, they maintained that 'we have no doubts that organizations must, and do adjust their strategies, technologies, structures, and processes to meet changing environmental demands.' Furthermore, they added that managerial perceptions of the environment are a key variable in deciding how to adjust to the environment.

Smart and Vertinsky (1984) asserted that modern organizations exist in turbulent environments which cause survival and growth threats. The relationship between strategy and environment was examined. Based on their findings, they emphasized that perception of the environment, and the cost to respond, are critical elements of success. Javidan (1984) examined the relationship between strategic planning and environmental perception. The result of the study implied that perception of the environment is a strong moderator for responding to the environment.

Cyrt and March (1963) found that organizations learn to adapt their behavior over time by changing their goals, refocusing their attention, revising procedures for search, as well as learning what to strive for in the environment whereas Miller (1969) asserted that systems are generally kept in tune with their environments by a process of mutual inputs and outputs, which helps to prevent inconsistencies in the environment from destroying the systems either by a collapse or explosion.

Eisenstadt (1969) asserted that the internal structure and the relationship a firm maintains with the environment in which it operates are affected by the firm's major goals, the place of the goals in the social structure as well as the type of dependence of the firm on external forces. Sullivan (1987) tested the environmental dependence hypothesis of Ansoff (1979) in his study on not-for-profit government agencies. He found that a reduction in subsidy dependence was accompanied by increase in efficiency and better market response.

Mitiku (1992) conducted her research in Ethiopia and studied the relationship between strategic behavior and the performance of 54 state-owned industrial NFP enterprises, with most of their environmental dependence generated through transactional income. She concluded that the performance of enterprises that had better alignment between the environmental turbulence, strategy, and capability was better than those of worse alignment.

Moussetis (1996) examined the alignment between firm's societal strategy and capability with turbulence of the regulatory environment of 133 for profit companies of the Fortune 500 corporate headquarters in Washington, DC. Moussetis confirmed that optimal performance occurred when the three variables of the Strategic Success Hypothesis aligned the turbulence level of the regulatory environment, the societal strategy, and capability.

Strategy

Ansoff (1984) defined the response of an organization or Environment serving Organization (ESO) to the environment as strategic thrust. Strategic thrust is composed of two elements, namely marketing strategy and innovation strategy.

Andrews (1980) defined strategy as the 'pattern of major objectives, purposes, or goals and essential policies and plans for achieving those goals, stated in such a way as to define what business a company is in or is to be and the kind of company it is or is to be.' The general manager's task is viewed in terms of four functions: supervising current operations, planning future operations, coordinating the functions and human capabilities of the organization, and making a distinctive personal contribution. Coordination of these functions is the primary job of the general manager: supervising the process for formulating, refining, and realizing the organization's strategy.

Argenti (1974: 121) described the philosophy and the technology of planning. He defined corporate planning as 'a systemic approach to clarify corporate objectives, make strategic decisions and check the progress of those decisions.' He maintained that the key distinction between strategic planning and other planning is the corporate nature of strategic planning.

Rothschild (1976: 125) approached strategic management from an investment standpoint. Strategy was defined as 'a statement of an organization's investment priorities, the management thrust, and the ways that it will use its strengths and correct its limitations to pursue the opportunities and avoid threats facing it.' Strategy is made up of three different levels: investment decisions, resources decisions, and a specific set of programs describing how resources will be employed to build on strengths and correct limitations.

Smith (1977: 65) defined strategy as 'the plan for getting the best returns from resources, the selection of the kind of business to engage in, and the scheme for obtaining a favorable position in the business field.' Strategy encompasses three areas:

1. Perspective strategy: the investigation of the nature of the market, industry, and environmental structures and the development of informational tools.
2. Optimizing strategy: the process of fitting the organizational programs into the industry structure and the way in which the resources can be utilized to maximum benefit.
3. Prospective strategy: a means for dealing with change either expected or unexpected and a plan for adjusting to new environmental developments. Guidelines were provided in order to minimize potential errors in strategy formulation.

Gluck et al. (1980: 154–161) postulated that the best firms are those which plan their future formally and explicitly. They stressed that their 'findings indicate that formal strategic planning does indeed evolve along similar lines in different companies.' Furthermore, extrapolations of past trends, and attempting to predict future political, economic, and social events, would be of great importance in order to provide the most appropriate strategy for the future.

Jauch et al. (1980) conducted an examination of the short-term success of 358 large business firms over a 45-year period. Their findings suggested that short-term success occurs when environment and strategic change are linked in the organization.

Miller and Friesen (1983: 221–235) investigated the strategy and environment relationship among two distinct samples. They emphasized that an increase in environmental change should be positively correlated with the strategy. Furthermore, their findings implied that positive correlations between strategy and environment are stronger in successful firms. In summation, they said that 'a third link, that between strategy and environment, must also be carefully managed.'

Capability

Capability is composed of four diagnostic elements: (1) managers, (2) climate, (3) competence, and (4) capacity (Ansoff 1979, 1984). The ability of an organization to sustain a certain level of strategic thrust is its general management capability.

Researchers express the concept of capability as being the organizational structure of a company. Structure is just one of the many elements of capability. Ansoff (1979: 79) incorporated structure as an attribute of 'general management competence,' which is a part of capability. He furthermore provided a conceptual framework for the integration of environment, strategy, and capability and their relation with performance.

Hatziatoniou (1986) examined the strategic posture of 59 firms in the USA engaged in different strategic business areas. The study found that optimum financial performance occurs when the environment, strategy, capability gap is smallest. Firms which had no gap were significantly different, in terms of their financial performance, from firms which had a gap, and they performed better than those with a gap.

Salameh (1987) examined the strategic posture and the financial performance of the banking industry in the United Arab Emirates. The study found that optimum overall financial performance occurred when levels of environmental turbulence, aggressiveness of strategy, and openness of capability matched each other. Furthermore, banks which were not strategically myopic outperformed banks which were strategically myopic.

Chabane (1987) studied restructuring and performance in Algerian state-owned enterprises. He found that the organizations that had aggressiveness of strategy and capability that were aligned with the prevailing level of turbulence performed better than those that were misaligned. Sullivan (1987) studied the relationship between proportion of income derived from subsidy and strategic performance. He found that the concepts and constructs of strategic management can be applied to public not-for-profit organizations and are meaningful in terms of their dependence on transaction or subsidy income. Numerous studies have tested H. I. Ansoff's strategic success hypothesis in numerous settings as follows:

1. Different industries.
2. Government Enterprises.
3. Not-for-profit organizations.

All the studies provided strong empirical support for the strategic success hypothesis of Ansoff. While the vast majority of the research cited above has been conducted in the private sector, certain concepts may be particularly relevant to not-for-profit organizations.

Another contribution to the field of strategic management is the resource dependency theory introduced by Pfeffer and Salancik (1978) is generally classified as belonging to the descriptive stakeholder school. Resource dependency theory provides a framework for determining the relative importance of the primary stakeholder groups of an organization given that management will attend to the needs of the key actors and will pay little attention to those stakeholder groups who do not have control over the critical resources.

Berman, Wicks et al. (1999: 491), suggested that '*attention to stakeholders' interests is necessary because it is the stakeholders that control resources that can facilitate or enhance the implementation of corporate decisions*'. Consequently, stakeholder groups tend to utilize their resource relationship with an organization to leverage their demands, and organizations likewise tend to pay attention to the demands of stakeholders who have control over critical resources.

The resource dependency theory is founded on managerial decisions being based on resource acquisition for the organization (Pfeffer and Salancik 1978). Pfeffer (1982) explicated this view as such; '*resource dependence theory suggests that organizational behavior theory becomes externally influenced because the focal organization must attend to the demands of those in the environment that provide resources necessary and important for its continued survival*' (p. 103).

Another contribution in the field of strategic management is the resource-based view (RBV) also referred to as resource-advantage theory, Barney (1991). The RBV is composed of elements from various social science fields. Essentially, the RBV is based on the firm's internal resources (tangible and intangible) as a central competitive asset pool that provides a long-term or sustainable advantage over competitors whereby the firm develops valuable, rare, imperfectly imitable and not easily substitutable strengths (VRIN criteria). Tangible resources are composed of assets such as financial and human resources, real property, equipment, branding, patents, trademark, etc. Intangible resources include firm's reputation/goodwill, culture, know-how/experience, relationships with suppliers and stakeholders (Lev 2001).

Mintzberg et al. (1999) conducted a comprehensive study of the many contributions in the field of strategic management and thereafter categorized them into ten schools as follows:

- The **DESIGN school**, which sees strategic management as a process of attaining a fit between the internal capabilities and external possibilities of an organization.
- The **PLANNING school**, which extols the virtues of formal strategic planning and arms itself with SWOT analyses and checklists.

- The **POSITIONING school**, heavily influenced by the ideas of Michael Porter, which stresses that strategy depends on the positioning of the firm in the market and within its industry.
- The **ENTREPRENEURIAL school**, which emphasizes the central role played by the leader.
- The **COGNITIVE school**, which looks inwards into the minds of strategists.
- The **LEARNING school**, which sees strategy as an emergent process—strategies emerge as people come to learn about a situation as well as their organization's capability of dealing with it.
- The **POWER school**, which views strategy emerging out of power games within the organization and outside it.
- The **CULTURAL school**, which views strategy formation as a process rooted in the social force of culture.
- The **ENVIRONMENTAL school**, which believes that a firm's strategy depends on events in the environment and the company's reaction to them.
- The **CONFIGURATION school**, which views strategy as a process of transforming the organization—it describes the relative stability of strategy, interrupted by occasional and dramatic leaps to new ones.

Part II

Planning Strategic Posture

Strategic posture planning is concerned with two challenges. One, which we call *competitive analysis*, deals with deciding on the way the firm will succeed in each strategic business area in which it intends to do business. We discuss this challenge in Chapters 6 and 10.

The second challenge, which we call *portfolio analysis,* is to integrate the firm's strategic intent in the respective strategic business areas into an overall strategy for the firm. Portfolio analysis is discussed in Chapter 11.

The remaining chapters of Part II discuss the overall perspective of strategic management in several specific settings.

6

Strategic Diagnosis

In this chapter, Ansoff describes the consequences of the evolving challenges to management of the business firm. One important consequence is differentiation of challenges among firms. This means that the tradition of universal prescriptions for management of all firms must give way to a tailored approach in which each firm identifies its own future challenges and develops its own responses. The first step in this tailored approach is the strategic diagnosis which determines the nature of a firm's strategic problem(s).

Two Key Problems for Strategic Management

Evolving environmental challenges surfaced in the USA during the mid-twentieth century: product-market shifts, developing nations, inadequacy of management capabilities, external sociopolitical pressures, and disruptive technology. Other developed countries arrived at the same challenges however their dates lagged by approximately fifteen years, Germany approximately ten years, Japan approximately twenty years.

By the 1980s, the challenges in the developed countries converged toward similar challenges. This convergence has been referred to as the common 'postindustrial predicament' of the developing nations.

While the country agendas converged, the agendas facing different firms within a country evolved at different rates.

© The Author(s) 2019
H. I. Ansoff et al., *Implanting Strategic Management*,
https://doi.org/10.1007/978-3-319-99599-1_6

1. As they faced the 1990s, a small minority of industries still confronts an agenda very similar to that of the first quarter of the century. The key challenge in such industries is to continue satisfying a basic demand for undifferentiated, reliable, unchanging products within the limits of a national market. The cement and funeral industries are examples of this minority.

2. A significant number of industries still confront the challenges of the second quarter of the century. Food processing, consumer durables, and low technology producer durables share the challenges of satisfying differentiated and continually changing needs of their customers.

3. A majority of industries must still face one or both of the challenges of the first half century but also must confront new challenges of the 2000s. The new challenges are numerous, discontinuous, diverse, and complex.

   Firms in such industries must:

   • Continuously survey the environment for signs of future discontinuity and potential surprises.
   • Cope with rapid saturation of markets.
   • Respond to frequent changes in competitive structure and dynamics.
   • Take advantage of opportunities in new growth industries.
   • Anticipate threats of invasion of their industry by alien technology.
   • Respond to global competition.
   • Adapt to political upheavals.
   • Respond to social pressures on the firm.
   • Cope with government regulations of business behavior.

4. A small (but growing) and important group of industries consists of the creators of economic and technological progress. These are the high-tech industries, born of novel technologies: nano-technologies, augmented technology, 3-D technology, six-core processors, solar fuel, atmospheric energy, etc. These are also new industries in the burgeoning service sector. Their challenge is to use leading-edge technologies to create products which serve previously unfilled needs of society, and thus create new industries.

Thus, firms will face different, continually changing challenges, and for many firms the challenges of tomorrow will be different from those of yesterday. This has two consequences for management:

1. The continuing evolution of the change agenda makes it dangerous to base future plans on successful responses to historical challenges.
2. There is no single prescription for future success which will apply to all firms.

As a result, management confronts two key problems:

1. Each firm needs to diagnose its unique pattern of future challenges, threats, and opportunities.
2. Each firm must design and implement its own unique response to these challenges.

This book is dedicated to enabling general management of a firm to develop unique, creative, thoughtful, and systematic solutions to these two problems.

Strategic Success Paradigm

Strategic diagnosis is a systematic approach to determining the changes that have to be made to a firm's strategy and its internal capability in order to assure the firm's success in its future environment.

The diagnostic procedure is derived from the *strategic success paradigm*, which has been validated by empirical research.

The strategic success paradigm states that a firm's performance potential is optimum when the following three conditions are met:

1. *Aggressiveness of the firm's strategic behavior matches the turbulence of its environment.*
2. *Responsiveness of the firm's capability matches the aggressiveness of its strategy.*
3. *The components of the firm's capability must be supportive of one another.*

In the following pages, Ansoff defines the concepts of environmental turbulence, strategic aggressiveness, and organizational responsiveness. (Management capability will be discussed in Chapter 7). We will next develop instruments by which turbulence, aggressiveness, and responsiveness can be estimated. Finally, we will describe a procedure for combining these assessments into a strategic diagnosis.

Environmental turbulence is a combined measure of the changeability and predictability of the firm's environment. We will describe it by five characteristics in three categories: *discontinuity, unpredictability,* and *instability.*

Discontinuity:

1. *Complexity* of the firm's environment.
2. Relative *novelty* of the successive challenges which the firm encounters in the environment.

Unpredictability:

1. *Rapidity of change,* the ratio of the speed with which challenges evolve in the environment to the speed of the firm's response.
2. *Visibility* of the future which assesses the adequacy and the timeliness of information about the future.

Instability:

1. *Frequency* of turbulence level shifts in the industry.

A scale of environmental turbulence is shown in Table 6.1. Level 1 turbulence describes a placid environment in which the following are the case:

- A firm can confine its attention to its historical marketplace.
- Successive challenges are a repetition of the past.
- Change is slower than the firm's ability to respond.
- The future is expected to replicate the past.

Table 6.1 Turbulence scale

Discontinuity	Complexity of the Environment	National Competitor w/ Economic Conditions	Plus	Global Regional Competitor w/ Technology effects	Plus	Global Competitor w/Social-Politcal effects
	Novelty of Change	No Change	Change is slow and incremental	Change occurs faster but still incremental	Change is discontinuous but an expected transition	Change is discontinuous but now completely unexpected
Unpredictability	Rapidity of Change	No Change	Change occurs slower than the firm can respond	Change occurs equal to the firms ability to respond	Change occurs more rapidly than the firm can respond	Change occurs catching the firm completely by surprise
	Visibility of Future Events	Complete visibility of future change events	Future change events are easy extrapolable	Future change events are predictable	Future change events become less predictable	Future change events are completely unpredictable
Instability	Frequency of Turbulence Level Shifts	No shifts due to no change	Low	Moderate	High	Multiple shifts per year
	Environmental Turbulence Level Scale	1	2	3	4	5

Level 1 turbulence is rarely observable in the free market economies in which natural forces of competition are at work. The reason is that the key to success in today's competitive environment is continual substitution of new products/services which are superior to the historical products/services. Firms which do not innovate do not survive.

While level 1 turbulence is rarely observable in a free market economy, the other levels, shown in Table 6.1, are all observable today. They have already been described (in order of increasing turbulence) by the five challenge agendas in this chapter (where they are numbered from 2 to 5 to correspond to the levels of turbulence). The turbulence scale can be used to diagnose the level of turbulence expected in the firm's environment over the coming years.

As we shall show in the following pages, at level 4 and above, active concern with strategic management becomes vital to a firm's success and, indeed, even its continued survival.

Strategic Aggressiveness

Strategic aggressiveness is described by two characteristics:

1. The *degree of discontinuity* from the past of the firm's new products/ services, competitive environments, and marketing strategies. The scale of discontinuity ranges from no change to incremental change, to change which is discontinuous for the firm but observable in the environment, to creative change which has not been observed previously.
2. *Timeliness* of introduction of the firm's new products/services relative to new products/services which have appeared on the market. Timeliness ranges from reactive to anticipatory, to innovative, to creative.

Table 6.2 describes the appropriate strategic aggressiveness which, according to the strategic success paradigm, is necessary for success at each turbulence level.

As previously discussed, level 1 aggressiveness is rarely observed in the business environment, but it is common in the not-for-profit organizations which do not change their products/services unless forced by a threat to their survival.

At level 2, the environment changes slowly and incrementally, a firm succeeds if it changes its products only in response to competitors' moves. In the absence of threats from competition, such firms stick to their historical

Table 6.2 Matching aggressiveness to turbulence

Turbulence level descriptor	Repetitive	Expanding Slow incremental	Changing fast incremental	Discontinuous Discontinuous Predictable	Surprising Discontinuous unpredictable
Strategic aggressiveness	**Stable** Based on Precedents	**Reactive** Incremental based on experience	**Anticipatory** Incremental based on extrapolation	**Entrepreneurial** Discontinuous based on expected futures	**Creative** Discontinuous based on creativity
Environmental turbulance level 1	1	2	3	4	5

products/services, while minimizing costs and underpricing competition. As discussed in the previous section, level 2 was typical of the business environment of the first part of the twentieth century.

At level 3, firms progressively improve their historical products/services in anticipation of the evolving needs of the customers. Firm's that are able to discover the secret of shaping and influencing the customer's wants capture a greater share of the market.

Level 4 aggressiveness is observed in firms whose environment is subject to frequent discontinuities and poor predictability. Level 4 aggressiveness is much more complex than on the other levels.

- Successful firms on level 4 continuously scan their environment in order to identify future economic, competitive, technological, social, and political discontinuities.
- The principle of 'sticking to one's knitting' is replaced with 'being where the action is.' The firm stays in an industry only as long as it expects the prospects to be attractive and its own competitive position to remain viable. When an industry loses attractiveness, or the firm can no longer compete, it exits the industry in a timely manner.
- The firm continually seeks and enters other industries in which the future looks bright and the firm can succeed.
- Thus, the firm continually and with foresight moves its resources from markets and industries which will become unattractive into growing and profitable industries of the future.
- In every industry in which it participates, the successful firm continually reassesses the competitive factors which will bring future success. Whenever the historical success strategies do not match the future success factors the firm either develops new strategies or leaves the industry.

The success formula on level 5 is straightforward: to remain a leader in developing products/services incorporating the cutting edge of innovation and technology.

To repeat the first part of the strategic success paradigm: to assure success, the aggressiveness level of the firm's strategic behavior must match the turbulence level of the environment.

Responsiveness of the Firm's Capability

In addition to strategic aggressiveness, the responsiveness of the firm's organizational capability must also be matched to the environmental turbulence.

The responsiveness appropriate to different turbulence levels is shown in Table 6.3. On level 1, where the environment is repetitive, and the optimal strategic behavior is change-rejecting, the optimal organization suppresses strategic change. The organization is highly structured with hierarchical, centralized authority.

On level 2, the efficiency-driven firm permits strategic change to occur, but only after operating management has failed to meet the firm's goals. The organization is introverted, focused on internal efficiency and productivity. Little attention is paid to the environment since it is assumed that minimization of cost will automatically assure success in the marketplace. The power center is usually in the production function. As a result, efficiency-driven firms are frequently referred to as *production-driven*.

Successful *market-driven* firms on level 3 are extroverted and future oriented. The focus is on serving the future needs of the firm's historical customers, using the historical strengths of the firm. The word 'our' is frequently heard in such firms our products, our technology, our customers. The firm's strategic planning is based on historical success strategies the marketing function typically drives the firm, hence the frequent use of the name *market-driven* to describe such firms.

A distinctive characteristic of an *environment-driven* firm on level 4 is that unlike the market-driven firm, it has no attachment to history. Future validity of historical success strategies is continually challenged and so is the future attractiveness of historically attractive markets.

Table 6.3 Matching responsiveness to turbulence

Turbulence Level Descriptor	Repetitive	Expanding Slow Incremental	Changing Fast Incremental	Discontinuous Discontinuous Predictable	Surprising Discontinuous Unpredictable
Responsiveness Of Capability	Custodial Based on Precedents	Production Efficiency Driven	Marketing Market Driven	Strategic Environment Driven	Flexible Seeks to Create the Environment
	Suppresses Change	Adapts to Change	Seeks familiar Change	Seeks New Change	Seeks Novel Change
	Seeks Stability	←	Seeks Operating Efficiency	→	Seeks Creativity
	Closed System	←	Seeks Strategic Effectiveness	→	Open System
Environmental Turbulence Level 1	1	2	3	4	5

Unlike in all other types of responsiveness, no single function guides the behavior of an environment-driven firm. Power over strategic activity is exercised by general managers who balance the contribution of the functional areas. This balance is determined by the nature of the future environmental challenges and not by political influence of a single function.

The *environment-creating* firms on level 5 have a feature in common with efficiency and market-driven firms: all three are usually driven by a single function. On level 4, this may be a creative market development function or a creative R&D department.

A characteristic which distinguishes an environment-creating firm from production or market-driven firms is its total commitment to creativity. The past is recognized only as something not to be repeated.

The lower section of Table 6.3 shows that the *strategic activity* (doing the right thing) and the operating activity (doing the thing right) compete for both resources and management attention at levels 3 and 4.

The last line in figure shows that on level 1 a successful organization is introverted and totally focused on internal problems. As the turbulence level rises, the organization becomes progressively extroverted.

*Strategic Diagnosis

Tables 6.1, 6.2, and 6.3 can be used to answer the two questions which are posed at the end of this chapter:

1. How to diagnose the future environmental challenges which will confront the firm? The answer to this question is diagnosis of future turbulence levels in the firm's environment.
2. How to determine the firm's strategic response which will assure success? The answers to this question are diagnoses of strategic aggressiveness and the organizational responsiveness which will match the future turbulence.

Strategic diagnosis is the procedure for answering the two questions. The following are the steps to the strategic diagnosis.

1. The first step is to segment the firm's environment into distinct strategic business areas which are likely to be on different turbulence levels. (The process of strategic segmentation will be discussed in detail in Chapter 8.)
2. The second step is to choose the time horizon for the turbulence diagnosis. This will vary from one strategic business area (SBA) to another. A

useful time horizon is the lead time needed in the SBA to develop a new generation of products/services.
3. The third step is to use Table 6.1 to identify the future level of turbulence for each business area.

This and the following steps are based on judgment as well as on forecasted data. Therefore, strategic diagnosis must be executed by line managers who have experience, understanding, and intuition about future trends in the respective business areas.

4. The fourth step is to repeat the procedure to determine the present turbulence level in each of the business areas.
5. The fifth step is to identify the strategic aggressiveness (using Table 6.2) and the responsiveness of capability (using Table 6.3) which will be needed for success in the future.
6. The sixth step is to identify the present aggressiveness and responsiveness of the firm.
7. The final step is to construct the firm's present and future turbulence–aggressiveness–responsiveness profiles.

An example of such profiles for a business area is illustrated in Fig. 6.1:

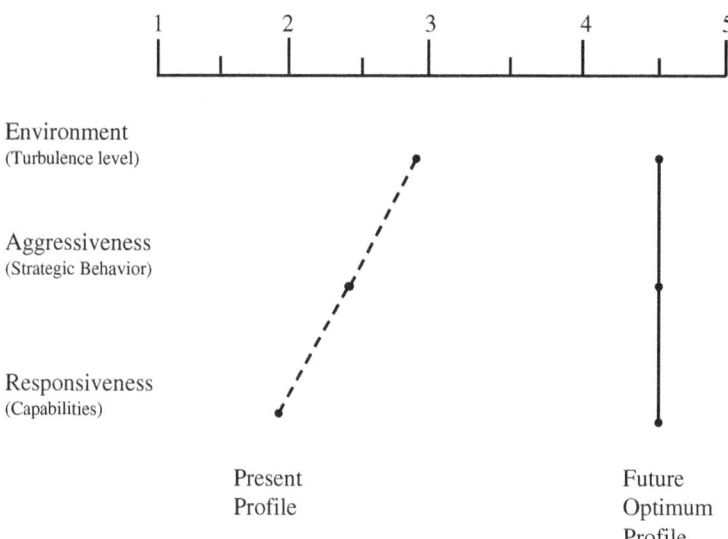

Fig. 6.1 Example of strategic diagnosis

- The figure shows that the present level 3 turbulence will move to level 4.5 in the future.
- The present aggressiveness and responsiveness are lagging behind the present turbulence suggesting that the firm is not a top competitor.
- However, it is too late to fix the present deficiencies. The focus must be on the gap between the present and future aggressiveness and responsiveness.
- The gaps in the example suggest that the firm faces a massive challenge of changing both its strategic behavior and its capability if it is to become a top competitor in the future.

During the past 40 years, several thousand managers around the world have been involved in executing the strategic diagnosis. The profiles illustrated in Fig. 6.1 are typical of a mediocre competitor. Leading competitors usually show a vertical line for the present profile. However, a majority of the participants, including managers of many leading international firms, showed a significant gap between the present and future profiles.

Short and Long Version of the Strategic Diagnosis

The strategic diagnosis discussed in the preceding section is a *short version* which determines whether a firm must change its historical strategic response in order to succeed in the future. But it offers no details of the changes which must be made in the firm's aggressiveness and responsiveness.

Chapter 7 presents a more detailed *long version* of strategic diagnosis which identifies specific changes in the strategic response of the firm.

Thus, the short version can be used for a quick identification of whether the firm has a strategic alignment problem, while the long version can be used to develop specific programs to solve the problem.

Validation of the Strategic Success Paradigm

Tables 6.1, 6.2, 6.3 are summarized in Table 6.4 which shows triplets of turbulence, aggressiveness, and capability responsiveness which will assure for the firm a potential for optimum performance. However, the turbulence–aggressiveness–responsiveness triplets are derived from the strategic success

Table 6.4 Matching triplets—aggressiveness and responsiveness with turbulence the optimize a firm's ROI

Turbulence level descriptor	Repetitive	Expanding	Changing	Discontinuous	Surprising
Strategic aggressiveness	Stable	Reactive	Anticipatory	Entrepreneurial	Creative
	Change based on precedents	Change based on experience	Incremental change based on extrapolation	Discontinuous new strategies based on observable alternatives	Novel, strategies based on creativity
Responsiveness of general man-agement capabilities	Stability seeking	Efficiency seeking	Market driven	Environment driven	Environment creating
Environmental turbulence levels	**1**	**2**	**3**	**4**	**5**

paradigm. As its name implies, a paradigm is defined as a new model, standard, or archetype in the way something is being done. In this case, the strategic success paradigm has been validated by applying it to business reality.

Conceptual Map of the Book

Strategic diagnosis identifies whether a firm need to change its strategic behavior to assure success in the future environment.

If the diagnosis confirms the need, the next step is to select and execute specific actions which will bring the firm's aggressiveness and responsiveness in line with the future environment. The rest of this book is devoted to discussing ways for making these decisions logically, systematically, and implementing them effectively.

To organize the discussion, we shall use a conceptual model for systematically managing a firm's adaptation to changing environments. The model is shown in Fig. 6.2. E_1 and E_2 are the present and future states of the environment and ΔE is the difference in the levels of turbulence.

The adaptation starts with a forecast of future growth/profitability in each of the firm's business areas and of the factors which will be key to success.

If the diagnosis predicts a change in the turbulence level, forecasting based on extrapolation of historical trends, which is commonly used in business firms, becomes invalid. It is necessary, therefore, to use non-extrapolative forecasting techniques. Furthermore, it is imperative to make the results of the new, unfamiliar forecasts acceptable to the key decision makers. This problem of strategic information is discussed later in the book.

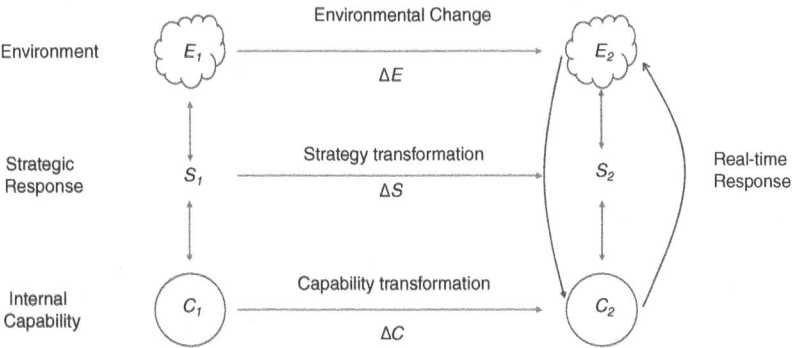

Fig. 6.2 Managing firm's adaptation to environment

The information is used to select the strategic response (S_2 on the figure) which will assure the firm's future success. In environments on level 4 and above, two types of response are found in today's practice. The first is *positioning response* which uses strategic planning to select the portfolio of business areas in which the firm will participate, and to develop the competitive strategies it will pursue in each area. The positioning response is later is Part II of the book.

The second type of response is the *real-time response*, which uses a technique called *strategic issue management*, to identify potentially unforeseen strategic threats and opportunities, to estimate their impact on the firm, and to develop and execute timely responses. Real-time response is discussed in Part V.

To assure effective implementation, the firm also needs to *design the capability* (C_2) which will enable it to initiate and support the new strategic responses. A firm has two different, complementary capabilities: *management capability* to identify, plan, and guide the strategic response; and *functional capability* to execute the response.

Management capability is discussed in Part III; functional capability is discussed later in Part II in conjunction with the positioning response.

The planned strategic response S_2 and the capability design C_2 must next be put into practice. Whenever the gap ΔC between the present and desired capability is discontinuous, implementation of change typically encounters *organizational resistance*. Part VI deals with the problems of diagnosing and managing resistance.

In summary, the conceptual model used in this book describes strategic management through four closely interrelated activities:

1. Strategic diagnosis which identifies the need for a new strategic response.
2. Strategic planning which determines the future strategic response.
3. Organizational design which plans the future organizational capability.
4. Change management which implements the response and capability plans.

Summary

The challenges of the postindustrial ere were first felt in the USA and then progressively arrive in other developed countries. The total challenge agenda for the 2000s is practically the same in these countries, but the parts of the challenge agenda confronted by different industries are different. As a result, it is no longer possible to devise a single prescription for response to the challenges which would apply to all industries and firms. Therefore, the first step in strategic management is to perform a strategic diagnosis which identifies the type of strategic aggressiveness and organizational responsiveness a particular firm needs to develop in order to meet the future challenges of its environment.

Exercises

1. Using the procedure found in this chapter, identify: (a) the turbulence level five to seven years from now, (b) necessary future strategic aggressiveness, and (c) necessary future organizational responsiveness for firms which aspire to be among the leading competitors in each of the following industries: automotive, artificial intelligence, commercialized space travel, banking, retailing, medicine, and any other industry with which you may be familiar.

2. For each industry, identify the following characteristics of the firm which will produce the necessary responsiveness:

   a. Profile of skills, talents, and risk propensity of the key managers.
   b. Characteristics of the organizational structure.
   c. Characteristics of the organizational culture.
   d. Basis of rewards and incentives for managers.

7

Concept of Organizational Capability

As previously discussed, the original approach to strategic planning, a new strategy was chosen to match the historical strengths of the firm. In a discontinuous environment, historical strength by definition becomes future weaknesses. It is necessary therefore to replace the strengths/weakness concept by a more general concept of organizational capability.

In this chapter, we develop this concept with particular emphasis on the general management capability.

Functional Capability

Environmental turbulence is described by the difference between present and future critical success factors within the SBA. The strategic aggressiveness is measured by the match between the characteristics of the firm's competitive strategy and the critical success factors. The responsiveness criterion is measured by the match between the critical capability success factors and the capability profile of the firm.

The capability profile is composed of the functional capabilities: marketing, R&D, HR, finance, production, etc., as well as the general management know-how (management of growth, diversification, and acquisition).

Invention of the functional capability occurred early in the history of the business firm when it was discovered that a firm runs more smoothly and more efficiently when the work of the firm is divided among specialized organizational units called *functions*, each of which possesses a distinctive

© The Author(s) 2019
H. I. Ansoff et al., *Implanting Strategic Management*,
https://doi.org/10.1007/978-3-319-99599-1_7

capability. DuPont managers made such subdivisions early in the twentieth century and referred to that process as 'putting like things together.'

The evolution of the functional capabilities followed shifts in the priority of different success factors. During the 1930s, low-cost production was the key to success in most industries. As a result, organizational builders focused on perfecting the production function: mass production technology in consumer industries, batch and continuous production in process industries, serial production in manufacturing of capital goods. Great progress was made in subdivision of work, plant layout, automation, equipment replacement, machine loading, inventory control, warehousing, and distribution and use of the learning curve. All this knowledge was brought together into a 'turnkey know-how' for timely and efficient creation of a complete production organization.

Starting in the 1940s, while concern with internal operations continued, the focus of attention shifted outward to markets. What had been a rather straightforward, if vigorous, sales activity, quickly became marketing, focused on recognizing, anticipating, and eventually shaping the needs of the customers. Attention turned to new product development, artificial obsolescence, shaping of customer needs and tastes. The newly developed capabilities included sales analysis, market research, consumer preference measurement techniques, salesmanship techniques, deployment of sales personnel, motivation of salesmen, advertising, promotion, and as in the case of operations, the design of a balanced marketing organization.

With the exception of technology-intensive industries, R&D activity played little more than a second role until after World War II, primarily focused on improving production and process technologies and on product durability. As the firm's attention increasingly focused on new product development, the focus of R&D shifted from durability and standardization to product differentiation, annual model changes, and artificial obsolescence. Thus, R&D increasingly became a handmaiden of the marketing function.

After World War II, R&D changed from a handmaiden to the leader. A torrent of technology unleashed by the war began to change the face of many industries, sent others into decline, and created new industries. The specter of an ungovernable 'R&D monster' turned management attention to innovation. What was previously regarded as a secondary and essentially unmanageable province of scientists and inventors increasingly became a key factor to success. As a result, the R&D function was progressively organized and structured; project selection, evaluation, and control techniques proliferated; budgeting and control of R&D were introduced; and leadership techniques for managing creative people and creative processes were developed.

A great deal has been learned about the nature of functional capability and about the capability building process.

The building blocks of each function are the same: skills, technology, facilities, equipment, shared knowledge, and know-how. But a capability is more than the sum of its parts, it possesses systemic properties. The key systemic properties are:

1. The manner in which tasks are subdivided. Highly subdivided, narrowly specified tasks produce a capability that is highly efficient but rigid. Aggregated, loosely defined tasks produce creativity at the cost of efficiency.
2. The manner in which the tasks are related to one another. Partitioned tasks produce functional stability, coupled tasks produce flexibility.
3. The organizational culture within the function shared norms, values, models of reality, rewards, incentives. A culture which is inimical to change contributes to efficiency but suppresses flexibility.
4. The power structure within and among functions, and the manner in which power is exercised. An autocratic structure contributes to stability and efficiency; shared power contributes to changeability but at the expense of efficiency.

These systemic characteristics are as important to the quality of a functional capability as the specific skills, technology, and capacity.

As we shall presently see, the same systemic characteristics are of even greater importance to the effectiveness of general management.

Evolution of General Management Capability

Another discovery made early in the history of the firm, which was comparable in importance to the invention of functional groupings, was that, after work was functionally subdivided, it was necessary to integrate, coordinate, and direct the functional efforts toward common goals. This integrative and coordinating task became known as *general management*.

Originally, general management was the exclusive prerogative of the top entrepreneur. However, as firms grew larger, the entrepreneur had increasingly to share his authority and responsibility with others. Today, general management is shared by members of the upper part of the organizational triangle where the necessary visibility and span of control are available for directing the overall thrust of the firm.

The entrepreneur was clearly the key actor during the creation of the modern firm. But as the firm turned its attention to perfecting its production function, the role of top management underwent a drastic change.

The inventors of the functional groupings in the DuPont Company saw the role as partitioning and standardizing the work of the firm. Once partitioned and standardized, the functions could run with a minimum of interference from general management. In fact, it was discovered the firm ran better when authority and responsibility were decentralized as near as possible to the level where the functional work of the firm was done. From this experience emerged the maximal decentralization principle which states that the top management of the firm should reduce its involvement in daily operations to a minimum and 'manage by exception,' involving itself in decision making only when unforeseen discontinuities and conflicts arise among functions.

So long as efficient production was the key to success, discontinuities were few and conflicts rare; the production function dominated the firm. As a result, corporate offices were minimally staffed and contributed little to the success of the firm.

When marketing emerged as a critical activity, the new marketing mentality focused on flexible response to the needs of the market, which interfered with the efficiency of standardized mass production.

As a result, conflicts arose between the production and the marketing functions, each trying to influence the firm's work in a direction which optimizes its own goals (maximal sales for marketing and minimal costs for production).

Therefore, top management increasingly had to play the role of an arbiter of the conflicts and optimizer of the opposing tendencies. The workload on general management grew and, as we shall see in Chapter 17, a new *divisional structure* was invented which introduced a new level of general management below the level of the headquarters.

As the R&D function grew in importance, general management workload increased again, because it now had to manage a three-way tug of war between marketing, production, and R&D. From management by exception, the role of general management evolved into one of an essential coordinator of the functional activities. Until the 1970s, while it was recognized that the functional capability was a complex combination of factors, the capability of general management remained personalized by the general manager, following the tradition established by the early entrepreneurs. When the role of the general management shifted to that of a functional coordinator, the profile of the successful general manager became one of a multifunctional expert.

Thus, the best way to qualify for a company's presidency was to be rotated through functional work assignments and then to understudy the incumbent president to get a feel for the complexity of such problems as setting prices, determining inventory and production levels, managing inter-functional conflicts, and developing key managers.

Business schools of the time reflected (and many still do) this perception of general management in their curricula. General management was treated as an empty box whose characteristics were totally determined by the functional inputs. A student was first exposed to the theory and practice of the respective functional skills and then to a series of integrative general management case studies augmented by complex computer simulations designed to replicate marketing, production, finance, and strategic decision making.

Since the middle of the century, as strategic response to the environment became increasingly important, it became evident in practice that general management *was* more than a simple sum of the functions. Just as knowledge of plumbing, structure, carpentry, electricity, heating, and air-conditioning for a house does not make an architect, neither does knowledge of the functions make a strategist. If anything, preoccupation with functional concerns produces a strategic myopia.

The problem-solving skills developed by functional management were recognized to be too structured and convergent for the job of the strategic manager, who must be a divergent, creative solver of ill-structured problems, and whose abilities should include be sensitivity to the environment, and skills in strategy analysis and in the design of strategically responsive structures. His leadership skills and style should be, in part, those of the entrepreneur: vision, risk-taking, change management, charisma and, in part, those of a political statesman.

As the strategic role of the general manager acquired importance, a curious paradox developed. The multifunctional manager clearly had to understand the functions of his firm and his industry, but the general manager was increasingly perceived as a generalist capable of giving strategic guidance to any firm in any industry.

Thus, a major US company saw nothing wrong in appointing a successful manager of its US consumer goods division to run a newly acquired computer subsidiary in France. The transfer did not succeed, not only because the business, the culture, and the social climate of the subsidiary were foreign to the manager, but also because he landed in the middle of a major political upheaval in the new country. This example was not singular. General managers who moved from low turbulence industries into fast-growing technology-intensive ones frequently found that their managerial skills were either insufficient or totally inadequate for managing in the new industry.

The personal experiences were matched by general ones. One source was disappointments in diversification. Numerous companies, having diversified into attractive but unfamiliar industries, found that the management style necessary for success in the new industry did not match that of the parent. Some firms found the mismatch to be serious enough to warrant divesting from the recent acquisition.

A second source of disappointment was frequent cases of the inability of a firm to adapt to the turbulence brought about by a technology substitution in its own industry.

Such experiences, combined with research finding, have led to the next step in the evolution of the concept of general management. The following aspects are becoming increasingly clear:

1. A general manager's capability is not universal. His successful performance in one environment is no guarantee that he will succeed in an environment which is on a different (higher or lower) level of turbulence.
2. General managers are only one, albeit critical, component of general management capability. As Chandler's studies have shown, other essential components are structure, the decision-making system, the information system, organizational climate, etc.
3. Different general management capabilities are appropriate to different environments.
4. The key characteristic of the environment which determines the characteristics of the general management capability is the level of the environmental turbulence (as compared to the key success factors which determine the appropriate functional capabilities).
5. The responsiveness of general management becomes a critical success factor when the firm needs or wants to make a discontinuous change in its strategy.
6. Since discontinuous change will be the rule rather than the exception, the quality of general management will be critical to the success and survival of the firm in the last part of the twentieth century.
7. When discontinuous changes are not only frequent but also rapid, as they will be during the last quarter of the century, the reactive unplanned adaptation of general management capability will be too slow. Therefore, the needs for changes of capability must be anticipated and installed in advance.

In the following pages, we shall develop a practical methodology for diagnosing the present capability, anticipating the need for change, and for determining the capability which must be put in place.

Definition of General Management Capability

General management is the organizational function *responsible for the overall performance of the firm*. This responsibility includes strategic positioning of the firm in its environment in a way which assures a coordinated performance toward its near-term objective. We now define capability of general management as *its propensity and its ability to engage in behavior which will optimize attainment of the firm's near- and long-term objectives.*

General management (as well as functional capability) can be assessed in two complementary ways. The first is by observing the characteristics of the firm's behavior; for example, whether the firm anticipates or reacts to discontinuities in the environment. We shall call this approach assessing the *responsiveness*. The other way is to identify the *capability profiles* of the firm which produce different types of responsiveness.

Table 7.1 shows that the responsiveness can be described by three capability attributes: climate, competence, and capacity. Each of the three is determined on the one hand by managers and on the other by the organization through which they work.

- *Climate* is the management propensity to respond in a particular way, for example, to welcome, control, or reject change.
- *Competence* is the management's ability to respond. For example, to anticipate change in a complex environment, the firm needs a sophisticated environmental surveillance system. Without it, the propensity to welcome change is an intent without the means.

Table 7.1 General management capability

	Managers	Organization
Climate	Mentality power	Culture
(will to respond)	position	Power structure
Competence	Talents	Structures
(ability to respond)	Skills	Systems
	Knowledge	Shared knowledge
Capacity	Personal	Organizational
(volume of response)		

- *Capacity* is the volume of work that the general management can handle. Its adequacy is related to the type of response used. For example, the number of general managers needed for change controlling management by exception is very much fewer than for vigorous change-generating strategic development.

Table 7.1 shows that the major determinants of the climate are the mentality/culture and the power positions/structure of the firm. The competence is determined by the abilities of managers on the one hand and the systemic abilities of the organization on the other. Organizational capacity can be measured by multiplying the work capacity of the individual managers (some produce 24 hours of work in 8 hours, and some play golf half of their working time) by the headcount.

The concept of capacity helps explain a part of the 'resistance to planning' problem which was encountered in introducing strategic planning into the firm. Typically, the new strategic work was 'dumped' on top of the operating workload, which already fully occupied the general managers' time. If, as was typically the case, at the time of introduction the capacity of general management was minimal, the strategic planning workload conflicted with the operations workload. For reasons which we shall be discussing in Part V, this conflict was typically resolved in favor of the operations work. The low priority accorded to the strategic work appeared as resistance.

The concept of competence helps explain another cause of the resistance to planning. It has been common to introduce strategic planning by means of one-day seminars during which general managers were converted into 'instant' strategic planners. Since a majority had no prior experience in strategic analysis, the quality of their plans was, at best, marginal. The poor quality of plans produced ineffective actions which again was perceived as resistance to planning.

The third source of resistance was the historical climate of the firm. Since at the time of introduction of strategic planning the climate was typically change controlling, both managers and organization rejected the change-generating' strategic management as irrelevant to the way things ought to be done.

The preceding discussion illustrates the important systemic property of general management capability which we have already observed in functional capability, namely which describes the way climate, competence, and capacity are matched. The overall capability is no stronger than its weakest attribute.

General Management Capability Profile

For diagnostic and planning purposes, we need to define the respective components of capability in greater detail than was done in Table 7.1. This is done below:

1. Managers

   (a) Mentality
   - The relative preoccupation with external vs. internal problems.
   - The past vs. future time orientation.
   - Propensity to take risks.
   - The manager's personal model of the world: What he perceives to be the critical success factors and behaviors.
   - Values, norms, and personal goals.

   (b) Power
   - The strength of his power position within the firm.
   - His ambition and drive to use power.

   (c) Competence
   - Talents/personality.
   - Problem-solving skills.
   - Leadership style/skills (e.g., political vs. custodial vs. inspirational vs. entrepreneurial vs. charismatic leadership).
   - Knowledge about the firm and about the environment.

   (d) Capacity
   - Personal work capacity.
   - Work habits (e.g., the typical 'workaholic').

2. Climate

   (e) Culture
   - The organizational attitude toward change: Whether the organization is hostile, passive, or predisposed to change.
   - The propensity toward risk: Whether, as a group, management avoids, tolerates or seeks risks, whether it is only comfortable with familiar risks, or whether it seeks novel ones.
   - The time perspective in which management perceives its problems: Whether it puts full reliance on past experience, prefers to deal with the present, or puts emphasis on the future.

- The action perspective: Whether organizational attention and energies are focused on internal operations or on the external environment.
- The goals of behavior: Whether it is stability, efficiency, effectiveness, growth, or innovation.
- The trigger of change: Whether a crisis or accumulation of unsatisfactory performance is necessary, or whether the firm continuously seeks change.
- The shared model of the world: perception of the critical success factors.

(f) Power
- The distribution of power among groups with different cultures.
- Stability of the power structure.
- Militancy of the power centers.
  (Not surprisingly, the group characteristics which determine the collective culture are quite similar to the behavioral attributes of individual key managers.)

3. Competence

(g) The organizational problem-solving skills and style: Whether they are based on precedents, trial and error, optimization of available alternatives, or creation of new alternatives.

(h) The problem-solving process: Whether it is compartmentalized and hierarchical, or firm-wide and problem-centered.

(i) The management process (informal as well as formal systems): Whether it controls to past performance, anticipates familiar futures, or creates new futures.

(j) The information used in managing, whether, it is derived from historical performance, extrapolation, or wide-ranging environmental surveillance.

(k) Organizational structure: the degree and type of complexity it can handle, its flexibility and adaptability.

(l) The rewards and incentives: Whether managers are rewarded for historical performance, growth, initiative, or creativity.

(m) The job definition: Whether it is narrowly circumscribed or open, encouraging venture and initiative.

(n) The technological aids to decision making (computation procedures, rules, models, computer programs, etc.): Whether they assist routine and repetition or innovation and change.

(o) Organizational capacity: Headcount of line and staff managers converted into volume of work which general management can produce.

An Illustrative Example

The above description of the components of capability permits us to illustrate the strategic success criterion: ***to assure optimal effectiveness of the capability profile, the components of the profile must be supportive of one another.*** Applying this criterion to the introduction of strategic planning, we would find the new system unwelcome and ineffective in a firm which has the following capability profile (Table 7.2).

In this case, the existing planning system is the only link which is out of balance with a capability for strategic responsiveness. As the reader will recall, the functional capability needed by a successful firm is determined by the critical capability success factors in the firm's marketplace.

On the other hand, the required general management capability of a firm is determined by the turbulence level of the firm's environment. In the following chapter, we present the long version of strategic diagnosis which can be used to relate the future turbulence in the firm's environment to the general management capability it must develop in order to succeed.

Table 7.2 Capability profile

Key managers:	Change Controllers
Culture:	Risk/change avoidance
Rewards:	for past performance
Information System:	Accounting data
Planning System:	Budgeting

But the following profile would welcome strategic planning and make it effective

Key managers:	Entrepreneurs
Culture:	Change seeking
Rewards:	For innovation/creativity
Planning System:	Long-range plannig

Summary

Successful firms entered the second half of the twentieth century with impressive strengths in the production, marketing, and R&D functions. The functions were supervised and coordinated by general management in the firms' upward thrust for growth.

From mid-century on, the firm increasingly had to turn attention to strategic repositioning of the firm in order to assure future profitability and offset maturity and decline. In the beginning, it was felt that the historical strengths would apply to the new strategic posture. But the strengths of yesteryear frequently turned into the weaknesses of today. Thus, as firms change their external strategies, they also have to change their internal capabilities,

When repositioning is discontinuous, then the general management capability to anticipate the need and to assure timely repositioning becomes the key to success. Thus, general management graduated from a secondary role of a coordinator of growth, to a vital role of developer of the firm's future.

Successful performance of this role requires a climate within the firm which welcomes and seeks change, a competence to anticipate, analyze, and select attractive opportunities.

This chapter lays a theory-based foundation for developing systematic general management capability by defining the components of a management capability profile.

Exercises

1. Arrange (and group if desirable) the fifteen capability elements in the general management capability section, in the order of their relative importance to effective action by general management. Which components would you consider vital?
2. If the firm needs to develop a new capability profile, in what order should the respective components be developed to assure a transition with the minimum of organizational resistance?
3. What programs of action would you initiate for the transition?
4. Refer to the turbulence scale, Table 6.1 and, using the profiles of general management capability, present in two columns the characteristics of the fifteen components appropriate to levels of turbulence 2 and 4.

8

Diagnosing Future General Management Capability

This chapter presents a procedure by which a firm can determine its future general management capability profile. The first version of this procedure appeared in 1976 (Ansoff et al. 1976-F). The revised procedure presented here has been repeatedly tested in practice with satisfactory results.

The Effect of Strategic Mismatch on Profit Potential

Previously, a short version of strategic diagnosis was introduced. At this point, a longer version of strategic diagnosis will be described which can be used to determine the specific action programs for developing the strategy and capability which will succeed in the future environment.

This chapter is based on one part of the strategic success paradigm introduced in Chapter 6. The part of interest at this point is the relation between turbulence and management capability. It states: **for optimum profitability, the responsiveness of general management capability must match the turbulence of the firm's environment.**

Tables 6.1 and 6.3 were used in the short version of strategic diagnosis to determine whether the firm's historical response to the environment will be adequate or whether the firm has a strategic problem.

A typical result of the short version of strategic diagnosis might produce information such as that illustrated in Fig. 8.1 which reflects the earlier Fig. 6.1.

© The Author(s) 2019
H. I. Ansoff et al., *Implanting Strategic Management*,
https://doi.org/10.1007/978-3-319-99599-1_8

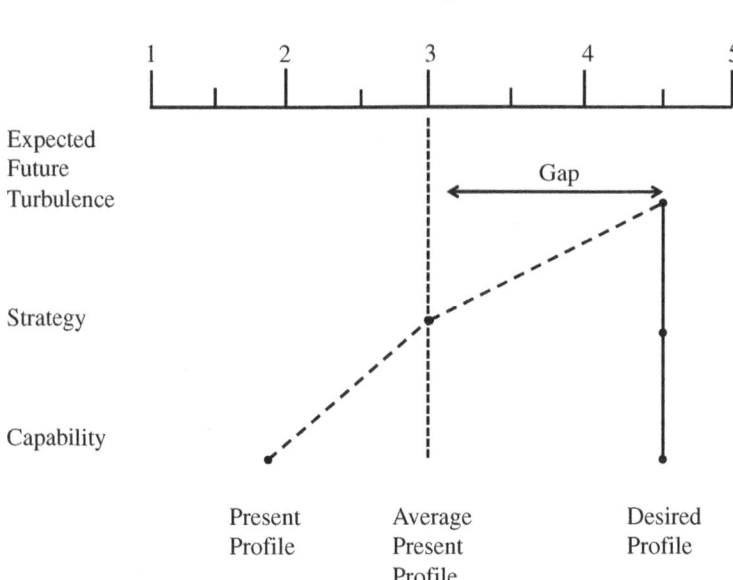

Fig. 8.1   Mismatch between present and desired future profiles

The impact of the gap shown in Fig. 8.1 on the firm's performance depends on the intensity of competition expected in the firm's environment. Figure 8.2 presents a general relationship of the dependence of the firm's return on investment and the average gap between the present and desired profiles.

The graph plots the firm's ROI potential as a function of the gap between the environmental turbulence and the firm's capability. Two hypothetical curves are shown: The upper curve is ROI in a market in which competition is weak. The lower curve shows the case of a strongly competitive environment.

The upper curve indicates that in weakly competitive environments, the penalty for being out of tune with the environmental turbulence is relatively small. But, in the case of intense competition, the firm's performance deteriorates rapidly. In the example shown, a gap of more than ±2 in a weakly competitive environment would degrade the firm's ROI potential to 75% of the optimum. But in an environment of intense competition, a gap of ±2 makes the firm chronically unprofitable, regardless of its competitive aggressiveness.

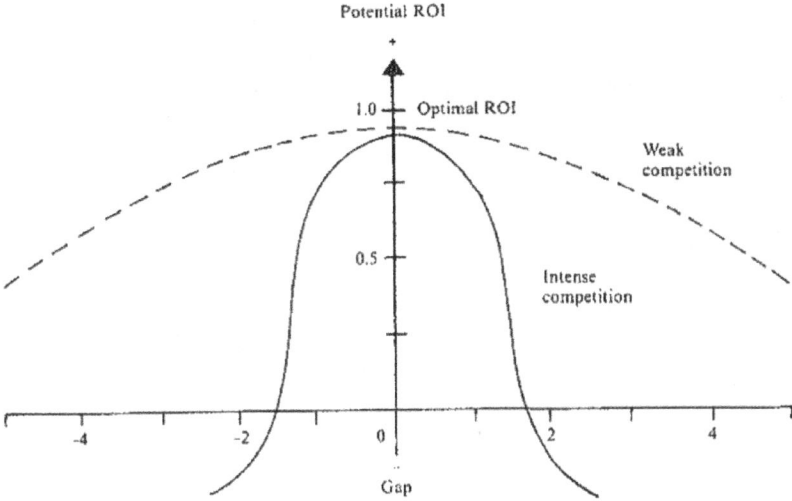

Fig. 8.2 Effect of strategic mismatch on profit potential

Figures 8.1 and 8.2 suggest that the decision to undertake the long version of the diagnosis depends on the competitive intensity which a firm expects to encounter in the environment.

If the short strategic diagnosis predicts a substantial capability gap, but management expects competition to be weak (e.g., the firm expects to occupy a near-monopoly position in the market), the need to undertake the long version of diagnosis would be relatively low in other words, the firm can remain a profitable performer even if its capability is out of tune with the environment.

On the other hand, if management expects competition to be intense, the 'intense competition' curve in Fig. 8.2 suggests immediate attention to the long version of diagnosis.

Differences Between the Long and Short Versions of Strategic Diagnosis

The short version describes general management by a single phrase which characterizes the kind of behavior (responsiveness) a particular capability will produce. In the long version, discussed in this chapter, we turn our attention to the components of capability which will be described in detail in the following pages.

This more detailed description serves three purposes:

1. It permits a better evaluation of the present capability of the firm.
2. It focuses attention on the specific components of capability which will need improvement.
3. The focus on the components makes it possible to identify programs which will be needed to improve the capability.

Just as in describing capability, the short version describes turbulence by a single phrase. In the long version, turbulence is analyzed in greater detail.

Another significant difference between the short and long versions is in the treatment of unpredictability. In the short version, it is implicitly assumed that future unpredictability is going to be low and it is possible to characterize future turbulence by a single number.

In the long version, this assumption is abandoned and a *range of probable turbulence* is estimated in a manner consistent with the dispersed positioning approach described in Chapter 10. Specifically, two estimates are made of the level of future turbulence: a low probable level and a high probable level.

*Step in a Strategic Diagnosis

In the following sections, we present a procedure for assessing the gaps between the firm's present capability profile and the future success profile. While the procedure may at first appear to be complicated, the reader can be reassured by the fact that it has been successfully used by many practicing managers.

More importantly, the reader can also rest assured that the diagnostic instruments have been validated by exhaustive research (see Salameh 1987-H; Hatziantoniou 1986-H; Sullivan 1987-H; Chabane 1987-H).

As discussed previously, most firms today do business in a number of different SBAs which have different characteristics and which, therefore, will require separate diagnoses. Therefore, the turbulence and capability responsiveness diagnoses should be conducted separately for each SBA. The following steps are followed:

1. Select a specific SBA for analysis.
2. Choose the future time horizon for the analysis. This will vary from one SBA to another. A useful time horizon is the lead time needed in the SBA

to develop a new generation of products/services or to introduce a novel technology.

3. Diagnose the future low probable turbulence in the selected SBA of the firm.
4. Diagnose the future high probable turbulence in the selected SBA of the firm.
5. Select the average of the lower and the average of the higher to describe the overall range of future turbulence.
6. Identify the present responsiveness of the firm's capability.
7. Diagnose the capability gap between capability and turbulence.
8. Choose the firm's future general management capability profile.

*Diagnosing Turbulence

Diagnosing future turbulence is, at best, an imprecise process. Although quantitative forecasts and multiple scenarios can provide a useful input to the diagnosis, the final estimate must be based on the judgment of managers who have a substantial record of experience in the SBA.

This leads to two conclusions about the process of turbulence diagnosis:

1. To enhance reliability of judgment, turbulence diagnosis is best performed by a group of managers who bring to the process a combination of unique experiences, knowledge, and viewpoints. An ideal team would consist of an SBU manager of the SBA being analyzed, and his key functional managers from R&D, marketing, finance, production, and corporate planning.
2. Secondly, the team should not be required to seek consensus on the precise level of future turbulence, but rather on a range within which the turbulence will probably fall. Thus, the group should seek consensus on the 'low probable' and 'high probable' values of future turbulence. Managers familiar with statistics can think of the *low* and high probable judgments as including the two-standard-deviation range of the probable future turbulence.

Table 8.1 can be used for diagnosing the expected level of future turbulence. As the left-hand column in the figure shows, the level of turbulence is determined by a configuration of competitive, economic, sociopolitical, and technological variables. Since the functional relationship among the variables is

Table 8.1 Worksheet for diagnosing the expected level of future turbulence

SBA:____	Level of Environmental Turbulence				
Attributes	1	2	3	4	5
Differentiation of marketing strategies	None	Low	Moderate	High	Revolutionary
Frequency of new marketing strategies	None	Low	Moderate	High	Revolutionary
Pressure by customers	None	Weak	Strong	Demanding	Threatening
Demand to industry capacity	> 1	> 1	Equal	< 1	< 1
Pressure by government	None	Weak	Strong	Demanding	Threatening
Pressure by environmentalists	None	Weak	Strong	Demanding	Threatening
Level of Product differentiation	None	Low	Moderate	High	Revolutionary
Frequency of new products in industry	None	Low	Moderate	High	High
Product life cycle	Long	Long	Moderate	Short	Very Short
Rate of change of technology affecting industry	Very Slow	Slow	Moderate	Fast	Discontinuous
Diversity of competing technologies	None	None	None	Several	Several
Critical marketing success factors	Control of Markets	Dominate Market Share	Image Differentiation	Best product at least cost	Breakthrough' Product
Critical innovation success factors	Cost Reduction	Product Adaptation	Product Improvement	Product Innovation	Creativity

Range of expected future turbulence
~3.0 ←————→ ~4.5

not known at the present time, we use a profile analysis method which is typically employed under such circumstances.

1. Since the list of variables changes from one SBA to another, in practical use of these and subsequent tables, the first step is to examine the list of attributes; delete any attributes which are not relevant to the particular SBA and add any that are missing.

   Repeated use of the tables by practicing managers has shown that only small modifications of the list are usually needed. For example, in defense-oriented industries, a major factor contributing to innovation turbulence might be 'level of government support of R&D.' For many strategic business areas in the western world, a key factor in marketing turbulence may be 'invasion by Chinese competitors.'

2. The second step is to circle two descriptions of each attribute in Table 8.1: The description which is judged to be the low probable, and the description which is judged the high probable in the future environment. The reader is reminded that the chosen descriptions should characterize the SBA during the chosen future period.

3. The third step is to average the low probable and high probable descriptions by drawing two vertical lines in the manner shown in Table 8.1. The pair of lines represents respectively, the possible low and the possible high level of expected future turbulence. Thus, the two lines enclose the range of turbulence which is expected to be observable in the SBA's future environment.

Table 8.2 Capability diagnosis

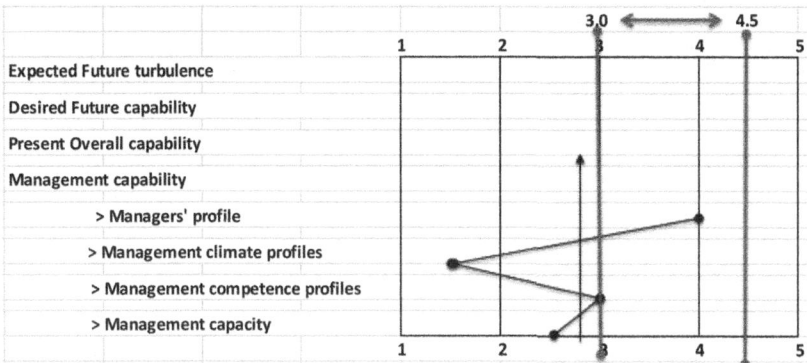

4. Make marks representing the low probable and high probable turbulence levels on the first line of Table 8.2, and draw two vertical lines as shown in the figure. In the example illustrated in Table 8.2, the future turbulence is expected to lie between 3.0 and 4.5.

*Diagnosing the General Management Capability of the Firm

For the purposes of capability diagnosis, general management capability is described by four components:

1. Managers' profiles (Table 8.3).
2. Management climate profiles (Table 8.4).
3. Management competence profiles (Table 8.5).
4. Management capacity (Table 8.6).

As the figures show, each part is further described by a number of attributes. Unlike in turbulence diagnosis which guesses at the future, capability diagnosis assesses the present state of the firm. Therefore, the team working on the diagnosis should reach a single value consensus on each attribute. (Disagreements which may arise will be due to differences in perceptions of reality and personal biases. We shall be discussing approaches to eliminating the biases and differences in perceptions later in this section.)

Table 8.3 Managers capability type attributes

Capability type / Attributes	Custodial 1	Production 2	Marketing 3	Strategic 4	Flexible 5
1. Mentality	Custodial	Production	Planning	Entrepreneurial	Creative
2. External vs. internal orientation	Introverted	→	Balanced	→	Extroverted
3. Time orientation	Precedent	History	Extrapolated future	New Futures	Invented futures
4. Model of success	Stability/repetition	Production efficiency	Balance of internal efficiency and marketing responsiveness	Investment in most profitable available opportunities	Creativity
5. Risk propensity	Reject	Accept familiar risks	Seek familiar risks	Seek unfamiliar risks	Seek novel risks
6. Power of general management	Strong	→	Moderate	→	Strong
7. Leadership style	Political	Disciplinary/controllership	Inspirational/common purpose	Charismatic	Creative
8. Problem solving	Trial/error	Diagnostic	Optimization	Alternative search	Alternative creation
9. Knowledge	Internal politics	Internal operations	Traditional markets/competitors/technology	Global opportunities	Emerging environment
10. Leadership skills	Political Custodial	Controllership	Goal achievement	Entrepreneurial	Charismatic

Table 8.4   Manager's climate profiles

Attributes \ Capability Type	Custodial 1	Production 2	Marketing 3	Strategic 4	Flexible 5
Attitude toward change	Don't challenge the system by initiating change	Adjust to difficult events as they happen	Plan ahead	If its new its good	Create the future
Risk Propensity	Avoid	Accept	Seek familiar risk	Seek unfamiliar risk	Seek novel risk
Time Perspective	Past	Present	Familiar Future	Perceivable Future	New Futures
Action Perspective	←——— Introverted ———→		←——————— Extroverted ———————→		
Change Trigger	Crisis	Unsatisfactory Results	Threats and Opportunities	Continued Search for change	
Initiative	Don't Volunteer'	Follow the Rules'	Run with the Ball'	Be a Self-Starter'	
Firm Power Structure	Centralized		Decentralized	Strong Corporate Office	
Model of Success	Stability	Efficient Performance	Effective Growth	Effective Diversification	Innovation

Table 8.5   Management competence profiles

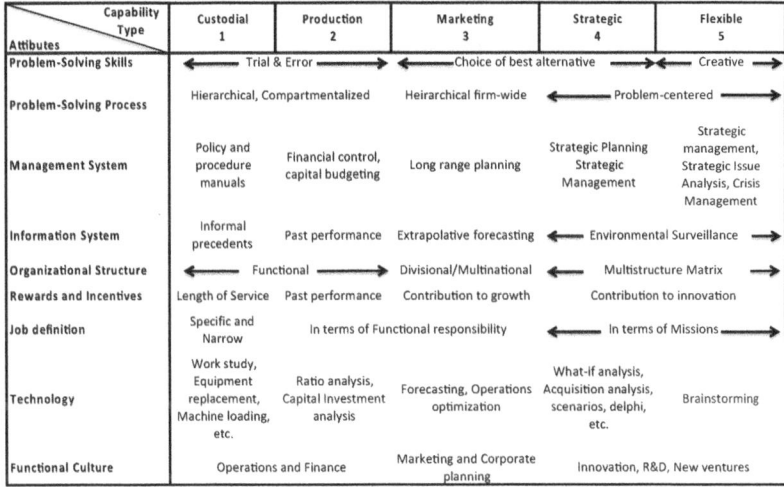

Attributes \ Capability Type	Custodial 1	Production 2	Marketing 3	Strategic 4	Flexible 5
Problem-Solving Skills	←——— Trial & Error ———→		←—— Choice of best alternative ——→		←— Creative —→
Problem-Solving Process	Hierarchical, Compartmentalized		Heirarchical firm-wide	←——— Problem-centered ———→	
Management System	Policy and procedure manuals	Financial control, capital budgeting	Long range planning	Strategic Planning Strategic Management	Strategic management, Strategic Issue Analysis, Crisis Management
Information System	Informal precedents	Past performance	Extrapolative forecasting	←— Environmental Surveillance —→	
Organizational Structure	←——— Functional ———→		Divisional/Multinational	←— Multistructure Matrix —→	
Rewards and Incentives	Length of Service	Past performance	Contribution to growth	Contribution to innovation	
Job definition	Specific and Narrow	In terms of Functional responsibility		←— In terms of Missions —→	
Technology	Work study, Equipment replacement, Machine loading, etc.	Ratio analysis, Capital Investment analysis	Forecasting, Operations optimization	What-if analysis, Acquisition analysis, scenarios, delphi, etc.	Brainstorming
Functional Culture	Operations and Finance		Marketing and Corporate planning	Innovation, R&D, New ventures	

1. The first step in diagnosis of capability is to use Tables 8.3, 8.4, 8.5, and 8.6 to identify and circle, on each figure, the description of each attribute which best describes the present capability of the firm.
2. The second step is to average the values of the attributes and draw a vertical line representing this average. Examples are shown in Tables 8.3, 8.4, 8.5, and 8.6.

Table 8.6 Management capacity

Capability type	Custodial 1	Production 2	Marketing 3	Strategic 4	Flexible 5
Levels of general management	Stability	Production	Capacity must be adequate for managing long range planning, production, marketing, R&D	Strategic portfolio production marketing R&D diversification	Creativity strategic portfolio production marketing R&D diversification novel ventures

1. Corporate line
2. Corporate staff
3. Divisional line
4. Divisional staff
5. Functional contributions to strategic management

3. The third step is to enter the average level of each attribute in the lower part of Table 8.2. The entries are then joined by a single line to produce a profile of the firm's capability.
4. The final step is to draw, on Table 8.2, a single vertical line which will be an approximate average of the points drawn in step 3 just above. Take the vertical line up until it connects with the line 'present overall capability.' The point of intersection represents the evaluation of the level of management's present capability.

A study of the illustration shows that the firm's present capability is well outside of the range of probable future turbulence.

Capability diagnosis may need to be performed by all management units which directly or indirectly affect the firm's strategic behavior in the SBA.

In a divisionally structured firm, in addition to the SBU management, divisional management, group level management (if any), and the corporate management may need to participate in the diagnosis.

The importance of involving general management units above the SBU level depends on the management style of the firm. If the style is conglomerate, in which upper levels of management do not interfere with strategic management of the SBU, only the SBU level diagnosis needs to be performed.

If the management style is synergistic, in which there is substantial guidance from above offered to the SBU managers, it may be necessary to make sure that capabilities of the higher management are responsive to the turbulence in the SBA under analysis (see Sect. 3.4.8).

As mentioned earlier, some parts of capability diagnosis, particularly those which evaluate skills, talents, perceptions, and attitudes, are subject to perceptual distortion and personal bias. As a result, there is a danger of producing a capability diagnosis which is biased toward the way individuals would like to be perceived, but which is not necessarily descriptive of the way in which they actually behave.

A method for minimizing distortions due to biases and misperceptions was pioneered by Revans. He applied this method to diagnoses of hospital management. The process involved two sister units from two similar hospitals, the unit which was to be diagnosed and another, similar unit.

Firstly, the unit from one of the hospitals evaluated itself. Secondly, it was evaluated by the peer; and thirdly, they jointly compared self and peer evaluations in an effort to eliminate biases. The roles were then reversed and the process repeated.

The Revans approach has been successfully applied to small business firms in New Zealand where top management groups from a pair of firms followed an identical procedure. The same method can be applied to 'sister' units in larger firms. An alternative, and preferable, method which is usable in synergistic firms, is to submit the results of a strategic diagnosis to the higher-level management for challenge, criticism, and modification.

*Choosing the Future Capability

The final step in strategic diagnosis is to select the firm's target future general management profile. According to the strategic success hypothesis, the future capability of the firm must match the future level of turbulence. However, Table 8.2 illustrates a likely case in which the range of probable future turbulence includes two turbulence levels, namely 3.0 and 4.5.

As the figure shows, the capabilities required by each of the turbulence levels are, respectively, marketing and strategic, which, as our previous discussion has shown (see Fig. 2.1.4), are very different from each other. Therefore, in cases when the range of future turbulence in Table 8.2 is greater than 1, it is not evident which of the two capabilities should be chosen as the target for the firm. This situation is similar to the one we encountered in which it was not possible to choose a specific target for the firm's competitive position in cases in which the region of uncertainty is large.

Thus, at the conclusion of the strategic diagnosis, management will be presented with one of two situations:

1. The range of possible future turbulence levels may be narrow enough to point to a specific capability type which the firm should develop. In this case, the future capability choice is unambiguous and made automatically by the strategic diagnosis.
2. The range may be wide enough to make it impossible to select a particular target capability for the firm. Such cases are typical in environments of low predictability. In such cases, the firm should avoid a commitment to a particular capability, a choice which it could live to regret. Instead, the choice is to follow a path of gradual step-by-step commitment.

The concept of gradual commitment will be discussed in Chapters 2.5 and 2.9. Applied to capability development, this concept involves the following actions (Tables 8.7 and 8.8):

Table 8.7 Managers' profiles

Attributes \ Capability Type	Custodial 1	Production 2	Marketing 3	Strategic 4	Flexible 5
Attitude toward change	Don't challenge the system by initiating change	Adjust to difficult events as they happen	Plan ahead	If its new its good	Create the future
Risk Propensity	Avoid	Accept	Seek familiar risk	Seek unfamiliar risk	Seek novel risk
Time Perspective	Past	Present	Familiar Future	Perceivable Future	New Futures
Action Perspective	← Introverted →		← Extroverted →		
Change Trigger	Crisis	Unsatisfactory Results	Threats and Opportunities	Continued Search for change	
Initiative	Don't Volunteer'	Follow the Rules'	Run with the Ball'	Be a Self-Starter'	
Firm Power Structure	Centralized		Decentralized	Strong Corporate Office	
Model of Success	Stability	Efficient Performance	Effective Growth	Effective Diversification	Innovation

Table 8.8 Management climate profiles

Attributes \ Capability Type	Custodial 1	Production 2	Marketing 3	Strategic 4	Flexible 5
Attitude toward change	Don't challenge the system by initiating change	Adjust to difficult events as they happen	Plan ahead	If its new its good	Create the future
Risk Propensity	Avoid	Accept	Seek familiar risk	Seek unfamiliar risk	Seek novel risk
Time Perspective	Past	Present	Familiar Future	Perceivable Future	New Futures
Action Perspective	← Introverted →		← Extroverted →		
Change Trigger	Crisis	Unsatisfactory Results	Threats and Opportunities	Continued Search for change	
Initiative	Don't Volunteer'	Follow the Rules'	Run with the Ball'	Be a Self-Starter'	
Firm Power Structure	Centralized		Decentralized	Strong Corporate Office	
Model of Success	Stability	Efficient Performance	Effective Growth	Effective Diversification	Innovation

1. Early steps in capability development should be 'general purpose'—applicable to a range of different capability profiles. For example, development of environmental surveillance capability.
2. Early steps should also be selected for their 'learning value'—the extent to which they contribute to a reduction of part of the range of uncertainty due to the firm's lack of available information about the future environment.
3. The firm's capability should be made flexible and adaptable to turbulence changes through development of:

   - Continuous scanning of the firm's environment for changes in the turbulence level (see Chapters 5.2, 5.3, and Sect. 1.3.6).
   - Sensitivity to changes in the environment.
   - Continual challenging of historical success precedents.
   - A flexible power structure.
   - Rewards which are focused on the future success of the firm.
   - Systems and structures which are flexible.
   - Continual re-evaluation of future prospects, strategies, and capabilities.

4. The firm's portfolio strategy should provide for a high level of strategic invulnerability (see Sect. 2.6.13).

To summarize the preceding discussion, when the firm confronts an environment in which the future level of turbulence cannot be predicted with confidence, the future capability must be developed through a gradual commitment approach accompanied by enhancement of the firm's responsiveness to surpriseful discontinuities (Tables 8.9 and 8.10).

The Multi-capability Problem

If the capability analysis described in the preceding sections were to be performed on a typical successful firm during the first half of the twentieth century, the number of SBAs would have been few, with one or two usually contributing a dominant percentage of the firm's profits. Most of the SBAs would have been in comparable stages of growth, with similar competitive challenges and, therefore, on the same turbulence level.

The present capability profiles of different units have been very similar. Thus, during the production-oriented period, key managers would all have shared the production mentality and skills, a firm-wide reward system would have rewarded production efficiency, and the budgeting/control system and

Table 8.9 Management competency profiles

Capability type / Attributes	Custodial 1	Production 2	Marketing 3	Strategic 4	Flexible 5
Problem-solving skills	Trial and error		Choice of best alternative		Creative
Problem-solving process	Hierarchical, compartmentalized		Heirarchical firm-wide	Problem-centered	
Management system	Policy and procedure manuals	Financial control, capital budgeting	Long range planning	Strategic planning strategic management	Strategic management, strategic issue analysis, crisis management
Information system	Informal precedents	Past performance	Extrapolative forecasting	Environmental surveillance	
Organizational structure	Functional		Divisional/ multinational	Multistructure matrix	
Rewards and incentives	Length of service	Past performance	Contribution to growth	Contribution to innovation	
Job definition	Specific and narrow	In terms of functional responsibility		In terms of missions	
Technology	Work study, equipment replacement, machine loading, etc.	Ratio analysis, capital investment analysis	Forecasting, operations optimization	What-if analysis, acquisition analysis, scenarios, delphi, etc.	Brainstorming
Functional culture	Operations and finance		Marketing and corporate planning		Innovation, R&D, new ventures

Table 8.10   Management capacity

Levels of General Management / Capability Type	Custodial 1	Production 2	Marketing 3	Strategic 4	Flexible 5
	Stability	Production	Capacity must be adequate for managing Long Range planning, Production, Marketing, R&D	Strategic Portfolio Production Marketing R&D Diversification	Creativity Strategic Portfolio Production Marketing R&D Diversification Novel Ventures
1. Corporate Line			*		
2. Corporate Staff		*			
3. Divisional Line		*			
4. Divisional Staff			*		
5. Functional contributions to strategic management			*		

◄——— Average management capability profile

functional structure would have assured attention on economies of scale and minimization of costs.

Applications of the capability analysis to firms in the 1990s often showed that the general management capability profile, although different from the first half century, was typically still uniform throughout the firm. All general managers are selected, developed, evaluated, and rewarded according to the same set of criteria. A single information/planning/control system is used to manage all units of the firm, and all parts of the firm are organized on the same principle (functional, divisional, etc.).

Analysis of the SBAs, though, typically produces a range of different turbulence levels and, therefore, the need for different capability profiles, only some of which match the profile of the firm.

In part, this is due to the fact that, since mid-century, SBA growth stages have become differentiated and their competitive, sociopolitical-economic-technological, turbulences have become different. In part, the diversity of needed capabilities is due to the fact that most medium and large firms have diversified from their original businesses. Furthermore, we will discuss in Chapter 2.6, that, to assure long-term success and survival, the firm's SBA portfolio *should* be a mix of different life cycle positions, different environments, and different technologies.

Thus, capability analysis frequently reveals that the firm should have not one but several different general management capabilities, each attuned to the needs of its diverse SBAs. As shown in Fig. 8.2, this need is made imperative by intense competition.

These imperative raises what we shall call the *multi-capability problem*: How can the needs for different management capability profiles be accommodated within a single firm?

One solution is to preserve the historically dominant capability attuned to the SBAs which are the major profit contributors and to accept suboptimal performance in other SBAs. The solution may produce satisfactory results, if the diversity of the portfolio is not great and the competition in them is weak (see Fig. 8.2). This solution offers the advantage of maximum simplicity, least confusion, an opportunity to develop managers imbued with the common culture of the firm, and easily transferable from one part of the firm to another.

A second solution is to reduce the diversity of the firm's SBAs through divestment to form a coherent portfolio which can be served equally well by the same general management capability. Drastic as it may appear, this solution was being used in the early 2000s by some firms which had been divesting from SBAs which did not fit their historical management capability. It was not unusual to read announcements that a diversified firm was divesting from a particular line of business because it did not fit the management style (e.g., Bayer, Merck, P&G, GE).

A third solution is to manage the firm as a genuine conglomerate in which each subsidiary company is left to develop its own capability profile. In this solution, there are no synergistic links among the subsidiaries, and the overall performance of the firm is a sum of the performances of the subsidiaries. The corporate capability is essentially legal and financial, and both strategic and operations management are left to the subsidiaries. When a subsidiary malfunction chronically, it is sold off, or its top management is replaced.

The fourth solution is to develop distinctive capabilities for different coherent clusters of SBAs, but to continue to manage the firm as a coherent and integrated whole. *This is the multi-capability solution.*

The multi-capability firm differs from a conglomerate in several fundamental aspects.

1. The firm is organized according to the SBU (see Chapter 11) with each SBU matched to a coherent SBA cluster. Each SBU is encouraged to develop a capability profile appropriate to its environment.
2. The corporate management continues to manage the firm strategically as an integrated SBA portfolio. It approves unit strategies, balances the overall strategic portfolio, allocates strategic resources on a global basis, including transfers of resources among SBUs, encourages and develops commonalities and synergies between strategies and capabilities of the distinctive units.

3. The capability profile of the corporate office is flexible, responsive to the different cultures, reward, and management styles of the SBUs.
4. The corporate office uses appropriate interface systems which permits it to integrate the results produced by the systems of the SBUs.

There is evidence that firms are beginning to use the multi-capability solution. For example, the Disney Company, regrouped itself into four different organizational segments, each responsive to a distinctive set of business areas.

Different firms will use different solutions to the multi-capability problem according to the management style and ambitions of their controlling managers. But there are also objective criteria which dictate different choices in different situations. These are illustrated in Table 8.11.

For an explanation of the capability design choices recommended in the figure, we need to refer to Fig. 8.2. That figure shows that, when competition is weak, a firm's performance in an SBA is relatively insensitive to the capability gap. If the diversity in turbulence levels among the firm's SBAs is small, use of the capability designed for the SBA which contributes a dominant percentage of the firm's profits will not substantially degrade the overall performance of the firm.

If the diversity of turbulence levels is high, the conglomerate organizational form is likely to produce a better average performance than the dominant form.

As Fig. 8.2 shows, when competition is strong, performance is highly sensitive to the size of the capability gap. If turbulence diversity is small, we will discuss in Chapter 11, divestment from non-synergetic SBAs becomes desirable.

Finally, if in strongly competitive environments, management desires to maintain a high level of diversity, the new multi-capability solution becomes desirable.

As Table 8.11 shows, the choice depends on the intensity of competition encountered in the firm's SBAs and the diversity of the SBA portfolio. The checks in the figure show the preferred choices.

Managing Strategic Posture Transformation

The complete strategic posture analysis will lead to one of two outcomes:

1. The case, which is unlikely today, in which there is no gap in either capability or strategic aggressiveness and, further, the future key success factors

Table 8.11 The capability choice

Competition	Weak		Strong	
Diversity of turbulence levels	Low	High	Low	High
Capability				
*Dominant	* ✓			
*Conglomerate		✓		
*Coherent portfolio			✓	
*Multi-capability				✓

are not expected to change significantly. This result gives the firm a clean bill of health: It is strategically ready for the future.

2. The more likely case in which one or more gaps exists: in strategic aggressiveness, in competitive posture, in portfolio, in competition.

When both strategy and capability changes are necessary, a logical approach would be to develop the necessary capabilities first, and change the strategic behavior subsequently. But, as will be recalled from the preceding chapter, Chandler's and other studies have shown that both strategy and capability transformation are multiyear processes which, on occasion, have lasted as many as ten to twenty years. During the 2020s, few firms will be able to afford the luxury of such slow sequential strategy-capability development.

Therefore, in practice, numerous strategy and capability programs will have to be conducted in parallel. As a result, the required organizational capacity and the budget needed for the programs will be substantial, and strategic work will come into conflict with the profit-making activities.

Furthermore, substantial changes in the strategic posture produce a phenomenon known *as* organizational resistance to change. Thus, the process of strategic posture transformation is complex, costly, and resistance laden. We shall discuss the management of this process in Part V.

Summary

When a firm's environment moves to a new turbulence level, the responsiveness of the firm's capability to the environment stimuli must also move to a different level. If the capability fails to keep pace with the environment, the firm is in danger of losing its competitive position and becoming unprofitable.

At this point in the book, it is appropriate to summarize the results of Parts I, II, and III, all of which have been devoted to the task of selecting the strategic posture that the firm will seek to occupy in the future environment.

The path we followed is traced in Fig. 8.3. The reader is encouraged to review the steps shown in the figure by referring to the appropriate part of the text.

Strategic diagnosis must be applied to each of the firm's important SBAs. In today's environment of diverse turbulence, a frequent result is that different SBAs require different capability profiles, thus raising the multi-capability problems. The solutions to the problems are: (1) to disregard them and maintain a dominant capability throughout the firm; (2) to compose the firm's SBA portfolio of SBAs which require similar capabilities; (3) to manage the firm as a conglomerate whose subsidiaries have distinct capabilities; and (4) to develop a multi-capability firm in which each SBU has a distinct capability profile and the corporate office manages the total strategic portfolio.

The choice of the solution depends on the diversity of turbulence among the firm's SBAs and on the intensity of competition in each.

The need and the extent of capability changes required by the firm can be determined by means of the strategic diagnosis which diagnoses future turbulence, the firm's present capability and determines the capability gap.

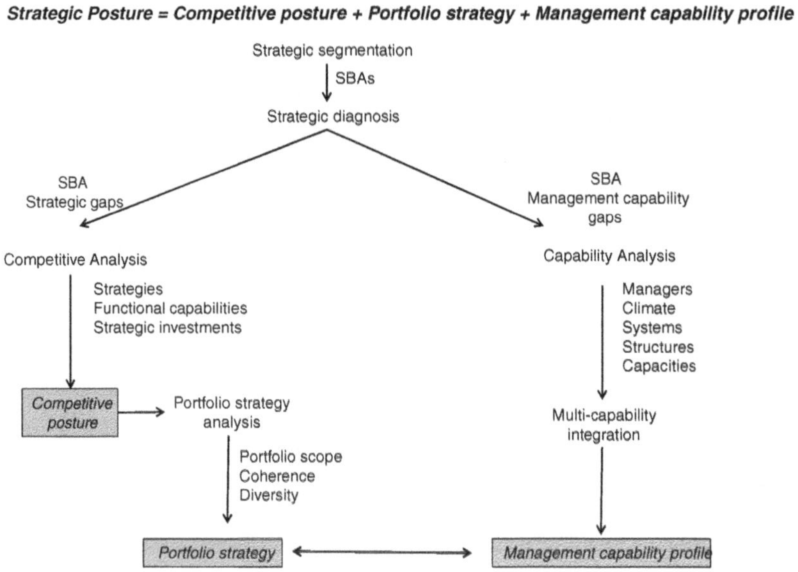

Fig. 8.3 Planning strategic posture

The choice of the future capability depends on the span of the range of expected future turbulence. If the span is narrow enough to point to a particular capability, the choice is clear. If the span is too wide, the solution is to use a process of gradual step-by-step development of the capability, accompanied by increasing the adaptability of the capabilities.

Exercises

1. Is the strategic posture analysis developed in this chapter applicable to nonprofit institutions such as a church or a hospital? If not, explain why. If yes, how would you apply the analysis to such organizations?
2. Using an organization familiar to you, or a case assigned by your tutor, make a complete strategic posture diagnosis following procedures given in Chapters 9–11.
3. Following the diagnosis, determine the new posture for the organization. Be specific about the criteria and the reasoning through which the new posture is chosen.
4. As a member of the corporate staff in a widely diversified large firm, you have been assigned the problems of developing pro and con arguments on the desirability of developing a multi-capability within the firm. Carry out your assignment.
5. If multi-capability is to be introduced, how would you go about selecting aspects of capability which should be left for determination by each SBU, and which should remain common throughout the firm? Give examples of each category.

9

Competitive Posture Analysis in Turbulent Environments

When systematic strategic planning was first introduced during the 1960s, the initial focus was on diversification of the firm. But as firms increasingly faced strategic challenges from technological turbulence, changing competition, saturation of growth, and sociopolitical pressures, it became evident that the problems posed by these challenges could not be resolved simply by adding new business areas to the firm.

As a result, in the 1970s the strategist's attention turned from diversification to optimizing the firm's competitive strategies in its historical businesses and then to optimizing the firm's total business portfolio. This shift was accelerated by the fact that the prospects for the different historical businesses of the firm became progressively differentiated from one another with respect to future growth, profitability, and strategic vulnerability.

A major conceptual contribution to strategic analysis was made by the Boston Consulting Group which introduced the well-known BCG matrix. Others elaborated the original concept into different and more comprehensive matrices. All of these matrices apply on turbulence levels 1–3. This chapter focuses on strategy formulation on turbulence levels 4–5.

© The Author(s) 2019
H. I. Ansoff et al., *Implanting Strategic Management*,
https://doi.org/10.1007/978-3-319-99599-1_9

Strategic Segmentation.

SBA and SBU

In the early approaches to strategy formulation, the first step was to identify 'the business that the firm is'. This summary statement reflected the common threads that gave the firm coherence and a distinctive character and, at the same time, put a boundary around its expansion and diversification ambitions. Thus, Theodore Levitt, who in the 1960s criticized railroads and petroleum companies for failing to articulate their business concepts, suggested that the former declare themselves to be in the 'transportation business' and the latter in the 'energy business'.

For early strategists, the definition of the 'business we are in' and identification of the firm's strengths and weaknesses constituted the extent of the attention paid to the historical businesses of the firm. By the 1960s, a majority of middle-sized and all large companies had become a complex assortment of product-market entries. While during the first half century most of the entries had shown positive and attractive growth, by the 1960s, the prospects had become mixed, ranging from excellent to declining. The differences were caused by differences in the stages of demand saturation, in geographic-economic-sociopolitical environments, in competitive climates, and in technological turbulence.

It became clear that diversification into new fields was not going to solve all of the firm's strategic problems, nor take advantage of all its opportunities, because many new challenges lay in the firm's historical business areas. As a result, strategic analysis increasingly placed emphasis on the prospects for the firm's historical portfolio of businesses, and the first step in such analysis became, not defining the 'business we are in' but identifying the multiplicity of distinct businesses of the firm.

In order to do this, management had to make a fundamental change in outlook. By the mid-century the firm's perspective had become introverted, 'inside out' the business prospects were viewed through the eyes of the different organizational units and the historical product lines of the firms. Future prospects were typically determined by extrapolating the historical performance of the firm's divisions. By the 1970s, though, a typical division was involved in an array of markets with very different prospects, and it was not uncommon for several divisions of a firm to be serving the same demand area. In turbulent environments, extrapolation of performance by organizational units became unreliable and, most importantly, failed to provide insights into the differences among the future prospects in different parts of the environment. Thus, it became necessary to shift to an 'outside-in' perspective: to analyze the environment of the firm in terms of the distinct areas of trends, threats, and opportunities which it offered to the firm.

A unit for such analysis is a *strategic business area* (SBA) which is a distinct segment of the environment in which the firm does (or may want to do) business. As the first step in strategy analysis, the respective SBAs are identified and analyzed without any references to the firm's structure or its current products. The outcome of such analysis is the growth/profitability/turbulence/technology prospects which the SBA will offer in the future to any competent competitor.

The ultimate use of SBAs is to enable management to make three key strategic decisions

1. In which SBAs will the firm do business in the future?
2. What competitive position will the firm occupy in each SBA?
3. What competitive strategy will the firm pursue to gain this position?

The pioneering work in developing the environment-centered perspective was done by R. McNamara and C. J. Hitch in the US Department of Defense who developed the 'mission slice'—the military counterpart of an SBA. In business, the pioneer was the General Electric Company which developed a complementary concept called strategic business unit (SBU) which is a unit of a firm which has the responsibility for developing the firm's strategic position in one or more SBAs. The concepts of SBA and SBU are compared in Fig. 9.1.

When the SBA–SBU approach is first introduced into a firm, an important question is how to structure the SBU operating unit relationship. For example, in the original application, Mr. McNamara found that his principal operating departments—Army, Navy, Air force, and Marines—all made overlapping and frequently conflicting contributions to the mission slices: strategic deterrence, air defense of the USA, limited warfare, etc. Mr. McNamara's solution was to create new units charged with strategic planning for the respective mission slices. The strategic decision made by these new SBUs was 'cross-walked' for implementation to the departments. Thus, in Mr. McNamara's scheme, the SBUs had only strategic planning responsibility, while the departments were responsible for strategy implementation. This split created conflicts and a lack of coordination, particularly because several departments frequently shared the responsibility for an SBA. For example, both the Navy (with its Polaris missile submarine) and the Air

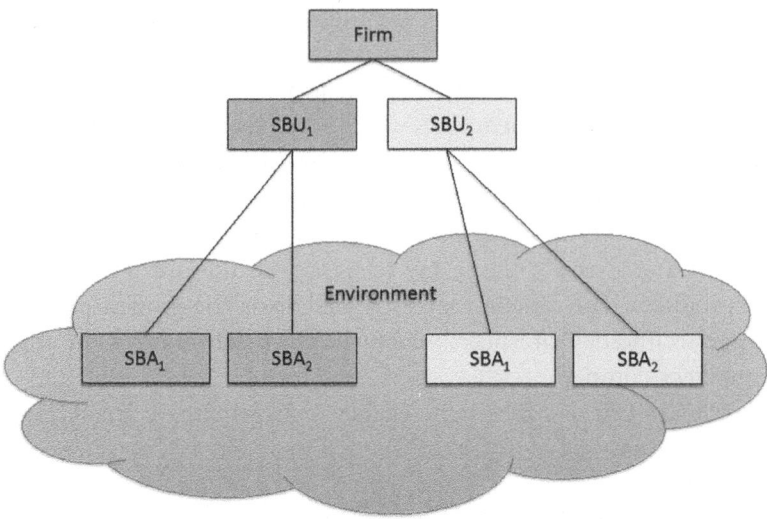

Fig. 9.1 SBA vs. SBU

force (with its Minuteman) were made responsible for developing products for the strategic deterrence mission.

To avoid such duality of strategic responsibility, the GE used a different solution. It undertook the difficult task of matching existing operating units to the firm's SBAs, thus making their SBUs responsible not only for strategy planning and implementation, but also for subsequent profit making. This approach eliminates the crosswalk and unifies profit and loss responsibility in an SBU. But, as GE and other companies have found, the historical organizational structure does not map simply onto the newly identified SBAs and the resulting responsibilities are not clear-cut and unambiguous.

A third solution is to reorganize the firm according to SBAs so that there is a one-to-one correspondence of SBAs and SBUs. This apparently simple solution runs into its own difficulties because effectiveness of strategic development, which is the organizational design criterion used in identifying SBUs, is only one of the key determinants of organizational structure. The others are the effective use of the firm's technology and the efficiency of profit making. A reorganization according to SBA, which maximizes the effectiveness of strategic behavior may, therefore, compromise the firm's profit-making performance, or it may be infeasible in light of technological considerations. (We shall be discussing the problem of accommodating strategic and operating activities within the organizational structure in Chapter 17.)

It can be seen from the above that the problem of allocating responsibilities for the firm's SBAs is far from simple and that solutions will differ from one case to another. Nevertheless, there is enough experience to show that the SBA–SBU concept is a necessary tool for giving a firm a clear view of its future environment, which is essential for effective strategic decisions.

Demand-Technology Life Cycle

During the first part of the twentieth century, most SBAs grew at positive and fairly steady rates. Although growth was interrupted by periodic recessions, the subsequent recoveries restored growth to the prerecession growth rates. Thus, firms developed the habit of comparing industries on the basis of their respective growth rates and of forecasting future performance by extrapolating historical trends.

From the 1930s on, the growth picture began to change. Some industries continued to prosper, for some growth slowed down, and some firms experienced sales declines in some of their SBAs. At the time this first happened, the deviations from the upward growth trend were seen as anomalies and the reasons for them were poorly understood. But the anomalies multiplied and by the mid-1970s a new perception of economic growth began to emerge.

This perception was based on what economists for many years called the *Gompert growth curve*. In practical applications, the curve has been renamed as the *demand- technology life cycle*. This cycle is illustrated in Fig. 9.2.

The upper curve of the figure, the *demand life cycle*, describes a typical evolution of demand from the day as previously unserved societal need (e.g., personal transportation, personal electronics, computers, and cell phones) begins to be served by products or services. As shown in both parts of the figure, the demand cycle can be subdivided into several distinctive parts:

1. *Emergence (E)*, a turbulent period during which an industry is born, and a number of aspiring competitors seek to capture leadership.
2. *Accelerating growth (G_1)* during which the surviving competitors enjoy the fruits of their victory. During G_1, the demand growth typically outpaces the growth of supply.
3. *Decelerating growth (G_2)* when early signs of saturation appear, and supply begins to exceed demand.
4. *Maturity (M)* when saturation is reached and there is a substantial overcapacity.

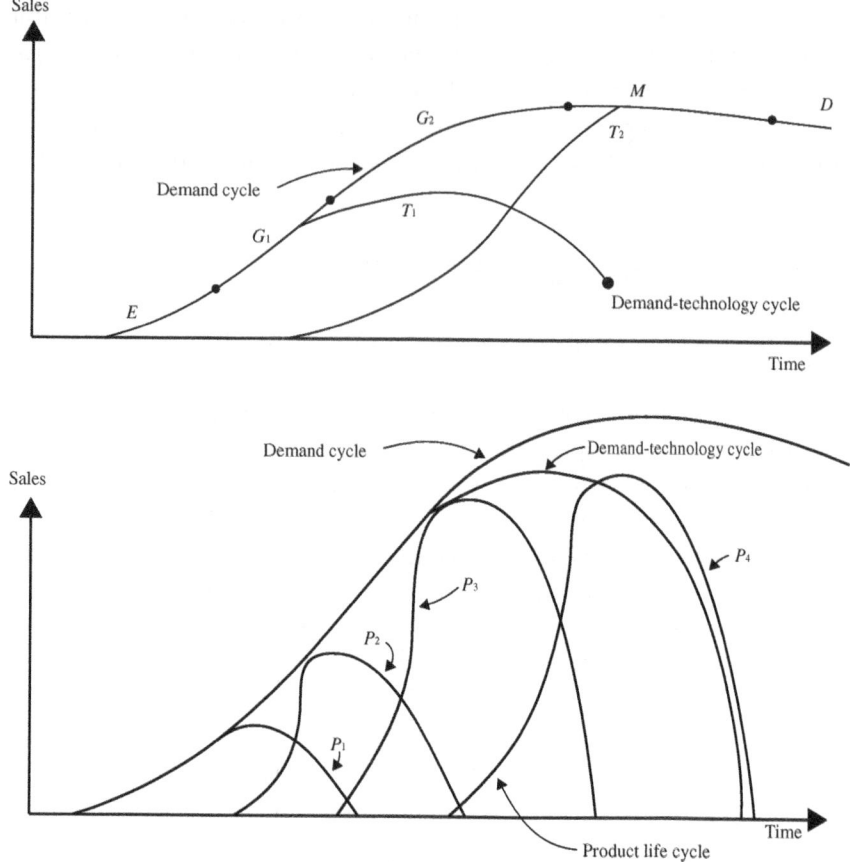

Fig. 9.2 Demand-technology-product life cycles

5. **Decline (D)** to a lower volume of demand (or to zero) which is determined by secular demographic and economic factors (such as growth rates in GNP or in population), and by the rates of product obsolescence or product consumption.

In the perspective of the demand life cycle, deceleration of growth and maturity appears not as aberrations but as inevitable consequences of economic development. The question is not whether an SBA will pass beyond G_1 but rather when it will do so, or, to put it differently, what will be the length of the demand cycle, measured from the beginning of emergence to the arrival of saturation.

Historical evidence suggests that the duration of industry life cycles has been shrinking, thanks largely to improvements in management and effectiveness of firms: improvements in speed of product development, effectiveness of marketing, and efficiency of distribution systems.

This observable shrinkage of time between the birth and saturation of an SBA poses several new and major challenges to management; a manager must expect to witness birth, growth, maturity, and decline in many of the firm's SBAs. As a result, if the firm is to maintain growth, then management must be continually concerned with adding new SBAs to the firm and divesting from SBAs which can no longer meet the firm's growth objectives. This is the first major challenge which, as we shall see later, is a concern central to strategic portfolio management.

The second challenge arises from the fact that, as a life cycle passes from one phase to another, the historical competitive strategies typically become ineffective.

This is illustrated in Fig. 9.3, which shows how the ***key success factors*** in an SBA change as demand moves into a new growth stage. For example, the advent of G_2 in the automotive industry, which occurred in the 1930s, caused a shift from undifferentiated products and competition on price to product differentiation and anticipation of customer needs. Figure 9.3 also shows that during E and G_1 the firm will succeed best if it focuses its energy on its domestic markets. But as growth begins to decelerate, internationalization to foreign SBAs, which are still in E and G_1 stages, begins to look increasingly attractive (see Chapter 14).

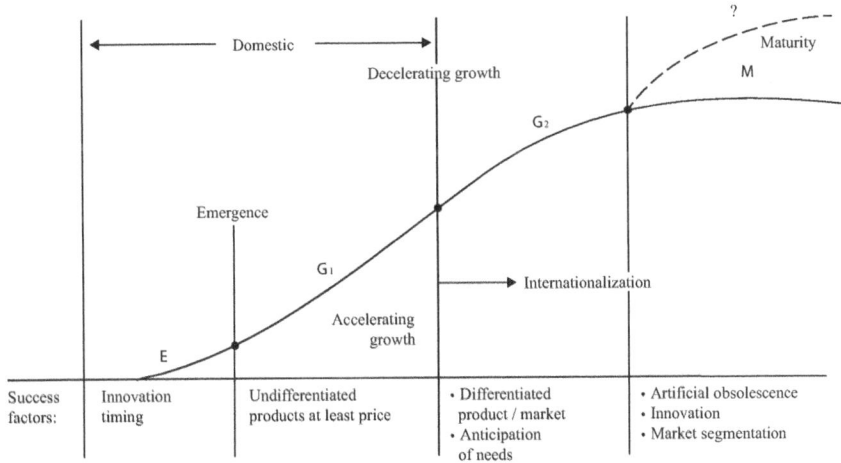

Fig. 9.3 Typical evolution of competitive strategy

Thus, the second challenge to management is to anticipate transitions in the stages of demand cycles and to revise the firm's strategy to respond to the changing competitive factors.

Returning to Fig. 9.2, the upper part shows another pair of life cycles. These are the demand-technology life cycles (labeled T_1 and T_2, respectively) which determine the demand for products/services *based on a particular technology.*

For example, in the mid-1990s the demand for handheld personal computers with a mobile operating system (smartphones) was still in the early G_1 stage, and growing at a rapid rate. Since the mid-1970s, this demand had been served by handheld wireless communication devices (illustrated as T_1). Toward the end of the 1990s, smartphone technology (T_2) began to displace handheld technology. Firms which clung to the historical technology (Nokia) began to lose market share. Curiously enough, the leading companies failed to make a transition to the smartphone technology. As a result, the demand for the relatively simple handheld technology was taken over by newcomers, such as Apple, Samsung, and BlackBerry.

One reason for this 'changing of the guard' is illustrated on the lower part of Fig. 9.2 where inside the demand-technology cycle are shown successive *product life cycles* based on the technology which originally served the demand.

If the technology is fertile (see Chapter 12), the research and development organization becomes a key contributor to success by developing a succession of products (P_1, P_2, P_3, etc.) which incorporate progressive technological improvements. As a result, the firm becomes *technology-driven* (see Chapter 12): The newest developments by the R&D department determine the pace of the firm's strategic development.

When, however, as shown in Fig. 9.2 the importance of the original technology begins to decline, the driving force of technology continues to proliferate products which are no longer competitive in the market place. Thus, in technologically turbulent environments, management needs to recognize early signs of technology obsolescence and assure that the R&D function does not continue to proliferate technologically obsolete products. Beyond implications for management of R&D, technology substitution has important consequences for the way in which a firm defines its SBAs. These consequences will be discussed in the next section.

SBA Segmentation

Experience has shown repeatedly that managers have difficulty in segmenting the firm's environment into SBAs. One reason is the difficulty many people have in changing an ingrained viewpoint: from viewing the environment through the eyes of the firm's traditional product line to viewing the environment as a *field of future needs* which any competitor may choose to address.

A procedure which has proved useful is to ask managers involved in SBA segmentation to avoid using the names or characteristics of the firm's products and focus attention on future threats and opportunities offered by the environment.

The left-hand column of Fig. 9.4 shows that an SBA is described by four dimensions:

1. A societal **need** for products or services. For example, personal transportation.
2. **Technology** which will serve this need in the future. For example, electric, fuel cell, or combustibles.

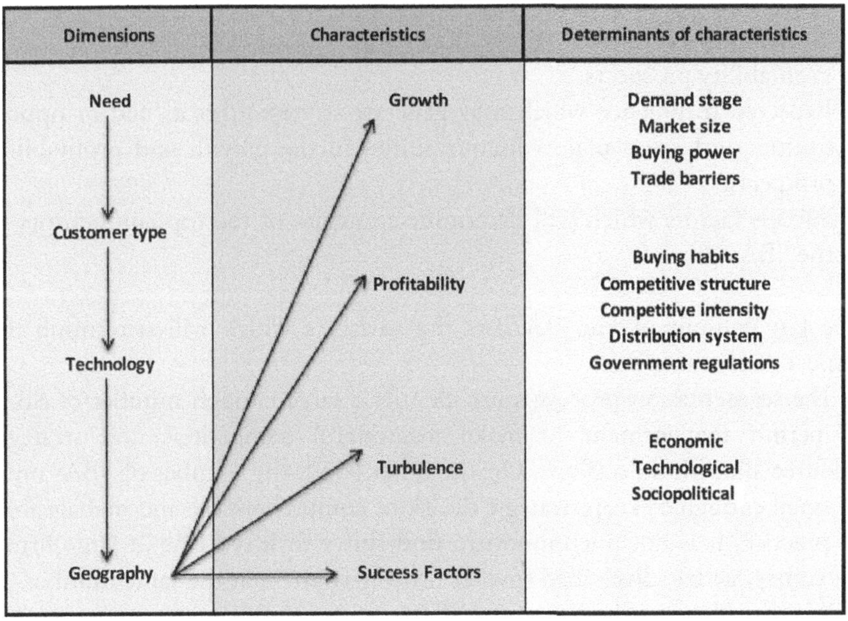

Dimensions	Characteristics	Determinants of characteristics
Need	Growth	Demand stage Market size Buying power Trade barriers
Customer type	Profitability	Buying habits Competitive structure Competitive intensity Distribution system Government regulations
Technology	Turbulence	Economic Technological Sociopolitical
Geography	Success Factors	

Fig. 9.4 Logic of SBA segmentation

3. The ***customer type*** which will have the need. For example, consumer, industrial, and government.
4. The ***geographic region*** in which the need will be served.

As the examples in 1 and 2 above show, in the environment of the 2000s, many needs of society will be served by competing technologies, with a new technology displacing the historical one. When this is expected to be the case, each need technology combination should be treated as a distinctive area of opportunity and, therefore, as a separate SBA. Thus, in our example, the need for fuel-cell technology would be an SBA which is different from the SBA of the same need served by electric technology.

The customer type is a category of organization or individuals which have the same need. The differences among customer types are determined by channels of distribution, buying habits, and/or special requirements for products which serve the need. A geographic region is determined by a distinctive economic entity, such as a country. However, whenever two or more adjoining countries have very similar economic and competitive environments, they may be consolidated into a single geographic region.

The second column of Fig. 9.4 lists the characteristics of performance, attainable by successful competitors in the SBA, which are used for comparison of SBAs:

1. Growth prospects.
2. Profitability prospects.
3. Expected turbulence which may generate strategic threats and/or opportunities and cause major discontinuities in the growth and profitability prospects.
4. Success factors which will determine strategies of the top competitors in the SBA.

The last column of Fig. 9.4 lists the variables which will determine the respective characteristics.

The segmentation process must identify a large enough number of SBAs to permit management to make meaningful competitive and strategic resource allocation decisions. On the other hand, the number of SBAs must be small enough to keep strategic decisions comprehensible and manageable. In practice, it is not uncommon to find thirty to fifty SBAs in large firms. Of course, widely diversified smaller firms may arrive at the same number.

We next illustrate the process of SBA segmentation by means of a concrete example, using Table 9.1. The firm chosen is in the automobile industry.

Table 9.1   SBA for Kinetic conversion transportation

Customer type	Technology	Geography			
	Kinetic conversion	US	EU	Asia/Pacific	Africa
Individual	Gasoline	←———	SBA_1 D	————————→	
	Diesel	←———	SBA_2 M	————————→	
	Hybrid	SBA_3 G_2	SBA_4 G_1	SBA_5 G_2	SBA_6 E
	Electric	←———	SBA_7 G_1	———→	
	Fuel Cell	SBA_8 E		SBA_9 E	
Commercial	Gasoline	←———	SBA_{10} D	———→	SBA_{11} M
	Diesel	←———	SBA_{12} M	————————→	
	Hybrid	SBA_{13} G_1	SBA_{14} E	SBA_{15} G_1	
	Electric	SBA_{16} G_1	SBA_{17} E	SBA_{18} E	

E= Emergence G_1= Accelerating Growth G_2 = Decelerating Growth   M = Maturity   D = Decline

Putting its product line aside, the need served as shown in the title of the figure, transportation. Two customer types of interest to the firm are domestic (individuals) and commercial. The basic technology is kinetic conversion, but within it, there are several possibilities: gasoline, diesel, hybrid, electric, and fuel cell. The firm in our example needs to consider, as a minimum, eighteen distinctive SBAs in making its strategic decisions. The estimates of the life cycle stage are all based on the near-term (five to seven) *years future stage of the demand*, as perceived at the time when the table was constructed.

Strategic Resource Areas

Systematic strategic planning was born in a resource-rich environment. Planners concentrated on choosing markets, technologies, geographic areas, and product lines which offered the most attractive prospects for the firm. They then translated the chosen strategies into requirements for monetary, human, and physical resources with the expectation that the treasurer, the personnel manager, and the purchasing manager would have no trouble in filling the requirements.

Recent events have cast doubts on the validity of this perspective. First, studies from the CATO institute have given the world a theoretical awareness of the finiteness of natural resources. Previous petroleum crisis showed how an escalation of resource costs can undermine and even make invalid the product-market strategy of a firm. Then, the worldwide recession of

2008 made money scarce and stopped growth for firms in which the cost of capital exceeds the return which the firm can earn on it.

The future prospects are for either physical or politically induced resource scarcities and constraints.

As a result, the trend today is to broaden the firm's strategic perspective to include resources, as well as market opportunities. Increasingly, resource constraints impose limits on what the firm can do in the product-market place. For some resource-constrained firms, the practical sequence for planning is now from the inputs to the outputs: first determining the resource availability and then using it as a guide in formulating the product-market strategy.

From the viewpoint of planning technology, the two-way feedback between resource and product-market strategies complicates the process, but poses no insuperable difficulties. More difficult, perhaps, will be the acceptance of the new outlook by managers. In the industrial age, growth vistas appeared limitless and the objectives were determined primarily by the aggressiveness and adventuresome of the managers. In the resource-constrained postindustrial universe, the managers have to balance what they *want* to do against what they *can* do. This does not necessarily mean a passive acceptance of resource limitations. There is as much room for ingenuity for development of entrepreneurial *resource strategies* as there is in the product-market technology strategies.

For firms confronted with strategic resource challenges, subdividing the firm's resource needs into the *strategic resource areas* (SRAs) is a useful first step in the formulation of the firm's resource strategy.

Strategic Influence Groups

In addition to constraints on input resources, the firm is increasingly subject to legal limitations, social pressures, and involvement of inside and outside non-management groups in the decisions and actions of the firm.

Up until the mid-1970s, this problem was viewed as a secondary one, lying outside the central concerns of corporate managers. The solution to the problem was seen as simple. The pressures on business were due to a 'misunderstanding' by the government and the public of the benefits which the firm brought to society and of the necessity of societal noninterference, if these benefits were to be produced. The solution lay through education, 'explaining free enterprise' to the public, and supporting the 'business viewpoint' through lobbying activity. This viewpoint was invariably and adamantly against all forms of constraints on managerial freedoms. To paraphrase President Ford, the solution was to 'get government out of business' hair'. But, progressively, constraints in one form or another have proliferated. The consuming public has turned from a docile and easily influenced purchaser into a demanding and suspicious critic; governments, particularly in Europe, have become increasingly directive; the public has become increasingly disenchanted with the firm.

Thus, from a peripheral problem, the relationship with society is evolving into a key one. In addition to business and resource strategies, firms will increasingly formulate *societal strategies*. The first step in societal strategy formulation is to sort out the many social-political influences into distinctive and different strategic influential groups (SIGs). (We shall be discussing the societal strategy problem of the firm in Chapter 13.)

To summarize the preceding three sections, success and survival of the firm in the 2020s will be determined by its ability to shift from its introverted focus on historical markets and products to an extroverted perception of the future trends, threats, and opportunities. The concepts of SBA, SRA, and SIG are useful complexity reduction tools for making this transition.

Strategic Information.

Environmental Surveillance as an Information Filter

The step following segmentation is to determine the future performance potential which will be available in each SBA to successful competitors. This performance is described by the characteristics shown in the middle column of Fig. 9.4 and determined by the variables described in the right-hand column.

In the early days of strategic planning, it was discovered that the extrapolative accounting-based information system, typically found in firms, was inadequate and misleading for forecasting performance in turbulent environments. As a result, numerous forecasting and environmental analysis techniques were developed, designed to capture nonlinearities, complexity, and unpredictability of future environments.

Figure 9.5 shows three groups of these techniques. As its title describes, the group of *forecasting techniques* is designed *to* develop future trends or identify significant probable future variables (in competitive analysis) and

°Forecasting (business, economic, demographic, sociological, technological)	Environmental Turbulence Level		
	1>2	3>4	4>5
Extrapolation			
Multiple regression			
Curve fitting			
Scenarios			
Corrected extrapolation			
Delphi			
Asymptotic analysis (building numerical methods to approximate equation solution)			
Threats/opportunities analysis			
Modeling of the environment			
Input/output			
Econometrics			
Cybernetics			
Stochastic			
Estimation of impact			
Impact analysis			
Cross-impact analysis			
Deductive analysis (project pattern)			
Force field analysis			

Fig. 9.5   Methods for evaluating the environment

events (in the Delphi technique). Scenarios are currently popular in strategic planning.

Modeling techniques construct a model of reality which can be manipulated by the planner to produce different futures by changing inputs and relationships among the variables within the model. A famous cybernetic model was used to predict probable futures of the world's ecological environment in the book *Limits of Growth* (Meadows 1972-G).

After forecasting or modeling has been used to make predictions about the firm's environment, it is next necessary to assess the impact of the results on the firm. This is the intent of the last group of techniques.

Impact analysis assesses the consequences of trends and events to the firm's performance, one at a time, while cross-impact assesses the extent and probability of a simultaneous coincidence of several events.

It is not our purpose in this book to acquaint the reader with the details of environmental analysis techniques; they can readily be found in a large body of literature on forecasting. Our purpose is to call attention to the limits of applicability of some of the techniques. This is illustrated in the three right-hand columns in Fig. 9.5, where the checks signify the conditions under which a technique will accurately reflect environmental reality. Thus, extrapolation (and its close cousins, multiple regression, and curve fitting) will accurately describe an extrapolable environment in which the historically determining variables, and relations among them, are expected to persist into the future. But, extrapolative techniques, as shown by the absence of checks in columns 2 and 3 in Fig. 9.5, will misrepresent the environment when the variables or the relationships change.

Thus, the environmental surveillance and analysis techniques can be viewed as a filter through which the environmental information must pass on its way into the firm. If the filter is sufficiently open to capture the full richness of the environment, the resulting image within the firm will be faithful to the external reality. If the filter is too restrictive, the data which find their way into the firm will distort and oversimplify reality. For example, during the 'Great Recession' when the housing bubble burst resulting in $8 trillion dollars of lost value, many firms around the world were using extrapolation-based long-range planning to anticipate the future. Understandably, little advanced indications of the surprise were given in the forecasts used by these firms.

The preceding discussion shows that the choice of the environmental surveillance technique is a decision of great importance which, if made improperly, can make the firm strategically myopic and result in the delayed reactive response discussed in the preceding chapter.

In practice, the choice of the techniques is frequently left to the staff who is environmental surveillance specialist. On the one hand, he lacks the breadth of perspective of the general manager, and on the other hand, his natural inclination is to use the technique in which he is trained. Thus, to paraphrase *Clemenceau*, the choice of the forecasting technique is too important to be left to the forecasters. The choice must be made by the general manager who is responsible for the development of a strategic business unit.

In making the choice, he need not, and cannot, become an expert in the details and processes of the respective techniques, but he must learn enough about the techniques to understand the restrictions which the respective filters impose on the firm's image of the external reality.

Mentality Filter

As firms began to use the new environmental surveillance techniques, a curious result was repeatedly observed. Whenever the information presented in the forecasts was consistent with the historical experience, the new data were quickly incorporated into management decisions. But when the data were at substantial variance, or contrary to historical experience, they were neglected or even rejected as irrelevant.

Thus, for example, when distribution of market shares shifted among the firm's historical competitors, management promptly took countermeasures. But, in market after market the inevitable arrival of Chinese competitors was disregarded until the Chinese arrived on the scene.

History is replete with examples of firm's failure to recognize an impeding discontinuity: Henry Ford's refusal to recognize the end of the single model era in the automotive industry, the formation of OPEC and the widespread effects on petroleum prices, and finally, the effects of e-commerce technology on the retail point-of-sale (POS) industry.

The instances of rejection of novel information are numerous enough to suggest the concept of another filter which is applied by the managers to whom surveillance data are addressed. We shall refer to it as the *mentality filter*. The explanation of this filter is readily found in sociological and psychological literature.

As managers respond to environmental stimuli, they encounter successes and failures. Over time, accumulation of the successes forms a conviction in the manager's mind about 'things that do work', and failures build a conviction about 'things that do not'. Together, the two sets of convictions evolve into a *success model* of the environment, or what psychologists call a *mindset*. The model contains the variables, relationships among them, and action alternatives which are believed to produce success in the environment. Very few managers attempt to make their mental success model explicit by writing it down, or programming it on a computer, but all experienced managers use such models in their daily decision-making work.

The model is essential for managing in a complex and changing environment. When complex information comes in, an experienced manager uses the model to reduce the complexity of the signals and to select appropriate responses. As a result, he reacts promptly and decisively. An inexperienced manager, without a developed and tested world model, becomes swamped by the volume and complexity of the information that comes in.

Thus, an articulated success model is an essential part of the equipment of a good manager. But it remains valid only so long as the variables and relationships in the environment remain unchanged. Whenever the environment undergoes a discontinuous change, as it did during the transition from the mass production to the mass marketing era, the manager's historical success model becomes the major obstacle to the firm's adaptation to the new reality.

The manager will filter novel signals which are not relevant to his historical experience and thus fail to perceive the shape of the new environment, the newly important variables, new relationships, and new success factors. As a result, he will delay accepting the new realities until they impact on the firm.

This leads to a widely observable paradox which is described in the phrase: 'success breeds failure' in a turbulent world, and the longer the record of successes of the preceding model, the more likely is the manager to cling to it in spite of novel information which is presented to him.

Thus, we can say that the manager's success model is a second filter which is applied to the incoming environmental data, and that this filter becomes critical whenever the environment moves from one turbulence level to another.

Development of Mentality

In business history, there were two periods of pervasive shifts in environmental turbulence which profoundly changed the character of the success model.

The first transition occurred early in the twentieth century when, entrepreneurial work being done, the key to success shifted to efficient production and distribution. The great founder-entrepreneurs, whose success model was based on creativity, vision, bold risk-taking, and enlargement of the strategic scope of the enterprise, became dysfunctional in the new mass production era in which efficiency of production, stability of the product line, economies of scale, and subdivision of labor became the critical factors of success.

As a result, entrepreneurs with strategic and creative mentalities were replaced by managers who had what came to be known as the *production mentality*.

The second transition started in the thirties, when the expansive growth of the first quarter century began to slow down and the success model shifted from the introverted efficiency-seeking production mentality to an extroverted *marketing mentality*, based on identifying and anticipating the needs of the market.

The transition to the marketing mentality was resisted by the entrenched production-minded managers. The transition was slow, accompanied by power struggles between the establishment and the new breed of power-hungry market-oriented managers.

The transition to the marketing orientation was easier in success-hungry firms, which had been 'also rans' during the mass production era, than it was in firms which had been the leaders. Thus, it was the 'small' General Motors which pioneered and succeeded in introducing the annual model change in the face of the insistence by Mr. Henry Ford on 'giving it to them in any color so long as it is black'.

A significant difference in the transition of the thirties was that, unlike during the preceding transition, the production managers were indispensable, as were the entrepreneurs. Thus, a new balance of power had to be established between the newly dominant marketing managers and the historically dominant production managers.

A third transition started in the USA in the 1960s, when a need began to grow for reintroduction of strategic and creative mentalities into the firm. But the circumstances accompanying the new transition were significantly different from the two preceding transitions.

Unlike in the 1930s, when there was little understanding of the fact that management mentality and corporate culture are the major obstacles to adaptation to new realities, today there is a widespread recognition of the importance of mentality/culture. The word culture, used here for reference to the *collective mentality of a firm*, commonly occurs in the business literature as a key variable in the strategic orientation of a firm. Furthermore, several systematic approaches have been developed to help managers to move to the strategic/creative mentality level.

One of these is a diagnostic approach which permits the firm to determine the type of mentality which the firm will need in the future, to diagnose the present mentality within the firm, and then to determine the mentality gap which will need to be closed in certain parts of the firm.

In Chapter 6, we provided a methodology for carrying out such diagnosis within the framework of the overall capability analysis. Table 9.2 extracts from this analysis the relationship between the environmental turbulence levels and the mentalities appropriate for success.

As the figure shows, for each environmental turbulence level there is an appropriate *success mentality*, which matches the success function at the turbulence level. The respective success functions are described briefly at the bottom of the figure.

This means, for example, that Mr. Henry Ford, who was a huge success in an expanding environment, would have been an obstacle to progress in the Apple company when it created an unpredictable environment in the per-

Table 9.2 Mentality and turbulence

Turbulence level	1 Repetitive	2 Expanding	3 Changing	4 Discontinuous	5 Surprising
Mentality	Custodial	Production	Marketing	Strategic	Creative/flexible
Success Function	Stability	Growth	Differentiation	Strategic Positioning	Creation of technology
Success Mentality	Repetition	Economies of scale	Response to markets	Flexibility	Markets, products

sonal computing industry by introducing the mass-produced PC. But Steve Jobs, the co-founder of Apple, would have been equally dysfunctional in the Ford Motor Company of the 1920s.

Recent experience shows that many firms which find themselves in a discontinuous or unpredictable environment have a difficult mentality-changing task, starting either from the production or from the marketing mentality.

Fortunately, in addition to diagnostic techniques, approaches are now available for helping selected managers develop a new mental success model. Thus, mentality change no longer has to occur through 'blood, sweat and tears' of an organic, unmanaged adaptation.

For enhancement of the creative mentality, creativity techniques are available, such as brainstorming, synectics, brain writing, etc. For enhancement of the strategic mentality, there are several mentality-changing techniques. Some of the early techniques, such as Trident (Davous and Deas in Ansoff et al. 1976-F) and strategic orientation round (SOR) developed by the Dutch Philips Company, are primarily oriented toward enhancing strategic mentality of managers. New techniques are dual purpose: They enhance strategic mentality of the participating managers in the course of producing effective strategic responses. We shall be discussing several of these techniques in Chapters 10, 19, 24, and 25.

Just as in the 1930s, the introduction of the strategic/creative mentalities is not a replacement but an addition process. If the entire management were to be converted to the new mentalities, the firm would become creative, but little efficient production would occur and little effective marketing would take place. The firm would be an excellent profit potential generator but very poor profit maker.

The additive character of the need is both an advantage and a problem. The advantage lies in the fact that only selected managers, those charged with the strategic development of the firm, need to undergo the mentality change. This limits the size of the task and permits a careful selection process to identify managers who have the talents and personality necessary to behave strategically.

The problem is the need to assure a constructive coexistence between several mentalities. We shall discuss a process and tools for assuring such coexistence in Chapter 25.

Strategic and Creative Mentalities

The strategic and creative mentalities are summarized in Table 9.2, but, since they will be new to many readers, they deserve a more detailed description.

- *Both are focused on the future.* In strategic mentality, the past is recognized and treated critically. Managers with strategic mentality are skillful in perceiving the underlying trends that will make the future different from the past. Managers with creative mentality make novel juxtapositions of historical trends and create new ideas.
- *Both subsist on novel unfamiliar change.* The strategic manager has no emotional or intellectual investment in history nor the future. His viewpoint was brilliantly described by CEO of General Motors, Alfred P. Sloan (A. P. Sloan, Jr. 1965-G) who said: 'The strategic aim of the enterprise is to produce a satisfactory return on investment; and, if the return is not satisfactory, ... then the resources should be allocated elsewhere'. Thus, the strategic manager has no sentimental attachment to 'our markets', 'our products', and 'our customers', which is typically found in the marketing mentality.

  The creative manager is focused on novelty. Typically, when asked who are your competitors, the creative managers' reply is, 'We have no competition. We are our own competition'.
- The strategic manager differs from the creative manager in his *preparedness to recognize that mentalities of others* (such as production managers) *are legitimate* and may make an important contribution to the success of the firm.

The creative manager, on the other hand, typically *cannot afford the luxury of ecumenism*, if he is to maximize the chance that his own unorthodox views are going to be accepted.

- In the matter of key success factors, the strategic manager *is skilled in identifying the small number of variables, in an unfamiliar and complex problem, which are critical to success.* The creator invents new success factors and variables.
- *Both are guided by an entrepreneurial drive:* a vision of a new future for the firm. Both are 'gamblers'. The strategic manager makes gambles only when they are in the best interest of the firm. The creative manager may gamble because of the excitement of novelty.
- *Both are tolerant of failure* in situations in which the risk has been taken with 'eyes open', with a full appreciation of the possibility of surprises. But they are intolerant of managers who avoid risks, or who walk into a risky situation with 'their eyes closed'. Both refuse to accept a one-time failure as a deterrent to trying again.

The characteristics of the successful strategic/creative manager have been aptly summarized in the Shell Company, where he is said to possess a helicopter mentality: the imaginative ability to rise above the many-variable complexity which novel challenges typically present, and to see the few basic variables and relationships which determine a successful response.

The Power Filter

As already discussed, environmental discontinuities frequently have major implications for the power structure. Thus, in the change from production to marketing orientation, a power transfer occurred from the production to the marketing departments. The current shift to the strategic orientation enhances the power of the corporate office (see Chapter 17), of the R&D department, and of the corporate planning department.

It is, therefore, natural for managers and departments, whose power base is threatened by a discontinuity, to minimize or even refuse to recognize the impact of the discontinuity on the firm. Frequently, such rejection is not an unscrupulous effort to preserve a position of power, come what may. The threatened power centers are usually also representatives of the historical mentality which had brought the original success to the firm. Therefore, they can exercise their blocking influence in good conscience and believe that they are acting for the good of the firm.

When the historical mentality in the firm is politically entrenched, the likelihood is high that, through repeated rejection of threatening environmental signals, the firm will drift into a crisis and will go bankrupt unless external influence and/or new management is brought in.

When the representatives of the new mentality have enough power to begin eroding the power of the dominant mentality, and if the threat/opportunity develops slowly enough, a protracted power struggle may bring about a shift of power as defenders of the old mentality/culture are repeatedly discredited by failure of their responses to arrest the decline of the firm's performance.

Thus, there is a third filter which can delay and impede acceptance of novel environmental signals. We shall call it the *power filter*.

Novel information will not find its way into management responses, unless the managers with the strategic/creative mentalities have the power to assure its acceptance.

For example, many 'progressive firms' invest substantial efforts in development of middle and lower managers. Either through in-company or external programs, these managers typically undergo a change in mentality, while the senior managers who send them to the programs continue to adhere to their historical mentality. When the middle managers return to work, their new mentality encounters hostility from their peers and indifference or rejection from their bosses.

Three patterns of reaction have been observed. In the first, the returnees conform to the historical mentality and forget their 'book-learning'. In the second, they leave the firm. In the third, they begin to fight the system, but are ineffective because they lack the necessary power base and skills in change management.

Therefore, to assure a firm-wide acceptance of a new mentality, it is essential that top management be the leading practitioners of this mentality.

A Model of Strategic Information

The problem of strategic information is summarized in Fig. 9.6. The signals and data about the future trends and possibilities in the environment are brought into the firm by means of environmental surveillance, forecasting, and analysis. The data that get into the firm are processed by the surveillance

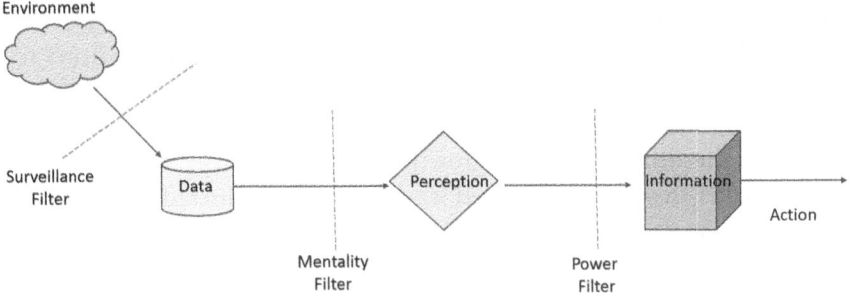

Fig. 9.6 Management information

filter, whose characteristics are determined by the forecasting/analysis techniques used by the firm.

For a faithful reflection of the environmental reality, it is necessary to use a technique which can capture the essential elements of that reality. The more complex the reality, the more comprehensive must be the technique.

Data brought into the firm do not become a part of information on which decisions are based until it passes two additional filters. The first is the mentality filter based on the mental success model which is used by managers to identify parts of the data which they perceive to be relevant.

Managers build their private success models through experience, trial and error, and successes and failures. When the environment is undergoing a discontinuous change, the historical success model becomes invalid and acts to block the newly relevant data. Thus, development in key managers of a mentality which will be responsive to future turbulence is a critical part of the strategic information problem. Today, techniques are available for both diagnosing the needed mentality and helping managers to acquire it.

The third filtering of data is imposed by the power structure. If the powerful managers lack *the* appropriate mentality, they will persist in preventing vital novel signals from affecting decisions. This explains the phenomenon of procrastination discussed in the last chapter.

Competitive Positioning.

The BCG Matrix

The BCG matrix, introduced by the Boston Consulting Group and shown in Fig. 9.7, offers a useful method for comparison of a firm's SBAs. From among the measures of prospects shown in Fig. 9.4, BCG chooses market growth rate as the single measure of the future SBA prospects. This is the vertical dimension of the matrix. The horizontal dimension is the firm's relative market share in relation to the share of the leading competitor which, in BCG's view, is the measure which determines the future relative competitive position of the firm. The future growth rate for each SBA *is* estimated, the relative market shares are computed, and each SBA is entered into the corresponding rectangle of Fig. 9.7.

A useful technique is to represent each SBA as a circle whose diameter is proportional to the expected size of the demand. A shadowed segment within the circle can represent the market share the firm expects to capture. Additional information which can be written alongside the circle is the percentage of sales and profits which the firm expects to derive from the SBA. The resulting scatter diagram presents a comprehensive view of the entire firm on a single piece of paper.

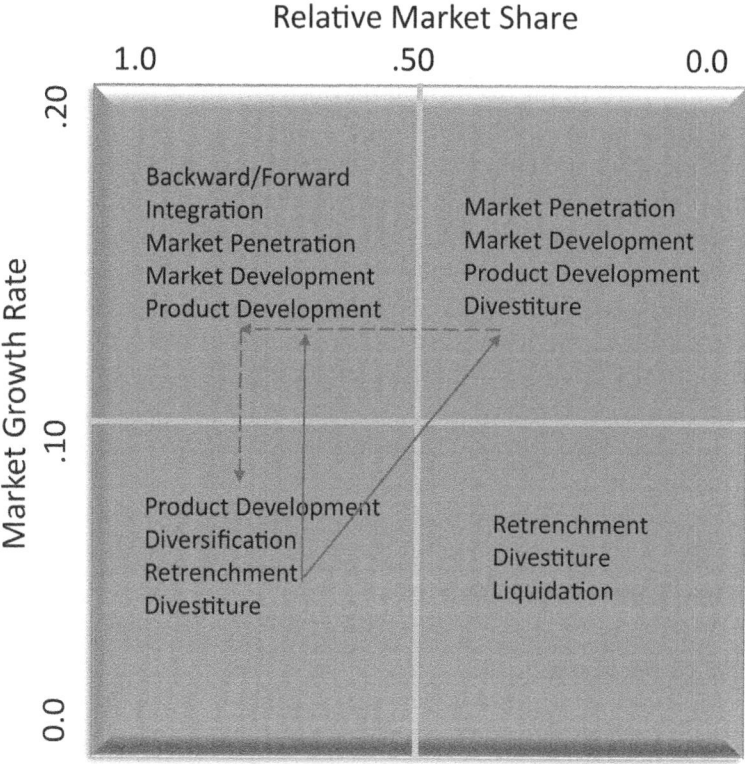

Fig. 9.7 The BCG matrix

The BCG diagram suggests decisions on future participation by the firm into the respective SBAs.

- The star should be cherished and reinforced.
- The dogs should probably be divested, unless there are compelling reasons for keeping them.
- The cash cows should be made to control (severely) their investments and send excess cash to the headquarters.
- The question marks need to be analyzed to see whether the investment necessary to convert them into stars is worthwhile.

As the dotted line indicates, the question marks may be promoted to stars, and the stars, because of eventual maturity, will become the cash cows of tomorrow. The solid arrows indicate the flows of cash from cash cows.

Thus, the BCG matrix is useful for two purposes: decisions on the desirable market share positions and allocation of strategic funds among the SBAs. Applications of the BCG matrix showed it to be a useful tool for making strategic position decisions about SBAs and for near-term strategic resource allocations. But experience also showed that the BCG matrix is applicable under very special conditions.

1. *The future prospects in all the firm's SBAs should be measurable by a single growth rate index.* This is true in SBAs which, for the foreseeable future, can be expected to remain in the same life cycle growth stage, and/or when the expected level of turbulence is low, which is another way of saying that the growth is not likely to be perturbed by unexpected events. But when the SBA is expected to move into another growth stage in the foreseeable future, and/or high-level turbulence is forecast, the single growth rate measure of prospects becomes inaccurate and dangerous.

What is even more dangerous is the implied assumption that high volume growth will necessarily lead to high profitability. In today's environment, SBAs which are technologically turbulent, or in which competition is cut-throat, may experience profitless growth.

2. The future competitive dynamics within the SBA should be such that *relative market share is the only determinant of its competitive strength.* This is true in the G_1 stage of growth, under conditions when technology is stable, the rate of growth of demand exceeds the rate of growth of supply, and competition is not cutthroat. But when these conditions do not hold

and/or an SBA is in G_2 or M, factors other than market share typically acquire dominant importance to continued competitive success.

The conclusion to be drawn from the above remarks is that before the BCG matrix is used, it is essential to make sure that the future prospects are adequately measured by volume growth and the firm's relative competitive position by its relative market share. Reference to Chapter 6 will suggest that these conditions exist when environmental turbulence is on levels 1 or 2. At these levels, the BCG has the advantage of simplicity and is an effective tool for analysis of the firm's portfolio.

When environmental turbulence rises above level 2, appropriately more complex measurements are needed for the two dimensions of the matrix. The growth rate should be replaced by the concept of SBA attractiveness, and relative market share by the firm's future extrapolated competitive position. In the next two sections, we show how to estimate the attractiveness and the competitive position, and in the section following, we shall use them to introduce a version of the matrix which takes explicit account of future uncertainty.

Estimating SBA Attractiveness

In a turbulent environment in which the length of demand-technology life cycle stages is shorter than the firm's planning horizon, the prospects in an SBA must be measured by several criteria:

1. Because of possible life cycle effects, two estimates of growth are needed, one for the remainder of the current growth stage and another for the following stage.
2. Because of probable changes in competitive dynamics, it should not be assumed that inherent profitability in the SBA will remain as in the past, or will positively correlate with future growth. It is possible for profitability to remain the same or to decrease as an SBA grows. Thus, two independent estimates of short- and long-term profitability are needed.
3. Because of probable social, political, economic, and technological shifts, estimation of attractiveness should take account of the future turbulence.

Thus, from a single measure of volume growth, used by BCG, the future attractiveness of an SBA becomes a complex combination of factors. Business and consulting firms have developed different ways of estimating the SBA attractiveness. One of these is briefly described in this section, and the logic of the approach is shown in Fig. 9.8.

1. The process starts with a *global forecast* of economic-sociopolitical-technological environments in which the SBAs of interest to the firm are located. A list of techniques for environmental forecasting was discussed in this chapter.
2. As the next step, an impact analysis of the key trends and contingencies on the respective SBAs is made. The result is a measure of the *probable future turbulence in the SBA*. This technique is described in this chapter. In making the estimate, it is important to recognize that turbulence manifests itself in two ways: welcome opportunities (*O*) which may develop in the SBA under analysis, and unwelcome threats (*T*).
3. Thirdly, both the historical growth and historical profitability *trends are extrapolated into the future*.
4. Next, the probable *changes in the historical demand trend* are estimated for each of the *demand determinants* which are illustrated in Table 9.3; +5 and −5 shifts represent major increases or decreases. Two profiles of the shifts in the intensity of the demand determinants are constructed: one for the near and another for the long term.
5. At the bottom of the figure, using the two profiles, a summary estimate is made of the *overall shifts of growth prospects* in the near and the long term. This estimate can be made by averaging the shifts in each line.

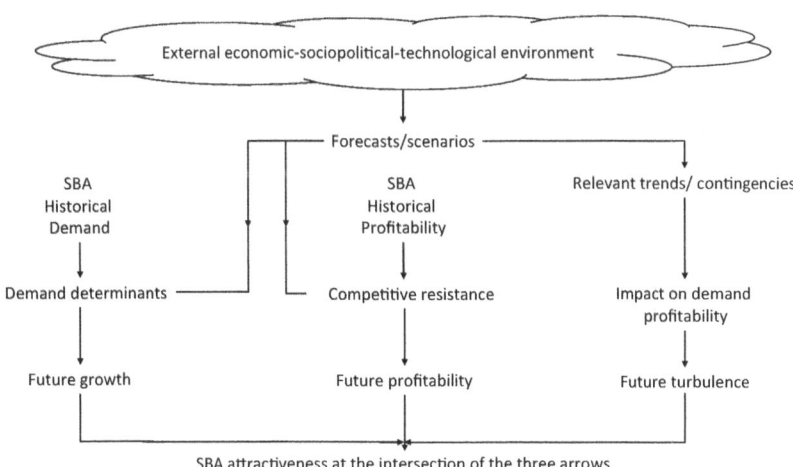

Fig. 9.8 Estimating SBA attractiveness

Table 9.3 Appraisal of changes in SBA prospects growth

	SBA name_____		
Attribute	**Shift in intensity***		
	|-5	0	+5|
1. Growth of relevant economic sector	decreased		increased
2. Growth of customer population	decreased		increased
3. Rate of geographic market expansion	shrinkage		expansion
4. Rate of product obsolescence	lower		higher
5. Rate of technological innovation	lower		higher
6. Rate of product innovation	lower		higher
7. Level of demand saturation	increased		decreased
8. Social acceptability of product/services	decreased		increased
9. Social acceptability of product/services	increased		decreased
10. Government regulation of costs	increased		decreased
11. Government regulation of growth	increased		decreased
12. Threats to growth/profitability	decreased		increased
Other factors which are relevant to the SBA:			
13	|_____|		
14	|_____|		
Overall shift in growth prospects	|-5	0	+5|
*If the future prospects will remain the same as in the past, check the midpoint of the scale (zero)			

A more sophisticated approach is to assign to each line an index of its relative importance to future growth, and then use the indices to compute weighted average shifts in the overall growth prospects.

6. The overall shift is applied to correct the extrapolation to produce *numerical estimates of future growth.*
7. A similar procedure is followed to estimate *the future shifts in the profitability* by estimating the change in the competitive resistance, using Table 9.4 and applying it to the extrapolated profits.
8. Returning to the bottom of Fig. 9.8, an *overall estimate is made of the future attractiveness of the SBA* by combining the growth (G), profitability (P), and turbulence prospects (T/0) in the following formula:

$$\text{SBA attractiveness} = \alpha G + \beta P + \gamma 0 - \delta T$$

where α, β, γ, and δ are coefficients whose sum is 1.0 and which are relative importance weights assigned by management to the respective contributions

Table 9.4 Shift in profitability of an SBA

Characteristics	Shift in intensity*		
SBA name_____			
	|-5	0	+5|
1. Fluctuation of profitability	|stable		highly variable|
2. Fluctuation of sales	|stable		highly variable|
3. Fluctuation of prices	|stable		highly variable|
4. Cyclicity of demand	|stable		highly variable|
5. Demand to capacity ratio	|very high		very low|
6. Market shares	|highly concentrated		distributed |
7. Stability of market shares	|stable		highly unstable|
8. Rate of product introduction	|rare		very frequent|
9. Length of product life cycles	|long		short|
10. Lead time to develop products	|long		short|
11. Research and development expenditures	|low		high|
12. Cost of entry/exit	|high		low |
13. Aggressiveness of leading competitors	|passive		aggressive|
14. Foreign competition	|weak		very strong |
15. Competition for resources	|weak		very strong |
16. Intensity of promotion/advertising	|low		very high|
17. After sales follow-up	|nonexistant		thorough|
18. Customer satisfaction	|very high		low |
19.Government regulation of competition	|nonexistant		strong |
20. Government regulation of products/services	|nonexistant		strong |
21. Consumer group pressures	|weak		very strong |

Other factors which are relevant to the SBA:

Overall shift, future shift in profitability	|-5	0	+5|

*If the future prospects will remain the same as in the past, check the midpoint of the scale (zero)

to attractiveness. These coefficients are the relative priorities of the firm's objectives (see Chapter 11).

Two independent estimates are to be made, one for the long and the other for the short term. The first of these estimates is used to replace the volume growth dimension in the BCG matrix. The second is used in the long-term portfolio balance which will be discussed in Chapter 11.

While a good deal more complex than the simple BCG measure of volume growth, the estimate of SBA attractiveness provides a more realistic basis for the comparison of the complex and interacting factors which determine the relative attractiveness of different SBAs to the firm.

Estimating Strategic Investment Ratio

Economic theory and common sense both suggest that the firm's profitability in an SBA will be proportional to the size of its investment. Experience shows that the profitability follows a curve similar to the one shown in Fig. 9.9, where the horizontal scale, labeled $I_{strategic}$, is the firm's total commitment of resources to an SBA, including not only facilities and equipment but also developing the firm's product and market position, in addition to the supporting capabilities in management, production, sales, etc.

As the figure shows, in each SBA there is a minimal *critical mass* which is the *strategic break-even point*. No matter how brilliant a firm's strategy, or how excellent its capability, a strategic investment below the critical mass level will not be profitable.

Critical mass is difficult to estimate and, until recently, has not been in the forefront of management attention. As a result, numerous well-intentioned plunges into new SBAs have floundered simply because the firm discovered, usually too late, that it did not have the resources to raise its investment in the SBA above the critical mass.

A current example of the importance of critical mass is the future prospects in the electric-automotive industry, which indicates that many of the present competitors will not be big enough to succeed in the global market of the next five years.

A firm which finds that the future critical mass in one of its SBAs is going to exceed substantially the resources of the firm has three possible solutions:

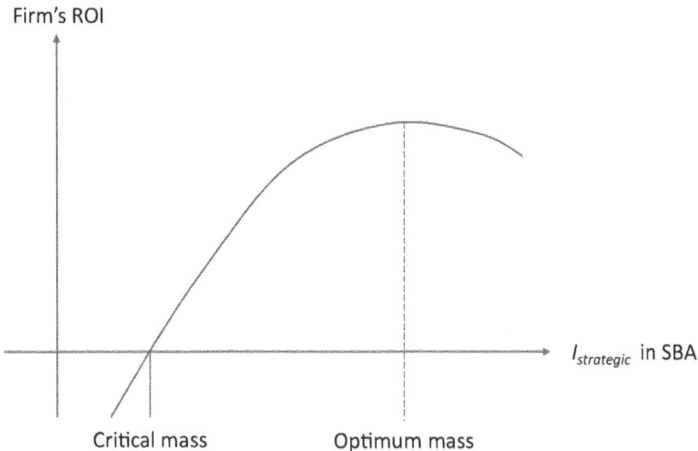

Fig. 9.9 Competitive position and strategic investment

1. To withdraw from the SBA rather than facing the inevitable losses.
2. Find a niche within the SBA. An example for a firm in the automotive industry would be to focus its business on a segment of the total demand for personal transportation, such as the demand for luxury transportation. In fact, this is the approach which the Volvo Company took in order to bring its resources in line with critical mass.
3. To form a *strategic alliance* with another firm (or firms). A recent dramatic example was an alliance between two companies: Nestle' company the Swiss food giant and Pastificio Rana from Italy. As announced by the two partners, the alliance was formed to pool complementary capabilities to enable them to exceed the critical mass of investment which will be required to succeed in the future global food business.

Figure 9.9 shows that there is also an *optimum mass* which is a level of investment beyond which profitability begins to decline due to decreased speed of organizational response and bureaucratization of the firm.

We shall use the ratio of a firm's expected profitability in an SBA to the optimal possible future profitability as one of the key factors which determine the firm's future competitive position in an SBA.

The following equation describes the future competitive position:

$$\text{FCP} = \frac{\text{ROI}_f}{\text{ROI}_{opt}} = \frac{I_f - I_{cr}}{I_{opt} - I_{cr}} \times \alpha \times \beta$$

where I_f is the firm's strategic investment level, $I_{cr,}$ critical mass level, and I_{opt}, the optimum level. We shall refer to the ratio on the right-hand side of the equation as the *strategic investment ratio*.

Expressed in words, the formula says that, provided the firm's strategy and capability are optimal ($\alpha = \beta = 1$), the firm's competitive position will be in proportion to the ratio of the firm's investment into an SBA to the level of investment which will produce optimal profitability. But, frequently, the firm's strategy and capability are not optimal. In such cases, the competitive position must be reduced by factors α *and* β which we shall discuss in the following sections.

As mentioned before, the recognition of the importance of the strategic investment level is relatively recent. Therefore, satisfactory techniques for estimating it are yet to be developed. A starting point is to identify the relevant categories of investment.

In estimating the firm's present strategic investment in the SBA, as well as the optimal mass, the following categories of investment should be considered:

1. *Investment in capacity.* This is the cost of facilities and equipment needed to provide the necessary capacity of: production facilities; distribution network; the marketing organization; and research and development.
2. *Investment in strategy.* This includes the costs of: strategic planning; market research; product development; and product launching.
3. Investments in capability: This includes the costs of: acquisition of personnel; training of personnel; acquisition of technology; and learning cost of development of competent functional organizations in each of the categories under item (1) above.

Thus, the first step in evaluating the firm's future competitive position in an SBA is to determine its future relative investment position by:

1. Estimating the firm's present and presently planned strategic investment by the firm.
2. Estimating the future critical and the optimal masses.
3. Determining the ratio of the firm's investment to the optimal investment, according to the formula presented above.

*Determining the Future Effectiveness of Present Strategy

The factor α in the equation in the preceding section is determined by the future effectiveness of the firm's present competitive strategy which the firm pursues in an SBA. The competitive strategy can be described, in part, by the following *sub-strategies:*

1. The firm's *growth thrust* which describes the way in which the firm will assure its future growth in an SBA.
   Growth thrust becomes an important component of strategy whenever the SBA growth prospects are not sufficient to meet the firm's growth objectives. Different ways in which a firm can exceed the market growth prospects are illustrated in the top line of Fig. 9.10.

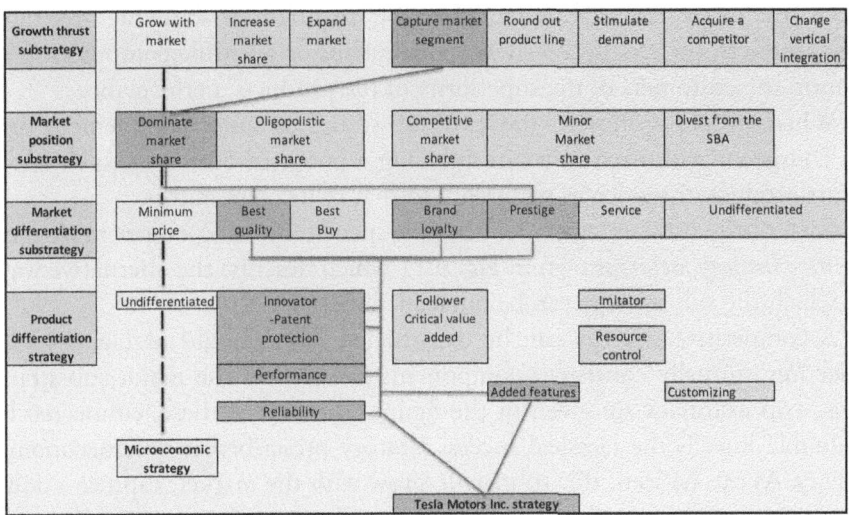

Fig. 9.10 Competitive strategy factors

2. *Market position* sub-strategy which describes the market share the firm will seek to occupy. Alternative choices are described in the second line of Fig. 9.10.

   Market position sub-strategy becomes the only component of competitive strategy in SBAs in which future growth is excellent and the demand is for undifferentiated products (such as cement).

3. *Market differentiation* sub-strategy which describes the distinctiveness of the firm's products/services which the firm will seek to establish in the minds of its customers. This is described in line three of Fig. 9.10.

4. *Product/service differentiation* sub-strategy which is the manner in which the firm will seek to differentiate its products/services from those of their competitors.

At first glance, product and market differentiation sub-strategies may appear to be identical. Brief reflection will show, however, that they are different. Thus, for example, promotion and advertising are commonly used to create distinctive images of virtually identical products (e.g., distinctive images of breakfast cornflake cereals).

On the other hand, the only 'marketing' required for some high-technology products, such as advanced weapon systems or scientific computers, is to inform the customers of the superiority of the products' performance.

When properly chosen, the two sub-strategies must complement and be consistent with each other in inducing a potential customer to choose a firm's product or service in preference to that of its competitors.

Each of the sub-strategies can be made specific by using one or more *competitive strategy factors* shown in Fig. 9.11 which describe the alternative ways in which the sub-strategy can be pursued.

A competitive strategy can be constructed with the aid of Fig. 9.10 by selecting mutually consistent components for each of the major sub-strategies. Two examples are given in the figure. The first of these, connected by a double line, is the classical success strategy prescribed in microeconomic theory. As can be seen, this strategy is 'grow with the market, capture a dominant market share, and offer an undifferentiated product at the minimum price'. As discussed before, this strategy works in a non-turbulent G_1 growth stage of the life cycle.

Another strategy, illustrated by the elements connected by the single lines, is the 'Tesla Motors' strategy: 'segment the market, occupy dominant share

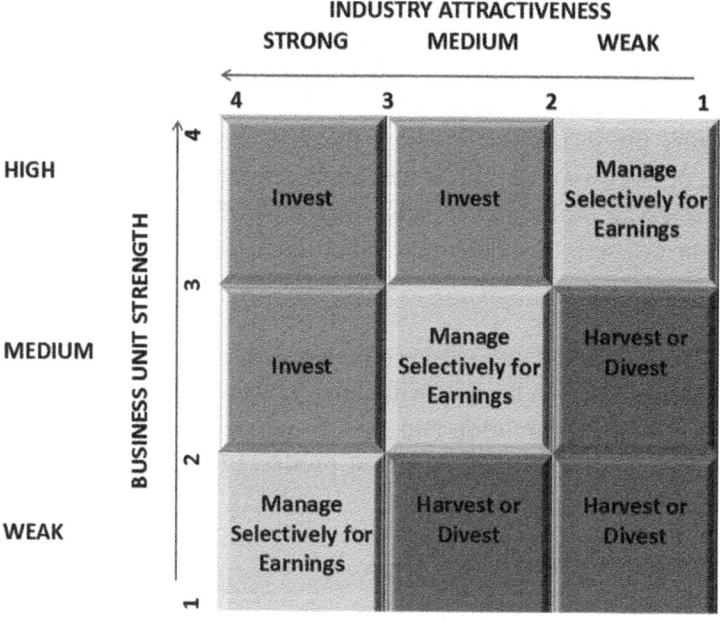

Fig. 9.11   The GE-McKinsey matrix

in your segment, offer service, performance features, and reliability which together project an image of exclusivity, comfort, and styling'.

This sample strategy illustrates the important fact that, to be effective, the sub-strategy components must be consistent with and supportive of one another. For example, the firm cannot hope to gain a dominant market share, if its growth strategy is to grow with the market. As another example, it is difficult, if not impossible, to pursue a minimum price sub-strategy while seeking to be a product innovator.

The future effectiveness of the firm's present strategy can be estimated as follows:

1. Using Fig. 9.10, select the elements of each sub-strategy which describe the firm's present strategy. Enter these into the second column of Table 9.5. The example in the figure illustrates the classic microeconomic strategy.
2. Construct a future success strategy by selecting from Fig. 9.6 a set of consistent elements which, in your judgment, will be used by top competitors in the SBA during the next five to seven years.
3. Estimate the future effectiveness ratio of the firm's sub-strategy relative to the success sub-strategy Si. In the example illustrated in Table 9.5, the growth sub-strategy ratio is estimated to be 0.2.
4. Average the ratios of the four sub-strategies to obtain the overall effectiveness ratio of the present strategy of the firm.
5. Follow the same procedure to construct two (or more) additional future success strategies, S_2 and S_1, which are expected to be comparably successful to S_1.
6. Determine the firm's overall effectiveness ratios for S_2 and S_3.
7. Compare the three effectiveness ratios. The largest ratio is the value of the factor a which should be used to substitute for the factor in the equation for determining the future competitive position. In the example in Table 9.5, the effectiveness of strategy S_1 is 0.55.

The success strategy which produces the highest effectiveness ratio is the closest to the present strategy and is, therefore, the optimal future strategy for the firm.

If the largest effectiveness ratio is close to one, the present and the optimal strategies are virtually identical, and little more than fine tuning needs to be applied to the present strategy.

Table 9.5 Determining future effectiveness of present strategy

Sub-strategies	Firm's present strategy: S_F	Future success strategies					
		S_1		S_2		S_3	
		Strategy element	Sub-strategy ratio $=\frac{S_F}{S_1}$	Strategy element	Sub-strategy ratio $=\frac{S_F}{S_2}$	Strategy element	Sub-strategy ratio $=\frac{S_F}{S_3}$
Growth thrust	Grow with the market	Increase market share	0.2				
Market position	Dominate market share	Competitive	0.5				
Market differentiation	Undifferentiated	Follower	0.5				
Product differentiation	Minimum price	Minimum price	1				
Firm's overall effectiveness ratio			0.55				

If the effectiveness ratio is substantially less than one, major changes in the present strategy will be required if the firm is to become one of the leading competitors in the SBA.

This completes our discussion of the strategy effectiveness ratio which was the α factor in the future competitive position equation presented at the end of this chapter. The equation can now be rewritten as follows:

$$\text{FCP} = \frac{\text{ROI}_f}{\text{ROI}_{\text{opt}}} = \frac{I_f - I_{cr}}{I_{\text{opt}} - I_{cr}} \times \frac{S_f}{S_{\text{opt}}} \times \beta$$

where S_f is the present strategy of the firm and S_{opt}, is the future success strategy in the SBA which is closest to S_f.

*Estimating Future Competitive Position

To explain the residual factor β, we turn our attention to the third determinant of the competitive position, the *capability* which the firm brings to the execution of strategy. A comprehensive list of capability factor choices is available for general management: finance, marketing, production, and R&D.

According to the strategic success paradigm discussed in Chapter 6, to assure optimum performance of a strategy, the firm's capability profile must match the strategy.

1. General management must focus its attention on growth and efficient production. It must also control and minimize disruptive changes which interfere with minimization of the unit costs of the product.
2. Financial management must manage cash and exercise strict controllership.
3. Marketing should focus on sales and on sales analysis.
4. Production is the key function under the microeconomic strategy. It must receive maximal support from general management and be focused on mass production and maximally cost-effective automation.
5. R&D is a potentially dangerous function under the microeconomic strategy. It must be limited to improvements in production technology and to incremental evolution of products in response to moves by competitors. R&D must be prevented from causing loss of economies of production.

Just as in the case of strategy, Table 9.6 can be used, first, to diagnose the firm's present capability, second, to determine the optimal capability which will be required for future success, and third, to determine the *capability ratio*. Table 9.6 is provided for this purpose.

1. In the second column, enter sub-capabilities which determine the firm's present capability profile.
2. In the third column, enter the profile necessary to support the optimum strategy which has been determined in Table 9.5.
3. In the last column, compute and average the ratios to produce the overall capability ratio.

The capability factor is the second residual β factor which remained to be explained at the end of the last section. Thus, the future competitive position can now be estimated.

4. Using the investment, the strategy, and the capability ratios, compute their product which is the future competitive position which the firm will occupy if it pursues the present strategy:

$$FCP = \text{Investment ratio} \times \text{Strategy ratio} \times \text{Capability ratio}$$
$$= \frac{I_f - I_{cr}}{I_{opt} - I_{cr}} \times \frac{S_f}{S_{opt}} \times \frac{C_f}{C_{opt}}$$

When all three of the ratios have the value of one, the firm's future competitive position will be outstanding, and it will be among the top performers in the SBA. When any factor is zero, the firm will not be profitable.

Readers who are not mathematically trained are warned that in the above formula the scale in between 1 and 0 is not linear, because the formula is in

Table 9.6 Determining the effectiveness of present capabilities

Capability components	Firm's present capability C_f	Capability needed for optimum strategy C_{opt}	Capability ratio $= \frac{C_f}{C_{opt}}$
General management			
Finance			
Marketing			
Production			
R&D			
Other			
Overall ratio			

the form of a product. To translate the numbers into positions in the matrix, the following approach can be used.

Compute a series of triple products of investment, strategy, and capability ratios and convert the results to 'good', 'average', or 'poor' evaluation of FCP. For example, assuming values for the three variables:

$$FCP = \text{Investment ratio} \times \text{Strategy ratio} \times \text{Capability ratio}$$
$$= 0.8 \times 0.8 \times 0.8$$
$$= 0.512$$

This figure or higher represents a *good* competitive position.

$$FCP = \text{Investment ratio} \times \text{Strategy ratio} \times \text{Capability ratio}$$
$$= 0.5 \times 0.5 \times 0.5$$
$$= 0.125$$

An FCP somewhere around this number range would represent an *average* competitive position.

$$FCP = \text{Investment ratio} \times \text{Strategy ratio} \times \text{Capability ratio}$$
$$= 0.25 \times 0.25 \times 0.25$$
$$= 0.016$$

An FCP somewhere around this number or lower would represent a *poor* competitive position. To summarize our discussion of the future competitive position (FCP), we stated that the FCP is determined by the following equation:

$$FCP = \frac{ROI_f}{ROI_{opt}}$$

where ROI_f is the ROI which the firm derives from an SBA, and ROI_{opt} is the ROI derived by the most successful competitor(s) in the SBA.

Expanding the equation into its principal components, we found:

$$\frac{ROI_f}{ROI_{opt}} = \frac{\text{Strategy}_f \times \text{Capability}_f \times \text{Strategy investment}_f}{\text{Strategy}_{opt} \times \text{Capability}_{opt} \times \text{Strategy investment}_{opt}}$$

The above equation can now be rewritten as follows:

$$\text{ROI}_f = \text{ROI}_{\text{opt}} \left[\frac{\text{Strategy}_f \times \text{Capability}_f \times \text{Strategy investment}_f}{\text{Strategy}_{\text{opt}} \times \text{Capability}_{\text{opt}} \times \text{Strategy investment}_{\text{opt}}} \right]$$

The term in brackets will be referred to as the firm's *relative competitive posture* in an SBA. Competitive posture is defined as the combination of factors which determines a firm's ROI in an SBA.

The GE-McKinsey Matrix

The results of the preceding two sections enable us to position the SBA in a version of the positioning matrix which meets the fundamental criticism which has been advanced against the BCG matrix, namely, that it uses oversimplified measurements along its two principal dimensions. The matrix, shown in Fig. 9.11, uses industry attractiveness to replace the BCG's market growth and business unit strength to replace the relative market share. The method of entering SBA data used in the BCG matrix applies also to this new matrix. We name it after the McKinsey company which was one of its co-inventors. As is shown in the new matrix, it is usable for the same types of decision as the preceding one.

Unlike the BCG, the new matrix is applicable in all stages of the *demand life cycle* and in a wide range of competitive climates (we shall be discussing its limitations in this chapter), but as the preceding pages have shown, the labor involved in using the new scales is considerable. Therefore, the Boston matrix remains a valid and simpler alternative for SBAs which expect stable non-turbulent growth and in which relative market share will determine the firm's competitive strength.

A criticism of early versions of both matrices is that they oversimplify the complex reality of the firm by dividing it into four neat piles. This objective was met by firms like Shell (and others) which began to use a 3 × 3 or even 4 × 4 format.

Such a matrix is illustrated in Fig. 9.11. As the figure shows, the finer subdivision robs the matrix of the appearance of unambiguous prescriptions found in three of the four cells of the 2 × 2 (optimized, milk, divest).

Both the BCG and the McKinsey matrices raise the natural question of the origin and validity of the commands contained in the matrix: optimize, divest, etc. The GE-McKinsey matrix increases the number of these commands to nine and also adds an additional question of how to choose between the alternative commands in each box (e.g., invest *or* hold). It does not answer the question of their validity though.

Furthermore, it is easy to construct situations in which the respective commands do not apply. For example, using the BCG matrix:

- A star may be inferior to other SBAs of the firm and should be milked by transferring resources to them.
- The future prospects of a cash cow SBA may be so poor that even the firm's superior competitive positive will produce no profits. Thus, there will be nothing to milk and divestment is indicated.
- The implications of the question mark are that it should be promoted to a star, but the firm may not have the necessary resources, or may be too far behind the competition to catch up in time, or may never recover the very high cost of catching up with the leading competitors.
- Finally, the dog may have very strong synergistic links with other SBAs and should be kept if only for the reason that it absorbs a part of the overhead which it shares with other/more attractive SBAs.

The preceding remarks suggest the desirability of replacing the arbitrary commands suggested in the matrices with a decision-making method which takes into account the realities of business in each particular situation. Such a method is described in the following section.

*Choosing the Preferred Competitive Position

The method bases the decision to change the firm's competitive position on the improvement in the return on investment which will be brought about by the change.

The four or nine cell matrix is replaced by a two-dimensional plot, with scales of attractiveness and competitive position ranging from 0.0 to 1.0.

This is demonstrated in Fig. 9.12 in which the extrapolated competitive position is ranked 0.2 and future SBA attractiveness is ranked 0.8

The decision process starts with management making a preliminary choice of the future competitive position in an SBA and analyzing the impact of this choice on the firm's return on the investment in the SBA. The figure illustrates a decision to try for a leading competitive position in this very attractive SBA.

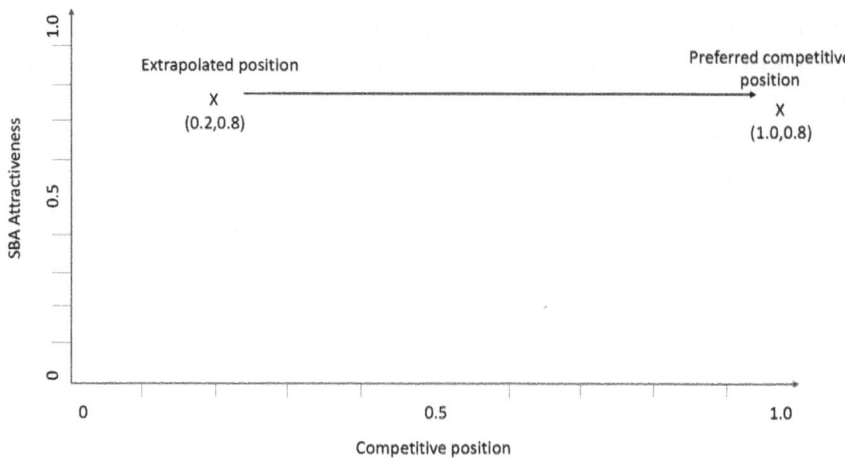

Fig. 9.12 SBA positioning plot

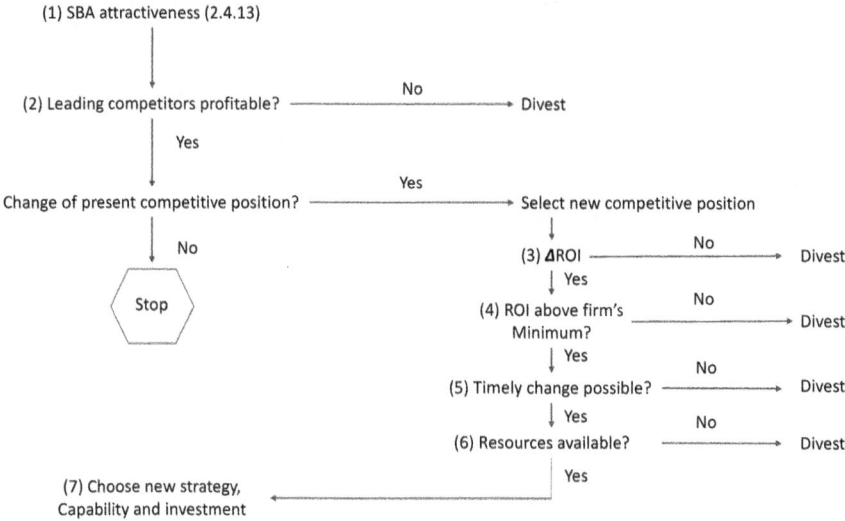

Fig. 9.13 Choosing the preferred competitive position

The steps in evaluating this decision are shown in Fig. 9.13 and discussed below.

1. The results derived in estimation the SBA attractiveness determine whether leading competitors in the SBA will be profitable.
   - If the leaders will not be profitable, the firm must divest from the SBA.
2. If the top competitors will be profitable, estimate:
   - P, which is the profit which will result from maintaining the present competitive position.
   - I, which is the firm's current investment in the SBA.
   - ΔI, the additional investment which will be required to reach the chosen competitive position.
   - ΔP, the increase in profit which will accrue to the firm.
3. Using the above estimates, compute:

$$\Delta \text{ROI} = \frac{P + \Delta P}{I + \Delta I} - \frac{P}{I}$$

   - If ΔROI is positive, move to the next step. If ROI is negative, change the target competitive position and try again.
   - If repeated trials for different competitive positions are all negative, the firm should not try to change its competitive position in the SBA.
4. Check the best possible ROI from the preceding step against the minimum ROI which the firm requires from all of its SBAs.
   - If the highest possible ROI is below the minimum acceptable to the firm, the firm must divest from the SBA.
5. If the ROI is acceptable, compare the time available to make the change in the position before market shares are preempted by competition, to the time needed by the firm to move to the new position (use the magnitude of the strategy and capability ratios in Table 9.5 and Fig. 9.10 as a guide).
   - If the firm is going to be too late to capture the desired market shares, a less ambitious target position may be tried, or
   - A decision must be made to divest from the SBA.

6. If the timing is right, make a feasibility test by comparing the resources which will be needed to attain the target position to the resources which will be available in the firm.
   - If the position change is unfeasible, either another target position should be tried, or
   - The firm must divest from the SBA.
7. If the change is feasible, the next step is to determine the strategy, capability, and strategic investment which will enable the firm to reach the chosen competitive position. This is discussed in the following section.

The procedures outlined above help management to make its positioning decisions on the basis of key business variables (ROI, resource availability, timing of market development, etc.) instead of arbitrary commands.

*Choosing the Competitive Posture

Referring to the competitive posture equation, the multiplicative relationship among strategy, capability, and investment means that the firm's ROI depends on all three, and that the ROI is severely reduced if one of the three components is mismatched.

Thus, a brilliant strategy and a matching capability design cannot be implemented if the investment is not available. Similarly, large amounts of money thrown at an SBA, without the guidance of strategy and capability, are highly unlikely to assure an attractive ROI for the firm.

A reader familiar with the early literature on strategic planning will recognize that the concept of competitive posture is quite new. In fact, even today, the bulk of research and literature is focused on the problem of strategy formulation.

The reason for the historical neglect of capability in determining the firm's success in an SBA is due to the fact that the original concept of strategic planning was formulated at a time when the environment of a majority of firms was on turbulence level 3. As discussed in Chapter 6, in level 3 environments the past is extrapolable into the future. As a result, historical strengths of the firm could be expected to remain strengths in the future and thus there was no need for concern with the firm's capability.

The reason for the historical neglect of strategic investment (the last factor in the posture equation) is due to the fact that firms were not financially constrained. Apple finds itself in this position of strength with a free cash flow of over $53 billion for 2018, allowing the firm to pick and choose its opportunities without the limitation of cash.

As the environment moved toward turbulence level 4, historical strengths typically became weaknesses. At the same time, firms increasingly found that financial demands from their SBAs exceeded the available resources (see the critical mass discussion). Thus, an effective strategy promised, but did not guarantee success.

To summarize, focus on strategy formulation and neglect of capability and strategic investment is justifiable under two conditions:

1. When the future turbulence level is expected to be on level 3 or lower.
2. When the available financial resources exceed the sum total of demands from the SBUs of the firm.

However, when the environment is expected to be on level 4 or higher, strategy formulation must be broadened to include design of the matching capability and determination of the level of investment which will be needed to enable the firm to implement the strategy and build the capability.

We next turn to selection of a firm's competitive posture in environments on turbulence levels 4 or higher. Fortunately, many of the results of the previous stages are useful at this point. Specifically, in the SBA under consideration:

1. The firm's present competitive posture has been diagnosed.
2. Several future alternative success postures have been identified.
3. The relative competitive position which the firm will seek to attain in the SBA has been chosen.

The above results are used as inputs to the selection of *optimum competitive posture* for the firm.

The steps are illustrated in Fig. 9.12:

1. The present strategy of the firm is compared to each of the future success strategies to identify the *success strategy which requires the minimum additional strategic investment by the firm.*
2. If the firm seeks to become a top competitor in the SBA, the minimum investment success strategy is relabeled the best fit strategy.

3. If the firm seeks a competitive position which is less than a leadership position in the SBA, the minimum investment strategy is scaled down appropriately and labeled best fit strategy.

The next step in analysis depends on the nature of the competitive environment which the firm expects to encounter in the SBA.

If the market is expected to be *multi-competitor*, which means that strategies of the firm's competitors will not significantly affect the success of the firm's own strategy, the best fit strategy is chosen as the *optimum strategy* for the firm. This is illustrated at the top of Fig. 9.13.

If the SBA's market is expected to be *oligopolistic* and competitors few, the firm's success is usually dependent on strategies of the other competitors. In this case, the best fit strategy may not be the optimal one for the firm and choice of the firm's preferred strategy must be made in light of the probable strategies of the competitors.

The two competitive situations are illustrated in Fig. 9.13. If, as shown on the left-hand side of the figure, the market is expected to be multi-competitor, the best fit strategy becomes the optimal strategy for the firm. If the market is expected to be oligopolistic, the 'game matrix' shown in the figure is used to estimate the success of the respective success strategies against the probable strategies of the competitors. The following procedure should be followed in this case:

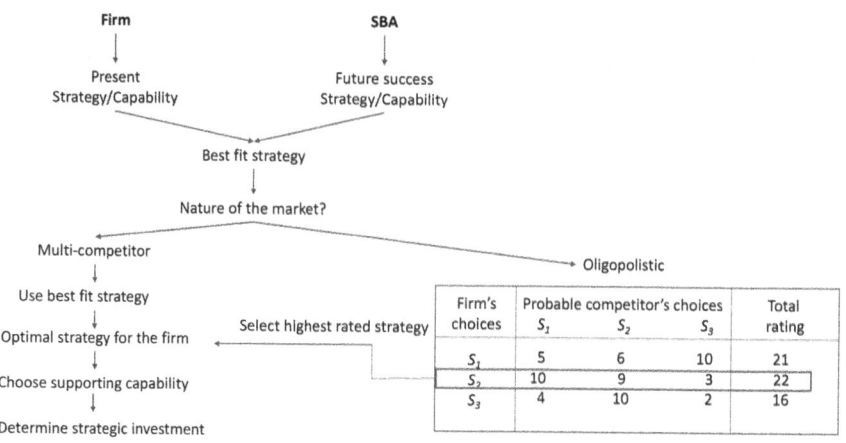

Fig. 9.14   Choosing best fit strategy

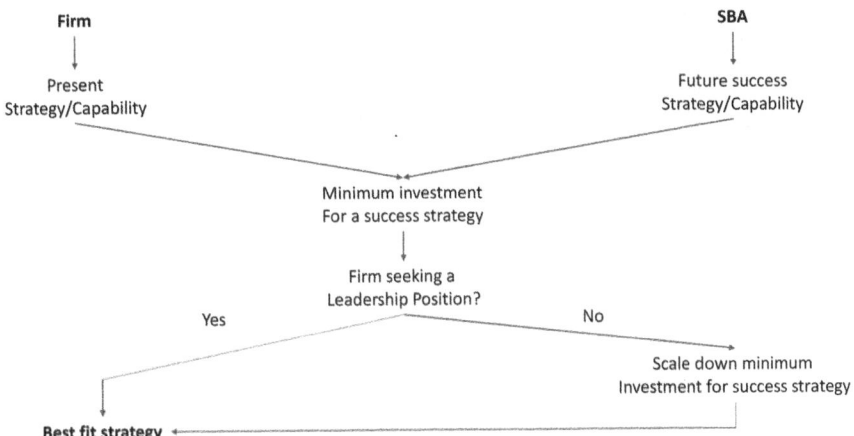

Fig. 9.15 Choosing the firm's competitive posture

1. Decide which of the success strategies are most likely to be used by the firm's most important competitors. The example in Fig. 9.14 shows that the competitors are expected to use different success strategies.
2. Estimate the success which the firm is expected to achieve if it uses each of the success strategies. An entry of 10 in Fig. 9.15 identifies the strategy which will be the most successful against the strategies adopted by the respective competitors.
3. Add the expected success ratings for each of the potential strategies for the firm and enter the result in the right-hand column of the matrix.

The strategy with the highest rating is the optimal strategy for the firm.

Once the optimal strategy has been chosen, the final step in competitive analysis is to determine the capability which will be needed to support the strategy and the required strategic investment.

This completes our discussion of competitive posture analysis. In the process, we have shown how to select the three contributors to the posture:

- Competitive strategy
- Organizational capability
- Strategic investment

Before the position is accepted for implementation, it is necessary to test it against several practical constraints, and this is discussed in the next section.

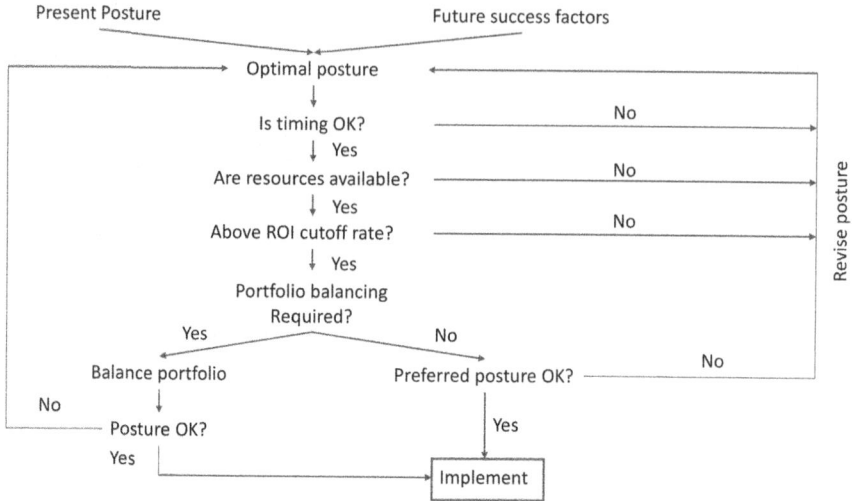

Fig. 9.16 Choosing the preferred posture

*Testing the Feasibility of the Preferred Posture

Figure 9.16 shows several tests to which the optimal posture must be subjected before being accepted for implementation.

1. The first is the timing test. This involves comparing the time which is needed to implement the posture to the time which is available before the market is preempted by competitors.

   If the required time exceeds the time available, the firm is in danger of being a late entry in the market, and the firm's ambitions in the SBA must be scaled down. As the figure shows, this is done by choosing a posture other than the optimum.

2. If the time test is passed, the next test is for availability of resources. If the required strategic investment cannot be provided by the firm, the optimum posture must be scaled down. This test is particularly important in SBAs which rave a high critical mass, or which are R&D or asset intensive.

3. If resources are available, the rate of return on investment promised by the optimum posture may be lower than the minimum rate which the firm normally requires from all of its SBAs. Again, this requires a revision of the posture.

4. Finally, a decision needs to be made whether a rebalancing of the entire SBA portfolio is necessary before the optimal posture is accepted for implementation. This situation typically arises when the strategic investment requirement of the SBA represents a significant portion of the firm's resources which will be available for future strategic investment. (The next section discusses portfolio rebalancing.)

*Balancing the SBA Portfolio

In comprehensive portfolio balancing, the financial resources required by all of the firm's SBAs are compared to one another. A procedure which can be used for portfolio balancing has been developed in the capital investment literature:

1. Rank the SBAs in the order of the expected ROI the firm can obtain from time feasible preferred positions.
2. Determine the total strategic investment resources which will be available to the firm during the next five to seven years. This will include investment available (above the needs of maintenance and replacement) from retained earnings, borrowings, and equity expansion.
3. Starting at the top of the ROI list, fund the successive SBAs to the optimum (or reduced optimum, because of timing) level and proceed until the money runs out.

Such mechanistic resource allocation process introduces infeasibilities and undesirable distortions:

- The analysis will almost certainly exclude funding for some SBAs which rank way down the list, because their near-term ROI is low, or even negative. And yet, these SBAs may be in the early stages of their life cycles and an important source of profit in the longer term. To correct such omissions, the procedure described above needs to be supplemented by a life cycle balance, which we shall discuss in the next chapter.
- The analysis may lead to the conclusion that an SBA should be retained and milked. Frequently, however, firms will find that such SBAs tie up scarce and trained managerial talent which can be put to more profitable use elsewhere in the firm. It may be advantageous to sell the cash cow to another firm and transfer the key talent to other SBAs.

These distortions can be avoided, if the procedure described above is supplemented by the following steps:

- If dog shares important overheads with other SBAs, a *synergy audit* (discussed in the next chapter) should be made to make sure that the penalty imposed on profitable SBAs by the liquidation of the dog will not offset the benefits of liquidation of the losses.
- Some of the SBAs funded for additional investment may be less attractive than diversification opportunities which will be uncovered during the period for which budgets are being committed. To provide for this, firms have used a twofold solution:

  a. A *cutoff ROI* rate is established below which the present SBAs are not funded for strategic investment. The same rate is used to screen diversification opportunities.
  b. A *strategic reserve* is set aside for funding future diversification opportunities.

- The comprehensive strategic investment allocation requires that all the SBAs be analyzed before the process starts. But in many firms, it is imperative to make decisions in certain SBAs at the early stages of the planning process, before all of the SBA analyses are completed. The cutoff rate of ROI described above is a useful approach in this case. It permits the SBA decision to be made without reference to all others.
- A development in one of the SBAs which does not justify a laborious re-examination of the entire portfolio may occur after the portfolio is balanced. Again, a cutoff rate of ROI is a solution.

The preceding discussion shows that there are two ways to decide on the optimal posture in an SBA. One is to perform a complete portfolio rebalance, and the other is to test the acceptability of an SBA's posture against the cutoff ROI rate.

When performed manually, a portfolio rebalance is a laborious and time-consuming process. The labor and the time can be reduced substantially by using an interactive computer model. But whether manual or computer-assisted, a complete portfolio rebalancing, if performed every time a new SBA is uncovered or an old SBA goes through a discontinuity, would produce instabilities in the firm's strategic work. Therefore, complete portfolio rebalancing should be used only on these occasions:

- Periodic (every three to five years) rebalancing.
- Whenever new environmental developments call for a rebalancing.

- Whenever a particular SBA presents threats or opportunities of a magnitude which upset the portfolio balance.

In between such major occasions, the cutoff rate of return should be used for individual SBAs. As shown in Fig. 9.16, the decision in both cases is either to reanalyze the optimal posture or to proceed with implementation of the optimal posture.

Limitation of Competitive Analysis

Competitive posture analysis based on the McKinsey type of matrix, described above, is applicable under a much wider range of conditions than analysis based on the BCG matrix. But it also has limitations. Three major limitations are:

1. The process of choice of the firm's future strategic posture described above is *anticipatory* in the sense that it is based on anticipating the future prospects and success factors, and positioning the firm to take advantage of them. But entrepreneurial firms not only do not limit themselves to anticipating the future, but also create novel futures: novel demands, novel products, and novel technologies. A procedure for handling novel technologies is described in Chapter 12.
2. The second limitation of the competitive positioning method described above is of a different nature. It originates with the way by which uncertainty and unpredictability are treated. The implied assumption in the above method is that the future state of an SBA can be predicted accurately enough to position it as a point (even if represented by a circle to show the size of the market), in one of the quadrants. In mathematical terms, this implies a dual assumption: (a) that the most probable prospects and competitive position *can* be estimated, and (b) that the probability of this estimate is so high that lower probability estimates can be neglected in making positioning decisions.
3. The third limitation is inherent not only in the positioning process but also in all logical analyses whose outcome affects lives of managers. The limitation comes from the fact that real-life managerial decision making contains three rationalities: the *cognitive* rationality based on the logic and facts; a *behavioral* rationality based on managers' perceptions and feelings; and a *political* rationality based on ambitions, power drives, and prestige.

The first two assumptions are not unreasonable when the expected turbulence level in the SBA is relatively low (between 1 and 3). However, as turbulence level increases, both assumptions lose validity. Above level 3, alternatives other than the most probable become just as likely (the probability distribution curve is no longer peaked at the most probable outcome).

Above level 4, not only are there several comparably probable alternatives, but the alternatives themselves are difficult to describe accurately enough to permit the firm to make a clear-cut posture choice.

Thus, the method of determining the future competitive position by using a single most probable estimate for each SBA becomes not only infeasible but also dangerous at higher turbulence levels.

To deal with positioning at high turbulence levels, it is necessary to introduce a major revision into the positioning method. We shall be describing such a revision in Chapter 10.

In processes, such as competitive positioning, in which all three rationalities are brought into play, facts, logic, and reason will be only some of the determinants of the outcome. For example, managers of dogs who stand to lose power, prestige, and even their jobs cannot be expected to be impartial in estimating the future prospects and future competitive positions of their divisions. Managers of cash cows, who frequently have a record of recent, distinguished successes behind them, will not submit easily to the conclusion that their operation ought to be milked. In bidding for continued strategic investment, they will use the often-heard argument that recovery of growth in their SBAs is 'just around the corner'. Managers in charge of new question marks without a record of success and without a power base are likely to be the losers in the resource allocation process, even if their SBAs are the savior stars of the future.

Thus, the limitation of the logical positioning process is that it is likely to become a *paralysis by analysis* in which conclusions are distorted by political forces, and implementation of politically and behaviorally threatening conclusions will languish.

This does not imply as some proponents of organic evolution are quick to suggest, that rational analysis should be abandoned in favor of a muddling through unsystematized progress. It implies that successful systematic strategic positioning will occur only when the behavioral and political rationalities are made a part of the process. We shall be discussing how this can be done in Part VI and in the next chapter.

Summary

When the different markets of the firm are all growing and are not turbulent, the future prospects can be determined through extrapolation of the historical trends. But when the growth prospects are mixed and turbulent, before future prospects can be estimated, it becomes necessary to segment the firm's environment into distinctive areas of trends, threats, and opportunities, which are called *strategic business areas* (SBAs). It further becomes necessary to identify units within the firm which are to be responsible for the strategic development of the respective business areas. Such units are called *strategic business units* (SBUs).

Complexity, uncertainties and turbulence in the resource technology and, sociopolitical environments may also make it desirable to segment these environments into *strategic resource areas* (SRAs), and *strategic influence groups* (SIGs), respectively.

The next step in strategic analysis is to determine the firm's prospects in each of the business areas. These are determined, in part, by the potential which will be available within the SBA to competent competitors, as measured by the future growth of demand in the SBA, profitability, and economic, technological, and sociopolitical turbulence.

The second determinant of the firm's prospects is its future competitive position within the SBA. This is measured by the product of three ratios: the ratio of the firm's investment relative to the optimum investment level for the SBA, the ratio of the firm's strategy to the optimal strategy, and the ratio of the firm's capability to the capability which will be needed by top competitors in the SBA.

Having determined its future prospects, the firm has the options of accepting the prospects, exiting from the SBA, or changing its future competitive position.

The choice among these alternatives is made in several steps:

1. The competitive position which management of the firm would like to occupy in the SBA is chosen.
2. The effects on the firm's ROI as a result of choosing this position in the SBA are computed.
3. If the ROI is satisfactory, the likelihood of a timely arrival in the new position is next tested.
4. Finally, availability of resources necessary to attain the chosen position is tested.

5. If all of the preceding tests yield positive results, the firm's strategy by which the new position will be reached, the necessary supporting capabilities and the required resources are chosen.
6. If one or more tests do not yield satisfactory results, a new competitive position is chosen and re-analysis is undertaken following the above steps.

Having selected its target competitive position, the firm needs to select the *competitive posture* which will enable it to attain this position. This is accomplished through the following steps:

1. Future success strategies in the SBA are compared to the firm's strategy to select the best fit strategy for the firm.
2. If the environment is expected to consist of many competitors, the best fit strategy is chosen.
3. If the environment is expected to be oligopolistic, the future success strategies are compared to the strategies which will probably be used by the most powerful competitors in the SBA. The success strategy which will perform best against all competitors is chosen as the strategy for the firm.
4. The capability and strategic investment which will be needed to assure success of the chosen strategy are selected.
5. The selected strategy is tested for timing, availability of resources, and rate of return on the firm's investment.
6. If necessary, the firm's entire SBA portfolio is rebalanced.

The method of strategic positioning described in this chapter has three major limitations:

1. It does not apply to creation of new SBAs,
2. It distorts environmental reality when turbulence levels are high, and
3. It neglects behavioral and political influences on the decision process. Consideration of these limitations is deferred until later.

Exercises

1. What is the difference between a strategic business area and a strategic business unit? How are the two related? What criteria should be applied to determine whether strategic segmentation of a firm has proceeded far enough? What conclusions would you draw when segmentation of a small firm produces a large number of SBAs?

2. Under what conditions does it make sense to organize the firm into SBUs each responsible for a cluster of coherent SBAs? Under what conditions does a dual structure (an SBU structure for the firm's strategic development and another structure for the profit-making activities) become necessary? What problems arise from using a dual structure?

3. Using a firm with which you are very familiar (or a case suggested by your instructor), segment the environment of the firm into SBA, SRA, and SIG.

   a. On what basis would you judge whether the firm is 'over diversified' or 'under diversified?'
   b. Choose one key SBA and follow the procedure outlined previously to estimate its future attractiveness.
   c. Estimate the strategic investment ratio in the SBA.
   d. Estimate the future competitive position of the firm and position the firm in the McKinsey matrix.

4. As a member of the corporate planning department, you have been given an assignment to assure that the firm's environmental surveillance, forecasting, and analysis system will reflect accurately the characteristics of its future environment.

   a. Outline the process of analysis by which the characteristics of the system should be determined.
   b. Prepare a preliminary list of specifications and criteria for the system.
   c. Describe the organizational structure for the system (roles, tasks, authority, responsibility, reporting relationships, etc.)
   d. Prepare a flowchart of environmental information through the system.

5. Under what conditions should the BCG matrix be used and when should the McKinsey matrix be used?

6. How would you go about competitive posture analysis of an SBA which is totally new?

7. How would you analyze the firm's future competitive position within an established SBA for which the firm has developed a revolutionary technology?

10

Dispersed Positioning in Competitive Analysis

This chapter is based on early research and collaboration between Ansoff and two of his German friends, Werner Kirsch, and Peter Roventa. Kirsch and Roventa's idea was that the concept of weak signals, which Ansoff developed for analyzing issues in highly turbulent environments, needs to be applied to strategic portfolio analysis. This chapter is based on the paper which resulted from this exciting collaboration [HIA].

The Original Approach to Portfolio Positioning

As discussed in Chapter 9, SBA positioning proceeds through typical steps. The first step is to identify the strategic business areas: product-market-technology combinations which subdivide the firm's environment into distinct areas of opportunity, threats, trends, and turbulence.

Next, the SBAs are positioned within the two-dimensional matrix. Determination of the SBA's future prospects is based on forecasts, scenarios, environmental modeling, etc. The future competitive position of the firm is estimated through analysis of trends in the competitive structure, success variables, market shares, client groups, etc.

The sources of data are publications, statistics, etc., but also purely subjective estimates of reality. It is only in rare cases that this analytic approach will produce a single unambiguous estimate. The usual case is a range of probable outcomes.

© The Author(s) 2019
H. I. Ansoff et al., *Implanting Strategic Management*,
https://doi.org/10.1007/978-3-319-99599-1_10

Therefore, as the next step, a group consensus process is used to select a commonly accepted position within this range. As the planner of one firm has stated: 'At the end of our discussion, there is a good consensus on what's green, red, or yellow.'

In the language of probability theory, the process is aimed at obtaining the most probable estimate of the SBA position in the matrix through a combination of analysis and subsequent consensus building. Typically, both the analysis and the consensus process are a responsibility of the planning staff and/or of the external consultants. The resulting matrix is presented to top management, which uses it to determine both the desired positions for each SBA and the overall portfolio balance. This obviously does not mean that top management accepts the point positioning presented to it without critical discussion and rearrangement of the matrix. But it does mean that top management does not participate in the positioning exercise and does not contribute its special insight and knowledge to the process.

Because it is built on most probable estimates which produce a point in the matrix, we shall now refer to this prevalent approach to portfolio analysis as *point-positioning*.

Criticism of Point Positioning

Four criticisms can be made of the currently prevalent practice of the point positioning approach:

1. The process forces evaluation to converge on a single, most probable point in the matrix, thus creating an appearance of certainty about the future which may be totally misleading.

   In highly predictable environments, the most probable estimate has a high probability of occurring, and the range of alternatives is relatively narrow. This means that the firm cannot be far wrong in accepting the probable estimate as the basis for action.

   Furthermore, since the signals are strong (see the preceding chapter), the action alternatives and their consequences are clear, and management can make a strong response to the most probable position.

   In high turbulence environments, the range of possible alternatives is wide, and the probability distribution tends to be flat, which means that the probability of the most probable alternative is not significantly higher than the probabilies of other alternatives. This means that the firm *can* go far wrong if it bases its strategy on the most probable case.

Furthermore, above turbulence level 4.5, signals become weak. Which means that, at decision time, the field of future alternatives may not be clear, or information about them is inadequate to make possible a strong unambiguous response.

When information is too vague to permit an unambiguous decision, management reaction must be accordingly cautious and tentative. The alternatives are: delaying the decision, hedging against several different possibilities, starting with weak responses, and making them progressively stronger as information improves.

Thus, the first criticism of the point positioning approach is that it does not provide the information necessary for strategic decisions in highly turbulent environments.

2. Positioning is frequently treated as a preparatory 'staff' process which does not involve the key decision makers. As a consequence, when the results are presented, the decision makers lack an understanding of the positioning process, of the assumptions underlying it, and of the model of reality which had been employed.

   In stable and low turbulence environments, the planners' estimates can be relied upon and are likely to be accepted, because they are based on a well understood and shared model of the future. But in the high turbulence transitional 2000s, predictions based on models developed from historical experience became suspect.

   Paradoxically, as discussed in Chapter 1 when planners create novel models, their predictions are also likely to be rejected by managers as impractical and irrelevant. A frequent result has been vividly summarized in a comment made to this author by a famous American consultant when he said: 'We pride ourselves in giving our clients good professional advice. But why don't the bastards follow it?'

   Thus, in highly turbulent environments, exclusion of key managers from the process of position analysis is highly likely to lead to rejection or neglect of the staff's advice.

3. Beyond prejudging the acceptance of the results, the absence of key managers from the process of portfolio positioning robs the process of the intuitive hunches and visions which experienced managers bring to problem solving.

   In an environment of steady turbulence, in which experience is a reliable guide to the future, such 'soft' perceptions of reality are frequently less reliable and useful than the analytic 'hard' data. But when the turbulence level changes or the complexity of the environment is increasing, novel possibilities must be visualized, new models of reality constructed, new visions formulated. Under such conditions, hard and soft data must be blended in the process of predicting the future. This cannot happen, unless entrepreneurial and creative managers become involved in the strategic positioning process.

4. The fourth criticism, closely related to the preceding, is that by forcing agreement on a single vision of the future, point positioning encourages within the firm a spirit of conformity at a time when divergences should be encouraged.

In summary, point positioning through staff analysis is a useful approach when the turbulence level is low and stable and the future is predictable. It becomes less effective, less useful, and even dangerous in highly turbulent environments. The basic criticisms are two: the inadequacy of the information for subtle and effective responses and the ineffectiveness of the line-staff roles in the process.

Dispersed Positioning

The concept of dispersed portfolio positioning falls into two related parts. The first is the analysis: The information that is generated, the way it is analyzed and presented, and the way it is used in decision making. The second part is the social process: The way managers organize and work together in performing the analysis and arriving at the decisions.

The analysis is based on a combination of both hard and soft data. *Hard data* are numerical, obtained from measurements and statistical data. They are processed by logical processes (models, estimates, forecasts). *Soft data* are views and opinions held by qualified individuals. They are qualitative. The conclusions drawn from soft data frequently cannot be supported by logical arguments.

In dispersed positioning, both hard and soft data are used, through a social/analytic process to be described in the following sections, to generate conclusions about the two dimensions in the positioning matrix: the SBA prospects and the firm's future competitive position in it.

The use of both hard and soft data offers two important and complementary advantages. The first is that it tests the validity of the historical hard data as a basis for making estimates for the future. The second is that it blends the hard and soft data into an overall estimate of the future.

As in point positioning, the future prospects in an SBA and the firm's future competitive position are estimated using the hard database. But throughout the estimation process, participating managers contribute their expertise, judgments and hunches about the inputs, the estimation process, and the outcomes.

The output of the process is not a single point judgment, but rather a range of alternatives. In predictable environments, the outputs are likely to be described by a smooth and narrow probability distribution, such as the one illustrated at the top left of Fig. 10.1. In this case, hard data will be dominant.

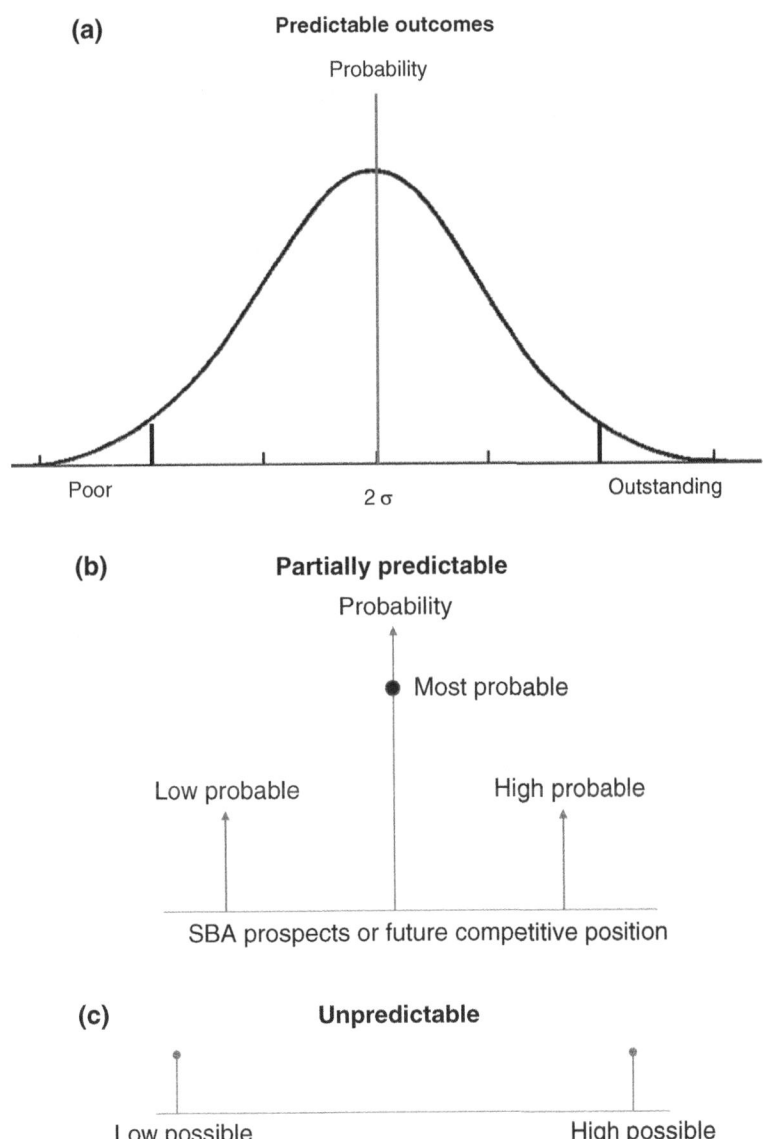

Fig. 10.1   Outcomes of positioning analysis

In less predictable environments, the best consensus that may be produced is on the most probable, high probable, and the low probable outcomes. This is illustrated in the top right of Fig. 10.1. (In statistical decision theory terms, the distance between the high and the low approximates the 2σ range.) Nothing can be said with confidence about the curve that connects the three estimates.

When signals are weak, and soft data dominates, the information shown at the bottom of the figure may be the best that is available: The outcomes will fall between two extremes, but no probabilities can be assigned to the extremes of the range, nor to the intermediate possibilities.

In all cases, the output is a range of probable future prospects and of competitive positions. Figure 10.2 illustrates the way the respective dispersion patterns would be represented for each SBA. SBA1 is a case in which the dispersion ranges are small enough to be representable by a point.

In SBA2, the range of uncertainty about the future prospects is narrow but the range of the future competitive positions is wide.

We shall refer to the rectangle formed by the estimates as the *region of uncertainty*. The region of uncertainty in SBA3 is large on both dimensions, but in SBA4, while it is certain that the firm's future competitive position is weak, there is much uncertainty about the firm's future prospects.

As the figure shows, the shape of the region of uncertainty tells at a glance the relative range of uncertainty in the respective estimates.

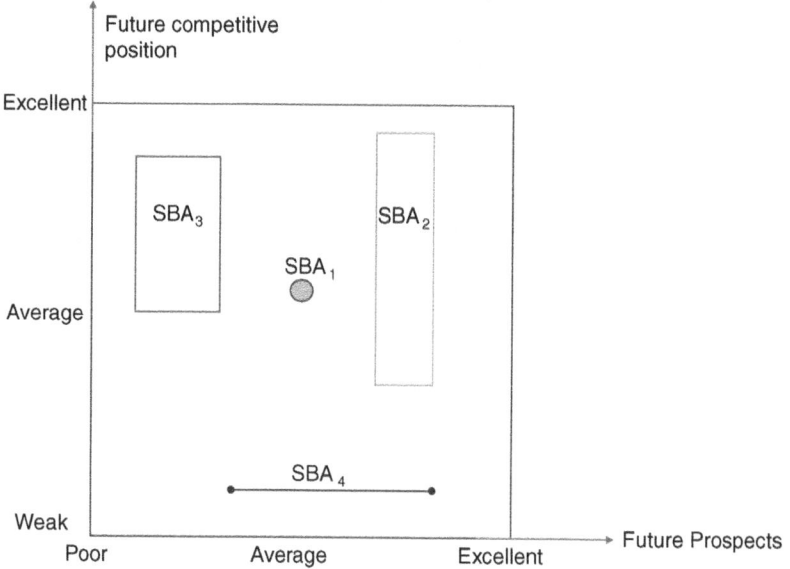

Fig. 10.2 Dispersion positioning

Using Dispersed Positioning to Enrich Decision Options

Dispersed positioning adds substantial cost and complexity to competitive analysis. In recent years, faced with growing complexity of management systems, some managers and writers reacted to the growth in complexity of strategic analysis by a call to 'keep it simple,' to return to management by experience and intuition.

Experienced managers will agree on the value of simplicity and the need to control costs, but will also warn against simplistic ways of attaining it. They will suggest that simplicity is not a 'free good': While making the manager's job simpler and less taxing, it may cause the firm to lose touch with the complexities of the external realities. As mentioned earlier, for continued success (and survival) in a turbulent environment, there is a requisite level of internal complexity which must be maintained to enable the firm to capture the nuances and variations in external trends, threats, and opportunities.

Nevertheless, the argument against unneeded complexity is valid. Therefore, a useful first step in portfolio analysis is to use strategic diagnosis to identify the turbulence level in the respective SBAs and to cluster the SBAs into two groups: Those that require dispersed analysis (turbulence levels 3.5–5.0), and those for which point positioning will be adequate (levels 1.0–3.5). The risk from over-emphasis on point positioning is small, because, if carefully conducted, the process of point analysis will quickly show a need for the more elaborate approach, and the SBA can be reclassified. The use of the positioning data in competitive decision making is illustrated in Fig. 10.3 and described below:

- Following strategic segmentation, low turbulence SBAs (levels 1–3) are submitted to the point positioning determination of the SBA prospects and the firm's competitive position.
- Following positioning, the future competitive posture is chosen and implemented.

For the high turbulence SBAs, the course of action depends on (a) the size of the region of uncertainty and (b) the urgency of making the response, which is determined by the anticipated pressure from competitors, and speed of change in the nature of customer demand.

- If the region of uncertainty is small and the urgency is high, immediate commitment is indicated, as in the case of low turbulence SBAs.
- If uncertainty is great and urgency is high, immediate commitment is similarly indicated.

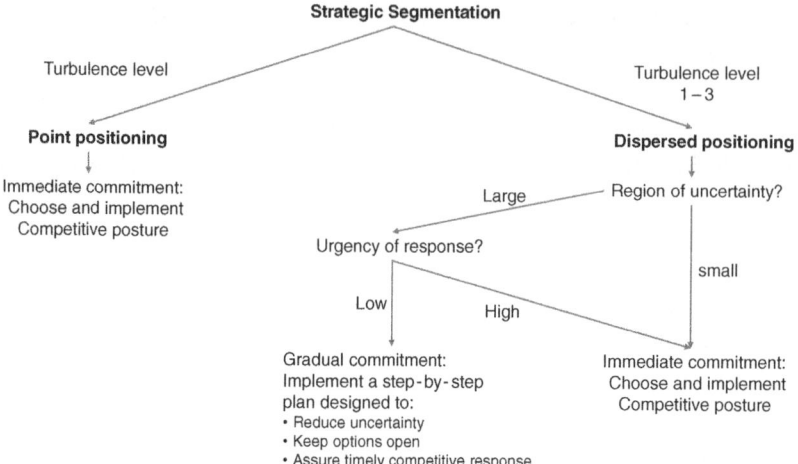

Fig. 10.3 Competitive analysis of turbulent environments

- If uncertainty is great and urgency low, a gradual commitment course is indicated.
- Rather than choose the final competitive position and posture, management makes provisional choices and launches a step-by-step process which is continually monitored and adjusted as the firm evolves toward a final competitive posture.

The preceding discussion shows that dispersed positioning adds a gradual commitment option which is important when the future is uncertain.

Strategic Control

In point positioning, a commitment is made to a strong response. Subsequent events may show that the environment has not developed as anticipated, or the chosen strategy may turn out to be not as successful as planned. Experience shows that once a firm commits to a strong response strategy it tends to stick to it, even in the face of disappointing results. Thus, strategic control is difficult under point positioning.

Through the option of gradual commitment, there is an opportunity for revising the SBA strategy as new data become available. If a strategy turns out to be unpromising, it can be revised or abandoned before major financial and psychological commitments have been made.

The region of uncertainty can be used for strategic control. If the region shrinks quickly with time, management can accelerate and sharpen the response strategy. An expansion of the region may mean mistakes in early estimates, or it may mean emergence of new, previously unperceived dimensions of turbulence, both of which may call for a revision of the response strategy.

Dispersed Positioning as an Instrument of Cultural Change

As discussed in Chapter 9, a firm's response to environmental change depends on three filters: A surveillance filter which determines what information is made available to the management, and the mentality and power filters which determine the portion of the available information to be used and the portion to be rejected as false or irrelevant (see Chapter 9 and Fig. 9.6).

We have shown in the preceding pages how the dispersion SBA analysis can be used to tune the firm's technological filter to a high level of unpredictability and turbulence, but the dispersion analysis is also an excellent tool for changing mentality and culture. The following features of dispersed positioning contribute to a cultural transformation:

1. The emphasis on introducing into the firm a faithful image of the environment with all of its uncertainties about the future.
2. The use of managerial judgment and intuition in an equal, and sometimes superior, role to quantitative analysis.
3. The encouragement of dialectic constructive confrontation of differences among managers, and the carryover of these differences into decision making.
4. The involvement of all managers who have relevant knowledge and/or responsibility for strategic action.

And yet, these advantages are easily lost if dispersion analysis is introduced and perceived as just another, even if superior, computational-analytic system for positioning SBAs within the matrix. A detailed discussion of how such misperceptions can be avoided will be presented in Part V.

Using Dispersed Positioning in Small and Medium-Sized Firms

Small and medium-sized firms typically have limited staff resources. The managers responsible for strategic decisions are also the key experts on the future prospects and the firm's competitive capabilities. Busy managers in such firms are prone to argue that concern with future uncertainties is a luxury which only the large firms can afford, and that small firms must keep things simple.

But the environment has no particular tolerance for small as opposed to large firms, and when the environment is turbulent, the unforeseen 'slings and arrows' of change can be much more damaging to small enterprises than they are to large ones. Thus, well managed small/medium enterprises have only two choices: either to stay out of turbulent environments, or to face up squarely to the consequences of uncertainty and turbulence.

Fortunately, dispersed positioning can give a small firm a realistic view of its environment at an affordable cost. The process can be organized as follows:

1. The key management group sets aside frequent periods (say half a day twice a month) for strategic deliberation and analysis.
2. As a first step this group subdivides the environment of the firm into SBAs.
3. Through discussion and argument, the group draws up a list of key trends, threats, and opportunities which are likely to affect both the future prospects in the SBA and the firm's competitive position within it.
4. Using an appropriate version of the positioning matrix, the group next positions within it the future prospects of the SBA, and the future position of the firm. A simple procedure is to ask each manager to make a judgment of low probable and high probable positions.
5. The managers next negotiate to determine low, probable, and high positions, each citing reasons and arguments for the positions. The results are plotted in the manner shown in Fig. 10.2.
6. It is of great importance that protocols be made of the views, the arguments, and positions taken by the respective managers. These protocols will be used later for strategic control of the decisions.
7. Once the group has worked through the positioning of the individual SBAs it will be ready to make concrete decisions in each SBA (see Chapter 1).
8. Once a cycle is complete, the management group continues to monitor the development of each SBA, reviews the progress of the decisions and makes control adjustments as necessary.

As can be seen, this approach is economical. It is also highly informal, permitting, and encouraging free expression of views and opinions. It is also an excellent team-building device for the group responsible for the future of the enterprise.

In some situations, it will be found that the power structure and/or presence of strong, dominant personalities will tend to bias the discussion according to personalities and not to facts. In this case, a relatively simple Delphi technique can be used to insulate judgments based on perceptions of facts from interpersonal influences.

As the preceding description shows, this approach to SBA analysis requires a minimum of assistance from either external or internal staff. However, when the system is first put in place, management would do well to seek outside expertise.

Using Dispersed Positioning in Large Firms

Large firms usually have staffs charged with environmental surveillance and analysis. Techniques such as extrapolative forecasts, scenario planning, impact and cross-impact analysis, environmental modeling, competitive analysis, competition modeling will be in use and will provide the hard database for dispersed positioning.

However, this database must meet the following conditions:

1. The surveillance techniques must match the environmental turbulence (see 'Strategic information' in Chapter 9.)
2. The database must capture the future uncertainties (in many firms only single line, most probable projections are used).
3. The surveillance must include weak as well as strong signals.
4. The forecasts, scenarios, etc. must be accompanied by statements of key assumptions, methodology and, particularly, explanation of the sources of the uncertainties.

Another characteristic of large firms is that there are a large number of staff and line managers throughout the firm whose jobs bring them into contact with the outside environment and who have valid intuitions and judgments about the impending changes. Such managers usually work in the 'interface' functions such as R&D, marketing, sales, purchasing, planning. This population offers a rich source of expertise which can be mobilized to augment and sometimes (in medium/large firms) replace the sophisticated analytic inputs by the staff.

The following procedure can be used to incorporate these valuable inputs into the work of SBA positioning:

1. *Environmental analysis* develops global forecasts of the firm's environment. (Scenarios are a popular tool. For other alternatives, see 'Strategic information' in Chapter 9).
2. *SBA segmentation* is performed and followed by a classification into two categories: SBAs for point positioning and SBAs for dispersed positioning.
3. Point positioning uses the classical staff-line relationship: Staff performs the analysis and submits the results for decision making to responsible line managers.
4. Dispersed positioning must blend hard and soft data, combine analysis and judgment, and allow for divergences in perceptions and judgments about the future. Because of these requirements, the conventional staff-line division of work is replaced by cooperative teamwork which involves line managers in both analysis and decision making.

   A typical team consists of the manager of a strategic business unit, chief functional managers and the planner. The team makes judgments about future prospects, success factors, and the firm's competitive position. Divergences of judgment arc encouraged but protocols are made of the reasons for the divergences. As its final output, the SBU team selects the optimal competitive posture for SBAs for which the SBU is responsible.
5. The proposed postures are submitted to the corporate management.

It is necessary to recognize that, unlike in a small firm, SBA positioning in a large firm is a complicated process involving many people. It is essential, therefore, to make sure of two things:

1. That the process is cost-effective and no more complex than necessary, and
2. That the 'noise' and distortion in the process are not responsible for the majority of the resulting dispersions (see Ansoff et al. 1980-F).

Summary

When environmental turbulence reaches level 4, point positioning matrices (such as BCG, McKinsey) become inadequate for capturing the range of uncertainty in the future environment.

The dispersed positioning technique 'brackets' the uncertainty and provides the information which permits management to choose between delaying action, a progressive response, or a forceful strategy.

Dispersed positioning offers a side benefit as a mentality-culture development tool. It is suitable for both small and large firms.

Exercises

1. Develop a procedure and a set of criteria by which the SBAs of a firm should be chosen for dispersed positioning analysis.
2. The senior management of your firm has decided to add dispersed positioning to the present positioning portfolio analysis. But it is apprehensive that the change will be perceived as 'another form-filling exercise,' just as the introduction of point positioning had been greeted some years ago. You are given the task of preparing a plan for the introduction of the new technique which will minimize the negative reaction, and at the same time enhance the strategic mentality of the participating managers.

11

Optimizing the Strategic Portfolio

Competitive posture analysis determines the future strategy and capability for each SBA of the firm and the strategic investment which will be required.

In this chapter, we enlarge our perspective from individual SBAs to their totality. The following questions are answered: (1) What are the alternative approaches to integrating and interrelating the SBAs? (2) Under which conditions should the respective approaches be chosen? (3) What are the principal components of an SBA portfolio strategy? (4) What are the objectives and goals commonly used by business firms? and (5) What are the processes by which the firm's SBA portfolio can be optimized?

Three Approaches to Portfolio Management

Analysis presented in the last chapter developed competitive postures for the firm's SBAs, one at a time. The next step in strategy formulation is to integrate the SBA results into an overall *strategic portfolio*.

Three different ways of managing the strategic portfolio are observed in practice:

1. To *manage by exception*: so long as satisfactory financial results are produced. The SBU (or divisional or subsidiary) managers are left to develop and implement their own strategic plans. Whenever the results turn unsatisfactory, corporate management applies one of the following corrections: financial controls, replacement of management, or divestment from the SBA.

© The Author(s) 2019
H. I. Ansoff et al., *Implanting Strategic Management*,
https://doi.org/10.1007/978-3-319-99599-1_11

2. The second way *to* manage the strategic portfolio is through portfolio balancing. Corporate management periodically examines SBU performance forecasts and allocates additional reserves to the most promising SBAs, cuts back investment in mediocre SBAs, and divests from SBAs which will be unprofitable for the firm (these are the dogs in Table 9.3).
3. The positioning matrices discussed in the previous chapter are very useful in portfolio balancing, since they plot the entire portfolio of the firm on a single sheet of paper and offer suggestions for repositioning of the strategic resources.
4. The third and most complex way to manage the SBA portfolio is through *portfolio optimizing*: corporate management formulates a corporate *portfolio strategy* which specifies portfolio evolution over time, new SBA additions, divestments similarities, and differences which will be maintained among the firm's SBAs.

A key difference between portfolio optimization and the other two portfolio management methods is that optimization *uses* the historical SBA portfolio as a point of departure for designing a different future for the firm, whereas both management by exception and strategic budgets accept the historical portfolio as the basic core of the firm's future business.

Which Approach to Use

Frequently, the portfolio management approach used by a firm is determined by the personal preferences and experience of the key corporate managers:

- Managers whose prior experience is in human resources management are likely to choose management by exception.
- Managers experienced in finance, legal, accounting, and production functions gravitate to portfolio budgeting.
- Managers from marketing and research and development are likely to opt for portfolio optimization. However, letting key managers' preferences be the only criteria in choosing the portfolio management style may endanger a firm's success and even survival. Other important determinants in the choice of the portfolio management method are the following:
- The objectives and goals of the firm.
- The characteristics of the future business environment in the firm's SBAs.
- The characteristics of the technological and political environments which surround the SBAs.

The following criteria should be added to the managerial propensities in selecting the portfolio management style for a firm:

Management by exception should be used only when *all* of the following conditions are met:

1. All SBAs of the firm offer comparable and attractive prospects.
2. Management is prepared to accept the sum total of the SBAs' prospects as the corporate goal.
3. It is safe to assume that no major surprises will occur in the firm's SBAs.
4. Management is not interested in establishing synergies among the firm's SBUs (or divisions, or subsidiaries).

Portfolio balancing must replace management by exception whenever all of the above conditions are met with the exception of condition 1, which becomes a case where SBAs of the firm have widely differing prospects. In this case, to assure efficient utilization of resources, corporate management *must* become active in strategic resource allocation among the SBAs.

Portfolio optimization becomes necessary under one or more of the following conditions:

1. Corporate management is entrepreneurial and seeks financial performance which substantially exceeds the sum total offered by the firm's present portfolio.
2. Corporate management seeks to develop a synergistic, coherent firm with an identifiable comparative advantage.
3. The firm's SBAs have different growth and profitability prospects. Some will be attractive in the near term and others in the long term.
4. The environment of the firm is expected to be unpredictable.

As can be seen from above, the imperative to optimize the firm's portfolio comes from two sources:

1. Preferences of the corporate management.
2. Prospects in the future markets of the firm.

Two approaches to portfolio optimization are observable in practice: informal/judgmental/intuitive and formal/analytic. In the spirit of this book, we will focus our attention on the latter.

Systematic optimization of a portfolio is based on two cornerstone concepts:

1. Portfolio strategy
2. Objectives and goals

We discuss these concepts in the following two sections.

Portfolio Strategy

Portfolio strategy is a set of decision rules which guide the composition and development of a firm's SBA portfolio. It consists of three sub-strategies: scope, coherence, and diversity.

Portfolio scope defines the boundaries and the development thrust of the strategic portfolio. The dimensions of the portfolio scope are shown in Fig. 11. 1.

Scope has two dimensions:

1. Evolution of the present portfolio:

- Assignment of priorities to the present SBAs which the firm intends to retain.
- Timing of divestment from SBAs from which the firm intends to exit.

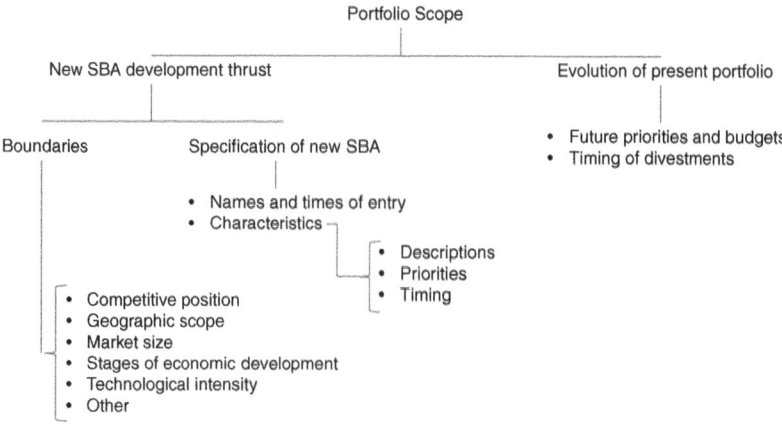

Fig. 11.1   Portfolio scope

2. Specification of new SBAs which the firm intends to enter:

- Names of SBAs which can be identified at this time and target entry dates.
- Types of SBAs unidentified at this time and which the firm will seek to identify.

As Fig. 11.1 shows, portfolio scope establishes the boundaries for such a search. The last column in the figure gives examples of the characteristics which firms use to define the search boundary. For example:

- Some firms intend *to do* business only in SBAs in which they can become one of the top competitors. This has immediate consequences *to* the size of the SBAs which the firm will enter. They must be small (or large) enough to take advantage of the firm's resource base.
- Some firms confine their interest to certain regions of the world and exclude others.

Portfolio coherence, the second portfolio sub-strategy, specifies the common threads (synergies) among three aspects of the firm:

1. Sharing of capabilities which will be developed and maintained among the productive functions of the firm, such as production, marketing, R&D, and purchasing. We shall refer to this aspect of coherence as the *functional synergy*.
2. Commonalities among the future competitive sub-strategies which the firm will pursue in its respective SBAs. For example, basing the market differentiation sub-strategies on 'best buy for the money' pricing *of* the firm's products or services. Since this is an environmentally visible aspect of the firm's coherence, it is a poor instrument for projecting a distinctive image to the firm's customer groups. We shall refer to this aspect of coherence as the *strategic synergy*.
3. Commonalities and complementarities between the capability of the corporate management and the general management of the firm's operating units. As we shall presently see, this aspect of complementarities is very important in highly competitive environments in which appropriate guidance and responsiveness from corporate management to the needs of SBA managers become a key determinant of the firm's success. We shall refer to this aspect of coherence as the *management synergy*.

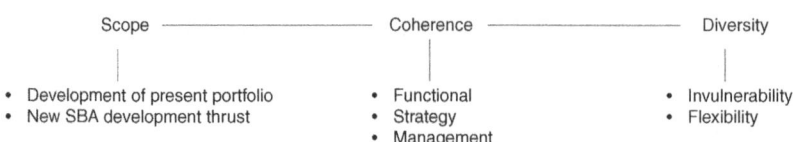

Fig. 11.2 Dimensions of portfolio strategy

Diversity, the third portfolio sub-strategy, specifies the differences which will be preserved among the firm's SBAs. The diversity may be among any or all of the following:

1. Geographical localities in which the firm does business.
2. Key technologies in the firm's respective SBAs.
3. Sociopolitical climates among the firm's SBAs.
4. Differing stages *of* economic development in the firm's various SBAs.

Figure 11.2 summarizes the dimensions of the portfolio strategy. The dimensions are general, and formulation of the strategy consists of making them specific for each firm. These specifics are determined by the characteristics of the performance which a firm seeks to achieve. Such characteristics are commonly called *goals* and *objectives*.

Mission, Goals, and Objectives

The firm is the primary instrument for generating society's economic wealth. Historically, the behavior of the firm was determined by the wealth aspirations of its owners, who were also its managers. During the twentieth century, owner-managers were replaced by professional managers employed by the firm. As these managers became powerful, they increasingly directed the firm in ways which satisfied their personal aspirations (for prestige, power, security, 'fun of the game,' etc.) which were different from aspirations of the owners.

After World War II, other constituencies (white- and blue-collar workers within the firm, environmental lobbies, suppliers, and governments from outside of the firm) increasingly forced the firm to serve their aspirations. As a result, today and in the future, the firm will be, in fact, a servant of many masters. This is contrary to the currently popular fiction in the USA that the firm should and does single-mindedly serve the interests of its owner-shareholders.

Therefore, a realistic process of formulating goals and objectives must start identifying the *mission* of the firm: the list of aspirations of the influential constituencies (commonly called stakeholders in the USA) which the firm serves. In Chapter 13, we will describe a process of stakeholder analysis under the title 'power field analysis.' This process can be used to determine the impact which each stakeholder group might exert in the determination of the mission of the firm.

Once the mission *is* formulated, the second step is to translate the mission into criteria which management can use for guiding the firm's performance. The results *of* this translation are the *goals and objectives of the firm.*

Predictably, while specific goals and objectives will differ among firms, they come from a common, master list. In general, however, business objectives fall into four distinct categories:

1. *Performance objectives* attained through activities which assure the desired trends of growth and profitability.
2. *Risk objectives* attained through activities which assure strategic invulnerability of the firm's growth and profitability on the one hand and the firm's participation in areas of major opportunities on the other.
3. *Synergy objectives* attained through activities which assure sharing *of* capabilities among the SBUs of the firm.
4. *Social objectives* include philanthropic activities which are outside the profit-making behavior and typically absorb a part of the profit made by the firm.

Each of the categories is discussed below.

Performance Objectives

It is a common practice in business firms to use two performance objectives:

1. The *growth* objective. The goal for the growth objective is typically expressed as the future *annual percentage growth rate* of sales.
2. The *profitability* objective. During the first half of the twentieth century, the commonly used goal, particularly in single industry firms, was expressed in terms of the ratio of profit to sales. Today, the general practice is to use the ratio of *net profit to the equity investment* as the profitability goal.

Risk Objectives

Performance objectives are sufficient in environments in which turbulence is low and unpredictable events are infrequent. In turbulent and 'surpriseful' environments, two risk objectives must be given serious consideration.

1. *One* of these is the *strategic invulnerability* objective which seeks to limit the damage to the firm's performance which may be caused by a strategic threat. It may be described as insurance against strategic surprises. Examples of strategic threats are:

   - Invasion of one or more of the firm's markets by new technologies.
   - Invasion of the firm's markets by new competitors.
   - Economic collapse of one or more regions in which the firm does business.
   - A political revolution which brings to power a government hostile to a market economy.
   - Nationalization of the firm's assets in one or more countries in which it does business.
   - Protectionist measures which limit the firm's access to one or more of its major markets.

The goal of the strategic invulnerability objective can be specified as the *maximum percentage of profits* which the firm will seek from any of its SBAs which are vulnerable to catastrophic surprises.

2. The second risk objective which must be given consideration is the *strategic opportunity* objective.

The invulnerability objective must be pursued by all prudent firms whose future is expected to be turbulent and surpriseful. Another risk objective is needed in firms whose management is entrepreneurial and seeks to position the firm in SBAs with potentially attractive strategic opportunities. We shall call this the strategic opportunity objective. Whereas the invulnerability objective seeks strategic insurance from threats, the opportunity objective places strategic bets on opportunities.

Examples of strategic opportunities are:

- Birth of a new industry spawned by a new technology.
- Major demographic shifts which create new markets.

- An economic growth takeoff in a developing country.
- Deregulation of an industry.
- Denationalization of an industry.
- A shift of power to a pro-business government.
- Emergence of a national industrial strategy.

The goal for the strategic opportunity objective can be specified as the *probable percentage of profits* which will be contributed by the firm's investments in future opportunity SBAs.

Synergy Objectives

Synergy objectives call for optimizing commonalities and sharing of resources and capabilities among the firm's SBUs. There are three possible synergy objectives:

1. The first is the *management synergy* objective which seeks to optimize the similarities between the capabilities of the corporate management and the managements of the respective SBUs. Examples of such similarities are skills in managing the following:

   - In highly turbulent environments.
   - High-technology businesses.
   - Market-driven businesses.
   - Aggressive strategic risk-taking businesses.
   - Mature businesses.

The goal of management synergy can be stated as the average degree of capability overlap between the corporate management capability and the SBU general management capabilities.

2. The second synergy objective is a *functional synergy* objective which seeks to maximize the common threads among functional capabilities in different parts of the firm.
   Examples of common threads are:

   - Technological know-how.
   - Product development skills.
   - Production facilities.
   - Purchasing know-how.

3. The third synergy objective is *strategy synergy* which seeks to maximize commonalities among the competitive strategies of the respective SBAs of the firm.

Social Objectives

Finally, firms which choose to serve constituencies whose needs cannot be satisfied entirely through economic performance would enunciate their *social objectives*.

These fall into two categories.

1. An *employee well-being* objective which seeks to serve the needs and aspirations of the employees of the firm. Examples are:

   a. Guarantee of job security.
   b. Providing opportunities for advancement.
   c. Assuring satisfying and self-fulfilling work.
   d. Respect for the individual.

As the above list suggests, the goals of the employee well-being objectives need to be formulated in different terms depending on the dimension of the well-being which the firm seeks to enhance.

2. *Societal* objectives which seek to respond to the needs of society such as education or preservation of the environment. These objectives are not necessarily enhanced by the growth and profit-seeking activities of the firm.

The goal of the societal objective may be expressed as the percentage of the firm's operating profits which will be used to pursue the various societal objectives.

The goals and objectives discussed in the preceding pages are summarized in Fig. 11.3.

The profusion of goals shown in the figure is a fairly recent phenomenon. During the first half of the twentieth century, growth was commonly the only goal pursued by the firm. In part, this was due to the fact that in those days superior growth inevitably produced superior profitability. This relationship between growth and profitability began to break down when some low-growth areas offered excellent profitability (e.g., in oligopolistic industries), and some exhibited the phenomenon of 'profitless prosperity' (excellent growth and very low to no profitability, as exampled in 2001 when General Motors offered

Objectives   **Goals**

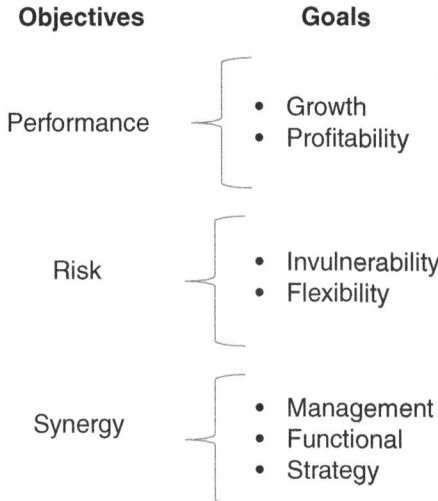

Fig. 11.3   Objectives and goals

rebates of up to $8000 as well as historically low financing on its SUVs, it was 'giving up its profit in exchange for sales volume').

Once the causal link between growth and profitability was broken, it becomes imperative to identify which of the two was the more important to the firm's prosperity and survival. Any student of business would immediately be able to identify profitability as the vital performance goal because a highly profitable low-growth firm can survive forever, but a high-growth, negatively profitable firm will soon go bankrupt.

This conclusion is supported by the action of a great many firms during the Great Recession (2008–2010) which used *strategic restructuring* (sometimes called strategic rationalization) to reduce the size of the firm through divestment from unprofitable SBAs and became impressive profit performers.

Figure 11.3 presents a master list of objectives/goals which are observed in business practice. In each firm, the objectives are determined by its mission. The goals established for particular objectives depend on two factors: the preferences of the stakeholders of the firm and the performance opportunities offered by the firm's markets.

As we shall presently see, determination of the goals, which respond to the stakeholders' preferences and which are at the same time realistic in light of the environmental opportunities, is a complex feedback process. An effective way to start this process is by determining a set of *provisional goals* which reflect the aspirations of the stakeholders of the firm.

Strategy, Objectives, and Corporate Vision

The driving forces of the firm are the goals and objectives: the performance which the firm will seek to achieve. Strategy is the means to attainment of the objectives. As the reader has probably observed, there is a marked coupling between the sub-strategies and the objectives in which each sub-strategy is the means by which the corresponding objective/goal is attained. This coupling is illustrated in Fig. 11.4.

The process of choosing the respective objectives–goals–sub-strategies is a complicated one due to conflicting influences erected by the determining forces. This is illustrated in Fig. 11.5. The four sources of these conflicting influences are:

1. The *environment* in which the firm does business which determines the maximum goals *which* the firm could attain in a particular SBA. As the figure shows, this environment is chosen by the portfolio strategy.
2. The *stakeholders* who determine the firm's mission and hence its objectives.
3. The firm's *future resources and present capabilities* which limit the range of strategies that the firm can afford.
4. The *key corporate managers* who set and control the firm's goals.

Corporate vision affects the choice of strategy; the firm's strategy chooses the environment; the environment determines the attainable objectives and goals; the goals affect the strategy and are subject to the resource constraints.

The role of corporate management is to strike a balance between vision, objectives, goals, and strategy which will result in the optimum attainment of the objectives for which they are held responsible by stakeholders. As the figure suggests, the triangular influence among environment, goals, and strategy makes such a balance a very complex process. In the following section, we show a process which reduces Fig. 11.5 to a linear process.

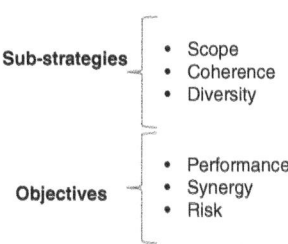

Sub-strategies
- Scope
- Coherence
- Diversity

Objectives
- Performance
- Synergy
- Risk

Fig. 11.4 Coupling of strategies and objectives

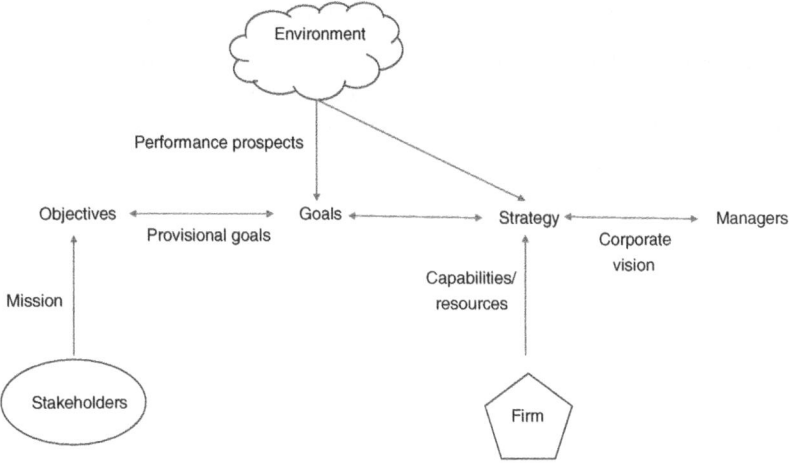

Fig. 11.5 Logic of portfolio analysis

But just as in the case of the provisional goals, the process must start by a diagnosis of the present portfolio strategy of the firm. This diagnosis is described for each sub-strategy in the following sections.

Portfolio Scope

Determining the scope of the firm's portfolio involves two tasks:

1. Assuring that the firm's future SBA portfolio is the best that the firm 'can buy for its money.'
2. Assuring that the firm meets its objectives both in the near and in the long term.

The problem of assuring a cost-effective portfolio is a relatively recent one. During the first half of the twentieth century, economies in the industrialized part of the world all enjoyed a continuous thrust of growth. To be sure, periodic recessions caused slowdowns, but every recession was usually followed by a recovery to the original growth curve. As a result, as late as in the 1960s, it was customary to characterize the quality of different industries by a single index: their growth rates. In addition, the growth rates were expected to remain the same for the indefinite future.

In the 1960s, it became increasingly evident that in all industries the growth was not an upward thrusting curve, but was an S-shaped curve, which we have called the demand-technology life cycle (see Chapter 9). This meant that every historically attractive SBA was in danger of becoming unattractive in the future, either because of saturation of demand or because of invasion of the SBA by an alien technology. As a result, corporate management was confronted with two problems:

1. Making sure that SBAs which will offer poor future prospects to the firm are divested in a timely manner.
2. Making sure that the growth/profitability deficiencies caused by the divested SBAs (and by SBAs whose future growth/profitability prospects are likely to be less attractive than in the past) are corrected through adding new SBAs to the firm's portfolio.

These two imperatives changed the firm's SBA portfolio from a permanent set of 'the businesses we are in' to a dynamically changing mix (not unlike a portfolio of stocks and bonds). The key concern in changing the mix is to assure that preoccupation with optimizing near-term performance does not depress investment in SBAs which will assure continuity of performance in the long term.

Life Cycle Portfolio Balance

The BCG, McKinsey, and dispersed positioning matrices discussed in Chapters 9 and 10 focus on optimizing the near-term performance of the firm. If the attractiveness analysis shows that the total prospects offered by the current SBA portfolio are unsatisfactory or that short-term prospects differ significantly from the long term, it is necessary to complement the positioning analysis with an appropriate long- vs. short-term portfolio balance.

The danger of failing to do so is illustrated in Fig. 11.6 which shows that firm A, whose near-term growth/profitability prospects are more attractive than those of firm B, is heading for a long-term disaster, whereas firm B promises a continuity of performance in the long term.

A convenient tool for balancing long- vs. short-term prospects is the *life cycle balance matrix*, shown in Fig. 11.7. Each SBA is positioned into a box which describes the respective near- and long-term life cycle position of the firm and the expected competitive positions. As shown, additional information is provided by representing each SBA by a circle whose diameter is the size of the market and a shaded segment which is the firm's market share.

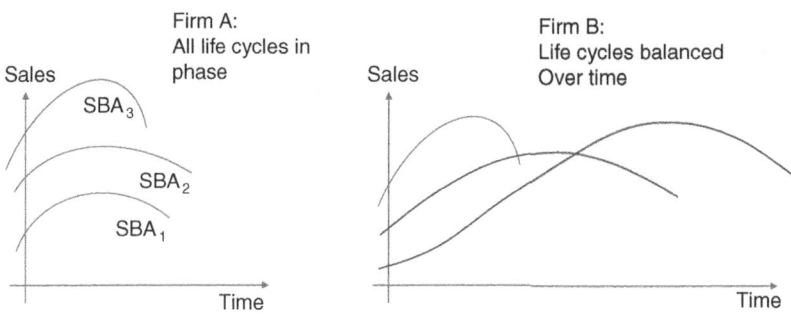

Fig. 11.6 Comparison of two SBA portfolios

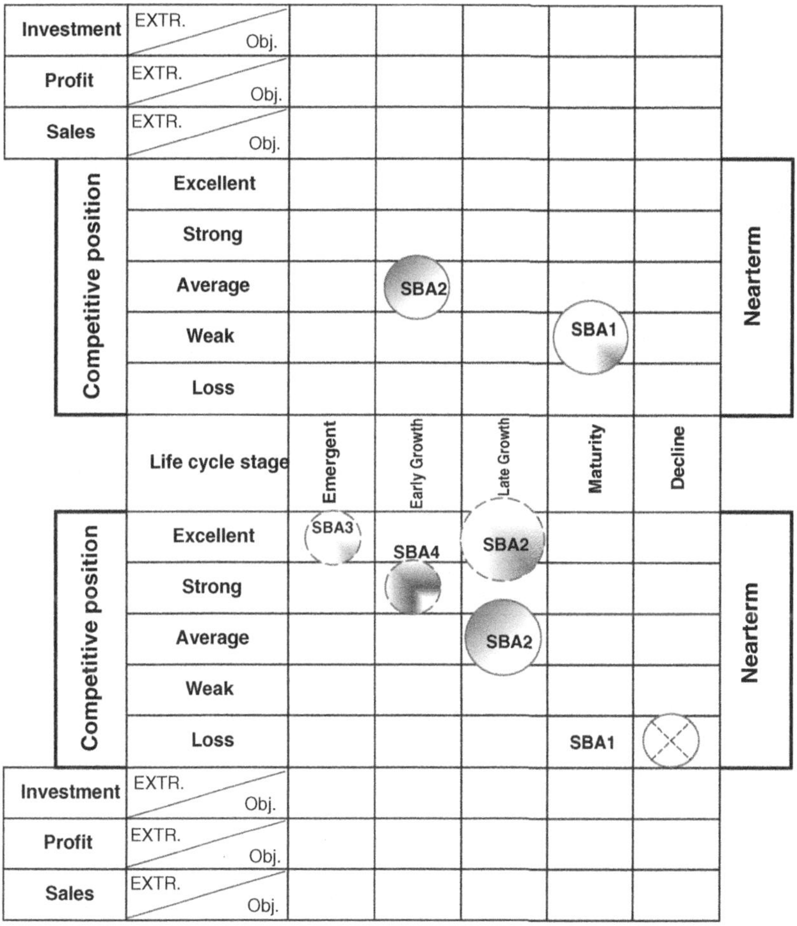

	Emergent	Early Growth	Late Growth	Maturity	Decline	
Investment — EXTR. / Obj.						
Profit — EXTR. / Obj.						
Sales — EXTR. / Obj.						
Competitive position — Excellent						Nearterm
Competitive position — Strong						Nearterm
Competitive position — Average	SBA2					Nearterm
Competitive position — Weak				SBA1		Nearterm
Competitive position — Loss						Nearterm
Life cycle stage	Emergent	Early Growth	Late Growth	Maturity	Decline	
Competitive position — Excellent	SBA3	SBA4	SBA2			Nearterm
Competitive position — Strong						Nearterm
Competitive position — Average			SBA2			Nearterm
Competitive position — Weak						Nearterm
Competitive position — Loss				SBA1	⊗	Nearterm
Investment — EXTR. / Obj.						
Profit — EXTR. / Obj.						
Sales — EXTR. / Obj.						

Fig. 11.7 Life cycle balance

The simple example illustrated in the figure shows a firm which has only two SBAs. Following our earlier example, this may be a technology firm who sells components in the US market (SBA1) and has established a strong position in one of the South American countries (SBA2).

The solid circle entries in the lower part of the table are the estimated long-term positions of the SBAs. The example suggests that the domestic market will shrink to replacement demand (because of technology substitution) and the firm's previous weak competitive position will degenerate into a loss. The South American market will expand and pass into late growth stage. If the firm continues its present marketing strategy, it will keep the market share, hence will have larger sales, and will retain its near-term competitive position.

In the example shown, the firm plans no changes in its strategic posture during the near term and devotes its energy to improving the long term. The dotted line crossing through SBA1 represents a decision to divest. The firm has made the drastic decision to get out of the shrinking, unprofitable domestic demand for components rather than try to master new technology. On the South American market, it plans to increase its market share and improve its competitive position from average to excellent. This decision corresponds to 'development of present portfolio' specification in the first line of Fig. 11.2.

After decisions are made about the present SBAs, it becomes obvious that in ten years' time, unless additions are made to the portfolio, the firm will have shrunk. The management decides that two new SBA entries must be in place in ten years' time: one in the emerging phase (SBA3) and another in the early growth (SBA4).

These are shown by dotted circles. The firm wants a significant market share in SBA4. In both SBAs, the total market must be small enough (indicated by the diameter of the circle) to permit the firm to become a significant competitor.

Nothing is said at this time about the specifics of these SBAs: What specific products will be developed, what markets, or what technologies will be acquired. But SBAJ and SBA4 are sufficiently specified to permit management to start a search for opportunities. This decision corresponds to 'new SBA development thrust' of Fig. 11.2.

*Balancing Life Cycle Positions

The preceding example can be translated into a step-by-step procedure for balancing the life cycle positions. The top and bottom lines of Fig. 11.7 will be used.

1. The first step is to spot the SBAs together with the necessary information into the respective near- and long-term boxes of the matrix. The information to be entered for each SBA (refer to Chapter 9) is the following:

   a. life cycle stage;
   b. future competitive position;
   c. size of the market (size of circle);
   d. firm's market share (the shaded part) as well as the sales the firm will derive from the SBA;
   e. the profits the firm expects from the SBA; and
   f. presently planned strategic investment in the SBA life cycle stage.

2. The second step is to summarize the sales and profits for each and enter the results into the 'extrapolated' half-boxes in the long- and short-term growth/profit lines. The summary of the summaries, which are expected average sales and profits of the firm over the near and long-term periods, are entered at the end of each line.

3. The third step is to determine the objectives for sales and profits for both the long term and near term and enter these into the lower half-boxes at the end of the 'objective' profit and sales lines. The objectives will be determined by:

   a. the aspirations and aggressiveness of the management and influential shareholders in the firm;
   b. the resources which will be available for closing the gap between the expected results and the objectives. These will be the *strategic investment* resources, over and above the resources which will be used to support near-term profit making.

4. The fourth step is to allocate the contributions to objectives among the life cycle stages, using two criteria:

   a. the annual contributions from SBAs in each life cycle stage must add up to the objectives for sales and profits;
   b. the overall portfolio must have continuity: There should be a sufficient commitment to emergence (which is frequently unprofitable) to assure later growth; enough in G_1 and G_2 to provide the backbone of profits and growth; and enough, but not too much, in maturity to provide cash flow for the firm.

5. The fifth step is to determine the presently planned pattern of the firm's investment in the respective life cycle stages. This can be done by adding up the presently anticipated investments, by stage, entering in the external part of the investment line and summing up the line.

6. The sixth step is to rebalance the investment by entering into the 'objective' line the investments that will be required in each stage to support the results of steps 3 and 4 above.
7. The seventh step is a resource feasibility check. This is done by adding and comparing the totals in the investment lines with the anticipated available strategic investment resources. If the total exceeds the resources, steps 3–7 must be repeated until the balance is attained.
8. The eighth and final step is to identify from Fig. 11.7 the characteristics of the portfolio changes which will be made. This will include contractions, expansions, divestments of the present SBAs, as well as targets, size, and profitability for new SBAs to be acquired in the respective life cycle stages. Thus, the *scope* (see Fig. 11.1) of the firm's strategic portfolio is specified.

It should not be assumed that all of the additions will be in the emergence and growth stages. A firm which already has a very strong investment in the emergence stage may, for example, seek additional entries into profitable low-risk maturity in order to develop a strong cash flow base.

The example discussed above involves a firm which has only two SBAs. In firms which have multiple SBAs, the 'eyeball' judgmental approach used in the example quickly becomes impossible as the number of SBAs increases. Here, as in the case of competitive analysis, an interactive computer program becomes desirable to help management master a level of complexity which cannot be spanned by an unassisted human mind.

Functional Synergy

The early prescription for strategic planning advised managers to start the process by identifying the holistic concept of 'the business we are in,' that is, identify the characteristics of coherence among the various SBAs of the firm.

As discussed in the preceding chapter, the modern approach starts with an anatomical analysis of the diverse businesses, in which the firm is already participating, using SBA/SBU concepts. But when the anatomic work of strategic segmentation is done, there still remains the question of *coherence*: What relationships should exist among the various SBUs and SBAs as the firm develops its portfolio over time (see Fig. 11.2).

Coherence is not an essential condition for a firm's survival or indeed for success, since many managements have successfully chosen to disregard coherence by building *conglomerate firms*.

A spectacular example is found in the Walt Disney Company, a widely diversified conglomerate whose businesses ranged from television to parks and resorts, to retail, to cruise lines, to movie studios, to cable broadcasting.

As the conglomerates blossomed, a different, larger, and also successful group of firms committed itself to coherence. Such firms included a specific definition of the 'business we are in,' in their strategies, and managed their growth and diversification according to this definition.

In the 1960s, a working concept called *synergy* was proposed for evaluating the coherence of the firm. As originally proposed, it was an extension of the principle of manufacturing economies of scale to a broader concept of *economies of overheads* which result from mutual *sharing of overheads* among the functional areas of the firm's SBUs.

Functional synergies may come from mutual sharing of facilities or competences. Subsequently, two additional types of synergy received increasing attention: *strategy synergy* and *general management synergy*.

The advantage claimed for functional synergy is that it produces a '2 + 2 = 5' effect, which is another way of saying that the combined return on investment of the firm is higher than the return which would result if each division (or SBU) operated without taking advantage of sharing and complementarity. (For a more complete discussion of the concept of functional synergy, see Ansoff [1988-B] and see *management synergy*.)

In the early days of the synergy concept, some observers of mergers and acquisitions claimed that synergy was not a useful concept, because potential synergies, diagnosed during merger investigations, failed to materialize after the merger. But subsequent experience showed that the difficulty lay not in the synergy concept, but in the failure by corporate managements to exercise sufficient authority to make sure that the potential synergies were realized by SBU managers, whose natural inclination is to 'row their own boat' and to avoid dependence on other parts of the firm.

It must be recognized, however, that the desire of SBU managers to avoid synergy is not capricious, because excessive sharing of capabilities with other SBU managers and with the corporate management can curtail the degree of freedom which a manager needs to respond quickly, decisively, and effectively to the demands of his environment. Therefore, the degree of sharing with other SBUs must stop short of the level at which SBU performance begins to be degraded. In later discussion, we shall refer to this level of synergy as the *maximum acceptable synergy level*.

Synergy was also challenged on the grounds that conglomerate firms seemed to perform as well as firms which insisted on coherence among their SBUs. To test this assertion, an empirical comparison of the performance of conglomerate and synergistic firms was made (Ansoff and Weston 1962-B). The conclusions showed that in good times synergistic firms did perform about as well as conglomerate ones. But under stress, and/or recession, synergistic firms were more resilient and maintained better performance than the conglomerates.

Experience with the concept of *functional synergy* suggests four conclusions:

1. Potentially, functional synergy is a powerful tool for assuring coherence of the firm which can substantially enhance its profitability.
2. However, synergy is inherently unstable.
3. Therefore, in synergy seeking firm's corporate management must make a continual effort to develop and maintain functional synergy.
4. The degree of synergy enforced by the corporate management must be below the maximum acceptable level in all of the SBUs.

Even a casual observation of the business scene reveals that, while many firms pursue synergy, many others use a conglomerate style of management, under which synergy receives little or no attention.

The style of management is a part of the *management vision* shared by the key corporate managers which describes the kind of firm they want to build in the future. This vision is typically determined by the personalities, training, and prior experience of the key managers. Thus, as an example, technically trained managers may be more likely to seek synergy and managers with a financial background more likely to opt for the conglomerate style.

However, if attention is focused on the long-term success of the firm, pursuit of synergy must also be determined by the future conditions in the marketplace. If the future is expected to be highly competitive and if synergy will be an important success factor, the preferences of the corporate management must yield to the demands of the market.

Experience shows many instances in which a failure to recognize the future need for synergy is a part of the strategic myopia which we have discussed in Chapter 9. The reader will recall from these sections that the mentalities of the key management group must be changed before unbiased attention can be given to the problem of synergy.

*Choosing Functional Synergy

Before starting analysis of synergy, it is vital to ascertain whether the key management group in the firm is interested in synergy. Further, it is vital to ascertain whether the key management is prepared to commit its energy to bringing about and subsequently to maintaining the synergy. If the response to either of the above questions is negative, it is highly likely that the synergy exercises will result in 'paralysis by analysis' and little synergy will be practiced within the firm.

If the response is positive, or provisionally positive, the synergy analysis described below should be carried out and the results presented to the key management group as part of the SBA portfolio strategy. The input into the functional synergy determination process is the functional capability plans developed by the firm's SBU managers during competitive analysis (see Fig. 9.10).

The first phase of the analysis determines the *present* and *maximum acceptable* firm-wide sharing of capabilities for each of the key functions: R&D, marketing, etc. This can be done with the aid of Fig. 11.8.

1. Enter the planned capability factors into column 1 (the reader will recall that the capability profile will consist of one or more *capability factors*).
2. For each success factor, estimate and enter into column 2 the percentage of the capacity of the factor which is presently shared by SBU1 with other SBUs of the firm.
3. In consultation and negotiation with the SBU manager determine in column 3 the maximum acceptable percentage of capability sharing which will not deprive him of the degree of freedom and control which he needs to succeed in managing his SBU.
4. As shown in Fig. 11.8, repeat the preceding steps for each SBU of the firm.
5. For each capability factor, compute the firm-wide average sharing of the capability factor. This is done both for the present capabilities and for the maximum acceptable capability sharing. The formulas for computing the averages are shown at the top of the last two columns of Fig. 11.8.

Function *(enter the name of the function)*				Firm wide capability factor sharing	
Column 1 planned capability factors (see figure 2.4.16)	SBU1 *(enter name)*		SBU2.........SBUn	Present = $\dfrac{1}{n}$ (PS)	Maximum = $\dfrac{1}{n}$ (MAS)
	Column 2 present % sharing = PS	Column 3 Maximum acceptable sharing = MAS			
1._____ 2._____ 3._____ 4._____			Repeat for other SBUs		
	Firm wide sharing of *(name of function)* capability			$\dfrac{1}{m}$ present	$\dfrac{1}{m}$ maximum

Fig. 11.8 Determining present and maximum functional capability sharing

6. Compute both present and maximum acceptable firm-wide sharing of the functional capability by averaging the last two columns and entering the results at the bottom of the respective columns.
7. Repeat steps 1–6 to obtain the average present and maximum acceptable firm-wide capability sharing for the other key functions of the firm which can benefit from functional synergy.

The firm-wide sharing estimates are used as two inputs into the synergy choice process illustrated in Fig. 11.9.

The third input is a list of *common capability threads*. A common capability thread is a capability factor which is common to two or more SBUs. If a capability factor is shared by only two SBUs, the common thread is said to be weak. If all SBUs share a factor, the common thread is very strong.

1. As shown in Fig. 11.9, the first step in the synergy choice process is to estimate the investment which would be required to increase the sharing from the present to the maximum acceptable level.
2. The second step estimates the improvement in the firm's profits from advancing them sharing to the maximum acceptable level. An experienced reader will readily recognize that accurate estimates of investment and profit improvements from synergy are at best very difficult to make. Therefore, approximate and qualitative estimates are the best that can be hoped for. Experienced line managers must participate in making these estimates.

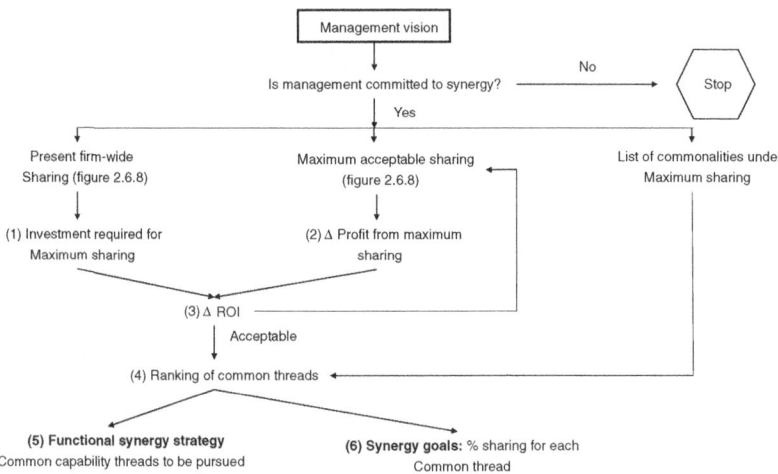

Fig. 11.9 Choosing functional synergy strategy and goals

3. The third step is to estimate the improvement in the firm's return on investment which will result from maximum acceptable capability sharing throughout the firm.

   If the increase in ROI is not acceptable to management, the maximum acceptable sharing level must be re-evaluated.

4. If the increase in ROI is acceptable to management, the fourth step is to rank the common capability thread factors according to their contributions to the profit improvement. A rough approximation is to rank them according to their average percentage of firm-wide sharing.

5. The fifth step is to select the high ranking common capability threads which the firm will vigorously pursue in its strategic development:

   a. by moving these threads from the present to maximum acceptable sharing level;

   b. by testing new SBAs which the firm plans to enter for their potential for strengthening the selected common capability threads.

   We shall refer to the list of the selected common threads as the functional synergy strategy of the firm.

6. The final step in functional synergy analysis is to establish a *synergy goal* for each common capability thread which is the firm-wide percentage of sharing which the firm will strive to achieve.

Synergy Among Strategies

Strategy synergy is described by the similarities among competitive strategies which a firm pursues in its respective SBAs.

One benefit of strategy synergy is that it creates a potential for functional synergies. Thus, a strategy synergy which insists that the market differentiation sub-strategies in all of the firm's SBAs should be to offer 'the best buy for the money' (see Fig. 9.9) creates a demand for the following functional common threads: low-cost production, quality cost-effective products, and 'no frills' distribution facilities.

Another benefit of strategy synergy is the contribution it makes to the image of the firm in the minds of managers, workers, customers, and investors. The managers and the workers perceive the 'best buy for the money' synergy as an element of the firm's culture: to offer high quality at the least possible price. Investors and investment advisors perceive 'where the firm is going' and what to expect from its behavior. As a result, they are better equipped to make decisions on whether to invest in the firm.

Conglomerate firms which do not have an articulated strategy synergy frequently invest substantial resources into trying to project a coherent image through logo images and advertising slogans (e.g., 'Let the power of the pyramid work for you').

*Choosing Strategy Synergy

As in the case of the functional synergy, strategy synergy is a part of the management vision of the firm.

The first step in analysis of strategy synergy is to determine whether strategy synergy is a part of the management vision. If the vision excludes strategy synergy, there is no need to proceed further. This is illustrated by the 'no' branch in Fig. 11.10.

If strategy synergy *is* a part of the management vision, two lists are prepared:

1. A list of the planned strategy common threads among SBA strategies. This list is prepared by comparing competitive strategies contained in the competitive posture plans for the respective SBAs.
2. A list of the preferred strategy common threads contained in the management vision.

Next, the planned and the preferred strategy common threads are compared:

1. If the lists are identical, the planned common threads become the strategy synergy of the firm, and synergy goals are set. These goals specify the SBAs of the firm in which the respective common threads will be made a part of the competitive strategies.
2. If the planned and preferred common thread lists are different, the corporate management group decides whether the management vision should be modified in light of the reality of the historical and planned competitive postures in the respective SBAs.

If the decision is to modify the management vision, the preferred common threads list is modified (as shown in the right-hand side of Fig. 11.10), and the planned common threads become the strategy synergy of the firm.

3. If the decision is to have the future strategy synergy comply with the management vision, the preferred common threads become the strategy synergy, and the goals are set accordingly.

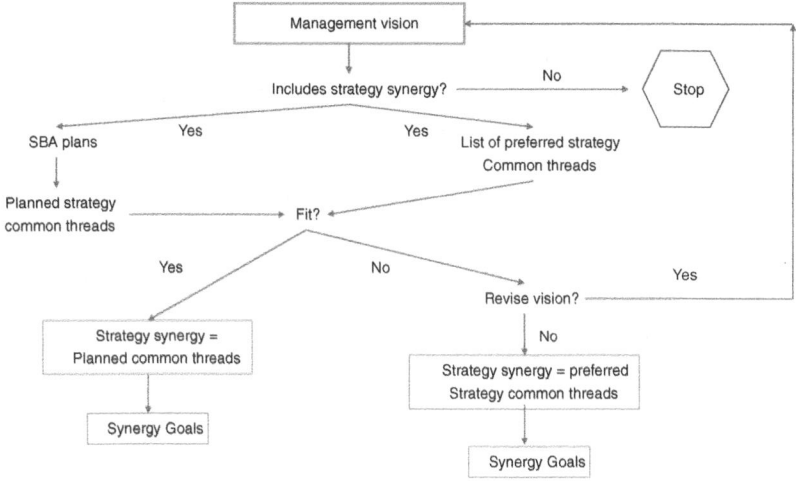

Fig. 11.10 Choosing strategy synergy

Management Synergy

During recent years, an increasing number of firms have engaged in strategic behavior which would have been unthinkable some twenty years ago: Instead of getting bigger, these firms got smaller by divesting from some of their business areas. As a result, profitability increased in a majority of these firms. Thus, growth was displaced from its position as the driving objective which was supposed to guarantee success of a firm. Two labels are being used in business literature to describe this phenomenon. One is 'going back to the core business,' and the other is 'strategic rationalization.' In announcing strategic rationalization moves, corporate managements typically say: 'We are divesting from these businesses because they do not fit our management style.'

One recent example of the largest reductions in the size is found with the General Electric Company. John Flannery, CEO, is continuing the divestments of GE units carrying on from Jack Welch's divestment plan of roughly one-third of the company. The divested parts, which were acquired by Flannery predecessors, were all in natural resource businesses. The reasons given by Mr. Welch and Flannery were that GE management had little competence or interest in managing low-technology, slow-growing, low-turbulence businesses. The future focus of the firm's portfolio strategy would be on growing, high-technology businesses.

This phenomenon calls attention to a third type of synergy which management must consider in planning the firm's future strategic development: *management synergy*. Management synergy is the degree of responsiveness of the corporate management capability to the needs of its respective SBAs. (The phenomenon of management synergy can be understood using concepts of strategic diagnosis which were developed in Chapter 6.)

The reader will recall that the empirically proved strategic success hypothesis states that a firm's performance in an SBA is optimized when the firm's organizational responsiveness matches the turbulence level in the SBA (see Table 6.4). As the gap between the responsiveness and the turbulence increases, the firm's performance progressively deteriorates (see Fig. 8.2). As was shown in Chapter 9, organizational responsiveness is determined by the management capability. Thus, as the gap between the turbulence level and management capability increases, the performance of a firm drops off.

A mismatch between turbulence and the corporate management capability has been one of the major causes of strategic rationalization. It typically occurred in firms which did business in several SBAs which were on different turbulence levels. The general management capability in such firms was typically aligned with SBAs called the *core business*, which were the original SBAs of the firm. Many other SBAs, which were on turbulence levels different from the turbulence in the core businesses, were receiving corporate guidance which was misaligned from the guidance needed to optimize the firm's success. In simpler words, *the noncore SBAs were being mismanaged by the corporate office.* As such mismanagement depressed the overall performance of the firm, many firms sought to solve this problem by divesting from the noncore SBAs.

A highly visible example of such behavior was the Exxon Corporation. At a time when its historical core SBAs in the petroleum business were on turbulence level 3, Exxon diversified into the office automation business which, at the time of the diversification move, was on turbulence levels ranging between 4 and 5. The diversification was spectacularly unsuccessful, and Exxon closed the office automation division some ten years later, but not before accumulating a huge financial loss in the division. Subsequent analyses of Exxon's venture into office automation, published in business literature, showed that the failure was due not to the quality of management or technology within the division, but to the failure of the corporate management to provide quick and appropriate response to the needs of the division.

To summarize the preceding discussion, the problem of management synergy arises in firms whose SBA portfolio contains SBAs on different turbulence levels, and different turbulence levels require different guidance from the corporate office. So far, we have focused discussion on one strategy for dealing with this problem: *strategic rationalization* through reducing the diversity of the firm's SBA portfolio to SBAs which experience the same turbulence, thus raising management synergy to the highest possible level.

Strategic rationalization has the advantage of simplicity. But by narrowing its portfolio, the firm pays the penalty of having to forego opportunities to gain protection from risk through diversity of its portfolio. In addition, the firm may lose the opportunity to position itself in the growth industries of the future which in their early days experience very high turbulence levels.

There are other strategies for solving the low management synergy problem:

1. One alternative is to disregard the problem of synergy and accept suboptimal performance from the noncore SBAs. Until recently, many firms have been content with this solution. This strategy is called the *dominant corporate capability strategy*.
2. Another strategy is to avoid the problem of management synergy by minimizing corporate management's influence on the strategic development of the SBAs. This is accomplished by delegating strategic authority to the general managers on the SBU level. As we have already discussed, this is the *conglomerate strategy* which has also been widely used.
3. A third alternative is the *multi-capability* strategy which seeks to design a multifaceted and flexible corporate management capable of 'tuning into' the SBA with which it is currently interacting. To date, there have been only a few instances of this strategy being successful. But in the complex world of the future, the multi-capability strategy will appear increasingly attractive, because it enables corporate management to remain an influential guide of the firm's strategic development without sacrificing the diversity of its strategic portfolio.

The three strategies described above are optimal under different conditions. A discussion of the procedure for choosing the best management synergy for a firm can be found in Chapter 9.

Formulating Coherence Strategy

The ultimate purpose of the coherence sub-strategy is to make the firm more profitable in its chosen strategic areas. However, pursuit of this purpose may be diluted by the *management vision* which, in part, is determined not only by the growth/profitability objectives of the firm but also by the personalities, drives, and experience of the key managers. Thus, a financially oriented chief executive officer, who enjoys the game of 'playing chess,' with companies as his pieces, may choose to neglect synergies in favor of a conglomerate assembly of unrelated operating units.

Discontinuities (description)	SBA, % of profit contributed										Repeat for all other SBAs	Cross-impact of each discontinuity			
	Opportunities					Threats									
	1 - Strength of impact	2 - Probability of impact	3 - Timing of impact	4 - Expected impact		5 - Strength of impact	6 - Probability of impact	7 - Timing of impact	8 - Expected impact			Opportunity.		Threat	
1._____ 2._____ 3._____ 4._____ 5._____				NT	LT				NT	LT	SBA2 SBAn	NT	LT	NT	LT
1. Use 0 - 10 for opportunity units (10 is a revolutionary impact). 2. Use 0 - 1 3. NT (near-term) = 0 - 5 yrs; LT (long-term) = 5 + yrs 4. Expected impact = impact x probability 5. Use 0 to -10	SBA flexibility index					SBA vulnerability index									

	NT	LT
Firm's flexibility		
Firm's Vulnerability		

Fig. 11.11 Estimating future diversity

Therefore, a realistic process for choosing the coherence sub-strategy must include a tradeoff between the management vision and the potential for profit-enhancing synergies. Figure 11.11 shows a schematic relationship among the factors which determine the coherence strategy:

1. The present functional, strategic, and management synergies of the firm.
2. The key success factors in the SBA competitive posture plans which offer opportunities for synergies.
3. The synergies desired in the corporate management vision.

The two-way arrows in the figure call attention to the fact that coherence strategy is the result of a tradeoff between the key success factors and synergy elements, which will optimize the firm's profitability, and the management vision, which reflects the style of the corporate management.

Portfolio Diversity

Portfolio scope and coherence are based on the probable trends of the firm's future, but the 'Great Recession' housing bubble highlighted the danger of exclusive reliance on probable trends. An economic event—lax lending standards in subprime mortgage loans contributed to high levels of household debt and the real estate bubble—introduced a discontinuity into the growth and profitability to many industries due to tightening of lending practices.

The 'Great Recession' caused strategic discontinuity that was particularly visible, because it was dramatic and its impact widespread. But a backward glance at the last thirty years shows a series of technological breakthroughs, political events, changes in market structure, and changes in consumer behavior which caught firms by surprise, frequently forcing them into crisis responses.

As our previous discussion of turbulence showed, there is a reason to expect that the incidence of strategic discontinuities will accelerate in the future. For some aggressive, risk-seeking managers, they present an opportunity to get in on the ground floor of new vistas and opportunities. For a majority of firms, though, discontinuities are an unpleasant fact of life which disrupt orderly progress and growth, and in the 2000s, this majority faces the problem of *strategic vulnerability* which needs to be controlled and reduced.

Discontinuities represent sharp breaks with the familiar past. Frequently, prior to their occurrence, their nature and extent of the impact can be defined only vaguely. Their very occurrence, as well as timing, remains uncertain before the event. As a result, it is difficult and sometimes impossible (see Part V) to plan and prepare for discontinuities in the same way one plans for trends.

Management has three options for dealing with surprising discontinuities:

1. The first option is to react to the discontinuity after it has begun to impact on the firm. In environments in which discontinuities impact slowly, relative to the firm's reaction time, this is a valid option. As our previous discussion has indicated, this option is effective on turbulence levels 1 and 2 (see Table 6.1).
2. The second option is to develop and use management systems which seek to anticipate and respond to discontinuities before they impact on the firm. Such systems become progressively necessary as the environmental turbulence rises above level 3. We have briefly discussed such systems in Chapter 2. We will discuss them in greater detail in Part IV.
3. The third option is to assure diversity of the firm's SBA portfolio so that surprising discontinuities will not exceed the impact which management is prepared to accept.

While options 1 and 2 are mutually exclusive, option 3 is complementary to the other two, but its usefulness is mainly under the conditions when option 2 becomes necessary, namely at turbulence levels above 3.

We have previously defined the components of the portfolio strategy which assure diversity as the *diversity strategy* (see Fig. 11.2). There are two complementary factors in this strategy: *external diversity* and *internal diversity*.

External diversity can have two objectives. The first is to assure a desired level of the firm's *invulnerability* to surprising threats. The other is to assure a desired level of *flexibility* which will enable the firm to capture surprising opportunities such as technological discoveries and favorable political changes.

The vulnerability objective is attained through two types of measure:

1. Making sure that the firm is not dependent on any one SBA to the extent to which a surprising threat will cripple the firm.
2. Assuring that the political/economic/competitive/technological environments of the firm's SBAs are different enough to make it unlikely that occurrence of a major threat in one would coincide with major threats in the other SBAs.

All firms, conservative and entrepreneurial alike, in environments above level 3, must give consideration to the invulnerability objective. The flexibility objective is a characteristic of the entrepreneurial firms. This objective is attained by positioning the firm in SBAs and in technologies which are expected to be turbulent and promise positive breakthroughs which will offer major opportunities to the firm. A current example of flexibility-seeking behavior is firms that have been taking positions in the biogenetic and artificial intelligence technologies.

Internal flexibility is attained by configuring the firm's resources, capacities, skills, and capability in such a way that, in case of need, they can be quickly and efficiently transferred from one SBA/SRA to another. The ultimate flexibility is, of course, total financial liquidity—having the firm's assets quickly convertible into money. But this path is possible only in the very few firms which are neither capital nor technology intensive. For most, the potential for enhancing internal flexibility is limited by the inherent convertibility of technology, skills, equipment, facilities, and inventories from one SBA/SRA to another.

*Analysis of Diversity

A quick assessment of the firm's potential strategic vulnerability is quite straightforward. A simple test is to determine the degree of concentration of the firm's profits and sales. This is illustrated in the Table 11.1, in which 80% of the sales and 77% of the profits come from three SBAs.

The high concentration of sales, profits, cash flow, and investment in the top three SBAs is cause for concern. However, it does not necessarily mean that the firm is strategically vulnerable. Therefore, a further analysis is indicated. A technique known as *impact analysis*, which is useful for this purpose, is illustrated in Fig. 11.10.

1. The first step is to enter into the first column a list of possible discontinuous events which may have a major impact on the firm. Today, most firms would list: political instabilities in many parts of the world, petroleum

Table 11.1 SBA performance

	% of sales	% of profits	% of cash flow	% of invested capital
Top SBA	40	52	45	35
Top two SBAs	62	70	68	55
Top three SBAs	81	77	82	60

politics, terrorism, inflation, technology of energy generation, changing consumer attitudes, changing attitudes toward work, government regulation of business, a growing demand for worker participation in decision, etc.

Many of these issues are shared by all firms, but each firm would find important issues which are specific to its industrial setting. Thus, firms in the automotive business would certainly add automotive safety legislation, production cost disparities among nations, and market protection measures as potential sources of major discontinuities.

2. The second step is to estimate the impact of each discontinuity on each SBA.

   a. At the top of Fig. 11.11, enter the average percentage of the firm's profits which has been contributed by each SBA during the past five years.
   b. Using a scale from 0 to 10, enter into the 'strength of impact' columns a number which describes the probable strength of each discontinuity's impact.
   c. Using a scale from 0.0 to 1.0, enter into the 'prob.' (probability) columns an estimate of the probability that the discontinuity will occur.
   d. In the columns labeled 'timing,' enter NT (near term) if the impact is expected to occur within the next five years. Enter LT (long term) if the impact is expected to occur beyond the next five years.
   e. For each SBA, compute the column average of 'expected impact' entries in column 4 and enter it at the bottom of the column. We will call this entry the *SBA flexibility index.*
   f. Repeat the above procedure for threat 'expected impact' entries (column 8) to compute the *SBA vulnerability index.* Enter the result at the bottom for each SBA.

3. The third step is to determine the firm's flexibility and vulnerability. They are computed (twice, once for flexibility and once for vulnerability) using the following equation:

$$\text{Flexibility/vulnerability} = \sum_{\text{SBA}} (\text{SBA flex./vulner.}) \times (\% \text{ profit contributed})$$

Enter the results at the bottom right-hand side of the figure.

4. The fourth step is to compute the cross-impact of each discontinuity on the firm. The cross-impact measures the firm-wide impact of each discontinuity.

a. Compute the *cross-impact* using the following equations:

$$\text{Opportunity cross-impact} = \sum_{\text{SBA}} \left(\begin{array}{c} \text{Expected opportunity impact on SBA} \\ \times \% \text{ profit contributed by SBA} \end{array} \right)$$

And

$$\text{Threat cross-impact} = \sum_{\text{SBA}} \left(\begin{array}{c} \text{Expected threat impact on SBA} \\ \times \% \text{ profit contributed by SBA} \end{array} \right)$$

b. Using the 'discontinuities' and the last four columns of Fig. 11.11, rank the discontinuities in the order of their potential impact on the firm. Enter the results in Fig. 11.12.

5. The fifth step in the diversity analysis is to compute the percentages of the firm's historical profits which will be exposed to different levels of vulnerability and flexibility.

a. In Fig. 11.13, against each value of the flexibility index, enter the name of SBAs at the respective index levels. (Obtain the index from Fig. 11.11.)
b. Alongside each SBA enter the percentage of historical profit contributed by it. (Obtain from top of Fig. 11.11.)
c. Add the profits for each level and enter into the 'total profit' column.

Discontinuities	NT* threat impact	Discontinuities	LT* threat impact	Discontinuities	NT* Opportunity impact	Discontinuities	LT* Opportunity impact
*Arrange in decending order							

Fig. 11.12 Cross-impact of discontinuities on the firm

Flexibility (+) Vulnerability (-) index	Flexibility (+)		Vulnerability (-)	
	SBA % profit	Total profit		Total profit
10 +,-			SBA 1/15%; SBA2/20%	35
9 +,-			SBA 3/10%	10
8 +,-				
7 +,-			SBA 4/35%	35
6 +,-				
5 +,-	SBA 1/ 25%	25		
4 +,-			SBA 5/10%	10
3 +,-	SBA 3/15%	15	SBA 6/10%	10
2 +,-	SBA 3/20%	20		
1 +,-				
0	SBA 2/20%; SBA 6/10% SBA 5/10%	40		
		100%		100%

Fig. 11.13 Percentage of profits at different levels of flexibility/vulnerability

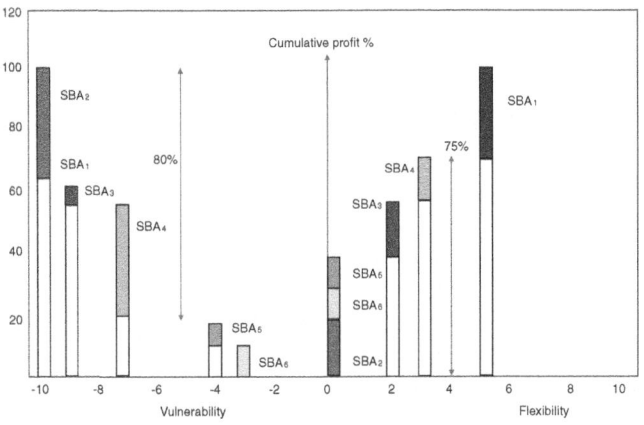

Fig. 11.14 Profit and vulnerability/flexibility levels

6. The sixth step is to construct a graph of the percentage of the firm's profit which will be exposed to different levels of vulnerability/flexibility.

   a. Using Fig. 11.13, construct a profile of profit distribution among different levels of vulnerability/flexibility in the manner illustrated in Fig. 11.14.

*Choosing Diversity Strategy

The profile illustrated in Fig. 11.14 shows a very vulnerable firm:

- Eighty percent of its historical profit came from four SBAs (SBA1, SBA2, SBAJ, and SBA4) which are likely to suffer a serious loss of profit.

- Thirty percent of the historical profit is likely to be transformed into losses in SBA1 and SBA2.

The flexibility picture is also unattractive:

- Seventy-five percent of the profits are in five (out of the total of six) SBAs, which, at best, are likely to experience only minor opportunities to increase profits as a result of opportunity breakthroughs.

The profile illustrated in Fig. 11.14 is characteristic of firms that have been historically successful in low-turbulence environments in which discontinuities have been rare and are now confronting a turbulent future. The remedial measures depend, in part, on the management vision of the firm. Conservatives' risk-averse managements would not be concerned with lack of flexibility, while entrepreneurial risk-seeking managers (who may have recently bought into this historically conservative firm) would emphasize flexibility.

While concern with flexibility may vary among firms, the grim vulnerability picture must be of concern to all firms because it threatens major losses of profit and even survival of the firm.

In developing a strategy for the future diversity of the firm's portfolio, management can take two different approaches:

1. One approach is to use a strategy which imposes the same limitations and expectations on all SBAs of the firm. Under this approach, the following complementary strategies may be chosen:

   a. Limit the percentage of profits which each SBA contributes to the corporate profit stream.
   b. Require that all SBAs comply with the same diversity limits.
   c. Require that all SBAs of the firm be highly likely (or highly unlikely) to be affected by specified discontinuities (e.g., technological breakthroughs or political upheavals).

This approach does not imply that a firm pursuing it is necessarily conservative. For example, technology-driven firms deliberately seek to confine themselves to SBAs on turbulence level 5 (see Chapter 6), in which the probability of breakthrough opportunity is very high.

Furthermore, uniformity of turbulence across SBAs enhances the management synergy (see section 'Management Synergy').

2. The second approach to formulation of the diversity strategy is to seek to maintain an average firm-wide vulnerability and flexibility, but allow different levels in different SBAs. Under this approach, the following complementary sub-strategies may be chosen:

a. Maintain average firm-wide levels of flexibility and vulnerability.
b. Specify percentage of future profits which will be contributed to the firm by SBAs in different flexibility/vulnerability categories.

This approach to diversity strategy gives management a greater freedom in selecting SBAs for the firm's future portfolio. However, as discussed in sections on management synergy and on multi-capability (see Chapter 9), SBAs with significantly different flexibility and vulnerability potentials require different styles of corporate management.

The same logic can be used in both approaches to arrive at the diversity strategy. One such logic is shown in Fig. 11.15.

There are three inputs to the analysis and it is completed in nine steps:

1. The *predicted diversity* which has been determined in the preceding section.
2. The *present diversity strategy* of the firm which is the logic which has guided the evolution of the firm's diversity. If the firm has no explicit statement of the strategy, the strategy can be inferred by analyzing the present SBA portfolio.

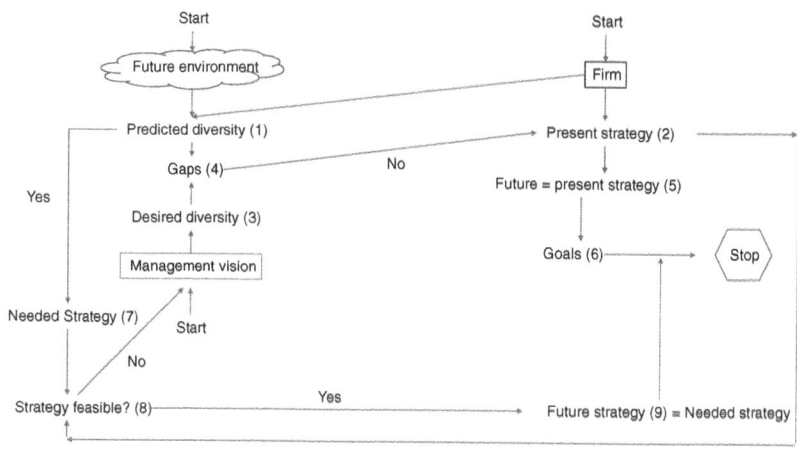

Fig. 11.15   Logic of diversity strategy formulation

3. The *future diversity* desired by the controlling management group. If the management vision of the firm does not include a statement of the desired level of diversity, it should be elicited from the key corporate managers.

4. The development of future strategy starts with a comparison of the predicted and desired diversity.

5. If there is no gap between the two diversities, the present strategy becomes the future diversity strategy of the firm.

6. The final step in this branch of analysis is to set future goals which are, in this case, the results of the predicted diversity analysis.

7. Returning to step 4, if there is a significant gap between the desired and predicted diversity, a *needed diversity strategy* is created which will assure attainment of the desired diversity.

8. Next, the *financial feasibility* of the strategy is tested, as well as its consistency with the other components of the portfolio strategy. For example, if the strategy synergy commits a firm to participation in turbulent high-tech SBAs, the diversity strategy should assure a high degree of flexibility.

   If the strategy is not feasible, it must be changed. The first step is to have the management vision modified, and the second step is to create a new needed strategy.

9. A needed strategy which is feasible becomes the future strategy of the firm and the appropriate goals are set.

Integrating Sub-strategies

We have completed a lengthy exploration of the dimensions of the portfolio strategy. To refresh the reader's memory, these dimensions and their components are:

Dimensions	Components
Portfolio scope	• Plan for evolution of the present portfolio • Plan for entry into new SBAs
Coherence	• Synergy among functional capabilities • Synergy among firm's strategies in its SBAs • Management synergy between corporate management capabilities and management capabilities required for the respective SBAs
Diversity	• Invulnerability of the portfolio to surprising threats • Flexibility of the portfolio for participating in unforeseen opportunities

In the preceding pages, we have developed logical procedures for determining the strategies for each of the above components. The next step is to integrate these strategies into the overall portfolio strategy.

The need to integrate arises from the fact that, as we have already discussed in analyzing the synergy strategies, the respective strategies are interdependent and must be made mutually supportive.

1. Thus, there is a strong link between the strategy and functional synergies. By defining the common strategy threads, the strategy synergy also defines the functional capabilities which will be needed to support the strategies.
2. Similarly, the strategy synergy defines the turbulence common threads. As we previously discussed, the strength of the turbulence threads determines the level of management synergy. As the reader will recall, a large diversity of turbulence levels among SBAs suggests a conglomerate organizational structure which has very weak management synergy.
3. Strategy synergy also interacts with the diversity synergy. The latter specifies the degree of dispersion of the firm's portfolio among SBAs which are subject to various surprising threats and opportunities which will require different response strategies. Thus, the higher the diversity, the more difficult is to identify common strategy threads.

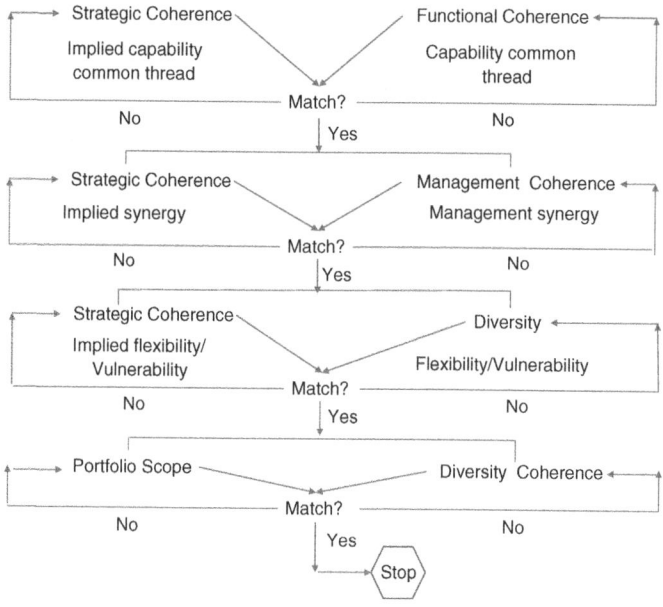

Fig. 11.16 Assuring consistency of portfolio strategy

4. The portfolio scope which specifics the SBAs in which the firm will do business in the future implicitly specifies both the diversity and coherence of the portfolio.

The preceding discussion shows need for a multistage reconciliation among the portfolio strategy components in order to assure coherence and effectiveness of the overall portfolio strategy. Figure 11.16 suggests a multistage procedure for effecting the reconciliation.

Alternative Approaches to Portfolio Optimization

The building blocks of portfolio optimization—the strategy and the objectives—described in the preceding sections can now be brought together in the process by which the optimum portfolio strategy is selected.

The problem is to select a portfolio strategy, from among several feasible strategic alternatives, which promises the best fulfillment of the firm's objectives. This problem is made complex by three major factors.

1. The objectives of the firm are *multidimensional*, aimed at optimizing several distinctive aspects of performance.
2. In the language of management science, the objectives are *not collinear*, which means that enhanced performance in pursuit of one of the objectives does not guarantee performance improvements on other objectives. On the contrary, performance on other objectives is typically reduced. For example, maximization of near-term performance depresses investment in the future and hence the long-term performance; or increase in strategic invulnerability and flexibility may depress growth and profitability.
3. Measurements of performance on respective objectives are *non-commensurate* which means that they are not directly comparable. For example, a 5% increase in the sales growth is not directly comparable to a 5% increase in the return on investment.

As a result of these complexities, it is not possible to construct a fully quantitative model which will automatically select the optimum portfolio for the firm. The process depends as much on managerial judgments as it does on quantitative data.

Two ways to insert judgment into the optimization process are described here. One is to ask the ultimate decision makers to make all the necessary judgments at the outset. For example: to assign priorities to the respective objectives. Once the judgments have been made, a computational model is constructed incorporating the judgments. The model is then 'run' in an optimizing mode so that it compares alternative strategies and determines the best portfolio strategy. The result is presented to management.

A modification of the above approach is to run the model in a what-if mode: The model is used as a 'black box' with alternative sets of inputs and assumptions made by management fed into the model to produce the best strategy. If the output is not satisfactory to management, a new set of inputs/assumptions is tried.

Both of the foregoing procedures are called *off-line* or *non-interactive* or *black box* approaches which means that management does not participate in the process by which the strategy is analyzed. Both approaches are consistent with the classic staff line roles in managerial decision making: The staff gathers the inputs, processes them, and presents the results to the line decision makers. The line managers provide judgmental inputs and preferences and accept or reject the results.

As the reader will readily recognize, the same approaches are typically used when external consultants replace the internal staff as data gatherers, analysts, and recommendation makers.

The optimizing mode has been widely used and continues to be used in business firms. The what-if mode came into use with the advent of the personal computer. Both methods proved to be effective in solving problems which produce no surprises to the decision makers, and are consistent with their model of the world and their mentality (see Chapter 9). But, experience shows that, when the solutions are contrary to the manager's world model and when these solutions recommend difficult organization— disrupting actions—the decision makers typically neglect or reject the recommendations. Examples of such decision-making situations are: divestment from an SBA which for many years had supplied a major profit stream to the firm, or acquisition of a new technology which is totally alien to the firm's R&D competence, or shifting of power from an historically entrenched function of the firm.

An explanation for this behavior has already been offered in Chapter 9 and will be elaborated upon in detail in Part V. For the present, it will suffice to recognize that such behavior occurs whenever the environment shifts from one level of turbulence to another. When this is the case, a third and different type of approach to portfolio optimization becomes necessary which involves the decision makers, together with the staff, in a step-by-step process of strategy analysis and decision making. We shall call this the *interactive strategy formulation* or the *on-line* approach to strategy optimization.

*Selecting the Optimum Strategy

Figure 11.17 presents the key steps in interactive portfolio optimization. The roles in the process are as follows:

1. Planning staff prepares essential inputs and facilitates the process of analysis and decision making.
2. The computer guides the logic of the process and performs computations.
3. Key corporate managers add their judgments and preferences, and progressively make a series of decisions which terminate in the choice of the portfolio strategy.

The steps in the process are as follows:

1. If, prior to portfolio optimization, the respective SBUs had prepared strategic plans for their SBAs, the corporate staff consolidates the SBA plans and diagnoses the proposed portfolio strategy implied by the plans.
2. If SBA plans are lacking, the present portfolio strategy is diagnosed. This is a staff responsibility.

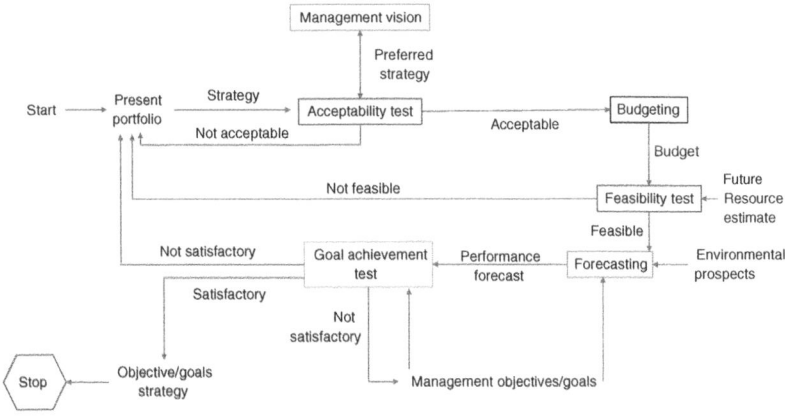

Fig. 11.17   Selecting optimum strategy

3. Assisted by staff, senior corporate managers, working as a group, formulate their collective strategic vision.
4. Assisted by the staff, the corporate managers compare the corporate vision with the proposed portfolio strategy. Lacking a proposed strategy, the comparison is made between the present strategy and the corporate vision.
5. If the strategy is responsive to the vision, the analysis moves to the next stage.
6. If there are minor discrepancies between the strategy and the vision, as the feedback arrow in Fig. 11.17 shows, the strategy is revised. If the discrepancies are major, a new proposed strategy is created by the staff.
7. The feedback is repeated as many times as necessary until the proposed strategy matches the vision. A way to minimize the number of the feedback passes is to have staff create several alternative strategies on the first pass.
8. The staff, assisted by the computer program, prepares the strategic investment budget required to implement the strategy(s).
9. The staff also prepares an estimate of the future resources which will be available for future strategic development of the firm.
10. Corporate managers compare the budget to the future resources and decide whether the strategy is feasible.
11. If the strategy is unfeasible, it is either scaled down (in the case of minor infeasibilities) or a new strategy is created.
12. New strategies are also created if the proposed strategy is feasible, but does not make full use of the future resources. In this case, the strategy is scaled up.

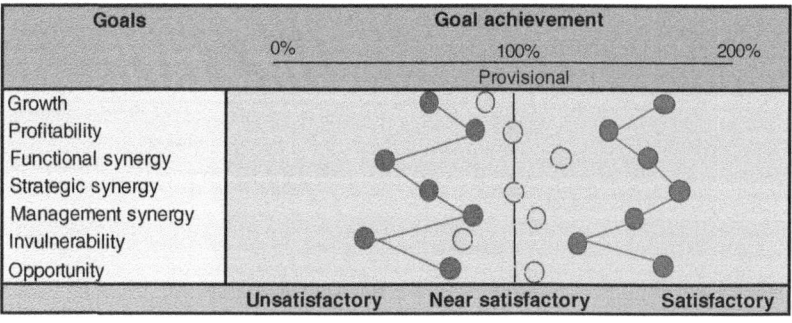

Fig. 11.18 Profiles of goal achievement

Fig. 11.19 Logic of strategy/goals

13. As the preceding discussion indicates, the process to this point can be applied to one strategy at a time or several alternative strategies.
14. Corporate managers assisted by the staff identify the firm's objectives and set provisional goals for each objective.
15. For each strategy which has passed the feasibility test, performance forecasts are prepared by staff for each objective.
16. The forecasts are compared to the provisional goals to produce goal achievement profiles for each objective. An example of a goal achievement profile is illustrated in Fig. 11.18, and the decision alternatives are illustrated in Fig. 11.19.
17. If there is no feasible strategy, whose performance is near or above the provisional profile, management makes one of the two decisions:

    a. To *create new provisional strategies* and submit them to the complete analysis.
    b. To reduce the provisional goal profile to the forecast profile. If this decision is made, portfolio optimization is completed.

18. If there is a near-satisfactory profile, as illustrated in Fig. 11.19, the provisional goal profile is modified and optimization is completed.
19. If there is a satisfactory profile which exceeds the provisional profile for every goal, the provisional goals are adjusted upward.
20. If the feasibility test produces more than one near-satisfactory profile, none of which clearly dominates the others, the final profile is chosen by assigning relative importance weights to respective goals and computing weighted profiles.

Overview of Strategic Posture Planning

The rather lengthy process of strategic analysis, discussed in this and the preceding chapter, is summarized in a logical flow form in Fig. 11.20.

As discussed before, the process starts not with identification of the 'business we are in,' but with an anatomic analysis of the businesses (SBAs) of the firm.

1. The first step is SBA segmentation which identifies the distinctive areas of opportunity in which the firm participates.
2. The second step is determination of prospects in each SBA (see Chapter 9) including near- and long-term growth, near- and long-term profitability, and economic/technological/sociopolitical turbulence.
3. The third step is identification of strategy and capability which the firm will pursue in each SBA. This starts with estimating the extrapolated future competitive position for each SBA (see 'estimating future competitive position' Chapter 9). These estimates are compared to the SBA prospects, using an appropriate matrix (BCG, McKinsey). The matrices are used to select the preferred competitive position and to then determine the preferred future investment level, strategy, and capability (see Chapter 9).

Readers will recall that early prescription for strategic planning asserted that strategic analysis cannot start until the management had made clear its objectives and goals. Experience in the use of strategic planning has shown

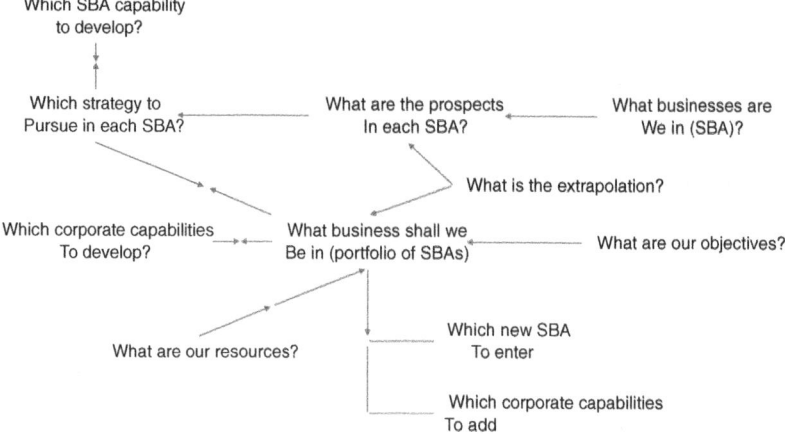

Fig. 11.20 Logic of strategic posture planning

that pragmatic managers are frequently not prepared to choose objectives and set goals until they have an idea of the future potential available to the firm. Given an estimate of the potential, aggressive managers can identify the priority objectives and set goals which are realistically above the present performance, but which require the firm to operate at full stretch. Less ambitious managers would set more moderate objectives.

Thus, the first line of Fig. 11.13 determines the maximum potential performance which the firm can attain within the limits of its present SBA portfolio. The determination of this potential does not depend on an early clarification of objectives and goals. As shown below the first line of the figure, however, objectives and goals become necessary for determining the shape and balance of the future SBA portfolio. A physical limit on goals and objectives will be set partly by the potential of the present competitive posture and partly by the strategic resources which will be available to the firm. As seen in the preceding sections, it is at this point that 'the business we will be in' can be realistically determined.

As the figure shows, the selection of the portfolio must be made in conjunction with the corporate (general management) capabilities. We shall be discussing corporate capability diagnosis and planning in Part III.

While the first line of the figure is a linear process, the lower part requires simultaneous consideration of several interacting factors. The outcomes of this interactive analysis are:

1. Identification of the future common threads ('the business we are in').
2. Establishment of performance objectives, goals, and their priorities.
3. Establishment of priorities among SBAs.
4. Strategic resource allocation among SBAs.
5. A program for the development of the SBA portfolio, including changes in emphasis, entries, and exits.
6. Identification of the characteristics of the new SBAs which the firm will seek to add to its portfolio.
7. A forecast of the resources which will be devoted to strategic development.

2.6.22 Summary of Techniques for Strategic Analysis

From the early days of strategic planning, an impressive development has been the evolution of new analytic approaches and techniques for portfolio analysis. A majority of these were developed within businesses and consulting firms. More recently, academia began to make contributions (such as dispersed positioning discussed in Part V). The principal techniques which are available today are listed in Fig. 11.21 together with the purposes for which they are intended.

As the figure shows, three distinctive types of matrix are available for position analysis and strategic resource allocation in the near term. We have discussed two of them in Chapter 9. The dispersed positioning matrix was discussed in Chapter 10.

In addition to the competitive posture analysis discussed in the preceding chapter, another popular approach is *PIMS* (profit impact of market strategies), developed by the General Electric Company and the Harvard Business School. It is based on a historical correlation of the firm's performance with key resource allocations and strategies used by firms in a given SBA.

The essential difference between PIMS and the competitive posture analysis approach is: PIMS uses historical data to establish future success behaviors, while the competitive posture analysis uses trend data and judgments of experienced managers. Thus, if the firm's future environment is confidently expected to be on turbulence level 3 or below, PIMS offers the advantage of conclusions drawn from a large data sample. But if turbulence is expected to be at level 4 or above, the more complex competitive posture analysis becomes necessary.

Tool	Purpose
BCG (Boston Consulting Group) GE-McKinsey Matrices, Dispersed positioning matrix	* Select competitive position for an SBA * Redistribute strategic resources among SBAs * Identify SBAs to be divested
Competitive analysis, PIMS	* Select strategy/capability for an SBA
Life cycle matrix	Balance: * Short vs. long-term prospects * investment into short vs. long-term * Identify new SBA needs
Diversity matrix	* Select vulnerability strategy * Select flexibility strategy
Synergy matrix	* Identify key synergies

Fig. 11.21 Tools for portfolio management

From Strategy to Action

The outcomes of the analyses in this and the preceding sections of this chapter are:

1. Specification of the future strategic posture (strategy, capability, and strategic investment) for the firm's historical SBAs.
2. A balanced portfolio which specifies the future composition of the portfolio, the synergies, the timing of SBA entry and exit, and the future strategic resource commitments.

As previously discussed, the SBA-by-SBA analysis, which must precede portfolio balance, leads to a preliminary choice of the preferred posture. The outcome of the portfolio balance may necessitate a modification of the posture in certain SBAs because of reduced or increased strategic resource allocations. This modification is indicated by the feedback arrow from portfolio to posture at the top of Fig. 11.22.

Once the future preferred posture of the historical SBAs is modified, the next step is to identify strategy, capability, and capacity development projects and to launch their implementation. This path is shown at the left of the figure. When the changes in posture are evolutionary and incremental, the process of R&D management, which is usually well developed within

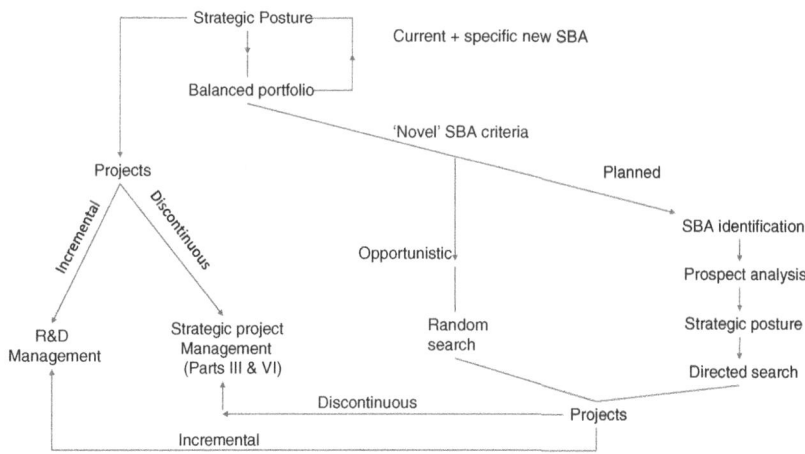

Fig. 11.22 Opportunistic vs. planned implementation

firms, assures effective implementation. But when the changes are massive and discontinuous, the 'conventional' decentralized R&D management runs into difficulties and a new way of managing implementation through strategic projects is needed (see Chapter 25).

SBAs new to the firm need to be treated differently, as outlined below:

1. It may be that during portfolio analysis, a range of attractive new SBAs is sufficiently well known to the firm to permit *planned selection* of specific new entries: for example, an entry into gene-splicing for cattle breeding, or an entry into the fifth-generation computers for scientific analysis.

   In this case, the firm can choose the preferred strategic posture for each of the new SBAs, following the procedure for already existing SBAs. This step is shown at the top of the figure by the 'specific new SBA' feedback arrow to posture analysis. The chosen strategic postures guide directed search for projects. As shown in the figure, these are assigned to R&D management.

2. Frequently, only a few or even no SBA alternatives will be identified at the time of portfolio balancing. Instead, *diversification criteria* are to be derived from the analysis of deficiencies in the current portfolio. The criteria specify characteristics of the 'novel SBA' which will be sought, for example, 'a large-scale entry into one or more new high-technology businesses, or in growing service businesses' (these are the criteria which have recently been enunciated in the General Electric Company).

Figure 11.22 shows two approaches to novel SBAs. In the *opportunistic approach*, shown on the left, the criteria for the desired SBAs are made known to people who are in a position to identify suitable opportunities. These will be the marketing, and R&D departments within the firm, and outside agents such as investment bankers and diversification brokers, who have frequent contacts with acquisition and merger possibilities.

The opportunities identified by these agents are typically screened, one at a time, on two sets of criteria. The first are the strategy criteria for new opportunities, and the second are the basic financial soundness and fit with the management of the firm.

The opportunistic approach is probably the dominant mode which has been used by firms in search of diversification. In many cases, particularly that of the conglomerate firms, the criteria which are enunciated to the public are in purely financial terms, without the benefit of prior portfolio analysis.

When acquisition opportunities are brought to the attention of the corporate management, it is typical in the opportunistic approach to focus evaluation on the merits of the particular acquisition opportunity rather than on the SBA which it represents. Further, the evaluation is based on the historical performance of the proposed acquisition, the quality of its management, and its fit with the parent firm.

So long as the acquisition comes from an SBA in which historical trends are safely extrapolable into the future, a historically successful performer can be expected to succeed in the future.

But in emerging SBAs, SBAs undergoing transition into a new life cycle stage, SBAs whose level of turbulence is expected to change in the future, and, particularly, in SBAs whose key success factors are expected to change significantly, historical success of the acquisition candidate is no guarantee of its future success nor of the future attractiveness of the SBA. If anything, as we shall see in Part III, the longer lasting the past success, the more likely it is that the acquisition candidate is headed for future difficulties.

Thus, by focusing on the historical characteristics of the proposed acquisition, with little understanding of the future of the SBA from which it comes, management takes great risks of acquiring a 'Cinderella.' History of the acquisition movement in the USA shows that the Cinderella effect has been a frequent phenomenon.

The alternative to the opportunistic approach is the *planned approach* shown on the right-hand side of Fig. 11.22.

1. A broad scope of potentially interesting SBAs is identified and then reduced to a relevant subset by application of the portfolio criteria.
2. The prospects of each new SBA in the set are analyzed in depth using the procedures of Chapter 1 or Chapter 10, and several new SBAs are selected for inclusion in the portfolio.
3. A preferred strategic posture is selected for each SBA.
4. A directed search is conducted for specific entries (such as companies available for acquisition or product lines) and each is subjected to a detailed analysis.
5. Entries which pass the strategic and financial criteria are next launched (through approaching attractive merger partners or initiating internal development projects).

As shown at the bottom of the figure, to ensure success, the implementation process has to be handled differently depending on whether the new entry is evolutionary or discontinuous from the firm's historical SBAs. The differences in handling will be discussed in detail in Parts II and V.

Under the planned approach, the firm does not enter an SBA until it has assured itself that the prospects are attractive and chances of success are good. Furthermore, the firm makes the entry in accordance with a pre-planned strategy.

Nevertheless, the planned approach has several disadvantages, as listed below:

1. An early limitation of the scope of interest may exclude potentially attractive SBAs. This was the case in a major diversification study in which the chosen scope (the entire manufacturing industry in the USA), which appeared to offer a comprehensive field of opportunities, turned out to exclude attractive internationalization opportunities as well as opportunities in the service industry.
2. The second disadvantage of the planned approach is its obvious high cost and duration. Therefore, it is usable primarily in large firms, which have the necessary resources and which seek major diversification.
3. The third disadvantage, which became increasingly prominent since the 1950s, is the growing unpredictability of the future, which makes it difficult to make accurate assessments of both prospects and opportunities.

Diversification Through Strategic Learning

The opportunistic and the planned approaches can readily be seen as extremes, whose respective merits have been argued for years in management literature: to plan or to muddle through, to use the 'right or the left side of the brain,' to act deliberately or to evolve organically, etc.

Given the complex realities of the remainder of the twenty-first century, this argument about the preferred extreme is simplistic. Complex and discontinuous reality and speed of change make it necessary to anticipate and to plan as far as possible, but the unpredictability also makes it necessary to make up for the shortcomings of planning by continually testing and learning from reality. Thus, a *synthesis of the opportunistic and planned approaches* is necessary. This synthesis must combine the advantages of rational analysis with a sensitivity and responsiveness to the unpredictable environment. Such synthesis is illustrated in Fig. 11.23.

Once the diversification needs and criteria have been identified, the next step is to determine whether these needs are pressing. If urgency is low, the

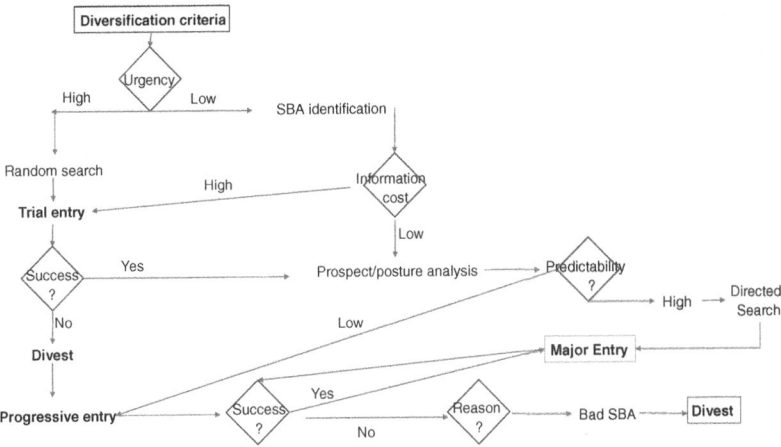

Fig. 11.23 Diversification through strategic learning

planned approach is taken: a comprehensive analysis aimed at identification of potential new SBAs. If urgency is high, 'random search' is started: The firm uses its many contacts with the environment to identify specific opportunities (typically mergers and acquisitions).

The choices of the approach are not mutually exclusive. For example, a firm which has a pressing near-term diversification need as well as long-term needs would use both approaches.

The random search, started at the left of Fig. 11.23, results in *trial entries* which, on the one hand, do not require major resources commitment and, on the other hand, permit quick strategic learning.

The operating profits obtained through the trial entry are not important at this point. What is important is the future attractiveness of the SBA and its general fit with the firm.

If the SBA turns out to be unattractive, the firm should divest from the trial entry. If it is attractive, the next step is to shift into the planning mode and formulate the preferred strategic posture.

Returning to the top of the right-hand side of the figure, the second step depends on the cost of acquiring the data needed to select the posture in an attractive SBA. At one extreme, the cost may be prohibitive or even infinite. The latter will be the case, for example, in SBAs which are in the early stage of emergence during which very little is known about the ultimate prospects, technology, and shape of competition.

If the cost of information is high, the firm should make a trial entry and monitor the evolution of information about opportunities in the SBA. If the cost of the SBA analysis is judged to be lower than the cost of trial entry, the next step is to formulate the preferred strategic posture, in the manner discussed earlier.

The posture analysis must shed light on the predictability of both the prospects and the firm's future success. For this reason, it is necessary to use the uncertainty preserving dispersed-portfolio positioning (see Chapter 2.4) rather than uncertainty reducing techniques, such as the BCG or GE matrices.

If the predictability is high, the firm can use directed search to identify a specific opportunity and make a major entry into the SBA.

If the SBA is unpredictable, as Fig. 11.23 shows, the firm is well advised to plan a progressive entry in several steps. At each step, strategic control is applied: (1) If the performance improves, the firm proceeds to the next step and eventually to a major entry; (2) if the results are poor, the question is raised whether the lack of success is due to the poor quality of the SBA or to a poorly chosen strategy. In the former case, divestment is considered; in the latter, a revision of the strategic posture is made.

Historically, a combination of a trial entry followed by progressive commitment has been used by firms which internationalized their operations by entering poorly understood foreign markets. We shall be discussing this process in Chapter 14.

The strategic learning process described above is clearly more complex, costly, and demanding, than either the opportunistic or planned processes. Returning to our scale of turbulence, the simpler opportunistic approach can be used safely on turbulence levels 1–2; the more complex planning approach becomes necessary between levels 2 and 3, and the complex strategic learning is essential for responding to turbulence levels above 4.

The reader will recognize that in strategic learning the time-honored concept that implementation follows planning disappears and is replaced by parallel planning and implementation. We shall be returning to the parallel planning/implementation management in Chapter 24.

2.6.25 New Workload for General Management

When systematic strategic analysis is introduced into a business firm, a substantial new workload is imposed on management. This workload consists not only of strategic planning but also of assuring the implementation of the new strategic departures.

The new strategic work comes in conflict with the daily profit-making activities. Experience has shown that unless new management capacity is provided and strategic responsibilities are clearly assigned, the conflict is typically resolved in favor of the profit-making work. We shall be discussing this problem in detail in Parts III and VI. In this section, we limit attention to the responsibilities for strategic analysis.

In the formative days of strategic planning, it appeared logical to concentrate strategic planning at the corporate levels of management. Experience quickly showed that, with one exception, this was an unworkable solution which typically produced a phenomenon which became known as 'paralysis by analysis': Plans made at the headquarters languished and remained unimplemented.

The exception was when the firm's strategic activity was confined to mergers and acquisitions. In this case, the corporate headquarters engage in a self-contained strategic activity: It both plans and executes the strategic moves.

Whenever strategic implementation was from within the firm, experience shows that the process of strategic development must be participative and interactive, which assigns important roles to both the corporate office and the SBUs.

A typical flow of planning between the corporate office and strategic business units is illustrated in Fig. 11.24. As seen from the figure, the corporate level sets the mission scopes for the SBUs, evaluates SBA strategies, and selects the corporate SBA portfolio. It also determines the diversifica-

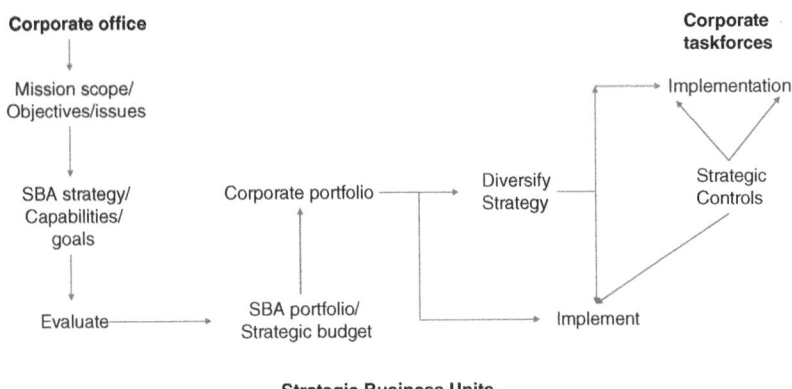

Fig. 11.24 Organizational flow of planning

tion/divestment strategy and sets up corporate taskforces for carrying out diversification/divestment.

The SBU managers are responsible for strategies and capabilities in SBAs assigned to them, for balancing their own portfolios, and for expanding these portfolios within the mission scope assigned to them.

A *strategic staff* is needed to support line executives at both levels: to design and supervise the planning process, provide environmental inputs, identify new portfolio opportunities, analyze SBAs and portfolios, and develop investment and divestment plans and budgets. (For a discussion of staff roles, see Sect. 4.3.11.)

But the work of the line executive is also voluminous. At the corporate level, this includes the following:

1. Assuring prompt recognition and timely responses to strategic challenges.
2. Assigning strategic responsibilities (missions) to the respective SBUs of the firm.
3. Setting the objectives and goals of the firm.
4. Selecting the corporate SBA, SRA, SIG portfolios.
5. Assuring transfers of strategic resources among the SBUs.
6. Selecting the mix of means for changing the portfolio: strategic development from within, as opposed to acquisitions and mergers.

What we have described above is the fully *strategic role* for the headquarters. It is in sharp contrast to two different roles which were prevalent prior to the 1960s and are still widely observable in practice.

One of these is the *operating role* in which the corporate office delegates strategy formulation and implementation to the SBU level and limits itself to resource allocation and development of the firm's resources and capabilities. This role is effective under the following conditions:

1. When the corporate management accepts the sum of its present SBU contributions as sufficient to meet the objectives of the firm.
2. When there are no transfers of strategic resources nor a need for cooperative efforts among the SBUs.

The other observable role is the *financial* or *conglomerate role*. The corporate office leaves strategy formulation and implementation, as well as organization building, to the SBUs (which are usually organized as subsidiaries) and limits itself to consolidation and monitoring of budgets and of financial performance, acquiring new subsidiaries, and divesting from subsidiaries which chronically malperform. This role is effective when all of the SBAs are growing, non-turbulent, and competition is not intense.

As already discussed in this chapter, the choice of the role to be played by the corporate office can be determined, in part, by the preferences, skills, and ambitions of the incumbent managers. But in the environment of the 2000s, the choice must also be determined by environmental conditions which the firm expects to confront in the future. If, as so often in the past, the firm expects a quiescent strategic environment, if its SBAs have promising long-term demand-technology cycles, if the sociopolitical pressures do not threaten, if technology is not expected to be turbulent, and if strategic input resources are secure—if all these conditions are satisfied, then corporate management is free to choose any of the three roles. In fact, the firm will probably be more successful if the corporate office stays out of the strategic role and does not 'meddle' with the SBUs.

If, however, the life cycles are short, technology turbulent, sociopolitical pressures are expected to be severe, and the SBUs compete for strategic resources, the corporate office must begin to take on strategic work which cannot be done at the lower levels and also make sure that the lower levels of general management take on comparably demanding strategic responsibilities. A failure to do so during the turbulent remainder of the twentieth century will imperil both success and survival of the firm. (For a detailed discussion of corporate line roles, see Chapter 17.)

Summary

When, as occurred during the first half of the century, the markets of the firm are in long growth stages, technologies are stable, and turbulence is low, management can focus its attention on optimizing near-term growth. If growth is optimized, profitability will follow, and long-term growth prospects are guaranteed.

However, as life cycles shorten and the environment becomes turbulent, profitability no longer follows growth, and near-term growth is no guarantee of long-term prospects. As a result, management has been giving increased attention to balancing investments into the near-term performance against investments into the long-term prospects.

As another result, the likelihood of both positive (opportunity) and negative (threat) discontinuities has made it necessary to minimize strategic risks through building into the portfolio internal and external flexibility. Third, increasing competitive pressures makes it increasingly necessary to optimize strategic effectiveness of the firm through synergies among the firm's SBAs.

If optimized separately, each of the three dimensions of performance (long- and near-term profitability, flexibility, and synergy) would depress the performance on the other two.

This chapter has presented a portfolio balance technique which permits a simultaneous consideration and balance among the three dimensions of performance as well as others which the firm may want to pursue.

It involves setting objectives and goals for each of the dimensions, assigning priorities to each, and then evaluating the total portfolio of SBAs for its individual and combined contribution to the objectives. If the contribution is unsatisfactory, the gaps in the portfolio are identified, and a new portfolio is specified and evaluated. The final portfolio is tested for feasibility against the firm's resources.

The chosen portfolio will specify the evolution of the firm's SBAs over time, including investments and withdrawals from the present SBAs, as well as characteristics of new SBAs which will be sought. In addition, the portfolio specifies the common threads (synergies) among the SBAs and SBUs which will be maintained and developed.

This and the preceding chapter have presented a systematic approach to strategic posture planning. The first major step is strategic segmentation (presented in Chapter 9) which analyzes the SBAs separately, chooses the firm's preferred posture in each, and determines strategic resource balance in the long term. The second major step is strategic integration, which develops the characteristics of the future portfolio in both the long and short term.

Strategic planning defines the future shape of the firm, but its only output is plans. The next step is to generate and take concrete steps which will implement the plans.

Historically, two approaches have been used for converting strategy into action. One of these is the *opportunistic approach* which dispenses with planning of entries and focuses on random generation of specific steps. The other is the *planned approach* which converts the portfolio strategy into preferred strategic posture for each of the firm's SBAs and uses directed search to develop new opportunities.

In the environment of the last quarter century, a third approach has become increasingly necessary. This is the *strategic learning approach* which dispenses with the usual sequence of implementation after planning and mixes planning and implementation steps according to the urgency felt by management, costs of developing the necessary information, and predictability of the future prospects in an SBA. The learning approach incorporates a process of *progressive commitment* by a firm, through which the firm simultaneously enters the marketplace and develops strategic information about the SBA.

The advent of systematic strategic analysis adds new workload and new roles to general management. Experience has shown that authority and responsibility for strategic development of the firm should be shared between the corporate office and the SBU managers, and that the strategic planning process should be both participative and interactive.

Exercises

1. Under what conditions does growth of a firm's sales cease to be a guarantee of profitability?
2. Why is there a conflict between short- and long-term focus of management attention? What is the nature of the conflict? How should it be resolved?
3. Identify five to ten probable discontinuities in the future environment which will pose major threats to firms in the developed nations. Select five industries which are most likely to be affected, and estimate the extent and the nature of the impact on each.
4. It has been argued that the conglomerate firm is the firm of the future. It has also been argued that it contributes nothing to the economic development of a country and is therefore socially undesirable. What is behind these arguments? What are your views on the future role of the conglomerate?

12

Strategic Dimensions of Technology

When the concept of strategy was first developing, the focus was on economic and competitive variables. R&D, like production, was treated as a functional area to which strategic decisions could be assigned for 'implementation.'

Since the 1950s, it has become increasingly evident that, in certain industries, technology was becoming a driving force which could shape the strategic future of an enterprise. But recognition of the strategic importance of technology has been slow in planning literature.

This chapter, based on an Ansoffian paper published in 1967 with John Stewart, was one of the early efforts to explore the impact of technology on strategy. The paper was a contribution to the efforts of one major consulting firm to enlarge its field of strategic consultancy to include technology-intensive firms.

The Role of Technology in Business Strategy

Emergence of Technology as a Competitive Tool

During the past 60 years, considerable attention has been directed to management of the R&D process: its organization, its planning and control, its budgeting, and, especially, the stimulation and management of creativity. The impact of technology on business strategies is more critical than it has ever been. Technology-intensive industries, such as chemicals, electronics,

© The Author(s) 2019
H. I. Ansoff et al., *Implanting Strategic Management*,
https://doi.org/10.1007/978-3-319-99599-1_12

pharmaceuticals, automotive or aerospace is frequently a driving force which determines the strategic future of the firm.

On the negative side, failure *to* recognize in time an impending technology substitution can result in a major loss of market share or, indeed, cause the firm to leave an industry in which it had enjoyed a profitable existence. On the positive side, technology can serve as a major and powerful tool through which a firm can gain and maintain a competitive dominance.

An outstanding example is found with Apple, which in 2007, in its strategic use of technology, introduced the first Apple iPhone during the 79th Academy Awards. The system made obsolete the existing cell phone technology and gave the company a major and lasting advantage over competition.

Recognition of the strategic importance of technology is growing. In many industries, R&D activities have grown to a point where today they rank among the top consumers of company funds. Chief executives, who once accepted R&D on faith, are no longer willing to let the technological tail go on 'wagging the corporate dog.' To some managers, R&D has become an ungovernable monster which must be harnessed.

Experience shows that the strategic success of firms is less sensitive to the specifics of a technology than to certain key technological variables which are common across the spectrum of technology-based industries. Firms which recognize and manage these variables will be more likely to succeed than those which let themselves be driven by the inner logic of the technological 'monster.'

In this chapter, we identify these variables and discuss ways in which they can be integrated with the processes of corporate strategy and capability planning.

Technological Turbulence

In Fig. 9.2, we referred to the importance of technological turbulence in the evolution of the demand life cycle. Figure 12.1 shows three possible levels of technological turbulence. The upper graph demonstrates a *stable, long-lived technology* which remains basically unchanged for the duration of the demand life cycle. This graph describes many of the first-generation industries which were founded at the end of the nineteenth century and began to reach maturity in the 1950s. During the accelerating growth stage G_1, the products offered by different competitors are similar and remain substantially unchanged. Competition is on product quality and price (as was, e.g., the case in the US automotive industry between 1900 and 1932).

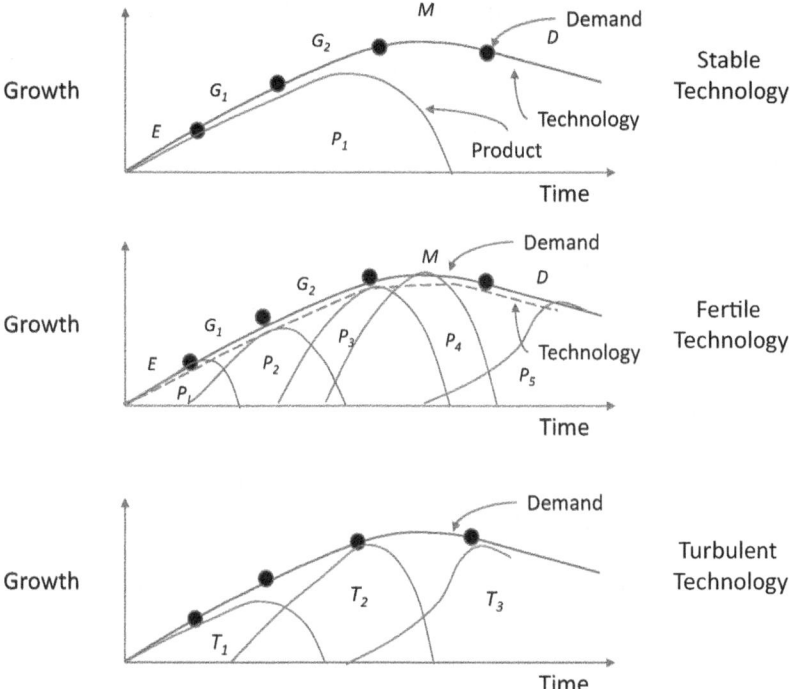

Fig. 12.1 Demand-technology-product life cycles

When product proliferation occurs during G_2, it is based on product features and design cosmetics rather than on technological advances in product performance.

The middle graph illustrates what we shall call *fertile technologies*. The basic technology is long-lived, but products proliferate, offering progressively better performance and broadening the field of application.

In fertile technologies (e.g., pharmaceutical industries today), product development becomes a critical factor in economic success. The newest and best-performing product captures the market. But, on the other hand, its leadership is likely to be short-lived due to challenges from similarly effective or superior products offered by competitors. As a result, firms are under constant pressure to innovate.

History shows that in technologically stable industries during period G_1 and G_2, growth of sales correlates with profitability. On the other hand, in technologically fertile industries, 'profitless prosperity' may occur: While growth is strong, profitability is either low or even negative, because intensive competition drives down the prices, and short product life cycles prevent firms from recovering their investment in the succeeding products/ services. This is what is happening today in the automotive and home entertainment industries, where intensive product proliferation is occurring in efforts to revive stagnating demand. At best, if the performance improvements are revolutionary, the new products may obsolete the current ones and effectively restart the demand life cycle. More typically, though, new products permit the successful firms to maintain or enlarge their market share at the expense of weaker competitors in a field of stagnant growth.

During maturity, product development is also used to diversify the firm into other less-saturated areas of demand.

The third graph on Fig. 12.1 demonstrates a *turbulent field of technology* in which, in addition to product proliferation, one or more basic technology substitutions take place within the life span of the demand life cycle.

The effects of technology substitution are further reaching than of product fertility, because they threaten obsolescence of the firm's entire investment in the preceding technology: in R&D know-how, in key scientific and technical personnel, and in processing and manufacturing facilities.

Within a firm, transition to the new technology is difficult, not only financially, but also *culturally* and *politically,* because the new technology challenges the historical success model held by both technologists and influential managers, and also threatens their position of power and influence in the firm (for a more detailed discussion of the resulting resistance to change, see Part V).

Experience shows that when the new technology is totally different from the old (such as the vacuum conduction and the solid-state technologies), firms frequently abandon the industry in which they were the original leaders. Thus, people familiar with today's electronics industry would have difficulty in remembering the names of the major vacuum tube manufacturers of some seventy years ago.

When the substitute technology belongs to the same knowledge stem as its substitute (as, e.g., in today's emergence of the biogenetic technology in the pharmaceutical industry), a firm will typically stay in the industry, but the problems of timely recognition and reaction remain. If the new technology is 'fast rising,' it is usually the historical leaders who fail to react and consequently lose their competitive position. This is illustrated by the recent slippage of the American automotive industry caused by the rapid advent of the new small-car technology.

The problem of transition to a new technology is further aggravated when technology is both fertile and turbulent. When a new technology surfaces, the firm is already deeply involved in the competitive struggle of product proliferation under the old technology. Its R&D program is committed to this struggle and becomes an obstacle to the firm's transition to the new technology.

Today, any historically stable industry can be changed overnight into a turbulent one by intrusion of an alien technology. This can occur at any stage of the demand life cycle, but is particularly challenging when it occurs during maturity, as is happening today in the automotive industry, where new technologies together with computer-assisted design and manufacturing are revolutionizing both product development and production. The challenge to management is to be realistic in the assessment of the consequences of the new technology. In a climate of concern and frustration with sluggish demand, it is easy to rationalize that the new technology will revolutionize the products and produce a large-scale revival of demand. This is not likely to occur, however, unless the advances are so revolutionary as to make obsolete the products which already saturate the marketplace. In the automotive industry, the 'automatic factory' is not likely to have such impact.

Influence and Role of R&D

Historical as well as theoretical analysis (Ansoff 1979-G) shows that during changes in the environmental turbulence, power is a determining factor in a firm's response. For example, the reason why many firms were slow and frequently late in shifting from the production to the marketing orientation, which occurred in the 1930s and 1940s, is traceable to the resistance to change by the entrenched production-oriented managers. On many occasions, the transition to the new orientation was achieved through political struggles and eventual power transfer to the marketing-minded managers.

Therefore, in technologically turbulent industries, an appropriate balance of influences within the firm is essential if two opposite and equally undesirable situations are to be avoided:

1. A situation in which the R&D function is dominated by others and unable to make its contribution to the strategic development of the firm; or
2. A situation in which the firm is driven by the historical technology at a time of technology substitution, or during a shift of critical success factors away from technology to production and/or marketing.

Table 12.1 illustrates the critical functional contributions and hence the power and influence roles appropriate to different technological environments.

In *technologically stable* industries, corporate general management is the critical driving force on two occasions: first, during emergence and, second, during maturity and decline. In between, experience has shown that the firm runs well if the function which is critical to the success of the firm is allowed to 'call the strategic shots.' During G_1, the production function and its mentality acquired a position of dominant power. During G_2 marketing took over.

Having made its original contribution in the establishment of the industry, R&D typically became a secondary supporting function until maturity, when it was frequently called upon by corporate management to play the savior.

The two lower parts of Table 12.1 show that in technologically active industries, R&D has a key role to play throughout the demand cycle. The essential distinction between the fertile and turbulent industries is that in the former the contribution of R&D is primarily through product and process development, while in the latter research becomes equally important. Since the nature of the two processes (as we shall discuss later in this chapter) is different and their values and goals are frequently contradictory, there is typically competition for influence within the R&D function. As in the case of the struggle between production and marketing, power gravitates to 'R' or to 'D' proportionally according to their historical contributions to the

Table 12.1 Critical success factors

Demand Stage		E	G 1	G 2	M	D
Technology	**Critical function**	Gen'l mgmt R&D	Production	Marketing	Gen'l mgmt R&D	Gen'l mgmt
Stable	**R&D contributio**	Innovation	Process improvement	Product development	Innovation	
Fertile	**Critical function**	◄——————— General management ———————► R&D ◄——— R&D + product+marketing. ——►R&D				
	R&D contributio	innovation ◄—— Process improvement —►Innovation ◄— Product development —►				
Turbulent	**Critical function**	◄——————— General management ———————► R&D ◄——— R&D + product+marketing. ——►R&D. R&D				
	R&D contributio n	◄——————— Technology substitution ———————► innovation Process improvement Innovation ◄— Product development —►				

firm's profitability. Usually, the 'D' activity is the winner which results in a built-in commitment to the historical technology. In times of technology substitution, the R&D department continues to proliferate products based on a technology which is in the process of becoming obsolete. This adherence to the historical technology can appropriately be named *technological myopia*.

Hence, during transitions from one technology to another, it becomes vital that general management exercise a driving influence to make sure that development of products based on the old technology is cut back and that the new technology is acquired by the firm.

Table 12.2 shows the circumstances which dictate different functional influences.

1. In technologically stable ('standardized') product environments, when the key success factor is the product price, production becomes the driving force in successful firms.
2. When response to, and persuasion of, customers is the key success factor (as in G_2 stage of low-technology consumer industries), the marketing function calls the shots.
3. In technology-intensive industries, when product performance is the key to success, and demand is not sensitive to price, R&D becomes dominant.

Table 12.2 Dominant power center for success

Management function Key success factors	Production	Marketing	R&D	Control	General management
Price	**				
Respond to market		**			
Product innovation			**		
Maximize cashflow				**	
Profit optimization	*	*	*		**
Technology substitution					**
Portfolio balance					**

4. In mature and well-ordered competitive environments, when maximization is the key to success, the influence variable shifts to control.
5. When more than one function makes comparable contributions to success, the key success factor is the firm's ability to optimize profits through trade-offs of typically conflicting influence and contribution of the functions. In this case, general management is the key to success.
6. As already mentioned, when technology substitution occurs, it is vital, not only to success but also to survival, that general management take control.
7. When the firm seeks success across several SBAs by balancing multiple objectives, control by general management is essential.

In the first four cases, as long as success depends on only one of the functions, general management can afford to delegate the deciding power over strategic development to the essential function. However, when the key success factors shift, general management first needs to anticipate the shift and, second, to assure a timely and effective transfer of influence among the functions.

Closing the Gap Between General Managers and Technologies

As the preceding section shows, in technology-intensive firms, general management must become involved in the management of that technology. All too frequently, though, such involvement is made difficult by a mutual lack of understanding between general management and the technologists.

As will be discussed in Chapter 15, during the first half of the century, preparation for the general management role typically included rotation of promising candidates through functional assignments in production, marketing, finance, and, less frequently, in R&D. This lesser frequency was due, in part, to the relatively minor importance assigned to R&D and, in part, to the fact that an expert knowledge of technology is required of R&D managers.

During the second half of the century, as technology progressively became a key to success, technologist-entrepreneurs became the controlling general managers in new companies founded on new technologies. An understanding of the intricacies, prospects, risk, and costs of technology comes naturally to such managers, and, if they had any knowledge gaps, their weaknesses came from a lack of expertise in marketing and manufacturing.

However, in numerous large firms, in which historically stable technologies became fertile and turbulent, and firms which chose to diversify into technology-intensive industries, general managers typically confronted several 'gaps' between themselves and the technologists, as listed below:

1. The *information gap* which arises from the fact that the vital, frequently vague, and difficult to quantify knowledge about prospects, risks, consequences, and costs of technology typically resides in researchers and development engineers. These *knowledge workers* are kept from contact with the strategists by several intervening layers of managers, who have neither competence nor interest in technology and who suppress and filter technological information.

One frequent consequence of the information gap is that general management makes R&D investment decisions on the basis of initial R&D project costs, without taking account of the usually massive range of downstream costs which must be incurred before a developed product or a new technique begins to make money in the market. This is akin to assessing the size of a 'technological iceberg' by the size of the peak visible above the surface of the water.

2. The *semantic gap* which arises from the difference in languages, concepts, and perception of success factors between the general managers and the R&D managers. In advocating new investment, R&D managers typically perceive technological variables as the critical success factors, and unless general management understands the technological claims and places them into overall commercial perspective, the firm may commit corporate resources to 'solutions in search of problems.'

An example of a general management misunderstanding of the state of the technology is offered by Microsoft and their Zune digital music player. In late 2001, Apple changed digital music forever with the launch of the iPod. Microsoft launched its rival, the Zune, five years later. Despite positive reviews, the Zune flopped due to its delayed entry, weak marketing efforts, and lack of support among major record labels. Sales never picked up, but Microsoft kept the Zune alive for six more generations before killing it off in 2012.

3. The *objectives/value gap*. The objective of the general manager is to produce an optimal return on the corporate resources. Technology is one

of the means for doing so and has no intrinsic value of its own. On the contrary, unless the manager is also a trained technologist, intricacies and complexities of technologies are something he prefers to avoid. The thrill of discovery and the elegance of solutions have no value for him.

By contrast, excitement of discovery, elegant solutions, and professional prestige are the objectives of a committed technologist, while concern with the ultimate return on the investment quickly becomes a negative value if it is used to prevent him from working on 'interesting' problems.

A consequence of the differences in values/objectives is a difference in perception of what constitutes a desirable product for the firm. For the technologist, a technologically feasible advance is reason enough to go to the market, while the general managers need to be convinced of its potential profitability.

The possible consequence of an objectives/value gap is illustrated in Fig. 12.2 by means of a buyer–seller 'game matrix.'

The upper right hand is a 'win-win' quadrant: The seller profits and the buyer benefits. We call it the *strategist's choice* because it forms a basis for a long-term profitable buyer–seller relationship.

Fig. 12.2 Buyer–seller 'game matrix'

In companies which are technology driven, in the sense that products developed by R&D are automatically placed on the market without prior estimates of their potential profitability, the upper left-hand *giveaway* situation may result. It is likely to occur under one or more of the following conditions:

1. When new technology is offered prematurely, before manufacturing costs have been brought in line with feasible market prices.
2. When the product is introduced before the market is ready to pay for the new technological advances.
3. When the size of the potential demand is not large enough to permit the firm to recover the development costs.
4. When the number of suppliers, attracted by demand-growth prospects, saturates the market.
5. Finally, and importantly, strategic giveaway will occur when the firm's technologists continue to proliferate products, using a technology which is rapidly being overtaken by a substitute technology, in which the firm *has* no competence.

The lower right-hand *buyer-beware* quadrant represents a 'win-lose' outcome: While the seller profits, the buyer does not get his money's worth. Historically, this has been a frequent case in low-technology consumer goods industries—a case which has led to the proliferation of consumer protection legislation. But this can equally occur in a technology-intensive industry when well-intentioned technologists, who have little understanding of client needs and cost-benefit relationships, force new products on clients. In such cases, 'technological fashion' rather than cost-benefits sells the successful products.

Finally, the lower left-hand *fool's paradise* may occur when enthusiastic technologists of the seller company convince the user technologists of the buyer of the technological advantages of their products. In this case, group has neither the competence nor the motivation to evaluate the bottom-line profitability consequences of this 'lose-lose' game.

One recent example of this is with the 'big box' retail stores (Sears, JC Penney and Macy's) with their 'hands-on' customer service and their symbiotic relationship with the mall owners where many of the big-box stores are located. The 'Big-box' retailers sold directly to consumers who enjoyed the experience of shopping-in-person and personal service, and the mall owners benefitted by having the big-box stores as anchors for the malls, drawing the larger customer volume.

However, all of this changed when the Internet became a shopping forum competing directly for the 'brick-and-mortar' customers. This new business model of online shopping was a difficult transition for the brick-and-mortar stores as such, it was a 'fool' paradise' to continue building malls for big-box retailers.

In order to survive, malls had to repurpose and create attractions like Mall of the America and ice rinks instead of relying on simply a selection of shopping experiences. This new approach is also in jeopardy as many of the new generation shoppers (Amazon shoppers) are not interested in malls or in-person shopping. Forcing both the mall owners and big-box retailer to once again rethink their competitive position with the consumer.

The preceding discussion reinforces the importance of active general management involvement in technology-based strategic decisions and hence the importance of bridging the information, the semantic and the value gaps. The following complementary steps can be taken to bridge them:

1. The mere awareness by general management of the dangers posed by the gaps is the first key step.
2. Assuring that the general management group responsible for strategy formulation includes competent up-to-date technologists.
3. Educating key R&D managers in strategic management.
4. Developing in general management expertise in using experts—skills of evaluating claims made by technologists.
5. Educating general managers in the dynamics and economics of the R&D process and in behavior of creative technologists.
6. Basing all major R&D investment on profitability estimates which include the entire stream of costs from research to market.
7. Developing direct communication channels between key knowledge workers and general managers.
8. Developing a technology surveillance system for general management.
9. Developing an R&D project management system within the firm which first encourages divergent creativity and then channels it into profitable development projects.
10. Including technological variables in the business strategy formulation.
11. Developing an explicit technology (R&D) strategy for the firm.

*2.7.5 Determining the Impact of Technology on Business Strategy

At the left-hand side of Table 12.3 are listed five key technology factors which affect business strategy: investment in R&D, competitive positioning, product dynamics, technology dynamics, and competitive-dynamics.

Under each factor, there are several elements which together determine what in Table 12.3 is called the *intensity* of the factor. The importance of the respective factors to the firm's future business ·strategy can be assessed as follows:

1. Assess the future intensity and relative importance of the respective technology factors to future success in a particular SBA.
2. Determine the gaps between the future environment and the firm's historical strategy.
3. Estimate the firm's future technological competitive position if the firm continues using its historical strategy. At this point, the technology factors must be integrated with the economic, competitive, social, and political factors. We shall demonstrate how this can be done in the following section.
4. Using the procedure discussed in detail in the preceding chapters, determine the desired competitive position.
5. Identify the changes in the technological strategy factors which should be made.
6. Check resource feasibility and timing of the changes.
7. Initiate change projects.

Table 12.3   Technological strategic factors

Factors (1)	Intensity (2)					Importance to future success (3)	Firm's strategy gap (4)	Firm's action priorities (5)
Investment in R&D								
1. R&D as % of profits	Low	I	I	I	High			
2. R as % of profits	Low	I	I	I	High			
3. D as % of profits	Low	I	I	I	High			
Competitive positioning								
4. Research leadership	Imitator		follower		innovator			
5. Product leadership	I	I	I	I	I			
6. Process leadership	I	I	I	I	I			
Product dynamics								
7. Frequency of new products	Low	I	I	I	High			
8. Length of life cycle	Long	I	I	I	Short			
9. Technological advance in successive products	Small	I	I	I	Large			
Technology dynamics								
10. Length of life cycle	Long	I	I	I	Short			
11. Frequency of new technologies	Low	I	I	I	High			
12. Number of competing technologies	One	I	I	I	Many			
Competitive dynamics								
13. Technological product differentiation	None	I	I	I	Large			
14. Technology as a competitive tool	Unimportant I		I	I	Key			
15. Competitive intensity	Low	I	I	I	Intense			
16. Forced product obsolescence	None.	I	I	I	Frequent			
17. Technological response to government regulations	Unimportant I		I	I	Key			
18. Technological response to consumer pressures	Unimportant I		I	I	Key			
Overall evaluation								
19. Technological turbulence	1	2	3	4	5			
20. Aggressiveness of firm's strategy	1	2	3	4	5			

Table 12.3 can be used as a worksheet, first, for determining the future environmental turbulence, secondly, the technological aggressiveness of the firm's strategy, and thirdly, the gaps and the action priorities. An example of the results of such analysis is presented in summary fashion in Fig. 12.3.

- The zigzag profile labeled future environment is the result of step 1 above.
- The zigzag firm's strategy is the diagnosis (step 2) of the historical strategy.
- The column next to the profiles is an evaluation of the relative importance of the respective factors to the future success in the environment.
- The strategic gap column is derived directly from the differences between the two zigzag profiles.
- The action priorities in the last column are determined in part by the gaps and in part by the particular strategy chosen by the firm.

So far, in this and the preceding sections, we have discussed a procedure for including technological factors in the formulation of the firm's *competitive strategy* for a given SBA. Similar modification should be made in formulation of the *portfolio strategy* whenever the firm participates in one or more turbulent technologies.

A technology impact analysis should be made following the procedure described in Chapter 11, and the SBA portfolio balanced to assure that, on the one hand, the firm's 'technological eggs' are not all in one vulnerable basket, and, on the other hand, the firm is not over-diversified to a point where it lacks the critical mass necessary in each of its different technologies.

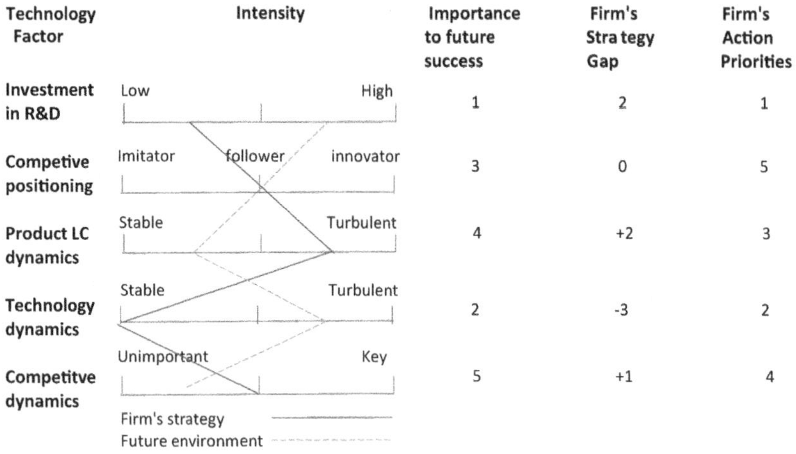

Technology Factor	Intensity		Importance to future success	Firm's Strategy Gap	Firm's Action Priorities
Investment in R&D	Low	High	1	2	1
Competive positioning	Imitator	follower	innovator	3	0	5
Product LC dynamics	Stable	Turbulent	4	+2	3
Technology dynamics	Stable	Turbulent	2	-3	2
Competitve dynamics	Unimportant	Key	5	+1	4

Firm's strategy ——————
Future environment --------

Fig. 12.3 Technological factors in strategy

Integrating Technology Factors into Competitive Strategy Formulation

Figure 12.4 illustrates the process. The first step is to match technological possibilities (state of the art) to needs which exist in society. As already discussed, in technology-driven firm's new *techno-feasible strategies* may originate from within R&D as 'solutions in search of problems' in the expectation that new developments will always find the market. In a preceding section (Fig. 12.2), we have already described the potential dangers of this approach. Therefore, techno-feasible strategies must be based as much on needs' analysis as on technological possibilities.

The next step—*econo-feasible strategies*—is to determine that, in the absence of competition and other constraints, a firm could make a profit from the innovation, because the potential customers have the purchasing power and are prepared to pay the price.

The next step, *competitive success postures*, uses the procedure described in Chapter 10. The procedure takes account of the dynamics of demand, expected competitive intensity, expected competitive offerings, and sociopolitical constraints and pressures. As a result of this analysis, a range of potential success postures is identified and their likely profitability is estimated.

The last step is to formulate the firm's *future competitive posture* in the manner described in Chapter 10.

The procedure described in Fig. 12.4 should be followed if a firm wishes to avoid a giveaway situation and/or the fool's paradise. The dotted line shown on the right of the figure describes the practice frequently followed by technology-intensive companies, particularly small ones, which do not have the marketing know-how and lack the resources for a systematic planning of strategy. This 'laboratory to the market' approach can be used with assurance only when the following conditions exist:

1. The firm is in possession of a highly unique technology.
2. There is an expressed customer desire for the technology.
3. The customers are prepared to pay any 'reasonable' price to obtain it.
4. The competition is weak.
5. The supply–demand relationship is highly favorable to the firm.

Unless these conditions are met, the firm will be taking high risks by plunging into the market with technically feasible but commercially unevaluated entries. When the investment in launching the new product is small, this risk may be well worth taking, and the firm may succeed on the average through a succession of successes and failures. When the R&D investment

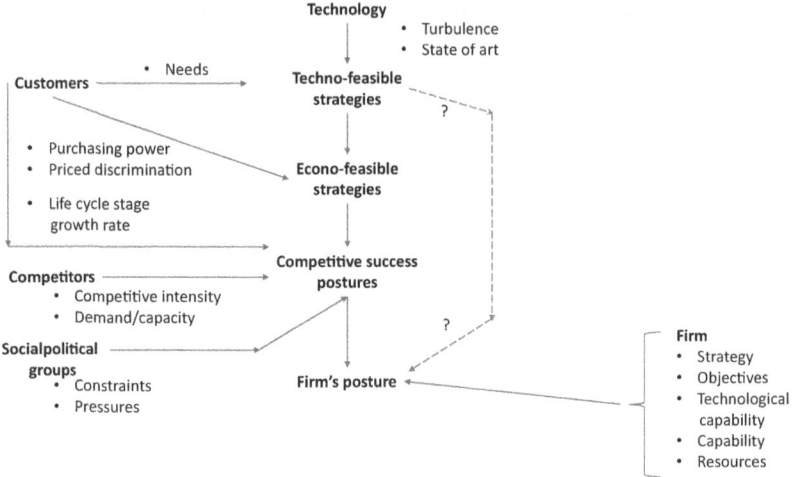

Fig. 12.4 Impact of technology on strategy

costs become substantial, though, a strong argument can be made in favor of allocating a part of the firm's resources to market research and strategy formulation, even if this means reducing the energy devoted to product/technology development.

The decision rule for choosing between the two alternatives is a classic one: whether the expected profitability from a succession of 'blind gambles' is likely to be greater or smaller than a succession of 'calculated risks.' Managers have found that this decision rule is easy to use, if one is willing to be content with qualitative judgments. But the use of this rule frequently becomes prohibitively costly if one insists on 'hard number' risk estimates.

If technological turbulence analysis (see Table 12.3) shows that the firm's technologies are turbulent, that they play an important role in the future success of the firm, and that R&D investment will be significant, it becomes desirable to synthesize the strategic variables into a statement of the firm's technology strategy. (A detailed discussion of technology strategy is beyond the scope of this book.)

Management Capability for Technology-Intensive Strategies

We next turn attention to the organizational capability needed to support the key technological factors in business strategy. Our concern shall be not with the specific technological knowledge and skills, but rather with the general management capabilities needed for successful development and implementation of the strategy.

2.7.7 R&D Investment Ratio

The size of the R&D investment ratio, as determined in Table 12.3, has important organizational consequences. High ratios are characteristic of technology-intensive industries such as pharmaceuticals, chemicals, and electronics; low ratios arc characteristic of non-intensive industries such as food, lumber, and cement. Most industries, of course, fall between the two extremes, for example, farm equipment and petroleum are near the middle of the range.

A high investment ratio puts four significant requirements on management:

1. Continuous evaluation of technology 'make or buy' decisions:

   • Whether to buy technology through licensing or through hiring consultants.
   • Whether to buy a company in order to acquire the latest technology in an unfamiliar field.
   • Whether to hire top people with the specific technical competence desired.
   • Whether to develop additional technical competence by internal training in order to stay competitive.

Where R&D investment ratio is low, it may be possible to develop technology within the company with relatively low risk of being outpaced by competition. High ratios allow less lead time and frequently make acquisition of technology a more attractive alternative. In any case, they call for constant review of the alternatives by a corporate-level group which is aware of the pace of development inside the company and which is also sensitive to significant competitive moves.

2. An adaptive organization, which can quickly shift to new product and process technologies either from external or internal sources. A major criterion of success in a high ratio organization is its ability to adapt to new technology smoothly without major disruption of its profitable performance.
3. Effective and flexible management of product innovation. This consists of:

   • Strategic control of product-market development which permits management to quickly cut off development projects which fail to come up to initial expectation.
   • Explicit R&D strategy. When development projects are many and originate in many places, and when the R&D budget is large, there is

a danger of misdirection, waste, and conflict in the development effort. There is further a danger of the historical thrust of technology becoming inconsistent and dysfunctional with the changing business strategy of the firm. Hence, the firm needs a clearly defined R&D strategy which is consistent with the business strategy.

- A well-developed project management system which coordinates and controls the project portfolio consistently with strategy and with annual corporate planning and control.

4. Close top management supervision of technical efforts. Since the company depends on technology for competitive survival, and commits substantial resources to it, senior managers need to understand cost and profit implications of technological developments. They need assurance that the thrust of technological development is consistent with objectives and the strategy of the firm.

The effect of a low R&D investment ratio is the converse of those described above. Technology can be developed internally within competitive lead times or, in some industries, purchased with the capital equipment into which technology has been incorporated by the manufacturer. Organization structure need not be highly adaptive; since technical developments are evolutionary, only occasional changes in structure will be needed. Resources devoted to technology need not be singled out because historical accounting data on expense and investment adequately reflect the impact of product or process replacements. Finally, marketing does not have to be closely coupled with the technological functions.

As discussed in the last chapter, the choice of the R&D investment ratio is partly determined by the technological turbulence and partly by the level of the firm's ambition in a given SBA. But in no case should the investment be below the *critical mass*.

Critical mass is not easy to measure, but a useful estimate can be obtained from arraying the profitability of a series of companies against their R&D budgets. Experienced R&D managers can be relied upon for estimates of the minimum technological effort necessary for the firm to remain technologically competitive (see Chapter 9). Since high-quality research personnel can generate a return out of all proportion to their number, quality as well as quantity affects the critical mass. Another complicating factor is the mix of disciplines found in the technical staff. Managers working with interdisciplinary groups have repeatedly noted that one mix of disciplines will result in higher innovation and output than another.

In technology and/or physical asset industries, the *project critical mass* must be a particular concern of top management of the firm, when it receives proposals for massive investments. It must not allow 'foot in the door tactics' of ambitious scientists and engineers committing the firm to large follow-on investments which the firm cannot afford to make.

2.7.8 R- vs. D-Intensive Organizations

When the firm makes a large investment in the innovation process, the nature of the organizational capability will differ significantly, depending on the relative importance of research vs. development investment. The concepts of 'research' and 'development' have become so closely linked in management thinking by the expression 'R&D' that important differences between them are often ignored in executive decision making. This becomes particularly apparent when companies attempt to apply the lessons of their research experience to problems in development, or vice versa.

We shall use the terms 'R-intensive' and 'D-intensive' to focus on basic and experimental research, on the one hand, and a focus on commercial product design on the other. As already discussed, the mix in most companies falls somewhere between the two extremes.

R-intensive organizations display six characteristics:

1. They work with *indefinite design specifications*. Management can identify the important areas of knowledge but cannot specify the results desired in the area. The task of the R-intensive organization is to discover new scientific facts and relationships which have potential commercial applications.
2. They tend to *'broadcast' objectives and market data among technical people* rather than channel-specific kinds of information to individuals. Being unable to present specific requirements to research, they use broadcast communication to stimulate creativity and generation of alternatives that will be consistent with top management's objectives and strategy.
3. They are *nondirective in work assignments*. Since design specifications in R-intensive companies are indefinite, and technical insight and potential contribution are individual rather than group attributes, managers must permit freedom for individual initiative and progress, rather than assign individuals to specific parts of a well-defined solution.
4. They maintain a *continuing project evaluation and selection process*. Research is constantly turning up alternative ideas and solutions. Moreover, a discovery by a competitor, or results achieved on a related

project, may render obsolete a piece of research or change its priority. This calls for a continuing revision of the project portfolio to permit changes in the status and priorities of projects.

5. They stress the *perception of the significance of results.* The consequences of research results are frequently not obvious. An essential skill of the strategic manager is his ability to recognize the technical or commercial implications of results. The history of invention is replete with instances, like that of Chemistry graduate student Jamie Link who was working on a silicon chip at the University of California in San Diego in 2003. The chip shattered. But, as it turned out, it was not a disaster. Link and her supervisor discovered that tiny bits of the chip were still sending signals, operating as tiny sensors. They called the self-assembling particles 'smart dust.' These microelectromechanical devices include sensors and computational ability. Hailed as one of the top inventions this century, it is used to monitor the purity of water, detect harmful chemicals in the air, and locate and destroy tumors in the body.

6. They value *innovation over efficiency.* Economy in performing research is less important than achieving a markedly better solution with clear market or profit advantages. Innovation is therefore encouraged, even at the sacrifice of efficiency, planning, or control.

By contrast, D-intensive organizations can usually be recognized by four characteristics:

1. *Well-defined design specifications.* The development objectives are reasonably clear, and performance tests can be specified early during design. The technical task is not to create new knowledge, as in research, but to reduce available knowledge to a commercially profitable solution.

2. *Highly directive supervision.* The work to be done is programmed from the beginning of design to successful testing; managers specify objectives, assign tasks, measure, and control performance. The relatively large number of people in the D-intensive projects—designers, test engineers, draftsmen, production engineers—calls for more coordination and 'people management' than in an R-intensive organization.

3. *Project management and control.* Unlike the R-intensive organization where many people work in parallel on the whole problem or on different aspects of the same problem, the D-intensive organization requires a programming of interlinked tasks, with controls which ensure that technical objectives are achieved with planned time and cost limits. When faced

with trade-off decisions between meeting deadlines and last-minute innovations, managers will frequently opt for entering the market on time.

4. *Vulnerability to disruption by change.* Given its high costs and relatively high manpower commitment and deadline pressures, a D-intensive project can be severely affected by midstream changes, in managerial or administrative changes, or in performance specifications. Studies by McKinsey and coworkers indicate that management or program changes contribute more heavily to cost, and schedule overruns, than do engineering or technical changes.

Given these differing characteristics, the hazards of managing a D-intensive organization with management concepts and controls suited to the R-intensive company, or vice versa, should be apparent. Consider the following example.

The president of a technically based electronics company was convinced that a strong research department was the key to innovative products and high profits. The department generated plenty of ideas, but few marketable products, a situation to which the president reacted by further increasing the research staff. The company's marketing, manufacturing, and financial managers began resigning in disgust. Profits dropped, so did the company's stock. Not long thereafter, the president was replaced by a new man from the outside. President no. 2 began strengthening the development-oriented functions that had atrophied during the research binge and hangover. Then, he began to trim the research staff which, by some estimates, was three times what the company could support. In the seven years since the advent of the new president, the company had successfully marketed a series of technically innovative products against strong competition. Its development, manufacturing, marketing, and financial functions became equal to its most formidable competition. The quality and management of research, despite a substantial staff reduction, have suffered no serious decline, but the management processes to support that research have been drastically altered.

2.7.9 Downstream Coupling

When the firm's strategy commits it to *aggressive product dynamics* (see Table 12.3), and when a blending and integration of the functional contributions are a critical success factor (see Table 12.2), the *downstream coupling* of the functional activities becomes an important factor in the success of the strategy.

In Fig. 12.5, we distinguish three degrees of coupling: high, moderate, and low. High coupling requires close interaction among the technical, manufacturing, and marketing functions of the business. Accurate and detailed market information is essential to adequate product-line planning. The selection of R&D projects is influenced heavily by manufacturing costs, availability of raw materials, abilities of the marketing organization, and countermoves by competition. Minimizing the disruptive effect of new product introductions on manufacturing is critical. Tight control of product quality is essential to successful customer applications and minimum service engineering effort. Finally, time pressure on all functions is usually acute.

Many technically based industries require exceptionally high coupling. In specialty plastics, for example, the functions of product and process development, production, and field technical service must be closely linked *by* a tightly knit communication, decision, and control process. In present-day electronics, integrated circuit producers find that they must work more closely with equipment designers, field service staff, and marketing planners than discrete component suppliers ever did.

In a highly coupled organization, management is usually concerned about the post-development downstream investments in marketing and production. The coupling-conscious management of one chemical company, wary of a proposed $6 million investment in development of a new chemical process, kept pressing for more information. The facts confirmed

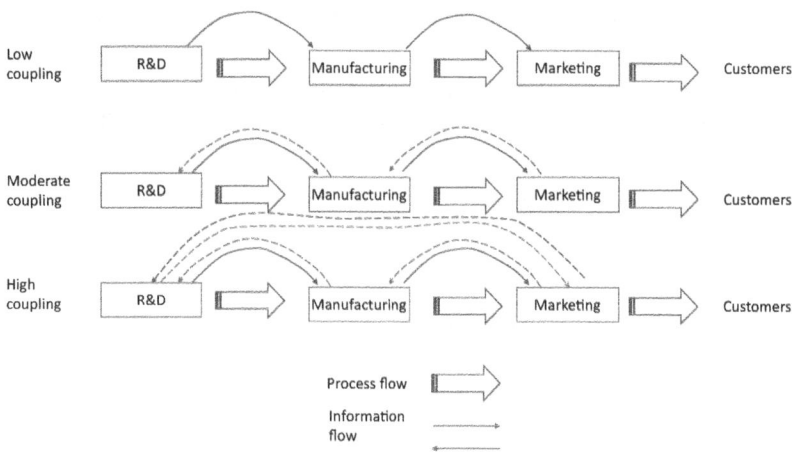

Fig. 12.5 Degrees of downstream coupling

their misgivings: More than $20 million of additional investment would be required before the parent company's target rate of return could be achieved. The $6 million 'down payment' was not approved.

In highly coupled companies, management must maintain a constant balance of influence among development, production, and technical service to the customer. If development becomes too strong, uneconomic or unreliable products or processes are rammed into manufacturing. If technical service is too powerful, future development is downgraded in the interest of extinguishing the fire-of-the-minute. Occasionally, manufacturing is strong enough to reject desirable product changes in the interest of maintaining high efficiencies, or to schedule output to maximize machine utilization rather than to meet customer commitments.

The correct balance among these three functions is dynamic rather than static. Changes in the company's competitive situation, technical strengths, and capacity utilization, among others, force management to keep readjusting the balance.

In an earlier section, we have already discussed the fact that when cooperation among the functions is essential, general management must take an active role in managing the development process. Closely coupled development is usually organized into projects, which introduces an additional complexity, since the project manager becomes an additional actor in inter-functional relations. Unless the role, responsibility, and power position of the project manager are clearly defined, the project system may reduce rather than improve the coupling and effectiveness of the development process. In a recent major consumer electronics breakthrough, based on technology substitution, the pioneering firm found that three of its major divisions had significant technological contributions to make to the final design. A project manager was appointed, but he lacked the status, the authority, and the control over the resources necessary to force cooperation in the face of the fierce competition which developed among the divisions. As a result, so much of the firm's energies were spent on the internal power struggles that schedules slipped severely and little attention was paid to the rate of competitive developments. The firm lost much of its advantage of being an early and imaginative innovator and arrived on the marketplace only to be confronted with vigorous competition from alternative technological approaches.

The lesson to be learned from this experience is that project management is complex and tricky, but it is the essential solution in closely coupled development processes. Fortunately, a large body of literature on project management is available, thanks to early pioneering work in the aerospace industry. In adapting this literature to the needs of a particular firm, attention should be given to assuring that the scope of responsibilities assigned to the project manager is commensurate with his power position and resources under his control.

Product Life Cycle

The concept of the product life cycle is too well known to require exposition here. Life cycles may vary in length from a few months (e.g., the finger fidget) to years or even decades (e.g., the wooden pencil). In technology-intensive businesses, the length of the cycle has important strategic implications, particularly for planning and control.

Speedy management action and response, high concurrency of activities in product introduction, and approximation rather than precision in technical objectives are characteristic of short-cycle companies.

Competitive intelligence is essential for early appraisal of competitive moves and countermoves. To succeed, a company needs to be among the first to bring out a new product or break into a new market, since competition thereafter will quickly force the prices down, depressing profit margins and return on investment. To continue to succeed, the pioneering firm should also be unsentimental and deliberate about 'killing its own successes' through timely substitution with the new generations of products.

To observers from slower-moving industries, the short-cycle company appears to be in perpetual chaos. It tends to favor short-circuit devices—such as product managers, project managers, or inter-functional committees—which speed up the inter-functional transfer of information. Faced with the choice of structuring the organization for economy or for rapid response, management will usually pick fast response, even at high cost. Many short-cycle companies, for example, maintain separate engineering and change organizations: These are nonexistent in companies with long product life cycles. Downstream coupling in a short-cycle business is usually very high. Manufacturing may begin to frame its plan, and marketing may set target dates for product introduction, before R&D planning is complete. This, in turn, means that the input to technical plans from marketing and manufacturing is much higher than in the long-cycle company. Engineering approaches must often be changed for manufacturing or marketing reasons, and much prior planning tends to be discarded in the process. Plans are often remade in the short-cycle company; the result is a series of increasingly accurate approximations of introduction dates, product specifications, and detailed plans for market introduction.

In a business with long product life cycles, the converse is generally true. With adequate time to learn about competitive market developments and to plan to counter them, there is less premium for unusual market sensitivity. In the long-cycle company, emphasis is on established procedure and routine. Organization is usually functional. Managerial decisions usually favor economy and efficiency at the expense of rapid response.

Planning is usually sequential—that is, detailed R&D is completed before the manufacturing and marketing planning is begun. Manufacturing and marketing are seldom deeply involved in technical planning. In fact, the technical staff may include market research specialists to help with the long-range R&D planning.

In long-cycle companies, marketing people are often unfamiliar with the specific technical problems or objectives. The marketing group tends to be volume oriented rather than response oriented, since new technical problems are rare and coupling between marketing and technical people is low.

As discussed previously, the life cycle length of successful products frequently changes. For example, in the information processing industry, as electronic computers replaced punched-card data processing equipment, the cycle shortened noticeably. One painful consequence of this shift was that many managers, who had been highly successful in the era of punched cards, were unable to adjust to the planning and control, organizational structure, and strategy implications of the shorter life cycle.

The same adjustment problem may arise when companies diversify. Thus, managers in the oil business often have trouble adjusting to the shorter cycle and the more rapid product obsolescence characteristic of the petrochemical business. The problem is still more acute for petrochemical managers whose companies integrate downstream, such as entering the plastics business—where some product introduction often takes place under near-crash conditions because life cycles are so short. To take a manager trained in the oil business, move him within a few years to a petrochemical subsidiary and then to a plastics operation is to subject his personal adaptability and the flexibility of his management methods and outlook to the severest possible test.

The life cycle conditioning that a manager receives is an asset to him in his present business, but might be a liability to him in a different business. When recruiting a key executive, presidents of non-technology-intensive companies too often go after a manager from the technically glamorous industries. Such a man, even though an outstanding performer in his old environment, may flounder for months or years in a new and different environment.

Distance to the State of Art

The state of the art has different meanings in research as compared to development. In research, it denotes the frontier at which investigators seek to discover new phenomena or to devise a solution to a previously unsolved problem. For development, it implies the less-rarefied zone where the validity of a theory or solution has already been proved, but a successful commercial application remains to be achieved. For development, in other words, the state of the art hinges heavily on economics and sociopolitical environment, as well as on technology.

The proximity of a company's technology to the state of the art has important implications for the management attitudes, behavior and competence. These implications may be considered under three headings: (1) rate of change, (2) unpredictability, and (3) use of historical precedents.

1. *Rate of change* increases as the company moves closer to the state of the art. If it is to remain successful, a company working near the state-of-the-art boundary must keep trying for rapid and frequent advances. At the same time, it must be alert to possible breakthroughs by competitors. Its market position is perpetually in jeopardy from technologically advanced competitors.

Top managers in such firms should be keenly aware of their dependence on a well-developed technological intelligence system. Surveillance of literature, attention to competitive developments, and attendance and participation in scientific societies should all be developed and encouraged. In addition, top managers should make a conscious personal effort to understand and keep abreast of the state of the art.

For companies well back from the boundary, radical breakthroughs are unlikely. Technical progress is evolutionary, with little innovation. Breakthroughs by immediate competitors are no serious threat; the danger is that breakthroughs in other industries and other technologies may obsolete the entire nature of technology.

2. *Unpredictability* is high for companies near the state-of-the-art boundary. Since their researchers are working in areas of partial knowledge, the nature and, even more, the timing of results are difficult to foresee. Flexible and adaptive planning of R&D, as well *as* of the firm's entire strategic development, is vital under low predictability.

Conversely, far from the boundary of the state of the art, where break-throughs are unlikely, predictability is high. Specific small improvements in products or processes can be foretold with confidence and timed with a high degree of accuracy; their achievement depends on the resources invested rather than on technical innovation.

3. *Use of historical precedents*, which underlies so much management activity, is not useful near the state-of-the-art boundary. Past experience supplies little guidance to help managers judge whether the technologists are doing a sound job, whether capital should be committed *to* a particular project, whether the project will have a long commercial life or whether, in fact, the entire effort will be profitable.

In view of the uncertainty and lack of precedent, senior executives cannot afford to demand infallibility in the decisions of the middle managers. For to do so is to stifle innovation. Therefore, firms near the state of the art must encourage imaginative risk taking, be prepared to reward venturesome behavior, and be tolerant of periodic failure. In such firms, rewards should be withheld from 'dependable' risk avoiders.

The implications of rate of change, predictability, and precedent are substantial in the areas of planning and control. Near the state of the art, a company *must* settle for more approximation and less precision in goals and standards, and the planning and control systems must be tailored accordingly. In such a company, judgment is critical, and precision is often specious.

Failure to take account of these implications may be exceedingly costly. In one diversified company, an electronics division devoted to the development and marketing of highly sophisticated microwave equipment was expected to plan as far ahead and in as much detail as the industrial products division did. When the division manager continued to protest that the requirement was unrealistic, he was replaced by an accountant. Within fifteen months, half of the technical people had left, and all momentum was gone from the R&D program.

Rapid change in the state of the art means rapid obsolescence *of* capital investment. Since even the most carefully analyzed investment decisions may turn out badly, rapid payback of investment and flexibility in capital facilities become crucial. In this situation, executives who take their one- and two-year plans very seriously may be justified in treating five-year planning as paper exercises.

Rapid change also means rapid obsolescence *of* the manager's knowledge and skills. The engineering director of an electronics company estimated that in twelve years four generations of managers had either relearned their technology or become obsolete. This point must be kept in mind when budgeting for renewal training of managers and technological personnel. Failure to stay abreast of technological development, too often neglected or regarded as 'superfluous,' results in erosion of both managerial and technical awareness and competence.

The need for flexible adaptation to technological change extends beyond individuals and the R&D function to marketing, production, and distribution. The entire firm must be a learning adaptive organism. For example, all the sales and application people have to undergo frequent retraining. Marketing must be technologically aware and ready to adapt marketing and promotion strategies to take advantage of technological advances. Production must be both ready and able to adapt to new processes, new tooling, and new equipment.

Summary

This chapter surveyed the impact of technology on a firm's business strategy. The key points may be stated briefly as follow:

- The impact of technology depends on the technological turbulence of the environment.
- In fertile and turbulent environments, R&D becomes a vital but, frequently, not the only critical function. Marketing, production, and financial controls may be equally important.
- In such cases, general management must play a key role in guiding and integrating the multifunction contributions toward the overall goals of the firm.
- In high-technology environments, general management must also avoid being driven by technology, on the one hand, and neglecting the opportunities offered by technology on the other.
- When technology substitution and proliferation take place, general management must play the crucial role of anticipating changes in technology and forcing timely technology substitution within the firm.
- When the environment is technologically turbulent, the business strategy formulation process must include a number of technological variables.

- Introduction of technological variables into the firm's strategy has far-reaching consequences on the organizational capability and, in particular, on the capabilities of general management.
- The success of the firm in a technologically turbulent environment depends, first, on matching the firm's strategy to the environmental turbulence and, second, on developing a capability which supports the chosen strategy.

A point of great importance to a firm's timely response to the environment, which has been demonstrated in the preceding discussion, is that the general management capability, which will be needed for a successful response, can be determined directly from an analysis of the future environment, and before the firm's strategy has been formulated and implemented. Thus, the necessary capability can be built parallel with or even ahead of strategy. We shall be returning to this point in Part III.

Exercises

1. Develop three lists of key industries which will be technologically stable, fertile, or turbulent during the next five years.
2. For industries on the turbulent list, identify the nature and the source of the future turbulence.
3. Map the fertile and turbulent industries into the appropriate quadrants of Fig. 12.2.
4. Select one industry from the turbulent list and using Table 12.3, construct their future turbulence profile.
5. For each of the selected turbulent industries, rank the future relative importance to success of: R&D, marketing, production, finance, and general management. Are there any other areas of the firm which will be critical to success? Give reasons for your ratings.

13

Societal Strategy for the Business Firm

Beginning in the 1950s, firms in the USA and Europe have come under increasing pressures from government, consumers, and environmental protection groups. In the USA, which remained firmly committed to the capitalist free market ideology, some firms responded to the challenge by embracing social causes and engaging in social audits aimed at establishing the firm as a responsible member of society. The majority of firms, though, made determined efforts to defeat legislation which curtailed managerial freedoms. But pressures to constrain profit-making activities continued.

The causes of the assault on the firm in a capitalist society have been variously interpreted. Many managers shared the view that society no longer understands how the free enterprise system works and the benefits it provides.

In this chapter, we explore the reasons which led the firm to its present social predicament and suggest a procedure by which each firm can formulate its own response strategy. As in the preceding two chapters, we shall find that the additional dimension of societal response requires development of significant additional and novel capabilities within the firm.

Introduction

Until recently in the USA, the approach of business managers to relating the firm to society was based on three fundamental propositions:

© The Author(s) 2019
H. I. Ansoff et al., *Implanting Strategic Management*,
https://doi.org/10.1007/978-3-319-99599-1_13

1. The first, enunciated in the USA by Charles Wilson, the president of General Motors from 1941 to 1953, was that 'what was good for GM is good for the country,' implying that the business firm is a faithful and responsive servant of its customers.
2. The second proposition was that 'the business of business is business,' or, to paraphrase Milton Friedman, to *ask* the firm to engage in an activity other than single-minded pursuit of profit, is a fundamentally subversive social doctrine.
3. The third proposition, based on the theory of Adam Smith, was that the public is best served when the pursuit of profit is conducted under minimum possible constraints from society—a condition known as 'free enterprise' in the USA.

Until the middle of the twentieth century, the principle of free enterprise was also accepted by the society surrounding the business firm. In part, it was accepted because entrepreneurial freedom was seen as an essential part of democratic freedoms and because free competition appeared as the optimal way to achieve the goals of fast economic growth.

From the early days of the Industrial Revolution, it became progressively evident that unrestrained behavior by the business firm produced grave social injustices. In response, society imposed a progression of restraints against such injustices: child labor laws, industrial safety, minimum wages, collusion, antitrust laws, etc. The cumulative effect of these restraints was such that, by the mid-twentieth century, it became increasingly difficult to define the meaning of the residual free enterprise.

From mid-century on, the attack on the firm accelerated, not only by governments, but also by consumers who became vociferous and critical. Confidence in business leadership progressively decreased, and the basic role of the firm in society was increasingly challenged. Today, many critics of the firm no longer accept free enterprise as an essential part of democracy, and/or challenge its relentless commitment to growth, and/or demand that the socially and physically polluting behavior of the firm be brought under control.

Business firms have responded on two fronts. The first was a defense against the proliferation of constraints on business behavior. These constraints were treated as a violation of the self-evident doctrine of free enterprise and were resisted and defeated whenever possible. As the hostile social climate continued to develop, the loss of public confidence in the firm was interpreted as an act of forgetfulness, a loss of public understanding of 'how free enterprise works.' Business firms, jointly and singly, mounted a vigorous educational campaign through public media, established chairs of free enterprise in business schools, encouraged teaching of microeconomics in secondary schools, etc.

On the second front, business responded to charges of physical and social pollution through 'social responsibility' programs: social audits, elements in conditions of working life, contribution to the welfare of the community, concern with business ethics.

During the past century of experience, the following appears to be evident:

1. Whatever the merits of the free enterprise doctrine, its defense has been ineffective. Since the beginning of the century, and at an accelerating rate since World War II, society has imposed controls on virtually every aspect of the firm (we illustrate these controls in detail later).
2. The claim typically advanced by business lobbies in public hearings—that all controls destroy the effectiveness of free enterprise—had been discredited. In fact, the business firm in capitalist countries has shown an amazing resiliency to proliferating constraints and continued to grow and prosper.
3. It is clear, however, that this resilience is not infinite; that at some point accumulated controls can 'break the camel's back.'
4. It appears that a reactive defense of the free enterprise doctrine is both impractical and dangerous. Impractical, because it is unlikely to arrest the accumulation of pressures on the firm: dangerous because, if the trend continues, the firm, like the proverbial baby, may be thrown out with the bathwater, its economic effectiveness drastically reduced by the surrounding constraints.
5. It is becoming increasingly clear that neither the 'explanation' of free enterprise nor social responsibility programs address the basic predicament of the firm, because, on both sides of the Atlantic, the real issue is not a return to idealized free enterprise but in determining the degrees of freedom that will permit the firm to optimize its contribution to society.

If the firm is to play a more effective role in the shaping of its future, it is necessary to set aside the historical assumption that the trouble stems from a loss of understanding of the free enterprise system and to inquire into the basic reasons for the present predicament. The results of such inquiry will suggest alternative response strategies.

Evolution of the Social Predicament

In a historical perspective, it is easy to understand both the virtuous posture and the sense of hurt and puzzlement which businessmen have felt under the recent societal onslaught. For over a hundred years, the firm has been the principal and successful instrument of social progress. Like most other social institutions, the firm is the result of an evolutionary trial and error process. No single mind conceived it and no single hand created it, but the evolution occurred in a congenial social environment whose basic values were the sanctity of private property and individual freedom, and whose key objective was economic progress. The firm gained its legitimacy from the laissez-faire theory of Adam Smith which asserts that the freedom of every man to pursue his selfish economic interest results, through the 'invisible hand,' in the maximum economic welfare for the society.

In this supportive environment, the firm evolved as one of the most impressive inventions made by man, it was in fact, a breeder of wealth with several impressive features as Fig. 13.1 shows:

1. It generates both goods and the buying power for the goods.
2. It supports the expansion of the social infrastructure and provides a return to the investors.
3. It creates jobs in three ways: in the firm itself; in the suppliers to the firm; and in the public sector.

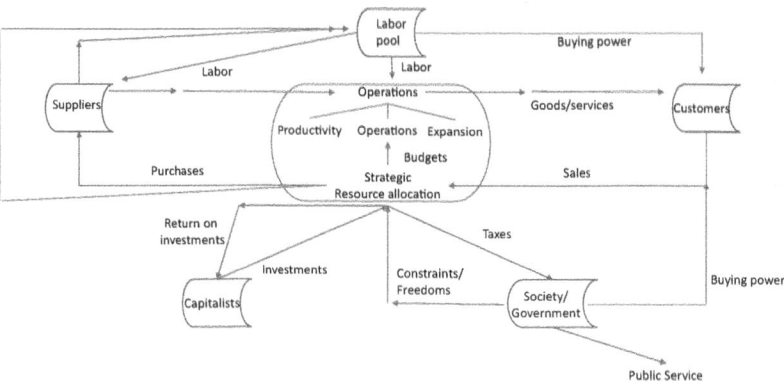

Fig. 13.1 Wealth-breeding reactor

4. It creates intricate interconnections between itself and its environment, making its success highly dependent on how and by whom the interconnections are controlled and regulated.
5. But the most impressive feature of this breeder reactor is that, while doing all of the above, it generates enough wealth for its own growth.

The 'invisible hand' doctrine states that, for optimal performance, the regulation must be left entirely to the management of the firm. History has provided us an example with the Soviet Union that an over-controlled firm becomes inefficient and wasteful. On the other hand, capitalist experience shows that, under minimal controls, the firm has generated more economic wealth than was generated in the prior history of man. Nevertheless, as the aggregate national wealth continued to grow, its distribution remained unequal. The growth was accompanied by ecological, social, and political pollution, as well as frequent fluctuations between prosperity and recessions. Further, when left unregulated, the business firm appeared to 'bite the hand that feeds it' by eliminating competition, creating monopolies, and thus destroying the 'invisible hand' which was the original justification for competitive freedom,

Over the years, the negative by-products of 'free enterprise' continued to cumulate. We have summarized these in Table 13.1 which gives examples of unresponsiveness to customer needs, imperfections and destruction of competition, violation of social norms, pollution, political interference, and failure to serve high-priority social needs. So long as society's primary concern was with economic growth, these negative by-products were tolerated in the name of progress.

Only where an excess became blatant and intolerable did society restrain it. But, shortly after World War II, capitalist countries arrived at a standard of living which saturated the economic needs of their influential citizens. For a substantial proportion of the population, the 'two chickens in every pot and two cars in every garage,' promised by Franklin D. Roosevelt in the 1930s, became a reality by the 1960s. The newly affluent society no longer had to tolerate business excesses and the firm's environment turned from benign to hostile. Attention shifted from the firm's economic contribution to its shortcomings. The firm ceased to be the sacred cow of economic progress and became, instead, a favorite target of control and criticism. Governments and the public united in actions to curb the negative by-products of the firm.

Table 13.1 What went wrong

	Examples
A. Negative by-products	
1. Poor response to customer needs	Monopoly pricing 'product misrepresentation', shoddy goods, 'buyer beware' behavior
2. Competition does not work as advertised	Very little genuine pram maximization 'oligopolistic' concentration, destruction of competition, growth for growth's sake, status quo seeking, resistance to innovation, collusion
3. Firm violates rules of social behavior	Prioe collusion, elimination of competition, bribes, political influence, dishonesty, discrimination
4. Harmful and undesirable social by-products	Inhuman work conditions, unequal distribution of wealth, environmental pollution, ecological imbalance, exhaustion of natural resources
5. Interference with national policy	Business interests vs. foreign policy, multinational vs. nation state, mililaiy-industrial complex vs. defense policy
6. Firm does not serve high priority social needs	Low cost housing, public transportation, health services, urban blight
B. Shift in societal values	Value shift from quality to quality of life, challenge to economic growth, disappearance of work ethic, suspicion and disapproval of business, emphasis on social infrastructure, social welfare, saturation of consumer demands
1. Economic growth no longer central national priority	
C. Change in ideology	Rejection of private ownership, rejection of the 'invisable hand' doctrine, national planning, demand for income redistrbution, nationalization of industry, participation by outsiders
1. Regection of capitalism as a social philosophy	

In the process, as Peter Drucker pointed out, the firm became a victim of its own success. Despite protestations against early constraints, it continued to grow and prosper as the constraints piled up. Thus, defense of free enterprise lost its credibility, society began to take it for granted that the firm will continue to grow and make money under any controls which may be imposed upon it.

In summary, the preceding discussion of the firm's predicament suggests that society's behavior is due to causes which are more fundamental than a misunderstanding of the workings and benefits of free enterprise. The negative reactions are threefold:

1. Firstly, there is an unwillingness to continue accepting the polluting by-products of laissez-faire.
2. Secondly, there is a refusal to accord an exclusive priority to economic progress.
3. Thirdly, there is either a rejection of capitalism as a societal ideology or a call for 'modernizing' capitalism in a way which purges it of its polluting aspects.

Because of different strengths of these three reactions in different parts of the world, business response strategies must be adjusted accordingly. In light of the trend 'toward modern capitalism,' US business is well advised to construct its defense on the capitalist ideology. But, instead of 'explaining' free enterprise it needs to join in defining a modern and viable meaning of capitalism. In Europe, where capitalism is not a universally accepted doctrine, the firm must negotiate its future *raison d'etre* through political processes which involve parties basically opposed to both free enterprise and private ownership.

In developing countries, where a promise of economic growth offered by free enterprise would, at first glance, appear attractive, private enterprise has to contend with alternative models of economic development offered by socialism. Further, the virtues of private ownership and competition must be made compatible with national pride and the desire for economic self-sufficiency.

The problem of positioning the firm in modern society is made difficult by the fact that the competing solutions which have been proposed are based on extreme doctrines. The free enterprise, capitalist doctrine asserts that a society's welfare is optimized if the firm is given *total* freedom to pursue its profit-seeking activities. The preceding remarks have shown that, historically, uncontrolled profit seeking leads to what Theodore Roosevelt called 'smash and grab imperialism.'

The opposing communist doctrine claims that society's welfare is to be attained through *total* central planning and control of the economic activity of a nation. Past events in Eastern Europe provide conclusive evidence that the application of the communist doctrine has produced a disastrous level of economic welfare in countries which have practiced the doctrine for more than three-quarters of a century.

The question for the countries operating under the respective doctrines, which are now moving in the direction of free enterprise, is how far can a society deregulate behavior of business firms without creating the conditions described in Table 13.1. Put somewhat differently, the two extreme doctrines have been shown by history to produce socially unacceptable consequences. A solution to this problem is to identify and articulate a doctrine which is not extreme and which is based on a balance between individual freedoms and public control. This type of doctrine has been given the name of a 'mixed economy' and has been discussed in detail by John Kenneth Galbraith in his book *The New Industrial State*.

Whatever mixed economy doctrine is formulated, it will of necessity be more complex than either of the historical extremal doctrines. The difficulty of gaining society's acceptance of a complex doctrine has been historically recorded by the demise of the Social Democratic Party in the UK, which advocated a mixed economy as a part of its platform and was not able to attract sufficient public support to permit the party to survive.

Alternative Scenarios

As in all planning efforts, the choice of business response to the societal predicament must be made in the perspective of future events. The following lists are four possible scenarios for the future of the firm:

1. Society will come to its senses.
2. Society will throw the baby out with the bathwater.
3. The firm will become a socioeconomic institution.
4. The firm will be replaced by new institutions.

Scenario 1 assumes that the negative impact of overregulation of business efficiency will become increasingly evident, and that society will arrest, and indeed reverse, the current regulatory trends before major damage is done. Proponents of this scenario can find support in the recent deregulation of the banking industry and net neutrality in the USA, and the blocking of a Euroskeptic government by Italy's President Sergio Mattarella.

Scenario 2 holds that, if the current trends continue, relief will not come until too late, after excessive constraints have caused major damage to the effectiveness of the business sector. When this occurs, business freedoms will be restored, but the recovery process will be prolonged and painful. Examples of firms in many European countries which are losing their competitive position as a result of excessive 'social overhead' costs illustrate how this scenario might develop. Another example is the growing pressure for employment maintenance which robs the firm of the essential control over its labor costs.

Scenario 3 holds that most of the present restrictions will not be removed, that further controls will be imposed, but that an equilibrium point will be reached at which economic efficiency will be balanced against other social imperatives. The firm will stop being a polluter, will become a responsive servant of the market, but it will remain an essentially economic instrument of society. This scenario is in line with the neo-capitalist approach advocated by writers such as John Kenneth Galbraith. Inevitably, it results in a large degree of central government planning.

Under scenario 3, the current trends are seen as a part of an irreversible process of repositioning the firm in the affluent postindustrial society. The profit-seeking objectives will be supplemented with noneconomic objectives, such as maintenance of employment, personally fulfilling work, non-managerial participation in decision making, provision of goods and services to inherently non-profitable areas of the economy, maintaining the welfare of the community, etc. This scenario sees the firm transformed from a purely economic to a socioeconomic instrument of society. Interestingly enough, institutionalization of the new values within the firm may reduce the need for centralized government planning and control. Thus, a new kind of invisible hand may come into existence. Proponents of this scenario can find support in the socio-audits and social responsibility programs already used by many leading firms.

Scenario 4, the most drastic one, draws on historical precedents. It assumes that the transition from the industrial to the postindustrial era is similar to prior turbulent transformations of society, such as the Fall of the Soviet Union, the Industrial Revolution, and the American Revolution. During such transitions, organizations which had served the needs of the prior era disappeared, and new ones 'arose from the ashes' to take their place. Under this scenario, the institution which will emerge in place of the firm will bear little resemblance to its predecessor.

Of the four scenarios, the optimistic scenario 1 and the apocalyptic scenario 4 call for a minimal managerial response. The historical reactive defense of free enterprise appears best designed for both hastening the good news and for retarding the apocalypse. Scenario 3 calls for a vigorous defense of the free enterprise system by responsible managers. Scenario 3 presents management with a basic choice: (1) to take Milton Fried man's advice, focus on the 'business of business,' and let others occupy themselves with shaping the role of the firm in society; (2) to take Geoffrey Barraclough's advice and join the government and the public in determining the future *raison d'etre* of the firm.

Historical behavior by management favors the former role; so, does the danger of loss of competitive edge as a result of undue preoccupation with sociopolitical questions; so, does business unfamiliarity with political processes.

In favor of involvement is the fact that the firm's behavior is now being shaped by people who have little understanding of what makes a firm work, what are its unique strengths and limitations, and what are its fragilities. By refusing to join the process, management increases the chances that both the economic and the social effectiveness of the firm will be severely impaired in the future.

It is not a purpose of this chapter to examine in detail the likelihood of the respective scenarios. However, it is important to underline the fact that commitment and response to one or more of the scenarios is one of the key strategic choices made by management. For this, choice may have as much influence on the future prosperity and survival of the firm as the choices of future markets and of technologies.

If the 'Barraclough' choice is made, the firm is confronted with the problem of formulating what it considers a viable alternative to the historical, and now very vague, doctrine of free enterprise. The procedure for formulating such a doctrine is significantly different from procedures involved in making business decisions. In the remainder of this chapter, we shall develop such a procedure.

Elements of the Legitimacy Strategy

The moment that management departs from insistence on exclusive focus on profitability and an uncompromising position against all constraints, it is no longer clear what should be the preferred objectives nor what the rules of the game (constraints and enablement's) are under which the firm can best attain them, nor what should be the process by which the firm should seek to legitimize the preferred objectives and rules.

It should be recognized that management has a limited influence over the final choice of objectives and the rules of the game. These are determined through a political process in which representatives of different ideologies negotiate, bargain, and use other available means of influence to make their respective viewpoints prevail. Thus, the analysis of the legitimacy strategy for the firm must bring together three key 'ingredients': (1) an analysis of the objectives; (2) an analysis of constraints; and (3) an analysis of the power field within which the firm must act.

These ingredients can be brought together to determine the *preferred* objectives and rules of the game (we shall call the combination the *preferred raison d'etre*), as well as the *probable* rules and objectives which will be the likely outcome of the political process after the firm has exerted its best efforts to make its viewpoint prevail.

In bargaining processes, which involve mutual give-and-take, it is inadvisable to announce the preferred position, unless its proponent has decisive power for making it accepted. Therefore, the firm further needs to formulate a *bargaining strategy* which also specifies the way it discloses its intentions, the types of action to be taken, the timing, and the coalition to be sought.

Aspirations Analysis

In Table 13.2, we show an approach to choosing the preferred objectives. Since the firm is an instrument of society, these objectives should reflect the aspirations of the constituencies whose interests the firm undertakes to serve. At the left of the figure, we show several constituencies which are directly affected by the behavior of the firm. In the second column, we illustrate the principal aspirations which each constituency expects the firm to fulfill. Two points should be noted:

- The first is that society is no longer content, as in the past, with the aspiration of economic growth, and now has other aspirations which frequently conflict with growth.
- Secondly, while managers are shown to share the owners' aspirations for profits and appreciation of equity, ample experience has shown that they frequently have other aspirations (e.g. for power, gambler's risk, security, recognition) which can run contrary to the profit drive. (In extreme cases, powerful managers have been known to play conglomerate 'chess games' with companies with very little apparent regard for profitability.)

It is for this reason that, in the body of the figure, we construct the 'entrepreneurial model' of the firm in which management 'challenges' are recognized, in addition to earnings growth and appreciation, as the first priority aspirations. The entrepreneurial model is of course the free enterprise Friedmanian model. It is to be noted that it does not concern itself explicitly with the aspirations of the customers (the assumption is that the invisible hand takes care of customer needs).

Table 13.2 Models for the firm's *Raison d'etre*

Alternative models

Constituency	Aspirations	Free enterprise	Prudent Capitalist	Philanthropic	Populist	Socialist	Preferred
Society	Economic growth	1	1	1			
	Tax income					1	
	Power equalization					1	
	Income equalization					1	
	Preservation of the environment		2			1	
	Resource conservation						
Community	Community welfare			2		1	
Share owners	Earnings growth	1	1	1		1	
	Share appreciation	1	1	1			
Lenders	Earnings stability		2				
Customers	Price quality						
	Choice		2				
	Stability						
Managers	Earnings growth	1	1	1			
	Challenge	1	1	1			
Employees	Employment						
	Wages				1	2	
	Leisure						
	Working conditions				1	2	
	Satisfying work						

In the next column, we show a 'prudent capitalist' model which responds to society's pressures for preservation of the environment and is secondarily responsive to the aspirations of the lenders and of the customers.

In the third column is the 'philanthropic' model, frequently observed in the USA, in which, after the profit is made entrepreneurially, a part of it is dispensed for community welfare.

The first three models are observable in business behavior. The fourth 'populist' model reflects the typical historical strategy of American labor unions which have focused on maximizing the aspirations of the employees but also, for practical reasons, place high priority on the growth of earnings.

The 'socialist' model, shown last, is intended to reflect the model preferred by governments rooted in socialist ideologies. Frequently, the prime focus is on the aggregate societal welfare, with employees' individual welfare being secondary.

The last column is left open for determination of the preferred aspirations to be served by the firm. These *preferred aspirations are the objectives of the firm* which guide its behavior. Since managers themselves are members of society, the ambient social pressures act to induce the firm to serve everybody. And, indeed, in public relations pronouncements some firms proclaim their intention to be equally responsive to all relevant stakeholders. Whether such announcements are made in good faith is a matter which does not concern us here, but, for practical purposes, it must be recognized that the respective aspirations are in conflict and cannot all be served equally. An example is the conflict between profitability and employment maintenance which is now a major issue in Europe. Hence, the choice of objectives should be limited to those aspirations which management believes the firm must serve (to respond to the most influential stakeholders) and is best qualified to serve.

Secondarily, the chosen objectives must be assigned priorities. The fulfillment of noneconomic priorities depends in the final analysis on the firm's solvency. Thus, whatever noneconomic objectives are added to the list, unless the firm makes an adequate profit, its survival will be imperiled and none of the other objectives can be served. This *centrality of the profit objective* is clearly understood by management and frequently missed by outsiders. It is reasonable to suggest, therefore, that the priorities should vary as a function of the profit level of the firm. In Fig. 13.2, we have shown an example of how priorities can be made to change with the profitability level.

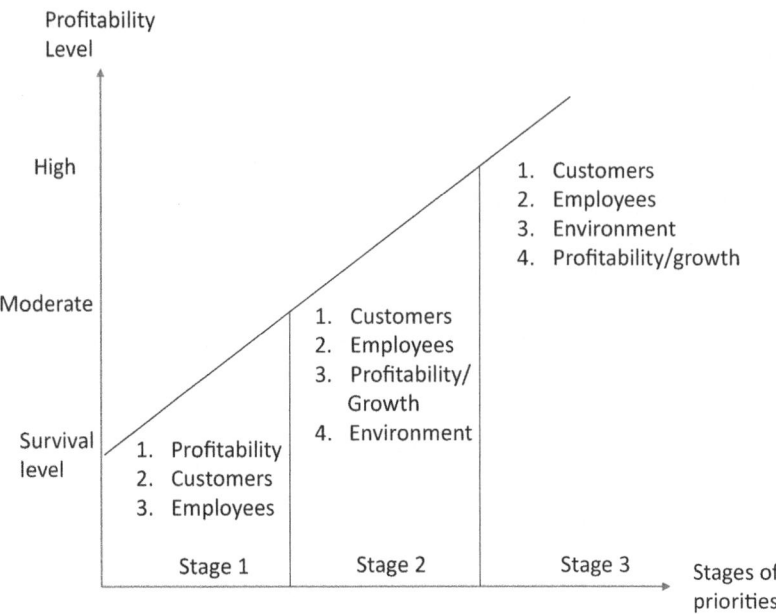

Fig. 13.2 Stages of priorities in a societally responsive firm

*Impact of Constraints

In the defense of free enterprise, it is assumed that all restraints on managerial behavior are equally damaging and are to be resisted. Experience has shown, though, that some constraints are less objectionable than others, and that some actually improve the profitability of the firm. For example, when foreign competition threatens, firms seek import protection from the government.

However, because of the historical rejection of all constraints, little is known today about the differential impact of different constraints on the firm's performance; research is badly needed in this area. Meanwhile, management will have to make its own evaluations.

One approach to such evaluation is to group the objectives chosen through aspirations analysis into three categories: profitability/growth objectives, objectives of responsiveness to the needs of the market, and objectives of social (nonprofit) responsiveness.

Figure 13.3 illustrates that the attainment of the respective group of objectives will be differently affected by different constraints. The three curves, without any claim at accuracy or universality, demonstrate how dif-

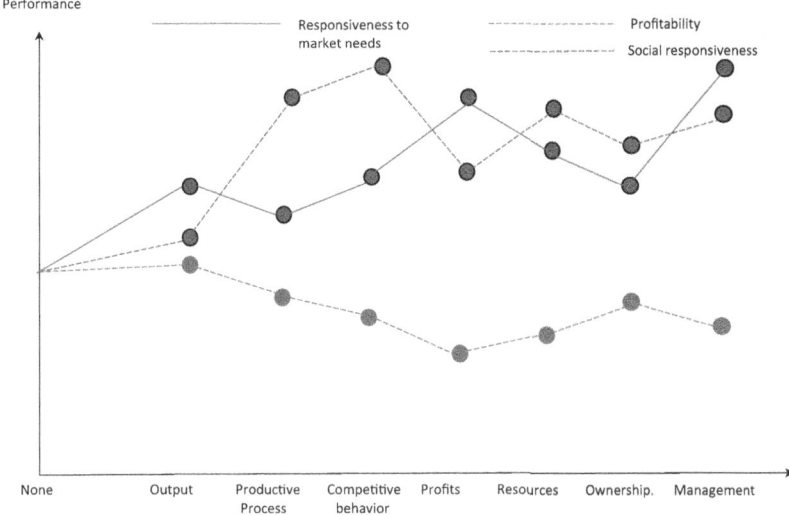

Fig. 13.3 Impact of controls/incentives on business performance

ferent controls can have opposing effects. For example, while the current restrictions on automotive performance in the USA may have a depressing effect on profitability, they can make a substantial contribution to the objective of environmental cleanliness.

Therefore, it is important for each firm to assess the real or potential impact of different constraints on the firm and to take a position on each constraint. A simple format for estimating the impact of the controls on a particular firm is shown in Table 13.3.

The purpose of the exercise is to establish the firm's position vis-à-vis the leverage controls.

1. In the left-hand column of Table 13.3 enter from the column labeled 'points of leverage' controls which now exist or are likely to be 'imposed' on the firm by the government, or exerted by society.
2. Across the top of Table 13.3 enter the firm's objectives from the column labeled 'preferred' in Table 13.2.
3. In the second column estimate the impact which the respective constraints will have, if imposed on the firm's attainment of its objectives. Use + 10 for constraints which would greatly improve the performance of the firm, 0 for no impact, and 10 for destructive impacts.
4. In the third column multiply the impact by the priority of the objective to produce the weighted impact.

Table 13.3 Estimating the importance of constraints

| Firm's Priority/ Objectives | O_1/P_1 | | O_2/P_2 | | O_3/P_3 | | $(I \times P)$ | * |
Constraints (Figure 2.3.8 Column 2)	Impact on the firm I	Weighted Impact	Impact on the firm I	Weighted Impact $I \times P$	Impact on the firm I	Weighted Impact	Overall Impact +	Firm's Position

* Alternative positions: 1). Defend at all costs 2). Use to bargain 3). Do not defend 4). Welcome control

5. Add the positive weighted impacts for each constraint and enter the overall impact into the third-to-last column.
6. Repeat the above steps for the negative impact. It is not unlikely that the overall impact will turn out to have both positive and negative effects.
7. The final and the important step is to choose the firm's attitude toward the respective constraints in dealing with regulatory bodies and social pressures. Four alternative positions are suggested at the bottom of the figure.

*Power Field Analysis

The firm's success in promoting its preferred legitimacy strategy will be determined through a political bargaining process with other groups which have the interest and the power to impose constraints on the firm. Therefore, the next step is to estimate the preferences which other influential constituencies are likely to advance during the bargaining process. The procedure is illustrated in Table 13.4 where the *raison d'etre* preferred by each constituency is estimated, followed by an estimate of the likely thrust behind the preferences. It is advisable to estimate the relative potential power of a constituency separately from the likely aggressiveness in the exercise of this power. For example, in the USA, the shareholders have enormous potential power, but their historical aggressiveness in asserting this power has been very low. Such high power, low aggressiveness groups are attractive potential partners in formation of coalitions. Political processes typically produce coalitions of constituencies whenever common objectives can be identified. In Table 13.5, we have shown mutual support and opposition to be found among constituencies. The diagonal entries indicate the aggressiveness exhibited by the respective constituencies in support of their interests. As our previous remarks indicate, there are substantial differences between the European and the American scenes. The entries in the table are for the observable American practice.

In any case, the entries are illustrative and each firm will have to make an evaluation of its own political setting. Once this is accomplished, the likely coalitions for and against the preferences of the respective constituencies can be determined as shown at the right of the figure.

Table 13.4 Power field analysis

Constituency	Objectives of the firm		Rules of the game		Relative power	Aggressiveness	Influence mechanisms	Probable thrusts	Strength of thrust
	Most preferred	Least preferred	Most preferred	Least preferred					
Management									
Employees									
Unions									
Shareholders									
Local government									
Central government									
Customers									
Others									

Table 13.5 Power field balance

Proponent Constituency	Respondent Constituency							Probable Coalitions	
	(1) Management	(2) Employees	(3) Unions	(4) Shareholders	(5) Local government	(6) Central government	(7) Other	For Proponent	Against
Management				0	0			1,4,2	2,3,5,6
Employees				0	0			2,3,6	1,4
Unions				0	0			2,3,5,6	2,5,6
Shareholders				0				1,4	
Local government			0					1,2,5,6	
Central government				0				2,3,5,6	1,4
Other									

Analysis of Legitimacy Strategy

In Fig. 13.4, we illustrate the manner in which the three preceding steps, the aspirations analysis, the impact of constraints, and the power field analysis, can be combined into the *legitimacy strategy* of the firm.

The power field analysis makes it possible to construct one or more scenarios which will describe the way the role of the firm is likely, in fact, to evolve. The selected objectives, together with the preferred rules of the game, define the preferred *raison d'etre* which the management would like to see emerge.

The probability is high that the preferred and the probable *raison d'etre* will differ, because of the influence of other constituencies which have distinctive sets of expectations for the firm. The task of management is to influence the evolution of events to bring the eventual *raison d'etre* as close as possible to the preferred position.

To accomplish this, the firm needs to follow a skillfully executed *bargaining strategy*: using the most effective means of influence at its disposal, engage in give-and-take bargaining with representatives of conflicting interests.

Thus, we can define the legitimacy strategy to consist of three components: (1) the preferred *raison d'etre*; (2) the forecasts of the probable *raison d'etre; and* (3) the bargaining strategy aimed at narrowing the gap between the probable and the preferred.

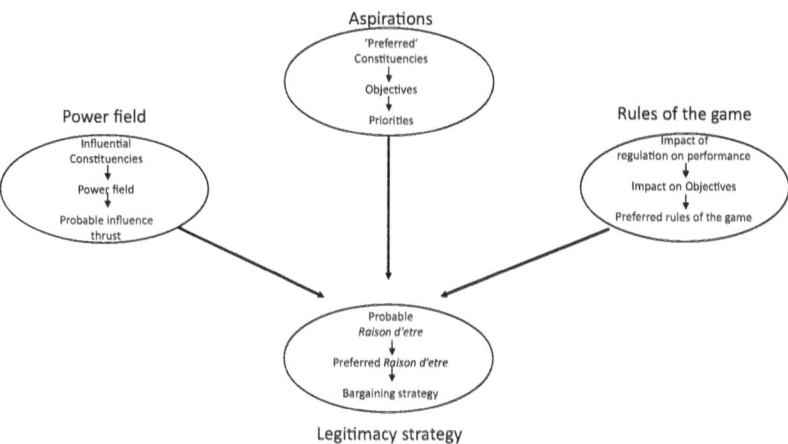

Fig. 13.4 Analysis of legitimacy strategy

Impact on Business and Social Responsibility Strategies

A firm can either choose to pursue an active legitimacy strategy by seeking to contribute to the process of defining its own future role in society, or it can remain a passive observer of the changes of its own role. In either case, an understanding of the scenarios of the probable *raison d'etre* is essential for the conduct of the traditional 'business of business'—the profit- and sales-seeking activities of the firm.

Today, there is hardly a business decision which is not seriously affected by sociopolitical considerations. For instance, after the accounting scandals of the early twenty-first century, the US Securities and Exchange Commission became more focused on corporate compliance and the government introduced the Sarbanes–Oxley compliance regulations of 2002. This was a response to the social environment that called for such change to make public companies more accountable.

Managerial decisions must now be made within the framework of some sort of control. The decisions on what product to make, where to sell it, how to sell it, how to price it, how to manufacture it, how to finance, and how to support it after sales are all subject to a variety of restraints and constraints. But beyond formal constraints, management must be increasingly aware of social reactions and consequences to its commercially inspired actions.

Numerous other instances are observable today on both sides of the Atlantic which show that the firm's business strategy can no longer be built only on 'dollars and cents' considerations and that, in the future, it will have to include political and social considerations along with the commercial ones.

Thus, dealing with the firm's societal predicament docs not stop with the legitimacy strategy. In the future, firms will increasingly need to develop three related strategies:

1. *A legitimacy strategy.* This is the strategy which the firm pursues in seeking to influence the rules of the game. The principal steps in its formulation are enclosed by the dashed line rectangle in Fig. 13.5.

This strategy, if successful, has a direct and important impact on the firm through creating rules of the game which make it easier to optimize its profit-seeking activity.

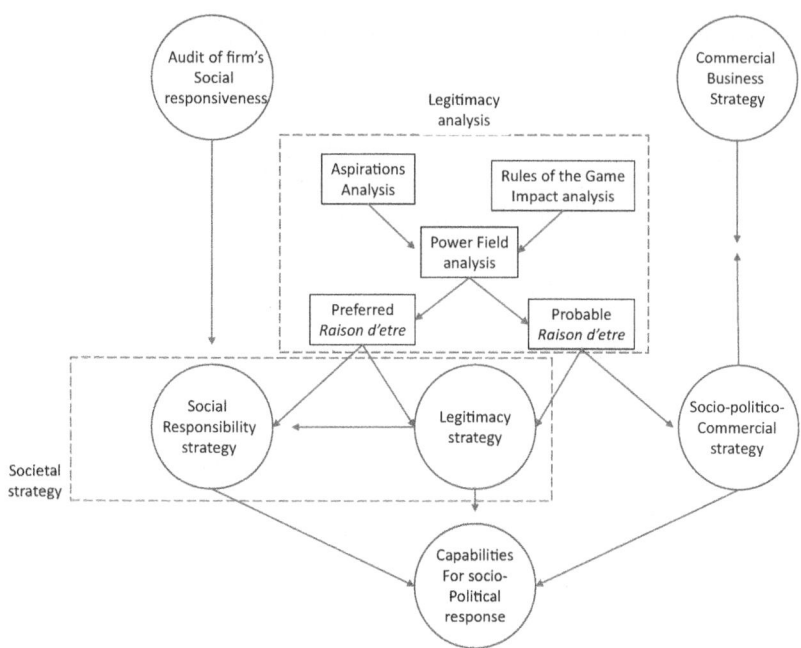

Fig. 13.5 Sociopolitical response analysis

2. *A social responsibility strategy.* An important part of this strategy is commonly called the firm's *code of ethics* which describes voluntary constraints which the firm undertakes to respect both in its intrafirm and environmental behavior (e.g., giving to employees 90 days' notice of permanent closure of the firm's plants or other facilities).

But a social responsibility strategy includes not only constraints but proactive behavior which the firm undertakes beyond its concern with growth and profit optimization (e.g., charitable contributions of money to social causes, or to building of the social infrastructure, or donation of management time to helping solve information management problems in a public school system).

Formulation of the social responsibility strategy is straightforward. It starts with *a social audit,* which is a diagnosis of the firm's present social responsibility strategy. This is followed by selection of social causes which management wishes to support, and then development of modalities which will be used to support those causes.

Pursuit of social responsibility may have an indirect impact on the firm's profit-seeking behavior. This impact is usually in the long term and is caused by the influence which the firm's behavior as a good and caring citizen has on customers' preferences for the firm's products.

A social responsibility strategy which is designed to maximize such influence has been called an *enlightened self-interest strategy*. But not all social responsibility strategies are undertaken in the spirit of enlightened self-interest. Some firms undertake social responsibility projects without an expectation that the costs incurred will eventually lead to higher profits.

3. The third strategy which reflects a firm's concern with societal forces is the *sociopolitico-commercial strategy* which is shown at the lower right of Fig. 13.5. As the figure shows, this strategy integrates the probable rules of the game *(raison d'etre)* with the firm's commercial business strategy.

As the two-way arrow on the right-hand side of Fig. 13.5 emphasizes, there is a two-way influence between the commercial business strategy and the sociopolitico-commercial strategy. As a result, the strategy formulation process is an integrated one in which sociopolitical variables are integrated into the stages of competitive and portfolio analysis. (An example of such inclusion is shown in Fig. 12.4 where the influences of sociopolitical groups are a factor in determination of future success postures.)

While the legitimacy strategy seeks to change the rules of the game, the sociopolitico-commercial strategy seeks to take the best advantage of the existing rules of the game under which the firm has to do business.

Need for New Management Capabilities

Generations of experience have prepared managers to believe that, on the one hand, the 'business of business is business' and, on the other, that the free enterprise ideology is superior to all other social ideologies. The knowledge and leadership skills of managers have been focused on making profit and their influence skills either on securing a consensus within a mutually acceptable ideology within the firm or 'explaining' the superiority of free enterprise to outsiders.

The information system which serves today's managers informs them about economic trends, technology, competition, customer preferences, and profitability performance. It is not equipped to provide an understanding of other ideologies, their perceptions of business, their strategies, the political process by which these strategies are implemented, nor is it equipped to track sociopolitical trends which impact on the firm. Some firms, which have become aware of this deficiency, have recently begun to use the issue management system (see Chapter 19) to develop a responsiveness to societal issues. Other firms, such as Shell, developed sociopolitical scenarios (see Chapter 10). Still others (such as General Electric) developed political risk assessment techniques for foreign investments.

However, experience shows that managers who receive sociopolitical information are both unwilling to recognize its relevance and incapable of using it effectively. Thus, when a firm decides to confront its societal challenges, it needs to develop a *societal response capability*. This includes the following:

1. An *ideological reorientation*. Managers need to understand ideologies other than free enterprise, recognize their legitimacy, and be prepared to change from a traditional dogmatic belief that free enterprise is the only truth to a more open ecumenical position which accepts the legitimacy of other ideological truths.
2. An *enlarged information-communication system* is needed which observes the social and political as well as the commercial world, learns the language of other constituencies, and translates business communications into other languages. Such a system also needs to be open to the environment, actively communicating with the constituencies both inside and outside the firm.
3. *Understanding of political processes and skills in political behavior.* Managers need to understand the differences between the consensual, uni-ideological, decision processes historically used within the firm, and multi-ideological decision processes in which no party holds deciding power. They need to acquire skills in preparation of political decisions, lobbying, coalition formation, bargaining, and the use of propaganda.
4. A *political action infrastructure*. Firms will need to build relationships and frameworks in which political action takes place; they need to define their political marketplace, just as in the early days of the industrial era they have defined the commercial marketplace.
5. The *reward and incentive* systems need to be changed to encourage effective and timely response to societal problems and opportunities.
6. *Changes in the firm's systems and structure* need to be made which provide the competence and the capacity for dealing with societal challenges.

The preceding remarks suggest that unless a firm attends to the task of building its societal action capability at an early stage, its societal response is likely to be ineffective and unproductive. (For further discussion of organizational capabilities, see Chapters 9 and 10.)

Summary

The societal predicament of the business firm has passed the stage at which it can be resolved by the dual strategy of resisting efforts to limit business freedoms, on the one hand, and educating the public about free enterprise, on the other.

The societal predicament is complex and multifaceted, and requires appropriately complex, multifaceted, and aggressive response strategies if private capitalism is to continue to play an effective role in future society. Management must approach its societal challenges with the same foresight, and in the same methodical and deliberate way in which it approaches its commercial challenges.

An essential input to a constructive legitimacy strategy is an understanding of both social and economic costs and benefits resulting from different controls and control mechanisms which society imposes on the firm.

Dealing with societal problems is very different from dealing with business opportunities. On the level of understanding, this requires a recognition of the many different perceptions, points of view, and different ideologies which different influential groups bring to their interactions with the firm. On the level of response, the firm needs managers who, by and large, are not found in firms today but who are capable of sensitive and unbiased analysis of political situations and skilled in the use of realities of power. Above all, management needs to take the role of constructive leadership in positioning the firm's role in the future society.

Exercises

1. a. Taking account of the latest sociopolitical developments, describe in detail the 'alternative scenarios' section. If necessary, add and describe in detail additional scenarios.
   b. Assign probabilities to the respective scenarios. Give reasons for your assignment.
   c. Identify the principle milestone events over the next five years which will help sharpen and revise the probability estimates.

2. For each scenario, develop and justify appropriate responses by firms. What should be done by each firm alone and what by groups of firms?

3. Select a firm well known to you, or use a case assigned by your tutor, to determine the 'elasticity' of the firm to different types of constraint and enablement. Use Table 13.3 as a worksheet.

4. a. Using Table 13.2, develop the appropriate *raison d'etre* for the above firm.
   b. Perform a power field analysis for the firm analyzed in exercise 3 above, employing Table 13.4.
   c. Following the format of Table 13.5, perform a power field analysis and identify the coalitions which the firm should form, and coalitions which are likely to oppose the firm.

5. a. What will be the problems and sources of resistance in developing the sociopolitical management capabilities? How can the resistance be minimized and maximum support assured for the capability development?
   b. Outline a related series of programs and actions which can be used to develop the capability?

14

Strategic Dimensions of Internationalization

The discussions covered in this chapter are based on research conducted by Dr. Ansoff and Markku Lahdenpaa. Most of the concepts and tools of strategic analysis developed in the preceding chapters are applicable to the problem of diversifying a firm from a domestic market to a larger international arena. There are, however, several additional variables which must be taken into account in formulating a cross-national strategy.

Distinctive Aspects of Internationalization

When a firm operates in a stable domestic environment, the primary focus of management attention is on the competitive and technological factors which determine success in the marketplace.

When such a firm moves abroad, its management expects to encounter new competitors and new competitive dynamics. But beyond the competitive variables, success in the new markets may equally be determined by a number of other factors which remain in the background (and are taken for granted) so long as the firm confines its attention to domestic markets.

One group of such factors is *economic*. The foreign environment may differ from the domestic in the level of economic development in the respective countries, in the size of the total market for the firm's products, in the degree of saturation of the market, etc. Another group of factors is *cultural*. The foreign SBA may differ in consumer tastes, buying habits, allocation of customer budgets, in the ability of the customers to use technologically

© The Author(s) 2019
H. I. Ansoff et al., *Implanting Strategic Management*,
https://doi.org/10.1007/978-3-319-99599-1_14

sophisticated products, etc. A third group is *political*. The government ideology in the new country may differ from the domestic. As a consequence, attitudes toward business will differ, *as* will the regulations, constraints, and enablement's under which the firm must operate.

A combination of economic, political, and cultural differences can easily be as important in the new marketplace as the competitive factors. A dramatic example is the history of the efforts by the firms in developed countries to enter the Third World markets. On the one hand, the enormous, latent demand in these countries was slow to develop because of slow growth of their economies; on the other, access to and profitability of the existing demand were frequently limited by local governments either committed to Marxist ideologies or run as military dictatorships.

Thus, when firm ventures abroad it must acquire a great deal more information than it needs for domestic commercial decisions.

One complicating factor is that firms which do not scan and analyze their domestic environments for broad economic, cultural, and sociopolitical trends have neither the appreciation nor the knowledge for acquiring such information.

It will be recalled from Chapters 11–13 that, when the domestic environment becomes turbulent, firms are forced to develop environmental surveillance capabilities. Thus, firms which have experienced domestic economic/technological/political turbulence are better prepared for internationalization than firms from a historically placid environment.

It follows that firms which seek to internationalize themselves, starting from a relatively placid environment, need to develop a new environmental surveillance and analysis capability.

For either type of firm, the problem is made difficult by the fact that much of the vital information about foreign environments may be non-quantifiable, or even not perceivable by a foreigner. Such information can only be acquired, either by a native, or by an individual who has lived in the foreign country long enough to have acquired what the Germans call *Fingerspitzengefühl* (fingertip feeling) for the critical but subtle success factors. In future discussions, we shall refer to such important un-verbalize able or unquantifiable perceptions as *implicit information* about a foreign strategic business area.

The strategic consequences of the above differences are the following:

1. Typically, the foreign entry will cost more and consume more time than a comparable diversification at home. Further, the objectives which can be attained through a foreign entry will be limited by the nature of the opportunities. For example, a move from a mature domestic to an

emerging demand cycle in another country will improve future profits but will not improve the current profitability. On the contrary, it will depress it because the emergence stage typically requires heavy near-term investments.

Therefore, it is important to identify the objectives and goals which are to be sought through internationalization and to make sure that internationalization is the preferred (or the only) way of attaining them. We shall discuss this problem in the following Sections.

2. The differences among the commercial and environmental success factors, the importance of implicit information, tax differences, currency and earnings barriers, and legal requirements for a local presence in the country—all of these factors may make it necessary for internationalizing firms to move beyond the role of an exporter, and to become a part of the local business community.

3. It is quite likely that product lines and marketing strategies which have proved successful on domestic markets may be suboptimal or even unsuccessful on foreign markets. It is essential, therefore, to choose between the two extremes of using identical strategies in all SBAs and designing tailored entries for each. This problem will be discussed later in this chapter.

4. When a firm moves to the multinational stage, where it seeks to balance the advantages of global product development and global economies of production against the imperatives of responsiveness to local market conditions, it becomes impossible to assign the overall strategic authority/responsibility to any single organizational unit or person. In multinational firms, it becomes necessary to develop a process by which conflicting objectives of country managers, product line managers, and production managers can be effectively negotiated and reconciled.

5. The very high cost of strategic information about foreign SBAs must be taken into account both in making profitability estimates and in formulating the strategy of commitment to internationalization:

   a. Whenever possible, the cost of learning about a new national market should be amortized over more than one SBA entry. This implies a strategy of developing a multi-SBA presence in a country.

   b. Firms found from experience that it is prudent to commit the firm gradually, making low-cost entries at first and learning from the experience before making further commitments. This means that the early entry should emphasize 'testing the strategic water' and put less than the usual emphasis on generation of early profits in the new country.

6. Finally, the management capability for carrying out an effective internationalization is different from the capability required to manage a purely domestic business. A detailed analysis of management capability is found in Chapter 7.

Objectives of Internationalization

Just as in domestic diversification, internationalization raises the question of the firm's objectives: the aspects of the firm's performance which the firm seeks to improve through internationalization. In both cases, it is important to be clear about what the objectives are, and whether the *strategic criteria* used in search and evaluation of alternatives will move the firm into SBAs which will satisfy the objectives. In the absence of objectives and criteria, firms frequently operate on the principle that the 'grass is greener in the neighbor's yard'; an attitude reinforced by ignorance about foreign environments. The behavior frequently leads to 'unanticipated results': The costs of internationalization greatly exceed budgets and operations fail to meet the profit objectives.

Among the objectives commonly sought through diversification/internationalization are the following:

1. *Growth in volume/size*

   • Sustain growth and avoid stagnation caused by saturation in the firm's historical SBAs.
   • Improve on the historical and still continuing growth.
   • Increase volume and size of the firm through entry into SBAs with comparable growth prospects.

The wave of diversification by US firms into European markets after World War II was prompted by the first and the second objectives. Many US firms were experiencing difficulties in sustaining historical growth rates, others had reached saturation. The European markets appeared to offer an attractive 'escape valve.' This was indeed the case, because Europe was just entering the 'consumer economy' which the USA entered in the 1930s.

Today there is a reverse move by many European firms which see the USA as a 'growth environment.' For example, many European retail firms have been acquiring food and consumer goods marketing chains in the USA. The only objective which can be served by such moves is the third one: Typically, the European firms are buying into maturity which is even more advanced than the maturity of the retailing businesses in Europe. Instead of buying into growth, they are buying volume.

2. *Improvement in profitability*

- Enhance long-term profitability prospects by entering SBAs in early growth stages.
- Enhance near-term profitability by entering currently profitable SBAs.
- Enhance/maintain near-term profitability through foreign SBAs which offer important synergies or economies of scale with domestic SBAs.

The pursuit of the first objective is exemplified by the acquisition by many important European pharmaceutical firms of small US firms in genetic engineering. The second is the obvious example of the Japanese invasion of the profitable computer markets. The third objective is pursued today in the increasingly global automotive market by firms whose domestic markets are no longer large enough to permit them to remain competitive with the four giants, unless their market becomes global in scope.

3. *Balance of the firm's strategic portfolio*

- Assure the firm's continued profitability/growth, both in the near and long term, by filling in the gaps in the firm's demand/technology life cycle portfolio. This is a more comprehensive objective than the preceding ones which, for implementation purposes, usually translates itself into one or more of the objectives described above.
- Assure the firm's future invulnerability to technological/economic/ sociopolitical cycles, upheavals, and discontinuities.

This last objective leads firms to position themselves in more than one technology and more than one sociopolitical system. It has been given as the reason for the moves to the USA by French firms which seek to reduce the current sociopolitical/economic uncertainties facing them in their own country.

An examination of the above list shows that, in many cases, most objectives can be met either through domestic diversification or through internationalization. In fact, the only objective unique to internationalization is the last one above.

Therefore, when contemplating internationalization, a firm is well advised to make a comparison of internationalization and diversification opportunities, since each offers its own advantages and disadvantages. Domestic diversification offers the advantage of familiar sociopolitical/cultural/economic environment, but incurs the risk and costs of entry into unfamiliar businesses. Internationalization offers the advantage of extending familiar businesses and the disadvantages and risks of having to learn about alien environments.

Objectives and Strategic Criteria

Listed across the top of Table 14.1 are a number of what we shall call *strategic criteria*: criteria which the firm uses in the search for and selection of foreign SBAs.

An examination of the list shows that most of the criteria are applicable to domestic as well as international environments. However, three criteria are unique to internationalization and deserve comment. These are:

1. Extension of the demand life cycle of the firm's products.
2. Extension of the useful life of the firm's technology.
3. Resource acquisition.

Table 14.1 Strategic criteria

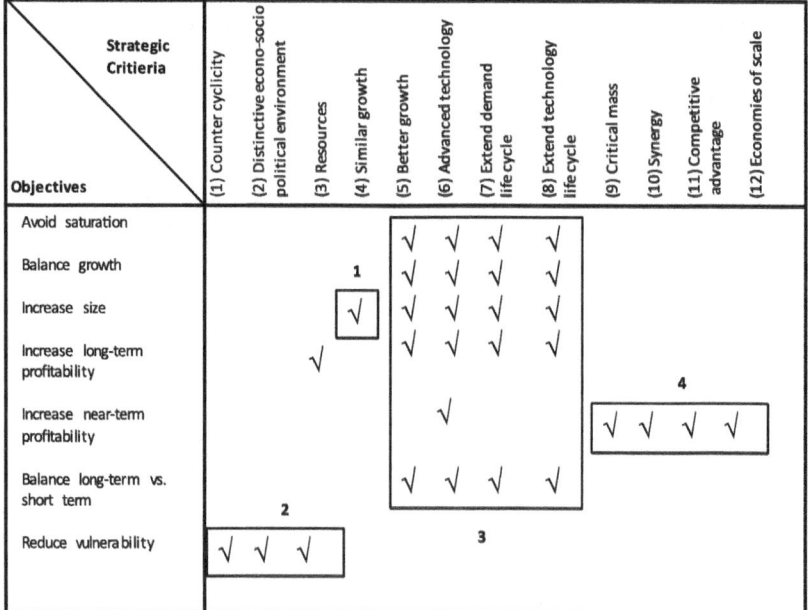

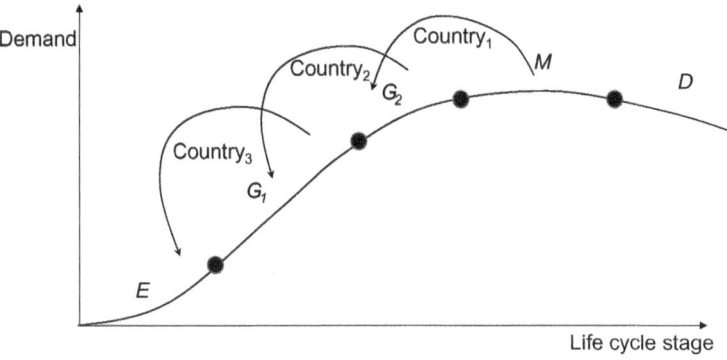

Fig. 14.1 Extending demand life cycle

Figure 14.1 shows the evolution of demand which typically occurs in a national market. The typical stages (see Chapter 2) are:

1. The technologically and competitively turbulent emergence, E.
2. The accelerating growth G_1 during which demand typically exceeds capacity.
3. The decelerating growth G_2 which is highly competitive.
4. The maturity M when demand reaches saturation.
5. Decline D in the rare cases when the original demand (e.g., pagers) declines or disappears.

During E and G_1 a firm's energies are typically absorbed by the domestic markets. But during G_2, when competition stiffens and growth decelerates, the extra costs of entry into a country where the demand is still in E or G_1 may be more than offset by the attractive growth and profitability opportunities. By the time domestic demand reaches M or D, the pressures to move to countries in earlier stages of growth become strong.

Thus, firms which anticipate and conduct their internationalization in accordance with demand stages can extend substantially the life cycle of a firm's product tine.

In industries in which the evolution of demand is accompanied by technology substitution (see Chapter 12), (e.g., in photography; pin-hole→ roll film→ 35 mm→ Polaroid→ digital), the useful life of a technology can be similarly expanded by transferring it to countries in lower stages of technological developments. This is illustrated in Fig. 14.2. Perhaps the best example is with the iPhone, as the product reaches the maturity stage in the

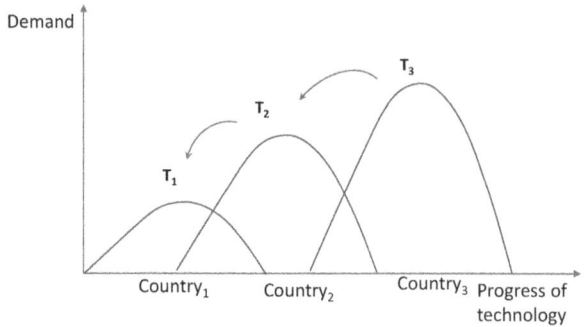

Fig. 14.2 Extending technology life cycle

developed country, it is exported to a country whose infrastructure can now support, thus extending the product life cycle.

But experience in developing countries shows that premature transfer of technology to countries which are not ready to take advantage of it can lead to disastrous results. Use of internationalization to acquire resources has been much in the news and requires little comment. For example, moving manufacturing to low labor costs areas, or processing facilities near to sites of natural resources, has been a popular strategy. Firms have learned, however, that the labor cost advantages are not static and that it is necessary to anticipate that, as low-cost countries develop economically, labor costs will rise to make local manufacturing less attractive. Firms have also learned that nationalization tendencies, or insistence by local governments on joint ownership, can make investment in local processing and manufacturing highly risky and ineffective.

Returning to Table 14.1, the checks inside the table show how different strategic criteria, listed across the top, contribute to different objectives, listed vertically. Four distinctive cases are boxed in:

- Box 1: The most restricted strategy is to internationalize into SBAs which have similar growth. This does not change the growth, profitability, or the portfolio balance of the firm.
- Box 2: Entry into countercyclical SBAs, entry into distinctive political/economic/technological environments, or assuring availability of resources are the criteria which reduce the firm's vulnerability.
- Box 3: The firm's near-term profitability is enhanced by SBAs which increase the size of the firm's global market position, offer synergies, economies of scale, or other comparative advantages.

- Box 4: Movement to better growth, and SBAs where technology is more advanced, and/or extending demand and technology life cycles are the most attractive strategic thrusts, because, as the figure shows, they have a comprehensive impact on the objectives.

Degrees of Internationalization

At the left of Table 14.2 are shown the typical stages in the internationalization of a firm: from export to international to multinational. Column 2 shows the activities in foreign countries, which cumulate as the firm progresses from export to the international stage.

As the figure shows, the move toward the international status is a decentralization process in which activities are progressively distributed among the countries in which the firm does business.

By contrast, the step toward the multinational status involves assumption of new and major strategic responsibilities by the corporate office. But, unlike the popular interpretation, in well-run multinationals, this is not a recentralization which takes authority away from the country managers and product line managers. It is rather an enlargement of the overall corporate perspective and introduction of new relationships among parts of the company.

Table 14.2 Stages of internationalization

(1) Stage	(2) Activity level	(3) Conditions that make activity necessary	(4) Strategic criteria met by activity	(5) Responsibility of Country manager
Export	Sell through agents	- Export small percentage of sales - No barriers to entry - Local demand > capacity	- Countercyclicity (1) - Distinct economic environment (2) - Access to similar growth (4) - Better growth (5) - Extend demand life cycle (7) - Economies of scale (12)	None
	Local sales office	- Export large percentage of sales - No barriers to entry - Demand = capacity - Competition is strong - After sales service important		Provide sales support
International	Local marketing	- Distinct environment - Differentiated marketing strategies - Intensive competition - Barriers to entry - Local cost advantage	- Distinct environments (2)	Maximize country sales
	Local production		- Access to resources (3)	Optimize profitability of assigned projects
	Local R&D	- Distinct marketing needs	- Advanced technology (6) - Extend technology life cycle (8)	
	Local diversification	- Local growth opportunities - Local financing	- Better growth (5) - Critical mass (9) - Synergy (10) - Competitive advantage (11)	Optimize profitability of assigned mission scope
Multinational	Global optimization of production/resources/R&D	- Global competition - Global scale critical mass - Global scale synergy advantages - Competition from globally optimized firms	- Economies of scale (12)	Contribute to global optimization
	Global diversification Global portfolio management		- Long-term vs. short-term portfolio balance - Global vulnerability balance - Global project optimization	Contribute to global strategy

In addition to retaining their own authority/responsibility scope, the lower managers are also made responsible for contributing to the global strategy of the firm.

As the figure shows, the first step toward the multinational stage is global optimization of the firm's product lines, technologies, production and distribution systems (see the following section).

The second step is global strategic planning, in which the strategic business area portfolio is optimized from a global perspective.

The progression through the stages shown in Table 14.2 is a typical pattern which has been observed in the past. It reflects a step-by-step learning process which many firms have followed as a result of the factors discussed in the distinct aspects of internationalization. But the pattern does not imply that all firms do or should follow the respective stages, nor that an internationalized firm must expect to progress inexorably to the multinational posture. It is interesting to note that many of the very large American firms have not yet progressed beyond the international stage. One reason for this is that the American market had been dynamic and large enough to permit firms to fulfill most of their objectives domestically.

Another reason is that the shift from the international to the multinational status requires a major organizational restructuring:

1. From what Howard Perlmutter called *ethnocentric* focus, in which domestic culture dominates the firm, to a *polycentric* perspective in which the distinction between foreign nationals and foreign culture on the one side, and domestic nationals and culture on the other, disappears, and the firm develops a cadre of multinational managers and a genuinely multinational culture. American managements, accustomed to operating on a huge and culturally uniform domestic market, have frequently exhibited 'cultural blindness' when moving to foreign markets.
2. The multinational stage also necessitates a shift to the *matrix* organizational form (see Chapter 17) in which the cherished and historically effective American concept of unity of authority and responsibility breaks down.

By contrast, limitations of the size of the domestic markets, the habit of doing business in culturally disparate environments, and a smaller commitment to the principle of unity of authority and responsibility have made it possible for major European firms to become fully multinational.

In part, the progression through stages of internationalization is forced by environmental conditions. The conditions which make each step necessary for success are shown in the third column of Table 14.2. The column shows, for example, that the firm can remain a successful exporter only so long as there are no barriers to entry, local products are undifferentiated and local market conditions are similar to the domestic market. When entry barriers appear, or local cost advantages become critical, the firm is forced to establish local manufacturing.

In general, a firm is forced beyond the export status whenever markets become differentiated, when entry barriers are high, and economies of size and synergies are global.

For a given firm, a quick diagnosis of the necessary degree of internationalization in a country can be determined by identifying the line in column 3 of Table 14.2 which best describes the conditions which exist in this country.

Column 3 determines the *forced choice* which a firm has to make in order to succeed. The *voluntary choice* of the stage of internationalization is determined by the strategic criteria of the firm. Column 4 of Table 14.2 shows the criteria which become possible at each activity level. (The numbers in parentheses refer to the numbering of the columns in Table 14.1.)

For a given firm, the degree of internationalization which will best meet the internationalization objectives of the firm can be determined in three steps:

1. Using the comprehensive list of objectives previously presented, determine the internationalization objectives of the firm.
2. Using Table 14.1, determine the consequent strategic criteria.
3. Using column 4 of Table 14.2, determine the degree of internationalization which will best meet the criteria.

The last column of Table 14.2 describes the progress of responsibilities which devolve on the country managers.

As the figure shows, the early steps in internationalization assign support and functional responsibilities to the country manager. He begins to acquire general management status when he is given the task of optimizing the profitability of the product line assigned to him. He reaches full general management responsibility when, on the one hand, he optimizes profitability in the mission scope assigned to him, and, on the other, contributes to the formulation of the global strategy of the firm. (As in the parent organization, the transition from a functional to general management perspective is not easy for a functionally trained and experienced manager.)

The arrival at the multinational status creates an anomaly: The local manager becomes completely responsible for the performance of the firm in his country markets, while the corporate office progressively turns to global optimization of products/technology/production/distribution and financing. This poses a dual problem:

1. How to make the trade-off between global economies of scale, made possible by optimization at the corporate level, and local market responsiveness, which requires products and market strategies tailored to the local conditions. We turn our attention to this problem in the following section.
2. How to assign authority, and responsibility, when both corporate level units (such as product development) and country managers have legitimately conflicting perspectives on the overall corporate strategy.

Global Synergies vs. Local Responsiveness

As a firm moves toward the multinational stage of development, a key issue is the trade-off between global strategies which take advantage, on the one hand, of synergies, economics of R&D, and economies of scale in production and, on the other hand, strategies tailored to local country markets, and which permit optimal responsiveness to the local conditions and opportunities.

These strategies vary across the following range:

1. *Global, standard* strategies which are applied equally to all SBAs. These may be optimal in undifferentiated product industries, such as natural gas, chemicals.
2. *Local, cosmetic* strategies under which a standard product and marketing strategy are locally modified through packaging, specialized advertising/promotion, etc.
3. *Tailored strategies for large SBAs, standard for small.* This is a mixed strategy, frequently observable in consumer product multinationals. It is used when the market size in a country reaches a level to permit local amortization of the product/market development costs. This type of strategy is forced on the firm in countries where the local government insists that the foreign entrant creates a distinct and integrated industrial entry in the host country.
4. *Interchangeability (modularity).* The firm develops its strategies on a building block principle which permits different blocks to be packaged in response to special local conditions. This attractive strategy is difficult to implement as evidenced by the time, cost, and energy that Volkswagen has invested in its 'world car' concept.

5. *SBA-specific* strategies are at the other extreme from global standard. A specialized strategy is developed for each SBA. This is the case of a multinational conglomerate which makes no attempt to relate similar divisions which operate in different countries.

In Table 14.3, we illustrate some of the key variables which determine the choice of the marketing strategy for a multi-nationally diversified firm. As the figure shows (line 1), a high level of non-transferable knowledge (implicit information) in an SBA forces a firm to develop a tailored strategy for the SBA as well as intense competition (line 2). The other factors which will drive the firm toward tailored strategies are: a variety of different competitive strategies in an SBA (high marketing strategy differentiation), frequent changes in the strategies (frequent shift of success factors), intense customer pressures and product discrimination.

At the bottom of the figure room is provided for additional key variables which may be important in a given SBA. As the preceding remarks suggest, a profile of the key factors must be constructed for each SBA and then the overall degree of strategy diversity chosen, using the process we shall describe below.

Table 14.4 shows a similar approach to the product-technology strategy. Tables 14.3 and 14.4 share the importance of non-transferable knowledge, but the other variables in Table 14.4 are concerned with the economic advantages and disadvantages of global product standards vs. distinctive products for each SBA.

Table 14.3 Diversity of marketing strategy

Preferred strategy types / Variables	Global standard	Local cosmetics.	Large SBAs tailored	Interchangeable	SBA specific
Importance of nontransferable knowledge	Low				High
Competition	Weak				Intense
Marketing strategy differentiation	None				High
Shift of key success factors	Slow				Frequent
Customer pressures/discrimination	Low				Intense
Size of SBA market in relation to cost of developing a tailored strategy	Small				Large
Other factors special to the SBA:					

Table 14.4 Diversity of product-technology strategy

Variables \ Preferred strategy types	Global standard	Local cosmetics.	Large SBAs tailored	Interchangeable	SBA specific
Importance of nontransferable knowledge	Low				High
Commonality of demand across SBAs	High				Low
Intra-SBA product variety	Low				High
Length of product life cycle	Long				Short
Differences in length of product life cycles	Small				Large
Ratio of global R&D to SBA sales volume	High				Low
Possibilities for interchangeability	Few				Many
Local government regulation of product characteristics	Weak				Intense
Size of SBA market in relations to R&D investment needed for tailored strategy	Small				Large
Other factors special to the SBA:					

A comparison of Tables 14.3 and 14.4 shows that a firm must develop tailored strategies for both technology-intensive and competitively turbulent SBAs. But, if the pressures for local responsiveness can only be met through investments, which are not justifiable on the grounds of potential profitability, the firm may do better to stay out of the SBA rather than try to apply standard products which are not responsive to the local needs.

In addition to marketing and product development, the third major strategic issue in a multinational is the location of the production facilities. The main alternatives are:

1. *Local* production in which each country supplies its own needs.
2. *Global network* in which production centers are established in certain countries, charged with the responsibility of producing for designated countries.
3. *Centralized* production in which a single center (not necessarily the country of the firm's headquarters) supplies global needs.

Table 14.5 shows a number of key factors which determine the choice of the appropriate production systems. When the economies of scale are high, and transportation and other distribution barriers are not important, centralized production is best located in a low-cost country.

However, as recent experience in the electronic industry has shown, low-cost countries do not remain the lowest cost producers forever. In the long term, the design of the production system must anticipate shifts in costs and resource availabilities. For this reason, a global network which can divide risks and anticipate geographic shifts will frequently be the preferred solution, particularly if it also takes account of legislative and economic barriers. In the language of cybernetics, the global network provides the *requisite variety* solution to a complex and dynamic problem.

*Choosing the Strategy

Conceptually, the diversity of the firm's marketing, product and production strategies should be chosen on the basis of a profitability analysis. The preferred strategy is one which will offer the best combined return on the investment over the lifetime of a product (or of a physical investment). In practice, though, the relevant variables (which include those of Tables 14.3, 14.4, and 14.5) are frequently difficult to quantify, the relations among them are poorly understood, and the uncertainties and risks are difficult to estimate.

In such situations, the technique of profile analysis used in the preceding chapters can offer a supplementary or even alternative approach to choosing the diversity of the marketing and the product-technology strategies and of the production/distribution system. (Readers who are mathematically minded will recognize that profile analysis assumes that return on the investment is a linear non-weighted function of the variables. If necessary, a refinement can be easily added by assigning relative priorities to the variables at the left-hand side of the respective figures.)

Table 14.5 Diversity of production system

Variables	Alternatives	Local	Global	Centralized
Economies of Scale		Low	Significant	High
Transportation costs		High	Significant	
Tariff barriers		High	Significant	
Balancing currency		Difficult	Significant	
Legislation enforcing local productions		Stringent	Significant	Permissive
Differential in labor costs		Low	Large	Low
Differential in response costs		Low	Significant	High
Other factors special to the firm production/ distribution problems				

The following procedure can be followed in determining the respective diversities:

1. Diagnose for each SBA the strategy profile which is optimal for the SBA, by constructing the appropriate profiles in Tables 14.3 and 14.4.
2. Determine the strategic importance of each SBA to the firm's future. This involves estimating its future contribution to the firm's objectives, particularly to profitability, growth, and strategic invulnerability. (The estimate may be numerical or made by relative ranking of the SBA. For further details refer to Chapter 11.)
3. Identify the large SBAs in which SBA-specific strategies are highly desirable.
4. Estimate whether (and when) profits from these SBAs will be large enough to justify SBA-specific strategies. When this point is reached, the strategy development responsibility and the necessary resource should be assigned to the local managers of these self-contained SBAs.
5. Use Table 14.5 in a similar manner to determine whether self-sufficient manufacturing and distribution responsibilities should also be assigned to these SBAs.
6. For the remainder of small SBAs, choose a common product-technology strategy for each of the major product lines of the firm. Also identify the common elements of the marketing strategies which will be enforced equally among small SBAs.
7. Without jeopardizing success in the large SBAs, establish the common elements of both strategies for both small and large SBAs. These will be the corporate strategies which will guide corporate level product-design and marketing strategy formulation.
8. By balancing the costs and benefits of economies of scale, transportation costs, resource availabilities, local technological know-how, and currency differences and transfer barriers against one another, design an optimal global manufacturing and distribution network.

Shared Authority/Responsibility

In an exporting company, 'standard' domestically developed products are offered in all markets and there are no distinctive marketing strategies for different countries.

In an international company, the country manager is either expected to formulate his own strategy for marketing a product mix assigned to him by the corporation, or is given the additional freedom to determine and develop the appropriate product mix for his country.

As discussed in the preceding section, in a multinational company the strategy is based on a three-way trade-off between the demands of the local marketplace, the synergistic advantages of global R&D, and the economies of a globally optimized production/distribution system.

The process of arriving at a globally optimal strategy is made difficult by the inherent split of strategic authority and responsibility between country managers, product-technology managers, and managers of the global production system. If each is allowed to optimize the strategies along the dimensions for which he is responsible, the global balance will be distorted in favor of his area of responsibility.

In the past, much of the historical success of business firms (particularly in the USA) has been ascribed to the *principle of unity of authority and responsibility*. According to this principle, the firm's performance will be optimal when certain key managers are given complete authority over decision making and implementation in areas assigned to them and are held responsible for the results.

Short of giving each country manager a total profit and loss responsibility (the case of the unrelated multicounty conglomerate described above), it is not possible to preserve this principle in a multinational firm. As a result, most multinationals have evolved three-dimensional matrix structures in which at least three key managers (and usually many more) must participate in joint-strategy formulation for each SBA for each country, and for the corporation as a whole.

While in a multinational matrix structure the principle of unity of authority/responsibility no longer applies, usually no formal substitute principle is put in its place. The strategic coordination is expected to occur through informal cooperation, based on mutual goodwill and a shared commitment to the global success of the firm. Experienced multinationals (such as Shell, Unilever, Nestle, IBM) have sought to assure mutual goodwill and commitment to the total enterprise by paying a great deal of attention to developing managers who share a common corporate *culture*. The result is a readily recognizable 'Shell manager' or an 'IBM manager' who resembles his colleagues and is distinct from managers of other firms.

As we shall be discussing in Part VI, development of a uniform corporate culture is a slow process. When strategic change is evolutionary and slow enough to permit timely cultural adaptation, assuring strategic consistency through shared culture and training is an effective method for resolving the inherent three-way conflict described above. But when strategic change becomes so discontinuous and fast, that cultural adaptation cannot keep pace with environmental change, experience shows that informal cooperation breaks down and the process of strategy formulation becomes dysfunctional and politically biased.

These difficulties can be ameliorated through strategic planning which develops new, commonly shared objectives as well as strategy guides for decision making (see Chapter 13).

Another very promising and complementary solution is to formalize strategic decision making by introducing a new principle of shared authority/responsibility. This new principle is based on a *role triangle* shown in Fig. 14.3.

The manager in role 1:

(a) is responsible for implementing strategic decisions assigned to him;
(b) is responsible for involving role 2 managers in a participative decision process;
(c) has the authority to make the final decision, whenever the participative process fails to produce consensus;
(d) is responsible for obtaining approval of the decision from role 3 manager.

The manager in role 2:

(a) is responsible for participating in the decision process;
(b) is responsible for voicing dissent to role 3 manager, if the final decision is not acceptable to him;
(c) has the authority to ask role 3 manager for relief from responsibilities which he feels he cannot discharge, because of the decision made by role 1 manager.

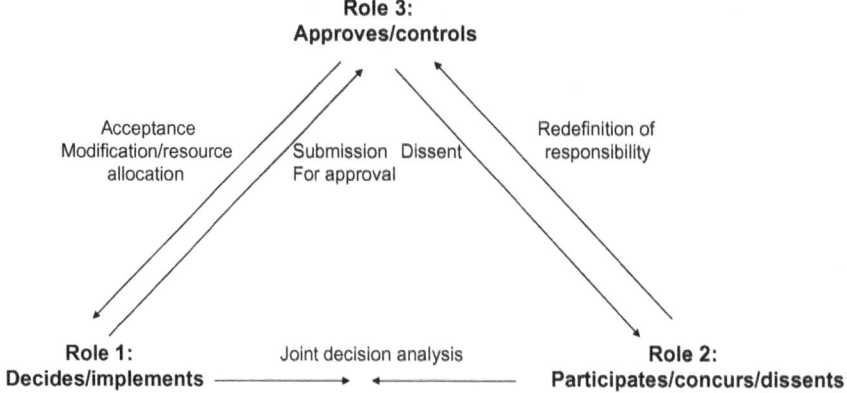

Fig. 14.3   Role triangle in shared authority/responsibility

The manager in role 3:

(a) has the authority to override the decisions of role 1 managers;
(b) is responsible for modifying the area of responsibility of role 2 manager, when requested to do so by the latter.

For example, the product group manager is responsible for implementing the product-technology strategy. Since the manager responsible for global production, and several country managers, will be affected by product strategy decisions, the product group manager must involve them in strategy formulation. If consensus is not reached, the product group manager makes the final decision and obtains approval from his superior (the company president or vice president for R&D).

The production manager and the relevant country managers are responsible for voicing their dissent to the president (or their respective superiors reporting to the president). They also have the responsibility to ask to be relieved of certain responsibilities which, in their opinion, they cannot carry out effectively, in view of the decision made by the product group manager.

The president (together with the respective vice presidents to whom the lower managers' report) has the authority to modify or reject the decision made by the product group manager. He is also responsible for redefining the responsibilities of the country managers and the production manager, as requested by them.

As can be seen from the above discussion, the shared authority/responsibility concept encourages consensus and consultation, but also provides for resolution of unavoidable conflicts and dissent.

Under the shared authority/responsibility concept, key managers will play different roles on different occasions, depending on the level and type of strategy being developed. This is illustrated in Table 14.5 which shows, for example, that a product division manager will play role 1 in product strategy decisions, and role 2 in marketing and production strategy formulation.

Table 14.6 also illustrates that, in corporate strategy decisions, corporate management should play role 1, the board of the company (using the word in the American sense) should play role 2, and the stakeholders should play role 3. In prevalent practice, corporate management approves its own strategy. This failure of the checks and balances implied by the shared authority/responsibility principle offers one explanation for the increasing frequency of myopic mismanagement by the corporate management of large firms.

Table 14.6 Examples of shared authority and responsibility

Roles Strategy type	1 Decides/implements	2 Partiipates/dissents	3 Approves/controls
Corporate	Corporate management	Board	Shareholders
Product-technology	Product manager	– Country manager – Production	Corporate management
Marketing	Country managers	– Product managers – Production managers	Corporate management
Production	Production managers	– Product managers – Country managers	Corporate management

Using a Progressive Commitment Process in Internationalization

As discussed previously, many firms internationalized by proceeding from exporting to progressive development of local marketing, manufacturing and R&D, to global design of the firm. An explanation for such a gradual approach is to be found in the cost of strategic information. As discussed, the cost of information for internationalization is very much higher than the cost of domestic information, and some of the vital knowledge about foreign environments can only be acquired through first-hand experience.

When a firm's internationalization strategy takes it to countries which are significantly different from the parent country, a *progressive commitment* approach becomes desirable for two complementary reasons:

1. The firm can learn by doing. Instead of investing in expensive market research, it invests in probing entries into an SBA and through experience acquires knowledge of the factors which are critical to success.
2. Progressive commitment permits the firm to control risk by controlling the size of exposure.

Figure 14.4 presents the steps which can be followed in a planned gradual commitment approach.

1. The first step is formulation of a global internationalization strategy which is in two parts.

   (a) The portfolio strategy is derived, first, by matching the firm's objectives to the strategic criteria and, second, by identifying geographic regions

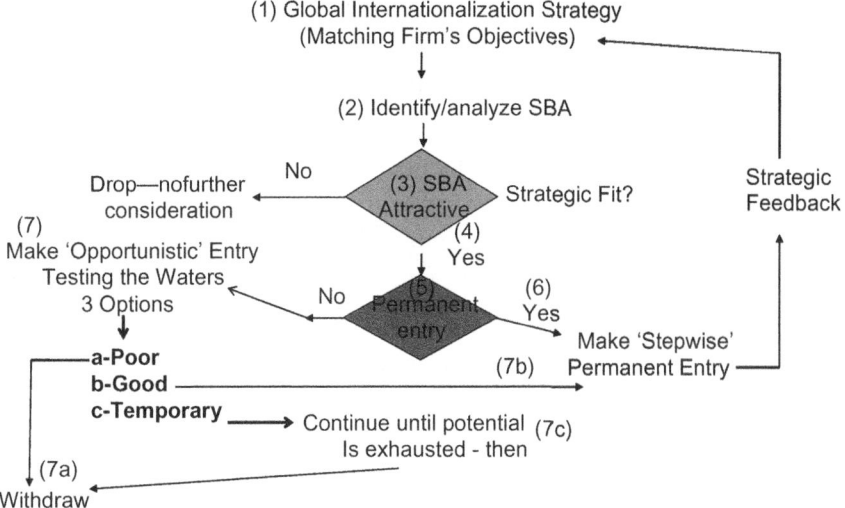

Fig. 14.4   Gradual commitment

and specific SBAs which match the criteria. The portfolio strategy will specify some strategic business areas which the firm proposes to enter (or leave), but it will also specify the broad geographic regions and the characteristics of the SBAs which the firm will seek to enter.

(b) The global strategy also includes specification of diversity of product-technology strategy, the marketing strategy, and the production/distribution strategy.

2. The second step is to launch a search for SBAs which fit the global strategy.
3. Each identified SBA is analyzed for its attractiveness on the basis of fit with the global strategy, fit with capabilities of the firm, feasibility, costs of entry, competitive intensity and the prospects for growth and profitability.
4. The procedure for such analysis has already been described in Chapters 10 and 11.

   It will lead to a twofold decision:

   (a) Whether to enter or leave the SB;
   (b) What specific competitive strategy to pursue.

5. However, in some cases information needed for a detailed analysis of an apparently attractive SBA may be prohibitively costly or even unavailable. Nevertheless, if such SBA appears very attractive, the firm may decide to make a low-cost opportunistic entry in order to 'test the water.' This

step is illustrated at the left of Fig. 14.4. For example, the firm may find distributors for its present products, or make a sales agreement with a local firm. As Fig. 14.4 shows, an opportunistic entry ends in one of three outcomes:

(a) quick withdrawal, because the SBA cannot be made profitable;
(b) withdrawal after the temporary profit opportunity is exhausted;
(c) conversion to a permanent entry, if the long-term profit potential turns out to be attractive.

6. The opportunistic entry should be designed and executed as a *strategic learning experience*. This means that, while the firm attempts to make sales in the SBA, the major emphasis is not on making profit but on learning whether the opportunistic entry is potentially profitable in the short and/ or in the long term.

7. It may turn out that, while there are no long-term prospects in an SBA, a satisfactory profit can be made in the near term. In this case, the decision should be to continue selling in the SBA while the potential lasts, but to keep resource commitments at a minimum. For example, the firm would not build local production facilities or make any other capital investments.

8. Returning to step 4, if sufficient information can be obtained at reasonable cost, which shows the SBA to be attractive, a permanent entry commitment can be made. Nevertheless, it is still advisable to proceed in steps using strategic learning at each step, but with more confidence and boldness, not only to confirm/deny the previous decisions, but also to modify the global internationalization strategy.

Management Capabilities for Internationalization

In the early stages of internationalization, the firm may make distribution agreements for export, or acquire distributing firms in foreign countries. While sales abroad may reach a high level, management capability changes little. The foreign sales are typically handled by an export department whose members develop and maintain foreign sales outlets and handle orders obtained from them.

If the export sales and profits continue to grow successfully, it is common to leave the total responsibility in the hands of the export department, while the corporate management devotes its attention to other matters. As a result, a paradoxical situation may arise in which the firm derives a substantial proportion of its sales and earnings from foreign countries whose social/economic/political/technological complexion is poorly (if at all) understood by the corporate management of the firm.

If such firms' internationalization proceeds beyond exporting to the various stages of local presence and eventually to the multinational stage, it becomes critical for management to recognize that success in multinational business requires a range of management capabilities which an exporting firm may not possess.

1. The organizational culture should be change-seeking, flexible, with low commitment to the 'way we've done it in the past,' and prepared for and welcoming unfamiliar opportunities. In the ethnic sense of the word, the culture should be receptive to foreign values, points of view, and ways of doing business.
2. Managers charged with internationalizing the firm should be entrepreneurial risk-takers, capable of identifying key success factors in an unfamiliar opportunity, tolerant of ambiguity, prepared to live with uncertainty, and to take calculated risks. They should be skilled in dealing with cultural/social/political factors which affect profit making in foreign countries.
3. The firm's information system should be global in scope, receptive to new and unfamiliar developments, and able to recognize important international differences. The information system should rely heavily on the local knowledge, perceptions, and judgments of managers who are 'on the spot' in different countries. It should contain not only economic/competitive, but also sociopolitical cultural data. It should not only contain quantitative but also qualitative judgment-based data.
4. Strategic planning should be decentralized to permit country managers not only to formulate and implement their own strategies, but also to contribute their special insights into the global strategy. Strategy formulation should analyze political risks and cultural differences.
5. The structure should be multifaceted, adaptable to different geographic conditions and different business areas.
6. Managers' roles should be defined according to the shared authority/responsibility principle.
7. The rewards and incentives should be multiple, some recognizing efficient profit making, some rewarding imagination and entrepreneurial risk-taking.

The system should be tolerant of the inevitable occasional failures which result from bold risk-taking.
8. The overall management capability should be flexible and capable of self-renewal in response to changing foreign opportunities and circumstances.

It can be seen from the above description that the profile of multinational management capability has much in common with the profile needed in a societally responsive firm. As was seen in Chapter 10, the multinational capability profile also has many similarities to the profile required for success in a turbulent domestic environment.

Summary

The following features of internationalization have been discussed in this chapter:

- The costs and risks of internationalization are high, as compared with domestic diversification. Therefore, we have argued that a firm seeking to internationalize itself should be clear about the objectives and the strategic thrusts it will pursue, and make sure that internationalization is the best way to pursue them.
- The internationalization process typically proceeds through a gradual commitment to a local business presence. We have described the advantages and imperatives of the various stages of presence.
- A major reason for the gradual commitment is the cost of information and ignorance about doing business in unfamiliar countries. We have described a stepwise procedure by which a firm can progressively commit itself.
- When a firm reaches the multinational status, it begins to optimize its global strategy through a trade-off between global economies and local responsiveness. We have suggested procedures for determining the preferred level of diversity of global product/technology, marketing, and production/distribution strategies.
- The principle of unity of authority/responsibility is very difficult to apply in a multinational. We have suggested a substitute principle of shared authority/responsibility.
- A major obstacle to successful internationalization is frequently the lack of an appropriate management capability. This deficiency is often

obscured by the fact that a firm which exports a large percentage of its sales perceives itself as already internationalized. We have identified the characteristics which management should have for successful internationalization.

Exercises

1. Prepare a checklist of new variables which should be added to a firm's domestic environmental surveillance system in order to give the firm information about significant trends, threats, and opportunities in foreign markets.

   a. In the checklist, identify the variables which belong in the category of implicit knowledge.
   b. How and by whom should the foreign data be collected?
   c. To whom, within the firm, should the data be distributed? How should the implicit knowledge be transferred to the headquarters of the firm?
   d. What should be done to assure that the recipients use the data in their strategic decision making?

2. In Table 14.1, checks are entered under each strategic criterion to shoe the contribution that the criterion makes to the respective objectives. Explain how internationalization entries make the contributions when they meet the following criteria: 3, 5, 6, 7, 9, 10. For which of the criteria will the contribution be automatic, once a foreign entry is made, and which require special management attention to realize the contribution?

3. Explain the essential differences between exporting, internationalized, and multinational firm.

4. Consider separately a firm in the following industries: steel, cosmetics, automotive, and passenger aircraft.

   a. For each industry, using Tables 14.3 and 14.4, prepare diversity profiles for the marketing and product-technology strategies.
   b. Assign relative importance to the variables in the first column and select the preferred strategy type.

5. For each industry in exercise 4 above, use Table 14.5 to select the preferred design for the production system of a firm which operates in many countries.

6. Compare advantages and disadvantages of centralized authority/responsibility and shared authority/responsibility principles.

   a. Prepare a checklist of factors under which one or the other principle should be used.

7. The German food giant Lidl has entered into the US market.

   a. Prepare a list of criteria which you think was used in making the following alternative entries types:
      i. A large-scale permanent entry.
      ii. Stepwise permanent entry.
      iii. Opportunistic entry.
   b. According to your criteria, which alternative should have been chosen?

Part III

Managers, Systems, Structure

15

General Managers for Diversified Firms

This chapter is based on a paper which Igor Ansoff wrote with Dick Brandenburg in 1967. In the paper, they predicted the qualifications which general managers would have to bring to their jobs during the last quarter of the twentieth century. Their principal predictions about complexities and diversity of demands on the general managers are currently observable in practice.

Management as a Problem-Solving Cycle

Management communication and influence are problem-solving activities which can be described as complex information processes. Hence, the role of a manager can be described through the following connected chain of activities.

1. Setting objectives for a given area of business activity.
2. Perception of problems and opportunities both inside and outside the activity. (This includes perception of present or future deviation from objectives, as well as of present or future prospects for raising the objectives.)
3. Diagnosis of problems and opportunities and their effect on the firm.
4. Generation of responses to the problems and opportunities.
5. Analysis of the probable consequences of the courses of action.
6. Selection of the preferred alternative.
7. Programming and budgeting the selected alternative.

© The Author(s) 2019
H. I. Ansoff et al., *Implanting Strategic Management*,
https://doi.org/10.1007/978-3-319-99599-1_15

8. Leadership in implementation including communication and motivation.
9. Measurement of performance in relation to the objectives.
10. Observation of significant trends and possible discontinuities both inside and outside the firm.
11. Recycling of some or all of the preceding steps.

Taken together, the eleven steps describe a complex and time-consuming process. In accordance with the strategic success hypothesis, all of these steps become necessary at turbulence levels 4 and above.

As the turbulence level decreases, a progressively smaller number of steps become necessary for successful management. Thus, at level 1 the nature and context of managers' tasks remain unchanged. The *management cycle* of Fig. 15.1 can be reduced to the *implementation cycle* of Fig. 15.2.

On turbulence level 2, the *control cycle* (Fig. 15.3), which uses steps 1, 2, 3, and 9, is added to the managers' work to monitor and control past performance of the firm in relation to the objectives.

In the *extrapolative planning cycle* (Fig. 15.4) steps 1, 2, 3, 7, and 10 are added to enable managers to make decisions, based on extrapolative

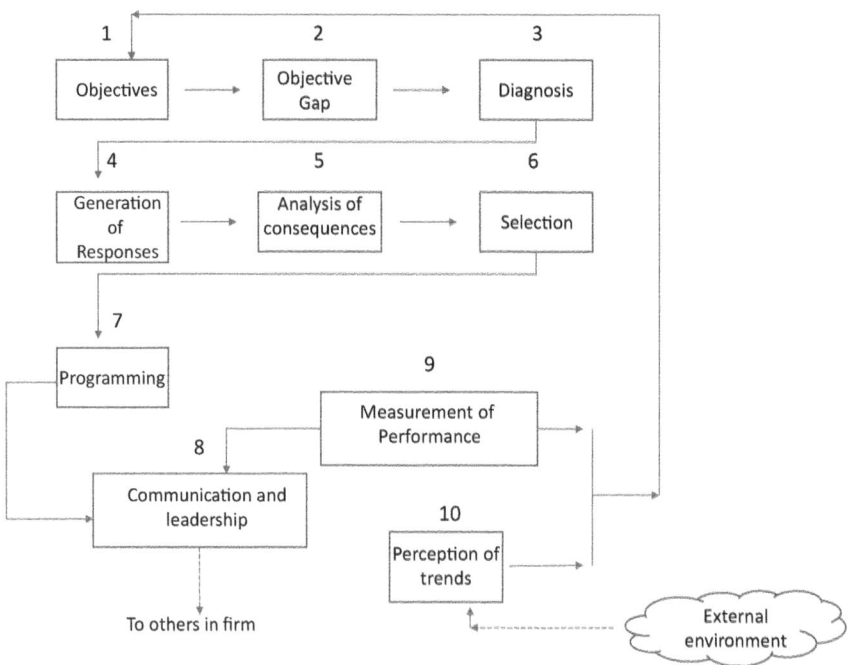

Fig. 15.1 Management cycle

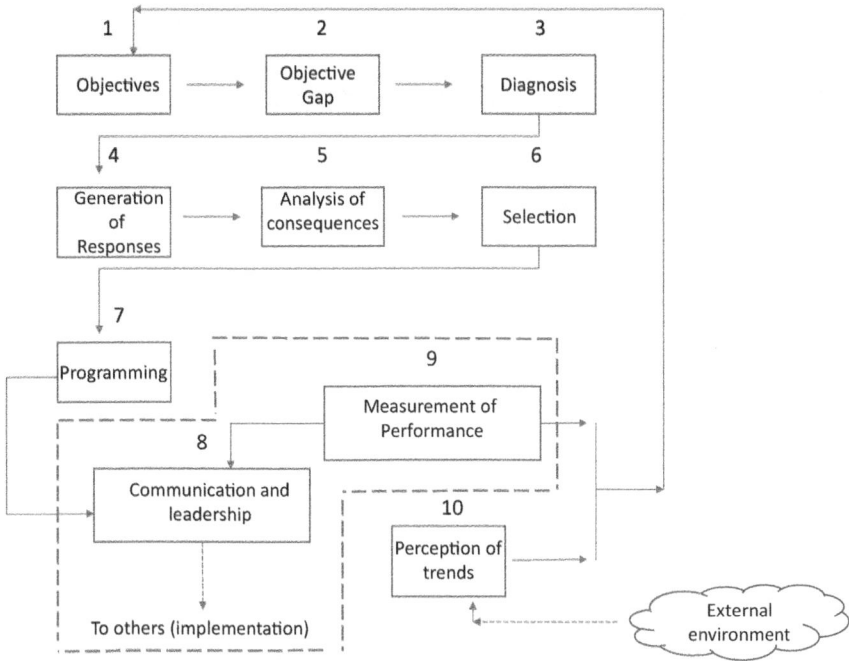

Fig. 15.2 Implementation cycle

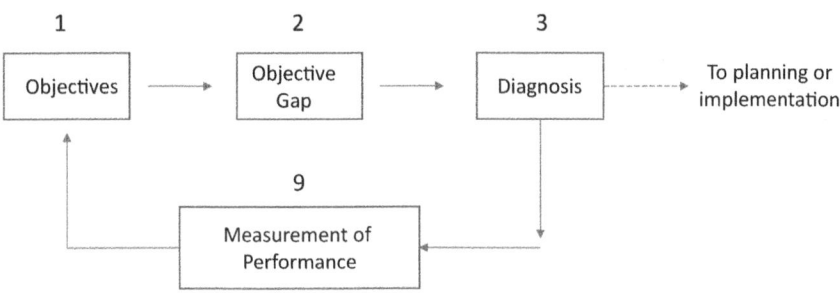

Fig. 15.3 Control cycle

forecasts of the firm's future. This cycle becomes important on turbulence level 3, but it complements, rather than replaces, the others.

Finally, on turbulence level 4 and above, the most complex cycle, *the strategic planning cycle* (Fig. 15.5) uses steps 10, 1, 2, 3, 4, 5, 6 to make decisions when step 10 indicates that the future will not be an extrapolation of the past, or when entrepreneurial management seeks to expand the firm beyond its historical boundaries. As a consequence, objectives in step 1 are

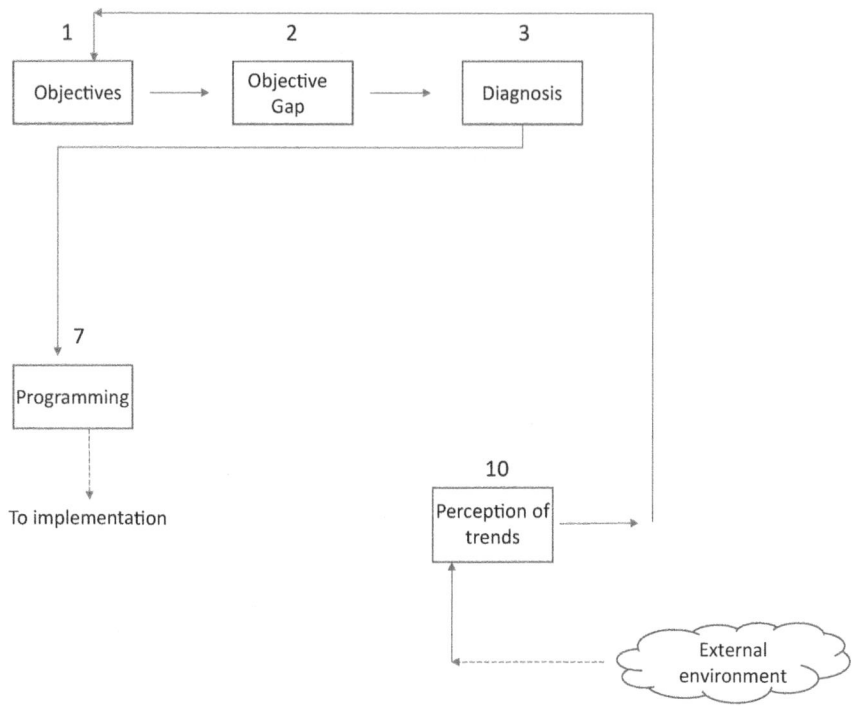

Fig. 15.4 Extrapolative cycle

thoroughly reexamined, a wide-ranging search (step 4) is made to generate new responses, and a full analysis of their consequences is made.

Manager Archetypes

Each sub-cycle delineates a distinct management role which calls for different knowledge, skills, and personal characteristics. We will refer to managers capable of filling such roles as archetypes (Table 15.1).

- Level 1—The **Custodian**—The *custodian* fills the implementation role that puts a premium on stability of the organization. The custodian rejects change and is comfortable living in the past using extrapolative data to base current and future decisions. Leadership is viewed as being centralized and political without which, decisions cannot be successfully put into action.
- Level 2—The **Controller**—This archetype requires a thorough understanding of the variables that are critical to the firm's success, a skill in

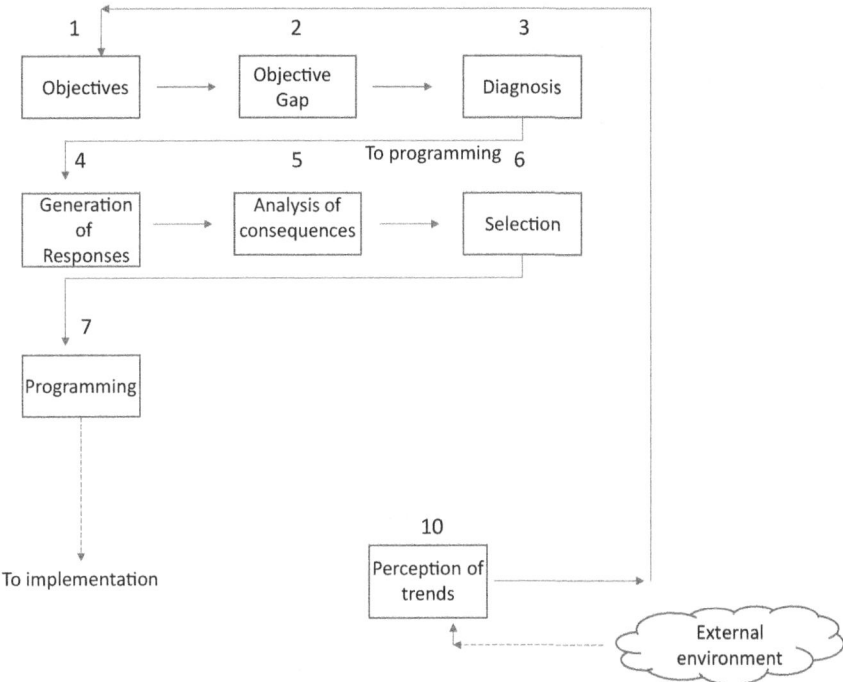

Fig. 15.5 The cycle

pinpointing the sources of trouble, and an ability to develop corrective courses of action. While aware of the human element, the controller does not allow personal loyalties and influences to obscure the substantive problems.

- Level 3—The **Planner**—The Planner is gregarious and an inspiration to men to do their best, objective with a preference for facts and logic making this archetype methodical, analytical, and future oriented through extrapolation.
- Level 4—The **Entrepreneur**—although future oriented, this archetype is somewhat different from the planner. Where the planner is concerned with extrapolating the historical dynamics of the firm into the future, the entrepreneur is concerned with *changing the dynamic*. Where the planner optimizes the future of the firm's present businesses, the entrepreneur seeks to enter new businesses and to diversify the firm. Where the planner projects the past into the future, the entrepreneur is an imaginative creator of new futures. Where the former archetypes are tough-minder and seeks to control risks, the entrepreneur is a willing risk-taker. A planner

Table 15.1 Managerial archetypes

Manager Archetype		Custodian	Controller	Planner	Entrepreneur/Intrapreneur	Creator
Motivation	Vision	Status quo	Minimize costs	Optimize profit	Optimal profit potential	Creation of new needs
	Mentality	Stability	Least price	Respond to customer	Strategic positioning	Creative innovation
	Aspirations	Prefers past	Present	Extrapolate for future	Predictable futures	Possible futures
	Aggressiveness	Stable	Reactive	Anticipatory	Entrepreneur	Creative
	Risk propensity	Suppress	Control	Comfortable with familiar	Seeks new risks	Prefers new risks
Competence	Power base	Command	Hold & maintain	Directives	Inclusive	Collaborative
	Problem solving	Control Change	Seeks efficiency	Optimizing processes	Opportunity finding	Opportunity Creating
	Leadership	Political	Rational	Inspirational	Charismatic	Visionary
	Knowledge	Internal politics	Internal operations	Historical markets	Global environment	Open to emerging possibilities
Environmental turbulence level		1	2	3	4	5

extrapolates the firm's goals. An entrepreneur sets new and challenging objectives.

The planner is a convergent problem solver who chooses among the available opportunities. The entrepreneur is a divergent problem solver who creates new opportunities.

- Level 5—The *Creator*—The creator is the evolution of the multimanager requiring a different set of skills and techniques than our previous managers. The creator will need to be part statesman and part system architect. When confronted with major decisions he is an expert in using experts for advice often times engaging them in a dialectic confrontation of opinions. As such, this will necessitate the creator manager to acquiring sufficient expertise about the respective fields in order to be able to judge whether the expert is using a method of analysis that is applicable to the real-world problem he is asked to solve.

    The creator manager emphasizes continuous planning and establishes a formal system for anticipatory, external environmental information gathering and rational analysis to create opportunities for the firm.

General Manager as the Man of the Moment

When all of the archetypal skills and talents are found in a single individual, we have a rare management genius who discharges each distinctive task with equal ease and excellence. However, as in other occupations, geniuses are rare. In high turbulence environments, when all of the archetypal abilities must be present, how is the managerial work to be handled?

One answer is provided by history. During the first industrial era of business, different roles were critical to the firm's success at different times. When industries were founded, the entrepreneurial role was critical. During the early growth stage, the administrator was critical to ensuring minimal cost, and hence market shares. During the late growth stage, the planner became essential, and maturity called for a return of the administrator controller to run a 'tight ship' and maximize the cash flow.

Historical evidence suggests a 'man of the moment' explanation for the way the needs for general managers were met. A combination of outstanding entrepreneurs, administrators, planners, or leaders has seldom been found simultaneously in a firm. Instead, a process of natural selection has brought to the top the archetype that was the most critical to a particular phase in the firm's life.

At the time, the original version of this chapter was written in 1967, it was possible to predict two things: (1) that the 'man of the moment' solution would become inadequate in the 1990s and (2) that new archetypes will be needed in the firm of the 1990s and beyond. In order to substantiate this prediction and outline solutions, Igor Ansoff and Dick Brandenburg used an earlier article which they wrote together to describe the shape of the future. From these characteristics, they derived the attributes of the contemporary and future manager.

The Firm of the Future

The shape of the firm of the future has been the subject of much speculation. From this speculation, we select four primary categories of change which will have an important impact on managers.

Today's managers are faced with complex competitive environments and organizational situations. Tomorrow's management will operate within a *much broader institutional perspective.*

1. The growing importance of business as a social force on the one hand and expanding governmental concern with social welfare on the other are forcing greater interaction between the firm and society. Increasingly, society will pose problems and assign priorities to the allocation of resources which will put the firm in competition and cooperation with other types of organizations, including government agencies, universities, nonprofit institutions, and foundations. New combinations of organizations will emerge to carry out the work of society, in which firms will be essential, though not always dominant, participants. New societal pressures, demands, and constraints on the firm will force general management to include societal variables in virtually every important decision. Objectives and value systems of the firm will be of active concern for tomorrow's management.

   • It is also evident that firms will operate within a greatly expanded geographic and political perspective, encompassing different sovereignties, cultures, and stages of economic development. Thus, the decision-making perspective will be further broadened to include cultural and political variables.
   • This transition to a broader perspective is by no means natural for general managers. Recent events have provided evidence of considerable

faltering and confusion on the part of today's management when confronted with strong reactions from society.

- None of the previously discussed management archetypes is equipped to deal with these new complexities. It appears that a new archetype is in the making: A *statesman general manager* who has a sense of history, knowledge of politics and understanding of cultures, and who is skilled in relating the firm to its sociopolitical environment and in making business decisions within an economic-social-political-cultural perspective. He must also be skilled in the use of political influence, negotiation and bargaining.

2. A second major trend -toward the firm of the future is the *information explosion.*

   The information explosion is coming in part from technology, in part from the diversity and global scope of the firm, in part from the expansion of the relevant decision variables and the consequent complexity of managerial decisions. The explosion is in both volume and in the substantive content of information needed by general management.

   The complex communication and decision patterns require a new level of organizational and system design skills. Not only will the processes be complex, but acquisition and management of this extensive and complex information process will require different skills and aptitudes and, therefore, a new general manager archetype. We will call him the *systems architect.*

3. A third related trend is the *growing complexity of the firm as a behavioral system.*

   Growing numbers of scientists and engineers, and the firm's growing dependence on research and development, will necessitate closing the gap between technologists and general managers. The growing reliance on complex decision support systems will necessitate greater rapport between staff management analysts and line managers. The size, complexity, and diversity of the firm will lead to further decentralization of decision making. Thus, as the firm becomes a more complex information system, it also becomes a complex behavioral system with diverse aspirations, values, norms, and cultures.

   This view of the future firm reverses earlier predictions that the age of technology will dehumanize management, centralize decision making, and reduce the number of managers through automation. It is true that the number of managers engaged in data processing tasks will decline. But these managers will be replaced by increasing numbers of decision makers, informational, management science, and technological experts.

The firm of the future will be people-intensive and will depend more than ever on human imagination, creativity, and initiative. What is lost to automation in the blue-collar population will be offset by creative contributions of general managers, scientists, technologists, and management scientists.

This trend suggests that the systems architect will need to be skilled, not only in information system design, but also in designing the behavioral environment of the firm.

4. The fourth major trend is the *growing discontinuity of environmental challenges.*

On the one hand, intense competition, faster global communication, and transportation will require more rapid responses to shifts in demand, competitive actions, product, and technology. On the other hand, novel products, new technologies, and novel marketing challenges will make changes more discontinuous from the past. Shrinking technology and demand life cycles will make strategic management a common, rather than an exceptional, method of assuring the firm's future profitability.

One consequence will be to increase the importance of the entrepreneur. Fewer decisions will be based on extrapolation of past experience. An increasing number will be novel, poorly structured decisions involving problems and opportunities new to the firm, requiring imaginative analysis and judgment, rather than decision rules based on historical experience. The flair, imagination, creativity, and risk propensity of the entrepreneur will become as essential as they were in the days of the Industrial Revolution.

However, the complexity of the challenges will make the entrepreneur increasingly dependent on contributions from a wide range of experts in areas in which he has limited personal expertise. Thus, in addition to being an imaginative risk-taker, the entrepreneur will have to become *an expert in using experts.*

Additionally, unlike the entrepreneur of the Industrial Revolution, the entrepreneur of the last quarter of the twentieth century has to effect departures from the historical path of the firm through an organization which is resistant to discontinuous change and the bolder and more imaginative the change, the greater is the resistance. Thus, in addition to creativity, risk propensity, and expertise in using experts, the entrepreneur will have to exhibit the skill of a charismatic discontinuous change manager.

The Work of General Managers

The preceding discussion includes a description of the work of general managers during the second half of the twentieth century and compares this work to the challenges of the first half of the twentieth century. Note that two new archetypes have been added: statesman and system architect.

The figure carries the following three major implications for the general manager:

1. As the plusses in the figure show, the general management work in the firm of the 1980/1990s is not a replacement but an enlargement of the volume of managerial work of the 1950s. As a result, the volume of work of a general manager is approaching a point at which he does not have enough hours in the day to attend to it. A partial solution is decentralization, but after the general manager has delegated all the responsibility he can legitimately pass to others, there is still more critical workload than he can handle effectively and expeditiously.

   The resulting management overload has already been felt at the chief executives' level, where the solution which has been emerging during the past several decades has been the creation of a corporate office.

2. Rapidly growing complexity of the executive decisions has meant increasing reliance on supporting staffs and on technologists who contribute a wide range of specialized knowledge and skills not possessed by the executive. The result is a knowledge/skill gap between line executives and the staffs. We shall discuss this problem in the following Section.

3. A single 'man of the moment' management archetype can no longer cope with the many interconnected complexities of the general management job. It is increasingly necessary, particularly in diversified firms, to assure the knowledge, skills, and talents of ail six archetypes.

Developing Expertise in Using Experts

As the preceding discussion suggests, key strategic decisions are increasingly dependent on contributions from a wide range of experts. The principal reasons are described below.

Firms are becoming more and more technologically intensive. This applies not only to the high-tech industries, but also to many others in which technology is becoming both a major investment and a critical success variable. This is supported by two business indices: the investment in plant and equipment, and investment in research and development. Both investment decisions present a curious paradox. As the size of the investment grows, so does its technical content and complexity. As the complexity grows, general management is less and less able to keep abreast of the full breadth of technical knowledge which underlies the investment decisions.

Thus, as general management risks increasing amounts of money, its understanding of the nature and consequences of the investment is decreasing. As a result, it must rely more and more on the knowledge and advice of many different technologists whose work is usually far removed from contact with top management and who traditionally have not been treated as a part of management. Thus, top management decision making on some of the most important issues is increasingly becoming a group decision process.

Another element of complexity is found in changing decision-making technology which translates technological and other inputs into the profit consequence. During the early part of this century, as firms grew in size and complexity, a layer of management called 'staff also grew in both size and importance'. Originally the role of the staff was to handle decision preparation through gathering, sorting, analyzing, and reporting information needed in decisions. Staff's role was to provide inputs, but not to participate in decisions. Staff managers generally possessed no unique decision-making skills which were not possessed by line managers. They represented an extension of general management, a set of sensory organs, rather than a unique capability.

This situation changed rapidly in the second part of the last century. A new kind of staff came into the firm who have knowledge not possessed by general managers. These are the data processing specialists and the scientific problem solvers, known as management scientists. The data processing specialists control the information inputs into decisions, and management scientists affect the analysis of decision consequences by the models they choose. Thus, in return for better inputs and analysis, the general manager has to relinquish control of important parts of the decision process.

One possible consequence is general management abdication of control over decisions. Some writers, for example Galbraith (Galbraith 1968-G), argue that in large, complex firms such abdication is inevitable and that, in fact, it has taken place. If abdication is to be avoided, general management will have to adopt and perfect a skill exhibited by some great managers: an expertise in using experts. Attaining such expertise by developing knowledge and skills equal to those of the numerous experts is obviously out of the question. Even if a general manager did nothing but attend school all of his lifetime, he could not begin to approach the scope of the required knowledge. Hence, the answer must lie in developing skills in evaluating the contribution of an expert without being able to understand the contribution in detail. At present, the understanding of what these skills are, and how they are to be acquired, is imperfect.

And the task is formidable. Yet, below are some ways to develop an expertise in using experts:

1. Experienced managers who work with technologists and scientists, frequently calibrate the experts who work with them. They do this by keeping track of the outcomes predicted by the experts and learn to bias their predictions toward higher or lower expectations. They may even assign special tasks to experts with a major purpose of verifying the reliability of the experts' predictions. The desire to surround oneself with reliable experts is one of the reasons why a general manager who is transferred to a new assignment usually prefers to take with them a core team of people with whom he had worked in the past.

2. Development of a skill in cross-ideological communication is very helpful in dealing with experts. As discussed earlier, managers and experts have norms and aspirations which they bring to their work. Understanding of these norms and of their influence on the behavior of experts is helpful in evaluating the proposals. One example, commonly found in high technology industries, is the fact that engineers trained in designing military hardware acquire the habit of designing to very high reliability standards with little regard for the cost of the product. When assigned the task of designing an industrial product, they typically follow this habit which produces designs which are noncompetitive commercially. Courses for developing cross-ideological communication skills have been developed and used successfully.

3. Experienced managers confronted with major decisions will frequently use the advice of several experts and may engage them in a dialectic confrontation of opinions.

4. Managers who must habitually rely on experts should acquire sufficient knowledge about the respective fields of expertise in order to be able to judge whether the expert is using a method of analysis which is applicable to the real-world problem he is asked to solve.

The Trend Toward Multiple General Managers

Once the manager makes sure that he or she is adequately supported by staff experts, they must bring to bear their own line of expertise to making the decision and its effective implementation. In an earlier section, we have concluded that turbulent environments require a simultaneous presence of all of the six-archetypal knowledge, skills, and talents, and that the historical, single-archetype 'man of the moment' solution will not work.

It is interesting to note, that in the original version of this chapter, Ansoff predicted that this problem would arise in the 1980s. And it did. An article in *Business Week* entitled 'A manager for each strategy' reported that numerous firms have recognized a shortage of entrepreneurs.

One distinguished manager, Walter Wriston, previous Chairman of the Board and CEO of the Citicorp banking firm (1967–1984), remedied the deficiency by recruiting entrepreneurs from nonbanking industries. The General Electric Company went further. It diagnosed its future need for the three types of general manager: entrepreneur, growth manager, and conservator, and proceeded to develop programs to identify and train each class of managers, and to design different career paths for each. This recognition of different general manager archetypes is a break with tradition which had been pioneered in the 1940s by leaders like Ralph Cordiner, chairman and chief executive officer of the General Electric Company from 1958 to 1963. This tradition holds that while, on the one hand, a general manager possesses a special knowledge which is over and above the knowledge of the firm's functions, on the other hand, this knowledge is universally applicable for handling all challenges encountered by the firm. Indeed, the tradition goes further and asserts that general management knowledge is fully transferable among industries.

Our earlier prediction of the breakdown of the traditions comes from the recognition that the range of knowledge, skills, and talents embraced by the six archetypes is found only in exceptional geniuses, and that the repertoire of a majority of managers is limited to one or two archetypal roles.

After recounting the recognition of the needs for different general managers, *Business Week* also recorded the fact that several senior managers who were interviewed felt that the multimanager problem did not exist, and an all-round general manager of the past will remain adequate for the future. Thus, the issue has been joined but not yet resolved.

If, as Ansoff believed, the issue is resolved in favor of the multiple general managers, their development and employment will pose several problems:

- One problem is that most management schools which claim to be different from one another do, in fact, develop the archetype we called the planner (and General Electric calls the growth manager). Given the very slow historical response of management schools to the needs of business (Ansoff 1973b-E), it is safe to predict that the initial task of developing differentiated managers will fall on leading firms, such as Apple, Google, Amazon.
- The evolution of the multimanager will require development of selection techniques, differentiated career paths, and different reward/incentive systems for the respective archetypes.
- The historical preference of many large firms for promotion from within may give way to the already observable practice of bringing in at the top some of the archetypes (such as the statesman), which are not easily developed by upward progression within the firm.
- The concept of a single chief executive will further give way to the concept of the corporate office, and the concept of unity of authority/responsibility to the concept of shared authority/responsibility.

Summary

Management is a complex problem-solving process which can be described in terms of ten modules: observation of trends, setting objectives, perception of threats/opportunities, diagnosis, generation of alternatives, selection of alternatives, programming and budgeting, guiding implementation, and measuring performance.

Over the years management developed sub-cycles composed of several of the modules, each addressed to a particular turbulence level in the environment. The implementation sub-cycle is the simplest, followed by control, extrapolative planning and entrepreneurial planning.

Managing each sub-cycle requires a distinct combination of knowledge, skills, talents, and personality. We have labeled types of general manager who possess the respective combinations as manager *archetypes*.

During the first half century, environmental challenges were such that one archetype at a time was adequate to assure the firm's success. Thus, entrepreneurs were succeeded by growth managers and were later replaced by controllers.

The challenges of the second half century require two new archetypes: statesman and system architect, as well as the entrepreneur, who has pretty much disappeared from medium and large firms. The need for these archetypes is no longer sequential. A reasonably diversified firm requires all of them simultaneously.

As a result of problem complexity and increasing technological intensity, each archetype is increasingly dependent on special knowledge of a variety of experts. Furthermore, the total volume of general management work has increased substantially as a result of the multiplicity and complexity of challenges, on the one hand, and increased size of the firm on the other.

The problem is, how will the general manager of the last quarter of the twentieth century handle the full diversity of the challenges. The problem of work overload has led, in many instances, to a replacement of the single chief executive by a multi-senior executive corporate office. The reliance on experts can be made more effective by developing in the general manager an expertise in using experts. The demand for a wide range of skills and talents, which is seldom found in a single person, has started a trend toward specialization of general managers in one or more archetypal roles.

Exercises

1. Prepare an archetype identification chart, under the heading of six archetypes (see Table 15.2) list the following characteristics for each: (1) leadership style; (2) problem-solving skills; (3) education background ('knowledge base'); (4) talents; and (5) personality traits.
2. Which archetype combinations are most likely to be found in a single person?
3. What variables should be taken into account in deciding what archetypes of general managers should be developed in a firm? Prepare an archetype selection chart. Under the name of each archetype, list the conditions under which the archetype is necessary in a firm.
4. Your firm is very large and widely diversified, it has been decided to start a multi-general management development program. Your assignment is to design the program.
5. Should the firm try to develop each archetype separately or should archetype combinations (types) be sought? What are these combinations?

    a. How should each type of manager be selected?
    b. How should they be trained?
    c. How should they be promoted?
    d. How should they be rewarded?
    e. What will be the problems of cooperation among the types? How should they be solved?

Table 15.2 The changing work of general managers

Firm of 1900–1960	Firm of 1960–2020
Archetype requirement	
Leader	Custodian
Administrator	Controller
Planner	Planner
	Entrepreneur
	Statesman
	System architect
Sequential	Archetype needs
	> Simultaneous
Content of decisions	
Operating issues, corportate policies	+ Strategy formulation, design of systems for strategy implementation
Exploitation of firm's current position	+ Innovation in patterns of firm's products, markets, and technology
Economic, technological, national, intraindustry perspective	> Economic, social-political, technological, multinational, multi-industry perspective
Decision process	
Emphasis on historical experience, judgment, past programs for solving familiar problems	> Emphasis on anticipation, rational analysis, pervasivie use of specialist experts, techniques for coping with novel decision situations
Personnel-intensive process	+ Technology-intensive process
Information for decisions	
Formal information systems for internal performance history	+ Formal systems for anticipatory, external environment information
One-way, top-down, flow of information	> Interactive, two-way communication channels linking managers and other professionals with knowledge workers
Computer systems emphasizing volume and fast response information for general management	+ Computer systems emphasizing richness, flexibility, and accessibility of information for general management
Emphasis on periodic operations plans, capital and operating expenditures budgets	+ Emphasis on continuous planning covering operations, projects, systems resource development. Control based on cost benefit forecasts
Organizational design criteria	
Continuous emphasis on efficiency, productivity in utilizing current resources and organization. Periodic emphasis on innovation in product-market patterns, technology	> Simultaneous, continuous emphasis on efficiency, productivity, and innovation
Emphasis on economies of scale	+ Emphasis on flexibility, adaptive response
Emphasis on best assignment of task within given organizational structure	+ Emphasis on best design of ad hoc organization to perform a given task

16

Selecting a Management System to Fit the Firm

Previously, we traced the evolution of the basic general management systems and presented Ansoff's 'quick and dirty' approach to choosing a system for a particular firm. We also dealt with the problem-solving logic embodied in each of the systems. In this chapter, Ansoff's attention turns to tailoring the system to the needs of a firm.

Systems and Structure

This chapter is concerned with formal management systems which are explicit arrangements for guiding and controlling the work of complex goal-seeking organizations. Within the USA, the prime inventor and developer of management systems has been the business firm. These inventions have occurred in response to both the growing size and complexity of internal operations and the growing turbulence of the firm's environment.

Since the turn of the century, the challenges have become more numerous and complex, the scope of the relevant environment has expanded, and the rate of change has accelerated. From the simple strategy of 'giving it to them in any color so long as it is black,' expounded by Henry Ford, management tasks have expanded to include global diversification, mastering the 'R&D monster,' coping with external sociopolitical pressures, and responding to growing demands for redesign of the working environment within the firm.

Previous chapters traced the evolution of systems in response to these challenges. Leading firms invented the respective systems, and other firms

© The Author(s) 2019
H. I. Ansoff et al., *Implanting Strategic Management*,
https://doi.org/10.1007/978-3-319-99599-1_16

have followed by adopting these inventions. The result of this process is an accumulation of close to a hundred years' worth of management technology.

Since each generation of systems was designed to respond to immediate and pressing problems, the overall development appeared to lack logical continuity. Successive systems were usually advertised as inventions superior to and superseding all previous approaches. Thus, long range planning which claimed to replace budgeting was in turn replaced by profit planning, only to be succeeded by strategic planning. The latter was declared old-fashioned when PPBS (planning-programming-budgeting system) was introduced.

In the perspective of history, two facts are clear:

1. System development has followed a coherent logic dictated by the changing character of the challenges which confronted management.
2. The succeeding systems usually were not so much replacement as enlargements and enrichments of the preceding ones.

These facts permit us now to treat the accumulated systems know-how, not as a collection of unrelated problem solutions, but as a coherent body of design technology. Using this technology, we shall develop in this chapter a building block approach to tailoring the system to the needs of a particular firm. As the first step, we shall analyze the dynamics and the components of the principal types of system. Secondly, we shall identify common building blocks and, thirdly, use these blocks to develop a procedure for system choice.

Systems vs. Structure

As mentioned above, one primary stimulus to system development was the changing external challenges. A study of the evolution of American business firms shows that, in addition to the environmental pressures, there has always been a persistent, internally generated drive to do things better and more efficiently. The result of these two drives has been a continual flow of new approaches to doing managerial work.

The earliest systematic arrangement of the managerial work originated in the second half of the nineteenth century, when the shape of the modern firm was emerging. One of the first systems developed was *standing policies and procedures*, typically embodied in a manual which can still be found in all firms today. The manual contains rules for decision making (policies) and steps to be followed (procedures) for a wide variety of repetitive, predictable but contingent activities, ranging from regulation of hours of work, to leaves of absence, to conduct of union negotiations.

Another early development was a formal grouping of the firm's logistic and managerial activities which became known as the *organizational structure*. The first formal structure to receive almost universal application grouped 'like logistic activities' in ways which permitted maximum economies of scale and specialization. During the following sixty years, this structure, which emerged around 1910 under the name of *functional structure*, was followed by a rich proliferation of structural alternatives, such as divisional structure, multinational structure, matrix structure, and innovative structure.

All of these organizational forms share with the functional form several common features:

1. They specified the responsibility, authority, tasks, and relationships assigned to organizational subgroups.
2. A structure once put in place was supposed to be 'permanent,' not to be changed in the foreseeable future. A change typically came after it became painfully evident that the prior structure had outlived its usefulness.
3. For the duration of an organizational form, and except for periodic minor reorganizations, the roles, relationships, and responsibility/authority assignments were considered fixed and applying to all activities in which a particular unit was engaged.
4. In the organizational design, nothing is said about the dynamics of work to be done within it: the division and flow of the tasks.
5. Thus, we can characterize organizational forms of semipermanent and static arrangements for grouping the productive work of the firm and assigning managerial roles for guiding this work.

On the left-hand side of Fig. 16.1, the vertical dotted line sketches the evolution of organizational structures which will be discussed in detail in the next chapter. The figure shows that, as the firm became more complex, dynamic elements were added to the structural design such as personal planning, information systems planning, and facilities planning. These were early precursors of the need for a balanced managerial capability, culminating in the integrated *capability planning* concept of the 1970s.

On the right of Fig. 16.1 are systems for managerial problem solving. By contrast to the structure, these systems are dynamic because they specify the flows and the timing of the problem-solving work through the organizational structure. It is on the problem-solving dynamic systems that we focus

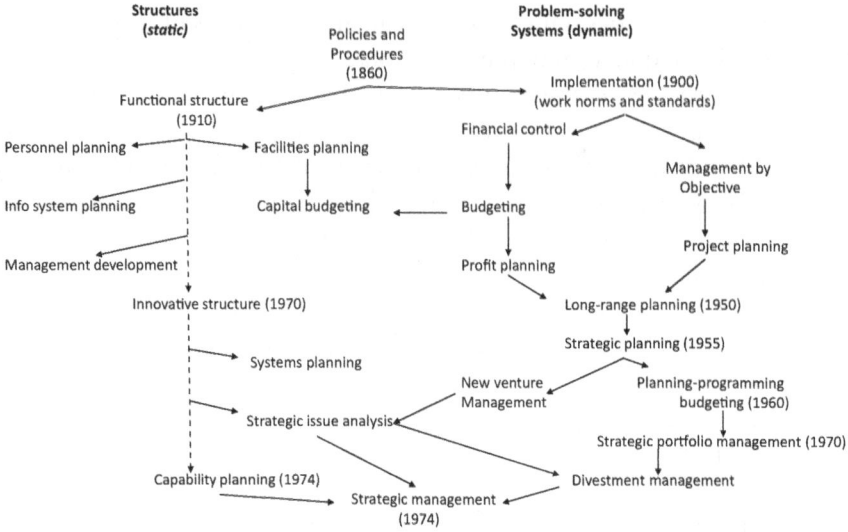

Fig. 16.1 Evolution of structure and systems

the rest of this chapter. We shall refer to them simply as *systems*. As shown in the right-hand side, systems are almost as old as structures and they, too, developed through trial and error.

Structure and systems can be seen as complementary arrangements for doing organizational work. One provides the static 'anatomy' of task assignment, and the other the dynamic 'physiology' by which the tasks are performed through competitive effort. Curiously enough, throughout the history of the firm, this close complementarity of systems and structure was rarely perceived. It is only recently that they became recognized as complementary components of the management capability vector.

Implementation Management

In this and the following two sections, we translate the language of Figs. 15.3, 15.4, and 15.5 into language useful in the design of systems.

A useful way to analyze systems is in terms of the contribution they make to the three-basic managerial sub-processes: planning, implementation, and control. Planning establishes purposes, guidelines, strategies, and constraints for the firm. Implementation is the process of causing the firm to behave in accordance with the purposes, guidelines, and strategies. Control evaluates the organization's performance and determines the needed adjustments in planning and implementation.

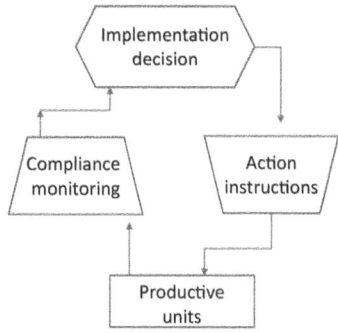

Fig. 16.2 Implementation management

In a firm whose throughput remains stable over longer periods of time (turbulence level 1), the implementation process shown in Fig. 16.2 is the dominant management activity. It is applied on the level of a department, a functional branch, such as marketing or production, or the entire firm. It consists of observation of how the unit has complied with previous instructions (*compliance monitoring*) and evaluating this information in terms of the need to issue further instructions (*implementation decision*). The box labeled 'action instructions' is a simple name for a complex management activity. It includes a twofold process of communicating to members of the unit the assigned tasks and—equally important—bringing about a willing acceptance of the instructions. This activity is one of the most difficult parts of the manager's job, entailing the intangible quality of leadership.

The implementation cycle depends on a personal assessment of progress, usually qualitative, made by the responsible managers. It may be adequate when the work of the units does not change over time, and all units are independent of one another.

Control Management

A control procedure, added to the implementation, is the next step in complexity of management. This is shown in Fig. 16.3 with the newly added steps indicated by the double-lined boxes. At this stage, the concept of *performance measurement* is introduced. To the previous qualitative assessment of how when the unit is applying itself to its tasks, control adds quantitative measurement and evaluation of what was accomplished. To facilitate this evaluation, historical experience is used to establish norms, quotas, and standards augmenting the personal judgments of the manager. The difference

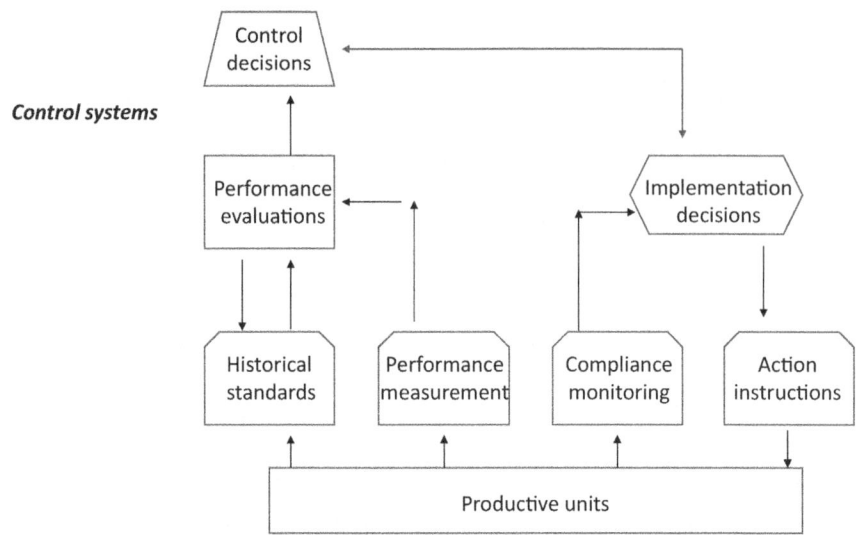

Fig. 16.3 Historical control management

between performance and the standards produces a *control signal*. A *control decision* is made and then translated into action instructions. Unlike in implementation management, which is qualitative, the action instructions in control management are both qualitative and quantitative. Furthermore, the quantitative record of performance also permits periodic revisions of the quotas and standards.

Thus, the control cycle augments rather than replacing the implementation cycle. Subjective judgment about the quality of performance and human attitudes in the latter is an important adjunct to quantitative measurements in the former.

This rather simple system was an important step in the evolution of formal management. It introduced objective measurement of performance, provided a tool for diagnosing and locating weaknesses, and a method for comparing the effectiveness of different units of the firm. Today, the historical control system is one of the indispensable (although, as we shall discuss below, obsolete) tools of management in large and complex firms.

The historical control system has obvious shortcomings. Since quotas and standards rest on experience, and since past performance is measured, control actions are geared to the history, rather than the future of the firm. Management by control thus inhibits aggressive, forward-looking exploitation of future opportunities.

Extrapolative Management

The next important development was the extrapolative management system shown in Fig. 16.4. The newly added boxes are indicated by the doubled outlines.

The fundamental difference between control and extrapolative management is that the former is based on historical experience, whereas the latter is based on extrapolation of the past into the future.

1. The first step is to use the historical trends as a basis for *environmental forecasts* of future trends in population, economy, technology, competition, and other factors. Using these *performance forecasts*, growth and profitability trends of the firm are prepared.
2. The second step is to compare the environmental and performance trends and to select goals for the firm. These are usually set above the performance trends in order to stimulate improvements on historical performance.
3. The third step is to convert the goals into coordinated *action programs* for various units of the firm. These programs specify schedules of actions, checkpoints, and milestones.
4. The action programs are then translated into *resource budgets* in terms of men, materials, money, and space needed to support the programs.

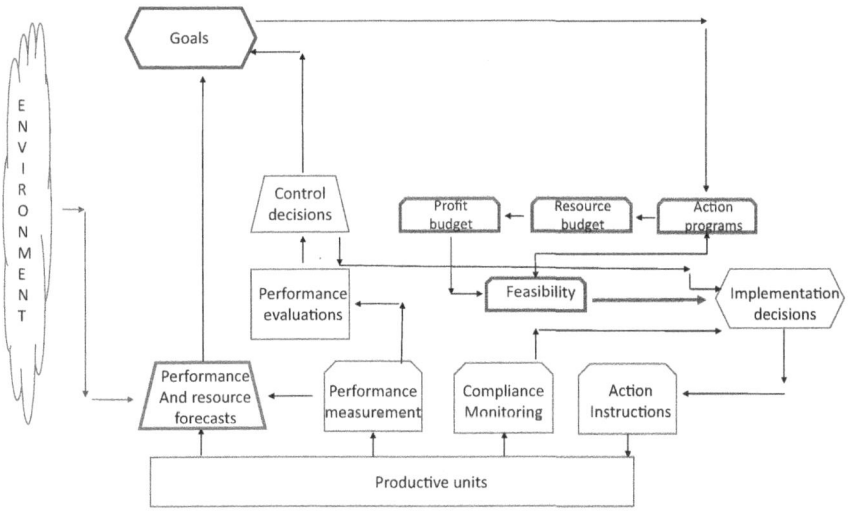

Fig. 16.4 Extrapolative management

5. The action programs and the resource budgets form the basis for *profit budgets*—measures of the net cost-effectiveness.
6. The final step in planning is to *check feasibility*—that is, to determine whether the projected results are satisfactory to the management and also whether the total resources needed by various units of the firm (money, borrowing power, executive talent) are available.

This simple-sounding set of activities turns out, in reality, to be difficult and complex. In part, this is because extrapolative management requires acquisition of a great deal of new information, development of new measurement techniques, and of scheduling and evaluation procedures. Moreover, extrapolative management requires active participation and support of all levels of management and supervision. To be effective, 1 it requires up, down, and lateral coordination, as well as leadership and support, from top management. But, most importantly, it requires a shift of the firm's mentality from an emphasis on the past to anticipation of the future.

As the figure also shows, programs and budget must be implemented and controlled. But both of these functions can now become forward-looking, based on what is to be done in the future and not on the results of the past. In *forward control*, emphasis shifts from deviations from the historical performance to measurement of the remaining difference between accomplishments to date and the goals which must be met by the end of the planning period. Correspondingly, implementation shifts from correcting historical errors to actions directed at meeting future goals.

As the figure shows, the control decision now has two possible options: (1) to correct performance or (2) to modify the goals if performance evaluation shows that the previously established goals are no longer realistic.

Figure 16.4 shows a popularly used extrapolative management system called long range planning (LRP). For reasons which will become apparent, we shall refer to the management system shown in Fig. 16.4 as *coherent long-range planning*. Several other extrapolative management systems have evolved and have been used in practice. Among these are the following:

- *Long-term budgeting.* This system does not make performance forecasts nor does it set performance goals. Instead, it periodically budgets resources allocated to the principal established activities of the firm. A flow diagram of the budgeting system can be obtained from Fig. 16.4 by deleting the environment, performance forecasting, goals, action programs, and profit budget boxes.

- We shall refer to an early version of long-term planning (LTP) as *anomalous long-range planning*. In this approach to planning, while the goals, programs, and budgets are focused on the future, the control system remains historic. In terms of Fig. 16.4, this means that the 'control decision' box is not connected to the 'goals' box.
- Another variant of the extrapolative management system, which we shall call *innovative long-range planning*, was invented in firms which were engaged in intensive product development activities and found that the historical approach of partitioning the firm's innovative process among the functional units of the firm was ineffective. As a result, such firms created project management units responsible for the innovative process.

In innovative long-term planning, two parallel extrapolative management activities are used. One set of activities is used for the operations of the firm's functional units, and the other for innovative activities executed by the project units.

If market demand remains structurally unchanged, if the firm's technology is long-lived, and if competitive structure and dynamics are stable, extrapolative management is the appropriate technique for managing the firm's future (on level 3 turbulence). However, if the firm faces saturation or decline of demand, or basic changes in the structure of its markets, or technological breakthroughs, or significant changes in the social/political environment, extrapolative management becomes not only an ineffective, but even a dangerous basis for managing. In response to these dangers, firms in the 1960s developed a more complex type of system which we shall call *entrepreneurial management*.

Entrepreneurial Management

In entrepreneurial management, a complex outer loop, shown in Fig. 16.5, is added.

First, extrapolative projections of the firm's present product/market position are replaced by non-extrapolative analysis of environmental trends and of probable threats and opportunities.

The trend and threat/opportunity analysis are combined into an estimate of the future prospects which will be available to the firm in the manner which was discussed in previous sections.

The analysis involves studies of: economic and social forces which determine demand for the firm's products; the nature of the competitive forces

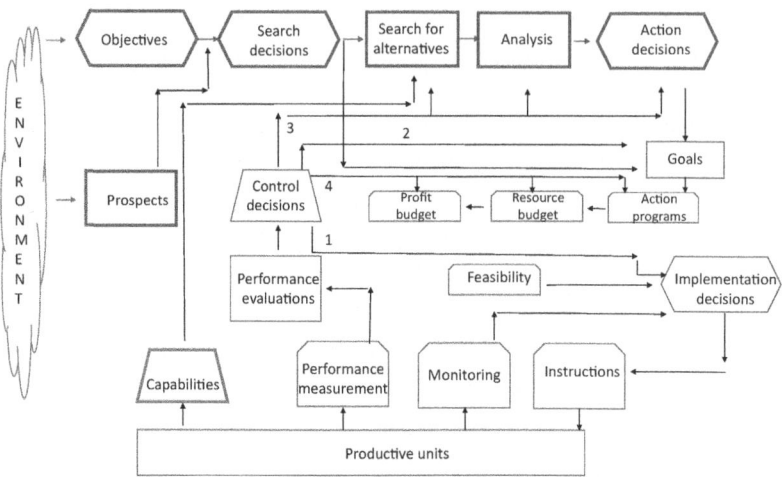

Fig. 16.5 Entrepreneurial management (project management, strategic planning, strategic posture planning, issue management)

which operate in its markets; and prospects for political and social changes which will affect the company and its environment. In technology-intensive industries, analysis of technological prospects is of particular importance.

Another new activity is a *capability diagnosis* analysis, which determines the profile of the capabilities of the firm.

Redefinition of the objectives of the firm becomes a subject of major concern when the firm moves from extrapolative to entrepreneurial management.

In extrapolative management, the objectives (dimensions of performance by which the firm's success is judged) remain stable over time, and the planning process starts with goals (levels of performance sought for the respective objectives).

In entrepreneurial management, the prospect of turbulence, discontinuities, and changing power alignment among influential stakeholders in the firm all make it necessary to redefine the objectives to which the firm aspires. A typical result is to change the relative priorities of the historical profit/growth objectives and to add flexibility and societal objectives.

- The strategic gap between the objectives and the prospects is determined in the box labeled 'search decision'. If the gap is acceptable to management, the next step is to set the goals which the firm will pursue for each of the objectives (see the box labeled 'goals').

- If the gap is unacceptable, the next step is to start a search for new strategic alternatives. As discussed in Part II, this may involve search for new competitive postures, or new SBAs or both.

As was discussed in Part II, the present capabilities of the firm are one of the important factors which direct the search.

- The *action decisions* dictate the shape of the new portfolio and appropriate competitive postures.

The prospects of the new portfolio are evaluated, new goals are set, and budgeting/implementation follows.

As Fig. 16.5 shows, under entrepreneurial management, the control function has four important options: (1) to correct performance, (2) to require a change in goals, (3) to require a re-examination of strategy, and (4) to require reprogramming of operations. These respective options are indicated by numbers 1–4 near the lines leaving the control box. Thus, in entrepreneurial management, control becomes not only forward but also strategic. Entrepreneurial management adds an outer strategic analysis loop to the extrapolative planning system. Its output is a set of new goals which are now based on analysis and not on extrapolation as before. These goals will be of two kinds: operating goals for near-term profit making and strategic goals for strategic development of the firm.

System Building Blocks

As shown in the captions of Figs. 16.3, 16.4, and 16.5, the control, extrapolative, and entrepreneurial management systems are basic types of systems. Each represents a family of systems shown in the caption of the respective figures. Within each type, the specific systems share a distinctive perception of the future environment of the firm.

- The control type assumes that the environment will change incrementally and slowly enough to leave sufficient time for after the fact response.
- The extrapolative type assumes that the future will be an extrapolation of the past that the change will be incremental, but too fast to permit after the fact reaction.
- The entrepreneurial type assumes that future events will be discontinuous from the past.

The figures show that, although different in intent, the systems are built of building blocks which perform identical functions in each system. These blocks are:

- Information input.
- Implementation (a combination of implementation decision and action instructions).
- Control (control decision plus performance evaluation).
- Budgeting (profit and resource budget).
- Programming.
- Planning (objectives, goals, search decision, search for alternatives, analysis, action decision).

*Choosing the System for the Firm

The left-hand column in Table 16.1 shows ten distinct management systems. All but one (surprise management) can be found today in business practice. As discussed previously, control, budgeting, anomalous, coherent long-range planning, and innovative long-range planning are widespread, and quasi-strategic planning, strategic planning, and strategic management are less widespread, but their use has been growing during the past ten years. Issue management is now receiving increasing attention, particularly in the USA, EU, and Asia.

Listed across the top of Table 16.1 are the six system building blocks which were identified in the preceding section. The entries describe the characteristics of each building block which are found in the respective systems. The first step in selecting the future system for a particular firm is to identify its present system.

With the exception of the anomalous long-range planning, all of the systems shown in the figure are balanced, which means that the building blocks match and support one another. In the anomalous long-range planning, planning is extrapolative but control is historical.

In practice, it may turn out that the firm's present system is unbalanced. This will become evident if the diagnosis does not fit into a single line or fits in the commonly observed line 3. Other observable examples of imbalance are strategic planning systems which lack a fully developed environmental surveillance input, or informal issue management systems which lack a decision-making structure.

Table 16.1 Typology of practical systems

System	Information	Implementation	Control	Budgeting	Programming	Decision-making
1. Control	Historical	Units	Historical	–	–	Corrective action
2. Budgeting	Extrapolative	Units	Historical	Short term	Milestones	Goals
3. Anomalous LRP	Extrapolative	Units	Historical	Long term	Programs	Goals
4. Coherent LRP	Extrapolative	Units	Forward	Long term	Programs	Goals
5. Innovative LRP	Extrapolative	+Projects	Forward	+Project budgets	+Project plans	+Projects
6. Quasi strategic planning	Environmental surveillance	+Projects	Forward	+Issue budgeting	+Project plans	+Issues
7. Strategic planning	+SBA prospects	+Projects	+Strategic	+Strategic budget	+Project plans	+Objectives +Strategies
8. Strategic management	+Internal surveillance	Change management	+Strategic	+Strategic budget	+Project plans	+Capabilities
9. Issue management	Singular events	Projects	+Strategic	Issues	+Project plans	Issues
10. Surprise management	Historical	Projects	+Strategic	Projects	Project plans	Damage repair

Shown across the top of Table 16.2 are conditions which determine the type of system needed by the firm. The first two columns describe the characteristics of the environment, and the second two the contributions the system makes to management of the firm.

The second step in selecting the system for a firm is to identify the line in Table 16.2 which will best respond to the needs of the firm during the next five to seven years. This is done by identifying the turbulence and environment conditions (in columns 2 and 3) which best describe the firm's future

Table 16.2 Choice of systems

System	Turbulence level	Environment	Problems solved	Contribution to management
1. Control	1	Repetitive	Complexity of work	Control of deviations
2. Budgeting	2	Expanding	Long lead times	Resource allocation
3. Anomalous LRP 4. Coherent LRP	3	Fast expanding	Rapid growth	Coordination of growth, management of profitability
5. Innovative LRP	3.5	Technological fertility competitive turbulence	Incremental adaptations	Management of incremental innovations
6. Quasi strategic planning	3.5	Fast expanding predictable discontinuities	+Response to discontinuities	+Management of turbulence
7. Strategic planning	4	Mixed dis-continuous prospects	Strategic positioning	Management of strategic innovation Strategic coherence Strategic allocation of resources
8. Strategic management	4.5	Novel dis-continuous prospects	+Capability development	Management of discontinu-ous strategic change
9. Issue management	4.5	Partially predictable surprising events	Avoidance of surprises	Management of partially predictable change
10. Surprise management	5	Surprises	Recovery from surprises	Orderly response to crisis

environment. A reader who has performed the turbulence diagnosis will have already performed this identification.

As Table 16.1 shows, systems 1–8 are progressively complex approaches to comprehensive management of the firm's future. Systems 9 and 10 complement the preceding ones in responding to singular events. Therefore, the firm's choice may include one of the lines from 1 to 8, plus 9, and/or 10.

Further, as you may recall from prior chapters, the firm may choose different management systems for different parts of the firm.

*Quick Readiness Diagnosis

As discussed in detail previously, the management system, even if it is responsive to the firm's needs, will be ineffective if other components of capability do not support it. Therefore, the choice of the preferred management system must be accompanied by a diagnosis of the state of readiness of the capability components. This may be a comprehensive strategic diagnosis or, as a minimum, by the quick readiness diagnosis shown in Table 16.3.

The scale from 0 to 10 on the right-hand side of the figure is a measure of progress toward the capability profile which must be in place if the new management system, selected in the preceding sections of this chapter, is to be fully effective.

Table 16.3 System readiness diagnosis

A value of 10 denotes a component which is ready to respond to the future needs of the firm. Zero denotes a state of the component which has nothing to contribute to the ultimate need. For example, a mark of O for the information base (item 5 in Table 16.3) means that no start has been made toward defining the information system which will be needed to support the new management system.

The left-hand profile shown by the crooked line in the figure illustrates the readiness of the present capability profile. This is in comparison with the straight line of all 10s, indicating that all components are fully ready to support the preferred future management system.

As the strategic diagnosis illustrates, the quick readiness diagnosis identifies the gaps between the present and the desired state of the management capability. The difference between the two procedures is that one is an elaborate, in-depth analysis, and the other is a 'quick and dirty' check on the state of the respective capability components, based on summary judgments and carried out by the managers responsible.

Roles and Responsibilities in Design and Use of Systems

During the era of long range planning, the principal functions of the planner were: (1) to provide forecasts; (2) to design and to install the system; (3) to monitor its operations; and (4) to coordinate and to integrate plans prepared by working managers. Thus, the working manager planned while the staff planner supervised the planning process.

Today, although process management has become even more important, the higher forms of planning demand a substantially expanded contribution from the planner.

As a result, planning and control staffs have been expanding in size, scope of responsibilities, and the range of competence and skills. Table 16.4 presents an up-to-date listing of the planning work required in a sophisticated strategic planning system.

This broad scope of activities suggests that it is no longer helpful to characterize 'the planner' in the singular, since there is more planning work than an individual can handle. Also, the new range of work requires a variety of knowledge and skills rarely found in a single individual. The traditional systems designer-expediter is still needed, but also required are the entrepreneurially minded new venture analyst, the analytic diagnostician-controller, a skilled forecaster-analyst, the computer model builder, and a skillful capability planner.

Table 16.4 Functions of a planning and control staff

Capability development	Decision analysis	Process control	Performance control	New venture management
Design of organizational structure	Environmental surveillance	Coordination of planning	Measurement of performance	Identification of opportunities
Design of planning systems and procedures	Forecasting threats and opportunities	Integration of plans	Diagnosis of deficiency	Analysis of opportunities
Management development modelling	Capability analysis	Evaluation of planning systems	Generate corrective actions	Acquisition and development of opportunities
Revision of planning systems Implementation of planning support systems Introduction of planning systems	Generation of alternatives Analysis of alternatives	Evaluation of plans	Analyze corrective actions Monitor corrective actions	

There is an important distinction to be made between these staff activities of the planning workers and the result-producing responsibilities of line managers. The responsibilities of the latter, as found in practice, are the following, to:

1. Assure that the management system is appropriate to the needs of the firm.
2. Assure that planning is integrated with implementation and control.
3. Make the necessary decisions and commitments in the course of the planning process.
4. Guide and control the implementation.
5. Assure that the firm attains the results specified in the plans.

Organizational Flow of Planning

In the early days, it seemed that the advent of formal planning would lead to the centralization of decision power. Early systems designers visualized that, eventually, all important planning decisions would be made in the corporate office, with the aid of high-speed computers.

Very quickly, this solution proved unworkable in practice. When centralized planning was attempted, the planning process became separated from the realities of day-to-day action; plans were neglected and disregarded by managers responsible for carrying them out; planning became largely an academic exercise. A *decentralized planning* concept emerged which directs that plans should be prepared by individuals responsible for executing them. Because this produced better results, it has been adopted in general practice.

Application of this principle makes it necessary to match systems decision points to the implementation responsibility points. But another problem arose: In what direction should planning flow? From the top of the firm down, or from the bottom up?

Since the entrepreneurial and social decisions are the higher-level decisions within which programming and budgeting must take place, the flow must start with strategic guidance from the top. But global guidance must be tailored by strategic inputs from the SBUs. As a result, the flow of planning in an effective system is neither top-down nor bottom-up. Instead, it combines the two flows and permits a constructive interaction between integrating guidelines from the top and entrepreneurial initiatives from below.

A new dimension of complexity is added in a multinational structure where divisions are typically replaced by product groups, and a new structural dimension of countries is added (see the next chapter). The directional flows of planning can be modified easily enough to add the country dimension, but the location of the strategic decision responsibility becomes unclear: Both countries and product groups have responsibility as well as important inputs to the strategic process. At the present time, three approaches to resolving the responsibility problem are found in practice:

1. The product groups are designated strategic business units (SBUs) and made responsible for strategic decisions; the countries contribute and consult.
2. Strategic plans are arrived at through shared authority/responsibility.
3. SBU responsibility is assigned according to the relative size and importance of the country market. When the latter becomes large enough to justify a separate product-line strategy, the SBU responsibility is shifted to the country.

The Human Dimensions of Systems

Early applications of strategic planning ran into resistance to planning both from line and staff managers. As systems became more sophisticated, the resistance to planning persisted.

The early solution for overcoming resistance to planning, offered in the literature, was to secure enthusiastic support from top management. Given the high degree of technological sophistication in modern planning, this is a strangely naive prescription: 'if managers do not plan willingly, threaten them with the displeasure of the big boss and tell them that he loves planning.'

An understanding of the causes of the resistance and more sophisticated ways of coping with it are now available. This understanding recognizes the profound social, psychological, and political ramifications of new systems which bring about a basic change in the way the firm perceives the environment, conducts its business, and distributes power among managers. Subsequent sections explore the origin of resistance to change and what can be done about reducing and managing it.

Contemporary and Future Trends

Given the history of and the rapidly changing challenges to the firm, it is certain that management systems will undergo major changes in the future. Several of the basic trends are already visible, as outlined below.

Tailored systems. In the past, a majority of firms put new systems in place when the preceding system no longer responded to the needs of management. Firms typically 'bought' a 'standard' system offered by one of the consulting firms or described in literature.

Today, the state of knowledge is at a point where it is possible to anticipate the future system needs and to tailor the system to the needs of the firm. Indeed, firms can anticipate their needs, tailor the system to them, and further develop plans for evolution of their systems over time.

Multi-systems. Most firms today find themselves operating in several environments which need different systemic responses. As a result, the presently monolithic concept of the single system for the entire firm is already giving way to a multi-system concept. Different parts of the firm will be encouraged to develop systems which meet their needs, but to design them to be compatible in a manner which permits consolidation and comparison at the corporate level.

Corporate capability perspective. Increasingly, as the strategic management perspective gains acceptance, management systems will be integrated into the overall concept of corporate capability. In particular, the intimate relationship between structure and systems will become recognized, and a combined dynamic-static concept of what we might call *strystems* will develop.

Planner vs. capability manager. The integrated capability perspective will lead to a closer relationship and cooperation among corporate staff functions (information, management development, organizational design, corporate planning, accounting, etc.). In the development of this relationship, the planner will be a strong contender for the 'chief of staff' role, responsible for harmonizing development of the corporate capability.

Sociopolitical perspective. Until recently, all systems were focused on the economic-technological-competitive behavior of the firm. Concern with sociopolitical variables is already evident in internal *social audits* and external *scenarios.* This concern will grow in three directions:

1. Adaptation of the systems to the new sociopolitical realities of worker participation within the firm and growing influence of external constituencies, such as consumer groups.
2. Broadening of strategy formulation, programming, and budgeting to take account of the sociopolitical variables which impact on the profit-making ability of the firm.
3. Enlarging systems to include systematic management of the firm's social responsibility and of concerns with the firm's 'legitimacy.'

Treatment of uncertainty and unpredictability. It is a curious fact that the prospects analysis in advanced systems has become increasingly *divergent*, seeking to capture the uncertainties and the differences among the possible futures (e.g. scenario analysis), while the decision processes have remained *convergent*, seeking to select the single course of action which the firm should follow. This has been particularly evident in the currently popular technique of portfolio analysis. In the future, increasing attention will be paid to matching the flexibility of the strategy to the uncertainty and unpredictability of the prospects. Earlier, we introduced a method of preserving a clear view of the future uncertainties in strategic portfolio analysis. This will lead to the concepts of *adaptive strategy*, greater emphasis on *flexible progressive commitment*, and increased use of *strategic control.*

Real-time systems. Until recently, all of the decision systems were periodic, operated usually on an annual planning cycle. In subsequent sections, we shall be discussing a new family of system designs which respond to challenges as they are perceived.

Flexible systems. Both flexible progressive commitment and real-time responsiveness of the firm depend on its flexibility. It is interesting to observe that, for reasons which were valid at the time, the design philosophy of systems, as well as of logistic facilities, was focused on single-purpose, low-cost designs. The current flexibility evolution, which is taking place on the shop floor, will spread to management. Management capability, including systems, will progressively become more flexible.

Summary

There are two organization-wide formal arrangements for organizing and directing management work: static structures, which assign tasks, authority, and responsibilities, and dynamic systems which prescribe the flow and the manner in which the tasks are to be performed.

During the twentieth century, three archetypal systems evolved: *Control*, which guides the firm on the basis of the historical performance, the *extrapolative* system, which is forward-looking and based on the assumption that the future can *be* predicted through extrapolation, and the *entrepreneurial* system, which expects the future to be discontinuous and surprising.

Each of the systems is made up of six building blocks: information, implementation, control, budgeting, programming, and planning decision.

These blocks are used in this chapter to describe ten practical systems, one for the control archetype, four for the extrapolative, and five for the entrepreneurial. Each system is uniquely suited to a particular environment and to particular needs of management. The system needed by the firm can be chosen by diagnosing the environment and the problems of the firm's management.

The evolution of increasingly complex systems has correspondingly broadened the demands on the planning staff which progressively became responsible for designing the systems, providing decision analysis and control data to line management, and participating in new venture identification and analysis.

The early arguments about centralization vs. decentralization and top-down vs. bottom-up flow of planning have been resolved through experience in favor of making implementers also responsible for planning and in favor of two-way flow of planning. When a substantial change in the management system is contemplated, it is advisable to perform a readiness diagnosis and arrange transition to the new system in a way which minimizes resistance and guarantees its acceptance by the organization.

Management systems are still in a process of evolution. Already visible are the trends toward tailored systems, several different systems within a firm, fusion of systems and structure into a concept of 'strystems,' emergence of the planner as the 'chief of staff' for capability development, broadening of systems to capture the sociopolitical perspective, emergence of adaptive and flexible strategies, and of real-time systems.

Exercises

1. The discussion in this book is focused on systems for the business firm. Which, if any, of the systems in Table 16.1 are applicable to: (1) hospitals, (2) churches, (3) universities, (4) the Congress of the USA, and (5) the White House? What additional characteristics should the systems possess to be useful in the respective institutions?
2. What problems and what resistance would be encountered in introducing the systems in exercise 1? What can and should be done to gain acceptance for the systems?
3. Under 'corporate capability perspective,' the concept of strystems is introduced. Define a system and construct an example. What advantages are offered by the concept of strystems?
4. What should be the future role of the corporate planner? What should be his responsibilities? What qualifications should he bring to his job?
5. Using an organization familiar to you, or a case assigned by your tutor, use Table 16.1 and to diagnose the present management system and to select the system which will be needed by the firm in the future.
6. Specify the changes which will need to be made in the present system. Who should be responsible for making them?

- Using Table 16.3, perform a system readiness diagnosis on the organization used in exercise 5.
- What changes should be made in the firm? Who should be responsible for them?

17

Designing the Firm's Structure

An extensive body of literature exists on the subject of organizational behavior and design. Most of it is theoretical, written in academic jargon. This chapter uses the language of business and focuses on organizational forms which have evolved in practice.

This chapter is an updated version of a paper which Richard Brandenburg and Igor Ansoff originally published in 1969. Ansoff noted that the original paper involved 'much hard work, argument, confrontation, and learning.' It must have had a significant impact on Ansoff. In the second edition of Implanting Strategic Management, Ansoff took the opportunity to thank Brandenburg for the contributions he made to his personal development and, in fact, to his career.

Evolution of Structure

In this chapter, we shift attention from the process by which management works to the shape of the firm, commonly called its *organizational structure*. As discussed in the previous chapter, the structure, like the systems, evolved in response to challenges.

As is shown across the top of the figure, two major stimuli to the evolution of structure were the growth of environmental complexity and the progressive accumulation of the critical success factors. In the 1900s, firms succeeded by minimizing the production costs, but in the 1980s, they also

© The Author(s) 2019
H. I. Ansoff et al., *Implanting Strategic Management*,
https://doi.org/10.1007/978-3-319-99599-1_17

need to be responsive marketers, skillful strategists aware of the sociopolitical environment and responsive to frequent shifts in major challenges.

The left-hand column of Table 17.1 shows that structure also had to respond to the evolving internal complexity of the firm. Part of the complexity developed in response to the changing external challenges. For example, deceleration of growth and arrival of maturity in the firms' historical SBAs forced them to diversify to multi-products and multi-markets. But much of the complexity was also self-created by entrepreneurial managers who continually sought to increase the size of the firm and to diversify it into a variety of businesses and countries.

Except for the last structure shown in the figure, the adaptive system, the names of the respective structural forms which evolved in response to challenges are now standard in management vocabulary. Each form is built on a different principle of grouping the managerial and the logistic activities of the firm. Thus, the functional structure is built on the principle of 'putting like things together.' The multinational (a form of matrix structure) is built on the principle of three-way balance: between responsiveness to local markets and competition, synergy among products and technologies, and efficiency of production.

Until recently, organizational forms were static and monolithic. A single organizing principle was applied to all parts of the firm, and once introduced, a new structure was expected to remain unchanged for a long time.

Table 17.1 Evolution of corporate structure

Time	1900	1930	1950	1980	2015
Environmental Challenges ⟶	Satisfaction of basic demand Acceleration of growth	Response to customer preferences Deceleration of growth	Internationalization Technology proliferation Saturation of growth	Global competition Stagflation limits on growth Socio-political pressures	Nationalization Technology Inflation Trade wars Socio-political pressures
Critical success factor	Low costs	Influence on customer	Innovation, diversification	Socio-political awareness, flexibility	Socio-political awareness, flexibility
Strategic complexity of the firm					
Single product line	Functional				
Multiproduct, multimarkets		Decentralized ⟶ Divisional division			
Multicountry, multiculture			International ⟶ Multinational division matrix ⟶		
Frequent and intensive strategic change		Project matrix ⟶		Dual structure ⟶	
Multi-life-cycle				Multistructure ⟶	
Response slower than speed of change				Adaptive 'strystem' ⟶	

In the late 1940s, an increasing rate of innovation gave birth to the first dynamic structure (project matrix).

In the late 1950s, the increasing rate of strategic activity gave rise to the dual structure in which the strategic (entrepreneurial and innovation) work is done through strategic substructure (based on SBUs) which is different from the substructure used for the operating (marketing and production) work.

The current high complexity of many firms has already given rise to the multi-structure in which distinctive clusters of the firm's SBAs are served by different structural configurations. Thus, one large Swedish multinational has three substructures: a multinational, a divisional, and a conglomerate.

As discussed before, although structure and systems are the complementary anatomy and physiology of the firm, until recently their respective evolutions proceeded in an uncoordinated manner. In times of low environmental turbulence, structural adaptation was usually the first response to new challenges. This has led to a common American saying 'when in doubt, reorganize.' New systems emerged later, after it became evident that the old systems worked poorly within the new structure.

As environmental turbulence grew, the order began to reverse. In previous chapters, we have argued that the appropriate choice in response to the new strategic challenge is not 'either structure or system.' All of the capability components are vital, and structure is only one of the contributors to organizational responsiveness. Therefore, in order to determine the contribution of structure, it is first necessary to understand the dimensions of responsiveness needed by a firm and then determine their implications for structure.

Organizational Responsiveness

In previous sections, we introduced the concept of responsiveness of capability which measures the ability of a firm's organization to respond effectively to a given level of environmental turbulence. We also defined the concept of capability, identified the components of the capability, and presented a method for choosing the types of component (one of them being organizational structure) which are appropriate for different levels of turbulence.

In this chapter, we focus on organizational structure and on the building blocks which make up a particular type of structure. Our further concern is with the way in which the building blocks fit together to produce a structure. For this purpose, we need another way of describing responsiveness of capability. We shall use the term *organizational responsiveness* which as the way a firm handles change. Organizational responsiveness is here described by the type of activity which either the total organization or a block supports effectively.

Four primary types of responsiveness, each of which serves a distinct goal of the firm, are:

1. *Operating responsiveness* which minimizes the operating cost of the firm.
2. *Competitive responsiveness* which optimizes the firm's profits.
3. *Innovative responsiveness* which develops the firm's near-term profit potential.
4. *Entrepreneurial responsiveness* which develops the firm's long-term profit potential.

For example, one of the organizational building blocks is the production function. The activities which it may be called upon to support may be minimization of production costs or balancing cost against responsiveness to market needs. At the level of the total organization, the behaviors which it may be called upon to support range from operating, to competitive, to innovative, to entrepreneurial.

As an example of the way building blocks relate to overall organizational behavior the reader will recall our earlier discussion of the effect that cost minimization by the production function has as a key to effective operating behavior.

In addition to the four types of responsiveness listed above, we will also examine the firm's *administrative responsiveness* which is its capability to support in an effective and timely manner the four environment-engaging behaviors.

For future diagnostic needs, we describe the characteristics which are observed in firms which are strong in the respective types of responsiveness. Table 17.2 shows that the goal of operating responsiveness is minimization of the costs of the firm's products. This is accomplished primarily through efficient production and supported by the minimal necessary marketing, R&D, and management. The underlying organizational structure is based on specialization of work, division of labor, and economies of scale, enunci ated in the eighteenth century by Adam Smith, elaborated in the twentieth century by Frederick Taylor, and converted to a huge practical success by Henry Ford.

In the modern and more complex firm, this principle is moderated by a compromise between economies of scale gained by geographic concentration and advantages of low local costs gained by dispersion of facilities.

Table 17.2 Operating and competitive responsiveness

Responsiveness goal	Operating (O) minimum cost	Rating	Competitive (O) optimal profit	Rating
Production activities	Cost minimization Division of work Economies of scale Automation Match of capacity to demand Other:		Compromise between cost and: Response to fluctuations in demand Timely response Standby capacity Timely delivery Other:	
	Average rating		**Average rating**	
Marketing activities	Sales aggressiveness Response to price competition Sales analysis Other:		Compromise between market responsiveness and cost minimization Response to/creation of needs Promotion/advertising Market research Sales aggressiveness Other:	
	Average rating		**Average rating**	
R&D activities	Product cost reduction Process improvement Product reliability Other:		Product cosmetics Sales support Cost reduction Reliability Other:	
	Average rating		**Average rating**	
Management activities	Minimal general management Maximal decentralization Specific roles Budgeting Financial control Control of change Rewards for low cost		Profit centers General management balances marketing vs. production Flexible roles Long range planning Management information systems Rewards for profitability	
	Average rating		**Average rating**	

Experience has shown that operating responsiveness is maximized when operations are standardized, the overheads are minimal, decisions are decentralized to the lowest possible level, and the size of management is kept at a minimum. This has become known as the *maximal decentralization principle*.

As the right-hand side of Table 17.2 shows, *competitive responsiveness* seeks to optimize the firm's near-term profitability. This is attained through cooperation between production and marketing and fast response to variations in demand and in competitive conditions. Many of the decisions are of an inter-functional nature and must be made rapidly, and the lines of communication between the logistic and management work must be short.

The purpose of decentralization is now to provide quick responsiveness to the markets, as well as maximal efficiency. This means a different pattern of decentralization than in the case of operating responsiveness. While functional decisions remain maximally decentralized, decisions on price setting, production levels product development, etc., are now raised to the general management levels. Corporate management involvement typically remains minimal, because it is too far removed from contact with market realities. The firm is subdivided into independent fully integrated organizational units (divisions), each with its own general management and each operating in distinct markets. Thus, economies of scale of unified production are sacrificed in favor of the need for quick and sensitive reaction to environmental fluctuations.

Operating and competitive responsiveness assure the profitability of the firm's present products in its present markets. By contrast, Table 17.3 describes two activities that develop the potential for future profitability of the firm.

The goal of the *innovation responsiveness* is to optimize the firm's development of new products and marketing strategies within the firm's SBAs. It supports what was termed the competitive positioning activity. The central function is research and development, but effective introduction of new products to the markets requires close cross-functional cooperation. The profit potential generating innovation work does not replace the operating profit-making work, but supplements it. As a result, the two types of work compete for time and attention from both management and the logistic functions.

Structural design consequences are the need to provide capacity dedicated to innovation work and to organizing capacity in a way which assures timely and effective multifunctional cooperation. Further, we shall discuss the typical solution which was developed by firms is a project management system.

Decentralization plays a distinct role in innovation responsiveness. Experience has shown that innovation responsiveness is highest when the project managers have the authority and the responsibility for the success of their projects, as well as a budget that enables them to buy the support needed from the functional areas.

Entrepreneurial responsiveness, described on the right-hand side of Table 17.3, assures the firm's long-term growth, profitability, and continuity through balancing the firm's SBA, SRA, and SIG portfolio. By comparison with innovation responsiveness, where the role of general management is to guide the natural dynamics of the firm's evolution, in entrepreneurial responsiveness general management must act as the creative brain of the firm.

When major concern with entrepreneurial effectiveness first surfaced at mid-century, an early solution was to locate the entrepreneurial work at the

Table 17.3 Innovation and entrepreneurial responsiveness

Responsiveness goal	Innovation (I) Near-term profit potential	Rating	Entrepreneurial (E) Long-term profit potential	Rating
Production activities	Speed of changeover to new products Other: Average rating		Speed of changeover to new technology Flexibility of facilities/equipment Flexibility of labor force Rapid response to discontinuities Other: Average rating	
Marketing activities	Anticipation of competitive trends New product introduction Anticipation of need trends Market expansion New product profitability analysis Other: Average rating		Anticipation o competitive discontinuities Novel product introduction Creative needs research Creative marketing concepts Other: Average rating	
R&D activities	New product development Anticipation of technological trends Timing of new products Profit-oriented product design Other: Average rating		Anticipation of technological discontinuities Creation of technologies and products Adaptation of novel technology Timing of creative products/Technology Other: Average rating	
Management activities	General management managers' innovation Project management system Rapid response to incremental changes Rewards for innovation Other: Average rating		Anticipation of turbulence General management managers' strategic portfolio SBU/SBA structure Managed diversification Strategic planning Capability planning Effective management of discontinuous change Timely response to turbulence Rewards for entrepreneurship Other: Average rating	
	Average rating			

corporate office and to assign to the middle and lower managers the task of guiding the day-to-day production and competitive activities. As a result of this perception, many firms limited strategic planning responsibilities to the corporate office.

Experience has shown that (with the exception of acquisitions and mergers) confining entrepreneurial concerns to the top levels of management is an ineffective and organizationally frustrating solution. Even the most brilliant entrepreneurial decisions will remain unimplemented unless they are connected, through the intermediate levels of management, to the logistic functions of the firm, which convert such decisions into new products, markets, new marketing activity, and new technologies.

Thus, experience showed that vertical connections between the 'brain' at the top of the firm and the 'body' of the logistic functions are vital if entrepreneurial activity is not to become a situation of 'paralysis by analysis.'

Thus, entrepreneurial responsiveness also needs to be decentralized. But in this case, the decentralization is not a process of pushing decisions as far down as possible, but rather a process of sharing of strategic responsibilities among several levels of general management. The maximal decentralization principle is replaced by the *principle of strategic visibility*: For each major strategic decision, authority/responsibility should be placed at the lowest level of the organization at which all of the variables relevant to this decision are visible.

The need for the 'brain-body' connection requires the involvement of significant numbers of managers throughout the managerial hierarchy and of workers in the functions. This has fundamental implications for structure. One of these, discussed in the preceding chapter, is the need for close inter-functional cooperation in the implementation of strategies. Another is the need for an adequate capacity for strategic work. A third is a need for capability for strategic work. Finally, strategic work must be protected from infringement of the day-to-day operating activities. All of these issues will be discussed in subsequent chapters.

In addition to the four primary types of organizational responsiveness discussed above, another type of responsiveness has become progressively more important to a firm's success during the second half of the twentieth century. This is *administrative responsiveness* which assures that:

- The firm's capability fully supports organizational behavior in one or more of the primary responsiveness modes which the firm is pursuing.
- The firm's capability is quickly adaptable to changes in the primary responsiveness modes.

In the past, when major administrative changes were infrequent and unplanned, they lagged behind the changes in the action types of responsiveness. As a result, when discontinuities occurred, there followed a significant period of time during which the administrative support was mismatched from the new behavior of the firm. Furthermore, since management attention *was* focused sequentially on one responsiveness at a time, the capability of the firm was single purpose, designed to support the dominant activity of the time. The structural consequences were that structures were single purpose and reactive, stable, and usually regarded as permanent.

Beginning in the mid-1990s, the administrative responsiveness required an anticipation of needs for new capabilities, rapid adaptation, and simultaneous accommodation within the firm of several distinctive types of capability. These characteristics are described in Table 17.4. As a result, structures must become anticipatory, dynamic, complex, flexible, and impermanent.

Fortunately, these demands on structure come at a time when new technologies make it possible to meet them. In particular, the emergence of computerized decision support systems makes possible flexible management structures which change to accommodate different types of decision process.

Table 17.4 Administrative responsiveness

Responsiveness	Administrative (A)	Rating
Goals	1. Effective support of O, C, I, E activity	
	2. Harmonious coexistance of O, C, I, E	
	3. Timely adaptation to O, C, I, E priorities and demands	
	Average rating	
Logistics (functional)	Capabilities match strategies	
	Rapid capability adaptation	
	Multipurpose capabilities	
	Capacity for innovation	
	Capacity for entrepreneurship	
	Capacities above critical mass	
	Other:	
	Average rating	
Management	Anticipation of capability needs	
	Anticipatory adaptation	
	Multipurpose capability	
	Capacity for innovation	
	Capacity for entrepreneurship	
	Capability adapts to turbulence	
	Responsiveness to discontinuities	
	Self-renewal capability	
	Other:	
	Average rating	

Earlier, we have suggested that this development will lead to an integration of systems and structure into 'strystems' which are comprehensive, flexible, and dynamic.

*Determining the Preferred Responsiveness

1. The first step in determining the preferred future responsiveness of the firm is to determine the profile of the present responsiveness. This should be done by evaluating the firm (using a scale from 5 to 0) on the respective characteristics. The ratings are averaged for each function.

   A rating of 5 means that the particular type of responsiveness maximizes its particular goal. A zero responsiveness denotes no contribution to the goal.

Thus, zero operating responsiveness denotes the highest cost producer in an industry, and a zero-competitive responsiveness denotes a chronically unsuccessful marketer.

   The overall average for each type of responsiveness should be entered into column 2 of Table 17.5.

2. The second step is to establish the desired priorities of the respective types of responsiveness as determined by the objectives of the firm.

The top lines of Figs. 3.3.2–3.3.4 show the objectives which are met by each type of responsiveness. These are transcribed in column 3 of Table 17.5. The next step is to enter in column 4 the firm's priorities for the respective objectives, using a scale of 10–0: 10 for the highest and 0 for objectives of no importance.

   It will be recalled that the flexibility objective means making the firm quickly responsive to novel threats and opportunities, while the diversity objective means diversifying the firm in a way which reduces its strategic vulnerability.

3. The third step is to determine the imperative responsiveness priorities required by the firm's environment.

During the first half century, when firms were in control of their environment, turbulence was low, predictability high, and the desired responsiveness and the preferred responsiveness would have been the same. But as firms lost

Table 17.5 Determining preferred responsiveness

Present		Desired		Imperative		Preferred	
Type of responsiveness (1)	Average responsiveness level (2)	Relevant objectives (3)	Firm's priorities (4)	Relevant turbulence category (5)	Priority weight (6)	Priority weight (7)	Responsiveness gap (8)
Operating		Near-term performance (minimize cost)		1–2			
Competitive		Near-term performance(optimal profit)		2–3			
Innovative		Near-term potential		3–4			
Entrepreneurial		Long-term potential		4–5			
Administrative		Adaptability		4–5			
Administrative		Capability match to responsiveness		1–5			

control, turbulence grew, and environment became unpredictable. The environment increasingly determined the characteristics of responsiveness which are essential for both success and survival. For example, the management of a firm may be focused on near-term profitability, but, if a significant proportion of the firm's profit comes from SBAs on turbulence levels 3 and above, the neglect of the longer-term perspective could jeopardize the firm's long-term survival. Therefore, responsible management cannot neglect building the responsiveness required by its high turbulence environments.

The relative importance of the respective types of responsiveness is determined by the following two factors:

(a) The percentage of the firm's profit which will depend on a particular type of responsiveness.
(b) The competitive intensity that the firm will encounter in making this profit.

The relative importance of the respective types of responsiveness can be determined through the following steps, with the aid of Table 17.6.

- Segment the firm's environment into SBAs.
- Diagnose the future turbulence level of each SBA.
- Group the SBAs into four turbulence level categories: 1–2, 2–3, 3–4, 4–5, and enter the names or numbers of the SBAs which belong in each category into column 2 of Table 17.6.
- Estimate the percentage of the total profits over the next seven to ten years expected from each SBA. (It is important not to neglect SBAs which are currently minor contributors, but which will become important in the long-term future.) Enter the profit percentages in column 3 of Table 17.6.
- For each SBA, estimate on a scale of 10–0 the level of competitive intensity expected during the following five to seven years. Enter the estimates in column 4 of Table 17.6.
- Multiply column 3 by column 4 to obtain the priority weight of the SBA; enter in column 5 of Table 17.6. Enter the priority weight for each category in column 6 of Table 17.5.
- Determine the imperative priority weight for diversity of the firm's capability by analyzing the spread of the other priority weights in column 6. If the spread is large, which means that most of the responsiveness types must be present in the firm, the priority weight for diversity should be close to 10. If one or two types of responsiveness cover or have dominant priority weights, the need for diversity should be low.

Table 17.6 Determining imperative responsiveness

Turbulence category (1)	SBA (2)	Percentage of profits (3)	Competitive intensity (4)	Priority weight (5)
1 - 2				
Total				
2 - 3				
Total				
3 - 4				
Total				
4 - 5				
Total				

- Select the larger priority rating of column 4 and column 6 and enter it in column 7 under preferred priority weight. The respective priority weights determine the priorities which should be assigned to developing the respective types of responsiveness listed in column 1 of Table 17.5.
- Subtract column 2 from the number 10 and enter the result in column 8 titled responsiveness gap. The respective gaps measure the relative amount of work which would be needed to build a responsiveness to the 100% level.

Patterns of Responsiveness

Table 17.7 shows the patterns which typically emerge from responsiveness analysis. Today, in a majority of firms, one type of responsiveness stands out as dominant. This is usually found in firms which grew to be large in a core business and then, either remained in this business or diversified into other fields.

The outcome of the preference analysis may indicate that the same type of responsiveness should remain dominant in the future. This will typically occur when the firm's objectives remain stable, when the SBA which contributes a majority of the firm's profits is expected to remain on the historical level of turbulence, and when competitive intensity in the minority SBAs is expected to remain low. In this case, *as* the figure shows, the indicated action is to reinforce the present pattern of capabilities by closing the respective gaps in the order of indicated priority.

Table 17.7 Patterns of responsiveness

Present	Preferred	Action
Dominant	– Same dominant	– Close responsiveness gap
	– Different dominant	– Redesign organization
	– Multiresponsiveness	– Build multiresponsiveness
		or
		– Contract firm's portfolio
Multiresponsiveness	– Dominant	– Redesign organization
	– Multiresponsiveness	– Close responsiveness gap

A frequent result in the environment of the 1980s was a shift from the historical level of turbulence in the key SBA of the firm. In such cases, responsiveness analysis produces a dominant preferred responsiveness which is different from the historical. Usually, the shift is from the historical operating or competitive responsiveness to innovative or entrepreneurial responsiveness. The indicated action is to shift the firm's capability to a profile which supports the new dominant responsiveness.

Another frequent result is a pattern of preferred responsiveness which no longer shows dominance. For example, all types of responsiveness have priority weights 5 or 4.

This will occur in cases when the firm is diversified to a point where several of its strategic business areas are expected to make comparable contributions to profits.

It will also occur whenever the competition in the SBAs which are minority profit contributors is expected to become very intense, which means that the firm cannot expect to remain profitable in these SBAs using the historical responsiveness pattern. In this case, the firm has two alternatives:

1. Build a multi-capability firm which can simultaneously accommodate different kinds of action responsiveness. This requires a high level of administrative flexibility and diversity.
2. The second alternative is to divest the firm from some of its SBAs in a way that reduces the range of responsiveness necessary for success. This alternative has been publicly espoused and pursued by a number of major firms.

The reader will recognize that the responsiveness analysis is an alternative and complementary method to the capability profile analysis. Just like the profile analysis, responsiveness analysis can be used to design each of the capability components. In the remaining sections of the chapter, we shall use the results of the responsiveness analysis for only one of the components, namely the organizational structure of the firm.

Dimensions of Organizational Design

Recall, early experience in creating workable organizational arrangements resulted in three functional groupings of the logistic work of the firm: production, marketing (originally called sales), and R&D. These follow the logical sequence of logistic work (creation—manufacturing—sales of products), and the capability of each function is distinct from the others. As we shall presently see, these functions became the basic building blocks in early organizational forms.

The next development came when innovation responsiveness became important, and it was discovered that the boundaries between the functions impeded the lateral interactions which are essential to rapid and effective innovation and change. In response, the concept of *project* was invented. Unlike the three functions which are permanent, projects are temporary, built around specific acts of innovation.

The functional building blocks acquired the name of *line Junctions* because they contribute directly to the profitability of the firm. As firms become large, the job of supplying common input requirements of the line functions was split off into *supporting staff functions*: personnel, purchasing, and accounting.

On the management side, the initial subdivision was between functional managers, charged with assuring the performance of their respective functions, and general managers, charged with assuring the overall performance or the organization. As firms became diversified and large, it became necessary to share general management responsibilities among a number of general managers. This was accomplished through the concept of the *profit center* in which a manager has complete profit and loss responsibility, full control of resources placed at their disposal, and authority to plan and conduct the profit center in a way which will optimize the objectives assigned to it.

The profit center concept was based on the *principle of unity of authority and responsibility*, which states that a manager's authority must be commensurate with his responsibility. In America, application of the principle has been shown, time and again, to produce superior performance.

The profit center was conceived during the first half century when innovative and entrepreneurial responsiveness were unimportant. Hence, the typical profit center responsibility was for near-term profitability (0 or C responsiveness), including the development and maintenance of the necessary capabilities.

When development of the future profitability potential became as important as near-term profit making, the concept of the profit center became vague. In some firms, the responsibility for innovation and entrepreneurship gravitated to other parts of management, and in some, it remained neglected precisely because the profit center responsibility remained, as before, confined to near-term profitability. Eventually, the ambiguity was resolved through the concept of the strategic business unit. An SBU can be described as a strategic profit center which is responsible for both near-term performance and for development of future potential.

In addition to the sharing of general management responsibilities, profit center managers had two other dimensions of responsibility:

1. On the dimension of responsiveness, some managers were assigned the responsibility for assuring profitable growth in the near term (a combination of operations and competitive responsiveness); others for assuring the long-term profit/growth potential (a combination of innovation and entrepreneurial responsiveness); and still others for development of the firm's capability (administrative responsiveness).
2. The second subdivision of responsibility was the performance of the principal steps of the managerial process: planning (decision making), implementation, and control.

Just as with logistic work, input-producing staff management responsibilities were separated from output-producing line management responsibilities. Among the management staff functions which appeared over the years are finance, organization planning, management development, management information systems, and corporate planning.

The organization building blocks discussed above are summarized in Table 17.8. Some of the items are asterisked to call attention to important recent developments.

The first of these was a transition of purchasing, in firms which found themselves resource constrained, from the status of a staff to a line function. This meant that from being a staff responder to the demands of the line functions, purchasing graduated to being a line contributor in determining what the demand for resources should be. In firms which are heavily dependent on scarce, expensive, or politically controlled resources, responsibility for strategic resources gravitated to the general management level.

The second and similar change occurred in the status of the finance function as a consequence of the high cost of borrowing, which in many cases exceeded the after-tax return which a firm could earn on borrowed money.

Under such circumstances, finance became a line function which provided a critical input to the strategic planning process of the firm.

The third change was a similar elevation of the traditional staff public relations to the line function of societal relations.

We shall next use the organizational building blocks to examine several organizational structures which have emerged in practice over the past one hundred and fifty years. It will be convenient to divide this examination into three parts:

1. We shall first deal with the different ways in which the building blocks have been put together.
2. Secondly, we shall examine different roles of corporate management.
3. Thirdly, we shall discuss the problems which have been encountered in defining the role of staff functions.

The Functional Form

The first modern organizational form evolved around the turn of this century in response to rapid growth and complexity of the firm. This *functional* form had received wide acceptance in industry and can still be found among smaller firms and in process industries.

The organizing principle was described by the management of the Du Pont Company which spoke of 'putting like activities together.' The functional form puts all production, marketing, research, and development activities under respective functional managers who report to a central

Table 17.8 Organizational building blocks

Logistics function		Key	
Line	**Staff**	A = Administrative	
Production distribution	Purchasing*	C = Competitive	
Marketing	Personnel	E = Entrepreneurial	
R&D	Accounting	I = Innovative	
Innovative/administrative projects	Data processing, etc.	O = Operating	
		* = Staff or line, depending on circumstances	

Manangement roles			
Line		**Staff**	
Line functional managers	General Mgrs	Logistic staff functional mgrs	Management staff managers
Profit center (O+C+)	Strategic development (I+E)	Public relations *	
SBU (O+C+I+E)	Operations (O+C)	Management development	
	Administration (A)	Finance	
	Strategic resources (A)	Organizational design	
	Societal relations (E)	Corporate planning	
		Management information system	
		Legal	
		Mergers/acquisitions, etc*	

headquarters. The headquarters is the only general management level of the firm, responsible for all decisions which involve functional interactions and interdependencies. In our terminology, this responsibility spans all of the types of responsiveness which the firm is called upon to exhibit. Thus, the headquarters is the one and only profit center.

The principal advantage of the functional form is its operating responsiveness which is attained through specialization of work according to the respective functions, economies of scale, overheads, and skills. So long as the firm remains single product, single market, and small, the functional form is also competitively responsive. The headquarters managers are in close touch with the market, lines of communication are short, and all of the decisions are about the unique product and market of the firm.

But competitive responsiveness drops off progressively as either the size of the firm, or the number of product-markets increases. Functional managers begin to encounter internal conflict of priorities among their respective product-markets. If synergies among the different products and markets are low, the advantages of scale and standardized skills are lost. When environmental fluctuations occur, functions come into conflict with one another, because each prefers to respond according to its distinctive perspective.

As a result, the workload on the headquarters grows, and its contact with the realities of the marketplace is diminished by the height of the management pyramid which intervenes between the headquarters and the logistic functions.

Innovative and entrepreneurial responsiveness are inherently poor in the functional form, because of their conflict with operating and competitive responsiveness. When general management is overloaded with decision workload, near-term profitability concerns preempt attention to the long-term development of the firm.

Similar priority conflicts occur and are similarly resolved within the functions. Recall, the problem is further aggravated by low downstream coupling among the functions. Lateral relations among them are not formalized, and each manager's responsibility (and rewards) for effective performance of his function comes in conflict with other functions.

As firms grew, and the environment moved from turbulence levels 1 and 2 toward 3 and 4, and as competitive and administrative responsiveness became increasingly important, progressive modifications were made in the functional form.

1. To handle the problems of overload, a *two-tier management* was introduced in the headquarters. The lower level was made responsible for day-to-day operations and the upper for long-term policy, which, in

our language, includes innovative, entrepreneurial, and administrative responsiveness.

2. Alleviation of the problem at the headquarters shifted *the* spotlight to the functional level. In response, *projects* were introduced. Innovation (such as new product development) or administrative projects (such as building a new headquarters) were organized by 'borrowing' resources from the respective functions for the duration of the project. Project managers were appointed, who typically had coordinating responsibility for assuring the progress of a project. In this staff role, the project managers reported to the chief operating manager at the headquarters.

3. In more recent times, firms which remained functionally organized and whose environment moved to levels 4–5 began to have difficulties with the entrepreneurial response. To solve this, SBA-based strategic planning was introduced in some firms to enhance the entrepreneurial responsiveness. While all of the above modifications helped, operating responsiveness remains the basic strength of the functional form, while the other types of responsiveness remained marginal. This is illustrated where the respective increments of responsiveness are rated on a scale 5–0.

It is for the reason of limited range of responsiveness that, around the 1920s, many firms moved to a different type of organizational structure. But in industries in which the economies of scale and specialization remained a critical success variable, the functional form, with its various modifications, is still used.

Functional form, together with all of the above modifications, is illustrated in the form of an organigram in Fig. 17.1. The letters E, A, etc., inside boxes identify responsibility for the respective types of responsiveness.

The Divisional Form

Among the firms which pioneered the second basic organizational form in the 1920s were Du Pont and General Motors. The form received relatively slow acceptance prior to World War II but spread rapidly after the war to a majority of large- and medium-sized corporations.

This divisional form evolved in response to the shortcomings of the functional form discussed above. For example, both General Motors and DuPont had grown and become diversified both in their products and in their markets. In the case of Du Pont, diversification had created a heterogeneous product which firmly put limits on realizable advantages of scale and at

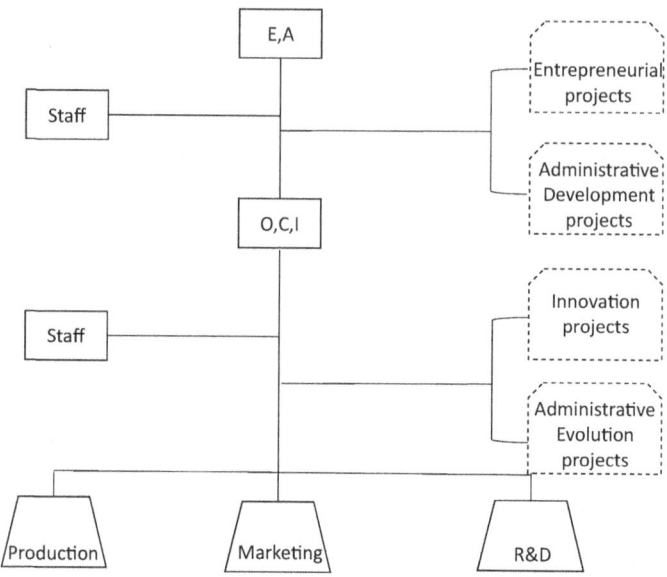

Fig. 17.1 Fully developed functional form

times produced negative synergy. Functional managers were making production, manufacturing, and development decisions over a range of distinctive products, many of which lay outside their competence; standard operating procedures, which were optimal for some products, were suboptimal for others. Under pressures of accelerated change, corporate managers were juggling decisions about a range of different business, while their total workload overloaded the corporate capacity and slowed down response.

The solution was to group the firm's activities according to the distinctive product markets and not according to functions. Each grouping, called a *division*, had its own functional capability. Thus, within the firm, there were as many marketing, production, and R&D departments as there were divisions. In fact, at first glance, the divisionalized firm appears as nothing more than an assemblage of a number of functional forms.

The distinctive feature of the divisional form comes from the respective roles played by the divisional managers and the headquarters.

Each division is a profit center, and its manager has a total authority/responsibility for assuring its performance. In the early days of the divisional form, this implied responsibility for the operating and competitive responsiveness. In theory, the headquarters kept the residual general management responsibilities: appointing and developing general managers, approving divisional budgets, controlling performance, allocating strategic resources, and obtaining external financing.

In frequent practice, when the corporate managers promoted themselves 'upstairs,' away from control of daily operations, they had difficulty in restraining themselves from meddling in the work of presumably autonomous division managers. As a result, physical distance of a division from corporate headquarters became a measure of how well the profit center concept worked in that division. This confusion of roles was further aggravated when changing environment made necessary greater innovative, entrepreneurial, and strategic responsiveness. We shall be exploring further the role of the corporate headquarters in the following section.

The multiplication of production, marketing, and R&D departments meant company-wide economies of scale were lost, and synergies minimized. The goal of minimal costs, inherent in operating responsiveness, was compromised in favor of increased competitive responsiveness which was made possible by elimination of conflicts and interference among different businesses, as well as the focus of the divisional managers on a single business. The responsiveness of the original 'pure' divisional form is rated. Over time, just like the functional form, the divisional form has undergone several significant modifications.

The loss of economies of scale was not taken lightly by the corporate managements, and they soon discovered that there were certain functions, such as purchasing or accounting, which were not vital to the effective functioning of a profit center, since they offered supporting inputs which had little importance on the divisional manager's profit optimizing decisions.

Thus, staff logistic functions were born and placed under control of the corporate office. The corporate office also tended to retain management staff functions, which either had no impact on the freedoms of divisional managers (such as public relations) or offered impartial advice (such as legal) to the divisional managers without infringing on their authority.

The theory of this solution was that staffs were responsive servants of the division managers. As we shall see presently, the practical reality was frequently different. Staffs developed a tendency to infringe on divisional authority. Thus, a first chink appeared in the principle of unity of authority and responsibility. We shall be discussing the role of staffs in a subsequent section.

The creation of corporate staffs offered some measure of economies of scale and helped enhance operating responsiveness. In some firms, in which economies of scale in production had an importance comparable to competitive responsiveness, a more drastic step was taken. The production activity was taken away from the divisions and consolidated into a profit center under a production general manager (usually a vice president).

In theory, just like the staffs, the production manager was supposed to be a responsive supplier of goods to the respective divisions which purchased from him. But the fact was that profit optimization behavior of manufacturing operations conflicted with optimal behaviors by marketing and R&D (e.g., production is optimized when manufacturing runs are long and products standardized, while marketing succeeds when production is responsive to frequent changes).

In an attempt to resolve this difficulty, the mechanism of *transfer pricing* was invented, under which manufacturing 'sold' its output to the divisions, and again in theory, the divisional managers were free to buy the products from the outside competitors. However, in practice, transfer pricing worked imperfectly because pressures from headquarters and loyalty to the firm made it very difficult for divisional managers to buy from outsiders, and the absence of the external market for the production output made transfer prices artificial and unrealistic.

As divisions became large, they encountered the problem which had also plagued the functional structure: the suppression of innovation by the operating activity. The solution, as in the functional form, was to add *project management* to the structure.

In some firms (particularly in the American aerospace industry) in which the innovation budget was a large percentage of the total budget, a separate profit center was developed which was named *project matrix substructure*. One dimension of the matrix is a pool of talent and facilities reserved for innovation work. The talent and skills for the innovation are drawn from this pool (and not from the divisions concerned with marketing and production) by projects which form the second dimension of the matrix. After the project is completed, the new product or market is transferred to the divisions for exploitation, the project is dissolved, and the resources are returned to the pool.

The project matrix substructure greatly enhances the innovation responsiveness of the firm because it protects innovation from conflict with operations and because it permits creation of highly specialized innovation capabilities within the profit center. But, like centralization of production, it creates lateral conflicts between the innovation profit center and the divisional and the production profit centers. The conflicts become particularly visible during the transfer of innovations to the exploitation activities.

In so-called R&D firms whose principal products are innovations or problem solving (e.g., consulting firms), or in firms whose economies of scale in production are insignificant, the project matrix structure can be highly effective as the basic organizational form. This means that the firm is subdivided into a capability group (frequently and confusingly called division) and a *project group.*

As firms diversified beyond national to international markets, a frequently used instrument was an *international division* charged with managing foreign activities.

So long as the international division remained a sales agent for the domestic products, it remained a marketing 'service' division and its objectives were in consonance with the domestic divisions. But, as the international division became concerned with responding to the unique demands of local markets and also began to establish foreign manufacturing and product development units, the international division manager came into conflict with the interests of the domestic division managers.

In the absence of a formal arrangement for shared authority/responsibility, this conflict could be avoided only through mutual and cooperative goodwill between the domestic and international operations. Typically, in tightly controlled American corporations in which each profit center is under pressure to optimize its own performance, the goodwill was difficult to maintain and conflict persisted. When foreign profits and sales became a significant part of the firm's total, firms began to turn to a new organizational form which we shall be discussing presently.

A recent structural development in the divisional structure has been the emergence of the *corporate office* as the top-level general management center of the firm. The emergence was triggered, on the one hand, by growing importance of strategic work at the corporate level and, on the other hand, by work overload on corporate management.

In the corporate office, the historically focal role of the chief executive, in which he personally makes all of the key corporate level decisions, is changed to a role in which he shares corporate level responsibility *and* authority with one or more managers, although he still retains a *primus inter pares* (first among equals) role in resolving conflicts which arise among the members of the office.

In the USA, where the principle of unity of authority and responsibility is strongly ingrained, the corporate office represents a further and important step away from the principle of unity of authority and responsibility. But in Europe, where the principle never acquired the same status, the corporate office sometimes appeared *as* an American reinvention of the long practiced *collegial management.*

The collegial, or corporate office, management is observable in two models. One of these, the *alter ego model*, makes the corporate office roles substitutable for one another. Thus, for example, the corporate office member who happens to be in town will make the decision about any matter which requires prompt corporate response. The other, *shared authority model*, assigns specific decision areas (e.g., for respective competitive, strategic, administrative, and societal responsiveness), to different members of the corporate office.

Collegial management is practiced effectively only in a minority of European enterprises. In many other enterprises, the top group is composed of powerful 'barons,' who use the political process to gain a favorable position for the part of the firm under their control. It can be argued that converting such politicized bodies into an effective corporate office is more difficult than instituting a corporate office in firms in which collegial management has not previously been practiced.

The growing need for strategic responsiveness produced another recent structural development. This was the evolution of the *dual structure* in which an strategic business unit (SBU) structure is added to the divisional structure. In the SEU substructure, certain managers, not necessarily the divisional managers, are made responsible for strategic development of clusters of coherent SBAs assigned to them. The dual structure presents an important departure from the historical practice under which there was only one permanent structure within the firm, through which all of the work of the firm was done. Under the dual structure, one structure is used for the profit-making activity of the firm and a different structure for the firm's strategic development.

Three alternative strategic roles are possible:

1. The manager becomes the strategic planner for his SBAs which makes him, in fact, an SBA and not SBU manager.
2. In a more powerful role, he has the resources, the budget, and the authority to carry strategic plans to the point of proven new products, new markets, new technology, and new capabilities, but he transfers the new profit potential to other managers who are responsible for realizing the profit.
3. Finally, if the SBU manager is also made responsible for profit making in his SBAs, he becomes a strategic profit center with a 'cradle to grave' responsibility for his SBAs.

The latter role suggests that a logical conclusion would not be to put in a dual structure but to reorganize the firm using the SBU as a unit.

This would mean regrouping the historical divisions of the firm according to coherent 'sub-portfolios' of SBAs and assigning strategic profit center responsibility to the SEU/divisional managers. This solution has considerable merit, provided the firm is not a multinational, and also provided that corporate economies of scale are not important to the firm's success.

To summarize, the original 'pure' divisional structure offered an effective response in SBAs on turbulence levels 2–3 in which competitive responsiveness is the key to success. Its essential difference from the functional form is that it decentralizes much of the general management responsibility to the divisional levels, thus putting general management in close touch with the marketplace.

As the need for innovation, entrepreneurial, and administrative responsiveness grew, a series of modifications was made to the pure divisional form. Each of these improved the overall responsiveness, but only at the cost of violating the time-hallowed principle of unity of authority and responsibility and creating potential conflicts among the different profit centers.

The Matrix Form

By the time the divisional form underwent all of the modifications described above, it also changed its character. The original basic form was strongly wedded to the principle of unity of authority and responsibility. By the time the sixth modification was introduced, authority and responsibility became so subdivided that the success of a profit center manager was determined to a substantial extent by variables controlled by other managers.

In recognition of this basic difference, the fully elaborated divisional form is given the distinctive name of *domestic matrix form*.

As the matrix form evolved, the inherent contradictions in managing profit centers whose managers do not have full control over their own performance frequently remained unrecognized. The corporate managers (particularly in the USA) continued to put pressure on each profit center manager to optimize his own performance and, at the same time, exhorted him to cooperate with other profit center managers, whose performance could only be optimized at his expense. For example, if the production profit center transfers its output to the marketing divisions at cost, its profit will be zero, while the marketing division's profit will be greatly enhanced. As a result, the new conflicts inherent in each new stage of modifications of the basic divisional form remained unresolved. In many firms which adopted the matrix form, the malfunctions due to conflicts were frequent enough to give it a bad reputation. As a result, some of these firms began to move back to simpler structures, and articles appeared which criticized the matrix form as impractical.

The preceding discussion suggests a different conclusion:

- Indeed, the matrix form should not be considered unless the firm needs the complex pattern of responsiveness which it makes possible.
- This pattern is potentially very impressive, with a high level of performance on all types of responsiveness.
- This potential is not likely to be realized unless corporate management takes the steps necessary to resolve conflicts and avoid dysfunctions caused by the split authority/responsibility inherent in the matrix structure.
- Two complementary approaches can be taken to avoid the dysfunctions:

  (a) Corporate management should recognize the unavoidable reality of the inter-profit center conflicts, anticipate their occurrence, and act to resolve them before the conflicts flare up.
  (b) A shared authority/responsibility substructure should be introduced alongside the matrix structure.

Table 17.9 shows two versions of the matrix structure: the domestic and the multinational. In the latter, the marketing profit centers (divisions) of the domestic form are replaced by the country profit centers. The multinational matrix structure became attractive when the diversity and importance of foreign operations reached a point at which the international division could no longer handle the full complexity from a domestic location. The role and the responsibilities of the country profit center are a good deal more complex than those of a domestic marketing division for the following reasons:

1. Each country organization operates in a distinct economic, political, and cultural environment, which creates distinct critical success factors to which the products and marketing strategies of the firm must be responsive.
2. Each country manager typically markets the entire product-technology scope of the firm.
3. Differences in the degree of market penetration result in different business approaches to the country market: Some country markets are offered standard products of the firm, some products have tailored features, and some are developed specifically for the local markets.

Table 17.9 Support by basic forms of different behaviors

Basic form	Modifications	Behaviors				
		Operating	Competitive	Innovative	Entrepreneurial	Administrative
Functional	1. Basic form	5	2	1	1	1
	2. Two-tier corporate management	4	2	1	2	2
	3. Project management**	4	3	3	2	2
	4. SBA-based planning	4	4	3	3	2
Divisional	1. Basic form	2	5	3	2	2
	2. Corporate staffs	3	5	3	2	3
	3. Centralized production	4	4	3	2	3
	4. Project matrix	4	4	4	2	4
	5. Corporate office	4	4	4	3	4
Domestic matrix	6. Dual structure	4	4	4	4	4
International matrix	7. Country profit centers	4	4	4	4	4
Multistructure	1. Holding	*	*	*	2	1
	2. Conglomerate	*	*	*	3	2
	3. Integrated	5	5	5	5	5

*Depends on structures of subsidiaries

**The ratings of each modification assumes that all the preceding modifications have been made

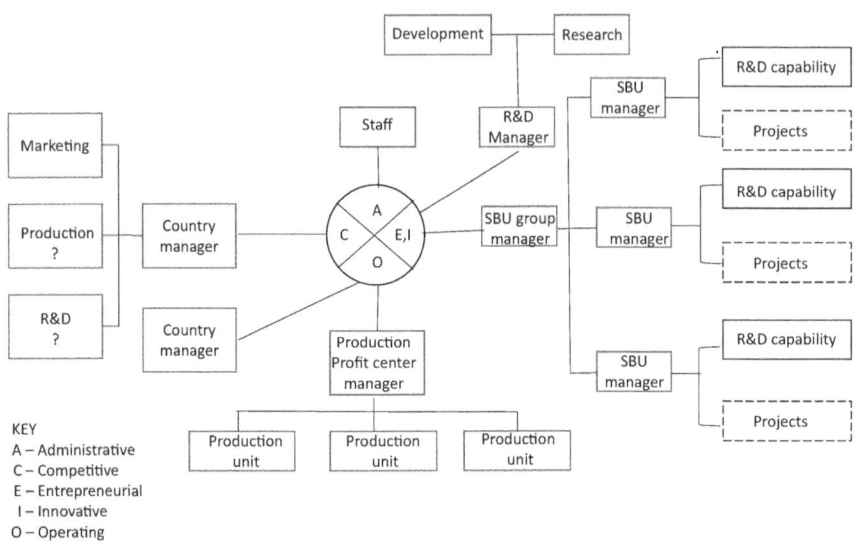

Fig. 17.2 Multinational matrix

4. A country manager is responsible for the performance of production units located in his country, but these units frequently produce for global consumption.

Figure 17.2 presents, in a somewhat unusual form, an organigram of the international matrix in which the question marks illustrate different roles which may be played by the country organizations. The modern SBU profit center is shown as the source of the firm's entrepreneurial and innovative responsiveness. Today, in many multinationals, the entrepreneurial responsibility is confined to the headquarters, and innovation is handled by separate product-technology centers.

The Multi-structure

The common feature of the fifteen organizational forms discussed in the preceding pages is that they are all *unistructural* in the sense that the same organizing principle applies to all parts of the firm. Broader unistructural firms are also typically uni-capability firms, which means that they use a single reward system, single planning system, share the same culture, etc. But, since the beginning of the modern firm, there have been multi-structure firms, made of units whose structures were not forced into a single mode. An ancient multi-structure is the *holding company* which owns shareholding positions in a number of firms and exercises no direct control over the way the subsidiaries are structured.

A more recent multi-structure, the *conglomerate*, emerged in the USA during the 1950s. A conglomerate typically consists of a number of subsidiaries wholly owned by the parent. The parent headquarters exercises financial control over the subsidiaries and offers assistance to the subsidiaries. It does not control the subsidiaries' strategies nor their structures. And neither, with two exceptions, does it insist on commonalities of capability except those necessary to enable the parent to consolidate and control the overall financial performance. These exceptions are common accounting and budgeting systems.

There is now a visible trend toward a multi-structure in firms in which the corporate management retains an active role in managing both strategic and operating performance but allows its groups, divisions, or profit centers to choose the structural form which is most responsive to their needs.

It is safe to predict that the multi-structural approach will be used increasingly in the future. This is for two reasons. First, the diversity of the firm and the competitive pressures of the environment will make it increasingly necessary to optimize the structure for each SBA of the firm. The second reason is that the job of managing a complex multi-structure from the headquarters will be made much easier by modern information technology.

The Role of the Headquarters

As was evident from the preceding discussion, the role of the corporate headquarters evolved alongside the evolution of organizational forms. As can be seen from the second column, there are at least twelve complementary roles which can be found at the headquarters. Of these roles, 2, 4, 7, and 10 are focused on control of the various dimensions of the firm's performances. Roles 1, 5, and 8 involve the corporate office in planning the overall future of the firm. In the remaining roles, 3, 6, 9, 11, and 12, the corporate office not only plans but also implements what it plans.

In these latter roles, the corporate 'staffs' (such as finance and administration) perform a vital 'line' function.

Table 17.10 gives further substance to the argument—which was made in this book on several previous occasions—that in a modern firm it is both

Table 17.10 Roles of corporate headquarters

Responsiveness	Roles	Applicable organizational forms
Financial	1. Investment in subsidiaries/ divisions	Holding, all other forms,
	2. Control of financial performance	Conglomerate, all other forms
	3. External financing	All forms
Operating (O+C)	4. Control of divisional profitability	Divisional, matrix
	5. Corporate profit optimization	Functional, divisional, matrix
Strategic (E+I)	6. Acquisitions, mergers, venture management	All forms
	7. Control of bottom-up management	Divisional, matrix
	8. Strategic portfolio management	Divisional, matrix, functional
	9. Societal response	All forms
Administrative	10. Accounting/rewards/senior management development	Conglomerate, divisional, matrix
	11. Corporate capability	Divisional, matrix
	12. Functional capability	Functional

meaningless and dangerous to build the top management on the maximal decentralization principle. Indeed, if the corporate headquarters is to be limited to controlling the firm's performance, a minimal size at the top will suffice. As planning and implementation roles are added, it becomes necessary to add the competence and capacity required to do the job.

The assumption of the roles by the headquarters is determined by two factors:

1. The preference by the top management for a loosely managed as opposed to a coherently managed firm. This choice is between the holding or conglomerate forms on the one side, and the functional, divisional matrix on the other.

2. The types of responsiveness required for success in the future environment. The corporate role profiles which are found in each of the organizational forms. The column labeled 'decentralized divisional' represents the original basis form of Table 17.9. As the entries in the column indicate, the decentralized divisional firm originally swung the production from one extreme to another: from the highly centralized role of the headquarters to the minimal control functions. As discussed in the preceding pages, over the years, the headquarters progressively assumed additional roles (Table 17.11).

Table 17.11 Corporate headquarters' role profiles for different organizational forms

Organizational form / Responsiveness	Holding	Conglomerate	Functional	Decentralized	Divisional	Matrix
Financial	1,3	1,2,3	1,2,3	1,2,3	1,2,3	1,2,3
Operating	–	–	5	4	4,5	4,5
Strategic	6	6,9*	6,8,9*	7	6,8,9	6,8,9
Administrative	–	10	10,11,12	10	10,11	10,11

* Typically only in response to external pressures

3.3.7 Staffs and Overhead Functions

In the preceding pages, we discussed two key aspects of organizational design: the choice of the organizational form and of the appropriate general management roles. A third key aspect is the incorporation into the firm of what, in American business language, are interchangeably called staff or overhead functions.

Probably, the earliest overhead activity to be institutionalized within the firm was accounting because it was essential both for measuring the performance of a firm and for assessing its financial health. This was quickly followed by creation of staff departments for maintenance, purchasing, personnel, legal, public relations, finance, etc.

All of these activities had two features in common: They provided essential inputs and support for the logistic and the management line functions, but their contribution per unit of the firm's production was very difficult to measure. This was partly due to the lack of measurement, and partly, because they typically have a critical mass, the overhead staff functions could not be expanded and contracted as readily as the direct labor costs incurred in the line functions. This made staffs difficult to control and manage, particularly because when left uncontrolled, they exhibited a Parkinsonian tendency to grow out of proportion to the needs of the firm.

This led, in the early part of this century, to the emergence of a control tool called the *minimal staff principle*. The principle states that the firm will be most profitable when the respective staff functions are reduced to an absolute minimum. In the USA, a yardstick called indirect (staff) to direct (line) personnel ratio became a standard tool for measuring organizational efficiency.

But, over time, staffs continued to proliferate. Most of the proliferation occurred in firms in which line management, beset with the growing diversity, complexity, novelty, and decision workload, increasingly required assistance for information gathering, preprocessing of decisions, expert advice, and development and maintenance of the increasingly complex administrative infrastructure of the firm. Among the new staff departments were: organizational planning, data processing, management information systems, management development, budgeting, financial planning, operations research, corporate planning, management system design, environmental surveillance, and forecasting.

In retrospect, it is now clear that the growth in the staff contributions had been related to the need for new types of organizational responsiveness. Without any attempt at comprehensiveness, Table 17.12 illustrates the cumulative staff inputs which became necessary as the responsiveness of the firm increased.

As the necessary staff inputs increased, the minimal staff principle progressively lost both its meaning and usefulness. It is true that, left uncontrolled and unmeasured, staffs (like other organizational units) exhibit a Parkinsonian tendency to become bloated out of proportion to the firm's needs. They also exhibit a tendency to pursue the goals and values of their respective professions *more* than the goals of the firm. But an arbitrary minimization of the indirect to the direct ratio is likely to 'cut off the nose to spite the face.' As the necessary staffs grow, firms will increasingly need methods for determining the size, type, and composition of staffs which, while avoiding the Parkinsonian tendencies, are needed to support line management. The technology for designing the *optimal staffs*, which will replace the minimal principle, is still in the developmental stages.

As staffs proliferate, a new approach is also needed to curb their historical tendency to exceed their intende roles.

The original conception of the role of the staff was to provide impartial inputs which in no way infringed on the prerogatives of line management. In practice, though, staffs exhibit several tendencies to infringe on these prerogatives, as follows:

1. Corporate staffs, charged with providing services to the lower levels of management, tend to present their advice, not as a neutral input, but as a compulsory 'corporate policy.'
2. Staffs charged with decision analysis in support of corporate management tend to use their private expertise and complexity of the analysis to obscure the issues and to bias the decision alternatives presented to the management.
3. Staffs charged with designing and operating the corporate structure and systems tend to design them to serve the needs of the corporate management and to neglect the needs of the other levels of management. This tendency has frequently been observed in corporate planning, with the

Table 17.12 Staff contributions to management

Type of behavior / Type of contribution	Information input	Decision analysis	Administrative design and operation
Operations	– Costs – Investments	– Work study – Financial performance – Capital investment	– Accounting system
Competitive	– Forecasts – Competitive behavior	– Sales analysis – Competition analysis – Operations analysis	– Organizational structure – Long-range planning – Management information system – Forecasting
Innovation	– Product market opportunities	– Market research – Technology assessment – R&D payoff	– Management development – R&D project management
Entrepreneurial	– Economic/tech-nological/social/political trends and discontinuities	– Competitive strategy – SBA portfolio – Capability design – Socio-political impact	– Strategic postur planning – Issue management – Strategic management – Crisis management – Environmental surveillance

result that planning is perceived as a form filling process for the benefit of the headquarters, and not as analysis which helps each manager to improve his own performance.

As staffs proliferated, and as dependence on their expertise increased, some observers were led to conclude that line management in large firms had become captives of their 'technocracies.' While it is a visible exaggeration to claim this for all firms, this phenomenon is observable, particularly in large firms in mature industries.

The solution to this problem is not clear at this point. Certainly, an important step is a clearer definition of the roles of staffs that is found in most situations. Beyond this, some observers have suggested that the line/staff distinction is obsolete, and that a rethinking and redefinition of the roles in the management process is in order. Other observers suggest that line management has to develop a new 'expertise in managing experts' and that it must devote increasing attention to management of the staff work in the manner similar to managing line operations.

Whatever the solution, it is clear today that the staffs and overhead functions will become an increasingly important factor in the success of the firm. In management, effective design of the automated office is becoming more important than its operating costs. Increasingly, complex decisions will be dependent on staff expertise and on decision models designed and operated by staffs.

Thus, as firms progressively become knowledge-, technology-, and capital-intensive, the historically labor-intensive, 'direct' functions are being replaced by 'indirect' functions as the keys to the firm's success.

*Redesigning the Structure

In the preceding pages, we have developed categories, concepts, and relationships which make it possible to diagnose the adequacy of the present structure for meeting the challenges of tomorrow and to determine the changes that need to be made.

In spite of the efforts to explore the complexities of organizational structure, the description in this chapter still falls short of illuminating the many nuances and complexities found in business firms. Therefore, the procedure presented below should be used with the understanding that it will produce a first approximation which will raise issues and questions about the firm's structural needs and require further detailed analysis.

The logic of the process is shown in Fig. 17.3.

1. Diagnose the present, the desired, the imperative, and the preferred responsiveness.
2. Determine whether the firm will need a unistructure or a multi-structure. If the future profit contribution is distributed among the different types of responsiveness, and if each type has a high preferred priority weight, consideration should be given to using a multi-structure.
3. Compare the preferred priorities of Table 17.5, with the ratings in Table 17.9 to determine the preferred form (or forms).
4. Using Table 17.9, diagnose the present form, and, comparing the preferred and the present forms, determine the changes in the form which should be made.
5. Using Figs. 3.3.12 and 3.3.13, identify the preferred corporate role profile(s).
6. Using the same tables, diagnose the present role profile and through comparison with the preferred profile, determine the changes in the profile.
7. Using Table 17.12, repeat the preceding two steps to determine the changes in the staff support.

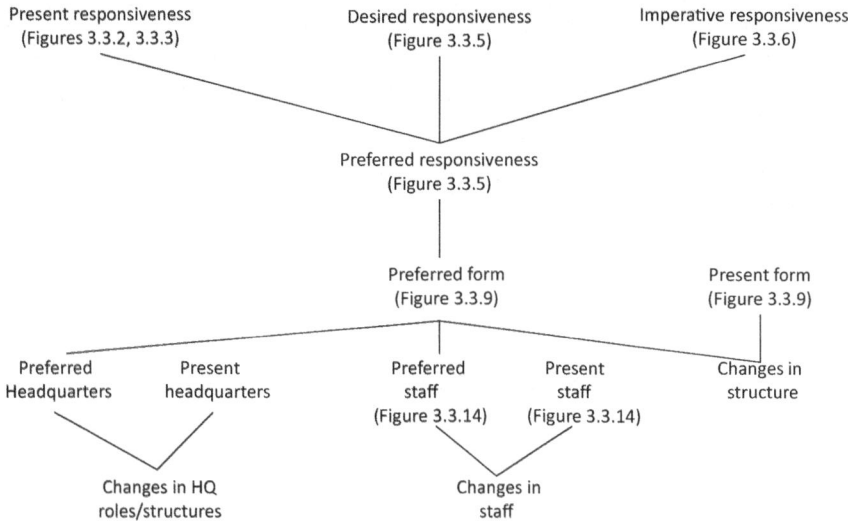

Fig. 17.3 Redesigning the structure

Summary

Structure is the arrangement of tasks, roles, authority, and responsibility through which a firm does its work. Throughout the history of the firm, structure evolved in response to the dual challenges of external diversity of the firm's strategic position and internal complexity of the firm. The progress has been from stable monolithic structures to dynamic multifaceted ones.

The purpose of structure is to support the firm's behavior. Therefore, the distinct types of behavior (responsiveness) in which the firm seeks to engage can be used to identify the structure it needs.

The types of responsiveness are: operating, competitive, innovative, entrepreneurial, and administrative.

In the history of the firm, four basic forms have evolved to date. These are listed below together with the primary dimension of their responsiveness:

Functional—operating responsiveness
Divisional—competitive responsiveness
Project matrix—innovative responsiveness
International matrix—strategic responsiveness
Multi-structure—responsiveness to different needs in different SBAs.

The relative importance of the different types of responsiveness to a firm can be determined, on the one hand, by the stylistic preferences of management and, on the other, by the turbulence characteristics of the firm's environment. This chapter presents a procedure by which management of a firm can determine the preferred responsiveness pattern and then use it to redesign the firm's structure.

Exercises

1. Textbooks on sociology recognize both formal and informal aspects of organizational structure. This chapter has been focused on the formal aspect. Define what is meant by an informal structure. When does it arise? How does it interact with the formal structure? What effect does it have on the firm? How can it be managed?
2. How does organizational structure of the firm differ from structures found in nonprofits? Choose a nonprofit firm with which you are familiar, draw its role and task structure, diagnose its responsiveness.
3. Using a firm with which you are familiar, or a case assigned by your tutor, follow the procedure on organizational responsiveness to determine the preferred structure for the firm.
4. What are the advantages and disadvantages of a multi-structure? What should be the roles, the tasks, the responsibilities, and the structure of the corporate office in a multi-structure?

Part IV

Real-Time Strategic Response

18

Management Response to Surprising Changes

In Parts III and IV, we focused attention on managerial responses which prepare the firm to face a difficult and changing future. Strategy prepares the firm to face its complex external environment, while corporate capability develops responsiveness to anticipated threats and opportunities.

Positioning the entire firm is typically a massive, slow, and periodic process which cannot respond to increasingly fast-developing threats and opportunities. In Part V, we turn attention to such fast, surprising events.

This introductory chapter is based on a paper written in 1978. Our purpose was to describe the character of surprising events and observable responses by different firms, as a basis from which to suggest improved systematic 'real-time' approaches.

Introduction

The bulk of managerial time in business firms is devoted to coping with uncertainties induced by the environment: competitors' moves, economic fluctuations, availability of raw materials, labor demands, etc. Most managers would agree that change has been their central preoccupation as far back as they can remember, and that managing change is the *raison d'etre* of management.

But, as we discussed in Part I, since the 1960s a new kind of turbulence has increasingly made it felt. Unlike the earlier changes, which arose out of uncertainties in one's own traditional business, the new turbulence came

© The Author(s) 2019
H. I. Ansoff et al., *Implanting Strategic Management*,
https://doi.org/10.1007/978-3-319-99599-1_18

from unaccustomed and unfamiliar sources: from foreign technologies, from foreign competitors, from governments.

An increasing number of such changes posed major threats or opportunities to the firm: obsolescence of the firm's technology, major loss of market share, drastic increase in the cost of doing business, a chance to get a major jump on competitors, or a ground floor entry into a new industry.

As discussed in Part I, the speed with which such threats and opportunities develop has been increasing to a point where the *periodic systems* which we have been discussing up to now, may no longer be capable of perceiving and responding to them fast enough, before the threat has made a major impact on the firm, or the opportunity has been missed.

In this part of the book, we turn attention to such unfamiliar, momentous, and fast changes. The concern of this chapter is to analyze and to construct descriptive models of the different ways in which firms respond to such changes.

Basic Model—Decisive Management

If a firm fails to respond to a threat, the losses caused by it will continue to accumulate in the manner shown by the curve labeled 'unchecked loss' in Fig. 18.1. But sooner or later, most firms will take countermeasures. In the figure, this occurs at time T_D. If the lost sales are irreplaceable, the solution is to stop the product line and to eliminate costs which no longer generate income. If more positive options are available, the solution is to develop new

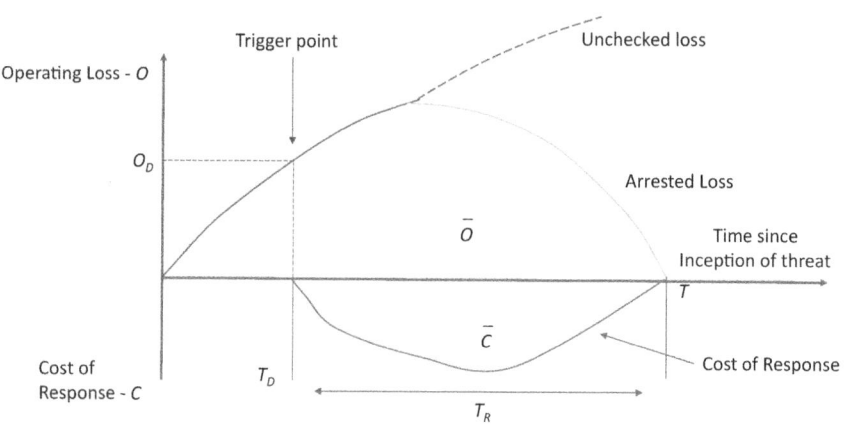

Fig. 18.1   Decisive management

products which will use capacities and capabilities made idle by the threat. A more difficult response is to divest from the obsolete products while, at the same time, replacing the lost profit with totally new products. The preferable alternative, though not always available, is to convert the threat into an opportunity: To devise a response which not only replaces but enhances profits and sales. Thus a firm with foresight, which anticipates the shift in the environment, can change to new products ahead of competitors and increase its market share at their expense.

The type of response and the timing of actions will differ among firms. In a frequent case, illustrated in Fig. 18.1, the response does not commence until after the threat has become a reality and the loss, O_D, is substantial. Once countermeasures are started, the loss is gradually brought to zero. In the meantime, divestment of plant, liquidation of inventory, reduction of workforce, etc., incur extraordinary costs over and above the normal cost of operations. Thus, while the threat is being arrested, during the period of response T_R, two streams of costs accumulate, as illustrated in the figure: Loss from unprofitable operations plus the cost of liquidating these operations.

By the time the threat is arrested at time T, the firm has incurred an accumulated operating loss $\bar{O}$, *measured* by the area under the upper curve, as well as the cost of arresting it, $\bar{C}$. Thus, the total loss is.

$$L_T = \bar{O} + \bar{C}.$$

The problem of strategic response is to minimize the loss L_T and, if possible, convert it into profit.

Reactive Management

When a discontinuity in the environment begins to affect a firm, its impact typically remains hidden within the normal fluctuations in performance. Unless the threat or opportunity has been identified out by a special forecast, the initial response is to treat it by actions which had in the past helped the firm to correct periodic reversals (such as cost reduction, efficiency improvements or sales aggressiveness).

When the historically successful actions repeatedly fail to work, it becomes evident that the firm is confronted with a new discontinuous threat. In Fig. 18.1, the time T_D is the *rational trigger point*. This is the point at which cumulated data show, with a high degree of confidence, that decline of performance will not be reversed and that special countermeasures are required.

Some firms (typically small and led by young, aggressive management) do not engage in environmental surveillance or forecasting. But they are quick to learn from the failure of conventional responses and are quick to cut their losses. This *decisive management* is illustrated in Fig. 18.1. As soon as the data show that cumulating loss of profit cannot be due to normal fluctuations, the management triggers a response. Management reacts at the rational trigger point T_D as shown in the figure.

In many other cases, particularly in large, established firms which have enjoyed a long history of success, the mere presence of persuasive data frequently <u>fails</u> to trigger prompt response. There are many historical cases of such firms which refused to recognize the 'writing on the wall' of the impact of a novel technology (e.g., replacement of mainframe computers by laptop computers and then by smartphones), or of a change in consumer preferences (e.g., the shift of American preferences from the 'gas guzzling monsters' to the small, fuel-efficient cars—and then back again periodically), or of major political realignments (e.g., the failure of many firms to pay attention to a scenario which predicted European integration or the rise of China's economic might).

In such cases, the start of response is delayed past the rational trigger T_D, by another Time of delay T_d, in the manner illustrated in Fig. 18.2. We can identify four contributing factors:

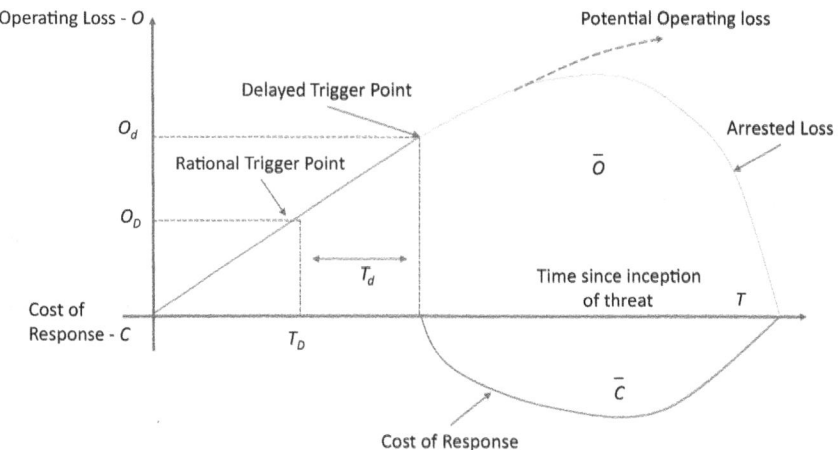

Fig. 18.2 Reactive management

1. A *management systems delay*, which typically occurs in large firms. It is due to the time consumed in observing, interpreting, collating, and transmitting information to responsible managers. The delay is also partly due to the time consumed by these managers in communicating with one another and establishing a common understanding, as well as the time necessary for processing the decisions among the responsible groups and decision levels.

2. A *verification delay* may be invoked because some managers will argue that, even though the level of impact has reached unacceptable proportions, there is never an ironclad assurance that the threat is real and that the impact is permanent. They will opt for waiting a little longer to see if the threat will 'blow over.'

3. A *political delay* may occur if certain managers, whose domain tributes to the crises, feel that recognition of a crisis will reflect on their reputation or will cause them to lose power. Even if they are convinced that the threat is real, they will fight a delaying action to avoid becoming scapegoats, to gain breathing space to develop a line of defense, or to set up a line of retreat.

4. An *unfamiliarity rejection delay* could contribute to the other three if, as is typical in many managerial cultures, the managers are trained to trust prior and familiar experiences and reject unfamiliar ones as improbable and invalid.

All four delays will postpone the response past the rational trigger point and will substantially increase the total cost to the firm. This response is *reactive management.*

Typically, neither the political resistance nor the unfamiliarity rejection is likely to be advanced overtly as the reasons for the delay, because both carry pejorative implications for the concerned managers. The justification is more likely to be given on the grounds of a need for verification, before a major organizational disruption is triggered off.

Planned Management

Both the decisive and the reactive behaviors occur after the fact: The response is triggered after the threat has inflicted tangible losses on the firms. Such behavior is not surprising in firms in which the internally available information is confined to historical events. Since many firms use historically based management information systems, decisive and reactive behaviors are widely observable in practice. In firms which engage in forecasting, one would expect to find anticipation of threats and opportunities to be matched by anticipatory response. But observation, as well as studies of the responses to the economic upheavals, shows that many firms which engage in forecasting exhibit the same procrastinating behavior as the reactive firms.

One reason for this can be found in the nature of the forecasted information. In many firms, forecasts of economic conditions, sales, earnings, and costs are extrapolations that project past performance patterns into the future. In these forecasts, the early impact of discontinuous departures from historical trends remains hidden behind the normal statistical fluctuations induced by economic and competitive activities. Only when the impact becomes large enough to stand out from the pattern does management become aware of the discontinuities. By this time, the advantages of anticipation may be lost.

A growing number of firms use techniques such as technological forecasting that is not based on extrapolation, structural economic forecasting, scenarios which identify threats and opportunities posed by strategic discontinuities. These approaches provide information and permit before-the-fact anticipatory responses. Given a time horizon that is far enough into the future, such forecasts enable the firm to complete its response before the threat can do any damage.

But, again, experience shows that in many firms, forecasts remain unheeded, and procrastination may last until after the threat has become a painful reality. For example, studies have shown that the presence forecasting scenarios that accurately predicted a discontinuity frequently made no difference: The responses were still after-the-fact, even when forecasts of the crisis were available to the management.

This case is illustrated in Fig. 18.3, which is called planned management. As the figure shows, the rational trigger point T_D is also the *forecasting horizon*. The firm should start its response as soon as the forecast has unambiguously identified an impending threat.

But, curiously enough, the procrastination delay T_d, which is found in reactive management (and is absent in decisive management) resurfaces in planned behavior. The same factors contribute, but for different reasons.

The systems delay is smaller in planned management. Unlike reactive management, where the information is derived secondhand from data intended to measure past performance, the threat or opportunity forecasting is primary input data. Typically, when forecasts are made, the individuals making them are not under pressure from other activities; they report their identification of the threats, either directly or through a small chain of command, to the responsible managers.

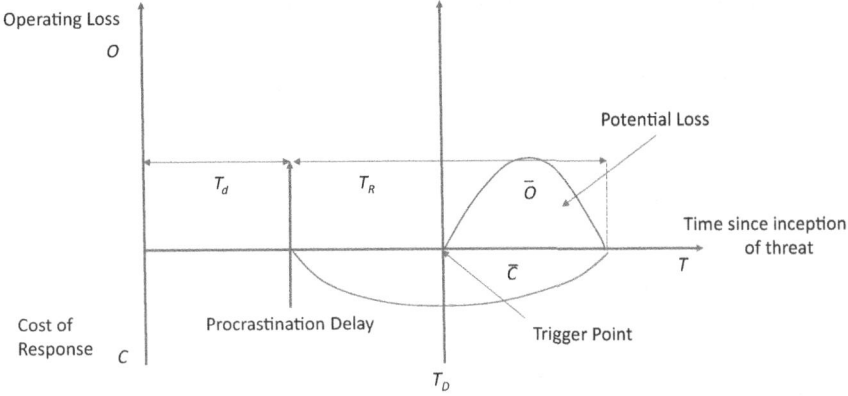

Fig. 18.3   Planned management

Offsetting the smaller system delay are potentially larger delays due to verification, political resistance, and unfamiliarity rejection. The fact that the triggering information is conjectural and no longer based on painful experience, as it is in reactive management, reinforces and provides justification for the natural delay tendencies.

The verification process, instead of questioning whether an observed result will persist, is now concerned with whether the threat will occur at all; and if it occurs, which course to follow. The defensive political tendencies of threatened managers are supported by the argument that it is imprudent and foolish to respond to 'mere speculations' about the future.

The threatened managers will be joined by others, who refuse to take seriously a vague threat which has no precedent in prior experience. The delays are psychological rather than political grounds. The delay mechanisms tend to counteract the potential advantages of forecasting.

The damage done depends on the relation between the three factors; the forecasting horizon T_D, the procrastination delay T_d, and the time required by the firm for response, T_R.

1. If the procrastination delay T_d is controlled, so that sufficient time is left to implement the response before the threat begins to impact, the optimal situation will result. On the one hand, the response is not premature and on the other, the only cost to the firm is the cost of implementing the response. This case can be described by the equation:

$$T_d = T_D - T_R$$

2. If a response is triggered before the threat begins to impact, but too late to complete the response before impact starts, the cost will be higher: a combination of cost of response and operating losses. The relationship in this case is:

$$T_d > T_D - T_R$$

3. If the procrastination delay T_d is excessive such that $T_d > T_D$, most of the advantages of forecasting are lost and the response moves into either a reactive or decisive category.
4. Finally, it may occur that the response time T_R is longer than the forecasting horizon T_D:

$$T_R > T_D$$

In this case, the response will not be completed before the threat begins to impact, even if procrastination T_d is eliminated,

In seeking to assure a timely, low-cost response to discontinuity, management can control (within limits) all of the three determining factors: the forecasting time horizon T_D, the response time T_R, and the procrastination T_d. In the following chapters, we shall explore all three possibilities.

We can now offer a concise summary of the preceding discussion. The three types of observable behavior (reactive, decisive, and planned) are typical points on a spectrum of *observable trigger behaviors* which change as the primary determining parameters vary. In the descriptive model of trigger behavior, which we have constructed in the preceding pages, we have recognized the following concepts:

1. The *rational trigger*, T_D, which is the point in time at which data is available within the firm to justify extraordinary response measures. T_D may be positive, after the threat has begun to impact on the firm, or negative, based on a 'reliable' forecast of a forthcoming threat.
2. The *actual trigger* adds the additional time delay for management decision making $T_D + T_d$ to determine the time at which management, in fact, turns attention to extraordinary counter-threat measures.
3. The additional time delay T_d is separable into two categories:

   a. *Management systems delay* incurred while interpreting and distributing the threat or opportunity information to influential managers.
   b. *Behavioral delay* due to verification, political resistance plus lack of will to deal with both threatening and unfamiliar prospects.

Thus, if the benefits of threat or opportunity forecasting are not to be lost, improvements in forecasting must be accompanied by comparable increases in managerial preparedness to accept the uncertainties and partial information of long-term forecasts.

Post-trigger Behaviors

The period between the first awareness of the threat and the point in time at which management begins coping with it may last months or even years. But it would be wrong to visualize the pre-trigger period as one of watchful inactivity. The daily life of management consists of problem solving: Coping with unwelcome deviations and planning to ensure future successes. During the pre-trigger period, this coping goes on as before: deficiencies are perceived, analyzed, and corrected, but all within established routines and programs of 'normal' activity. The significance of the trigger point is that it ushers in extraordinary, non-routine, drastic measures.

It is useful to divide these extraordinary measures into two classes:

1. The first-class copes with *discontinuous* changes in the firm's relationship to the environment, in its internal dynamics, or in its value system. Discontinuities such as diversification into new businesses, divestment from major product lines, major reorganizations, introduction of strategic planning systems—all exemplify such measures which change the 'face of the firm,' alter perspectives, introduce new ways of life. These changes are *strategic measures.*
2. The second-class stops short of changing familiar relationships. Nevertheless, they are drastic enough: An unusual major sales promotion, a substantial price-cut to revive flagging sales, a major write-off of assets, disposal of large amounts of obsolete inventories, replacement of obsolete plant, a freeze on hiring, arresting management development programs, or cutback in Research and Development (R&D) expenditure. These are extraordinary *operating measures.*

In many firms, the operating measures (while drastic in their impact) will be familiar and acceptable either because they have been tried before or because their impact can be forecast with confidence. Strategic measures will be acceptable only in firms which have previously made drastic strategic change a way of life. For those who have historically confined themselves to incremental change, drastic strategic measures appear strange, risky, and threatening.

The management response, typical of *reactive management* which has been widely explored in strategic planning literature, is illustrated in Fig. 18.4. The initial assumption is that the difficulty can be overcome through familiar, but drastic, operating countermeasures. A series of measures are tried sequentially starting with ones which have been successful in the past.

If none of the countermeasures produces a sufficient improvement, the tendency is to conclude that the situation is out of the firm's control, but that the environmental disturbance is temporary, and that if the firm holds out long enough the problem will go away. The firm turns from countermeasures to retrenchment. The 'game plan' is no longer to address the threat but to weather it. Typically, 'non-essential' activities such as management development are the first ones to suffer. Secondly, future-oriented activities, such as R&D and capital investment, are decreased; thirdly, expenses supporting current operations are cut down.

It is only if the losses continue in spite of both operating countermeasures and retrenchment that a reactive firm turns to strategic remedies. Meanwhile, a great deal of time has been lost, substantial losses accumulated, and extra costs incurred.

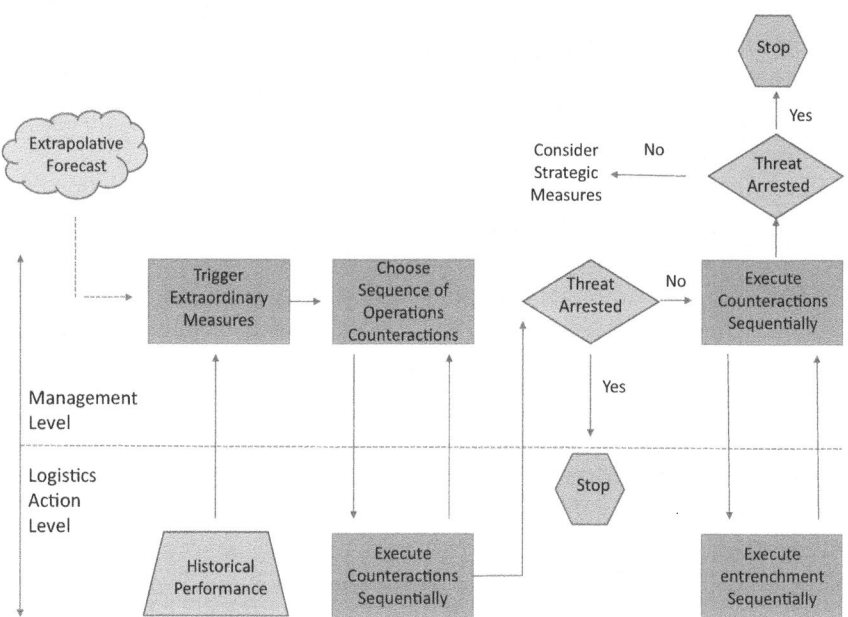

Fig. 18.4 Sequential response to threats in a reactive firm

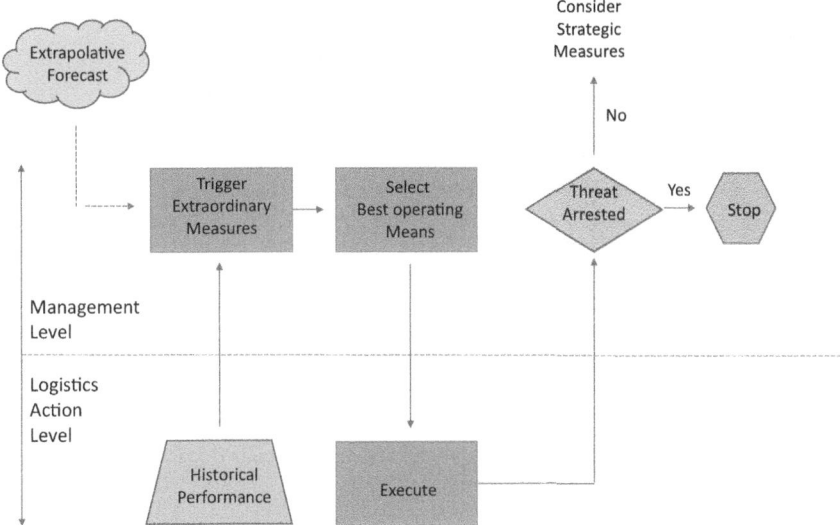

Fig. 18.5 Response to threats in a decisive firm

This sequence will not be changed substantially if extrapolative forecasting and even long-range planning exist in the firm (see the upper left-hand corner of Fig. 18.4).

In a decisive firm, the initial response to operating measures is also typical as shown in Fig. 18.5. The decisive firm is still unwilling and unprepared to face unfamiliar strategic threats. But instead of sequencing responses, the firm analyzes, selects and executes the best combination of counteractions and retrenchments. Once these prove futile, it moves decisively to strategic countermeasures.

Finally, Fig. 18.6 models the *planned management* behavior. Extrapolative forecasting is augmented by environmental surveillance that searches for threats or opportunities. The diagnosis simultaneously considers operating and strategic remedies. The organization has the capacity to execute both in parallel.

Comparison of Behaviors

The key differences between Figs. 18.4, 18.5, and 18.6 arise from the manner in which managerial decisions are sequenced. Management has two sequencing decisions to make:

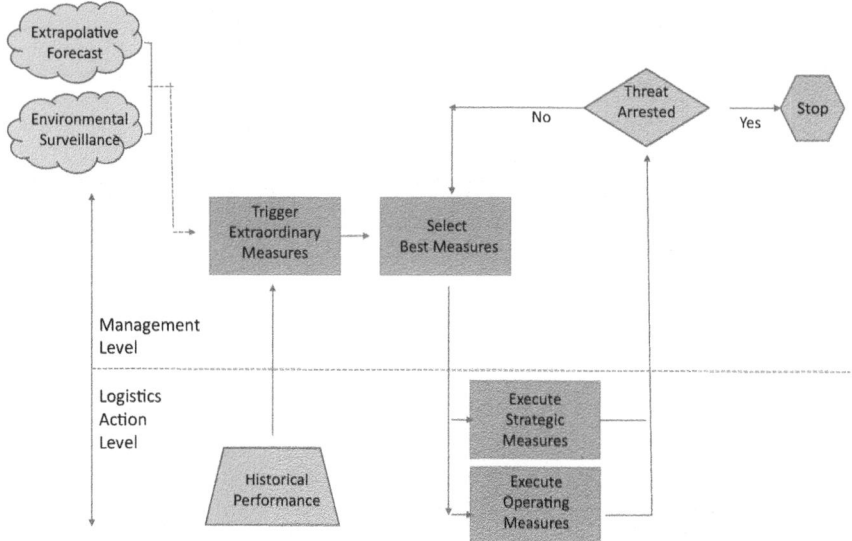

Fig. 18.6 Response to threats in an entrepreneurial planning firm

1. The sequence in which the strategic and operating problems are addressed.
2. The sequence in which the specific measures are taken within each problem.

The reactive behavior is *doubly sequential.* Strategic response does not commence until after the operating options have been exhausted. When operating responses are being explored, each action is tried sequentially—one at a time. This behavior is an experience-dependent trial and error process.

Decisive management is *sequential-parallel:* operating measures then strategic actions are addressed sequentially, but when it comes to specific operating actions, an analytic approach is used. Alternatives are identified and compared. If necessary, several measures are implemented in parallel.

Planned management is a *parallel-parallel approach.* Both the type of response and the measures are chosen through comparisons and analysis. A number of action programs can be initiated in parallel.

Figure 5.1.7 brings together the three types of management behavior. All three modes of behavior are observable in practice. Since this book is concerned with prescriptive advice, the question is 'what mode of response management should a firm be advised to pursue?'

The answer, indicated in the bottom two lines of the figure, is that *the cost-effective choice depends on the level of environmental turbulence.* Reactive response is adequate at turbulence levels 1–2 when the speed of change is slow and strategic discontinuities are rare. At turbulence levels 2–3, strategic discontinuities are infrequent, but the speed of change makes it advisable to establish a rapid management response. Strategic discontinuities are frequent at levels 4–5—both operating and strategic responses must be made expeditiously.

Summary

When a discontinuous change impacts on the firm, two costs are incurred: The cumulative loss of profit and the cost incurred in halting or reversing the loss. The management problem is to minimize the sum of the two losses by restoring profitability of affected product lines or by shutting down the operations that support them.

Observation and research both reveal three types of management behavior. In the reactive behavior, response is delayed until the impact of change has become painful and threatening. Once the response is triggered, the first efforts are 'heroic' operating changes and retrenchment. Operating actions are tried one at a time, and only when they have been exhausted, does attention turn to strategic countermeasures.

In decisive management, the response is triggered when the impact of change has become unambiguous. The additional procrastination observed in the reactive management is avoided. Operating countermeasures are tried first, but in a planned systematic manner. Once the operating actions have been exhausted, the firm turns attention to a strategic response.

Planned behavior differs from the preceding two in the fact that operating and strategic countermeasures are considered at the outset. A proper combination is implemented in parallel.

In both reactive and planned behavior, there is frequently an additional period of procrastination beyond the point at which the importance of the threat has become clear. This procrastination is composed of a systemic delay (due to data processing and decision making) and a behavioral delay (due to resistance from the power structure and resistance from managers who refuse to accept evidence which is at variance with experience). In planned management, the procrastination delay can waste the time advantage offered by forecasting and planning.

All these behaviors have their place in the repertoire of management responses to threats and opportunities. In slowly changing environments, reactive management, while costly, can avert disaster. As the environment becomes more and more turbulent, it becomes necessary to use the decisive response or the planned response, if the firm is to avoid a disastrous impact.

Exercises

1. Compare the three behaviors described in Table 18.1 with the capability profiles presented in Chapter 8. What are the similarities and what are the differences? Which capability profiles does a firm need to assure reactive, decisive, and planned behaviors, respectively?
2. Prepare detailed checklists of the factors which contribute to the systemic, procrastination, political, and unfamiliarity delays. What measures can be taken within the firm to minimize each of the delays?
3. What steps can be taken to reduce the delay T_R?

Table 18.1   Comparison of behavior in confronting a strategic threat

Management behavior / Period	Reactive	Decisive	Planned
Pre-trigger phase	Delay trigger past threshold until sure of threat	Act when rational threshold is reached	Act in advance of threat
Post-trigger phase	–Assume threat as operating –Respond sequentially –Try past operational successes –Try retrenchment –Turn to strategic response	–Assume threat as operating –Select optimal operating responses –Try responses –Turn to strategic response	–Diagnose nature of threat –Select both optimal strategic and operating responses –Try strategic and operating responses
Conditions for best cost effectiveness	Strategically and operationally continuous environment	Strategically continuous operationally fluctuating environment	Both strategically and operationally discontinuous
Appropriate turbulence level	1–2	2–3	3–5

19

Strategic Issue Management

We turn attention from describing surprising changes to a system for detecting, analyzing, and responding to them. This system is now receiving increasing attention from firms.

Why Strategic Issue Management?

A *strategic issue* is a future development, either inside or outside of the organization, which is likely to have an important impact on the ability of the enterprise to meet its objectives. An issue may be welcome: An *opportunity* to be grasped in the environment, or an internal *strength* which can be exploited to advantage. Or it can be unwelcome: an external *threat*, or an internal *weakness* which imperils continuing success, even survival of the enterprise. Frequently, external threats, because they signal significant discontinuities in the environment, can be converted into opportunities by aggressive and entrepreneurial management. In fact, such ability to convert threats into opportunities has been one of the most prized characteristics in the history of US management.

The concept of strategic issues evolved from strategic planning. When strategic planning was first introduced, the expectation was that strategies would be revised annually. But experience quickly showed this to be both impractical and unnecessary. Impractical because strategy revision is an energy- and time-absorbing exercise. If conducted annually it overloads management capacity. Unnecessary because a strategy is a long-term thrust

© The Author(s) 2019
H. I. Ansoff et al., *Implanting Strategic Management*,
https://doi.org/10.1007/978-3-319-99599-1_19

which takes several years to implement. Instead of improving a strategy, annual revisions will cause vacillations in managerial behavior and prevent a fair test of the strategy.

As this understanding grew, business firms began to space comprehensive revisions of strategies several years apart. In the beginning of each year's planning cycle, a review of last year's progress focused attention on business areas which had encountered important strategic issues. A comprehensive analysis of environmental trends and prospects identifies additional strategic issues. Resolution of these strategy- and environment-derived issues becomes the central preoccupation of the annual planning process. Thus, *strategic issue analysis* (analysis of impact and response to significant developments) was added to strategy analysis (determination of thrusts for the future development of the enterprise).

In recent years, two considerations have made it desirable to separate strategic issue analysis from the annual strategic planning cycle. The first is that some organizations either cannot afford, or do not need, the cumbersome paraphernalia of annual strategic planning. The former is the case of smaller enterprises which must cope with environmental turbulence, but do not have the managerial capacity nor resources for comprehensive planning. The latter is the case of an enterprise whose basic strategic thrusts arc clear and relatively stable, but whose environment is turbulent.

The second factor has been a growing incidence of events which come from unexpected sources and impact quickly on the organization. The combination of speed and novelty of such issues may make them too fast to permit timely perception and response within the annual planning system. Some of these issues, which occur between planning cycles, may impact too quickly to be delayed until the next cycle; others, which occur during the planning cycle, may impact before the planning period is over.

When one or both of these factors are present, it becomes desirable to separate issue resolution from the annual planning cycle.

What Is a Strategic Issue Management System?

A strategic issue management system (SIM) is a systematic procedure for early identification and *fast* response to surprising changes both inside and outside an organization.

Early identification can be promoted in the following ways:

- Unlike budget control, long-range planning and strategic planning systems, which address issues during an annual planning period, SIM is 'real time'—continuously alert to strategic issues throughout the year. In practice, this continuous engagement requires periodic reviews (say monthly) and maintaining a list of key strategic issues.
- SIM also requires continuous surveillance, both inside and outside the enterprise for 'fast' issues which may arise between the reviews. When issues arise, a 'red light signal' alerts management of the need for immediate attention.

Fast response to rapidly moving trends can be fostered in the following complementary ways:

- The responsibility for managing the system is assumed by a senior management group which has the resources and the authority to initiate prompt action without unnecessary delays.
- If necessary, SIM cuts across normal hierarchical organizational lines. The senior management group assigns responsibility for individual issues directly to units which are best equipped to deal with the issue, even if this means reaching across several hierarchical levels. If, as is often the case, an issue is not specific to one unit, an ad hoc project is formed, composed of both affected and expert individuals. Resources are assigned directly to the project, and the project reports directly to the senior management group.
- The assigned responsibilities are not for planning the response but for resolving the issue. Thus, SIM is a management *action system* (not only for planning). With several projects underway and continuous updating and revision of the strategic issue list, the usual separation between planning and implementation periods is not visible in an SIM.

There are a number of ways in which responsibilities for the system can be assigned. One way is illustrated in Fig. 19.1 which divides responsibilities among three groups:

1. A *staff* group which is concerned with detection of trends, evaluation of their impact and timing, assessing the time required for response and alerting decision makers about sudden and important issues. This group is also responsible for maintaining a 'war room'—an up-to-date display of the key issue list, their priorities and the status of the projects. The staff group concerns itself with monitoring the progress of the various projects toward their assigned objectives.

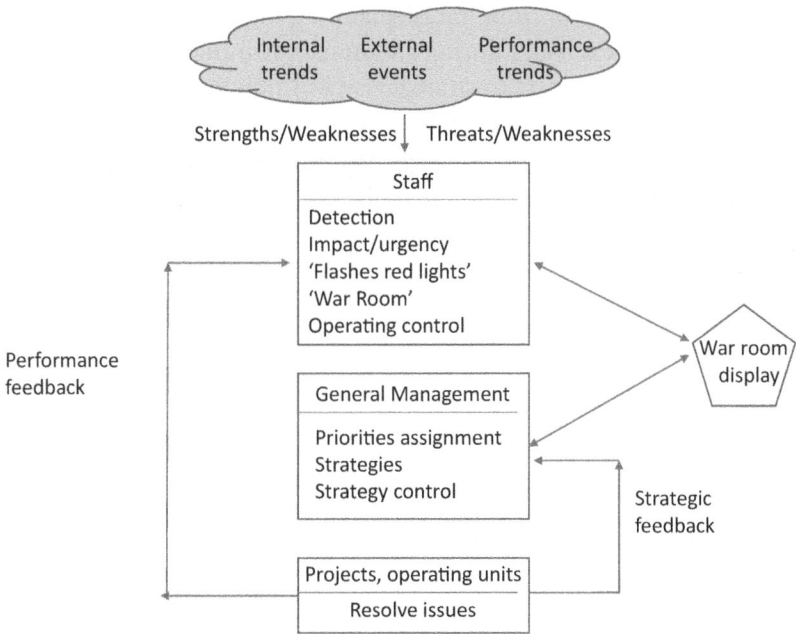

Fig. 19.1 Strategic issue management system

In Fig. 19.1, the term 'staff' is in quotation marks because this surveillance-interpretation-measurement function will be handled differently in different settings. In a large organization a separate staff department, probably a part of the larger planning department, may be given the job of issue analysis. In a small firm, two or three top managers can periodically put on 'staff hats' for the purpose of systematically reviewing the strategic issues, preferably with part-time help of one of the few available assistants.

2. The second approach is a *general management* group (which in a small firm may be the same as the staff group) which is responsible for assessing the relative importance of the issues, selecting the key strategic issue list, deciding on how the respective issues are to be treated, and assigning responsibilities for their resolution.
3. The third group of participants are the workers—the units or ad hoc projects which have been assigned the responsibility for specific issues. On occasion, when the strategy of response to an issue is not clear, these groups may be asked to act as planners and to submit action recommendations. But the success of SIM depends on making the projects responsible for action, not just planning for issues. Experience shows that, unless this role is clearly established, SIM may degenerate into 'paralysis by [repeated] analysis.'

Since urgent issue projects will frequently be started before their dimensions and implications are fully understood, the early stages will progressively make clear the *strategic dimensions* of the issue: the extent of its impact and the urgency. As work progresses, attention will progressively shift to the *operating results*.

Therefore, as Fig. 19.1 shows, it is important to assess success of the project teams not only for their operating results but also for their success in clarifying the strategic implications. If general management fails to exercise strategic control, projects tend to acquire a life of their own and continue even after it becomes clear that their impact on the firm will not be significant.

Issue Identification

The principal steps in issue analysis are shown in Fig. 19.2. The first step is issue identification. As the figure shows, there are three sources of information about impending strategic issues: trends in the external environment, trends within the organization, and trends in its performance. Tables 19.1, 19.2, and 19.3 contain representative lists of these trends. Table 19.1 shows a list of possible environmental trends which may be of importance to firms in developed and developing countries. Table 19.2 is a list of internal characteristics which may change over time and typically give rise to strategic issues. Table 19.3 is a list of typical objectives (performance attributes) by which organizations may measure their successes and failures.

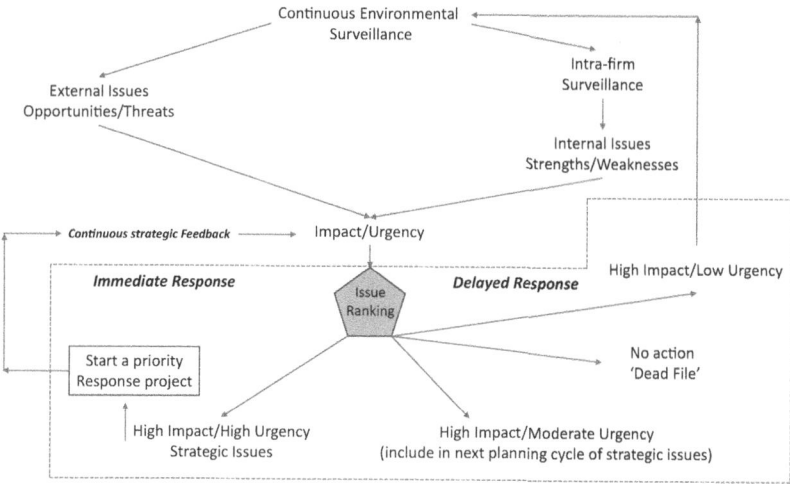

Fig. 19.2   Strategic issue analysis

Table 19.1   Environmental trends

1.	Trends in the global market place (protectionism ie. 'America First' vs. free trade)
2.	Growth of govenment as a customer
3.	Economic growth of Pacific rim countries
4.	Chinese challenge
5.	Loss of American competitiveness
6.	Economic and political trends in developing countries
7.	Monetary trends
8.	Inflationary trends
9.	Emergence of the multinational firm
10.	Developing technology
11.	Size as a competitive tool
12.	Saturation of growth
13.	Technological breakthrough
14.	Growth in the service sector
15.	Affluency of consumers
16.	Changes in age distribution of consumers
17.	Selling to reluctant consumers
18.	Social attitudes toward business
19.	Government controls
20.	Consumer pressures
21.	Union pressures
22.	Concern with ecology
23.	Impact of 'zero-growth' advocates
24.	Shortening of product life cycles
25.	Intra-European nationalism
26.	Conflict between multinational firms and national interests
27.	Public distrust of business
28.	Difficulty in forecasting
29.	Strategic surprises
30.	Competition from developing nations
31.	Changing work attitudes

All organizations (both for-profit and not-for-profit) which find themselves in a complex and rapidly changing environment should identify major environmental trends. It is particularly important to identify possible major future discontinuities which have the potential for a major impact on the organization. Table 19.1 provides a starting point for issue identification. The procedure is to cross out the issues which are not relevant to the firm and to add others which are identified from scanning of the environment.

Table 19.2   Internal trends

1.	Size
2.	Complexity
3.	Structure
4.	Systems
5.	Communications
6.	Power structure
7.	Role definition
8.	Centralization/decentralization
9.	Values and norms
10.	Management style
11.	Management competence
12.	Logistic (workforce) competence
13.	Capital intensity
14.	Technological intensity
15.	Product diversification
16.	Market diversification
17.	Technology diversification
18.	Other

Table 19.3   Objectives

1.	Growth
2.	Profitability
3.	Cyclical stability
4.	Flexibility
5.	Invulnerability to environmental surprises
6.	Solvency
7.	Debt/equity
8.	Invulnerability to hostile take over
9.	Competitive leadership
10.	Innovativeness
11.	Market share
12.	Internal social climate
13.	External social responsiveness
14.	Good citizenship
15.	Work satisfaction
16.	Responsiveness to aspirations of internal constituencies (identify both constituency and aspirations)
	a.
	b.
	c.
	d.
17.	Responsiveness to external constituencies
	a.
	b.
	c.
	d.
18.	Other

In large and complex firms, environmental surveillance should be supplemented by identification of important <u>internal</u> trends and events which are expected to have a significant impact on organizational performance. This is necessary because, when an organization passes a certain size and complexity, general management begins to lose track of the developments in culture, managers, structure, systems, and capacity, which can have both positive and negative impact on the efficiency and/or on the responsiveness to the environment.

Internal trend identification becomes particularly important in fast-growing small and medium-sized firms, because at certain sizes, major weaknesses develop in organizational capability to handle new complexities brought about by size. For example, the passage from small to medium is typically accompanied by a loss of control and perspective by the founding entrepreneur. Table 19.2 provides a starting list of internal trends.

The list of objectives, shown in Table 19.3, can be used to develop important additional information about issues. To use this list for issue management, the first step is to identify the objectives which the firm is pursuing and the relative priorities which are assigned to them. Typically, this will reduce the long list of Table 19.3 to no more than four or five lines.

Once the objectives are identified they can be compared to the performance trends. In firms with systematic annual planning, the objectives and trends will already be available in the form of forecasts. A comparison of performance objectives to forecasts will be a part of the annual planning cycle.

The comparison identifies what in Fig. 19.2 is called the *objectives gap*: anticipated deficiencies in future performance. The gaps are usually *diagnosed* to determine the causes. Many of the causes are can be traced to inefficiencies in performance or ineffectiveness of the firm's strategy, and corrections are programmed into annual plans. But some causes will be traceable to environmental threats or to organizational weaknesses. Such environmental threats or internal weaknesses would be added to the list of issues, to be treated outside (but in parallel with) the annual planning-implementation process.

In summary, threats, opportunities plus future strengths and weaknesses can be identified from the three sources shown at the top of Fig. 19.2. The performance trends can be analyzed during regular performance reviews, but environmental trends and internal trends should be scanned continuously throughout the year to ensure identification of sudden, fast-moving and potentially surpriseful changes.

*Estimating Impact/Urgency

Returning to Fig. 19.2, the next step (at the center of the figure) is to assess the potential future impact of the trends on the future performance of the enterprise. The ideal approach is to estimate impact on the attainment of the firm's objectives, which have been identified in Table 19.3. But in many practical situations, the necessary information may not be available or the method for making the estimate may not be clear. A practical substitute is to use management judgment to assign a number (say, on a scale of +10 to −10) to the impact of each trend or event. The estimate is arrived at by a group of 'experts'—including managers and outsiders to the firm who possess the relevant knowledge and experience. In addition to the impact, it is also necessary to estimate the *probability and timing of the impact strength.*

The impact may be positive or negative or both. The latter case may indicate either a range of uncertainty in the evaluation or the expectation that the trend will be both beneficial (in meeting some of the objectives) and harmful (in depressing performance on other objectives).

In Table 19.4, a simple format is provided for recording the preceding steps of the analysis. Next, an estimate is made of the *urgency* for each trend or event. This is obtained by comparing the probable timing of the impact of the event with the time needed by the firm for a timely response. (A procedure for estimating urgency will be presented in the next chapter.) A three-point scale is useful for classification of urgency:

1. If the difference between the timing of the event and the response time is such that the firm must respond immediately, the event is labeled *urgent.*
2. If the response can be delayed until the next planning cycle (but not much longer), the event is labeled *delayable.*
3. If, according to the present estimates, the response can be delayed indefinitely until better estimates of impact can be made, the event is labeled *postponable.*

Table 19.4 Impact/urgency of environmental trends

Trends	Impact	Time before impact	Needed response time	Urgency	Issue assignment

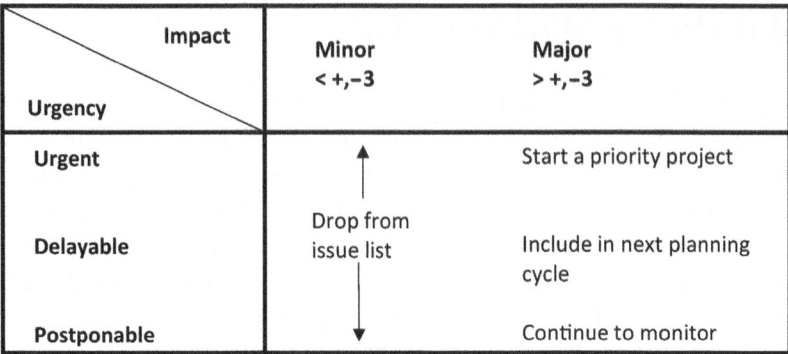

Fig. 19.3 Issue assignment

Based on the estimates of impact and urgency, the next step is to assign issues to one of four categories illustrated in Fig. 19.4 (see also the lower portion of Fig. 19.2).

Issues whose impact is low (±3 or less on the level of 10) are assigned to the minor impact category and dropped from further consideration. The remaining major issues are subdivided into the three categories shown in Fig. 19.3: Urgent, Delayable, or Postponable.

The process is completed by describing the nature of threats and opportunities posed by the each issue. Threats and opportunities should be arranged in the order of priority according to their expected impact. The result is the *key issue list* of the firm, which is used in managing the issue system. It is changed and updated as some issues are resolved, others dropped because their impact turns out to be minor, and new issues are added as a result of issue surveillance.

The key issue list helps solve a problem which is commonly encountered when issues are analyzed for the first time. The problem is that the number of issues exceeds the firm's capacity to respond. The key issue identification procedure helps reduce the size of the list and also assigns priorities within the limits of the available resources.

The procedure described above is based on the *impact analysis* technique, which analyzes one event or trend at a time and does not concern itself with their interdependence.

A somewhat more complex procedure called *cross-impact analysis* can be added in order to estimate the likelihood of simultaneous occurrence of several events or trends. The cross-impact analysis produces clusters of events/trends which are likely to impact together on the firm and permits identification of probable future *disaster scenarios* in which the firm may be severely damaged by a series of threats or weaknesses. It also allows for *opportunity scenarios* (futures in which the firm will enjoy a series of attractive opportunities/strengths).

*Coupling Opportunities and Threats to Strengths and Weaknesses

Impact analysis and cross-impact analysis respond to issues on the basis of their urgency and impact on the firm.

A complementary approach is described by the acronym SWOT (strengths, weaknesses, opportunities, and threats). SWOT identifies the threats and opportunities posed by each issue and match them to the historical strengths and weakness of the firm. The matching process is illustrated in the matrix shown in Table 19.5.

1. Opportunities which can be captured using the firm's relevant strengths are given high priority.
2. Opportunities which require capabilities which are weak in the firm are not pursued.
3. Threats which can be avoided using the firm's strengths are vigorously avoided.
4. Capabilities which are too weak for response to serious threats are built up and converted into strengths.

Table 19.5 The SWOT matrix

The SWOT matrix		Opportunities $O_1 O_2 O_3 O_4$	Threats $T_1 T_2 T_3 T_4$
Strengths	S_1	High priority response	High priority response
	S_2		
	S_3		
	S_4		
Weaknesses	T_1	Do not respond	Convert weaknesses (in capabilities) into strengths
	T_2		
	T_3		
	T_4		

Thus, the outcomes of the SWOT analysis are decisions on opportunities which will be pursued, threats which will be countered, and organizational weaknesses which will be remedied. The underlying assumption in the SWOT analysis is that the historical strengths and weaknesses will remain strengths and weaknesses in the future. The reader will recall from the strategic diagnosis (see Chapter 6) that this assumption remains valid up to turbulence level 3. Beyond level 3, it is highly probable that some historical strengths may become future weaknesses and vice versa.

*The Eurequip Matrix

Figure 19.4 shows a modification of the SWOT matrix which does not assume permanence of historical strengths or weaknesses and can, therefore, be used at turbulence levels 4 and 5. The Eurequip matrix is named to recognize the French consulting firm who developed it.

The matrix has two cases. The *positive synergy case* shown at the top has a positive interdependence where both strengths and weaknesses turn out to be useful for pursuing future opportunities or minimizing the impact of the threats. The entries in the matrix indicate the kinds of shift that are desirable in the priorities previously established by estimation of impact. For example, when a historical strength of the firm is applicable to the development of an opportunity, two consequences follow:

1. the opportunity is likely to yield better than average positive impact and
2. the strength will appear more attractive than it did before. The result is to increase the expectations and the priorities assigned to both.

An interesting result, shown in the lower left cell of the matrix in case 1, is the possible discovery that certain capabilities which had been previously regarded as weaknesses will become strengths in the perspective of new threats and opportunities. Instead of being eliminated, these 'weaknesses' should be enhanced. For example, a lack of tight cost controls and of clearly defined vertical lines of authority/responsibility, which in the past may have inhibited organizational efficiency, may become advantages if new opportunities demand fast organizational response and entrepreneurial risk-taking. As another example, the absence of a well-developed financial controller function, a weakness in the mass production age, made it easy to introduce more advanced forms of planning and control which are essential in the turbulent postindustrial environment.

Case I Positive synergy: Strengths and/or weaknesses are applicable to responding to threats/opportunities

The SWOT Matrix		Opportunities				Threats			
		1	2	3	4	1	2	3	4
Strengths	1	(a) Highest priority on opportunity (b) Increase priority of building strengths				(a) Reduce priority of threat (b) Maintain priority of building strength			
	2								
	3								
	4								
Weaknesses	1	(a) High priority on opportunity (b) Enhance 'weakness'				(a) Reduce priority of threat (b) Enhance 'weakness'			
	2								
	3								
	4								

Case II Negative synergy: neither strengths nor weaknesses help deal with threats/opportunities

The SWOT Matrix		Opportunities				Threats			
		1	2	3	4	1	2	3	4
Strengths	1	(a) Low priority on opportunity (b) Low priority on strengths				(a) Increased priority on threats (b) Low priority on strengths			
	2								
	3								
	4								
Weaknesses	1	(a) Low priority on opportunities (b) Priority on elimination of relevant weaknesses				(a) Increase priority on threats (b) Priority on elimination of relevant weaknesses			
	2								
	3								
	4								
New Capabilities	1	(a) Assign high priority to building new strengths				(a) High priority on new strengths			
	2								
	3								
	4								

Fig. 19.4 Interdependence between T/O and S/W

The *negative synergy case* in the lower matrix of Fig. 19.4 illustrates the consequence of the negative cross-impact. Historical strengths become less attractive, threats must be taken more seriously than in the past, new opportunities lose appeal. A very important consequence to negative synergy is the *need to identify new capabilities* which must be developed in order to cope with new environmental challenges.

The results of the dual matrix analysis are summarized in Table 19.6 (which is a modification of Table 19.4). As shown in the figure, impact and urgency estimates will usually change as a result of evaluation of SWOT synergies. For example, high-positive synergy will increase the positive impact and reduce the negative impact. Negative synergy will have the opposite effect.

Table 19.6 Impact/urgency of threat/opportunities after synergy analysis

Trends	Impact		Urgency		Threats	Opportunities	Firm's decision
	Before synergy evaluation	After synergy evaluation	Before synergy evaluation	After synergy evaluation			

In summary, SWOT analysis is a sequel to the issue urgency and impact analysis which enables management to identify specific threats and opportunities to which it will respond. The simpler version of SWOT (Table 19.5) should be used in environments on turbulence levels 1–3. The more complex version (Fig. 19.4) should be used at turbulence levels 4–5.

Periodic Planning and Strategic Issue Management

SIM has emerged to fill a gap in periodic planning and not to replace it. The two types of system have complementary purposes. Periodic planning concerns itself with determining the basic thrusts of an enterprise and assuring coherence and cooperation among different parts of a complex enterprise. SIM deals with deviations from these thrusts which may occur as a result of new opportunities, threats, strengths, and weaknesses.

An organization which is well-coordinated (or too small to have coordination problems) and which has well-developed and promising strategic thrusts may need only a simple periodic planning system such as financial control or long-range planning. But if the external or internal environments are turbulent, the organization should use SIM.

When both future thrust and turbulence present problems, then a comprehensive strategic planning system must be coupled with SIM. In this case, it is dangerous to limit the organization to SIM without the accompanying strategic planning. For example, if the major prospects of an organization are on a declining trend, SIM is likely to make its descent into bankruptcy more elegant than it would be without the system. The use of SIM would also create a false sense of security. The choice of the appropriate systems can be made with the aid of Table 19.7.

Table 19.7 Environmental and choice of systems

Environment / System	Discontinuous	Surprising	Both
Strategic planning	✓		✓
SIM		✓	✓

A way to couple the strategic planning and SIM systems is illustrated in Fig. 19.5. At the outset of the period, the annual planning cycle picks up the strategic issues from SIM and includes them in comprehensive company-wide planning. The final outputs of the planning are: (1) a set of *operating programs and budgets* for ongoing operations, which are aimed at meeting the near-term performance objectives and goals, and (2) a number of strategic issues translated into *change programs and budgets*. The latter are addressed at changing either the strategic thrusts of the enterprise or its internal capabilities that contribute to future *performance potential.*

As Fig. 19.5 shows, the change programs generated by periodic planning become a part of a larger group of temporary projects; the other part being generated by SIM throughout the year. An important conclusion suggested by the figure is that the process shown in Fig. 19.5 can be used to manage *all* of the projects of the enterprise. When used in this enlarged capacity, it is called a *project management system* (see Chapters 17 and 25).

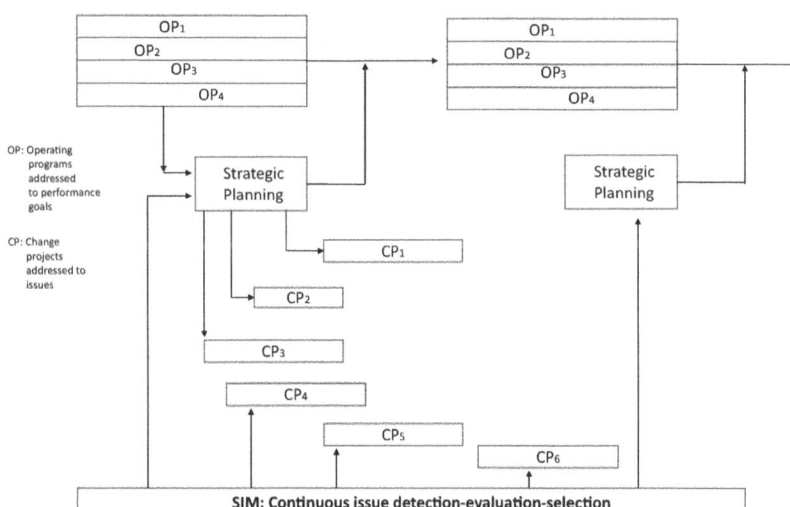

Fig. 19.5 Continuing issue detection-evaluation-selection

The Behavioral Factor

At first glance, SIM appears to be an easy system to put in place and to manage. It is lightweight, with a minimum of the 'make-work' often observed in periodic planning systems. In addition, SIM addresses pressing problems, it is compatible with other systems and organizational structures, it is responsive to change and does not have many of the bureaucratic self-perpetuating tendencies observed other planning systems.

But installation and acceptance of SIM are not likely to be simple. The difficulties come from two sources. The first is refusal of the top management group to submit itself to the discipline of SIM. Periodic planning is frequently used for organizing 'the others' in the enterprise. If top management refuses to become a part of the process, periodic planning can still make a useful contribution to the enterprise. But if top management pays lip service to SIM (and, e.g., appoints a staff planner to manage the war room), then SIM will not work.

Refusal to take charge is frequently coupled with the mentality problem discussed in the last chapter—a refusal by top management to accept new and unfamiliar issues as relevant to the business of the enterprise.

Therefore, acceptance of SIM by top management is the major problem to solve. The solution is a 'sales campaign' by the 'converted' subgroup of general managers. Careful education and an involvement in confrontation of issues by the top group are more promising courses of action. In cases when the new realities require a transformation of mentality of key managers, the firm will probably need external help. We will have more to say about this in Part V.

Summary

Strategic issue management offers the following advantages:

1. Timely anticipation of new developments.
2. A quick internal reaction time.
3. Response to problems which may arise from any source (economic, political, social, or technological).
4. A 'lightweight' system, not affected by organizational size and complexity.
5. Compatibility with most organizational structures and systems.

There are several analytic techniques for SIM:

1. Use of simple environmental impact analysis.
2. Use of cross-impact analysis.
3. Use of the issue ranking approach in Table 19.4.
4. Adding the Eurequip matrix to the approach (Table 19.6).

There is no one correct SIM technique for all situations and any one of them can significantly improve the responsiveness of the organization to external turbulence and internal complexity.

Three rules can be used to guide the choice of SIM for a particular organization:

1. The approach must be *responsive* to the complexity of the challenges.
2. The approach must be as *simple* as the complexity permits.
3. The approach must be *feasible* within the resources of the enterprise.

The advantages of SIM described in this chapter are that SIM can be used by organizations of any size and SIM requires very little prior experience with formal management systems.

The principal limitation of the SIM system is that while it reacts to departures from the historical dynamics, it does not focus management attention on rethinking and redefining these dynamics as is done in periodic strategic planning.

Strategic issue management cannot be made to work unless key managers in the organization accept a central role in the system. Getting key managers to submit themselves to the discipline demanded by the system and getting them to react to strategic issues which do not conform to historical experience are the two most difficult problems of introducing SIM into organizations.

Exercises

1. As a member of the corporate planning staff, you have been asked to prepare a recommendation on whether your firm should install a strategic issue management system. What questions would you pose, what data would you gather, and how would you analyze them in order to prepare the recommendation?
2. Using an organization well known to you or a case assigned by your instructor, follow the logic of Fig. 19.2 to arrive at the key issue list.

20

Using Weak Signals

As speed of change accelerates, it becomes increasingly difficult to predict changes with sufficient accuracy and reliability to permit a timely full-scale response. This chapter, based on a paper published in 1975, anticipated the current interest in weak signals which permit a firm to respond to poorly predictable events.

Why Weak Signals?

Strategic issue management, discussed in the last chapter, enhances the timeliness of the organization's response in three ways: (1) It detects surprising changes in real time as they become evident; (2) it responds in real time without waiting for the annual planning exercise; and (3) it uses a cross-organizational task force approach which expedites the resolution of issues.

Real-time detection of strategic issues increases the time available for response. But, recalling the discussion of Chapter 2, as the speed of surprising changes increases, the predictability drops. This means that by the time information about the change becomes sufficient to permit a well-considered response, the time remaining may be inadequate to complete the response before the threat strikes, or an opportunity is missed.

Thus, there is a paradox: If the firm waits until information is adequate for a decisive response it will be increasingly surprised by crises; if it accepts vague information, the content will not be specific enough for a thorough analysis and a well-considered response to the issue.

© The Author(s) 2019
H. I. Ansoff et al., *Implanting Strategic Management*,
https://doi.org/10.1007/978-3-319-99599-1_20

A solution to this paradox is to change the approach for using strategic information. Instead of waiting for sufficient information to accumulate, an organization can determine what immediate steps in planning and action are feasible now. As clearer strategic information becomes available in the course of the evolution of a threat or opportunity, additional, more decisive steps can be taken.

Early in the life of a threat, when the information is vague and the organization's future course is unclear, the responses will be correspondingly unfocussed, aimed at increasing the strategic flexibility of the firm. As information becomes more precise, so will the firm's response, eventually terminating in a direct action to counter the threat or exploit the opportunity. But the prior buildup of flexibility will allow this action to occur sooner; the action will be better planned and executed.

This approach is called the *graduated response through amplification and response to weak signals*. In this section, a practical method for graduated response will be proposed. The first task is to explore the range of weak signals that can be typically expected from a strategic discontinuity.

States of Knowledge

In strategic planning, the information required for evaluating the impact of threats and opportunities (T/Os) seems to be imperfect because of the uncertainties in both their occurrence and probable course. A closer look shows that while uncertainty exists, the information is very content-rich: The threat has to be well-enough understood to compute the possible profit consequences and the responses well-enough developed to estimate both their costs and their mitigating effects on the threat.

It is reasonable to expect this knowledge from a T/O which arises from a familiar, prior experience. This will be the case when a competitor introduces a new marketing approach, a new product, or a new pricing strategy. But when the T/O is discontinuous (such as the impact of laser technology on land surveying or of large-scale integration on electronic components), in the early stages the nature, impact, and possible responses are unclear. Frequently it is not even clear whether the discontinuity will develop into a threat or an opportunity.

Thus, when a threat or opportunity first appears on the horizon, the organization must be prepared to deal with very vague information, which will eventually develop and improve with time.

This progression may be described by five states of knowledge. These are illustrated in Table 20.1 where level 5 (the highest state of knowledge) contains exactly the information required for strategic planning. Enough is known to compute both the probable profit impact of the discontinuity and the profit impact of the response.

At the other extreme, level 1 is the highest state of ignorance that can be of use to management. All that is known is that some threats and opportunities will undoubtedly arise, but their shape, nature, and source are not yet known. In today's political and economic fog of uncertainty, many firms find themselves in this state of ignorance. Having experienced shocks of change in the recent past, managers are convinced that new ones are coming, but they cannot identify the source. State of knowledge on level 2 improves matters somewhat. For example, in the 1980s, it was generally recognized that small 'desktop' computers had great potential for the electronics industry. But the invention of the specific discontinuities, such as portable laptop computers, the integration of computers with wireless communication, high computing power in small mobile devices, and the explosion of software applications, was still several years off. The source of the T/O was clear (state 2), but not the T/O itself. As various technologies reached the prototype stage, the knowledge was raised to level 3, but at the outset the ramifications of the technological tidal wave were unclear, as were the defensive and aggressive responses that different firms were eventually to make.

When the firms developed and made their initial responses and knowledge was raised to level 4, the eventual investments and profits were not yet visible. Pioneering firms were investing boldly in the new technology with little experience to guide them, in high hopes that their entrepreneurial risks would pay off. Level 5 was not reached until knowledge of computer processing, telecommunications, software design, and the Internet were sufficient to make reasonable predictions of the ultimate technology and its profitability. But by then, the leaders were entrenched, and those who originally held back had to pay a high cost of entry into the industry.

Strong and Weak Signals

In Table 20.1, as the number of 'Yes' entries in each row grows, ignorance is reduced and information is increased as a T/O evolves from level 1 to level 5. A variable of crucial importance is the time remaining at level 5 before the full impact of a T/O will be felt by the organization. For a threat, this is the

Table 20.1 States of knowledge under discontinuity

Information content \ States of Knowledge	(1) Sense of threat/opportunity	(2) Source of threat/opportunity	(3) T/O defined	(4) Response defined	(5) Outcome
Conviction that discontinuities are impending	Yes	Yes	Yes	Yes	Yes
Area of organization is identified which is the source of discontinuity	No	Yes	Yes	Yes	Yes
Characteristics of threat, nature of impact, general gravity of impact, timing of impact	No	No	Yes	Yes	Yes
Response identified: TIMING, action programs, budgets	No	No	No	Yes	Yes
Profit impact and consequences of response are computable	No	No	No	No	Yes

time remaining before maximum loss of profit has occurred; for an opportunity, it is the time before competitive responses by other firms will have progressed to a point at which an attempt by a new competitor to join the market is doomed to be unsuccessful and unprofitable. The time remaining must be compared with the response time required by the organization to avert the threat or capture the opportunity.

If the time remaining at knowledge level 5 is insufficient, then the organization can try to start its response at a lower knowledge level. However, below level 5 there is not enough information to make reliable estimates of the impact and of the effectiveness of response to permit a commitment to an irreversible, unambiguous response. Instead of making a definite commitment to a course of action, management must choose steps which prepare the organization for the ultimate response and, at the same time, keep the options open.

The situation in which knowledge level 5 is reached and the time remaining to act is sufficient for a calculated response is known as a *strong signal problem*. In contrast, the situation case when the time to act is insufficient when knowledge level 5 is reached is the *weak signal problem*.

The strategic issue management procedure developed in the preceding chapter was based on strong signals. In this chapter, we discuss the modifications in the procedure necessary to make it applicable to the weak signal problem.

Gaining Acceptance for Weak Signal Management

Perhaps the most important step is to convert senior managers, who must manage the system, to acceptance of the weak signal approach. Strategic and creative managers would have little difficulty with the concept because, as we discussed in Chapter 9, theirs is essentially a 'weak signal mentality' (see section 'Strategic and Creative Mentalities'). Therefore, strategic and creative managers must be 'sold' not so much on the weak signal concept as on the idea that a systematic management of weak signals is desirable.

The argument to be used is that in the modern turbulent world, weak signals are numerous and frequently novel, and that it will be dangerous to continue handling them in an ad hoc manner.

Managers with mentalities other than strategic or creative will have difficulty in accepting the very concept of weak signals, because their experience (and that of several generations of their teachers and mentors) is based on strong signals. Therefore, selling the concept to them will encounter strong resistance.

In Part V, we offer suggestions for overcoming this resistance and changing the mentality of such managers.

Detection of Weak Signals

Use of weak signals means that individuals responsible for identifying issues must begin to listen for early warning of threats and opportunities. For example, in the list of Table 19.1, item 29 (strategic surprises) must be expanded into more specific descriptions.

In recent years, potential surprise sources would include: global terrorism, globalization and integration of production of markets, the explosive rise of economies in Asia (especially China), chronic unemployment, relations between the 'have' (developed) and 'have not' (developing) nations, consequences of stagnant growth, new methods of energy production, etc. In addition to these global trends, every industry on a high turbulence level would have its own portentous weak signals. For example, the automation of financial institutions and the impact of global integrated production in the automotive industry are weak signals.

Detection of weak signals requires sensitivity as well as expertise on the part of the observers. This means that the detection net must be cast wide, and numerous people involved in addition to the corporate staff charged with managing issues. One source of the detectors are sociopolitical, economic, and technological experts who are outside the firm. Many large firms already have advisory groups which provide weak signal inputs on a systematic basis.

Another source of external weak signals are the individuals (both managers and workers) who serve in the interface functions such as marketing, purchasing, legal, public relations, or R&D. A source of internal weak signals are staff individuals who have broad contacts inside the firm: personnel and management developers, organizational and strategic planners, etc.

*Estimating Impact

The procedure for estimating the impact of threats and opportunities using strong signals was discussed developed in Chapter 19. This approach will be enlarged to accommodate weak signals. It will be recalled from Table 19.4 that when using strong signals, the impact of a trend on the organization can usually be estimated. In the weak signal case, it becomes desirable to estimate the impact SBA by SBA.

The methodology must first recognize the state of knowledge about a trend or event. Then the approach is to provide some latitude in the accuracy of the estimates. On lower levels of knowledge when less is known, trusted judgment or expert opinion techniques such as Delphi can be used. On higher levels of knowledge when more is known, quantitative forecasting and modeling techniques become feasible.

A format for impact estimation is shown in Table 20.2. This figure illustrates a simple case of a firm with four SBAs and one important signal per SBA. As seen across the top, each trend is placed in a column, according to its state of knowledge (1 through 5). It is further described along with three characteristics:

1. Whether it is a threat, opportunity, or both.
2. The time remaining, ranging from high probable estimate to low probable estimate (meaning, in statistical language, a *2-sigma* range).
3. The range of impact on profits presently derived from the SBA (again ranging from high probable to low probable). The entries represent the fractions by which the profit will be increased or decreased.

The range of timing and profit impact estimates becomes wider as ignorance increases. Thus, the impact on SBA_2 which is ten to fifteen years off may turn either into a threat or an opportunity, but it is clear that the impact is likely to be very serious. Clearly, this discontinuity needs watching closely.

Table 20.2 Threat/opportunity weak signal analysis

State of knowledge →	(1) Sense	(2) Source	(3) T/O defined	(4) Response defined	(5) Outcome defined
SBA	% of Profit				
SBA1	50		Threat 1–3 years 0.15–0.40		
SBA2	30	T/O 10–15 years + 0.30 to −0.30			
SBA3	15			Opportunity 1–2 years 0.35–0.40	
SBA4	5	Opportunity 3–7 years 0.08–0.18			

On the other hand, the profit estimates for the opportunity in SBA$_3$ can be estimated within a narrow range of both occurrence and impact.

Alternative Response Strategies

Just as we have expanded the states of information to include poorer knowledge, we need to enlarge the repertoire of responses to permit appropriate actions to weak signals. This is shown in Fig. 20.1 where management options are subdivided into two groups: responses that change the firm's relationship with the *environment* and responses that change the internal *capability* of the firm. For each group, there are three progressively stronger strategies: one that enhances the firm's awareness and understanding; one that increases the firm's flexibility; and one that directly responds to the threat or opportunity. Thus, the table provides a total of six response strategies.

The strongest *external action* strategy directly acts to counter threats or exploit opportunities. It includes selection of the type of action, preparation of programs and budgets, and implementation. The end result is a threat averted or an opportunity captured in the form of an enhanced potential for future profits.

As discussed in Part III, external direct strategic action must be supported by development of the appropriate *internal readiness* shown in the lower box under the direct response heading.

The earliest response to a threat or opportunity is offered by the pair of *awareness* strategies, shown in the right-hand column of the figure. In most firms, a degree of environmental awareness is provided through economic

Response Strategies / Domain Of Response	Direct Response	Flexibility	Awareness
Relationship to Environment	External action (Strategic Planning and Implementation	External Flexibility	Environmental Awareness
Internal Capability	Internal readiness (capability planning and implementation)	Internal Flexibility	Self-awareness

Fig. 20.1 Alternative response strategies

forecasting, sales forecasting, and analysis of competitive behavior. But all of these measures are frequently extrapolative, based on a smooth extension of the past into the future, and do not provide information about strategic discontinuities.

To broaden the awareness to include discontinuities, the firm must add special types of environment analysis, such as environmental monitoring, technological forecasting, sociopolitical forecasting, and SWOT analysis (see Chapter 10).

Starting the awareness activities in the firm does not require concrete information about threats and opportunities. The highest state of ignorance (a sense of threat) is adequate to justify a program for enhancing the firm's environment awareness. A sense of threat is also adequate for starting many of the self-awareness measures, such as capacity audits, strength/weakness assessments, and financial modeling of the firm.

The flexibility strategy shown in the middle column of Fig. 20.1 differs from the direct action strategies in that its end product is an enhanced responsiveness, rather than tangible changes in profits and growth. The external flexibility sub-strategy is concerned with diversifying the firm in the environment in a way which puts the firm in a position to participate in major opportunities which may arise in turbulent SBAs but also minimizes the impact of catastrophic reversals which may occur in an SBA.

Formulation of the external flexibility strategy is part of the strategic flexibility planning process, where it is usually assumed to require level 5 information input. But measures such as balance of technological, business, and political-geographical risks can be planned and implemented if the state of knowledge is no better than level 2—long before the nature of the threat becomes concrete.

Finally, *Internal flexibility* is concerned with configuring the resources and capabilities of the firm to permit quick and efficient repositioning to new products and new markets, whenever the need arises. One important element is the flexibility of the managers, including awareness of the environment, psychological readiness to face unpleasant and unfamiliar events, ability to solve unfamiliar problems, and creativity. Another element is the flexibility of the managerial systems and structure to permit quick and efficient response to change. A third element is the flexibility of logistic resources and systems such as resource liquidity, diversification of work skills, modular capacities, and so forth.

Unlike external flexibility, internal flexibility has received relatively little attention from strategic planners. But it can be a crucial ingredient in strategic preparedness. In the area of managerial flexibility, the preparation of managers for strategic thinking and action is now recognized as essential and vital if the firm is to anticipate and deal with the growing turbulence of the environment.

Flexibility of the logistic resources has received even less attention than managerial flexibility. As strategic change accelerates, logistic flexibility will become increasingly important. As with external flexibility, the mere knowledge of the sources of threats and opportunities is sufficient to start a rigorous program of logistic preparedness.

Feasible Responses

The preceding discussion shows that if management is receptive to weak signals, much can be done long before the threat becomes tangible and concrete. The possibilities are summarized in Fig. 20.2 in which the shaded portions represent the areas of feasible response. The partly shaded boxes mean that some, but not all, of the particular type of measure becomes feasible at the particular state of knowledge. As seen in the figure, all of the environment awareness measures, all of internal flexibility, and a substantial portion of external flexibility can be put in place before the threat becomes clear and definite.

As Fig. 20.2 shows, for direct response strategy (bottom rows), it is necessary to have a good idea of the threat or opportunity. But even a sufficiently

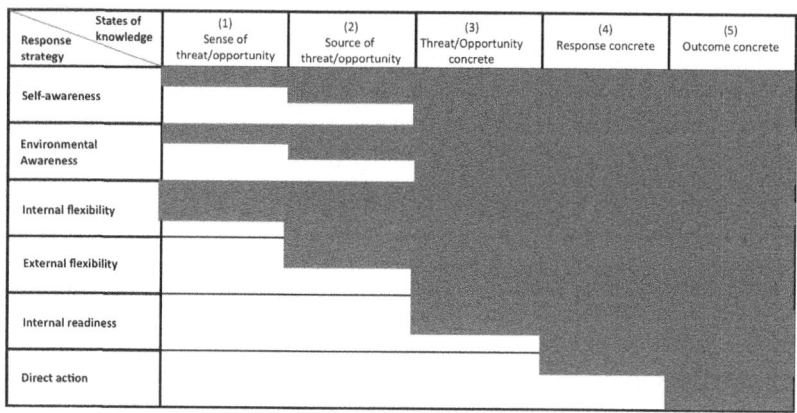

Fig. 20.2 Feasible ranges of response strategies (shaded areas)

clear idea of the origin and shape of a threat or opportunity is sufficient to launch a substantial program of internal readiness measures, including acquisition of necessary technological, production, and marketing skills, new product development and development of sources of supply.

Even direct external action need not await information that makes possible reliable cash and profit flow calculations. This is where entrepreneurial risk-takers become differentiated from cautious followers. Adventurous firms will typically launch their entry into a new industry at knowledge level 4, before the technology, market, and competition are well-enough defined to permit such calculations. More conservative firms will prefer to wait on the sidelines until the situation is better defined.

Dynamics of Response

Each of the six response strategies makes a contribution to the organization's ability to handle strategic discontinuities. Each requires a different length of time for implementation. The total length of time for responding to a specific threat or opportunity depends on the prior preparedness of the firm, the vigor with which the firm responds, and the sequence in which the programs of action are put in place.

Conventional strategic planning proceeds from direct response, to flexibility, to awareness. Figure 20.2 and the preceding discussion suggest the reverse sequence: awareness, to flexibility, to direct response which enables the firm to start response much earlier, and finish earlier, utilizing weak signals.

Figure 20.3 illustrates the dynamics of the firm's response, using this latter sequence. The vertical scale shows the time needed by the firm to complete the response, that is, to eliminate or stabilize operating losses or to make viable a new opportunity. The horizontal scale lists the states of preparedness from which it may start. The curves show the obvious advantage of prior readiness: The better prepared the firm when it starts, the less time it will need to complete the response.

The upper curve of Fig. 20.3 traces the *normal response* in which the threat or opportunity is treated routinely by existing processes, structures, systems, and procedures. The lower solid curve, the ad hoc *crash response*, shows the time savings that can be gained when everything possible is done to speed up the response—normal rules and procedures are suspended, other priorities are pushed into the background, organizational lines are crossed, activities are duplicated, overtime is incurred, and so forth.

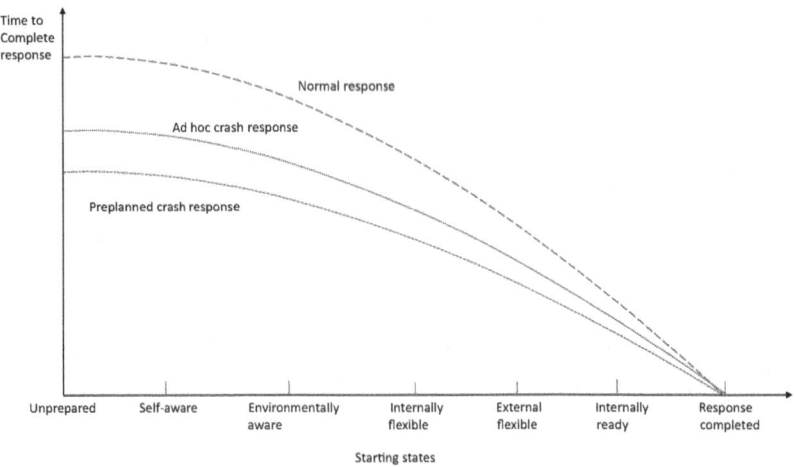

Fig. 20.3 Internal dynamics of response

The mere 'pulling out of stops' is not the only emergency procedure open to the organization. In spite of best efforts to anticipate threats and opportunities, an organization may still expect to be confronted with sudden, fast-developing threats. In this case, investment in a program of training in crisis management is worthwhile. The result will be to lower the response time to the level labeled *pre-planned crisis response* (see Chapter 2).

The envelope of response times defined by the three curves in Fig. 20.3 will differ among organizations and differ from one threat or opportunity to another. Size, complexity, and rigidity of organization structure will lengthen the response times while the nature of the threat or opportunity will be equally influential. Important factors will be the size of the discontinuity as well as its degree of unfamiliarity. Both of these factors determine the magnitude of the response effort. Next, a procedure is proposed that will translate the theoretical curves of Fig. 20.3 into practical application.

*Preparedness Diagnosis

Table 20.2 indicated that at a given time, the state of knowledge will differ from SBA to SBA. Consequently, the range of possible responses will also differ. Therefore, first step is to determine the feasible responses for each SBA and its threat or opportunity.

Continuing with the example of Table 20.2, we have chosen SBA_1 which had a single, clearly visible threat. A reference to the feasibility table of Fig. 20.2 shows that five or six response strategies are feasible in this advanced stage of information. This is recorded as F (feasible) or I (infeasible) in the second column of Fig. 20.4.

The next step is to diagnose the firm's current state of readiness in each of the feasible strategies. The result is shown in column three of Fig. 20.4. Letting 100% represent the maximum that can be done to respond to the threat or opportunity in the current level of knowledge, the entry is an estimate of the current readiness in each of the categories.

The 15% entry for self-awareness suggests that, while the threat is concrete enough, the organization has done relatively little to determine the usefulness of its own capability for dealing with the threat. On the other hand, the organization appears to be well advanced in understanding the market, the potential competition, and the future.

To continue with the example, the low rating on internal flexibility shows that the firm's resources and facilities are highly specialized while the slightly higher status for external flexibility indicates that the organization's profits are largely dependent on current technology and that it is highly threatened by new technology.

The next and critical step in the procedure is to estimate the time the firm will need to move the state of readiness to the 100% level for each of the preparedness categories. The estimate is made for each category for both normal and crash responses. In the last row of Fig. 20.4 a summary estimate is made, looking at four to eight years to achieve a completed response.

SBA₁	Feasibility	Status	Effort expended			
			Crash		Normal	
			Time (yrs)	Cost (x current profit)	Time (yrs)	Cost (x current profit)
Self-awareness	F	0% ●————100%	3		6	
Environmental awareness	F	0% ————●—100%	1		2	
Internal flexibility	F	0% ●————100%	2		4	
External flexibility	F	0% ——●——100%	4		8	
Internal readiness	F (Partial)	0% ————●——100%	2		4	
Direct action	I	0% ————————100%	2		4	
Completed response	✕	0% ——————●—100%	4 yrs	4.0	8 yrs	1.0

Fig. 20.4 Preparedness diagnosis

In our example, this might have meant divesting from the SBA in the old technology, possibly narrowing the firm's scope to a market in which the old technology will continue to be competitive, or making a successful entry into the new technology line of business.

The final step in readiness diagnosis is to estimate the cost-effectiveness of the total response. The cost of the response is shown in the last row of the figure as a fraction of the percentage of current profits contributed by the SBA. If, as shown in Fig. 20.4, a crash program will cost four times the current profits, and if the response will prevent a loss of 0.15–0.40 of this profit annually (see Table 20.2), the investment will amortize itself in 10–27 years. The cost-effectiveness is low, which suggests that the threat should be written off and allowed to run its course. On the other hand, the normal response (if it turns out to be timely enough) costing 1.0 times current profits will be much more cost-effective, because the amortization period will be only 2.5–7 years.

*Opportunity-Vulnerability Profile

The preceding discussion suggests two conclusions. First, the decision to respond should not be based on response costs alone, nor on the amount of profit loss or gain that is at stake. Rather, it should be based on the return on the costs incurred. We used the simple but useful payback measure of this return. With better data (particularly in the advanced states of knowledge), other measures can be employed. By doing this, ill-advised spending is avoided, especially when the threat looms large and the temptation is to respond directly, no matter what the costs.

Second, the selection of the appropriate action, in the range between normal and crash response, cannot be made independently of the timing of the threat. A comparison of the timing is provided by the *opportunity/vulnerability profile* shown in Fig. 20.5. This figure combines the results of the threat and opportunity analysis with the readiness diagnosis.

The shaded rectangles enclose the regions of probable impact on each SBA. Rectangles below the horizontal axis will result in losses in profitability due to threats; those above the line indicate gains offered by opportunities. The height of the rectangle spans the probable range of gain or loss. The base spans the probable times when impact of the discontinuity will reach critical level. Both dimensions are obtained from the threat and opportunity analysis presented earlier in Table 20.2.

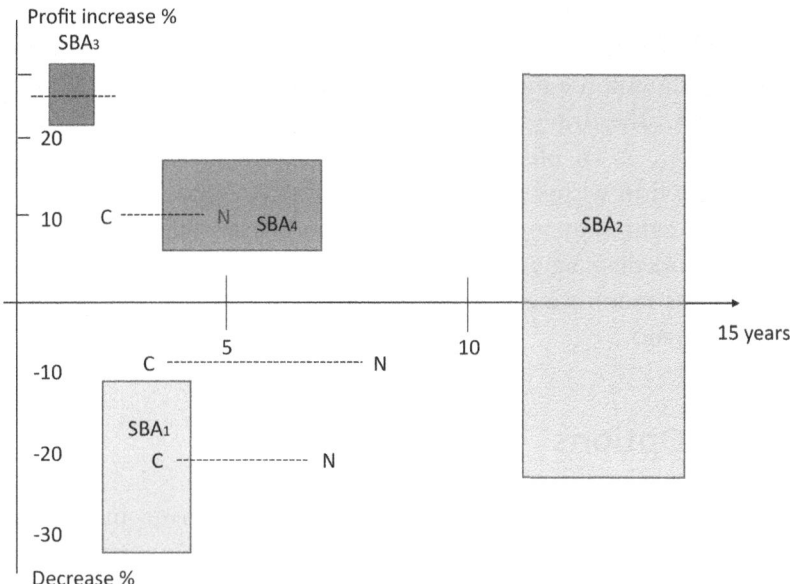

Fig. 20.5 Opportunity/vulnerability profile

The horizontal, dotted lines in Fig. 20.5 were obtained from the readiness diagnosis (Fig. 20.4). They span the time of probable completion of successful response. Thus, the normal response for SBA_3 would be late, but the firm can assure itself of capturing the opportunity through a crash program. SBA_2 is safe—normal response will capture the threat or opportunity, provided the firm continues to monitor the development of the contingency. SBA_1 is in trouble because even a crash response may be late; it looks like a surprise in the making.

These examples show that timing of the threat does not by itself determine the priority of the respective responses. The priorities are determined in part by the urgency (the difference between the timing of the threat and the time needed for response). In our example, both SBA_1 and SBA_4 are expected to reach critical impact at about the same time. But because of the longer response time needed, SBA_1 must be handled on an all-out crisis response basis, while a moderately urgent response will suffice for SBA_4. The priorities are also determined by the potential cost-effectiveness of the responses determined in the manner discussed in the preceding section.

The opportunity profile provides an overall perspective on significant strategic changes in the firm's future. The firm needs to check the impact of

SBA_1 because if unchecked, a minimum of 15% and a maximum of 40% of the profit will be lost. Since timely response to this threat will be difficult, either the crash response must be used, or the firm should start a withdrawal from the SBA. The firm *must* use a crash response to capture the opportunity in SBA_3, as an offsetting insurance against possible loss in SBA_1. Further, if the firm wishes to capture the attractive opportunity in SBA_4, it needs to start right away to avoid a crash response later. Only SBA_2 seems to call for no immediate aggressive action. But its potential impact is so great that a vigorous monitoring program should be spotlighted on the development of this trend.

Decision Options

Previously in Fig. 20.5, we saw that priority assignment in strong signal management divides the issues into four categories: no action, continued monitoring, delayed action until the next periodic planning cycle, and immediate action through priority projects.

Weak signal management adds another important option, which we have already explored in Chapters 11 and 14. This is the strategic learning or gradual commitment option under which the firm responds, step-by-step, as the issue progresses to higher states of knowledge.

The decision process in weak signal strategic issue management is illustrated in Fig. 20.6. If the potential impact has been estimated as major, the

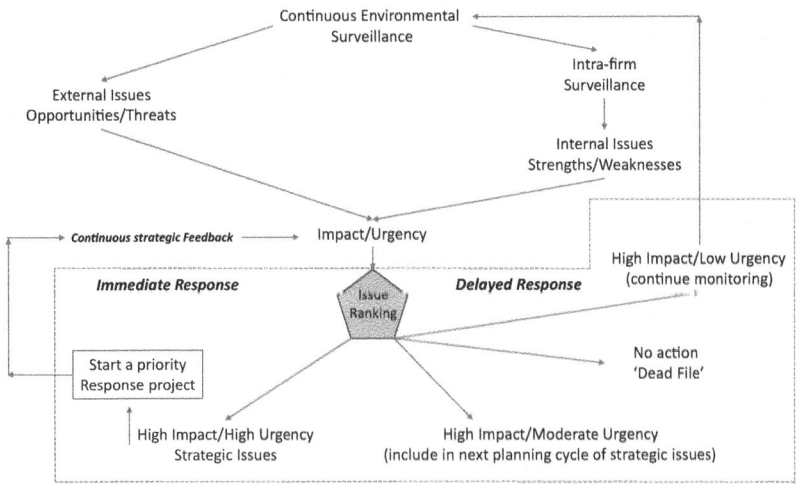

Fig. 20.6 Priority assignment in weak signal SIM

next question is whether the signal is strong or weak. In both cases, the next step is an evaluation of urgency. As the figure shows, delayable and post-ponable issues lead to the same action priorities for both strong and weak signals. But there is a significant difference when the issue is urgent—strong signal issues trigger a priority project, while the weak signal issues must be treated through a gradual commitment project.

The reader may recall, the process of strategic learning (stepwise response) was covered in more detail in Chapter 5.

*Choice Among Periodic Planning, Strong Signal and Weak Signal Management

As discussed in conjunction with Fig. 20.3, short of a crisis response, there are two modes in which a firm can respond to the environment: the normal response in which the established periodic planning and implementation systems are used, and the ad hoc crash response which crosses established lines and uses ad hoc task forces to produce a rapid response. The time periods required to complete a response in these modes are called *normal response time (T)* and *issue management response time (T₁)*.

The choice of the response depends on the speed with which a threat or opportunity develops in the environment. This is illustrated in Fig. 20.7. The vertical scale is the state of information which is available about a threat or opportunity. It will be recalled that knowledge level 5 (see Table 20.1) is

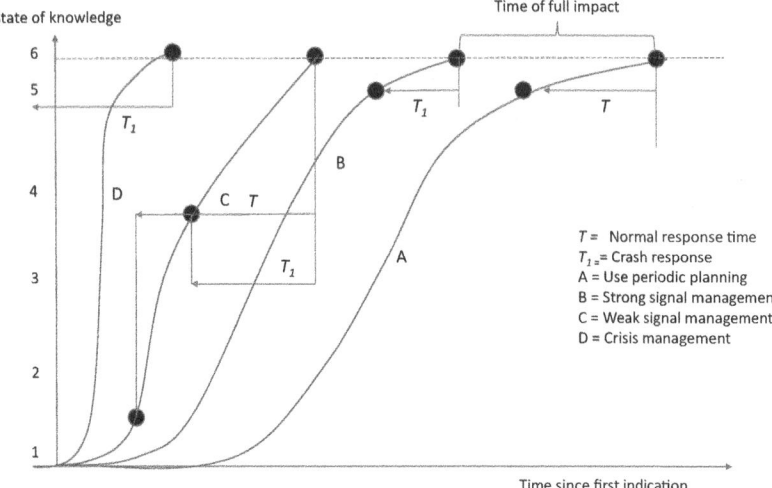

Fig. 20.7 Choosing the system

when enough information is available to compute the impact of a threat or opportunity and the consequences of responses (even though probabilities may have to be assigned to each of the computations). In Fig. 20.7, we have added level 6 at which the computation of impact is converted into reality and it is too late to respond.

The horizontal scale is the time which elapses since level 1 awareness has been reached about a threat or opportunity. The figure shows four threats or opportunities which develop at different speeds. Event A is the slowest and event D is the fastest. The arrival of each curve at level 6 is its time of full impact.

The figure shows that the slow curve A arrives at level 5 in time to permit the normal response. In this case, there is no need for an issue management system and the threat or opportunity can be handled by the periodic planning and implementation system.

In the case of curve B, the threat or opportunity arrives at level 5 too late to permit the firm to use the periodic planning system. But the response will be timely if strong signal issue management is used.

Curve C arrives at level 5 too late for strong signal issue management. As the figure shows, the normal response would have to be started between knowledge levels 1 and 2 and issue response at knowledge level 3.5. In this case, a weak signal detection system must be used.

Curve D is a threat or opportunity which is an *unavoidable surprise*, because even the issue response would have to be started before the sense of impending threat or opportunity (knowledge level l) is perceivable in the environment.

If analysis of future turbulence indicates that significant threats or opportunities are likely to occur which will be faster than the speed of the issue response by the firm, management should give serious consideration to developing a crisis management system.

For mathematically inclined readers, the preceding remarks can be summarized as follows. If we label the time remaining from knowledge level 5 to full impact (level 6) δ, and the time from the inception of threat to full impact F:

If $T < \delta$, use only periodic planning.

If $T > \delta$ and $T_1 < \delta$, use strong signal issue management.

If $T_1 > \delta < F$, use weak signal issue management.

If $T_1 > F$, use crisis management.

Summary

When environmental turbulence rises above level 4 (see Chapter 6) important threats and opportunities develop so very fast. If the organization waits until the impact and consequences can be accurately estimated, it will be too late to launch a timely response. In such cases, it becomes necessary to start the response while information is still incomplete. Such partial information is referred to as 'weak signals.'

Knowledge about each threat or opportunity will progress through several stages: First there is a sense of turbulence in the environment, and then the probable source of the threat or opportunity is identified. At some point, specific threat or opportunity becomes concrete enough to describe, but not sufficiently defined to estimate the full consequences for the organization. At the next stage of knowledge, it becomes possible to develop responses to the threat or opportunity, even though information is still unavailable to estimate the profit consequences. Profit consequences can be estimated at the final stage, but the estimates are still uncertain, which means that a probability must be assigned. Eventually certainty is reached, when the impact of the threat or opportunity has been reflected in the firm's performance.

Managing by weak signals requires that the individuals involved in detecting signals are sensitized and trained to be open to a wide range of incoming data. In addition, the detected signals must be classified according to their state of knowledge, and best possible estimates made of their probable impact and timing. The lower the level of knowledge, the wider will be the range of impact and timing estimates.

At each stage of knowledge, weak signal responses are possible which progressively prepare the organization to deal with the threat or opportunity. The advantage of taking early action is that it permits the organization to make timely responses which would be missed if the firm were to wait for them to become fully developed.

In addition to starting early, the organization can improve its timeliness by using special task forces.

The choice of whether and how to respond should be determined by comparing the timing of the threat or opportunity versus the time required for the response. Also, the gain to the firm by responding should be compared to the cost of making the response.

Weak signal management is one of three alternatives for dealing with threats and opportunities. The others are strong signal management and periodic planning. The choice of the systems to be used is determined by speed of threats and opportunities, as compared to the speed of response of each system. When the threat or opportunity speed becomes too high for periodic planning, strong signal issue management should be added. When strong signal issue management becomes too slow, it should be replaced by weak signal issue management.

Exercises

1. You are a member of the corporate planning staff in a large diversified pharmaceutical company. The V.P. of Planning says to you: 'As a result of the Tylenol crisis, I am convinced that we should introduce weak signal issue management. But this cannot be done unless the top management committee is sufficiently convinced of its possible advantages to devote its time to managing the system. Will you please prepare a 30-minute briefing to be presented to the management committee which will explain in clear terms what weak signal issue management is, why should it be used in our firm, how should it be used, what benefits will it bring about?' Your assignment is to prepare a series of briefing charts and a text which will accompany them.

2. Your briefing has been well accepted, and the management committee now wants to know how the system is to be put in place, who should be involved, how it will run, what it will cost, what problems are likely to be encountered, how long it will take to put in place. Your assignment is to prepare a plan for introducing the system into the firm which will answer all of these questions.

3. Develop a list of the five most important weak signals which should be considered by the firms in the following industries:

   Pharmaceuticals
   Steel
   Banking
   Health
   Education
   Information Systems.

4. For each of the chosen industries, prepare an opportunity/vulnerability profile, using the format of Fig. 20.5.

Part V

Managing Strategic Change

21

Behavioral Resistance to Change

In the second edition of Implanting Strategic Management, Ansoff and McDonnell introduced this chapter with a quote from Machiavelli. In his famous book The Prince, Machiavelli said: 'There is nothing more difficult to take in hand, more perilous to conduct, or more uncertain of success than to take a lead in the introduction of a new order of things, because the innovation has for enemies all those who have done well under the old conditions and lukewarm defenders in those who may do well under new.' They recognized this prophetic statement as capturing the essence of one major source of resistance to strategic discontinuities. This chapter will examine the nature of the 'order of things' and offer suggestions for managing it.

Sources of Resistance.

The Phenomenon of Resistance

Since the emergence of systematic management of strategy, attention of both practitioners and students has been focused on two aspects:

1. The first is the logic and techniques of strategy analysis (*strategy formulation*).
2. The second is the design of a systematic process (*strategic planning*) through which managers interact and contribute to the formulation of strategy.

Prescriptions, which were developed for strategic planning, were based on three underlying assumptions.

© The Author(s) 2019
H. I. Ansoff et al., *Implanting Strategic Management*,
https://doi.org/10.1007/978-3-319-99599-1_21

1. The first was that 'reasonable people will do reasonable things' and that managers will, therefore, welcome new ways of thinking and will cooperate wholeheartedly. When, in practice, the new strategic thinking encountered 'resistance to planning,' this was viewed as a temporary aberration due to ignorance, to be removed by strong endorsement of planning by top management.
2. Since the firm had justly earned a reputation for implementation of decisions, the second assumption was that the key problem in strategy was to make the right decisions, and that existing systems and procedures would effectively translate strategic decisions into actions.
3. The third key assumption was that strategy formulation and strategy implementation are sequential and independent activities. Hence, concern with implementation could start after the strategic decisions were made and thus not interfere with the already difficult and complex strategic decision process.

Cumulated experience of the past twenty-five years has cast serious doubts on all three assumptions. When firms diversified into novel markets and technologies, the costs of the new ventures typically exceeded estimates, unanticipated delays were encountered, and the organization exhibited resistance to the new departures. In the field of mergers and acquisitions, case after case led to disappointments. New acquisitions, which were profitable before the merger, mysteriously became unprofitable afterward; key managers acquired through merger tended to leave the firm, in spite of attractive financial inducements; synergies anticipated from mergers failed to materialize.

When top management decided to place strategic decision making on a systematic basis, by introducing strategic planning, the organization resisted the new system. Once introduced, many systems exhibited 'paralysis by analysis' or 'death in the drawer,' in which planning languished, or strategies never connected with the marketplace. In addition, there was a common tendency to squeeze the system out of the firm and to return to earlier, less-radical, approaches to decision making. Expressions of support by top management had the effect of temporary coercion. So long as top management applied strong pressure, the organization compiled; but when the support was removed, or top management attention shifted to other priorities, resistance resurfaced.

In summary, practical experience shows that significant changes in a firm's strategic orientation, whether introduced through formal strategic planning or as an informal process, encounter organizational resistance. Four conclusions follow from experience:

1. 'Reasonable people *do not* do reasonable things,' if by reasonable, we mean analytically logical things. Resistance to planning is not a superficial phenomenon; it has a logic of its own, and it cannot be removed by exhortations from top managers.
2. Implementation of strategy does not automatically follow strategy formulation. It exhibits its own resistance, which can invalidate the planning effort.
3. Treatment of strategy planning and implementation as two sequential and independent processes is an artificial convenience, which neglects the fact that the way planning is done has a determining effect on the eventual implementability of decisions.
4. Resistance to change is not confined to introduction of strategic planning. It occurs whenever an organizational change introduces a discontinuous departure from the historical behavior, culture, and power structure.

Thus, significant strategic reorientations evoke resistance not only to planning but also to the entire change process. Resistance is not an aberration but a fundamental problem which deserves attention comparable to that historically given to strategy formulation.

Resistance Defined

By resistance, we shall mean a multifaceted phenomenon, which introduces unanticipated delays, costs, and instabilities into the process of a strategic change. Resistance manifests itself throughout the history of a change. During the change process, all of the following may occur:

1. Procrastination and delays in triggering the process of change.
2. Unforeseen implementation delays and inefficiencies which slow down the change and make it cost more than originally anticipated.
3. Efforts within the organization to sabotage the change or to 'absorb' it in the welter of other priorities.

After the change has been installed, the following may occur:

1. There is a typical performance lag. The change is slow in producing the anticipated results.
2. There are efforts within the organization to roll back the effects of the change to the pre-change status.

1. **Rejection** – "There is nothing wrong with us that a long production run wouldn't cure."
2. **Procrastination** – "Tomorrow we'll get organized and plan."
3. **Indecision** – "Death in the drawer."
4. **Lack of implementation follow-up** – "Paralysis by analysis."
5. **Strategic ineffectiveness** – "The more trucks we sell, the more money we lose."
6. **Sabotage** – "What the boss doesn't know won't hurt her."
7. **Regression** – "Let's end this and get back to some real work!"

Fig. 21.1 Seven symptoms of resistance

When firms make a major revision of the external strategy, the internal capability becomes maladapted and performance suffers. We have suggested that a firm's strategic response to the environment will be more timely and effective, if capability is developed in conjunction with the new strategy which it will support. But while the performance will be more effective after the capability is installed, the *process* of capability installation more than doubles the organization-disturbing workload (as compared to installing a new strategy), and the impending discontinuities in culture and power structure become more visible. As a result, strategic posture planning will encounter even higher resistance than strategic planning.

Seen from the point of view of a strategy analyst, resistance is a manifestation of the 'irrationality' of an organization, a refusal to recognize new dimensions of reality, to reason logically, and to carry out the consequences of logical deductions (Fig. 21.1).

But seen from the viewpoint of a behavioral or a political scientist, resistance is a natural manifestation of different rationalities, according to which groups and individuals interact with one another. In the following sections, we identify the sources and the rules of these rationalities.

Resistance and Rate of Change

Noting that a key characteristic of resistance can be inferred from Machiavelli's quotation cited at the opening of this chapter, Ansoff noted 'Resistance to change is proportional to the degree of discontinuity in the culture and/or the power structure introduced by the change. For a given discontinuity, the resistance will be inversely proportional to the time over which the change is spread' (Ansoff 1979-G).

In business language, culture is frequently described as the 'management orientation' or 'management mentality.' Thus, under 'production orientation,' efficiency of production is the key norm, and success is perceived to come from being able to offer, at the lowest prices, durable undifferentiated products. For example, in the 1930s and 1940s, when production orientation ceased to be the key to success, and marketing-oriented response became necessary, management typically persisted in their 'production mentality.' They clung to historical success experiences and resisted a transition to a new model of reality based on the marketing concept.

The resistance was further augmented by the fact that the transition to the marketing orientation was accompanied by a discontinuity in the power structure: a passing of influence and power from production to the marketing parts of the organization. Thus, when cultural change is accompanied by a shift of power, resistance is compounded.

The second part of the above proposition about the speed of the change is based, in part, on the fact that, when change is introduced gradually, only one part of an organization at a time is affected, resistance is local, and does not receive support from the unaffected parts of the enterprise.

Furthermore, individuals and groups will resist change in proportion to the degree of threat and discomfort introduced by the *current increment of change*. This is another way of saying that, in resisting change, the affected individuals typically take the near-term view of its consequences and seldom concern themselves with the cumulative impact of all of the future increments.

As a summary, we present in Table 21.1 the contributing effects of cultural and political resistance. As the figure shows, not all strategic changes necessarily provoke resistance: Groups and individuals whose culture is reinforced by the change, and/or who stand to gain power, welcome the change and give it support. In Machiavelli's words, they usually 'stand to gain under the new order.' But, as he points out, their support is frequently 'lukewarm.' In the following sections, we shall be exploring the reasons for this attitude, and how those who stand to gain can be won over to more active support. We can generalize Table 21.1 by means of a single symbolic equation where ΔC and ΔP are the signs of the cultural and political disturbance implied by the change, and ΔT is the period over which the change is introduced.

Table 21.1 Effects of power and cultural implications on behavioral resistance

Implications of change ⟶ ↓	Politically Threatening	Politically Neutral	Politically Welcome
Change in Culture	Greatest Resistance	Depends on size of cultural change	Depends on size of cultural change
Culturally Acceptable	Depends on Size of threat	Least Resistance	Positive Reinforcement

The equation expresses in symbols the verbal proposition at the beginning of this section.

$$R \text{ behavior } \propto \pm \frac{(\Delta C + \Delta P)}{\Delta T}$$

An Illustrative Example

A contrast between two similar changes, one of which induced severe resistance and the other did not, is offered by the recent histories of long range planning and strategic planning as we discussed earlier. Both were invented within a few years of each other, but their track records are very different.

As noted earlier, long range planning (LRP), introduced in the 1950s, is a method for extrapolating the firm's past into the future. Rather than violate, LRP elaborates and confirms the historical model of reality and culture.

Its political consequences are minor, since it is a 'bottom-up' process and does not threaten the established power structure. On the contrary, long range planning permits the powerful groups to reinforce their historical claims on resources, and weak groups remain weak. Long range planning quickly became popular, and, within a few years, surveys began to show that a majority of medium and large firms had adopted LRP.

The history of strategic planning (SP) is different. Despite initial enthusiasm and popularity given to it by articles and seminars, acceptance of strategic planning has been slow, and it was not until the late 1970s that leading firms began to settle into a systematic practice of strategic planning. Since then, there have been numerous instances in which strategic planning, after having been introduced by enthusiastic management, either became a process of 'paralysis by analysis,' or was gradually sabotaged and disappeared from the organization.

The reason for this dramatic difference is that strategic planning typically attacks *both* the cultural and the political order of things. Its very purpose is to replace the historical model of reality, and its power implications are to increase influence and power of general management levels. In light of the proposition presented at the beginning of this section, this explains the strong resistance against strategic planning.

Resistance by Individuals

The causes of resistance can be traced to reactions by individuals on the one hand and to common actions by groups of individuals, on the other.

Both experience and literature on psychology show that individuals will resist change when it makes them insecure. This occurs in the following situations:

- When a manager is uncertain about the impact and implication of the change.
- When he is called upon to take risks which are uncongenial to him.
- When a manager feels that the change may make him redundant.
- When he feels incompetent to perform in the new role defined by the change.
- When he feels that he will lose face with his peers.
- When he is incapable and/or unwilling to learn new skills and behavior.

Individuals will also resist change when their position of power is threatened. This occurs in the following situations:

- When a manager expects his share in organizational rewards to be reduced.
- When he feels that the change will diminish his position of influence over organizational decisions.
- When it will diminish his control over organizational resources.
- When it will diminish his personal prestige and reputation.

But not all managers are alike. Some are personally secure; some are prone to anxiety; some are proud, and others less so; some actively seek power and prestige, and others are indifferent to the trappings of power; some are born leaders, and some are content to follow; and some are set in their ways, and others are open to change and are eager learners. Thus, the way in which managers will react to change will depend on the strength of their personality and their personal flexibility. Therefore, for a given change in culture and power, the resistance by a manager will depend on:

- the strength of their convictions
- their preparedness to defend themselves
- their power drive, and
- their predisposition to learn and change.

Group Resistance

Group reactions to change are traceable, in the last analysis, to the views and convictions of individuals. But, as likely as not, these may be individuals who have long left the organization. Thus, group culture and group power have an existence of their own. Further, they have stability and permanence which exceed those of most individuals. It is much easier to remove or shunt aside an individual who is a major block to progress, than it is to change the culture of a group, or deprive it of power.

Both sociological literature and practical experience show the following:

- Groups of managers who share common tasks and preoccupations develop, over a period of time, commonalities of behavior and outlook.
- They establish norms and values which reward certain types of behavior and punish others. For example, in some firms and in bureaucracies, the slogan 'we don't rock the boat' has the power of an edict. In innovative firms, the key norm is: 'if it's not new it's not good.'
- They develop a consensus on information that is pertinent to their common tasks and information that is irrelevant. For example, there has been a long tradition in business firms that political and social phenomena are not relevant to managerial concerns, because the 'business of business is business.'
- They develop a consensus, sociologists call it *model of reality*, on which behaviors produce desirable results and which do not. Thus, during the first part of the century, there was a prevalent view that the way to maximize profits was through producing the cheapest standardized product.
- They develop an allegiance to the common culture described above, and they will jointly defend it against encroachment of influence of other cultures.

Political science literature, as well as common observation, shows that groups behave in the following ways:

- They coalesce and act as power centers within the rest of the organization.
- They seek to accumulate power and influence.
- They defend their power positions.

Groups will resist a change in proportion to which it:

- Threatens the power of the group.
- Violates accepted values and norms.
- Is based on information which is regarded as irrelevant.
- Is based on a model of reality which differs from the model held valid by the group.

Organizational Loyalty

Described above are what may be called the selfish reactions of groups and individuals in response to threats to their power, security, and culture. These reactions may be modified by a concern for the welfare of the organization as a whole.

A dramatic and often observed example is behavior of organizations under a survival crisis, when cultural/political resistance is suspended for the duration, and everyone rallies around efforts to assure organizational survival. Equally well documented is the revival of cultural/political pressures, once survival appears assured. We shall call this phenomenon an expression of *negative loyalty* to the organization under which resistance is diminished in proportion to the perceived imminence of a survival crisis.

Negative loyalty, which is sometimes described as the *survival drive*, is typically observed in all-purposive organizations, both profit and nonprofit oriented. In firms, and some mission-oriented nonprofits, there is also the phenomenon of *positive loyalty*: diminution of cultural/political resistance in proportion to the positive contribution to the organization's performance expected from a strategic change.

Thus, during changes aimed at averting organizational disaster, the cultural/political resistance is moderated in proportion to the following:

1. Perceived nearness of a survival crisis.
2. The level of negative loyalty which individuals and groups have for the organization.

During changes aimed at improving organizational performance, cultural/political resistance will be moderated and may change to positive support in proportion to the following:

1. The degree of improvement in performance promised by the change.
2. The level of positive loyalty within the organization.

Perception vs. Reality

Under normal conditions, it is trivial to say that people react to what they perceive. But during resistance-inducing changes, the gap between perception and reality can substantially and unnecessarily increase the level of resistance.

The originators and proponents of a change are reacting to novel environmental signals, whose impact is portentous but unclear. The response alternatives are difficult to identify, and their consequences are seen, at best, vaguely in broad strategic terms. The commitment to making a drastic departure from the familiar, and usually successful past, takes courage, 'an overall view' of the problem, and a conviction that comfortable historical alternatives are not the proper response to the challenge.

Individuals capable of this kind of long-term vision and courage are rare. In business, they are called entrepreneurs; in political life, they are statesmen. They are helped toward the decision by the knowledge that it is their responsibility to make it and by access to the best available information.

Typically, these individuals are at the top levels of the management hierarchy and they deliberate and make momentous decisions within a small circle of peers. But the implementation of the decision and the burden of the consequences rest on the entire organization.

The announcement of the decision typically comes as a shock and a surprise to managers outside the privileged circle. They have had no prior exposure to the warnings of the necessity of the change and no relevant framework for evaluating its desirability and its consequences. Under these conditions, the following tendencies are likely to occur:

1. A tendency to conclude that the change is unnecessary and irrelevant. The strength of this conclusion will vary in proportion to the extent to which it contradicts historical experience.
2. A tendency to exaggerate the negative impact of the change by the affected individuals/groups.
3. A tendency by individuals/groups, who will not be affected by the change, to assume that they also will suffer.
4. A tendency to underestimate the positive benefits of the change on the one hand, and the costs of inaction on the other.

Thus, when the originators of change warn the organization of the imminence of crisis, they are at first suspected of 'crying wolf.'

On the other hand, once the reality of a crisis is accepted, there is a tendency to overreact, to panic. This is the point at which negative loyalty manifests itself fully. Individuals who want the organization to survive will close ranks behind the change. Those who are not loyal will jump ship, and some, who are hostile, will plot to deepen the crisis.

When an organization is in the process of recovery from a crisis, there is a tendency for a premature resurgence of resistance to the very change that is bringing about salvation. Thus, reactions to change are based on perception of the necessity and the impact of change.

The Cultural-Political Field

In today's society, there are few organizations in which the power structure is monolithic, concentrated in a single person or group, with a uniform culture pervading the organization. Most organizations are multicultural and have multiple power centers. Therefore, a given change will elicit a multiplicity of reactions, varying from strong support to total rejection.

In most organizations, and particularly in the firm, we would expect to find each power center to be identified with a particular culture. In the firm, these centers will typically be organizational units which are responsible for a particular type of work, e.g. production units, marketing units, and LRP units. As has been discussed in Part III, the nature of the work of the respective units gives a distinctive cast to their cultures.

The extent to which the resistance-arousing factors discussed in the preceding pages are translated into active opposition to change will depend on the strength of *cultural and political drives* of power centers. By cultural drive, we mean the preparedness to defend a center's cultural convictions, and by political drive, we mean the use of power to impose these conditions on others.

A strong cultural drive will trigger an exercise of power. Society is generally tolerant of such behavior in support of one's convictions. But society is less tolerant of the use of power in the absence of strong cultural convictions. Individuals and groups using it are regarded as 'power hungry' and the process as an exercise of 'naked power.'

Some groups/individuals will have *weak cultures* in the sense that they lack the strength of their convictions, are easily influenced by others, and do not assert themselves. Some others will have strong convictions, will defend themselves, but will not attempt to influence others. These are referred to as strong *non-proselyting cultures*.

Finally, some are *militant cultures* which seek to impose their 'truth' on the rest of the world. They are the ones who make active use of all the influence and power available to them.

Thus, resistance/support for a change will vary from one part of an organization to another. The active manifestation of support/resistance will be determined by the strength of the power and cultural drives at different power centers.

Summary of Contributing Factors

The preceding sections we have discussed a number of factors which determine the behavioral and political rationality. All of these factors have been amply discussed in the literature on psychology, sociology, and political science; they are also easily recognizable from managerial experience. Hence, the phenomenon of resistance to change has no surprises or mysteries, but it is complex because of the multiplicity of factors that contribute to it.

Briefly summarizing, we found that the level of resistance to change is determined by the following factors:

1. The degree of discontinuity in the historical culture and power structure implied by the change.
2. The length of the period over which the change is introduced.
3. The threats/insecurities/loss of prestige/loss of power implied for key individuals.
4. The expected contribution by the change to the success/survival of the organization.
5. The strength of positive/negative loyalty toward the organization felt by the participants.
6. The strength of the cultural and power drives at the respective power centers.

We have recognized that the contribution of factors 1–4 is determined by the perception by managers of the relevance and the consequences of the change, and that this perception is frequently at variance with reality. Therefore, because of distorted perception, resistance will usually be higher than is justified by the facts of the situation.

Managing Resistance

From Reactive to Proactive Management

Major strategic changes are frequently introduced without regard to the consequent resistance. The change is planned, 'explained' to those who are responsible for carrying it out, and then launched. When implementation lags and inefficiencies occur, they are treated one at a time, typically on the level of the change process and not at the roots and sources of the resistance.

Control meetings are convened to diagnose deficiencies. Remedies are addressed to the process and not to the underlying fears, frustrations, and opposition of individuals. Power is used to overcome deficiencies: Orders are given to reluctant groups/individuals, punishment is meted out for slipped schedules, and cost overruns.

Although inefficient, such an unplanned process eventually produces results, provided the proponents of change have the necessary power potential; the more drastic the change, the more power is needed. If sufficient power is lacking, or if the change managers run out of 'power chips' during the process, the change grinds to a halt, and the organization returns to pre-change 'business as usual.'

If power is adequate to complete the change, the change remains unstable and requires continuing application of power against hostile power centers and the hostile cultures. If change proponents relax their vigilance prematurely, a rollback to the 'good old times' takes place.

This muddling through approach sufficed in the days when strategic discontinuities were rare, and the pace of change was slow. As the environment becomes more turbulent, managers will need to manage change in a more expeditious and effective manner.

Using the results of the first part of this chapter, presented next are a series of measures which can be used to anticipate, manage, and control behavioral resistance.

Building a Launching Platform

Whenever a strategic change requires significant discontinuities in the culture and/or power structure of the firm, time, costs, and dysfunctions will be saved if management 'makes haste slowly.'

A desirable first step, preliminary to strategy planning and implementation, is to prepare the ground through a series of measures aimed at the following:

1. Minimizing the startup resistance.
2. Marshaling a power base sufficient to give the change momentum and continuity.

3. Preparing a detailed plan for the change process which assigns responsibilities, resources, steps, and interactions through which the change will be carried out.
4. Designing into the plan behavioral features which optimize the acceptance and support for the new strategies and capabilities.

We shall refer to this pre-launching process as building the launching platform. It is similar to the preparatory work done by politicians in preparation for launching a campaign or legislative proposal.

Diagnosing the Nature of Change

The first step in building the platform is to perform a preliminary *resistance diagnosis* which determines the following:

1. Whether the expected discontinuity is singular and will not recur in the near future or whether it is one of a series which will recur and represents an environmental shift to a new level of turbulence. (In Chapter 22, we shall discuss the importance of this assessment.)
2. The time available to the firm (as determined by the speed of change in the environment) for an effective response to the discontinuity (this information, critical to the scheduling of change, will be used in Chapter 23).
3. The extent of the changes in the capability which will be needed to provide support for the new strategy. A simplified version of the procedure, outlined in Chapter 22, can be used for diagnosing these changes, but on an aggregate level, without going through a detailed SBA by SBA analysis.
4. The units of the organization which will be affected by the change.

The second step is a *behavioral diagnosis* which determines:

1. The extent of political/cultural disturbance which will occur in the affected units.
2. The key individuals who will support/resist change and the reasons for their position.
3. The support/resistance by culturally/politically coherent groups.
4. The relative importance of individuals/groups to the success of the change.

The result of the behavioral diagnosis can be superimposed on the organizational chart to produce a *cultural/political support/resistance map*.

Building a Supportive Climate

Using the resistance map, the following measures can be taken to eliminate unnecessary resistance:

1. Eliminate misperceptions and exaggeration by making clear throughout the firm the need/opportunity and the beneficial consequence of the change to the firm's performance. Groups/individuals which are expected to resist will need special attention, but the entire organization should also be informed.
2. Eliminate or reduce fears and anxieties by making clear to groups/individuals the positive/negative impact of the change on them.
3. Use the political information from the map to build a pro-change power base, as follows:

   a. To the extent possible within the available time, make changes in the power structure which will increase the power behind the change.
   b. Form a coalition of those who will benefit from the change. In particular, seek to enlist the would-be 'lukewarm' supporters.
   c. Offer rewards for support of the change.
   d. Neutralize key points of potential resistance through side bargains and payments.

Designing Behavioral Features into the Plan for Change

1. To the extent possible, exclude from the process individuals/groups who will continue to resist the change.
2. Include in decision making all individuals who will be involved in implementing the change.
3. Individuals responsible for the success of implementation should also be made responsible for making the corresponding decisions.
4. Spread the change over the longest possible time which is compatible with the urgency of the external developments.
5. If time permits, use the contagion approach:

   (a) Start change with groups which are committed to the change.
   (b) Reward and recognize them.
   (c) After their initial successes, spread the change to other units.

6. Do not assume that managers have the knowledge and skills in solving problems which are novel to them. Build into the plan the necessary education and training programs. This will not only produce effective solutions, but will also relieve fears and anxieties and thus enhance acceptance.

Behavioral Management of the Process

The platform will optimize the launching conditions, but will not guarantee completion of the change. During the period of platform building, there is seldom enough time to change attitudes, values, norms, and perceptions of reality, which will create a consistently welcoming and receptive atmosphere. The preliminary political maneuvers, while assuring a launching base, will not create a stable pro-change power structure.

Therefore, the behavioral change process must be managed as follows:

1. Monitor and anticipate the sources of resistance during the change.
2. Marshall and use sufficient power to overcome the resistance.
3. Provide participants in the process with necessary new knowledge, concepts, and problem-solving skills.
4. Alongside strategy projects, start projects aimed at transforming culture and power structure.
5. Monitor and control the parallel development of new strategy and new capabilities. If strategy gets too far ahead and generates strong resistance, it may be necessary to stop strategy development temporarily and focus energies on gaining acceptance of the progress made thus far.
6. After the new strategy has been translated into new product/market positions, diagnose the state of the capability. If, as is frequently the case, the capability is not yet fully developed, the capability projects must be continued until the new culture and power structure are supportive of the new strategy. We shall refer to this residual capability development as the *institutionalization of a change*.
7. If the strategic shocks are going to repeat, the firm will have to go through a continual series of change management exercises. Hence, management must institutionalize not a particular change, but an ongoing change process. This requires development of the following:

   (a) Managers who are seekers or creators of change, skilled in charismatic leadership.

(b) Power shared by entrepreneurs, general managers, creative R&D and marketing managers.

(c) A change-seeking culture in which historical models of the world are definitionally suspect.

(d) A high level of positive loyalty throughout the firm, an adventure-seeking *esprit de corp.*

Summary

Behavioral resistance is a natural reaction by groups and individuals to changes which threaten their culture and position of power.

Resistance to change is proportional to the size of the discontinuities introduced into culture and power and inversely proportional to the speed of introduction.

The level of resistance is reduced by the extent of positive/negative loyalty which groups and individuals exhibit toward the organization. The reduction in resistance is proportional to the perceived contribution to the survival/success of the organization. Experience shows that both survival threats and contributions to success tend to be underestimated.

In managing resistance, a useful approach is to start by building a launching platform. This involves: a strategic diagnosis, a behavioral diagnosis, eliminating unnecessary resistance, forming a pro-change power base, and designing resistance- reducing features into the plan for the change.

Once the change is launched, the residual resistance should be anticipated and necessary power applied to overcome it. Whenever the change in strategy is completed before the changes in the capability, capability building should be continued until the change is institutionalized.

If diagnosis reveals that the impending discontinuity is singular, and not likely to be followed by others, the change should be planned as a one-time experience. If discontinuities are likely to recur, a strategic or flexible capability profile should be developed within the firm (see Part II).

Exercises

1. As the director of corporate planning, you have been given an assignment by the president to prepare your firm for a transition from LRP to strategic posture planning. The president is well aware of the difficulties which

had been encountered by other firms and wants to maximize acceptance of the new system.

Prepare a detailed plan for what is to be done, by whom, and how prior to and including the launching date. The firm has had LRP for ten years; its financial performance has consistently been satisfactory; and no major environmental discontinuities are expected.

2. As the president of a firm, you have become aware that your major division which has in the past contributed 50% of the sales and 35% of the profit is headed for disaster within three years because of a rapidly developing technology substitution. In spite of your efforts to persuade them, your conviction is not shared by your associates, either at the corporate or divisional levels. They see the recent leveling off of the division's performance as a temporary phenomenon caused by the general recession.

3. The firm has been operated under a decentralized divisional structure in which the corporate management has served as a coordinator and financial controller of the firm's performance; the firm has an established LRP system. What are the alternative courses of action available to you? How can you implement them?

4. Your firm is in a highly turbulent environment, and the top management expects several significant discontinuities to occur during the next five years which will require significant changes in mentality, culture, and the power structure. The management wants to minimize the internal disruptions and the inefficiencies which may occur during these changes. As a senior corporate planner, you have been asked to design an internal monitoring and control process which will enable the management to anticipate and respond to cultural and political resistance.

5. Prepare a detailed design for such process. Who will be involved? What data will be collected? How will the data be collected? How will they be evaluated? Who will make the decisions and when? How will the decisions be implemented?

22

Systemic Resistance

We next turn attention to another type of resistance which we shall call systemic. The two types of resistance are concurrent during the history of a change and they produce similar effects: delays, unanticipated costs, chronic malperformance of new strategies. But, the basic causes are different. One comes from active opposition to change and the other from the passive incompetence of the organization.

Duality of Organizational Activity

Firms engage in two different and complementary types of activity:

1. To succeed and survive in the *near-term*, they must make their products/services attractive to their customers. In the firm, this means efficient manufacturing, effective marketing, efficient distribution, reliable after-sales performance, etc.
2. To survive and succeed in the *long-term*, firms typically seek to increase and expand their market penetration through aggressive competition, expansion of capacity, investment in improved production technology.

This activity, aimed at assuring both the current and the future profitability of the firm's historical lines of business, has been named the *operating activity* by some writers, *competitive activity* by others. As noted earlier, during the first half of the twentieth century, the competitive activity absorbed the

© The Author(s) 2019
H. I. Ansoff et al., *Implanting Strategic Management*,
https://doi.org/10.1007/978-3-319-99599-1_22

bulk of the budgets and of managerial attention. It was highly productive, because the environment offered what appeared to be unlimited opportunities for growth.

During the first half of the twentieth century, growth horizons became increasingly limited. As a result, firms turned their attention to a second activity, called *strategic activity*, aimed at changing their historical business through development of novel products, entry into previously unserved markets, diversifying into new businesses and new technologies.

During the second half of the twentieth century, strategic activity received only a minor portion of the budget and of managerial attention. Typically, it was confined to incremental product modifications; major strategic discontinuities were regarded *as* once-in-a-lifetime upheavals, to be dealt with whenever they arose.

During the second half of the twentieth century, preoccupation with the strategic activity grew progressively and, with it, the strategic budget grew to a point where strategic activity became a serious competitor for management attention.

Strategic Capacity

As the preoccupation with strategy grew, the operating problems did not slacken. On the contrary, the intensified competition and development of global markets in the twenty-first century made them more challenging and complex. Therefore, the total demand on management time grew rapidly.

Whenever the new strategy required new technological or marketing or production know-how, the need for new production capacities was readily perceived and accommodated. But, curiously, the need for new managerial capacities was neglected and increases in the strategic work were 'dropped' on top of the expanding operating challenges, thus creating an overload on the management system.

For example, during the introduction of strategic planning, it is typically standard practice to add the very substantial amount of the new planning work to the other responsibilities of the already-pressed managers. Since in medium or large sized firms a typical planning cycle takes at least seven months of each year, the new workload was, to all intents and purposes, continuing and substantial.

When the results of planning needed to be implemented, strategic projects were similarly assigned as 'extracurricular' activity to line managers and other personnel who were already loaded with operating concerns.

Predictably, in the absence of adequate capacity, something had to give, and in most cases, it was the strategic activity that gave precedence and priority to the operating work. So, typical was this behavior that Herbert Simon, one of the great researchers in the behavior of organizations, formulated 'Gresham's Law of Planning' which states that routine, repetitive, and historically familiar operating activities tend to displace novel, episodic strategic activities.

The resulting shortage of capacity for strategic work predictably affects the results. Deadlines are slipped, strategic planners developed 'planning fatigue,' strategic projects suffered from slipped schedules and cost overruns, and many disappeared 'down the chute' within the organizational maze.

Thus, the following propositions about the *systemic resistance* are attributed to *strategic overload*:

1. Whenever both operating and strategic work compete for management attention, the former drives out the latter.
2. At any given time, systemic resistance will be proportional to the difference between the capacity required by new strategic work and the capacity available to handle it.
3. Whenever the strategic budget is increased significantly, without an accompanying increase in the managerial capacity, the strategic overload will cause delays, cost overruns, and strategic project failures in proportion to the speed with which the strategic budget is builtup.

At first glance, it appears desirable in the near term, while the strategic capacity is being developed, to reserve some of the operating capacity to the strategic work. But this solution is likely to rise, rather than lower, the resistance; the reason being that operating units are poorly equipped to perform strategic work.

Operating vs. Strategic Capability

Alongside the implicit assumption that management capacity is elastic enough to absorb major increases, another implicit assumption has been that general management capability is universal, and that a capability developed for solving operating problems is applicable to the strategic work. For example, it has been assumed that successful managers of growth and profitability can instantly become effective entrepreneurs. Yet, our discussion shows this is not the case.

The Comparison of Capabilities summarizes the typical management capability profiles needed for effective support of, respectively, strategic and operating work. An examination of the figure readily shows that the operating capability profile is geared to support profit making, efficiency-serving, change-controlling behavior. By contrast, strategic capability supports investment in future profits (and thus incurs current loss) through generation of change.

As depicted in the figure, all six components of capability are not only different, but frequently contradictory. Thus, the typical operating incentive system, which reward historical and current performance, would suppress strategic activity, which depresses profits in the short term. A manager skillful in current profit making would be reluctant to take risks on novel ideas and would lack skills in managing strategic projects, as well as in managing creative people. The long-range planning and control system of operations management would not be capable of identifying and evaluating novel opportunities, nor of controlling strategic expenditures. The reader can readily see for himself how the operating information system, organizational structure, and power structure would similarly act to suppress strategic activities.

The Comparison of Capabilities helps explain the rejections, inefficiencies, and delays which occur when strategic tasks are imposed on the operating capability. Further, the figure suggests that these inefficiencies will be due not only to cultural/political rejection and overload, but also to *inapplicability of operations management skills to strategic work*. Thus, forcefully borrowing operating capacity for strategic work does not solve the problem, unless the borrowed managers and their staffs are already trained in strategic decision making, implementation, and control.

When the strategic budget becomes large and strategic work important, additional capacity will, of necessity, have to be built. But because of the Gresham's law phenomenon, the expanding operating priorities will continue to preempt the new capacity, unless dear-cut managerial arrangements (through job definitions and possibly structural change) are made to protect the strategic activity.

This becomes particularly important in the implementation and control phases of strategic work, because it involves many more managers than the strategic decision making. Thus:

1. If strategic work is assigned to operating units, without developing their strategic capabilities, the strategic incompetence will compound the priority conflict and the overload.

2. Unless new capacity, which is added to accommodate growing strategic work, is dedicated to this work and protected from operating priorities, there will be a tendency to preempt the new capacity for operating concerns.

In summary, we have identified three contributors to systemic resistance:

1. Priority conflict which suppresses strategic activity in favor of operations.
2. Strategic overload which creates bottlenecks, costs, and slippages.
3. Strategic incompetence which in addition to costs and slippages produces unrealistic and suboptimal strategies.

This last component of systemic resistance needs to be discussed further—a matter to which we now turn our attention.

Resistance and the Capability Gap

The right-hand column of Fig. 22.1 is a generic description of strategic capability. Its basic characteristics are that it is change-generating, by contrast to the operating capability which is change-controlling, and that it is directed toward creating new future profit potential for the firm, whereas the operating activity is focused on exploiting the existing potential.

As discussed, the pure operating and strategic behavior are extremes of the range of behaviors observable in practice, which range from incremental reaction after the fact to creation of novel products, technologies, and demands. Between the two extremes, we have defined several intermediate levels of progressively increasing aggressiveness of behavior. As you will recall, for every level of aggressiveness there is a distinct strategic capability which gives best support. Low aggressiveness is best supported by management capability which filters out radical changes, places high reliance on historical experience, and which is introverted—focused more on the internal management than on the relationship to the environment. As aggressiveness rises, the successive capability profiles are more receptive to change, more skillful in managing it, more open to the environment.

In Chapter 2.3, we have constructed matching strategic aggressiveness—management capability profiles. The same figure has been reproduced as Table 22.1.

The left-hand column of the figure shows pure operating behavior in which no strategic change takes place. This is optimal for the stable environment. As the turbulence rises, so does the aggressiveness of the strategy; and the supporting capability becomes increasingly change-seeking and open to the environment.

	Operating	Strategic
Culture	-Production/marketing orientation: success = aggressive competition + efficient production	- Strategic/flexibility orientation: success = invention + anticipation/ creation of needs
Manager	-Profit-maker -Goal achiever -Controller	-Entrepreneur -Innovator -Charismatic leader
Management System	-LRP/budgeting -Historical performance control	-Strategic planning/SIM -Strategic management -Strategic control
Information	Demand/profitability trends	-New threats/opportunities
Structure	-Functional/divisional -Stable	-Project/matrix -Dynamic
Power	-Decentralized -In production/marketing	-In general management -In new ventures -In strategic planning

Fig. 22.1 Comparison of Capabilities

A strategy-capability match will result in optimal behavior and, therefore, will not contribute to the resistance. When a mismatch occurs, resistance will rise in proportion to the degree of mismatch.

During the process of strategy change, resistance will arise whenever the change is planted into an unready ground, that is, whenever the change in strategy outpaces the accommodation of the managerial capability. If, after the new strategy becomes operational, there is a residual mismatch or imbalance of capability, resistance will cause chronic ineffectiveness of the new strategy.

We are now in a position to advance three more basic propositions regarding systemic resistance:

1. Systemic resistance will occur whenever strategic aggressiveness and capability are mismatched.
2. Systemic resistance will occur during a change in strategy if development of capability lags behind the development of strategy. The resistance will be proportional to the gap between the two.
3. Systemic resistance will occur whenever the components of capability are mismatched to one another.

Table 22.1 Matching triplets—aggressiveness and responsiveness with turbulence which optimizes a firm's ROI

Turbulence level descriptor	Repetitive	Expanding	Changing	Discontinuous	Surprising
Strategic aggressiveness	Stable Change based on precedents	Reactive Change based on experience	Anticipatory Incremental change based on extrapolation	Entrepreneurial Discontinuous new Strategies based on observable alternatives	Creative Novel, Strategies based on creativity
Responsiveness of general management capabilities	Stability seeking	Efficiency seeking	Market driven	Environment driven	Environment creating
Environmental turbulence levels	1	2	3	4	5

In Table 22.2, we combine the effect of the *overload resistance* which occurs when workload exceeds capacity, with *incompetence resistance* which is due to a mismatch between strategic behavior and the supporting capability.

Resistance-Inducing Sequence

In addition to neglecting the needs for new capacity and capability, many firms also disregard the effect of sequencing of the change on resistance. This has been repeatedly illustrated by a typical sequence of events used to introduce strategic planning into a firm. This sequence is shown in Fig. 22.2.

The introduction typically starts with appointment of a corporate strategic planner; development of a calendar and sequence of events, preparation of planning formats and procedures; and launching of the planning process, usually by means of a one-day seminar involving managers who are expected to participate.

As the Fig. 22.2 illustrates, this causes confusion and poses threats to the existing power structure and to individuals. Much of this is due to a combination of lack of understanding, lack of planning competence on the part of the involved managers, and anxieties about the impact of planning on the organization. The result is a high-level of both systemic and behavioral resistance.

Frequently, the first problem to surface from the welter of confusion is that good profit-making managers are not necessarily good strategic planners. They need to learn the purposes, the concepts, the terminology, the techniques of analysis before they can intelligently fill the planning forms. Once this deficiency is uncovered, usually through the poor quality of submitted plans, training is organized as a remedy.

Once the managers have acquired planning know-how, they begin to complain about what IBM has labeled the GIGO (garbage in garbage out) phenomenon: The information necessary for strategic decisions is lacking, and managers complain about having to invent meaningless facts and figures. Measures are next taken to develop a strategic database through environmental surveillance, forecasting, impact analysis, etc.

By now, planning may be on its third annual cycle, and it is increasingly perceived that the successive cycles tend to be 'paralysis by analysis': plans are made but, mysteriously, the new strategies do not find their way to the marketplace. This leads to a belated recognition that the operating implementation and control system tends to sidetrack and reject strategic activity.

Table 22.2 Combining capability and capacity effects on systemic resistance

Change in Statergy / Change in Stategic Budget	Small	Large
Small	Low resistance	Incompetence resistance
Large	Overload resistance	Both incompetence and overload resistance

As mentioned earlier, planning is usually introduced as an extracurricular activity into the lives of already busy managers. After four or five cycles of planning, it is recognized that this activity is highly time-consuming, and may consume as much as seven months out of the year. It becomes evident that managers are getting 'planning fatigue.'

After adequate capacity for strategic work has been provided, it is typically discovered that, since the inception of planning, the reward and incentives system has remained unchanged. Or, it may be discovered that the planning system and the organizational structure are in conflict, a situation which often occurs whenever strategic planning is introduced on top of a functional structure.

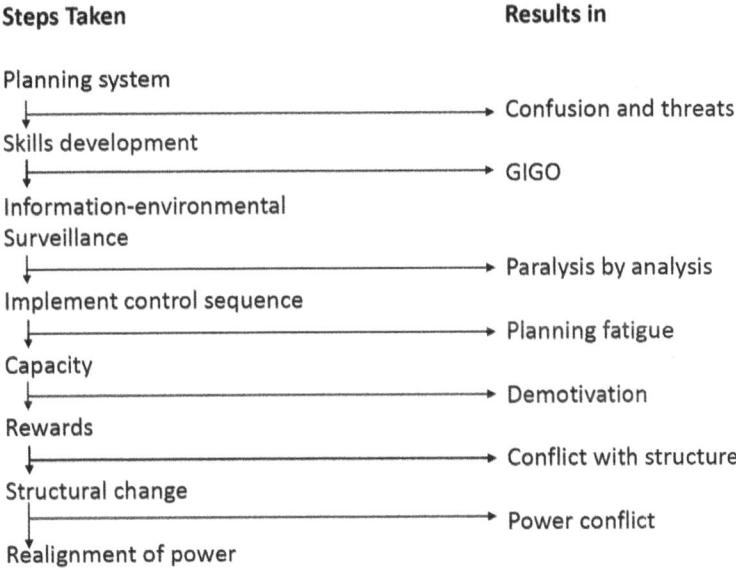

Steps Taken   **Results in**

Planning system → Confusion and threats

Skills development → GIGO

Information-environmental Surveillance → Paralysis by analysis

Implement control sequence → Planning fatigue

Capacity → Demotivation

Rewards → Conflict with structure

Structural change → Power conflict

Realignment of power

Fig. 22.2 Steps in resistance-inducing sequence

After the fifth or sixth planning cycle, powerful groups and individuals, who continue to be threatened by planning, but have been biding their time, begin to use the planning fatigue to squeeze planning out of the organization. It becomes clear that a realignment of the power structure is necessary in order to assure continued survival of the new system.

Ansoff's repeated experiences in observing the reactions of battle-scarred planners as outlined in the 'Steps in Resistance-inducing Sequence' lead him to state that 'the sequence presented is not as much of a caricature as it may appear to uninitiated readers.'

Thus, the historically typical introduction of planning has been, as the title of the figure suggests, through a *resistance inducing sequence*: A partial systemic change is imposed on the firm. It triggers behavioral resistance. The cause of the resistance is diagnosed as a systemic deficiency. The correction of the deficiency triggers new behavioral resistance and a new systemic change.

In the process, the system may not survive in the organization. A typical point of demise is the inability of top management to resolve the paralysis by analysis. This occurs because the operations implementation system, which is typically hierarchical and incremental with respect to past experience, cannot handle non-hierarchical, non-extrapolative, and high-risk strategic decisions.

Motivating Change Sequence

Understanding of the causes of the behavioral and systemic resistance, we now construct an alternative sequence which, instead of generating resistance to strategic planning, minimizes it throughout the process.

In the course of a discontinuous strategic change, three major component changes occur:

1. A change in strategy which introduces new products and markets.
2. A change in the systemic competence which includes systems, structure, skills, and knowledge.
3. A behavioral change which includes norms, perceptions, values, models of the world, and distribution of power.

Figure 22.3 illustrates how the sequencing of these changes affects the resistance. The upper part shows how resistance evolves if the sequence strategy → systems → behavior is used to introduce change.

If changes in systems are delayed until after strategy is in place, both systemic and behavioral resistance will persist throughout strategy introduction.

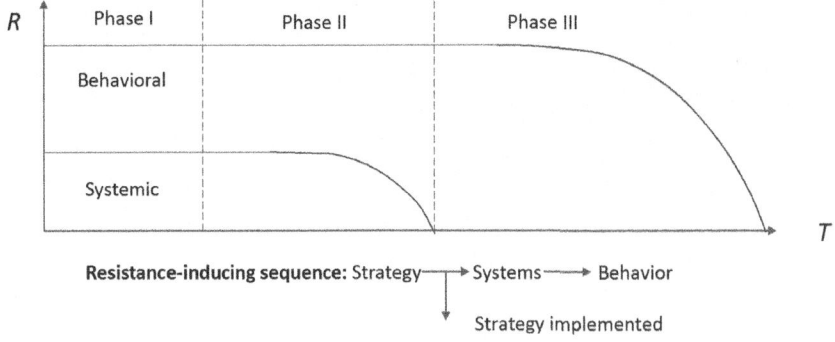

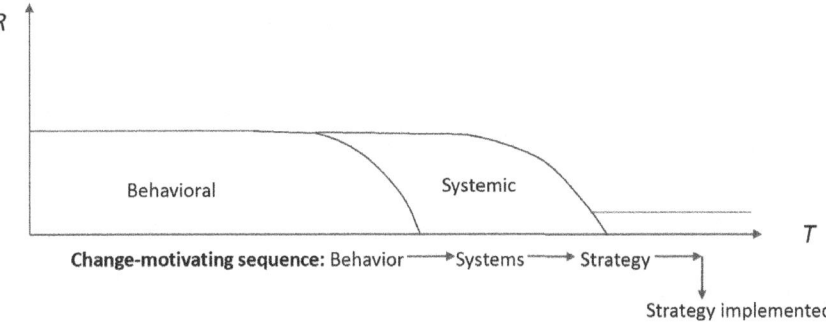

Fig. 22.3 Resistance and sequence

As systems are changed during the second phase, behavioral resistance will persist, and will not start to drop off until the third phase, when attention is turned to culture and power structure.

If, as in many historical cases, the third phase is neglected, and culture and power are not given attention, behavioral resistance will persist. As we shall learn in the next section, continuing application of power will be necessary if the new strategy and systemic arrangements are to stay in place.

If, as frequently occurred in the past, top management relaxes its vigilance after phase two, the behavioral resistance begins to erode the strategic gains and may result in a rollback of the entire strategy.

Thus, we can refer to strategy → systems → behavior as the *maximum resistance sequence.*

The lower part of Fig. 22.3 shows the opposite behavior → systems → strategy sequence. As the graph shows, by making behavioral changes before the systemic, management can delay the systemic resistance. After the behavioral acceptance is gained, and systemic competence is in place, implementation of strategy encounters no resistance. Thus, behavior → systems → strategy is the *minimum resistance sequence.*

Figure 22.4 illustrates how the minimum sequence can be implemented through a sequential series of steps. Comparing it with Fig. 22.2, you will note that instead of progressive erection of new barriers to change, the minimum sequence builds acceptance of change.

Attractive as it may appear, the minimum sequence has an obvious drawback; the implantation of strategy is delayed until after the behavioral and systemic changes have been made. By contrast, the maximum resistance sequence changes strategy in the shortest possible time.

This explains the importance of the second step in the resistance diagnosis. In a practical situation, the choice between the two sequences will have to be made as a function of the urgency of the strategic challenge posed by the environment.

But the choice does not have to gravitate to either extreme. As an example, while developing a power base and a mentality which will support and encourage change, it would also be possible to begin development of both the capacity and skills for planning. An examination of Fig. 22.4 suggests that it is possible to follow *parallel paths* which will be mutually

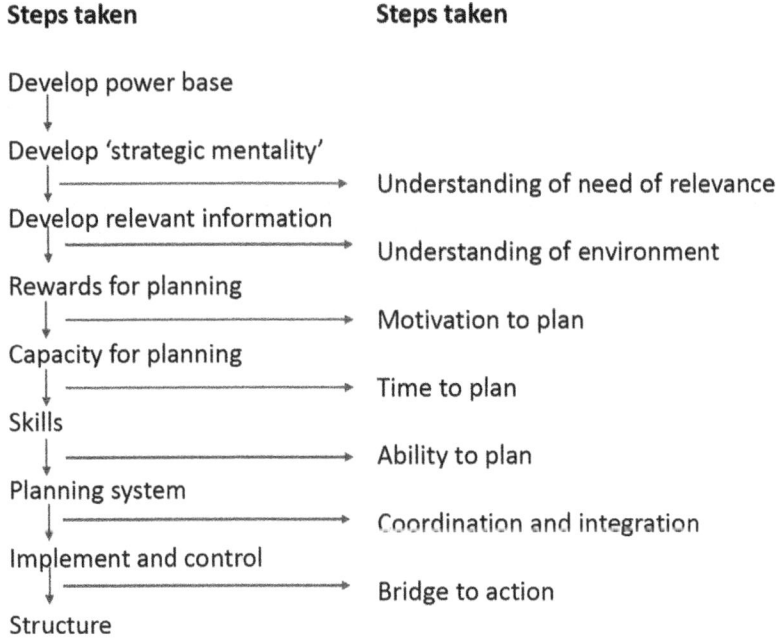

Steps taken   **Steps taken**

Develop power base

Develop 'strategic mentality'
                                   Understanding of need of relevance
Develop relevant information
                                   Understanding of environment
Rewards for planning
                                   Motivation to plan
Capacity for planning
                                   Time to plan
Skills
                                   Ability to plan
Planning system
                                   Coordination and integration
Implement and control
                                   Bridge to action
Structure

Fig. 22.4 Steps in change-motivating sequence

reinforcing, thus substantially reducing the total time required. The choice of how much should be done in parallel will depend, on the one hand, on the urgency of the external change, and, on the other, on the energy and capacity which the management can devote to the process. We shall discuss this parallel resistance-reducing sequence further along in this chapter.

Resistance and Power

In many organizations, it is rare that all of the behavioral resistance to discontinuous change can be converted into positive support of change. Typically, this only occurs, as previously mentioned, when an organization is in a survival crisis and everyone rallies around a change which promises salvation. Yet, it can also occur when a charismatic leader fires everyone's imagination by a vision of a 'promised land' or conquest of 'a mortal enemy.' Under most other circumstances, even after resistance has been reduced to a minimum, there will be points (individuals and groups) of nonreducible resistance against change.

Therefore, the change-initiating group must muster enough power to overcome the residual behavioral resistance. The amount of power (or strength of authority) that needed will be proportional to the level of resistance to be overcome.

If the power is insufficient to launch the process, the change will never get off the ground. If the 'power chips' get used up in the process, the change will fizzle out during the process.

When resistance to planning was first encountered in the early days of strategic planning, the need for power to overcome the resistance was quickly recognized. A practical conclusion was reached that, to succeed, strategy change must have the wholehearted support and attention of top management. But this power was used to impose the new strategy on the firm and not to reduce the behavioral resistance. As a result, the managerial pressure and support of the new strategy had to be maintained continuously if the strategy was to remain in place. In many cases, after several years of active support, the attention of top management shifted to other pressing concerns. When this occurred, cultural and political opposition resurfaced, and succeeded in 'rolling back' the new strategy, or suppressing the new strategic planning system.

Less frequently, when top management remains firmly committed to planning for a long time, a process of *cultural and political adaptation* gradually takes place: pro-planning managers replace those who opposed it, a new culture supportive of the planning emerges, individuals learn to live and be comfortable with the new view of the world. When this occurs, the new strategy and its supporting capabilities become gradually *institutionalized*. But this is a slow process which may take five to ten years.

Designing Systemic Features into the Plan for Change

Earlier, we described a number of behavioral features which can minimize behavioral resistance during the change process. Additional discussion in this chapter has suggested the following features which minimize the systemic resistance:

1. Provide a dedicated capacity for the change process by budgeting for it, assigning specific shares of individuals' time, and programming capacity buildup.
2. Integrate management development programs into the change process. One way to do this is to preface the change with a training course. A more effective way is to divide the change into distinct steps (modules) and preface each module with a training experience.
3. To the maximum extent possible, use the sequence: behavior development $\rightarrow$ systemic buildup $\rightarrow$ strategic action.
4. Stretch the duration of change to the longest possible period which will still assure effective and timely response to the environmental challenge.

Summary

Systemic resistance to change occurs when operating and strategic activities within the firm compete for organizational capacity. Unless special provisions are made, operating work tends to preempt the strategic work. Systemic resistance also occurs when organizational competence is unsuited for supporting the strategic aggressiveness of the firm.

Systemic resistance will be proportional to the mismatch between the available and required strategic capacity, and to the mismatch between the aggressiveness of the new strategic behavior and the existing systemic competence. Systemic resistance will be inversely proportional to the speed with which change is introduced.

A third source of both systemic and behavioral resistance is the sequencing of the steps during a change. When the sequence strategy systemic competence behavioral modification is followed, the resistance will be maximal. When the sequence is reversed, the resistance is minimal.

In most cases, the launching platform will reduce, but not eliminate resistance. A combination of behavioral and systemic resistance will persist through the change process. Therefore, sufficient power must be mustered to assure successful completion of a discontinuous change. The duration of the change should be matched to the available time, adequate capacity should be provided, provisions made for training managers in strategic analysis.

Exercises

1. What is a strategic budget?

   a. What should be the principal categories of a strategic budget?
   b. What should be the process of strategic budgeting?
   c. What principal factors should determine the size of a strategic budget of a firm?
   d. In the absence of a formal strategic budgeting process, how is the de facto strategic budget determined in a firm?

2. What are the key ingredients of strategic capacity?

   a. How should the volume of the needed capacity be determined?
   b. What are the ways of protecting strategic capacity from encroachment of the operating activities?

3. How could you go about determining the time available to the firm for effecting its response to a strategic discontinuity?

4. Using a selected organization, design a graphical presentation of the cultural/political map of the firm. What information should be presented on the map? How would you use the map?

23

Alternative Methods for Managing a Discontinuous Change

The preceding two section chapters described the attitude toward resistance which has historically been found in firms and most other organizations. This attitude can be summed up, to borrow from Senator Moynahan, as 'benign neglect.' Firms introduce new strategies without anticipating, nor providing, for the resistance, and they deal with it reactively when it arises.

Ansoff noted 'this attitude may be justified when the changes in strategy are evolutionary, minor and incremental, because the level of resistance to these will not be significant enough to warrant special attention. But as discontinuous strategy changes become frequent, the costs and delays due to resistance will increasingly focus the firm's attention on managing the transition process.'

In this chapter, we present four approaches toward managing discontinuous changes, compare their advantages and disadvantages, and propose a method for selecting the approach that is appropriate to a given situation.

Coercive Change Management

The preceding discussion has shown that, when strategic planning is introduced into a firm, support and influence by top management is typically used to overcome resistance to planning. Further, implementation of the new strategy is the first and initial concern, followed by a step-by-step recognition of the systemic deficiencies. Discovery of the need to change culture and power (if it comes at all) comes last.

© The Author(s) 2019
H. I. Ansoff et al., *Implanting Strategic Management*,
https://doi.org/10.1007/978-3-319-99599-1_23

We shall refer to such a method of introducing discontinuous change, which follows a resistance inducing sequence and uses power to overcome resistance, as a *coercive change process*.

Experience shows that coercive change is expensive and socially disruptive, but it offers the advantage of a rapid strategic response. Thus, the coercive approach must be used when urgency is high and rapid response is essential.

But given an understanding of the nature of resistance, it need not be the brute force approach typically used in the past. Even under pressures of time, resistance can be managed and costs minimized. The typical pitfalls in the brute force approach are:

1. Failure, prior to the change, to muster be amount of power necessary to assure its completion. The result is frustration of the change, which peters out before the new strategy is in place.
2. Failure to anticipate the sources and strength of behavioral resistance. The results are unanticipated confusion, costs, and delay.
3. Failure to attack its root causes, when resistance surfaces. The result is paralysis by analysis.
4. Premature removal of the political support behind the change. The result is regression of the change.
5. Failure to follow up implementation instructions issued to resisting units/individuals. The result is sabotage of the change.
6. Failure to recognize the need for new competence, and capacity. The results are suppression of change in favor of operating concerns, low quality of strategic decisions, and ineffective implementation.

The pitfalls can be avoided, and the coercive change made more effective, through the following measures:

1. Before launching the change, the organization must identify the potential sources of cultural and political resistance/support by performing a behavioral diagnosis.
2. Build the necessary political platform for the change, that is, muster enough power behind it to assure successful completion.
3. During the change, managers must monitor the process for incipient signs of resistance and deal with them before the resistance erupts.
4. After the strategy change is made, turn attention to capability/capacity, and continue to apply power until the new strategy and capability match, and the change is institutionalized within the firm.

If a firm using the coercive approach lacks a strategic planning capability, it can save time by using external consultants for strategy formulation. It should be kept in mind, however, that if the consultants recommend changes which impact on the culture and the power structure, they will be unpopular. Top management will need to apply continuous pressure and follow up to assure implementation of the consultants' advice.

Adaptive Change

Firms and other organizations which are not subjected to strategic shocks do, nevertheless, go through discontinuous strategic changes, this occurs through step-by-step accumulation of incremental changes which, over a long period of time, add up to transformation of culture, power structure, and competence. This is a process which sociologist calls *organic adaptation* which is unmanaged from the top and occurs in response to successive environmental stimuli, or to unsatisfactory performance by the firm, or, more rarely, it is brought about by creative forces within the firm. The successive adaptations are usually arrived at through trial and error.

If the change is spread over a long period of time, at any given time the resistance will be low, but not absent, because even incremental departures from the 'historical order of things' induce organizational dysfunctions and conflicts. But the required power is correspondingly low and applied by the proponents of the change who are usually below the top management level. The conflicts are resolved through compromises, bargains, power shifts.

We shall refer to introduction of a discontinuous strategic change through a series of incremental steps spread over time as an *adaptive change process*. It is slow but has the virtue of minimizing the level of resistance at any given time. Even though it may be argued that this amounts to spreading pain over time, the adaptive response belongs in the repertoire of valid responses, because it makes change possible under conditions when very little power is available to the proponents of change.

Like the coercive approach, adaptive change can be made more effective if it is managed. The suggestions made in the preceding section for improving *the* effectiveness of coercive change apply equally in this case. In addition, adaptive change should be made to follow the *change motivating sequence*. It will be recalled that this requires that changes in climate, mentality and power be made first, systemic changes in competence and capacity should follow, and strategy is changed only when the organization is ready and winning.

Crisis Management

During the last quarter of the twentieth century, there is an increasing likelihood that the firm will fail to perceive some rapidly developing and novel discontinuities until they forcefully impact on the firm. When a change appears to imperil the firm's survival and places the firm under severe time pressures, the firm is confronted with a crisis.

When a crisis strikes, behavioral resistance is replaced by support. But solutions are not obvious, and time pressures are great. The initial task of top management is not to cope with resistance but to prevent panic and to generate a rapid and effective response.

However, as the firm emerges from the crisis, management must anticipate and counteract premature revival of resistance which usually accompanies early signs of recovery.

Frequently, a group of key managers convinces itself of the inevitability of an impending crisis while the rest of the firm does not yet see it coming. If this group has sufficient power and influence, it must take recourse to a coercive response. The suggestions made earlier for effective use of coercive power apply, except that they must be executed under severe time pressures.

When a crisis is imminent, the managers who perceive its advent ahead of the rest of the organization have the following options:

1. Make a determined effort to convince others of the inevitability of the crisis and launch an anticipatory response.
2. Resign oneself to the inevitability of the crisis and prepare to play the savior role when the crisis arrives.
3. Trigger off an early artificial crisis, usually by inventing an external enemy, who threatens survival of the firm. This is an approach which has been used by political leaders throughout history.

The first two alternatives are less risky than the third, which carries not only high personal risk *for* the leaders, but also severe ethical implications inherent in creating an artificial crisis which will not necessarily transform itself into a real one. But its advantages are that it drastically reduces resistance, engenders support for the solution, and enhances the chances of a successful recovery.

Managed Resistance ('Accordion') Method

Of the three approaches discussed above, crisis management should be reserved for emergencies. The coercive and the adaptive approaches are each an extreme way for dealing with change. The coercive approach is a 'damn the torpedoes, full speed ahead' way of overpowering resistance. Even when optimally managed, it is costly, disruptive and conflict-ridden, but it is a necessary solution under conditions of high urgency. The adaptive approach is a 'Rome was not built in a day' way of introducing change: it minimizes resistance, but it is too slow under conditions of environmental urgency.

Hence, there is a need for an intermediate approach which works under conditions of moderate urgency and which can be implemented within the time limits dictated by the environment. We shall call this approach, the *managed resistance*, or *'accordion,' method* for managing a discontinuous change. We describe it in detail in the following two chapters. Its salient characteristics are the following:

1. It is *applicable under conditions of moderate urgency* when there is more time than necessary for the coercive method and not enough for the adaptive.
2. The *duration of the change is tailored* to the available time. As urgency increases, the method moves toward the coercive extreme. As urgency decreases, it approaches the adaptive change. Hence its name 'accordion' to describe the stretchable property.
3. This accordion property is made possible by the use of a modular approach: the *planning process is subdivided into modules*; at the end of each module appropriate implementation projects are launched.
4. The conventional idea, that planning and implementation must be sequential, is abandoned in favor of *parallel planning and implementation*.
5. *Resistance is minimized and controlled*; first, by building a launching platform; second, by using the change motivating sequence within each module; third, by developing implementability during the planning process; and, fourth, by controlling resistance during the change process.

The advantage of the managed resistance method is that it tailors the firm's response to the external timing imperatives on the one hand, and to the internal power realities on the other. The disadvantage is that it is more complex than either of the extreme approaches. Furthermore, it requires continual attention from top management.

Because the know-how necessary for designing and conducting such a complex process will often be lacking in the firm, outside assistance will be needed. However, the contribution of the outside consultants must be different from the coercive method. One of the key features of the accordion method, a feature which is essential for enhancing the acceptance of change, is that the implementers must also be planners.

Hence the roles of the consultants are: to assist in the design of the process, to supply tools of analysis, to train managers, to help monitor the process, to play the devil's advocate.

Comparison of Methods

Table 23.1 compares the advantages and shortcomings of several methods. We need to recall that all of these methods are 'heavyweight,' requiring considerable attention and energy from management, and that they become useful and necessary only when the change in strategy requires what Machiavelli called, introduction of 'a new order of things.'

As the figure shows, because of the high failure risk, crisis management is an undesirable substitute for the coercive method, but it has to be used whenever the management either fails to anticipate a crisis, or does not have enough power to force a timely response.

The adaptive approach is the slowest, but it provokes the least resistance and requires the least commitment of managerial attention and resources. It is useful in environments in which threats/trends/opportunities are highly predictable and the urgency is therefore low.

Table 23.1 Comparison of change methods

Method	Applicability	Advantage	Shortcomings
Coercive	–High urgency	–Speed	–High resistance
Adaptive	–Low urgency	–Low resistance	–Slow
Crisis	–Survival threat	–Low resistance	–Extreme time pressure
			–Failure risk
Managed resistance	–Medium urgency	–Low resistance	–Complexity
	–Recurrent discontinuities	–Tailored to time	
		–Comprehensive capability change	

The managed resistance ('accordion') method is to be preferred whenever urgency is not so great as to require the coercive change. Its chief advantage is that it strikes the best possible tradeoff between reducing resistance and use of power, within the limits of the available time.

As the figure shows, the managed resistance method is also effective under conditions when the environmental discontinuity is not singular but repetitive and the firm needs to develop a permanent change-responsive strategic capability. It is also more effective than the brute force introduction of strategic planning which has repeatedly been used in the past.

*Choosing the Appropriate Method

The logical procedure illustrated in Fig. 23.1 can be used in choosing a method to be used to push a major discontinuous change through the firm.

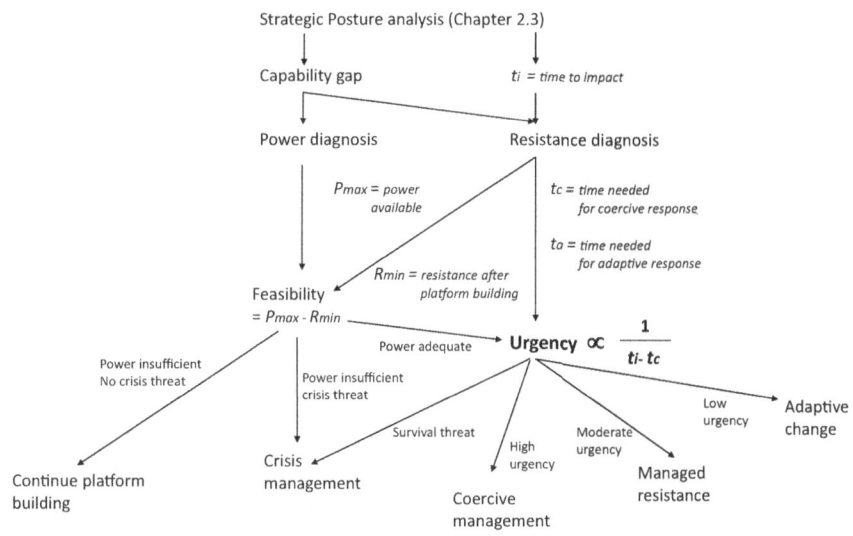

Fig. 23.1 Choice of change method

1. Use the strategic posture analysis of to determine the gap between the management capability of the firm and the capability needed to introduce and support the change.
2. Taking into account the speed with which the change is expected to develop and the probable competitive dynamics, estimate the time to impact (t_1) for a timely response (if the change is an opportunity, t_i will depend on whether the firm intends to adopt a position of leadership, or to become a follower).
3. Make power and resistance diagnoses to determine:

   a. The maximum power base (P_{max})
   b. The minimum resistance (R_{min}) which will have to be overcome after platform-building.

4. Estimate the time t, which the firm would need for response. Also, estimate time t, needed for adaptive response.
5. Compare the power base P_{max} to the resistance R_{min} and decide whether the available power is sufficient to push the change through the firm using the adaptive method.
6. If the power is insufficient, and failure to introduce the change will trigger a crisis, one or more preparatory approaches described in Sect. 6.3.3 should be taken.
7. If the power is insufficient, but the change will not trigger a crisis, continue building support until it reaches the minimum necessary level to assure pushing the change through the firm.

$$\text{Urgency} \propto \frac{1}{t_i - t_c}$$

8. If P_{max} is adequate, the next step is to estimate the urgency by using the following relationship.
9. Choose the response approach according to the following rules:

   a. If $t_1 > t_a$ use the adaptive method.
   b. If $t_a > t_c$ use the managed resistance.
   c. If $t_i \approx t_c$ use the coercive method.
   d. If $t_i < t_c$ prepare for a crisis.

The preceding conclusions determine the minimal level of aggressiveness which management needs to pursue for timely change. When a choice is available, the level of aggressiveness above the minimum is determined by the following factors:

1. *Management style*: authoritarian managers will prefer to move decisively and forcefully and will prefer shorter change processes; participative managers will prolong the process as long as possible in the interests of minimizing resistance.
2. The choice will be influenced by the *uncertainties* in the time available t_j. It may be difficult to estimate with precision the time by which a market must be entered in order to capture the emerging demand, or when a new competitive response must be in place before the firm loses its market share. When the uncertainty in the estimates is large, management will incline toward high power and short duration.
3. The choice of the method will also be influenced by the *entrepreneurial risk propensity of the management*, particularly in the case of opportunities. There is usually a tradeoff between early entries into the marketplace, which may secure a position of leadership for the firm, but which may turn out to be premature and costly, and delayed entries by the 'also-rans,' who cannot hope for leadership but are less prone to fail. Entrepreneurial managers will choose to move more forcefully. Cautious managers will stretch change over time.

Summary

There are three commonly observable methods by which organizations address discontinuous change: (1) coercive, which rapidly forces the change on the firm; (2) adaptive, which spreads the change over time; (3) crisis response, to survival threats under extreme time pressure. All three approaches are useful components of the management response repertoire, each appropriate under different conditions.

Historically, all three methods have usually been used without deliberate efforts by management to diagnose and manage resistance. The suggestions offered for resistance management in can be applied, to different degrees, in all three approaches, and thus make them more efficient and less disruptive.

When power is lacking or urgency is immediate, crisis management should be used. When power is adequate and the change is urgent, the coercive method is appropriate. When urgency is low, the adaptive method is attractive because it minimizes resistance and hence the need for power.

For conditions of moderate urgency, a new method, not normally observable in practice, called the managed resistance method, becomes attractive. It is to be described in detail in the next chapter.

Exercises

1. Prepare a procedure for estimating the time 1 (see Fig. 23.1), which is available to the firm for responding to change. How will the estimate be affected by the risk propensity of the key managers?

    a. Discuss the advantages and disadvantages of triggering off an artificial crisis.
    b. How can an artificial crisis be made credible to the organization?

2. During recovery from a crisis, what should be done to prevent an early resurgence of behavioral resistance?
3. The management of your firm has decided that a major and unpopular change must be pushed through the firm.

The firm is an electronic component manufacturer, with a long record of success, whose position is being rapidly eroded by a new technology. The top management intends to cut out the major historical product line, reduce the present market's scope to the still profitable segments, and make a crash effort to enter the new technology.

Your assignment is to prepare part of the transition plan for activities which will make the change as painless as possible.

24

Managed Resistance ('Accordion') Method for Introducing a Discontinuous Change

In Chapters 21 and 22, we identified the causes of resistance and made some general suggestions for reducing it. In Chapter 23, we identified three 'natural' methods for managing change which usually occur without deliberate management of resistance. Ansoff's suggestions for managing resistance can be applied to all three methods, but they apply particularly to a fourth 'synthetic' method, which he coined managed *resistance*, or the 'accordion' method. This chapter will describe the accordion method in detail.

Application of Resistance Management to the Alternative Methods

The ideal application for the suggestions made in Chapters 21, 22, is to the adaptive method. The availability of time makes it possible to extend the duration of launching platform building until both the behavioral and the systemic resistance are eliminated, and the new strategy can be launched in a receptive and welcoming atmosphere.

Since the platform is built gradually, step-by-step, capacity is no problem. Throughout the process, resistance can be kept low and little power is needed. The platform building activity starts an organizational contagion process which gradually spreads through the firm, resulting in a pro-change culture, power structure, and competence.

Because of the pressures of time, the least opportunity to apply resistance reduction is in the coercive method. Nevertheless, its effectiveness can

© The Author(s) 2019
H. I. Ansoff et al., *Implanting Strategic Management*,
https://doi.org/10.1007/978-3-319-99599-1_24

be increased if a resistance/power diagnosis is made at the outset, and if resistance is anticipated and managed throughout the process. In particular, when malfunctions and delays occur, they should be traced to their behavioral and/or systemic origins and treated at the roots, not through superficial exholiation to higher performance or through meting out punishment to wrongdoers.

During a crisis, management benefits from reduction of behavioral resistance and can focus its attention on the strategic response and on systemic changes. But, as discussed, management must remain aware that resistance typically recurs before the crisis is over. Therefore, it is important to keep the organization informed of actual progress and to dampen premature enthusiasms about recovery.

It is the managed resistance ('accordion') method that offers a major opportunity to apply the lessons of change management learned.

We start its discussion by comparing typical Western and Japanese approaches to decision making.

Japanese and Western Decision Making

American managers who have engaged in business negotiations in Japan frequently report a common and, to them, frustrating experience. Coming from a culture which places high premium on decisiveness, they are frustrated by the apparent disregard for speed in decision-making exhibited by their Japanese counterparts. They find it difficult to force the joint planning to a decision point, and they are surprised to learn, that before this point is reached, their Japanese counterparts frequently launch certain implementation steps. They are further surprised to find that, once the decision is reached, implementation of the Japanese commitment is likely to proceed faster and with less resistance than for the Americans.

We have summarized these impressions in Fig. 24.1 as models of American and Japanese strategic action. As the figure shows, the Japanese take advantage of a longer decision phase to gain commitment to the decision and to launch early implementation. They reap the overall benefit of a shorter strategic action cycle.

The Japanese practice is a result of a long and distinctive cultural heritage, which is different from the Western culture. Therefore, it would be imprudent to imitate it slavishly. However, two features of the Japanese approach can be usefully translated into Western practice. These are:

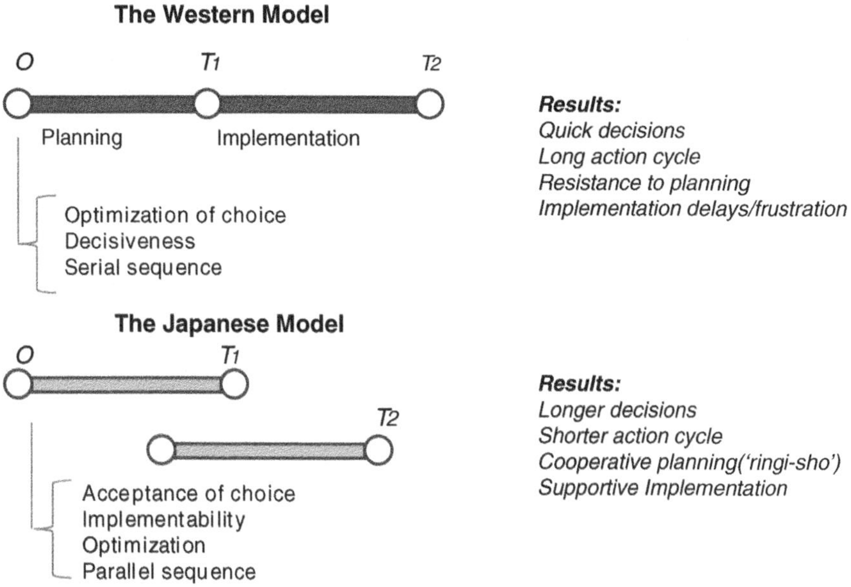

The Western Model

O   T₁   T₂

Planning   Implementation

Optimization of choice
Decisiveness
Serial sequence

Results:
Quick decisions
Long action cycle
Resistance to planning
Implementation delays/frustration

The Japanese Model

O   T₁

                                    T₂

Acceptance of choice
Implementability
Optimization
Parallel sequence

Results:
Longer decisions
Shorter action cycle
Cooperative planning('ringi-sho')
Supportive Implementation

Fig. 24.1 Japanese vs. Western models of strategic action

1. the concern with behavioral acceptance of new strategies from the very beginning of the decision process, and
2. the early launching of projects before planning is completed, resulting in parallel planning/implementation activity.

Building the Launching Platform

The 'accordion' method is illustrated in the somewhat complex Fig. 24.2. As discussed in the preceding chapters, building the launching platform for the change is the first step. Perhaps it is not necessary in the Japanese setting, where there is managerial allegiance to the firm and to superiors, and consensus is a powerful social norm, which is exemplified by a popular Japanese saying: 'When a nail is crooked, we hammer it in.'

But, as we have discussed, the Western culture is individualistic and consensus is not a generally accepted norm. Therefore, *platform building* becomes essential whenever the strategic change is discontinuous and likely to encounter resistance.

The launching platform is a set of preconditions which achieves a power-resistance balance necessary for launching of the change. The platform

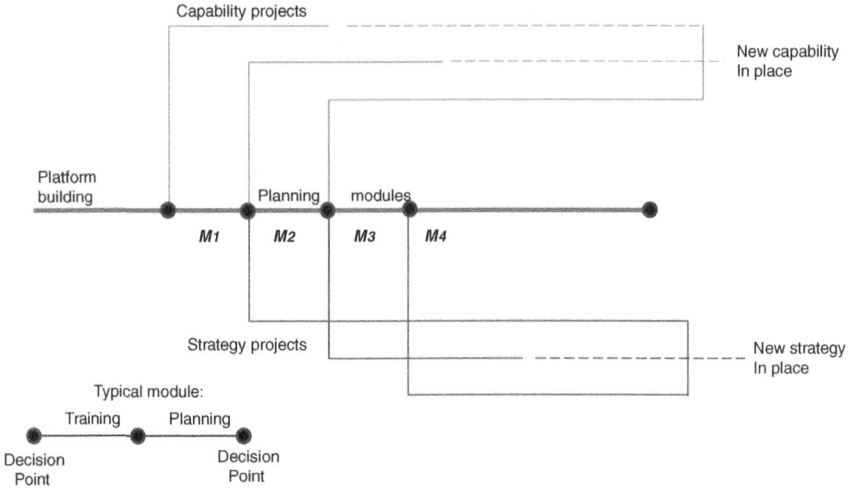

Fig. 24.2 'Accordion' method for introduction of change

makes it possible to 'lead the horse to water' (start planning) but does not necessarily assure that 'the horse will drink' (accept and implement the plan). This means that the resistance reducing efforts during platform building will reduce it only enough to permit a successful launching, and that resistance monitoring and control must continue while the change takes place.

The reader is referred to Chapter 21 for detailed suggestions for the behavioral component of the launching platform. In summary, these include:

1. Cultural/social changes which minimize apprehensions, enhance understanding of the need and of the impact of the change, and assure positive support for it.
2. Political changes which minimize resistance from people who are expected to oppose the change, as well as creation of a pro-change coalition, powerful enough to overcome the resistance to the startup.
3. Design of the change process in a way which minimizes resistance and builds acceptability for the change.

The reader is further referred to Chapter 22 for suggestions for the systemic component of the launching platform. These include:

1. Freeing the time of busy managers for involvement with the new strategy.
2. Protecting this time from infringement of operating activities.
3. Identifying and involving individuals who are best qualified and supportive of the change.
4. Design of the change process in a way which minimizes systemic resistance.
5. Timing of the change process, so as to produce timely results in the marketplace.

As discussed earlier, strategic change has typically been triggered by introduction of a formal strategic planning system. We suggest that this is premature for two reasons: First, one of the purposes of the initial problem solving is to determine whether the firm needs strategic planning or some other system. Thus, introducing the strategic planning at the outset is akin to putting the cart before the horse.

Second, and more importantly, the formal system focuses attention on the procedures, responsibilities, and relationships at a time when attention should be focused on rapid resolution of pressing strategic problems.

In summary, building the launching platform includes the following steps:

1. A strategic diagnosis of the strategic problems and of their urgency.
2. A behavioral diagnosis of the cultural and political resistance/support to be expected.
3. A reduction of cultural resistance and mustering of political support to a point where a sufficient power base exists to launch the change.
4. Preparation of a plan by which the diagnosed problems are to be resolved.

Platform building requires introspective and unbiased recognition of the cultural, political, systemic, and strategic deficiencies in the firm. Such introspection is difficult, at best disturbing, and at worst, threatening. As discussed in Chapter 18, typical responses to strategic challenges are tensions, procrastination, refusal to face reality, preoccupations with superficial problems instead of real ones.

Therefore, external help is frequently needed to assist management to make an impartial behavioral, systemic, and strategic diagnosis and to build a realistic platform for change.

Preparing a Modular Plan for Change

According to the Japanese lesson, the 'accordion' is designed to two requirements:

1. Behavioral acceptance building must start from the beginning of the planning process;
2. Planning must be conducted in a way which permits early launching of implementation projects.

As shown in Fig. 24.2, both of these requirements can be met by a modular design of the planning process. Eleven planning modules, which have been used in this book for a comprehensive strategic posture planning, are described in Table 24.1. In traditional strategic planning, modules 1–7 are usually used in the sequence shown in the figure and are treated as parts of an uninterrupted planning process. In the modular approach, the modules are selected and sequenced according to the problems determined during the resistance diagnosis.

For example, if strategic diagnosis identifies improvement in the firm's competitive posture as the problem, the sequence of modules should be $2 \rightarrow 5 \rightarrow 6$. If the problem is internationalization of the firm, the sequence should be $3 \rightarrow 7 \rightarrow 8 \rightarrow 9$. As the right-hand column of Table 24.1 shows, each module can further be subdivided into submodules either for serial or sequential execution by the planning groups.

Thus, as the first step, using the priorities indicated by the strategic diagnosis, management should select the particular modules and module sequence which will resolve the problems diagnosed during the platform building in the most expeditious manner, without unnecessary planning 'makework.'

The next step in the modular design is to identify the skills which will be needed by the participants in the planning process. These are shown in the third column of Table 24.1.

The execution of each module is planned in two parts. The first is *training*, which equips the participants with the knowledge and skills necessary for analysis and decision. The second is the *planning*, which yields appropriate action decisions at the end of each module.

Since implementation projects will be launched at the end of each module, training during early modules must also focus on *project implementation skills*: gaining acceptance for novel departures, diagnosing and managing

Table 24.1 Planning modules

Module	Planning module	Submodules/skills required
1	Platform building	Cultural diagnosis
		Power diagnosis
		Strategic diagnosis
		Master planning
2	Analysis of prospects	SBA segmentation
		Environmental forecasting
		SBA prospects analysis
		Turbulence analysis
3	Setting objectives	Stakeholder identification
		Power field mapping
		Participative objectives setting
4	Assessing resources	Financial audit
		Human resource audit
		Strategic raw materials audit
5	Choosing competitive posture	Key success factor analysis
		Competitive posture determination
		Competitive posture choice
6	Portfolio balancing	Life cycle balancing
		Synergy diagnosis
		Flexibility diagnosis
7	Choosing diversification posture	Gap analysis
		Search criteria/methods
		Opportunity evaluation
		Integration planning
		Capability needs
		Progressive response
8	Corporate capability needs	Strategic posture diagnosis
		Multicapability design
9	Corporate capability design	Planning system
		Issue management system
		Organizational structure
		Management selection
		Reward system
		Project management
		Environmental surveillance
		Information system
		Dual system
		Dual structure
10	Real-time response	Issue management system selection
		Issue identification
		Impact/urgency analysis
		Progressive commitment
11	Behavioral transformation	Mentality development
		Cultural transformation
		Resistance management
		Institutionalization

resistance, forming pro-change coalitions, protecting strategic work from encroachment from daily operating tasks.

The use of two-part modules (first learn, then apply the new knowledge) integrates management development into the strategic action process and avoids forcing managers into the role of 'instant planners.' This results in improved quality of decisions, as well as reduction of the resistance to planning.

As shown at the bottom of Fig. 24.2, decisions are made at the end of each module. These are of two kinds: (1) approval of conclusions of the module (e.g., agreement on SBA segmentation) and (2) selection of implementation project which should be launched at this time (e.g., an early decision to start divestment from the obvious 'dogs' in the firm's portfolio).

In summary, modular design of the planning process includes the following.

Use of the resistance diagnosis.

1. Selection and sequencing of the modules.
2. Training at the beginning of each module.
3. Decision points at the end of each module.

Building Implementability into Planning

It is common practice in Western decision making to focus on the substance of the decision, its merits and disadvantages, and to pay little attention to the way the individuals involved feel and react. For example, in a typical introduction of strategic planning, little effort is devoted to making it clear to the participants why strategic planning is necessary, how it will affect them personally, what benefits it will bring, how it should be used in the manager's daily work. Nor is any special effort made to make the results of planning understandable and acceptable to the nonparticipants in the planning process who, nevertheless, will be key to successful implementation.

It is also common practice to treat managers as instant planners, to give them forms to fill, without giving them an understanding of the nature of strategic thinking and developing their skills in strategic analysis.

A typical result of such disregard of the human aspect of planning is a feeling by the involved managers that planning is done for 'them' at the headquarters, that it has little to do with their own problems, that it is a form filling exercise, which distracts them from their daily responsibilities. Hence, a lack of commitment and resistance to planning.

The above results are typical in cases when planning is treated as a purely problem solving, analytic exercise. However, when the planning process is designed to deal with both problem solving and behavioral development, the results have been a dramatic opposite. Instead of demotivation and lack of commitment, managers develop a new *strategic mentality*, an understanding of the importance and relevance of the strategic problems to their daily work, and a willingness to deal with them. And they regard the planning process as a useful tool for solving these problems. We shall refer to the process of including behavioral development in the planning process as *building implementability into planning*.

The steps which can enhance implementability are the following:

1. Involvement of all managers, working in groups, who will be responsible for implementation, as well as of managers and other individuals (e.g., R&D experts) who make key contributions to the decision process. Strategic participation does not mean strategic decentralization. On the contrary, the upper and lower levels of the involved management each have their own strategic thing to do, as well as joint problems to solve. Experience has shown that involvement and continued contribution by the top management is a key factor in ensuring organizational acceptance. It should be noted that involvement and contribution are not the same thing as enthusiastic but passive pronouncements in favor of planning, which have been advocated as an early antidote to resistance. It is essential that top management should have its own planning tasks and that it makes decisions at the end of each planning module.

2. During the planning process, information on reasons for planning, and the expected outcomes, and the impact of the change on the organization are communicated and discussed with individuals who will be involved in the implementation. Further, general bulletins are sent to nonparticipants who will, or feel that they will, be affected by the strategy changes.

3. Before each planning and implementation module, education and training are given to the participants in the relevant concepts, skills, and techniques.

4. The planning process is focused on solving problems identified during the strategy diagnosis. Mechanistic filling of planning forms for the benefit of the headquarters is avoided.

5. Problem-solving techniques and procedures are kept simple, compatible with the level of knowledge, and skills of the participants. The emphasis is on the understanding of the logic of the problem and not on technical sophistication of the solution. This point is of particular importance, because experience has shown that, if the details get to be too numerous

and technical, managers can no longer see the wood for the trees and become demotivated and frustrated.

6. Planning tasks assigned to each group of managers should have a real impact on their own jobs.

7. To the extent possible, new strategic information (which is different from the usual operating information supplied by the accounting system) is provided to the planning groups. However, the state of strategic information is frequently so poor that planning would have to be delayed substantially, if a fully adequate strategic database is to be a prerequisite. In such cases development of a strategic database should be one of the early projects. Until the project is completed, planning should rely on the experience and judgment of qualified managers.

8. If the necessary resources and capacity are available, implementation of planning is not delayed until the plan is complete and approved. Instead, implementation projects are launched early in the manner to be described later.

Controlling the Planning Process

In the accordion method, the planning process has two aims: to make realistic and timely decisions and to build acceptance and enthusiasm for implementation of these decisions. For effective control of resistance, it is essential that the *decision milestones* at the end of each module should match the appropriate *acceptance milestones*. This is referred to as *behavioral control* at the top of Fig. 24.2.

The problem is illustrated in Fig. 24.3. The horizontal axis represents the sequence of the planning modules M_1, M_2, etc., and the dots are the decision milestones at the end of each module. The vertical axes are the levels of acceptance (acceptance milestones) which are essential for organizational acceptance of the results of each planning module.

Line B is a case in which enthusiasm for and acceptance of change are built faster than the substantive progress. This is the case of frustration through inaction which had been observed in firms at the end of behavioral OD (organizational development) experiences. Being a purely behavioral technique, OD builds organizational acceptance of change, but produces no decisions, nor launches any strategy changes. A phrase heard on such occasions is 'now that we have our human problems solved, why don't the profits go up?'

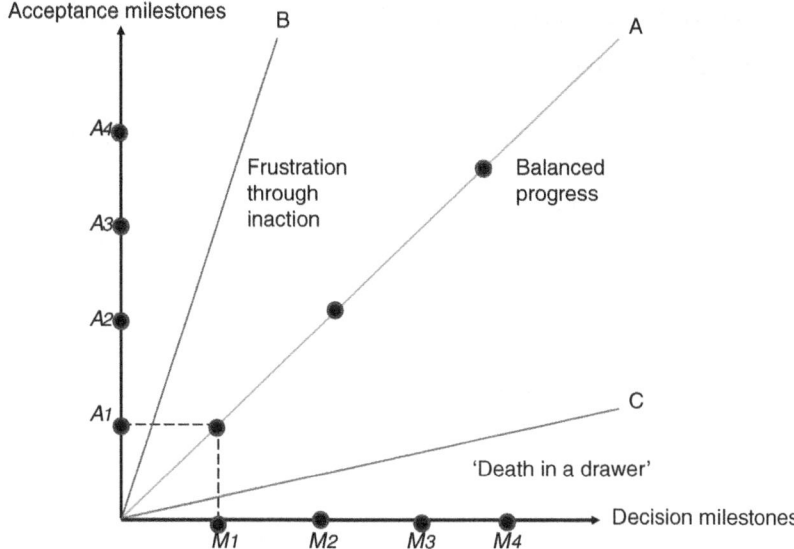

Fig. 24.3 Control of implementability

Line C represents the previously discussed historical experience in strategic planning, which is the 'death in the drawer': Plans are made but they lack the necessary acceptance and implementation is blocked.

The corrective actions are clearly different in the two cases. In the former, vigorous planning should be launched; in the latter, efforts should be focused on reducing resistance.

The forty-five-degree line represents a line of balanced *progress*. As planning progresses, acceptance of the results is raised in step, thus enabling prompt and effective implementation.

The parallel progress is monitored, and if progress along one of the axes lags behind the other, appropriate corrective measures are taken before implementation projects are launched.

Thus, it is necessary to monitor and control the joint progress toward decisions and toward organizational acceptance of these decisions. Experience has shown that this is best accomplished by a *process management team*, composed of the strategic planners and outside consultants, who are expert in behavioral process management (Ten Dam and Siffert, in Ansoff et al. 1982-D).

Progressive Decision Making and Early Implementation

In the customary approach to planning, final decisions and the launching of implementation are delayed until the plans are completed and approved by management at the end of the planning cycle. The reasoning usually is: 'We cannot decide until after all options have been made clear, and we cannot start implementation until after the decisions have been made.'

In the accordion method, a different approach is taken. At the end of each module, it usually becomes clear that certain actions will have to be taken, regardless of the conclusions of the subsequent planning steps. For example, at the end of module 2 (analysis of prospects) it usually becomes evident that the firm's environmental surveillance capability is deficient and must be improved as quickly as possible. At the end of the competitive strategy analysis (module 5) it may become evident that the firm has no future in certain of its traditional SBAs and should quickly proceed with divestment to avoid further losses.

In such cases, nothing is to be gained from delaying actions which will eventually have to be taken anyway. In the accordion method, appropriate projects are launched at the end of each module. This offers several advantages;

1. The spacing of decisions over time creates an evenly spaced decision workload on top management, as compared with the typical decision overload which occurs at plan approval time.
2. Early launching of projects similarly spreads implementation workload over time and assures earlier completion of the overall change process.
3. Implementation conducted in parallel with planning provides valuable feedback on the validity of the planning decisions and assumptions.
4. Early experience with decision-implementation develops and perfects the strategic decision/implementation capability in advance of the major decisions which will be made at the end of the planning process.
5. The option of early decisions/implementation permits management to control the duration of the overall change process and thus tailor it to the time that is available for making the change.

The major drawbacks of the early decisions/implementation are the additional workload it puts on management and on the implementers, as well as the increased complexity of the overall process. Therefore, it is not always feasible to launch all of the projects made possible by the early decisions.

Institutionalizing a New Strategy

As illustrated in Fig. 24.2, because of external market pressures, a new strategy is likely to be in place before the capacity/capability needed for its effective exploitation have been fully developed, and before the power structure and culture have become supportive.

As already discussed on several occasions, such premature termination of capability developments produces two effects:

1. The strategy chronically fails to reach full profitability.
2. The hidden and pent-up resistance surfaces and attempts to rollback the change.

Therefore, to assure stability and full profitability of a new strategy, the behavioral development and competence/capacity projects must be continued to completion after the new strategy has been launched on the marketplace.

Summary

In Western countries, the three 'natural' methods for managing discontinuous change (coercive, adaptive, and crisis response) follow a serial problem-solving paradigm which was developed by the rationalist philosophers and, in particular, by Descartes. Applied and elaborated in management practice, this paradigm prescribes that planning must precede implementation, that planning must be decisive and performed expeditiously, and that it should be exclusively focused on selecting the optimum course of action. Concern with implementation should be delayed until after planning has been completed.

A comparison of this paradigm with Japanese practice shows that the Japanese solve problems differently: They use a parallel planning/implementation process, and use the planning process not only to arrive at the optimal decision but also to assure its cultural and political acceptance. As a result, their planning process lasts longer, but the implementation is quicker and change takes less time.

In this chapter, the parallel approach is adapted to the Western culture to design a method for systematic management of a discontinuous change. This method consists of the following elements:

1. Building a launching platform for the change.
2. Using a modular process, interspersed with decision points to plan the change.
3. Building management training into each module.
4. Building implementability into the planning process through participation, communication, focus on solving problems relevant to the planners, simplicity of problem-solving routines, involvement of top management in planning, and early development of the strategic database.
5. Monitoring and controlling the planning process to assure that each planning module has reached acceptability before it is launched.
6. Launching implementation projects after each module.
7. Institutionalizing the change through development of necessary competence/capacity and a supportive culture/power structure.

An important feature of the change management method described above, which gives it the name 'accordion method,' is that it permits management to expand or contract the duration of the change in response to the urgency dictated by the environment.

Exercise

The manager of your division, to whom you report, wants to make a major strategic reorientation. The new orientation is not clear, but he has convinced himself that the present prospects of the division are for stagnation and eventual decline. He further feels that the decline is not far off and that the division must be turned around within five years.

He has read the preceding four chapters, is impressed, but feels frustrated with the fact that 'simple' things are made to appear complicated.

1. Your assignment is to prepare a 45-minute presentation and a two-page memorandum which will help the manager decide what to do, and how he should proceed in launching a major strategic orientation of your division.

25

Institutionalizing Strategic Responsiveness

While the preceding chapter was concerned with effective 'pushing' of a discontinuous change through the firm and assuring its effectiveness and stability; in this chapter, we turn attention to converting the firm into a habitual strategic actor.

Introduction

In the early days of concern with strategy, the need for a discontinuous repositioning of the firm in the environment was seen as a 'one time' exercise. The firm had a spectacular fifty years of success, thanks to the initial positioning by the entrepreneurs of the nineteenth century. Therefore, it seemed in the 1950s that a major re-adaptation would serve the firm's needs for another fifty years. Since the 1990s, and the increasing effect on industry by technology, it has become increasingly clear that for many firms, periodic, or even continual, strategic repositioning must become a way of life. These are firms which operate in environments on turbulence levels 4 and above.

Previously, we identified the characteristics of the management capability profile which the firm needs to become a habitual strategic actor. The characteristics of this profile are compared to the profile of operating profit-making capability. A comparison of the two profiles shows that the two capabilities are not only different, but inimical to each other.

As discussed on several earlier occasions, the introduction of strategic responsiveness is not a process of replacing operating responsiveness. If

© The Author(s) 2019
H. I. Ansoff et al., *Implanting Strategic Management*,
https://doi.org/10.1007/978-3-319-99599-1_25

this were done, the firm would become a devoted generator of future profit potential without any means of converting the potential into current profits. Thus, the problem, expressed in the language of Lawrence and Lorsch, is to assure a balance of differentiation and integration between the strategic and operating activities within the firm. The remainder of this chapter is devoted to concrete measures for solving this problem.

Why Strategic Planning Does Not Work

Since many firms which seek to institutionalize strategic responsiveness depart from a disappointing experience with strategic planning, it is helpful to start with a summary of the reasons why strategic planning does not work, and then proceed to a discussion of remedial measures.

The reasons, and the observed symptoms of malfunction, are summarized once again in the first and second columns of Table 25.1.

The first three are systemic reasons: the lack of strategic implementation and control mechanism, the capacity and priority conflict between strategic and profit-making work, and the lack of a strategic database.

Table 25.1 Why strategic planning does not work

Reason	Symptoms	Solutions
1. Strategic planning is not a complete system	–Paralysis by analysis –Frustration through inaction	–Dual management system –Strategic control –Rewards
2. Strategic activity competes with operations	–Tomorrow we will organize and plan	–Strategic budget –More general management –Dual management structure
3. MIS does not provide strategic information	–Garbage in/garbage out GIGO	–Environmental forecasting analysis system
4. Managers lack strategic management skills	–Strategic form-filling for corporate benefit	–Trainig in strategic decision-making/ implementation
5. Threat to power structure/culture/ mentality	–Resistance to change –Let's get back to real work	–Pro-change power structure –Pro-change mentality/ culture –Participative planning –Resistance management

Reason four is both behavioral and systemic, since the lack of understanding and skills leads managers both to resist planning and to perform it ineffectively. The fifth reason is the behavioral resistance to a change in the order of things.

Listed in the right-hand column is a series of measures which can eliminate the deficiencies indicated in the first column. In the light of our earlier discussion, some of the solutions are already well explored: training of managers, environmental forecasting, need for more general managers, and participative planning. The remaining measures deserve further exploration.

Dual Management System

Earlier, we explored a dual system of responsibility which becomes necessary whenever strategic activity is an important user of investment funds. Responsibilities for profit making are assigned to the operating units, and responsibilities for strategic development to strategic business units.

In some organizational arrangements, it may turn out that certain managers are assigned both responsibilities and, as a result are, in Drucker's terminology, fully profit and loss responsibility. But whenever the strategic activity level is high, it becomes desirable to install a *dual system* through which such managers participate in the profit making and the strategic work. Such a system is illustrated in Fig. 25.1.

The strategic planning process produces two sets of goals and objectives: *operating*, for the near-term profit making, and *strategic* for development of future profit potential. As Fig. 25.1 shows, in the dual system the goals,

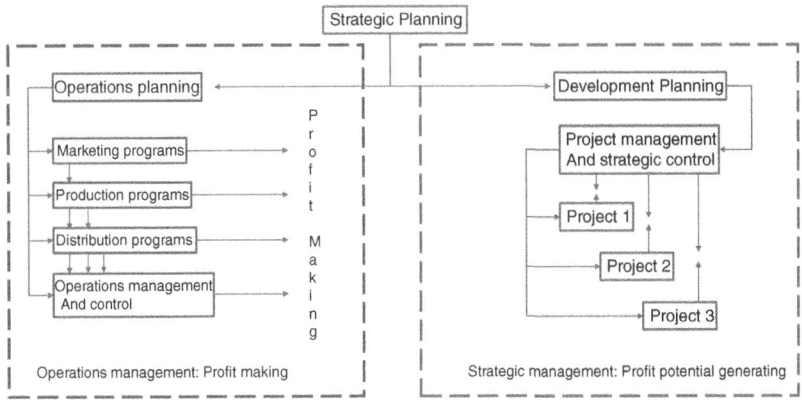

Fig. 25.1 Dual system

objectives, and strategies are next used to generate two sets of action plans and supporting budgets. The profit goals are converted into operations plans, and the profit potential goals into innovation (sometimes called development) plans.

The operations plan is a set of operating programs and budgets which are prepared for each operating unit in marketing, production, etc. A distinctive characteristic of these programs/budgets is that they have the same and repetitive time horizon, usually one year in detail and, frequently, three to five years specified in less detail.

The innovation plan contains *projects* which differ from the programs in four significant ways:

1. They have different time horizons and different durations.
2. As shown in the figure, they are not launched all at once but are spread throughout the year.
3. Most importantly, the projects are problem, and not unit, focused.
4. Unlike the operating units, the projects are impermanent. They are launched when needed, and disbanded when their strategic goal is achieved.

As discussed earlier, experience has shown that the *operations control system*, which is used for managing implementation of operating programs and budgets, is ineffective and even inimical to managing strategic projects and is, in fact, one of the major causes of paralysis by analysis. Therefore, the dual system uses a separate project management and control system.

As shown at the bottom of Fig. 25.1, in addition to managing projects generated through strategic planning, the project management and strategic control system provides a natural home for projects generated by the issue management process (see Chapter 19).

Strategic Control and Strategic Rewards

The distinctive character of strategic control is illustrated in Fig. 25.2, which represents a typical cash flow profile for a strategic move, such as introduction of a new product line, conversion to a new technology, or entry into a new SBA.

The process starts with planning and is followed by product-technology development, market research, market testing, building production, marketing and distribution capabilities. The project terminates after a full-scale market entry has been made.

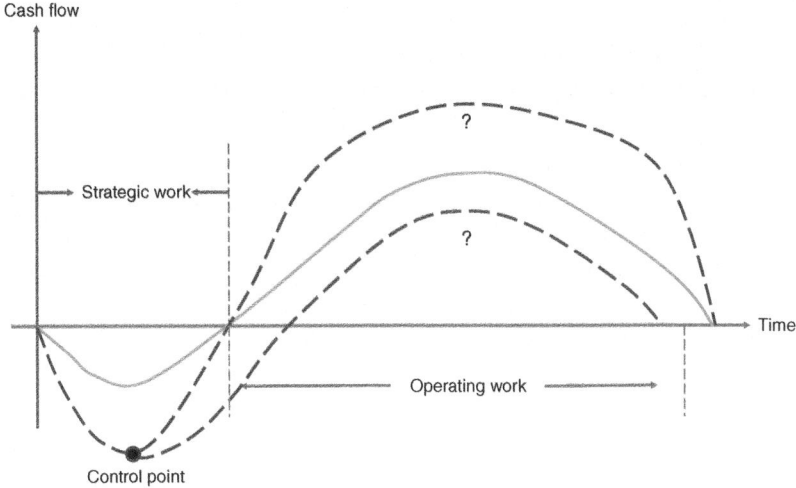

Fig. 25.2 Control of strategic projects

The part of the solid curve, which lies below the horizontal axis in Fig. 25.2, traces the negative cash flow which is generated by all of these strategic activities.

Roughly around the point where cash flow turns positive, the exploitation of the new entry is turned over to an operating unit, which makes profits and cash from the potential generated by the strategic project.

The original decision to launch the project is based on the ratio of the area under the solid curve, above the horizontal axis, to the area below. This ratio is a measure of the return on the firm's investment over the lifetime of the entry.

In most cases, when the strategic project is launched, many uncertainties surround its probable outcome. Therefore, the solid cash flow line is highly conjectural and probability is very high that the actual course of events will not follow the line.

Suppose that the actual evolution follows the lower dotted line in the figure, and that a major review of the project is about to take place at the control point, say, three years after the project was started.

If the operating control philosophy decisions that are based on a comparison of past accomplishments with the plan are followed, the project is clearly in deep trouble because of the 100% cost overrun.

But from the strategic point of view, the historical performance is much less relevant than the future prospects, which can now be assessed better than was possible three years ago, when the project was started.

If the new assessment of the future follows the lower dotted line in the figure, the project is indeed a disaster. Not only did the project manager grossly overspend, but he also delayed transition to the operational status to a point where the firm will be late in the market and will, therefore, not be able to recover its investment.

On the other hand, if the best estimate at the control points follows the upper dotted line, the project promises to be a success in spite of the cost overruns and, possibly, precisely due to the fact that the larger early invest-ment increased the size of the positive profit area.

The preceding discussion suggests the following principles for strategic control:

1. Because of uncertainties and imprecision of estimates, a strategic pro-ject can easily (and frequently does) become a 'free-spending boondog-gle.' This must be prevented, and costs must be tracked against promised accomplishments. But unlike the typical practice in operating control, the focus must be on ultimate cost-benefits and not on tracking the budget. In fact, if early progress shows promise of very high benefits related to costs, it may be desirable to encourage overspending of the original budget.
2. At each control point, an estimate should be made of the return on investment over the project lifetime. So long as the return remains above the cutoff rate of return, the project should be continued. When the return falls below the cutoff level, a comparison should be made with other opportunities and serious consideration given to discontinuing the project.

Unlike operations control, strategic control is based on uncertain and some-times vague estimates and not on concrete results. Strategic control is as much an entrepreneurial decision process as the original decision to launch the project. Therefore, a manager who belongs to the controller archetype will not have either the risk-taking propensity, or the requisite skills for the job. The role of the strategic controller must be played by an entrepreneur who will not only encourage but also participate in the entrepreneurial risk-taking.

The strategic controller must also be a tough-minded change manager. He must continuously be aware that members of the project are frequently driven by excitement of discovery, fun of the game, allegiance to the pro-ject team, and they are quite likely to be indifferent to the ultimate profit-ability of the strategic move, particularly since they are unlikely to bear the responsibility for the ultimate profit making. Therefore, the strategic controller must be prepared to be ruthless in terminating the project once he has convinced himself that the project will not be profitable.

It should be clear from the preceding discussion that the rewards for past performance used in operating control are not only inapplicable but are suppressive in strategic project management. The characteristics of the appropriate reward system should include the following:

1. Entrepreneurial risk-taking must be encouraged. This means, in part, that project failure must not be indiscriminately penalized. On the contrary, failure to fail periodically should be punished, as a sign of a lack of entrepreneurial spirit.
2. In part, entrepreneurship can be encouraged and rewarded through freedom to undertake projects without bureaucratic and lengthy approval procedures. Firms which have succeeded in encouraging entrepreneurship have set up budget pools on which entrepreneurs can draw freely, provided they do not exceed a set limit for a project. Once the limit has been reached, the project is either approved by higher management or it is written off.
3. Private entrepreneurs frequently take the risk because they expect to get rich. There is no reason why the same incentive cannot be offered in large companies. In some firms, inventors participate in the royalties on their inventions. Similarly, entrepreneurs can be made participants in the ultimate success or failure of their projects.
4. As discussed repeatedly in this book, strategic activity is stifled and demotivated by the necessarily bureaucratic rules of the profit-making activities. Some firms have solved this conflict by setting up strategic 'skunk works,' isolated from the bureaucracy and free to engage in creative strategic work.
5. Finally, for entrepreneurially minded managers who are frustrated by the overload of operating work provision, time to engage in strategic activity is a significant motivator.

Dual Budgeting

Returning to Table 25.1 the second reason given for the ineffectiveness of strategic planning is the competition for capacity between strategic and operating work, which usually is resolved in favor of the latter.

An effective way to protect strategic work is to separate the total budget of the firm into two parts: an *operating and a strategic budget*. This is illustrated in Fig. 25.3, where expected profit contributions from each budget are plotted against time. As can be seen in the figure, each of the budgets is further subdivided according to activities which make distinctive contributions to profits:

The operating budget is divided into the following categories:

1. Support of continued profit making using the current capacity of the firm.
2. The investment in capacity expansion.
3. The investment in increasing profits through cost reduction.

The strategic budget categories are:

1. Investment in improvement of competitive posture in the present SBAs.
2. Addition of related SBAs through geographic expansion.
3. Addition of new SBAs (and divestment from undesirable ones).

The *dual budget* offers the following advantages:

1. It effectively sets aside resources for strategic work and thus protects strategic work from operating encroachment.
2. The subdivision into the major budgets helps balance the investment in near-term vs. long-term profitability.
3. The particular graphic presentation is helpful in assessing the wisdom of allocation among the sub-activities. If the respective sub-budget categories are written into the figure, the sizes of the profit wedges can be instantly

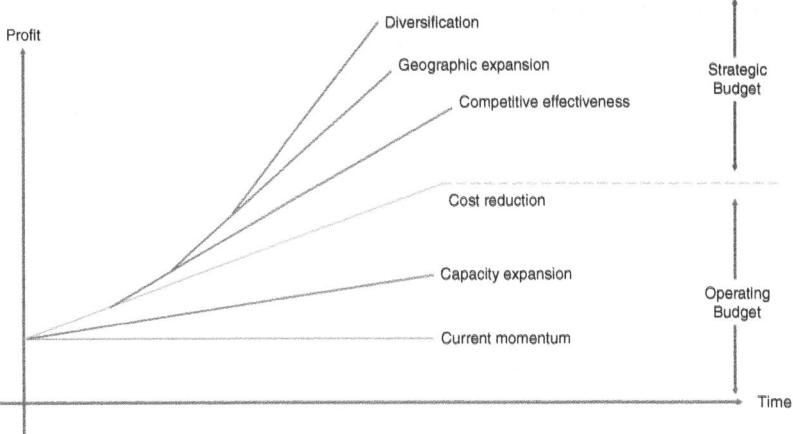

Fig. 25.3 Dual budget

compared with the budgets assigned to them to produce the return on the respective investments. For example, if profit improvement through capacity expansion turns out to be a relatively narrow wedge, but will absorb a substantial percentage of the operating budget, the wisdom of capacity expansion immediately comes into question.

4. Finally, the graphic presentation shows the comparative timing of the respective profit contributions.

Thus, dual budgeting emerges as a major tool for managing the future of a firm, whenever the size of the strategic budget becomes a significant portion of the total.

Dual Structure

The ultimate way to protect the strategic work is to subdivide the firm into two parts as shown in Fig. 25.4. As the figure shows, units which are in growing or mature profit or cash-generating positions are grouped under an operations manager, and SBUs concerned with developing new SBAs are grouped under a strategic development manager. The organizational arrangement of Fig. 25.4 is very similar to that commonly used in multinational companies. Although Fig. 25.4 does not show it, the two parts report to a headquarters.

There are two ways to make the grouping:

1. To assign *all* strategic activities to strategic development, including evolutionary R&D for the present SBAs. The operating group is limited to manufacturing, distribution, and marketing. This, in fact, is the model which has been used for many years in the Soviet Union with highly unsatisfactory results. The reason is that the strategic development becomes technology driven with little concern for either the producibility of the prototypes which is delivered to the factories, or for the needs of the market.
2. A subtler approach is to leave the operating group in control of the new strategic development of the existing SBAs and to confine the strategic development group to development of new businesses.

The problem with the second arrangement is that, in Western firms, the transfer of the new businesses generated by the strategic development group to the operations is difficult for two reasons: the cultural NIH (not invented here) reaction by the operating managers, and their fear that the new businesses will depress profits in the short run, and will make it difficult to meet the near-term profit objectives.

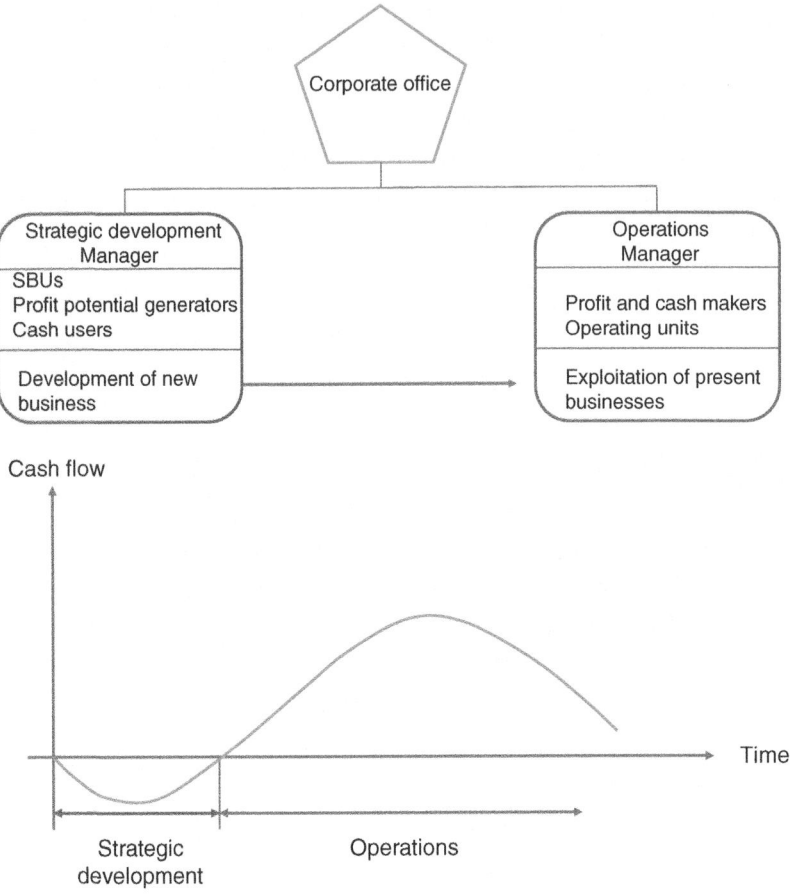

Fig. 25.4 Dual structure

As you may recall, one way to resolve the conflict is to introduce shared authority and responsibility into the strategic development decisions. Another solution is to require that the strategic development group offer the operating group 'the right of first refusal' on all promising new business ventures. But, should the operating group refuse, the strategic development group is free to set up new operating divisions or companies. Experience shows that the fear of turning down attractive opportunities brings a strong pressure on the operators to consider the new businesses seriously.

Aside from providing dedicated capacity for strategic work, the dual structure solution has one other important advantage. It permits the company to build two independent and internally consistent management capability profiles which do not come into conflict during daily work.

Institutionalizing Strategic Culture and Power Structure

The last reason for failure of strategic planning given in Table 25.1 is the threat it poses to the established culture and power structure. Table 25.2 shows five types of action which, over time, remove the threat and convert the resistance into active support.

Exemplary behavior by top management requires much more than the usual protestations of support for planning. In fact, if the protestations are not accompanied by strategic behavior by top management in its daily work, management will be discredited and the protestations demotivating. In a recent company seminar on strategic management, one highly respected and successful third level manager said: 'I will believe all this only when I see them [top management group] practicing it in the next planning review.'

The *exemplary behavior* includes:

1. Participation in the same strategic training that is given to the lower level managers. In practice, top managers are frequently reluctant 'to go back to school.'
2. Involvement in the strategic planning process. This includes defining mission scopes of the SBUs, issuing strategic guidelines, setting corporate objectives and goals, balancing corporate portfolio, and allocating strategic resources.
3. During planning reviews, focusing attention on evaluation and review of strategies and strategic progress, and minimizing involvement in budgeting and programming problems.
4. During performance reviews focusing attention on evolution of strategies and strategic projects.
5. In daily contacts with lower level managers discussing all problems in the perspective of the strategies of the firm. This is not to say that operating

Table 25.2 Changing resistance into support

Results \ Actions	Exemplary behavior by top management	Rewards/ Punishment	Participative planning/strategic communication	Skills, concepts, language, model of reality	Realignment of power
Strategic culture/ mentality	✓ ✓	✓ ✓	✓ ✓	✓ ✓	✓ ✓
Pro-change power structure	✓	✓			✓ ✓
Incentives	✓	✓ ✓	✓	✓	

problems are not discussed, but it does mean that such discussions are related to the strategic perspective.

6. Giving verbal recognition to entrepreneurial and strategic behavior by lower level managers.

As Table 25.2 shows, exemplary behavior is a powerful tool for creating a strategic culture/mentality in the firm. By choosing people to whom it gives special assignments, top management can also significantly affect the de facto power structure.

The other four types of action shown in Table 25.2 have been discussed in the preceding pages. When they are brought together in the figure, it becomes apparent that each produces more than one result. It also becomes apparent that the firm's culture is shaped by all of the action areas.

Managing the Institutionalization Process

If all the measures described in the right-hand column of Table 25.1 are put in place, the firm's strategic behavior will be institutionalized. This means that it will have the behavioral will and the systemic competence for strategic action, and that strategic activity is assured a coexistence alongside daily profit-making activities.

But it is clear from the preceding discussion that institutionalization is a massive and time-consuming process. If strategy development is delayed until institutionalization is completed, as much as ten years may elapse before the firm starts changing its strategy. In cases in which such delay is not acceptable, the adaptive, serial behavior systems strategy sequence must be replaced by a parallel sequence.

The managed resistance approach described in the last chapter, where it was discussed in the context of making a discrete continuous change, is easily adaptable to a major strategic posture transformation, which involves both a strategic repositioning in the environment and a comprehensive transformation of the capability.

All of the planning modules of Table 24.1 are relevant in this case. This means that the planning process becomes lengthy. In one early application in a medium sized high technology company, the first complete pass at planning was organized into five modules and conducted over a period of a year (see Ten Dam and Siffert, in Ansoff et al. 1982-D).

The sequencing of the modules is arranged so as to start both strategy and capability projects after early planning modules. Thus, institutionalization occurs in parallel with strategy change.

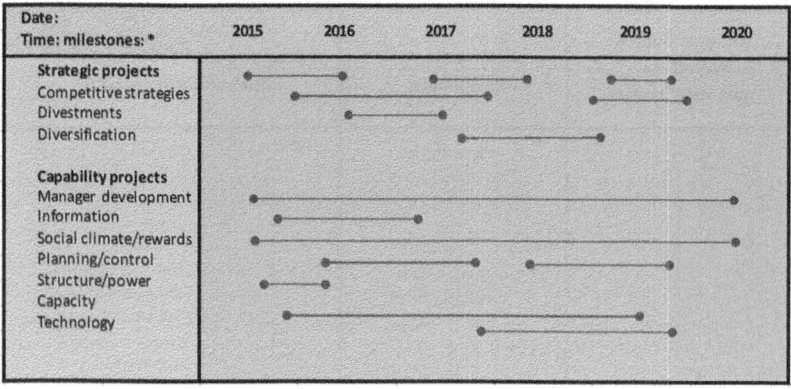

Fig. 25.5 Master plan for strategy development

The resulting projects are numerous, and conflicts will easily result, unless they are coordinated and arranged in a motivating change sequence.

An instrument for managing the interrelated projects is illustrated in a *master plan* in Fig. 25.5. The program illustrated in the figure is scheduled over five years. It is highly probable that during this period significant environmental events will occur, which will either confirm or cast doubts on the validity, or content, or the timing of the projects programmed in 1987.

It is, therefore, necessary to exercise strategic control over the program. In the illustration, major milestone events should be identified at the top as the principal control points.

The body of the master plan is presented in the form of a Gantt chart: Each line represents a project, and the length of the line spans the life of the project.

How Far to Institutionalize

As Fig. 25.5 illustrates, a complete institutionalization of a strategic behavior is a massive and a costly process. Therefore, it should be undertaken only in cases in which management intends to devote major resources to continuous strategic activity.

In cases in which the strategic change needs of the firm are less extensive, partial institutionalization is the cost-effective approach. This may range from developing strategic mentality in key managers, which will assure timely perception of strategic discontinuities, to developing an ad hoc response capability, to strategic issues, to a systematic comprehensive strategic posture management capability.

The range of choices is illustrated in Fig. 25.6. As the figure shows, two factors determine the needed degree of institutionalization: the proportion of the

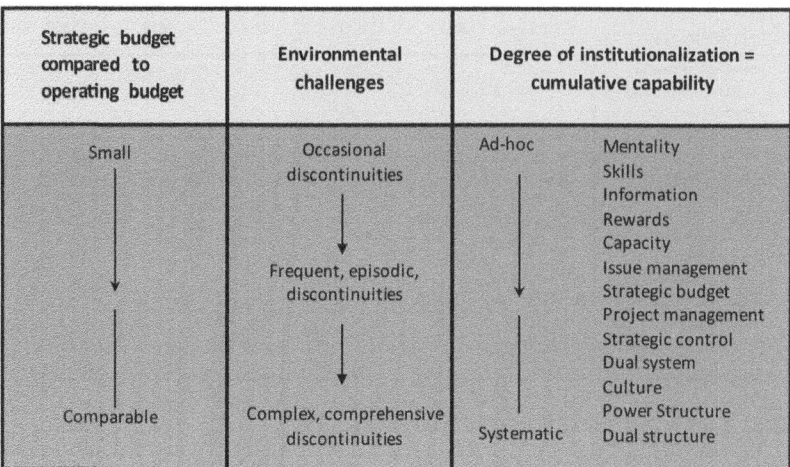

Strategic budget compared to operating budget	Environmental challenges	Degree of institutionalization = cumulative capability	
Small	Occasional discontinuities	Ad-hoc	Mentality Skills Information Rewards Capacity
	Frequent, episodic, discontinuities		Issue management Strategic budget Project management Strategic control Dual system Culture
Comparable	Complex, comprehensive discontinuities	Systematic	Power Structure Dual structure

Fig. 25.6 Choice of institutionalization

firm's budget devoted to strategic development, and the nature of the discontinuities expected to occur in the environment. As shown at the right, a capability for an ad hoc response to episodic discontinuities requires substantially less institutionalization than a comprehensive strategic positioning system.

Summary

Strategic responsiveness can be institutionalized within a firm through a series of related measures which jointly protect strategic work from the operational, make the strategic work more effective, and create a change supporting climate within the firm. These measures are:

1. Introducing a dual management system under which management and control of strategic projects is separated from the operations control systems.
2. Basing strategic control on the future prospects and not on past performance.
3. Basing rewards for strategic activity on encouragement of entrepreneurship and risk-taking.
4. Subdividing the firm's total budget into strategic operating budgets.
5. Subdividing the firm into an operating group, charged with optimizing profitability, and a strategic development group charged with generation of new businesses.

6. Focusing behavior of top management on the strategic development of the firm.
7. Involving in strategic planning all managers who will be responsible for implementation. Informing others who will participate in the implementation.
8. Training managers in strategic management, developing a 'strategic language' and a shared strategic model of reality.
9. Putting in positions of power managers with strategic mentality and drive.

*Checklist for Managing Change

1. *Building the launching platform*

- Perform strategic diagnosis.
- Prepare political/cultural resistance map.
- Mobilize political support for change.
- Identify and mobilize relevant talent.
- Inform and reassure individuals/groups.
- Select an approach appropriate to the realities of timing, resistance, and power.
- Get external help for diagnosis.

2. *Designing the change process*

- Focus process design on resolving strategic challenges.
- Design the process for implementability.
- Use modular design.
- Build in strategic decision making at the end of each module.
- Provide for early implementation.

3. *Protecting process from conflict with operations*

- Assign clear responsibilities.
- Budget the change.
- Provide managerial capacity for strategic activity.
- Reward strategic activity.

4. *Designing implementability into process*

- Train individuals in strategic decision making and implementation at the beginning of each module.
- Involve responsible managers and relevant experts in the decision process.

- Progressively inform all affected individuals.
- Let managers work on problems which are relevant to their jobs.
- Control complexity of analysis to be compatible with manager's knowledge and skills.
- Provide relevant strategic information.

5. *Managing the ongoing process*

- Conduct planning and implementation as parallel activities.
- Control the planning process to assure balanced progress on making of decisions and on their acceptance.
- Launch implementation projects as early as circumstances permit.

6. *Institutionalizing the new strategy*

- Use a strategy development master plan to manage the process.
- After strategy is in place, continue climate-building until the new culture and the power structure naturally support the strategy.
- Continue capability-building until all the elements of capability are balanced and effectively support the strategy.

7. *Institutionalizing strategic responsiveness*

Introduce:

- A dual management system.
- Strategic control.
- Strategic rewards.
- Strategic budget.
- Dual structure.
- Exemplary strategic behavior by top management.
- Key managers with strategic mentality and entrepreneurial skills.

Exercises

Develop a job description for the manager of strategic projects and a description for the job of the strategic controller.

1. In operations, it is usual to have different people charged with management of operations and with operations control. What should be the case in strategic management? Give your reasons.
2. Describe the database which is necessary for effective strategic control.

3. How should this database be generated?
4. Develop a checklist for strategic control of projects.
5. Describe in detail a strategic reward and incentive system for a firm in which strategic projects are costly and typically have long duration.
6. What problems will be encountered in introducing strategic budgeting into a firm? How can they be solved?
7. Discuss in detail the advantages and disadvantages of a dual structure.
8. Prepare a list of conditions under which a dual structure should be adopted.

You are given an assignment by top management to prepare a plan for converting the firm's culture from production oriented to the strategic. The firm is a large internationalized producer of farm machinery.

1. Develop a strategy for the cultural change.
2. Prepare a plan consisting of phased programs and major milestones.
3. Prepare a list of major problems which will be encountered and suggest solutions.
4. Defend the timing which you suggest for completing the cultural change.

Glossary

Accordion method A method for managing change in which: (a) planning and implementation are conducted in parallel and (b) the duration of the change is expanded or contracted according to the urgency of the challenge.

Ad hoc management A management process in which response to challenges is systematic but without reference to an overall plan or strategy (*see* organic adaptation and planned management).

Aggressiveness of strategy Degree of discontinuity between successive strategic projects.

Business strategy A strategy of the firm addressed to optimizing its financial performance.

Capability (Firms' or managers') motivation, competence, capacity to manage change.

Functional Capability of the firm's functions, e.g., marketing, R&D, personnel.

General management Capability of the units charged with general management responsibility.

Organizational The predisposition and the ability of a firm to engage in a particular type of behavior.

Vector Attributes of capability: managers, climate, competence, capacity.

Capacity Part of the capability vector. The volume of work which can be handled by an organizational unit per unit of time.

Cash cow An SBA in which the firm minimizes investment and maximizes cash flow to other SBAs.

Change management

Coercive Introduction of a change by using force to overcome organizational resistance.

Crisis Introduction of a change at a time when the firm is in a state of crisis.

H. I. Ansoff et al., *Implanting Strategic Management*, https://doi.org/10.1007/978-3-319-99599-1

Change sequence

Motivating A sequence which minimizes resistance and optimizes support for a change.

Resistance inducing A sequence of steps which maximize resistance during a change.

Climate The part of capability which determines the firm's predisposition for a particular type of behavior.

Competence The part of capability which determines the firm's ability to make effective a particular type of behavior.

Competitive position Profitability of the firm in an SBA relative to the most successful competitors.

Competitive posture The combination of the competitive strategy, capability, and strategic investment which a firm commits to an SBA.

Competitive strategy The unique position (niche) which a firm seeks to occupy in an SBA. Consists of: growth thrust, market position, product differentiation, and market differentiation.

Conglomerate firm A firm in which: (a) major business units operate independently of one another (a zero-synergy firm); (b) corporate office manages the business units on the basis of their financial performance (*see* synergistic firm and multi-capability firm).

Contingency perspective A perspective on the firm's behavior which recognizes that the choice and the outcome of behavior differ according to differences in the conditions under which behavior takes place.

Critical mass The minimum level of strategic investment in an SBA which assures potential profitability. A strategic breakeven point.

Critical success factors A element of the competitive posture which is essential for assuring a leading competitive position in an SBA.

Cultural-political field A map of the probable support/resistance which groups/individuals are expected to offer to a change.

Culture (a) A perception of the critical success factors shared by a unit of the firm. (b) Norms and values applied to selection of strategic projects.

Demand life cycle Curve of the evolution of demand in an SBA.

Demand-technology life cycle A curve of evolution of demand in an SBA for products/services based on a particular technology.

Discontinuity An event which does not follow from extrapolation of a series of preceding events.

Discontinuous change A change which cannot be handled by the historical capability of the firm.

Dispersed positioning The positioning of an SBA in a BCG or McKinsey matrix in a way which shows differences in predictability among SBAs (*see point* positioning).

Downstream coupling Degree of interaction between research and development, production, and marketing functions of the firm.

Dual budgeting Preparation of separate operating and strategic budgets during a firm's budgeting process.

Dual management system A management planning and control system which has distinctive strategic management and operations subsystems.

Dual structure An organizational structure which has distinctive substructures for operations and strategic work.

Eurequip matrix A matrix used in issue management to evaluate the interrelationship between the external threats/opportunities and internal strengths and weaknesses of the firm.

Filter Screening of the information observable in the environment before it becomes the basis for managerial decisions.

Mentality/cultural Filter introduced by culture of organizational units and by mentality of key managers.

Political Filter introduced by influential units or managers.

Technological Filter introduced by the choice of the environmental analysis / forecasting technique.

Gap

Current momentum The difference between extrapolation of the firm's performance and performance projection based on environmental analysis.

Current potential The difference between projection based on environmental analysis and performance possible if the firm optimizes its competitive posture.

Diversification The difference between the optimal performance inherent in the firm's present strategic portfolio and the objectives of the firm.

General management The management groups and individuals responsible for the overall success of all or a part of the firm.

Growth thrust A component of competitive strategy which specifies the source of the firm's future growth.

Implementability of plans/decisions The degree of organizational support for planned changes.

Institutionalization of change The process of developing organizational capability to a point where it is fully supportive of a new mode of behavior.

Key success factors An element or the competitive posture which is essential for assuring profitability in an SBA.

Launching platform Measures taken to prepare a firm for launching a discontinuous change.

Legitimacy of the firm Degree of response of a firm's behavior to its stakeholders' expectations.

Life cycle matrix A matrix showing the distribution of the firm's SBAs according to their demand-technology life cycle stages.

Long range planning (LRP) A systematic procedure for long-term goal setting, programming, and budgeting based on an extrapolative forecast.

Loyalty Support given by a participant in the firm to actions expected to assure success and survival, even though these actions may be contrary to the participant's aspirations.

Management

Decisive Management which responds promptly and decisively once a challenge begins to affect the performance of a firm.

Entrepreneurial Planned management based on examination of novel alternatives.

Extrapolative Planned management based on extrapolation of alternatives used in the past.

Planned Management which anticipates challenge and prepares its responses in advance.

Reactive Management which procrastinates beyond the initial impact and responds only when a challenge begins to have a serious impact on the firm's performance.

Market differentiation A component of competitive strategy. The way in which a firm differentiates itself from competitors in the eyes of its customers.

Market position A component of competitive strategy. The relative market share position that a firm seeks to establish in relation to its competitors.

McKinsey matrix A matrix for evaluating SBAs which uses SBA attractiveness and firm's competitive position as the principle dimensions.

Mentality The mental map, or model, of reality which a manager uses to guide his behavior.

Multi-capability firm A firm in which: (a) major organizational units develop distinctive management capabilities suitable for their respective environments. (b) corporate management integrates and controls the strategies of the units.

Objectives Criteria used to select a firm's activities and to evaluate performance.

Opportunity/vulnerability profile A graphical presentation which shows the spread in the probable impact of threats and opportunities on the firm, the spread of the probable timing of the impact, and the time required by the firm for response.

Optimum mass Level of strategic investment in an SBA at which the return to the firm is optimum, provided the firm uses optimal strategy and has optimal capability.

Organic adaptation Strategic adaptation in reaction to stimuli without guidance from general management.

PIMS A methodology for identifying key success variables based on extrapolation of performance of large samples of similar firms.

Planned management of change A process which consists of building a launching platform, managing resistance, and institutionalizing the change.

Point positioning The positioning of an SBA in a BCG or McKinsey matrix at the most probable points on the scales of SBA attractiveness and competitive position.

Portfolio

Coherent A portfolio strategy which calls for SBAs which can be managed by the same management capability.

Strategy A description of the SBAs in which the firm proposes to participate, enter, and exit as well as of the synergies which will be maintained among them. Definition of 'the business we arc in.' The 'vision' of the firm.

PPBS Planning-programming-budgeting system which is a strategic planning system first introduced by Robert McNamara into the US Department of Defense.

Predictability The degree of accuracy with which an impending event can be described at the time when a firm must start a response, if the response is to be completed in time for the arrival of the event.

Product differentiation A component of competitive strategy. The way a firm differentiates its products from those of competitors.

Progressive commitment A series of strategic moves of increasing degrees of commitment.

Raison d'etre The basis for a firm's legitimacy described by the objectives it pursues and the rules of the game under which it operates.

Requisite variety An organizational response to the environment whose complexity matches the complexity of the environment.

Resistance to change Active and passive opposition to a change which produces cost overruns, delays, distortions, or rejection of a change.

Behavioral Resistance to change by individuals or groups.

Systemic Resistance to change which is induced by lack of organizational competence or capacity for handling it.

Responsiveness of management capability The degree to which management of the firm responds to new and unfamiliar signals from the environment.

ROI, marginal The improvement in the return in the investment from an SBA which the firm can obtain by a given change in its strategic posture.

Rules of the game The set of constraints and enablement's by society (such as subsidies) under which a firm conducts its activities.

SBA (strategic business area) An area of business opportunity defined by a distinctive demand-technology life cycle curve.

SBA Attractiveness A composite measure of attractiveness of an SBA to successful competitors. The measure is composed of growth, profitability, and turbulence prospects.

SBU (strategic business unit) A unit of the firm which is responsible for strategic development of one or more SBAs.

Shared authority responsibility A formal organizational arrangement under which several managers share authority and responsibility for strategic actions.

SIG (strategic influence group) A social group or an institution which has expectations of the firm and the power to influence the firm's behavior.

Signal

Strong A development whose probable impact can be accurately described sufficiently in advance to permit a timely response by the firm.

Weak A development about which only partial information is available at the moment when response must be launched, if it is to be completed before the development impacts on the firm.

Social responsibility strategy A strategy of the firm addressed to objectives other than economic performance.

Societal strategy A strategy of the firm for relating the firm to its sociopolitical environment (the SIGs). Consists of legitimacy strategy, social responsibility strategy, and the preferred rules of the game.

SRA (strategic resource area) A source of supply to the firm which is essential to the success of its business strategy.

Stakeholder An SIG or an individual who has expectations of the firm and the influence to support them.

Star An SBA which has outstanding attractiveness and in which the firm expects to have an outstanding competitive position.

Strategic budget The budget committed to the strategic development of a firm.

Strategic control Modification of a strategic project based on evaluation of its lifetime contribution to the firm and to the firm's strategy.

Strategic development Process within a firm which lasts from conception to the point of establishment of a new profitable product/service in an SBA.

Strategic investment A firm's investment in its strategic posture in an SBA. Includes investments in strategy, capability, and capacity.

Strategic issue A development which is likely to have a significant impact on the performance of a firm.

Strategic learning A process in which feedback from strategic moves is used to modify the firm's strategy.

Strategic management A process for managing a firm's relationship with its environment Consists of strategic planning capability planning, and management of change.

Strategic planning A systematic procedure for entrepreneurial management which bases the firm's future strategy on examination of novel alternatives.

Strategic posture A combination of portfolio strategy with competitive postures in the firm's SBAs.

Strategic project A project devoted to strategic development of the firm, including product/service development, capability development, societal response development, etc.

Strategic surprise A development which arrives unanticipated which is novel to the firm, and holds prospects of a major impact on performance.

Synergy Sharing of capabilities among units of the firm which produces performance which is greater than the performance which can be obtained if the units operate independently of one another. The '2 + 2 = 5' effect.

Synergistic firm A firm in which corporate management seeks to optimize synergy.

Technology

Fertile A technology characterized by frequent product innovations.

Stable A technology which remains unchanged from inception to the maturity stage of a demand life cycle.

Turbulent A technology whose life cycle is short relative to the length of the demand life cycle.

Turbulence Changeability in an environment characterized by the degree of novelty of challenges and the speed with which they develop.

Level A combined measure of the degree of novelty of challenges and their speed relative to the response time of firms.

Negative Turbulence which poses threats to the firm.

Positive Turbulence which presents opportunities to the firm.

Wildcat An SBA which has outstanding attractiveness and in which the firm's competitive position is weak.

Bibliography

The bibliographic references presented below are arranged by categories commonly found in management literature and not according to the logic of this book.

Each category is referenced back to the parts of the book in which relevant subjects are discussed.

A—Strategic Information	Ch. 12, 13
B—Strategy Formulation	Part II, Ch. 6,12, 13,14
C—Strategic Planning and Control	Ch. 2, 6, 8, 10, 11, 14, 16, 20, 25
D—Managing Change	Ch. 8, 11, 14, 23, 24, 25
E—Organizational Capability	Ch. 7, 8, 9, 12, 13, 14, 15,16,17
F—Strategic Management	Intro. Ch. 6, Ch. 1, 3, 5, 8
G—Organizational Behavior	Ch. 1, 5, 8, 12, 14, 18, 19, 21, 22
H—Strategic Diagnosis	Ch. 6
I—Real-Time Response	Ch. 2, 9, 18, 19, 20

Part A Strategic Information

Ackerman, R. W. (1975). *The Social Challenge to Business*. Cambridge, MA: Harvard University Press.

Allen, M. G. (1976). *Strategic problems facing today's corporate planner*. Presentation to the Academy of Management, Kansas City, Missouri, August.

Ansoff, H. I. (1965, September/October). The firm of the future. *Harvard Business Review*.

Ansoff, H. I. (1973). The next twenty years in management education. *The Library Quarterly, 43*(4), 293–328.

© The Editor(s) (if applicable) and The Author(s), under
exclusive licence to Springer Nature Switzerland AG 2019
H. I. Ansoff et al., *Implanting Strategic Management*,
https://doi.org/10.1007/978-3-319-99599-1

Ansoff, H. I. (1976, September). Interview: 'Shortcomings of strategic planning'. *International Management.*

Ayres, R. (1969). *Technological Forecasting and Long Range Planning.* New York: McGraw-Hill.

Bright, J. R. (1970, January/February). Evaluating signals of technological change. *Harvard Business Review.*

Brown, J. (1976). *Perceived environmental uncertainty and the two-step flow process of scientific and technical communication in research and development laboratories* (Doctoral dissertation). Indiana University.

Buer, R., & Fenn, D. H., Jr. (1972). *The Corporate Social Audit.* New York: Russel Sage Foundation.

Butler, W., & Kavesh, R. A. (1974). *Techniques of Business Forecasting.* Englewood Cliffs, NJ: Prentice Hall.

Carrol, A. B., & Beller, G. W. (1975). Landmarks in the evolution of social audit. *Academy of Management Journal, 18*(3), 589–599.

Cetron, M. J. (1971). *Industrial Applications of Technological Forecasting.* New York: Wiley.

Chambers, J. C., Mullick, S. K., & Smith, D. D. (1976, July/August). How to choose the right forecasting technique. *Harvard Business Review.*

Collings, R. L. (1968). *Scanning the environment for strategic information* (Doctoral dissertation). Harvard University.

The Conference Board. (1978). *Planning Under Uncertainty: Multiple Scenario and Contingency Planning.* New York: The Conference Board.

Dalkey, N. D., & Rourke, D. L. (1971, February). *Experimentation Assessment of Delphi Procedures with Group Value Judgments.* Santa Monica, CA: The RAND Corp., R-612-ARPA.

Drucker, P. F. (1980). *Managing in Turbulent Times.* London: Heinemann.

Drucker, P. F. (1981). *The Changing World of the Executive.* New York: Time Books.

Emery, F. E., & Trist, E. L. (1965). The causal texture of organizational environments. *Human Relations, 18*(9), 21–32.

Evered, R. (1976). A typology of explicative models. *Technological Forecasting and Social Change, 9*(3), 257–277.

Everitt, B. (1975). *Cluster Analysis.* London: Heinemann.

Fahey, L., & King, W. R. (1977). Environmental scanning for corporate planning. *Business Horizons, 20*(4), 61–71.

Farmer, R. N. (1973). Looking backward at looking forward. *Business Horizons, 16*(1), 21–28.

Jantsch, E. (1973). Forecasting and systems approach: A frame of reference. *Management Science, 19*(12), 1345–1462.

Kahn, H., & Pepper, T. (1979). *The Japanese Challenge: The Success of Failure of Economic Success.* New York: Crowell.

Keegan, W. J. (1974). Multinational scanning: A study of information sources utilized by headquarters executives in multinational companies. *Administrative Science Quarterly, 19*(3), 411–421.

Kefalas, A., & Schoderbek, P. (1973). Scanning the business environment: Some empirical results. *Journal of the American Institute for Decision Sciences, 4*(1), 63–74.

King, W., & Cleland, D. (1977). Information for more effective strategic planning. *Long Range Planning, 10*(1), 59–64.

Lebell, D., & Krasner, O. J. (1977). Selecting environmental forecasting techniques from business planning requirements. *Academy of Management Review, 2*(3), 373–383.

Linneman, R., & Klein, H. E. (1978). The use of multiple scenarios by US industrial corporations. *Long Range Planning, 11.*

Radford, K. S. (1978). *Information Systems for Strategic Decisions.* Reston, VA: Reston.

Rodriguez, J. I. (1977). *The design and evaluation of a strategic issue competitive information system* (Doctoral dissertation). University of Pittsburgh.

Sackman, H. (1975). *Delphi Critique: Expert Opinion Forecasting and Group Process.* Lexington, MA: Lexington Books.

Simon, H. A. (1969). *The Sciences of the Artificial.* Cambridge, MA: MIT Press.

Turoff, M. (1970). The design of a policy Delphi. *Technical Forecasting and Social Change, 2*(2), 149–171.

Utterback, J. M., & Brown, J. W. (1972). Monitoring for technological opportunities. *Business Horizons, 15*(5), 5–15.

Utterback, J. M., & Burack, E. H. (1975). Identification of technological threats and opportunities by firms. *Technological Forecasting and Social Change, 8*(I), 7–21.

Utterback, J., & Kim, L. (1979). *Discontinuities in product and process innovation.* Paper presented at the ORSA/TIMS Joint National Meeting, Milwaukee, Wisconsin.

Wagle, B. (1969). The use of models for environmental forecasting and corporate planning. *Operational Research Quarterly, 20*(3), 327–336.

Wilson, I. H. (1974). Socio-political forecasting: A new dimension to strategic planning. *Michigan Business Review, 26*(4), 15–25.

Wilson, I. H. (1976). *Corporate Environments of the future: Planning for the major change* (Special Study No. 61). New York: Presidents Association.

Zetner, R. D. (1975, October 6). Scenarios in forecasting. *C and E News.*

Zetner, R. D. (1982). Scenarios: Past, present and future. *Long Range Planning, 15*(3), 12–20.

Part B Strategy Formulation

Abaroni, Y. (1966). *The Foreign Investment Decision Process.* Boston, MA: Harvard University Press.

Abell, D. F. (1975). *Competitive market strategies: Some generalizations and hypotheses* (Report No. 75-107). Cambridge, MA: Marketing Science Institute.

Abell, D. F. (1980). *Defining the Business: The Starting Point of Strategic Planning.* Englewood Cliffs, NJ: Prentice Hall.

Abell, D. F., & Hammond, J. S. (1979). *Strategic Market Planning, Problems and Analytical Approaches.* Englewood Cliffs, NJ: Prentice Hall.

Ackerman, R. W. (1973, July/August). How companies respond to social demands. *Harvard Business Review.*

Ackerman, R. W. (1975). *Managing Corporate Responsibility.* Boston: Harvard University Press.

Adizes, I., & Weston, J. F. (1973). Comparative models of social responsibility. *Academy of Management Journal, 16*(1), 112–128.

Amara, R. C. (1972). Toward a framework for national goals and policy research. *Policy Sciences, 3*(1), 59–69.

Anderson, C. R., & Paine, F. T. (1977). *PIMS: A re-examination.* Presentation to Academy Management, Orlando, Florida, August.

Andrews, K. R. (1980). *The Concept of Corporate Strategy* (Rev. ed.). Homewood, IL: Dow-Jones/Irwin.

Anshen, M. (1970). Changing the social contract: A role for business. *Columbia Journal of World Business, 5,* 6–14.

Anshen, M. (1974). *Managing the Socially Responsible Corporation.* New York: Macmillan.

Anshen, M. (1980). *Corporate Strategies for Social Performance.* New York: Macmillan.

Ansoff, H. I. (1957a). *A model for diversification.* Paper presented at the Fifth Annual Meeting of the Operations Research Society of America, May 9–10.

Ansoff, H. I. (1957b, September/October). Strategies for diversification. *Harvard Business Review.*

Ansoff, H. I. (1962, September). Company objectives: Blueprint-or-blue sky. *Management Review,* 85–90.

Ansoff, H. I. (1964a). A quasi-analytic approach to the business policy problem. *Management Technology, IV*(1), 1–77.

Ansoff, H. I. (1964b). Evaluation of applied research in business firms. In J. R. Bright (Ed.), *Proceedings on the Conference on Technological Planning on the Corporate Level.* Homewood, IL: Richard D. Irwin.

Ansoff, H. I. (1969a). *Business Strategy.* Harmondsworth: Penguin Books.

Ansoff, H. I. (1969b). Issues in national policy on growth of firms. In J. F. Weston & S. Peltzman (Eds.), *Public Policy Towards Mergers.* Pacific Palisades, CA: Goodyear.

Ansoff, H. I. (1971). Strategy as a tool for coping with change. *Journal of Business Policy, 1*(Summer), 3–7.

Ansoff, H. I. (1978, September). *Proposal for research and future legitimacy (role) of the businessfirm in Europe* (H. I. Ansoff, Anders, & G. Hedlund, Eds.; EIASM Working Paper 78-45).

Ansoff, H. I. (1979a, January). *Strategic Business Areas*. Tehokas Yritys: Johtamistoimen, Ammattilehti.

Ansoff, H. I. (1979b). *Societal strategy for the business firm* (EIASM Working Paper 79-24).

Ansoff, H. I. (1988). *The New Corporate Strategy*. New York: Wiley (Published originally as *Corporate Strategy*. New York: McGraw-Hill, 1965).

Ansoff, H. I., Andersen, T., Norton, F., & Weston, J. F. (1956). Planning for diversification through merger. *California Management Review, 1*(4), 24–35.

Ansoff, H. I., Avner, J., Brandenburg, R., Portner, F., & Radosevich, R. (1970). Does planning pay? The effect of planning on success of acquisitions in American firms. *Long Range Planning, 3*(2), 2–7.

Ansoff, H. I., & Brandenburg, R. (1967). Research and development planning. In H. B. Maynard (Ed.), *Handbook of Business Administration*. New York: McGraw-Hill.

Ansoff, H. I., & Lebell, D. (1971). Institutional factors in strategic decision-making. *Journal of Business Policy, 1*(Spring).

Ansoff, H. I., & Leontiades, J. (1976). Strategic portfolio management. *Journal of General Management, 4*(1), 13–29.

Ansoff, H. I., & Stewart, J. M. (1967, November/December). Strategies for a technology-based business. *Harvard Business Review*.

Ansoff, H. I., & Weston, J. F. (1962). Merger objectives and organization structure. *Review of Economics and Business, 2*(3), 49–58.

Baker, R., & Susbauer, J. C. (1977). *New venture development and corporate growth strategy and tactics* (Unpublished Working Paper).

Ball, B. C., & Lorange, P. (1978). *Managing your strategic responsiveness to the environment* (Sloan School Working Paper). Cambridge: Sloan School of Management, MIT.

Bauer, R. A., & Gergen, K. J. (1968). *The Study of Policy Formation*. New York: Free Press.

Baumhart, R. (1968). *Ethics in Business*. New York: Holt, Rinehart and Winston.

Baumol, W. J., Likert, R., Wallich, H. C., & McGowan, J. J. (1970). *A New Rationale for Corporate Social Policy*. New York: Committee for Economic Development.

Berg, N. A. (1963). *The allocation of strategic funds in a large diversified company* (Doctoral dissertation). Harvard Business School.

Berg, N. A. (1965, May/June). Strategic planning in conglomerate companies. *Harvard Business Review*.

Berry, C. (1975). *Corporate Growth and Diversification*. Princeton, NJ: Princeton University Press.

Bettauer, A. (1967, April/May). Strategy for divestments. *Harvard Business Review*.

Bettis, R. A., & Hall, W. K. (1981). Strategic portfolio management in the multibusiness firm. *California Management Review, 24*(Fall), 23–38.

Boston Consulting Group. (1971). *Growth and Financial Strategies.* Boston, MA: Boston Consulting Group.

Bower, J. L. (1962). *Managing the Resource Allocation Process: A Study of Corporate Planning and Investment.* Homewood, IL: Richard D. Irwin.

Bower, M. (1966). *The Will to Manage.* New York: McGraw Hill.

Bower, J. L. (1967). *Strategy as a problem-solving theory of business planning* (Report No. BP894). Boston, MA: Intercollegiate Case Clearing House.

Bowman, E. H. (1974). Epistemology, corporate strategy and academe. *Sloan Management Review, 5*(2), 35–50.

Braybrooke, D., & Lindblom, C. E. (1963). *A Strategy of Decision.* New York: Free Press.

Buckley, J. W. (1971, December). Goa! Process system integration in management. *Business Horizons.*

Business Week. (1972, July 8). GE's new strategy for faster growth.

Buzzell, R. D., Gale, B. T., & Sultan, R. G. M. (1975, January/Febraury). Market share key to profitability. *Harvard Business Review.*

Buzzell, R. D., & Wiersema, F. (1981, January/Febraury). Successful share building strategies. *Harvard Business Review.*

Buzzell, R. D., & Wiersema, F. (1983, January/Febraury). Is vertical integration profitable? *Harvard Business Review.*

Cadbury, G. A. H. (1968). The company environment and social responsibility. In G. A. Bull (Ed.), *The Director's Handbook.* New York: McGraw-Hill.

Camillus, J. C. (1973). *Formal planning: Creativity vs. control* (Doctoral dissertation). Harvard University.

Carroll, A. B. (1973). An organizational need: Forecasting and planning for the social environment. *Managerial Planning, 21*(6), 11–13.

Carroll, S. J., & Tosi, H. L., Jr. (1971). Relationship of characteristics of the review process to the success of the MBO approach. *Journal of Business, 44,* 299–305.

Carter, E. E. (1972, July/August). What are the risks in risk analysis? *Harvard Business Review.*

Carter, E. E. (1974). *Portfolio Aspects of Corporate Capital Budgeting.* Lexington, MA: Heath.

Carter, E. E. (1977). Designing the capital budgeting process. In P. C. Nystrom & W. H. Starbuck (Eds.), *Prescriptive Models of Organization.* Amsterdam: North-Holland.

Carter, E. E., & Cohen, K. J. (1972). Portfolio aspects of strategic planning. *Journal of Business Policy, 2*(Summer), 8–30.

Caves, R. E., & Porter, M. E. (1977). From entry barriers to mobility barriers: Conjectural decisions and contrived deterrence to new competition. *Quarterly Journal of Economics, 91*(2), 241–262.

Channon, D. (1977a). Strategy formulation as an analytical process. *International Studies of Management and Organization, 7*(Summer), 41–57.

Channon, D. (1977b). *Use and abuse of analytical techniques for strategy making.* TIMS Conference, Athens.

Charnock, J. (1975). Can hospitals be managed by objectives? *Journal of General Management, 2*(Winter), 36–47.

Churchman, C. W. (1964). Managerial acceptance of scientific recommendations. *California Management Review, 7*(Fall), 31–38.

Churchman, C. W., & Schainblatt, A. H. (1965a). The researcher and the manager: A dialectic of implementation. *Management Science,* 11(4), B-1–C-50.

Churchman, C. W., & Schainblatt, A. H. (1965b). Commentary on the researcher and the manager. *Management Science, 12*(2), B-2.

Clark, C. D. (1969). New directions in professional business education. In P. Drucker (Ed.), *Preparing Business; Leaders Today.* Englewood Cliffs, NJ: Prentice Hall.

Clifford, D. K., Jr. (1973, September/October). Growth pains of the threshold company. *Harvard Business Review.*

Conrad, C. (1974). University goals: An operative approach. *Journal of Higher Education, 45*(7), 504–516.

Cooper, A. C., & Schendel, D. E. (1971). Strategy determination in manufacturing firms: Concepts and research findings. *Proceedings of the American Marketing Association Fall Conference,* August/September.

Davis, J. V. (1974). The strategic divestment decision. *Long Range Planning, 7*(1), 15–18.

Day, G. S. (1971). Diagnosing the product portfolio. *Journal of Marketing, 41*(2), 29–38.

Donaldson, G. (1969). *Strategy for Financial Mobility.* Boston: Harvard Business School.

Emshoff, J. R., & Mitroff, I. I. (1979). On strategic assumption-making: A dialectical approach to policy and planning. *Academy of Management Review, 4*(1), 1–12.

Enthoven, A. C. (1969). Analysis, judgement and computers: Their use in complex problems. *Business Horizons, 12*(4), 29–36.

Ferguson, C. R. (1974). *Measuring Corporate Strategy.* Homewood, IL: Dow-Jones/ Irwin.

Fischer, D. W. (1983). Strategies toward political pressures: A typology of firm responses. *Academy of Management Review, 8*(1), 71–78.

Gibson, R. E. (1966). The strategy of corporate research and development. *California Management Review, 9*(Fall), 33–42.

Gilmore, F. F. (1973, May/June). Formulating strategy in smaller companies. *Harvard Business Review.*

Granger, C. H. (1964, May/June). The hierarchy of objectives. *Harvard Business Review.*

Hall, W. K. (1978). SBUs: Hot new topic in the management of diversification. *Business Horizons, 21*(1), 17–25

Hall, W. K. (1980, September). Survival strategies in a hostile environment. *Harvard Business Review*.

Hammermesh, R. G., Anderson, M. J., & Harris, J. R. (1978, May/June). Strategies for low market share businesses. *Harvard Business Review*.

Harrigan, K. R. (1980). *Strategies for Declining Businesses*. Lexington, MA: Heath.

Haspeslagh, P. (1982, January/February). Portfolio planning: Uses and limits. *Harvard Business Review*.

Henzler, H. (1982). Functional dogmas that frustrate strategy. *McKinsey Quarterly* (Winter), 23–35.

Hewkin, J. W. M., & Kempner, T. (1968, December). Is corporate planning necessary? *BIM Information Summary*.

Heyne, P. T. (1971). The freemarket system is the best guide for corporate decisions. *Financial Analysts Journal, 27*(5), 26–27.

Hofer, C. E., & Schendel, D. E. (1978). *Strategy Formulation: Analytical Concepts*. St Paul: West Publishing Co.

Kotler, P. (1965). Competitive strategies for new product marketing over the life cycle. *Management Science, 12*(4), B-49–C-112.

Leontiades, J. (1980). *Strategies for Diversification and Change*. Boston: Little Brown.

Macmillan, I. C. (1978). *Strategy Formulation: Political Concepts*. St Paul: West Publishing Co.

Mintzberg, H. (1973a). *The Nature of Managerial Work*. New York: Harper & Row.

Mintzberg, H. (1973b). Strategy making in three modes. *California Management Review, 16*(2), 44–53.

Mintzberg, H., Raisinghani, D., & Theoret, A. (1976). The structure of "unstructured" decision processes. *Administrative Science Quarterly, 21*(2), 246–276.

Mitroff, I. I. (1971). A communication model of dialectical inquiring systems—A strategy for strategic planning. *Management Science, 17*(10), B-569–B-704.

Mitroff, I. I., Barabba, V., & Kilmann, R. (1977). The application of behavioral and philosophical techniques to strategic planning: A case of a large federal agency. *Management Science, 24*(1), 1–120.

Nees, D. (1981). Increase your divestment effectiveness. *Strategic Management Journal, 2*(2), 119–130.

Normann, R. (1977). *Management for Growth*. New York: Wiley.

Porter, M. E. (1980). *Competitive Strategy: Techniques for Analyzing Industries and Competitors*. New York: Free Press.

Prahalad, C. K. (1976, July/August). Strategic choices in diversified MNCs. *Harvard Business Review*.

Richards, M. D. (1973). An exploratory study of strategic failure. *Academy of Management Proceedings, 33*(1), 40–46.

Rothschild, W. E. (1979). *Strategic Alternatives: Selection, Development and Implementation*. New York: AMACOM.

Salter, M. A., & Weinhold, W. A. (1979). *Diversification Through Acquisition*. New York: Free Press.

Scheiffer, F. (1974). Planning for the unexpected. *McKinsey Quarterly* (Spring).

Schendel, D. E., Atton, R., & Riggs, J. (1974, August). *Corporate turnaround strategies* (Working Paper). Purdue University.

Schendel, D. E., & Patton, G. R. (1976). Corporate stagnation and turnaround. *Journal of Economics and Business, 28*(Spring/Summer), 236–241.

Schoeffler, S., Buzzell, R. D., & Hzeany, D. F. (1974, March/April). Impact of strategic planning on profit performance. *Harvard Business Review.*

Simon, H. A. (1964). On the concept of organizational goal. *Administrative Science Quarterly, 9*(1), 1–22.

Steiner, G. (1969). *Strategic Factors in Business Success.* New York: Financial Executives Research Foundation.

Tabatoni, T. (1972). Le Plan Strategique Face aux Contraintes Sociopolitiques. *Le Management.*

Thomas, D. R. E. (1978, July/August). Strategy is different in-service businesses. *Harvard Business Review.*

Tilles, S. (1963, July/August). How to evaluate corporate strategy. *Harvard Business Review.*

Twiss, B. C. (1970). Strategy for research and development. *Long Range Planning, 3*(1), 57–62.

Vancil, R. F. (1976). Strategy formulation in complex organizations. *Sloan Management Review, 17*(Winter), 1.

Vickers, G. (1973). Values, norms and politics. *Policy Sciences, 4*(1), 103–111.

Part C Strategic Planning and Control

Ackerman, R. W. (1977). The role of corporate planning executive. In P. Lorange & R. Vancil (Eds.), *Strategic Planning Systems.* Englewood Cliffs, NJ: Prentice Hall.

Ackoff, R. L. (1970). *A Concept of Corporate Planning.* New York: Wiley.

Ansoff, H. I. (1964). Planning as a practical management tool. *Financial Executive, 32,* 34–37.

Ansoff, H. I. (1967a). The expanding role of the computer in managerial decision-making. *Informatie, 9,* 46–64.

Ansoff, H. I. (1967b). A quasi-analytic method for long range planning. In M. Alexis & C. Wilson (Eds.), *Organizational Decision Making.* Englewood Cliffs, NJ: Prentice Hall.

Ansoff, H. I. (1969). Long range planning in perspective. In *Proceedings of the 15th CIOS International Management Congress.* Tokyo: Kogakusha Co.

Ansoff, H. I. (1972). Dolgosrochnone plainrovanie v perspective. In G. K. Popov (Ed.), *Sovremennye Tendenzyi v Upravlenti v Capitalisticheskich Stranakh* (pp. 51–72). Moscow: Izdatelstvo Progress.

Ansoff, H. I. (1975). *The state of practice in management systems* (EIASM Report, Working Paper 75-11)

Ansoff, H. I. (1976, September). Interview: 'Shortcomings of strategic planning'. *International Management*.

Ansoff, H. I. (1977). The state of practice in planning systems. *Sloan Management Review, 18*(Winter), 1–24

Ansoff, H. I. (1979). Planned management of turbulent change. *Encyclopedia of Professional Management*. New York: McGraw-Hill.

Ansoff, H. I., & Brandenburg, R. G. (1967). A program of research in business planning. *Management Science, 13*(6), B-219–C-180.

Ansoff, H. I., Avner, J., Brandenburg, R., Portner, F., & Radosevich, R. (1970). Does planning pay? The effect of planning on success of acquisitions in American firms. *Long Range Planning, 3*(2), 2–7.

Ansoff, H. I., Brandenburg, R. J., Portner, F. E., & Radosevich, H. R. (1971). *Acquisition: Behavior of US Manufacturing Firms 1946–65*. Nashville, TN: Vanderbilt University Press.

Ansoff, H. I., & Thanheiser, H. T. (1978, March). *Corporate planning: A comparative view of the evolution and current practice in the United States and Western Europe* (EIASM Working Paper 78-JO). Brussels.

Baker, R. J., & Susbauer, J. C. (1975). The venture formation/development process: A framework for evaluation of venture assistance experiments. In *Proceedings of Project ISEED*. Milwaukee, WI: Project ISEED Ltd.

Bales, C. F. (1977). Strategic control: The president's paradox. *Business Horizons, 20*(4), 17–28.

Bower, J. L. (1970). Planning within the firm. *American Economic Review, 18*(3), 1.

Business Week. (1975, April 28). Corporate planning: Piercing fog in the executive suite.

Camillus, J. C. (1975). Evaluating the benefits of formal planning systems. *Long Range Planning, 8*(3), 33–40.

Camillus, J. C., & Grant, J. H. (1980). Operational planning: The integration of programming and budgeting. *Academy of Management Review, 5*(3), 369–379.

Casasco, J. A. (1970). *Corporate planning models for university management* (Report no. 4). Washington, DC: ERIC Clearing House on Higher Education.

Cash, H. W., & Revie, J. M. (1971). Long range planner and acquisition planning. In R. F. Vancil (Ed.), *Formal Planning Systems*. Boston: Graduate School of Business Administration, Harvard University.

Channon, D. (1976). *Strategic planning portfolio models: Practical progress and problems in practice* (Unpublished Paper). Manchester Business School.

Channon, D. F., & Jalland, R. M. (1978). *Multinational Strategic Planning*. New York: Macmillan.

Coyle, R. G. (1973). Systems dynamics: An approach to policy formulation. *Journal of Business Policy, 3*(Spring), 40–48.

de la Brie, J. (1978). *General electric's approach to strategic planning*. Paper presented at North American Society for Corporate Planning Conference, Hofstra University.

Greiner, L. E. (1970). Integrating formal planning into organizations. In F. J. Aguilar, et al. (Eds.), *Formal Planning Systems*. Boston: Graduate School of Business Administration, Harvard University.

Grinyer, P. H., & Norburn, D. (1974). Strategic planning in 21 U.K. companies. *Long Range Planning, 7*(4), 80–88.

Henry, H. W. (1977). Formal planning in major US corporations. *Long Range Planning, 10*(5), 40–45.

Hofer, C. W. (1976). Research on strategic planning: A survey of past studies and suggestions for future efforts. *Journal of Economics and Business, 28*(Spring/Summer), 261–286.

Holloway, C., & Pearce, J. A., II. (1982). Computer assisted strategic planning. *Long Range Planning, 15*(4), 56–63.

Horovitz, J. (1979). Strategic control: A new task for top management. *Long Range Planning, 12*(3), 2–7.

Humble, J. W. (1969). Corporate planning and management by objectives. *Long Range Planning, 1*(4), 36–43.

Hurst, E. G. (1982). Controlling strategic plans. In P. Lorange (Ed.), *Implementation of Strategic Planning*. Englewood Cliffs, NJ: Prentice Hall.

Hussey, D. E. (1974). Corporate planning for a church. *Long Range Planning, 7*(2), 61–64.

Lorange, P. (1977). *An analytical scheme for the assessment of diversified company's corporate planning system: Needs, capabilities, effectiveness* (Working Paper 964-977). Cambridge, MA: Sloan School of Management.

Lorange, P., & Vacil, R. F. (1977). *Strategic Planning Systems*. Englewood Cliffs, NJ: Prentice Hall.

Mintzberg, H. (1973). *The Nature of Managerial Work*. New York: Harper & Row.

Mintzberg, H. (1976, July/August). Planning on the left side and management on the right. *Harvard Business Review*.

Naumes, W. (1971). *Effects of responsive computer interaction in the strategic planning process* (Doctoral dissertation). Stanford University.

Ringbakk, K. A. (1971). Why planning fails. *European Business, 29*(Spring), 15–27.

Schick, A. (1969). Systems politics and systems budgeting. *Public Administration Review, 29*(2), 137–151.

Schick, A. (1973). A death in the bureaucracy: The demise of federal PPB. *Public Administration Review, 33*(2), 146–156.

Simmons, W. W. (1976). A strategic planning program for the next decade. *Advanced Management Journal, 3*(Winter), 45–49.

Steiner, G. A. (1969). *Top Management Planning*. New York: Macmillan.

Steiner, G. A. (1977). *Strategic Managerial Planning*. Oxford, OH: Planning Executive Institute.

Steiner, G. A. (1979). *Strategic Planning: What Every Manager Must Know*. New York: Free Press.

Stewart, R. F. (1963). *A Framework for Business Planning* (Report No. 162). Long Range Planning Service. Menlo Park, CA: Stanford Research Institute.

Strategic Planning Institute. (1977). *Guide to Portfolio Analysis.* Cambridge, MA: Strategic Planning Institute.

Thanheiser, H., & Patel, P. (1977). *Eine Eimperische Studie der Strategischen Planung in Diversifizierten Deutschen Unlerneem.* Paris, France: INSEAD.

Wilson, I. H. (1974). Reforming the strategic planning process: Integration of social and business needs. *Long Range Planning, 7*(5), 2–6.

Part D Managing Change

Allen, T. (1977). *Managing the Flow of Technology.* Cambridge: MIT Press.

Ansoff, H. I. (1964). *Integrating the Individual and the Organization.* New York: Wiley.

Ansoff, H. I. (1968). The innovative firm. *Long Range Planning, 1*(2), 26–27.

Ansoff, H. I. (1970). *Intervention Theory and Method.* Reading, MA: Addison-Wesley.

Ansoff, H. I. (1980a, July). *Managing the process of discontinuous change. Part 1: Behavioral resistance* (EIASM Working Paper 80-26).

Ansoff, H. I. (1980b,September) *Managing the process of discontinuous change. Part 2: Systematic resistance* (EIASM Working Paper 80-36).

Ansoff, H. I. (1980c, October). *Managing the process of discontinuous change. Part 3: Alternative approaches* (EIASM Working Paper 80-37).

Ansoff, H. I. (1980d, October). *Managing the process of discontinuous change. Part 4: The learning action approach* (EIASM Working Paper 80-38).

Ansoff, H. I., Bosman, A., & Storm, P. (1982). *Understanding and Managing Strategic Change.* Amsterdam: Elsevier/North-Holland.

Argyris, C. (1973, March/April). The CEO's behavior: Key to organizational development. *Harvard Business Review.*

Argyris, C. (1981). *Management and Organizational Development: The Path from XA to YB.* New York: McGraw-Hill.

Ashby, W. R. (1956). *Introduction to Cybernetics.* New York: Wiley.

Barron, F. (1969). *Creative Person and Creative Process.* New York: Holt, Rinehart and Winston.

Beckhard, R. D. (1969). *Organization Development: Strategies and Models.* Reading, MA: Addison-Wesley.

Blalock, H. (1969). *Theory Construction.* Englewood Cliffs, NJ: Prentice Hall.

Bogdan, R., & Taylor, S. J. (1975). *Introduction to Qualitative Research Methods.* New York: Wiley.

Buchanan, B. (1974). Building organizational commitment: The socialization of managers in work organizations. *Administrative Science Quarterly, 19*(4), 533–546.

Buchanan, B. (1975). To walk an extra mile: The whats, whens and whys of organizational commitment. *Organizational Dynamics, 3*(Spring), 67–80.

Burns, T., & Stalker, G. M. (1961). *The Management of Innovation*. London: Tavistock Press.

Campbell, D. T., & Stanley, J. C. (1963). *Experimental and Quasi Experimental Designs for Research*. Chicago: Rand McNally.

Chin, R., & Benne, K. (1976). General strategies for effecting changes in human systems. In W. Nennis, et al. (Eds.), *The Planning Change*. New York: Holt, Rinehart and Winston.

Coch, L., & French, J. R. P., Jr. (1966). Overcoming resistance to changes. In H. Proshanski & B. Seidcnberg (Eds.), *Basic Studies in Social Psychology*. New York: Holt, Rinehart and Winston.

Crozier, M. (1973). *Les problemes humaines qne osent Jes structures de l'enterprise dans unc societe en changement*. Paper presented at Cannes Colloquium, March.

Durkheim, E. (1983). *The Rules of Sociological Method*. New York: Free Press.

Farris, G. F. (1971). *Colleque roles and innovation in scientific teams*. Sloan School of Management (Working Paper 552-71). Cambridge: MIT Press.

Green, J., & Jones, T. (1981). Strategic development as a means of organizational change: Four case histories. *Long Range Planning, 14*(3), 58–67.

Hamblin, R. L. (1958). Leadership and crises. *Sociometry, 21*(4), 322–335.

Keen, P. G. W. (1975). *The Implementation of Computer-Based Decision Aids*. Cambridge, MA: Center for Information Systems Research, Sloan School of Management.

Lee, D. (1976). *Strategic decision making in a management game: An experimental study of objectives setting and consistency in complex decision making* (Working Paper WP 887-76). Cambridge, MA: Sloan School of Management.

Lorange, P. (1978). Implementation of strategic planning systems. In A. C. Hax (Ed.), *Studies in Operations Management*. New York: Elsevier/North-Holland.

Lundberg, O., & Richards, M. D. (1972). A relationship between cognitive style and complex decision making: Implications for business policy. *Academy of Management Proceedings* (1), 95–98.

MacCrimmon, K. R. (1974). Managerial decision-making. In J. W. McGuire (Ed.), *Contemporary Management: Issues and Viewpoints*. Englewood Cliffs, NJ: Prentice Hall.

McCaskey, M. (1982). *Managing Ambiguity*. Marshfield, MA: Pitman.

McClelland, D. (1975). *Power: The Inner Experience*. New York: Irvington.

McGregor, D. (1967). *The Professional Manager*. New York: McGraw-Hill.

Michael, D. N. (1973). *On Learning to Plan and Planning to Learn*. San Francisco: Jossey-Bass.

Mumford, E., & Pettigrew, A. (1975). *Implementing Strategic Decisions*. London: Longman.

Pfeffer, J., & Salancik, J. (1977). Who gets power and how they hold onto it. *Organizational Dynamics, 5*(Winter), 3–21.

Rubin, J. Z., & Brown, B. R. (1975). *The Social Psychology of Bargaining and Negotiation.* New York: Academic Press.

Sackman, H., & Citrebaum, R. L. (1972). *On-line Planning: Towards Creative Problem Solving.* Englewood Cliffs, NJ: Prentice Hall.

Schein, E. H., & Bennis, W. G. (1967). *Personal and Organization Change Through Group Methods.* New York: Wiley.

Taylor, D. E. (1979). Strategic planning as an organizational change process: Some guidelines from practice. *Long Range Planning, 12*(5), 43–53.

Weick, K. (1977). Enactment processes in organizations. In B. Staw & G. Salancik (Eds.), *New Directions in Organizational Behavior.* Chicago: St Clair Press.

Zaid, M. N. (1970). *Organizational Change.* Chicago: University of Chicago Press.

Zaltman, G., & Duncan, R. T. (1977). *Strategies for Planned Change.* New York: Wiley/Interscience.

Part E Organizational Capability

Abernathy, W. J., & Utterback, J. (1975). *Innovation and the evolving structure of the firm* (Working Paper 75-IR). Harvard Business School.

Ackoff, R. L. (1974). *Redesigning the Future: A Systems Approach to Societal Problems.* New York: Wiley.

Ackoff, R. L. (1981). *Creating the Corporate Future.* New York: Wiley.

Aiken, M., & Hage, J. (1968). Organizational interdependence and intra-organizational structure. *American Sociological Review, 39*(6), 912–930.

Allen, S. A. (1976). *A taxonomy of organizational chokes in divisionalized companies* (Working Paper). IMEDE.

Ansoff, H. I. (1963). Management participation in diversification. *Proceedings of Client Conference.* Menlo Park, CA: Long Range Planning Service, Stanford Research Institute.

Ansoff, H. I. (1964). Evaluation of applied research in business firms. In J. R. Bright (Ed.), *Proceedings of the Conference on Technological Planning on the Corporate Level.* Homewood, IL: Richard D. Irwin.

Ansoff, H. I. (1973a). Corporate structure, present and future. *Proceedings of the Third International Conference on Corporate Planning, Brussels* (EIASM Working Paper 74-4).

Ansoff, H. I. (1973b). The next twenty years in management education. *The Library Quarterly, 43*(4), 293–328.

Ansoff, H. I. (1974a). *Functions of the executive office in a large conglomerate* (EIASM Working Paper 75-42).

Ansoff, H. I. (1974b, October). La structure de l'enterprise aujourd'hui et domain. *Cahier de Fondation National pour l'Enseignement de la Gestion,* No. 9.

Ansoff, H. I. (1975a). The knowledge professional in the post-industrial era. *Bedrifjskunde, Jaargang, 47,* 88.

Ansoff, H. I. (1975b, February). La structure de l'enterprise, aujourd 'hui et demain (premiere partie). *Cheft, Revue Suisse du Management.*

Ansoff, H. I. (1975c). The future of corporate structure. *Journal of General Management* (Autumn).

Ansoff, H. I. (1978). *Corporate capability for managing change* (SRI Business Intelligence Program, Research Report No. 610).

Ansoff, H. I. (1979). *Aspirations and culture in strategic behavior* (EIASM Working Paper No. 79-12).

Ansoff, H. I., & Brandenburg, R. G. (1967). Design of optimal business planning system: A study proposal. *Journal for Cybernetics of Planning and Organizations.* March.

Ansoff, H. I., & Brandenburg, R. G. (1969). *The general manager of the future.* Paper presented at the Alumni Conference, Carnegie Institute of Technology, April, 1967; published in *California Management Review, 11*(3).

Ansoff, H. I., & Brandenburg, R. G. (1971). A language for organizational design. *Management Science, 17*(12), B-717.

Anyon, G. J. (1973). *Entrepreneurial Dimensions of Management.* Wynnewood: Livingston.

Barnard. C. I. (1938). *The Functions of the Executive.* Cambridge, MA: Harvard University Press.

Ballalia Lotz and Associates. (1969). *A Decade of Change in Top Management Organization and Executive Job Title.* New York: The Firm.

Benson, J. K. (1975). The interorganizational network as a political economy. *Administrative Science Quarterly, 20*(2), 229–249.

Berg, N. A. (1969, November/December). What's different about conglomerate management? *Harvard Business Review.*

Berg, N. A. (1973). Corporate role in diversified companies. In B. Taylor & K. Macmillan (Eds.), *Business Policy: Teaching and Research.* New York: Wiley.

Boettingcr, H. M. (1973). The management challenge. In E. C. Bursk (Ed.), *Challenge to Leadership.* New York: Free Press.

Bower, J. L., & Prahalad, C. K. (1978). *Power in the Multinationals.* Homewood, IL: Richard D. Irwin.

Boyatizis. R. (1981). *The Competent Manager.* New York: Wiley.

Brown, C. C., & Smith, E. E. (1958). *The Director Looks at His Job.* New York: Columbia University Press.

Brown, J., & O'Connor, R. (1974). *Planning and the Corporate Planning Director.* New York: National Industrial Conference Board.

Burck, C. (1976, May). A group profile of the Fortune 500 chief executive. *Fortune.*

Business Week. (1980, February). Wanted: A manager to fit each strategy, pp. 166–173.

Business Week. (1980, July 21). Putting excellence into management, pp. 196–197.

Child, J. (1977). *Organization: A Guide for Managers and Administrators.* New York: Harper & Row.

Child, J., & Ellis, T. (1973). Predictors of variations in managerial roles. *Human Relations, 26*(2), 227–250.

Churchman, C. W. (1971). *The Design of Inquiry Systems*. New York: Basic Books.

Clark, B. R. (1972). The organizational saga in higher education. *Administrative Science Quarterly, 17*(2), 178–184.

Conference Board Studies. (1969). *The Chief Executive and His Job*. The Conference Board Studies in Personnel Policy, no. 214.

Cordiner, R. J. (1956). *New Frontiers for Professional Managers*. New York: McGraw-Hill.

Dale, E. (1952). *Planning and Developing the Company Organization Structure*. New York: American Management Association.

Dalton, G., Barnes, L. B., & Zaleznik, A. (1968). *The Distribution of Authority in Formal Organizations*. Boston: Harvard University Press.

Davis, S. M., & Lawrence, P. R. (1978, May/June). Problems of matrix organizations. *Harvard Business Review, 56*.

Deal, T. E., & Kennedy, A. A. (1982). *Corporate Cultures: The Rites and Rituals of Corporate Life*. Reading, MA: Addison-Wesley.

England, G. W. (1967). Personal value systems of American managers. *Academy of Management Journal, 10*(1), 53–68.

Fast, N. (1977). *The evolution of corporate new venture divisions* (Doctoral dissertation). Harvard University.

Fortune. (1965). Harnessing the R&D monster, *81*(1).

Franko, L. (1974). The move toward a multidivisional structure in European organizations. *Administrative Science Quarterly, 19*(4), 493–506.

Galbraith, J. R. (1968). Achieving integration through information systems. *Academy of Management Proceedings* (1).

Galbraith, J. R. (1970). Environmental and technological determinants of organizational design: A case study. In P. R. Lurch & J. W. Lawrence (Eds.), *Studies in Organizational Design*. Homewood, IL: Richard D. Irwin.

Galbraith, J. R. (1971). Matrix organization designs. *Business Horizons, 14*(1), 29–40.

Galbraith, J. R. (1972). *Organizational Design*. Reading, MA: Addison-Wesley.

Galbraith, J. R. (1973). *Designing Complex Organizations*. Reading, MA: Addison-Wesley.

Galbraith, J. R. (1974). Matrix organization design: How to combine functional and project forms. *Business Horizons, 14*(Summer), 29–40.

Galbraith, J., & Nathanson, D. A. (1978). *Strategy Implementation: The Role of Structure and Process*. St Paul: West.

Goggin, W. (1974, January/February). How the multidimensional structure works at Dow-Corning. *Harvard Business Review*.

Harrell, T. W. (1961). *Managers Performance and Personality*. Dallas: Southwest Publishing Co.

Harrison, R. (1972, May). Understanding your organization's character. *Harvard Business Review*.

Heron, R. P., & Friesen, D. (1973). Growth and development of college administrative structures. *Research in Higher Education, 1*(4), 333–346.

Hickey, W. J. (1972). The functions of the hospital board of directors. *Hospital Administration 17*(Summer), 43–52.

Hickson, D., Pugh, D., & Pheysey, D. (1969). Operations technology and organizational structure. *Administrative Science Quarterly, 14*(3), 378.

Hill, R., & Hlavacek, J. (1972). The venture team: A new concept in marketing organization. *Journal of Marketing, 36*(3), 44–50.

Hlavacek, J. D., & Thompson, V. A. (1973). Bureaucracy and new product innovation. *Academy of Management Journal, 16*(3), 361–372.

Hofer, C. W., et al. (1979). GEs evolving management system. *Strategic Management: A Casebook*. St Paul: West.

Hornaday, J. A., & Bunker, C. S. (1970). The nature of the entrepreneur. *Personnel Psychology, 23*(Spring), 47–54.

Jacoby, N. (1969, July). The conglomerate corporation. *The Center Magazine*.

Kelly, L., & Reeser, C. (1973). The persistence of culture as a determinant of differentiated attitudes on the part of American managers of Japanese ancestry. *Academy of Management Journal, 16*(1), 67–76.

Khandwall, P. N. (1973). Effect of competition on the structure of top management/control. *Academy of Management Journal, 16*(2), 285–295.

Kilman, R., & Mitroff, I. (1976). On organization stories: An approach to the designing and analysis of organizations through myths and stories. In P. Kilman & D. P. Slevin (Eds.), *The Management of Organization Design* (Vol. I). Amsterdam: Elsevier/North-Holland.

Labovitz, G. H. (1971). Organizing for adaptation. *Business Horizons, 14*(3), 19–26.

Levinson, H. (1968). *The Exceptional Executive: A Psychological Conception*. Boston: Harvard University Press.

Livingstone, J. S. (1971, January/February). Myth of the well-educated manager. *Harvard Business Review*.

Long, L. E. (1982). *Design and Strategy for Corporate Information Services*. Englewood Cliffs, NJ: Prentice Hall.

Lorsch, J. W. (1965). *Product Innovation and Organization*. New York: Macmillan.

Mintzberg, H. (1979). *The Structure of Organizations*. Englewood Cliffs, NJ: Prentice Hall.

Mintzberg, H. (1980). *Leadership: Beyond establishment views*. From a presentation at the Sixth Biennial Leadership Symposium at Southern Illinois University at Carbondale.

Mintzberg, H. (1981, January/February). Organization design: Fashion or fit? *Harvard Business Review*.

National Industrial Conference Board. (1967). *Corporate Directorship Practices* (Studies in Business Policy no. 125).

Ohmae, K. (1982). *The Mind of the Strategist: The Art of Japanese Management.* New York: McGraw-Hill.

Osmond, N. (1971). Top management: Its tasks, roles and skills. *Journal of Business Policy, 2*(Winter), 2–21.

Ouchi, W. G. (1977). The relationship between organizational structure and organizational control. *Administrative Science Quarterly, 22*(1), 95.

Post, J. E., Murray, E. A., Jr., Dickie, R. B., & Mahon, J. F. (1982). The public affairs function in American corporations: Development and relations with corporate planning. *Long Range Planning, 15*(2), 12–21.

Rhenaman, E. (1973). *Organization Theory for Long-Range Planning.* New York: Wiley.

Schein, E. (1972). *The general manager: A profile.* Distinguished Management Scholar Lecture given at the Eastern Academy of Management.

Schendel, D. E. (1977). *Designing of strategic planning systems.* Institute for Research in the Behavioral, Economic and Management Sciences, Working Paper 616, Purdue University.

Shank, J. E., Niblock, E. G., & Sandells, W. T. (1973, January/February). Balance creativity and practicality in formal planning. *Harvard Business Review.*

Shetty, Y. K., & Perry, N. S., Jr. (1976). Are top executives transferable across companies? *Business Horizons, 19*(3), 23–28.

Smith, N. R. (1967). *The Entrepreneur and His Firm: The Relationship Between Type of Man and Type of Company.* East Lansing, MI: Graduate School of Business Administration, Michigan State University.

Steiner, G. A. (1981). A new class of chief executive officer. *Long Range Planning, 14*(4), 10–20.

Stieglitz, H. (1970, September). The chief executive's job and the size of the company. *The Conference Board Record.*

Sussman, J. A. (1979). Making it to the top: A career profile of the senior executive. *Management Review, 68*(7), 14–21.

Swann, K. (1975). Entrepreneurship in large companies. *Journal of General Management, 2*(Summer), 48–54.

Swayne, C., & Tucker, W. (1973). *The Effective Entrepreneur.* Morristown, NJ: General Learning Press.

Taylor, C. W. (1972). *Climate for Creativity.* Elmsford, NY: Pergamon.

Vance, S. C. (1972). Toward a collegial office of the president. *California Management Review, 15*(Fall), 106–116.

Wainer, H. A., & Rubin, I. M. (1969). Motivation of research and development entrepreneurs: Determinants of company success. *Journal of Applied Psychology, 53*(3), 178–184.

Westfall, S. (1969). Stimulating corporation entrepreneurship in US industry. *Academy of Management Journal, 12*(2), 235–246.

Zald, M. N. (1969). The power and functions of boards of directors: A theoretical synthesis. *American Journal of Sociology, 75*(1), 97–111.

Part F Strategic Management

Ansoff, H. I. (1968). Vers une theorie straiegique des entreprises (Toward a strategic theory of the firm). *Economies et Societes, II*(3).

Ansoff, H. I. (1972). The concept of strategic management. *Journal of Business Policy, 2*(4), 2–7.

Ansoff, H. I. (1976). Managing strategic surprise by response to weak signals. *California Management Review, 18*(Winter), 21–33.

Ansoff, H. I. (1978). Management in unpredictable environments. *The Intercontinental Advanced Management Report, I*(7).

Ansoff, H. I. (1979a). *ABC of strategic management* (EIASM Working Paper 79-25).

Ansoff, H. I. (1979b). Changing shape of the strategic problem. *Journal of General Management, 4*(4), 42–58.

Ansoff, H. I. (1979c). Planned management of turbulent change. *Encyclopedia of Professional Management.* New York: McGraw-Hill.

Ansoff, H. I. (1979d). *Strategic Management.* New York: Wiley.

Ansoff, H. I. (1980). Strategic issue management. *Strategic Management Journal, 1*(2), 131–148.

Ansoff, H. I., Declerck, R. P., & Hayes, R. L. (1976). *From Strategic Planning to Strategic Management.* New York: Wiley.

Ansoff, H. I., Eppink, D., & Gomer, H. (1978). Management of strategic surprise and discontinuity: Improving managerial decisiveness. *Marknads Vetande, Utgiven av Sveriges Marknadsforbund, 4/78* argang 9.

Ansoff, H. I., Kirsch, W., & Roventa, P. (1980). *Dispersed positioning in strategic portfolio analysis* (EIASM Working Paper 80-12).

Ansoff, H. I., Kirsch, W., & Roventa, P. (1983). Unschärfenpositionierung in der Strategischen Portfolio Analyse. In *Bausteine Strategischen Managements.* Berlin and New York: Walter de Gruyter.

Banks, R. L., & Wheelwright, S. C. (1979, May/June). Operations vs. strategy: Trading tomorrow for today. *Harvard Business Review.*

Brown, J. K. (1979). *This Business of Issues: Coping with the Company's Environments.* New York: The Conference Board.

Cannon, W. M. (1972). Organization design: Shaping structure to strategy. *McKinsey Quarterly, 9*(Summer), 25–32.

Chandler, A. D., Jr. (1962). *Strategy and Structure: Chapters in the History of the American Industrial Enterprise.* Cambridge: MIT Press.

Channon, D. (1973). *The Strategy and Structure of British Elllerprise*. Boston: Harvard University Press.

Child, J. (1972). Organizational structure, environment and performance: The role of strategic choice. *Sociology, 6*(1), 1–22.

Child, J. (1974). Managerial and organizational factors associated with company performance—Part I. *Journal of Management Studies, 11*(3), 175–189.

Child, J. (1975). Managerial and organizational factors associated with company performance—Part II. *Journal of Management Studies, 12*(1–2), 12–27.

Child, J., & Mansfield, R. (1972). Technology, size and organization structure. *Sociology, 6*(3), 369–393.

Clifford, D. K., Jr. (1973). *Managing the Threshold Company*. New York: McKinsey.

De Woot, P. (1970). *Strategie et Management*. Paris: Dunod.

Doz, Y. (1976). *National policies and multinational management* (Doctoral dissertation). Harvard University.

Eppink, D. J. (1978a). Planning for strategic flexibility. *Long Range Planning, 11*(4), 9–15.

Eppink, D. J. (1978b). *Managing the unforeseen: A study of flexibility* (Doctoral dissertation). Free University, Amsterdam.

Frankenhoff, W. P., & Granger, C. H. (1971). Strategic management: A new managerial concept for an era of rapid change. *Long Range Planning, 3*(3), 7–12.

Lawrence, P. R., & Lorsch, J. W. (1967). *Organization and Environment: Managing Differentiation and Integration*. Boston: Graduate School of Business, Harvard University.

Miles, R. E., & Snow, C. (1978). *Environmental Strategy and Organization Structure*. New York: McGraw-Hill.

Pascale, R. T., & Athos, A. G. (1981). *The Art of Japanese Management: Applications for American Executives*. New York: Simon and Schuster.

Pitts, R. A. (1977). Strategies and structures for diversification. *Academy of Management Journal, 20*(2), 197–208.

Rumelt, R. P. (1974). *Strategy, Structure and Economic Performance*. Boston: Graduate School of Business Administration, Harvard University.

Schendel, D. E., & Hatten, K. J. (1972). Business policy or strategic management: A broader view for an emerging discipline. *Academy of Management Proceedings* (1), 99–102

Schendel, D. E., & Hofer, C. W. (1978). *Strategic Management: A New View on Business Policy and Planning*. Boston: Little Brown.

Steinbruner, J. D. (1974). *The Cybernetic Theory of Decision*. Princeton, NJ: Princeton University Press.

Steiner, G. A., & Ryan, W. G. (1968). *Industrial Project Management*. New York: Macmillan.

Thomas, J. M. (1969). Expertness upon creativity of members of brainstorming groups. *Journal of Applied Psychology, 53*, 159–163.

Thomas, J. M., & Bennis, W. G. (1972). *Management of Change and Conflict*. Harmondsworth: Penguin.

Part G Organizational Behavior

Abell, P. (1975). *Organizations as Bargaining and Influence Systems*. London: Heinemann.

Ackoff, R. L. (1972). *On Purposeful System*. Chicago: Aldine.

Allison, G. T. (1968). *Policy process and politics* (Doctoral dissertation). Harvard University.

Allison, G. T. (1971). *Essence of Decision: Explaining the Cuban Missile Crisis*. Boston: Little Brown.

Ammer, D. S. (1970). Has big business lost the entrepreneurial touch? *Business Horizons, 13*(6), 37–46.

Anderson, C., & Paine, F. T. (1975). Managerial perceptions and strategic behavior. *Academy of Management Journal, 18*(4), 811–823.

Ansoff, H. I. (1975). *An applied managerial theory of strategic behavior* (EIASM Working Paper 75-12).

Ansoff, H. I. (1979). *Strategic Management*. London: Macmillan and New York: Wiley.

Applebaum, R. P. (1970). *Theories of Social Change*. Chicago: Markham.

Argenti, J. (1976). *Corporate Collapse: The Causes and Symptoms*. New York: Wiley.

Argyris, C. (1952). *The Impact of Budgets on People*. Controllership Foundation: New York.

Argyris, C. (1965). *Organization and Innovation*. New York: Irwin.

Argyris, C. (1973). Personality and organization theory revisited. *Administrative Science Quarterly, 18*(2), 141–167.

Argyris, C., & Donald, S. (1974). *Theory and Practice*. San Francisco: Jossey-Bass.

Arrow, K. J. (1975). *The Limits of Organization*. New York: Norton.

Baumol, W. J. (1967). *Business Behavior, Values and Growth*. New York: Harcourt, Brace and World Inc.

Baumol, W. J. (1968). Entrepreneurship in economic theory. *American Economic Review, 58*(2), 64–71.

Beckwith, B. P. (1967). *The Next 5000 Years*. New York: Exposition Press.

Beer, S. (1981). *The Brain of the Firm*. New York: Wiley.

Bell, D. (1971). The corporation and society in the 1970s. *The Public Interest, 24*(Summer), 5.

Bell, D. (1973). *The Coming of Post-industrial Society*. New York: Basic Books.

Bell, D., et al. (1967). Toward the year 2000: Work in progress. *Daedalus* (Summer).

Bennis, W. G. (1966). *Changing Organizations*. New York: McGraw-Hill.

Berle, A. A., & Means, G. C. (1968). *The Modern Corporation and Private Property* (Rev. ed.). New York: Harcourt, Brace and World Inc.

Beylc, T. L., & Lathrop, G. T. (1970). *Planning and Politics*. New York: Odyssey Press.

Blau, P. (1963). *The Dynamics of Bureaucracy*. Chicago: University of Chicago Press.

Blau, P. (1974). *On the Nature of Organizations*. New York: Wiley.

Blumberg, P. I. (1971). The politicalization of the corporation. *The Business Lawyer, 51*, 425.

Boulden, J. B. (1969). Merger negotiations: A decision model. *Business Horizons, 12*(1), 21–28.

Boulding, K. E. (1950). *A Reconstruction of Economics*. New York: Wiley.

Boulding, K. E. (1970). *Economics as a Science*. New York: McGraw-Hill.

Bower, J. L. (1971). Descriptive decision theory from the "administrative" viewpoint. In R. A. Bauer & K. J. Gergen (Eds.), *The Study of Policy Formation*. New York: Free Press.

Brief, A. P., Delbecq, A. L., Filley, A. C., & Huber, G. P. (1976). Elite structure and attitudes. *Administration and Society, 8*(2), 227–248.

Brook, M. Z., & Van Beusekom, M. (1979). *International Corporate Planning*. London: Pitman.

Burgelman, R. (1983). A model of the interaction of strategic behavior, corporate context and the concept of strategy. *Academy of Management Review, 8*(1), 61–70.

Carlson, S. (1951). *Executive Behavior: A Study of the Work Load and the Working Methods of Managing Directors*. Stockholm: Stromberg.

Carroll, T. H. (1958). *Collegiate Business Education in the Next Quarter Century*. Morgantown: West Virginia University Pres.

Chandler, A. D., Jr. (1977). *The Visible Hand*. Cambridge, MA: Harvard University Press.

Child, J. (1973). Strategies of control and organizational behavior. *Administrative Science Quarterly, 18*, 1–17.

Child, J., & Keiser, A. (1981). The development of organizations over time. In P. Nystrom & W. Starbuck (Eds.), *The Handbook of Organizational Design* (Vol. I). Oxford: Oxford University Press.

Clark, J., Freeman, C., & Soete, L. (1980). *Long Waves and Technological Developments in the 20th Century*. University of Sussex SPRU.

Clegg, S. R. (1975). *Power, Rule and Domination: A Critical and Empirical Understanding of Power in Sociological Theory and Organizational Life*. London: Routledge.

Cooper, A. C. (1973). Technical entrepreneurship: What do we know? *R&D Management, 3*(2), 59–64.

Crozier, M. (1964). *The Bureaucratic Phenomenon*. Chicago: University of Chicago Press.

Crozier, M. (1968). Le problème de!'innovation dans les organisations economiques. *Sociologie de Travail, 10*.

Cyert, R. M., & March, J. G. (1963). *A Behavioral Theory of the Firm*. Englewood Cliffs, NJ: Prentice Hall.

De Woot, P. (1962). *La Fonction d'Enterprise: Formes Nouvelles el Progrb Economique.* Louvain: Editions Nauwelaerts.

Drucker, P. F. (1970). *Technology, Management and Society.* New York: Heinemann.

Duncan, R. B. (1972). Characteristics of organizational environments and perceived environmental uncertainty. *Administrative Science Quarterly, 17*(3), 313–327.

Emery, F. E., & Trist, E. L. (1973). *Towards a Social Ecology.* New York: Plenum Press.

Fiedler, F. E. (1967). *A Theory of Leadership Effectiveness.* New York: McGraw-Hill.

Forester, J. W. (1961). *Industrial Dynamics.* Cambridge: MIT Press.

Galbraith, J. K. (1968). *The New Industrial State.* Harmondsworlh: Penguin.

Galbraith, J. K. (1969). *The Affluent Society* (2nd ed.). Boston: Houghton Mifflin.

Greiner, L. E. (1967, May/June). Patterns of organizational change. *Harvard Business Review.*

Greiner, L. E. (1972, July/August). Evolution and revolution as organizations grow. *Harvard Business Review.*

Haire, M., Giselli, A. E., & Porter, L. W. (1966). *Managerial Thinking: An International Study.* New York: Wiley.

Hansen, H. (1965). *Patterns of Discovery.* Cambridge: Cambridge University Press.

Hatten, K. J. (1974). *Strategic models in the brewing industry* (Doctoral dissertation). Purdue University.

Heyvaert, H. (1973). *Strategie el Innovation dans l'Enterprise.* Universite Catholique de Louvain.

Hickson, D. J., Hinings, C. R., Lee, C. A., Schneck, R. E., & Pcnnings, J. M. (1971). A strategic contingencies theory of interorganizational power. *Administrative Science Quarterly, 16,* 216–229.

Hinings, C. R., Hickson, D. J., Pennings, J. M., & Schneck, R. E. (1974). Structural conditions of interorganizational power. *Administrative Science Quarterly, 19*(l), 22–44.

Jacoby, N. H. (1973). *Corporate Power and Social Responsibility: A Blueprint for the Future.* New York: Macmillan.

Jantsch, E., & Waddington, C. H. (1976). *Evolution and Consciousness: Human Systems in Transition.* Reading, MA: Addison-Wesley.

de Jouvenel, M. (1972). *Du Pouvoir-Histoire Naturelle de sa Croissance.* Paris: Hachette.

Kuhn, R. S. (1972). Scientific paradigms. In B. Barnes (Ed.), *Sociology of Science* (pp. 80–104). Harmondsworth: Penguin.

Lindblom, C. E. (1959). The science of muddling through. *Public Administration Review, 19*(Spring), 79–88.

Lindblom, C. E. (1968). *The Policy Making Process.* Englewood Cliffs, NJ: Prentice Hall.

Lodge, G. C. (1975). *The New American Ideology.* New York: Knopf.

Lorsch, J. W., & Allen, S. A., III. (1973). *Managing Diversity and Interdependence: An Organizational Study of Multidivisional Firms.* Boston: Harvard University Press.

Lorsch, J. W., & Morse, J. J. (1974). *Organizations and Their Members: A Contingency Approach.* New York: Harper & Row.

Macmillan, I. C. (1974). Business strategies for political action. *Journal of General Management, 1*(1), 51–63.

Mansfield, E. (1961). Technical change and the rate of imitation. *Econometrica, 29*(4), 741–766.

March, J. G., & Simon, H. A. (1958). *Organizations.* New York: Wiley.

Marquis, D. G. (1969). The anatomy of successful innovations. *Innovation, 1,* 28–37.

Meadows, D., et al. (1972). *The Limits of Growth.* New York: Universe Books.

Mensch, G. (1978). *The Stalemate of Technology.* Cambridge: Ballingen.

Mintzberg, H. (1979). Organizational power goals: A skeletal theory. In D. E. Schendel & C. W. Hofer (Eds.), *Strategic Management: A New View of Business Policy and Planning.* Boston: Little Brown.

Nagashima, Y. (1976). Response of Japanese companies to environmental changes. *Long Range Planning, 9*(1), 20–28.

Nystrom, P., & Starbuck, W. H. (1977). *Prescriptive Models of Organizations.* Amsterdam: North-Holland.

Ouchi, W. (1981). *Theory 'Z'.* Reading, MA: Addison-Wesley.

Perrow, C. (1968). Technology and structural changes in the business firms. In B. C. Roberts (Ed.), *Industrial Relations: Contemporary Issues.* New York: Macmillan.

Perrow, C. (1973). The short and glorious history of organizational theory. *Organizational Dynamics, 2*(Summer), 3–15.

Pettigrew, A. M. (1973). *The Politics of Organizational Decision Making.* London: Tavistock Press.

Pfeffer, J. (1981). Management as symbolic action. *Research in Organizational Behavior* (Vol. 3). Greenwich, CT: JAI Press.

Pfeffer, J., & Salancik, G. R. (1974). Organizational decision making as a political process: The case of a university budget. *Administrative Science Quarterly, 19*(2), 135–151.

Popper, K. (1959). *The Logic of Scientific Discovery.* London: Hutchinson.

Quinn, J. B. (1980). *Strategies for Change: Logical Incrementalism.* Homewood, IL: Richard D. Irwin.

Rosenberg, N. (1972). *Technology and American Growth.* New York: Harper Torch Books.

Ross, J., & Kami, M. J. (1973). *Corporate Management in Crises: Why the Mighty Fall.* Englewood Cliffs, NJ: Prentice Hall.

Sahal, D. (1981). *Patterns of Technological Innovation.* Reading, MA: Addison-Wesley.

Schelling, T. C. (1960). *The Strategy of Conflict*. New York: Oxford University Press.

Schien, E. (1965). *Organizational Psychology*. Englewood Cliffs, NJ: Prentice Hall.

Selznick, P. (1957). *Leadership in Administration*. New York: Harper & Row.

Simon, Ha. (1959). *Administrative Behavior*. New York: Macmillan.

Sloan, A. P., Jr. (1965). *My Years with General Motors*. New York: McFadden.

Sullivan, J. J. (1983). A critique of theory "Z". *Academy of Management Review, 8*(1), 132–142.

Thompson, J. D. (1967). *Organizations in Action*. New York: McGraw-Hill.

Ullrich, R. A. (1972). *A Theoretical Model of Human Behavior in Organizations: An Eclectic Approach*. Morristown: General Learning Corporation.

Utterback, J. M. (1971). The process of technological innovation: A study of the organization and development of ideas for new scientific instruments. *IEEE Transactions on Engineering Management, 18*(4), 124–131.

Weinshall, T. D. (1977). *Culture and Management*. Harmondsworth: Penguin.

Whitehead, A. N. (1958). *The Function of Reason*. Boston: Beacon Press.

Zaleznik, A. (1970, May/June). Power and politics in organized life. *Harvard Business Review*.

Zaleznik, A., & de Uries, K. (1975). *Power and the Corporate Mind*. Boston: Houghton Mifflin.

Part H Strategic Diagnosis

Chabane, H. (1987). *Restructuring and performance in Algerian state-owned enterprises: A strategic management study* (Doctoral dissertation). United States International University, San Diego, California.

Gutu, J. (1990). *Strategic management of state-owned corporations (parastatals): An investigation of environmental dependence for resources by parastatals in Kenya* (Doctoral dissertation). United States International University, San Diego, California.

Hatziantoniou, P. (1986). *The relationship of environmental turbulence, corporate strategic profile, and company performance* (Doctoral dissertation). United States International University, San Diego, California.

Jaja, R. (1989). *Technology and banking: Implications of technology myopia on banking performance* (Doctoral dissertation). United States International University, San Diego, California.

Lewis, A. O. (1989). *Strategic posture and financial performance of the banking industry in California in a strategic management study* (Doctoral dissertation). United States International University, San Diego, California.

Peters, T. J., & Waterman, R. H., Jr. (1982). *In Search of Excellence*. New York: Harper & Row.

Salameh, T. T. (1987). *Strategic posture analysis and financial performance of the banking industry in the United Arab Emirates: A strategic management study*

(Doctoral dissertation). United States International University, San Diego, California.

Sullivan, P. A. (1987). *The relationship between proportion of income derived from subsidy and strategic performance of a federal agency under the commercial activities program* (Doctoral dissertation). United States International University, San Diego, California.

Part I Real-Time Response

Ansoff, H. I. (1985). Conceptual underpinnings of systematic strategic management. *European Journal of Operational Research* (Netherlands), *19*(1), 2–19.

Beaudoin, T. (1988). Planning for the worst: Crisis planning. *Management Review, 77*(8), 7.

Bhattacharya, K. (1985). Crisis management: Getting out of a tight corner. *Accountancy, 96*(1107), 77–82.

Blair, C. (1986). Scanning the corporate horizon: Public affairs in the strategically managed organization. *Canadian Business Review, 13*(3), 33–36.

Crane, T. Y. (1987). How to prevent a crisis. *New Management, 5*(1), 36–41.

Dutton, J. E., & Duncan, R. B. (1987). The creation of momentum for change through the process of strategic issue diagnosis. *Strategic Management Journal, 8*(3), 279–295.

Dutton, J. E., & Ottensmeyer, E. (1987). Strategic issue management systems: Forms, functions, and contexts. *Academy of Management Review, 12*(2), 355–365.

Dutton, J. E., Fahey, L., & Narayanan, V. K. (1983). Toward understanding strategic issue diagnosis. *Strategic Management Journal, 4*(4), 307–323.

Health, Robert L. and Associates. (1988). *Strategic Issue Management.* San Francisco: Jossey-Bass.

Logsdon, J. M., & Palmer, D. R. (1988). Issues management and ethics. *Journal of Business Ethics* (Netherlands), *7*(3), 191–198.

Miller, W. H. (1987). Issue management: No longer a sideshow. *Industry Week, 235*(3), 125–129

Mitroff, I. L., Shirvasta, P., & Udwadia, F. E. (1987). Effective crisis management. *Academy of Management Executive, 1*(4), 283–292.

Muller, R. (1985). Corporate crisis management. *Long Range Planning, 18*(5), 38–48.

Nelson, R. A., & Heath, R. L. (1986). A system model for corporate issues management. *Public Relations Quarterly, 31*(3), 20–24.

Power, C. (1988, September 26). *At Johnson & Johnson, a mistake can be a badge of honor* (Industrial/ Technology Edition).

Quarantelli, E. L. (1988). Disaster crisis management: A summary of research findings. *Journal of Management Studies, 25*(4), 373–385.

Renfro, W. L. (1987). Issues management: The evolving corporate role. *Futures, 19*(5), 545–554.

Schneider, B. L. (1985). Issue management—It counts! *United States Banker* (NE regional edition), *96*(6), 41–42.

Shrivastava, P., & Mitroff, I. I. (1987). Strategic management of corporate crises. *Columbia Journal of World Business, 22*(1), 5–11.

Stroup, M. A. (1986). Questioning assumptions: One company's answer to the planner's nemesis. *Planning Review, 14*(5), 10–15.

Stroup, M. A. (1988). Environmental scanning at Monsanto. *Planning Review, 16*(4), 24–27.

Wartick, S. L. (1988). How issue management contributes to corporate performance. *Business Forum, 13* (2), 16.

Wartick, S. L., & Rude, R. E. (1986). Issue management: Corporate function? *California Management Review, 29*(1), 124–140.

Weick, K. E. (1988). Enacted sensemaking in crisis situations. *Journal of Management Studies, 25*(4), 305–317.

Weiner, E., & Brown, A. (1986). Stakeholder analysis for effective issue management. *Planning Review, 14*(3), 27–31.

Index

© The Editor(s) (if applicable) and The Author(s), under
exclusive licence to Springer Nature Switzerland AG 2019
H. I. Ansoff et al., *Implanting Strategic Management*,
https://doi.org/10.1007/978-3-319-99599-1

The manufacturer's authorised representative in the EU is Springer
Nature Customer Service Centre GmbH, Europaplatz 3, 69115 Heidelberg,
Germany. If you have any concerns regarding our products, please
contact ProductSafety@springernature.com

Printed and bound by CPI Group (UK) Ltd, Croydon, CR0 4YY

27/04/2026

02097607-0004